Western Civilization
A Brief History
Fifth Edition

Western Civilization

A Brief History

Fifth Edition

Marvin Perry

Baruch College City University of New York

George W. Bock, *Editorial Associate*

Houghton Mifflin Company   Boston   New York

Editor-in-Chief: *Jean Woy*
Senior Sponsoring Editor: *Nancy Blaine*
Senior Developmental Editor: *Julie Dunn*
Editorial Associate: *Annette Fantasia*
Senior Project Editor: *Jane Lee*
Senior Art and Design Coordinator: *Jill Haber*
Senior Photo Editor: *Jennifer Meyer Dare*
Composition Buyer: *Sarah Ambrose*
Senior Manufacturing Coordinator: *Priscilla Bailey*
Senior Marketing Manager: *Sandra McGuire*
Marketing Assistant: *Ilana Gordon*

Cover Image: Portrait of Gabriele D'Annunzi. Credit: Archive Iconographica, S. A./Corbis.

Printed in the U.S.A.

Library of Congress Control Number: 2003116063

ISBN: 0-618-37033-1

3456789-MV-07 06 05

Contents

Maps

Chronologies

Preface

Western civilization is a grand but tragic drama. The West has forged the instruments of reason that make possible a rational comprehension of physical nature and human culture, conceived the idea of political liberty, and recognized the intrinsic worth of the individual. But the modern West, though it has unravelled nature's mysteries, has been less successful at finding rational solutions to social ills and conflicts between nations. Science, a great achievement of the Western intellect, while improving conditions of life, has also produced weapons of mass destruction. Though the West has pioneered in the protection of human rights, it has also produced totalitarian regimes that have trampled on individual freedom and human dignity. And although the West has demonstrated a commitment to human equality, it has also practiced brutal racism.

Western Civilization: A Brief History, Fifth Edition, is an abridged version of *Western Civilization: Ideas, Politics, and Society,* Seventh Edition. Like the longer text, this volume examines the Western tradition—those unique patterns of thought and systems of values that constitute the Western heritage. While focusing on key ideas and broad themes, the text also provides economic, political, and social history for students in Western civilization courses.

The text is written with the conviction that history is not a meaningless tale. Without a knowledge of history, men and women cannot fully know themselves, for all human beings have been shaped by institutions and values inherited from the past. Without an awareness of the historical evolution of reason and freedom, the dominant ideals of Western civilization, commitment to these ideals will diminish. Without a knowledge of history, the West cannot fully comprehend or adequately cope with the problems that burden its civilization and the world.

In attempting to make sense out of the past, the author has been careful to avoid superficial generalizations that oversimplify historical events and forces and arrange history into too neat a structure. But the text does strive to interpret and synthesize in order to provide students with a frame of reference with which to comprehend the principal events and eras in Western history.

Changes in the Fifth Edition

For the fifth edition, most chapters have been reworked to some extent. The numerous carefully selected modifications and additions significantly enhance the text. Some changes deepen the book's conceptual character; others provide useful and illustrative historical details.

In Chapter 1, "The Ancient Near East," a deliberate effort has been made to upgrade the end piece, "The Religious Orientation of the Ancient Near East." The discussions of Hebrew religious-ethical thought and the end piece, "The Legacy of the Ancient Jews," have been enriched in Chapter 2, "The Hebrews." In Chapter 3, "The Greeks," material was added on early Greek philosophy, the Sophists, Socrates, Plato, the Stoics, and drama and the end piece, "The Greek Achievement: Reason, Freedom, Humanism," was upgraded. In Chapter 4, "Rome," the discussions of republican politics and slavery were broadened as was the discussion on the signs of trouble during the Pax Romana that ultimately contributed to Rome's demise. Several topics have been given more attention in Chapter 5, "Early Christianity," including Jesus's Jewish background and the new religion's appeal. In addition, the concluding essay, "Christianity and Classical Humanism: Alternative World-Views," has been enriched. The most significant changes in the two chapters on the Middle Ages are expanded treatments of the Byzantine legacy, Islamic society and culture, and literature in the Latin West; as in several other chapters the conceptual framework of the end piece, "The Middle Ages and the Modern World: Continuity and Discontinuity," was strengthened. Chapter 8, "Transition to the Modern Age" features enlarged sections on "The Renaissance Outlook," "Renaissance Art," and "The Lutheran Revolt." Chapter 10, "Intellectual Transformation: The Scientific Revolution and the Age of Enlightenment," contains additional material on the philosophes' critique of religion. Chapter 11, "The Era of the French Revolution: Affirmation of Liberty and Equality," features expanded sections on "A Bourgeois Revolution?" and "Reforms of the National Assembly" and greater attention to Robespierre and the Terror. Here too, the conceptual quality of the end piece, "The Meaning of the French Revolution," has been upgraded. The treatment of Romanticism and nationalism has been deepened in Chapter 13, "Thought and Culture in the Early Nineteenth Century." Also revised is the section, "Revolutions of 1848: An Assessment," in Chapter 14, "The Surge of Liberalism and Nationalism." The most notable change in Chapter 15, "Thought and Culture in the Mid-Nineteenth Century," is the expanded treatment of Social Darwinism. Chapter 16, "Europe in the Late Nineteenth Century," draws out more implications of German

Volkish thought. In Chapter 17, "Modern Consciousness," the discussion of Nietzsche, Weber, and modernism has improved; also improved is the end piece, "The Enlightenment Tradition in Disarray." Several qualitative changes dealing with the causes and conduct of the war have been incorporated into Chapter 18, "World War I: The West in Despair." The most important additions to the chapter are found in the treatment of the Russian Revolution and in the end piece, "The War and European Consciousness." In Chapter 19, "The Era of Totalitarianism," the analyses of the nature of totalitarianism, Stalin's dictatorship, fascism's nature and appeal, the Weimar Republic, and Hitler's rise to power have each been improved. Chapter 20, "World War II: Western Civilization in the Balance," now has expanded treatment of the events leading up to the war, the New Order Germany imposed on conquered Europe, the Holocaust, and two major turning points of the war—the battle of Stalingrad and D-Day; the end piece, "The Legacy of World War II," has also been improved. In extensively reworking the concluding chapter, "The West in a Global Age," considerable attention has been given to international terrorism, in particular the tragedy of September 11th and the U.S. invasion of Afghanistan and Iraq. Finally, the art essays have been revised and now include a new section on contemporary art.

Distinctive Features

This brief edition was prepared for Western Civilization courses that run for one term only, for instructors who like to supplement the main text with primary source readers, novels, or monographs, and for humanities courses in which additional works on literature and art will be assigned. In abbreviating the longer text by about a third, the number of chapters has been reduced from 34 to 21. The emphasis on the history of ideas and culture has been retained, but the amount of detail has of necessity been reduced.

The text contains several pedagogical features. Chapter introductions provide comprehensive overviews of key themes and give a sense of direction and coherence to the flow of history. Chronologies at the beginning of most chapters show the sequence of important events discussed in the chapter. Many chapters contain concluding essays that treat the larger meaning of the material. Facts have been carefully selected to illustrate key relationships and concepts and to avoid overwhelming students with unrelated and disconnected data. Each chapter concludes with an annotated bibliography and review questions. The questions refer students to principal points and aim at eliciting thoughtful answers.

This text is published in both single-volume and two-volume editions. Volume I treats the period from the first civilizations in the Near East through the age of Enlightenment in the eighteenth century (Chapters 1–10). Volume II covers the period from the Renaissance and the Reformation to the contemporary age (Chapters 8–21), and incorporates the last three chapters in Volume I: "Transition to the Modern Age: Renaissance and Reformation," "Political and Economic Transformation: National States, Overseas Expansion, Commercial Revolution," and "Intellectual Transformation: The Scientific Revolution and the Age of Enlightenment." Volume II also contains a comprehensive introduction that surveys the ancient world and the Middle Ages; the introduction is designed particularly for students who have not taken the first half of the course.

Ancillaries

Learning and teaching ancillaries, including the *History Companion, Instructor's Manual with Test Items,* and *Map Transparencies,* also contribute to the text's usefulness.

New to this addition is the *History Companion,* which consists of three components:

The *Instructor Companion* is a free, searchable CD-ROM featuring hundreds of historical images and maps in PowerPoint format. Each image is accompanied by notes that place it in its proper historical context and tips for ways it can be presented in the classroom. The CD also includes the *HM Testing* program, a computerized version of the *Test Items* to enable instructors to alter, replace, or add questions, as well as resources from the *Instructor's Resource Manual.*

The *Student Research Compnaion* is a free web-based tool with 100 interactive maps and 500 primary sources. The primary sources include headnotes that provide pertinent background information and questions that students can answer and email to their instructors.

The *Student Study Companion* is a free online study guide that contains chapter outlines, review questions, the ACE self-testing program, web activities, matching exercises, and web links.

The *Instructor's Manual with Test Items* was prepared for the brief edition by Professor Diane Moczar of Northern Virginia Community College. The *Manual* contains chapter outlines, learning objectives, lecture topics, a film/video bibliography, essay and discussion questions, identifications, and multiple-choice questions and answers. In addition, a set of map transparencies is available on adoption.

Acknowledgments

In preparing this abridgment, I have made extensive use of the chapters written by my colleagues for *Western Civilization: Ideas, Politics, and Society.* Chapter 8, "Transition to the Modern Age: Renaissance and Reformation," and Chapter 9, "Political and Economic Transformation: National States, Overseas Expansion, Commercial Revolution," are based largely on James R. Jacob's and Margaret C. Jacob's chapters in the longer volume. Parts of Chapter 12, "The Industrial Revolution: The Transformation of Society," and of Chapter 16, "Europe in the Late Nineteenth Century: Modernization, Nationalism, Imperialism," are drawn from Myrna Chase's chapters. Material on tsarist Russia and the Soviet Union and the concluding chapter, "The West in a Global Age," are based very much on Theodore H. Von Laue's contribution to the larger text. To a lesser or greater extent, my colleagues' material has been abridged, restructured, and rewritten to meet the needs of this volume. Therefore, I alone am responsible for all interpretations and any errors. I wish to thank my colleagues for their gracious permission to use their words and thoughts.

I am also grateful to the staff of Houghton Mifflin Company who lent their considerable talents to the project. In particular, I wish to thank Jane Lee, project editor, for her careful attention to detail, Susan Zorn, whose copyediting skills are reflected in the final manuscript, and Julie Dunn, developmental editor, who supervised the project. I am especially grateful to my friend George Bock who read the manuscript with an eye for organization, major concepts, and essential relationships. As ever, I am grateful to my wife Phyllis G. Perry for her encouragement.

M. P.

Introduction

The Foundations of Western Civilization

Western civilization is a blending of two traditions that emerged in the ancient world: the Judeo-Christian and the Greco-Roman. Before these traditions took shape, the drama of civilization was well advanced, having arisen some five thousand years ago in Mesopotamia and Egypt.

Religion was the central force in these first civilizations in the Near East. Religion provided explanations for the operations of nature, justified traditional rules of morality, and helped people to deal with their fear of death. Law was considered sacred, a commandment of the gods. Religion united people in the common enterprises needed for survival, such as the construction of irrigation works. Religion also promoted creative achievement in art, literature, and science. In addition, the power of rulers, who were regarded as gods or as agents of the gods, derived from religious traditions. The many achievements of the Egyptians and the Mesopotamians were inherited and assimilated by both the Greeks and the Hebrews, the spiritual ancestors of Western civilization. But Greeks and Hebrews also rejected and transformed elements of the older Near Eastern traditions and conceived a new view of God, nature, and the individual.

THE HEBREWS

By asserting that God was one, sovereign, transcendent, and good, the Hebrews effected a religious revolution that separated them forever from the world-views of the Mesopotamians and Egyptians. This new conception of God led to a new awareness of the individual. In confronting God, the Hebrews developed an awareness of *self*, or *I*. The individual became conscious of his or her moral autonomy and personal worth. The Hebrews believed that God had bestowed on his people the capacity for moral freedom—they could choose between good and evil. Fundamental to Hebrew belief was the insistence that God had created human beings to be free moral agents. God did not want people to grovel before him, but to fulfill their moral potential by freely making the choice to follow, or not to follow, God's law. Thus, the Hebrews originated the idea of moral freedom—that each individual is responsible for his or her own actions. Inherited by Christianity, this idea of moral autonomy is central to the Western tradition.

The Hebrew conception of ethical monotheism, with its stress on human dignity, is one source of the Western tradition. The other source derives from the ancient Greeks; they originated scientific and philosophic thought and conceived both the idea and the practice of political freedom.

THE GREEKS

In the Near East, religion dominated political activity, and following the mandates of the gods was a ruler's first responsibility. What made Greek political life different from that of earlier civilizations—and gives it enduring significance—was the Greeks' gradual realization that community problems were caused by human beings and required human solutions. The Greeks came to understand law as an achievement of the rational mind, rather than as an edict imposed by the gods. In the process, they also originated the idea of political freedom and created democratic institutions.

Greece comprised small, independent city-states. In the fifth century B.C., the city-state (polis) was in its maturity. A self-governing community, it expressed the will of free citizens, not the desires of gods, hereditary kings, or priests. The democratic orientation of the city-states was best exemplified by Athens, which was also the leading cultural center of Greece. In the Assembly, which was open to all adult male citizens, Athenians debated and voted on key issues of state.

In addition to the idea of political freedom, the Greeks conceived a new way of viewing nature and human society. The first speculative philosophers emerged during the sixth century B.C. in Greek cities located in Ionia in Asia Minor. Curious about the basic composition of nature and dissatisfied with earlier legends about creation, the Ionians sought physical, rather than mythico-religious, explanations for natural occurrences.

During this search these early philosophers arrived at a new concept of nature and a new method of inquiry. They maintained that nature was not manipulated by arbitrary and willful gods and that it was not governed by blind chance. The Ionians said that underlying the seeming chaos of nature were principles of order, that is, general rules that could be ascertained by the human mind. This discovery marks the beginning of scientific thought. It made possible theoretical thinking and the systematization of knowledge. This is distinct from the mere observation and collection of data. Greek mathematicians, for example, organized the Egyptians' practical experience with land measurements into the logical and coherent science of geometry. In another instance, the Greeks used the data collected by Babylonian priests, who observed the heavens because they believed that the stars revealed their gods' wishes. The Greeks' purpose was not religious—they sought to discover the geometrical laws underlying the motion of heavenly bodies. At the same time, Greek physicians drew a distinction between medicine and magic, and began to examine human illness in an empirical and rational way. By the fifth century the Greek mind had applied reason to the physical world and to all human activities. This emphasis on reason marks a turning point for human civilization.

In their effort to understand the external world, early Greek thinkers had created the tools of reason. Greek philosophers now began a rational investigation of the human being and the human community. The key figure in this development was Socrates.

Socrates' central concern was the perfection of individual human character, the achievement of moral excellence. Excellence of character was achieved, said Socrates, when individuals regulated their lives according to objective standards arrived at through rational reflection, that is, when reason became the formative, guiding, and ruling agency of the soul. Socrates wanted to subject all human beliefs and behavior to the clear light of reason and in this way to remove ethics from the realm of authority, tradition, dogma, superstition, and myth. He believed that reason was the only proper guide to the most crucial problem of human existence—the question of good and evil.

Plato, Socrates' most important disciple, used his master's teachings to create a comprehensive system of philosophy that embraced the world of nature and the social world. Socrates had taught that there were universal standards of right and justice and that these were arrived at through thought. Building on the insights of his teacher, Plato insisted on the existence of a higher world of reality, independent of the world of things experienced every day. This higher reality, he said, is the realm of Ideas or Forms—unchanging, eternal, absolute, and universal standards of beauty, goodness, justice, and so forth. Truth resides in this world of Forms and not in the world revealed through the human senses.

Aristotle, Plato's student, was the leading expert of his time in every field of knowledge, with the possible exception of mathematics. Aristotle objected to Plato's devaluing of the material world. Possessing a scientist's curiosity to understand the facts of nature, Aristotle appreciated the world of phenomena, of concrete things, and respected knowledge obtained through the senses. Like Plato, Aristotle believed that understanding universal principles is the ultimate aim of knowledge. But unlike Plato, Aristotle held that to obtain such knowledge, the individual must study the world of facts and objects revealed through sight, hearing, and touch. Aristotle adapted Plato's stress on universal principles to the requirements of natural science.

By discovering theoretical reason, by defining political freedom, and by affirming the worth and potential of human personality, the Greeks broke with the past and founded the rational and humanist tradition of the West. "Had Greek civilization never existed," said poet W. H. Auden, "we would never have become fully conscious, which is to say that we would never have become, for better or worse, fully human."[1]

The Hellenistic Age

By 338 B.C., Philip of Macedonia (a kingdom to the north of Greece) had extended his dominion over the Greek city-states. After the assassination of Philip in 336 B.C., his twenty-year-old son Alexander succeeded to the throne. Fiery, proud, and ambitious, Alexander sought to conquer the vast Persian Empire. Winning every battle, Alexander's army carved an empire that stretched from Greece to India. In 323 B.C., Alexander not yet thirty-three years of age, died of a fever. His generals engaged in a long and bitter struggle to succeed him. As none of the generals or their heirs could predominate, Alexander's empire was fractured into separate states.

The period from the early Greek city-states that emerged in 800 B.C. until the death of Alexander the Great in 323 B.C. is called the *Hellenic Age*. The next stage in the evolution of Greek civilization (*Hellenism*) is called the *Hellenistic Age*. It ended in 30 B.C. when Egypt, the last major Hellenistic state, fell to Rome.

Although the Hellenistic Age had absorbed the heritage of classical (Hellenic) Greece, its style of civilization changed. During the first phase of Hellenism, the polis had been the center of political life. The polis had given the individual identity, and it was believed that only within the polis could a Greek live a good and civilized life. During the Hellenistic Age, this situation changed. The city-state was eclipsed in power and importance by kingdoms and empires. While cities retained a large measure of autonomy in domestic affairs, they had lost their freedom of action in foreign affairs. No longer were they the self-sufficient and independent communities of the Hellenic period.

Hellenistic society was characterized by a mingling of peoples and an interchange of cultures. As a result of Alexander's conquests, tens of thousands of Greek soldiers, merchants, and administrators settled in eastern lands. Greek traditions spread to the Near East, and Mesopotamian, Hebrew, and Persian traditions—particularly religious beliefs—moved westward. Cities were founded in the east patterned after the city-states of Greece. The ruling class in each Hellenistic city was united by a common Hellenism that overcame national, linguistic, and racial distinctions.

During the Hellenistic Age, Greek scientific achievement reached its height. Hellenistic scientists attempted a rational analysis of nature, engaged in research, organized knowledge in logical fashion, devised procedures for mathematical proof, separated medicine from magic, grasped the theory of experiment, and applied scientific principles to mechanical devices. Hellenistic science, says historian Benjamin Farrington, stood "on the threshold of the modern world. When modern science began in the sixteenth century, it took up where the Greeks left off."[2]

Hellenistic philosophers preserved the rational tradition of Greek philosophy. Like their Hellenic predecessors, they regarded the cosmos as governed by universal principles intelligible to the rational mind. The most important philosophy in the Hellenistic world was Stoicism. By teaching that the world constituted a single society, Stoicism gave theoretical expression to the worldmindedness of the age. Stoicism with its concept of a world-state offered an answer to the problems of the loss of community and the alienation caused by the decline of the city-state. By stressing inner strength in dealing with life's misfortunes, Stoicism offered an avenue to individual happiness in a world fraught with uncertainty.

At the core of Stoicism was the belief that the universe contained a principle of order: the *logos* (reason). This ruling principle permeated all things; it accounted for the orderliness of nature. Because people were part of the universe, said the Stoics, they also shared in the logos that operated throughout the cosmos. Since reason was common to all, human beings were essentially brothers and fundamentally equal.

Stoicism had an enduring impact on the Western mind. To some Roman political theorists, their Empire fulfilled the Stoic ideal of a world community in which people of different nationalities held citizenship and were governed by a worldwide law that accorded with the law of reason or natural law. Stoic beliefs—such as all human beings are members of one family; each person is significant; distinctions of rank are of no account; and human law should not conflict with natural law—were incorporated into Roman jurisprudence, Christian thought, and modern liberalism. There is continuity between Stoic thought and the principle of inalienable rights stated in the American Declaration of Independence.

ROME

Rome, conqueror of the Mediterranean world and transmitter of Hellenism, inherited the universalist tendencies of the Hellenistic Age and embodied them in its law and institutions. Roman history falls into two periods: the Republic, which began in 509 B.C. with the overthrow of the Etruscan monarchy; and the Empire, which started in 27 B.C. when Octavian became, in effect, the first Roman emperor.

The Roman Republic

The history of the Roman Republic was marked by three principal developments: the struggle between patricians and plebeians, the conquest of Italy and the Mediterranean world, and the civil wars. At the beginning of the fifth century B.C., Rome was dominated by *patricians* (the landowning aristocrats). The *plebeians* (commoners) had many grievances; these included enslavement for debt, discrimination in the courts, prevention of intermarriage with patricians, lack of political representation, and the absence of a written code of laws.

Resentful of their inferior status, the plebeians organized and waged a struggle for political, legal, and social equality. They were resisted every step of the way by the patricians, who wanted to preserve their dominance. The plebeians had one decisive weapon: their threat to secede from Rome, that is, not to pay taxes, work, nor serve in the army. Realizing that Rome, which was constantly involved in warfare on the Italian peninsula, could not endure without plebeian help, the pragmatic patricians begrudgingly made concessions. Thus the plebeians slowly gained legal equality.

Although many plebeian grievances were resolved and the plebeians gained the right to sit in the Senate, the principal organ of government, Rome was still ruled by an upper class. Power was concentrated in a ruling oligarchy consisting of patricians and influential plebeians who had joined forces with the old nobility.

By 146 B.C., Rome had become the dominant power in the Mediterranean world. Roman expansion occurred in three main stages: the uniting of the Italian peninsula, which gave Rome the manpower that transformed it from a city-state into a great power; the struggle with Carthage, from which Rome emerged as ruler of the Western Mediterranean; and the subjugation of the Hellenistic states of the Eastern Mediterranean, which brought Romans into close contact with Greek civilization.

A crucial consequence of expansion was Roman contact with the legal experience of other peoples. Roman jurists, demonstrating the Roman virtues of pragmatism and common sense, selectively incorporated elements of the legal codes and traditions of these nations into Roman law. Thus Roman jurists gradually and empirically fashioned the *jus gentium,* the law of nations or peoples.

Roman jurists then identified the jus gentium with the natural law (*jus naturale*) of the Stoics. The jurists said that law should accord with rational principles inherent in nature—universal norms capable of being discerned by rational people. The law of nations—Roman civil law (the law of the Roman state) combined with principles drawn from Greek and other sources—eventually replaced much of the local law in the Empire. This evolution of a universal code of law that gave expression to the Stoic principles of common rationality and humanity was the great achievement of Roman rule.

Another consequence of expansion was increased contact with Greek culture. Gradually the Romans acquired knowledge about scientific thought, philosophy, medicine, and geography from Greece. Adopting the humanist outlook of the Greeks, the Romans came to value human intelligence and eloquent and graceful prose and oratory. Rome creatively assimilated the Greek achievement and transmitted it to others, thereby extending the orbit of Hellenism.

During Rome's march to empire, all its classes had demonstrated a magnificent spirit in fighting foreign wars. With Carthage and Macedonia no longer threats to Rome, this cooperation deteriorated. Rome became torn apart by internal dissension during the first century B.C.

Julius Caesar, a popular military commander, gained control of the government. Caesar believed that only strong and enlightened leadership could permanently end the civil warfare destroying Rome. Rome's ruling class feared that Caesar would destroy the Republic and turn Rome into a monarchy. Regarding themselves as defenders of republican liberties and senatorial leadership, aristocratic conspirators assassinated Caesar in 44 B.C. The murder of Caesar plunged Rome into renewed civil war. Finally, in 31 B.C., Octavian, Caesar's adopted son, defeated his rivals and emerged as master of Rome. Four years later, Octavian, now called Augustus, became in effect the first Roman emperor.

The Roman Empire

The rule of Augustus signified the end of the Roman Republic and the beginning of the Roman Empire, the termination of aristocratic politics and the emergence of one-man rule. Under Augustus the power of the ruler was disguised; in ensuing generations, however, emperors would wield absolute power openly.

Augustus was by no means a self-seeking tyrant, but a creative statesman. His reforms rescued a dying Roman world and inaugurated Rome's greatest age. For the next two hundred years the Mediterranean world enjoyed the blessings of the *Pax Romana*, the Roman peace.

The ancient world had never experienced such a long period of peace, order, efficient administration, and prosperity. The Romans called the Pax Romana a "Time of Happiness." It was the fulfillment of Rome's mission—the creation of a world-state that provided peace, security, ordered civilization, and the rule of law. The cities of the Roman Empire served as centers of Greco-Roman civilization, which spread to the furthest reaches of the Mediterranean. Roman citizenship, gradually granted, was finally extended to virtually all free men by an edict in A.D. 212.

In the third century, the ordered civilization of the Pax Romana ended. The Roman Empire was plunged into military anarchy, as generals supported by their soldiers fought for the throne. Germanic tribesmen broke through the deteriorating border defenses to raid, loot, and destroy. Economic problems caused cities, the centers of civilization, to decay. Increasingly people turned away from the humanist values

of Greco-Roman civilization and embraced Near Eastern religions that offered a sense of belonging, a promise of immortality, and relief from earthly misery.

The emperors Diocletian (285–305) and Constantine (306–337) tried to contain the forces of disintegration by tightening the reins of government and squeezing more taxes out of the citizens. In the process they divided the Empire into eastern and western halves, and transformed Rome into a bureaucratic, regimented, and militarized state.

Diocletian and Constantine had given Rome a reprieve, but in the last part of the fourth century, the problem of guarding the frontier grew more acute. At the very end of 406, the borders finally collapsed; numerous German tribes overran the Empire's western provinces. In 410 and again in 455, Rome was sacked by Germanic invaders. German soldiers in the pay of Rome gained control of the government and dictated the choice of emperor. In 476, German officers overthrew the Roman Emperor Romulus and placed a fellow German on the throne. This act is traditionally regarded as the end of the Roman Empire in the West.

EARLY CHRISTIANITY

When the Roman Empire was in decline, a new religion, Christianity, was sweeping across the Mediterranean world. Christianity was based on the life, death, and teachings of Jesus, a Palestinian Jew who was executed by the Roman authorities. Jesus was heir to the ethical monotheism of the Hebrew prophets. He also taught the imminent coming of the reign of God and the need for people to repent their sins—to transform themselves morally in order to enter God's kingdom. People must love God and their fellow human beings.

In the time immediately following the crucifixion of Jesus, his followers were almost exclusively Jews, who could more appropriately be called Jewish-Christians. To the first members of the Christian movement, Jesus was both a prophet who proclaimed God's power and purpose and the Messiah whose coming heralded a new age. To Paul, another Jewish-Christian, Jesus was the redeemer who held out the promise of salvation to the entire world; the new Christian community was the true fulfillment of Judaism. And Saint Paul carried this message to Jews and especially to non-Jews (Gentiles).

The Christian message of a divine Savior, a concerned Father, and brotherly love inspired men and women who were dissatisfied with the world of here-and-now, who felt no attachment to city or Empire, who derived no inspiration from philosophy, and who suffered from a profound sense of loneliness. Christianity offered the individual what the city and the Roman world-state could not: a personal relationship with God, a promise of eternal life, and membership in a community of the faithful (the church) who cared for each other.

Unable to crush Christianity by persecution, Roman emperors decided to gain the support of the growing number of Christians within the Empire. By A.D. 392, Theodosius I had made Christianity the state religion of the Empire and declared the worship of pagan gods illegal.

The Judeo-Christian and Greco-Roman traditions are the two principal components of Western civilization. Both traditions valued the individual. For classical humanism, individual worth derived from the human capacity to reason, to shape character and life according to rational standards. Christianity also places great stress on the individual. It teaches that God cares for each person and wants people to behave righteously, and that He made them morally autonomous.

Despite their common emphasis on the individual, the Judeo-Christian and Greco-Roman traditions essentially have different worldviews. With the victory of Christianity, the ultimate goal of life shifted away from achieving excellence in this world through the full and creative development of human talent, toward attaining salvation in a heavenly city. For Christians, a person's worldly accomplishments counted very little if he or she did not accept God and his revelation. Greek classicism held that there was no authority higher than reason; Christianity taught that without God as the starting point, knowledge is formless, purposeless, and error-prone.

But Christian thinkers did not seek to eradicate the rational tradition of Greece. Rather, they sought to fit Greek philosophy into a Christian framework. In doing so, Christians performed a task of immense historical significance—the preservation of Greek philosophy.

THE MIDDLE AGES

The triumph of Christianity and the establishment of Germanic kingdoms on once-Roman lands constituted a new phase in Western history: the end of the ancient world and the beginning of the Middle Ages. In the ancient world the locus of Greco-Roman civilization was the Mediterranean Sea. The heartland of medieval civilization shifted to the north, to regions of Europe that Greco-Roman civilization had barely penetrated.

The Early Middle Ages

During the Early Middle Ages (500–1050), a common civilization evolved with Christianity at the center, Rome as the spiritual capital, and Latin as the language of intellectual life. The opening centuries of the Middle Ages were marked by a decline in trade, town life, central authority, and learning. The Germans were culturally unprepared to breathe new life into classical civilization. A new civilization with its own distinctive style was taking root, however. It consisted of Greco-Roman survivals, the native traditions of the Germans, and the Christian outlook.

Christianity was the integrating principle of the Middle Ages, and the church its dominant institution. People came to see themselves as participants in a great drama of salvation. There was only one truth—God's revelation to humanity. There was only one avenue to heaven—the church. To the medieval mind, society without the church was as inconceivable as life without the Christian view of God. By teaching a higher morality, the church tamed the warrior habits of the Germanic peoples. By copying and preserving ancient texts, monks kept alive elements of the high civilization of Greece and Rome.

One German people, the Franks, built a viable kingdom with major centers in France and the Rhine Valley of Germany. Under Charlemagne, who ruled from 768 to 814, the Frankish empire reached its height. On Christmas day in the year 800, Pope Leo crowned Charlemagne as "Emperor of the Romans." The title signified that the tradition of a world empire still survived, despite the demise of the Roman Empire three hundred years earlier. Because the pope crowned Charlemagne, this act meant that the emperor had a spiritual responsibility to spread and defend the faith.

The crowning of a German ruler as emperor of the Romans by the head of the church represented the merging of German, Christian, and Roman elements—the essential characteristic of medieval civilization. This blending of traditions was also evident on a cultural plane, for Charlemagne, a German warrior-king, showed respect for classical learning and Christianity, both non-Germanic traditions. During his reign, a distinct European civilization took root, but it was centuries away from fruition.

Charlemagne's successors could not hold the empire together, and it disintegrated. As central authority waned, large landowners began to exercise authority over their own regions. Furthering this movement toward localism and decentralization were simultaneous invasions by Muslims, Vikings from Scandinavia, and Magyars originally from Western Asia. They devastated villages, destroyed ports, and killed many people. Trade was at a standstill, coins no longer circulated, and untended farms became wastelands. The European economy collapsed, the political authority of kings disappeared, and cultural life and learning withered.

During these times, large landowners, or lords, wielded power formerly held by kings over their subjects, an arrangement called *feudalism*. Arising during a period of collapsing central authority, invasion, scanty public revenues, and declining commerce and town life, feudalism attempted to provide some order and security. A principal feature of feudalism was the practice of *vassalage,* in which a man in a solemn ceremony pledged loyalty to a lord. The lord received military service from his vassal, and the vassal obtained land, called a *fief,* from his lord.

Feudalism was built on an economic foundation known as *manorialism.* A village community (manor), consisting of serfs bound to the land, became the essential agricultural arrangement in medieval society. In return for protection and the right to cultivate fields, serfs owed obligations to their lords, and their personal freedom was restricted in a variety of ways.

Manorialism and feudalism presupposed an unchanging social order with a rigid system of estates, or orders—clergy who prayed, lords who fought, and peasants who toiled. The revival of an urban economy and the re-emergence of the king's authority in the High Middle Ages (1050 to 1300) would undermine feudal and manorial relationships.

The High Middle Ages

By the end of the eleventh century, Europe showed many signs of recovery and vitality. The invasions of Magyars and Vikings had ended, and kings and powerful lords imposed greater order in their territories. Improvements in technology and the clearing of new lands increased agricultural production. More food, the fortunate absence of plagues, and the limited nature of feudal warfare contributed to a population increase.

Expanding agricultural production, the end of Viking attacks, greater political stability, and a larger population revived commerce. In the twelfth and thirteenth centuries, local, regional, and long-distance trade gained such a momentum that some historians describe the period as a commercial revolution that surpassed commerce in the Roman Empire during the Pax Romana.

In the eleventh century, towns re-emerged throughout Europe, and in the next century became active centers of commerce and intellectual life. Socially, economically, and culturally, towns were a new and revolutionary force. Towns contributed to the decline of manorialism because they provided new opportunities for commoners, apart from food-producing.

A new class (the middle class) of merchants and artisans appeared; unlike the lords and serfs, the members of this class were not affiliated with the land. Townspeople possessed a value system different from that of lords, serfs, or clerics. Whereas the clergy prepared people for heaven, the feudal lords fought and hunted, and the serfs toiled in small villages, townspeople engaged in business and had money and freedom. Townspeople were freeing themselves from the prejudices of both feudal aristocrats, who considered trade and manual work degrading, and the clergy, who cursed the pursuit of riches as an obstacle to salvation. Townspeople were critical, dynamic, and progressive—a force for change.

Other signs of growing vitality in Latin Christendom (western and central Europe) were the greater order and security provided by the emergence of states. While feudalism fostered a Europe that was split into many local regions, each ruled by a lord, the church envisioned a vast Christian commonwealth, *Respublica Christiana,* guided by the papacy. During the High Middle Ages, the ideal of a universal Christian community seemed close to fruition. Never again would Europe possess such spiritual unity.

But forces were propelling Europe into a different direction. Aided by educated and trained officials who enforced royal law, tried people in royal courts, and collected royal taxes, kings enlarged their territories and slowly fashioned strong central governments. Gradually, subjects began to transfer their prime loyalty away from the church and their lords to the person of the king. In the process the foundations of European states were laid. Not all areas followed the same pattern. England and France achieved a large measure of unity during the Middle Ages; Germany and Italy remained divided into numerous independent territories.

Accompanying economic recovery and political stability in the High Middle Ages was a growing spiritual vitality. This vigor was marked by several developments. The common people showed greater devotion to the church. Within the church, reform movements attacked clerical abuses, and the papacy grew more powerful. Holy wars against the Muslims (the Crusades) drew the Christian community closer together. During this period, the church with great determination tried to make society follow divine standards, that is, to shape all institutions according to a comprehensive Christian outlook.

European economic and religious vitality was paralleled by a cultural flowering in philosophy, literature, and the visual arts. Creative intellects achieved on a cultural level what the papacy accomplished on an institutional level—the integration of society around a Christian viewpoint. The High Middle Ages saw the restoration of some learning of the ancient world, the rise of universities, the emergence of an original form of architecture (the Gothic), and the creation of an imposing system of thought (scholasticism).

Medieval theologian-philosophers called *scholastics* fashioned Christian teachings into an all-embracing philosophy that represented the spiritual essence of medieval civilization. They achieved what Christian thinkers in the Roman Empire had initiated and what learned men of the Early Middle Ages were groping for: a synthesis of Greek philosophy and Christian revelation.

The Late Middle Ages

By the opening of the fourteenth century, Latin Christendom had experienced more than 250 years of growth, but during the late Middle Ages, roughly the fourteenth and early fifteenth centuries, medieval civilization declined. The fourteenth century, an age of adversity, was marked by crop failures, famine, population decline, plagues, stagnating production, unemployment, inflation, devastating warfare, abandoned villages, and violent rebellions by the poor and weak of towns and countryside, who were ruthlessly suppressed by the upper classes. This century witnessed flights into mysticism, outbreaks of mass hysteria, and massacres of Jews; it was an age of pessimism and general insecurity. The papacy declined in power, heresy proliferated, and the synthesis of faith and reason erected by the Christian thinkers during the High Middle Ages began to disintegrate. All these developments were signs that the stable and coherent civilization of the thirteenth century was drawing to a close.

But the decline of medieval civilization in the fourteenth century brought no new dark age to Europe. Its economic and political institutions and technological skills had grown too strong. Instead, the waning of the Middle Ages opened up possibilities for another stage in Western civilization—the modern age.

The Middle Ages and the Modern World: Continuity and Discontinuity

In innumerable ways the modern world is linked to the Middle Ages. European cities, the middle class, the state system, English common law, universities—all had their origins in the Middle Ages. During the Middle Ages, important advances were made in business practices, such as double-entry bookkeeping and the growth of credit and banking facilities. By translating and commenting on the writings of Greek philosophers and scientists, medieval scholars preserved a priceless intellectual heritage without which the modern mind could never have evolved. During the Middle Ages, Europeans began to lead the rest of the world in the development of technology.

Medieval philosophers, believing that God's law was superior to the decrees of states, provided a theoretical basis for opposing tyrannical kings who violated Christian principles. The idea that both the ruler and the ruled are bound by a higher law would become a principal element of modern liberal thought. The Christian stress on the sacred worth of the individual and on the higher law of God has never ceased to influence Western civilization. The Christian commandment to "love thy neighbor" has permeated modern reform movements.

Feudalism also contributed to the history of liberty. The idea evolved that law should not be imposed by an absolute monarch, but requires the collaboration of king and subjects; that a king too should be bound by the law; and that lords should have the right to resist a monarch who violates agreements. Related to this development was the emergence of representative institutions, notably the English Parliament. The king was expected to consult its members on matters concerning the realm's affairs.

Despite these concrete elements of continuity, the characteristic outlook of the Middle Ages is much different from that of the modern world. Religion was the integrating feature of the Middle Ages, whereas science and secularism determine the modern outlook. Medieval thought began with the existence of God and the truth of his revelation as interpreted by the church, which set the standards and defined the purposes for human endeavor.

The medieval mind rejected the fundamental principle of Greek philosophy and modern thought—the autonomy of reason. Without the guidance of revealed truth, reason was seen as feeble. Unlike either ancient or modern thinkers, medieval scholars believed ultimately that reason alone could not provide a unified view of nature or society. To understand nature, law, morality, or the state, it was necessary to know its relationship to a supernatural order, a higher world.

In the modern view, both nature and the human intellect are self-sufficient. Nature is a mathematical system that operates without miracles or any other form of divine intervention. To comprehend nature and society, the mind needs no divine assistance; it accepts no authority above reason. The modern mind finds it unacceptable to reject conclusions of science on the basis of clerical authority and revelation, or to base politics, law, and economics on religion; it rejects the medieval division of the universe into a heavenly realm of perfection and a lower earthly realm. Scientific and secular attitudes have driven Christianity and faith from their central position to the periphery of human concerns.

The transformation of the medieval worldview based on religion into the modern view based on science and secularism occurred over a span of four centuries. We shall now examine the movements that helped shape the modern world: the Renaissance, the Reformation, the Commercial Revolution, the growth of national states, the Scientific Revolution, the Enlightenment, and the Industrial Revolution.

Notes

1. W. H. Auden, ed., *The Portable Greek Reader* (New York: Viking, 1952), p. 38.

2. Benjamin Farrington, *Greek Science* (Baltimore: Penguin Books, 1961), p. 301.

Western Civilization

A Brief History

Fifth Edition

Geography of Europe

The map on the following pages shows the continent of Europe and the countries around the Mediterranean Sea, together with the physical features of the land such as major rivers and other bodies of water, mountains and changes of elevation, and the names of countries and their capitals. A knowledge of the geography of this area will help give a sense of the relationship between geography and history, of how the characteristics of the terrain and the availability of rivers and other bodies of water affected the movement of people and the relationship between people and environment throughout history.

Europe is the smallest continent in the world with the exception of Australia. The other continents are Africa, Asia, North America, South America, and Antarctica. The continent of Europe, which can be viewed as the western extension of the Asian landmass, is distinctive in its configuration. Peninsulas make up a significant portion of the continent's land area. This feature gives Europe an unusually long coastline, equal in distance to one and a half times around the equator (37,877 miles). Europe's western boundary is the Atlantic Ocean, while the Ural Mountains, Ural River, and Caspian Sea—in Russia and Kazakhstan—form its eastern boundary. Europe extends southward to the Caucasus Mountains, the Black Sea, and the Mediterranean Sea. The continent extends to the Arctic Ocean in the north. Off the mainland but considered by geographers to be part of Europe are thousands of islands, most notably the British Isles to the northwest.

North Americans are often surprised to discover the small size of the European continent. The geographic area of France, for example, is less than that of Texas; England is similar in size to Alabama. The distance from London to Paris is about the same as from New York to Boston; the distance from Berlin to Moscow is comparable to that of Chicago to Denver. And the entire continent of Europe is about the size of Canada.

MAJOR PENINSULAS AND ISLANDS   There are five major European peninsulas: the Iberian (Portugal and Spain); the Apennine (Italy); the Balkan (Albania, Bulgaria, Greece, and parts of the former Yugoslavian republics and Turkey); the Scandinavian (Norway and Sweden); and Jutland (Denmark). Ireland and the United Kingdom of England, Wales, and Scotland make up the British Isles. Major islands of the Mediterranean Sea include the Balearic Islands, Corsica, Sardinia, Sicily, Crete, and Cyprus.

SEAS, LAKES, AND RIVERS   Europe's irregular coastline encloses large areas of the surrounding waters into bays, gulfs, and seas. In the Mediterranean Sea are located, from west to east, the Tyrrhenian Sea (between Italy and Sicily, and Sardinia and Corsica), the Adriatic Sea (between Italy and the former Yugoslavian republics), the Ionian Sea (between Italy and Greece), and the Aegean Sea (between Greece and Turkey).

The Baltic Sea, in the north, is bordered by Finland, Estonia, Latvia, Lithuania, Poland, Germany, and Sweden, and connected by narrow channels to the North Sea, which lies between Great Britain and the countries of the northwestern mainland. The English Channel separates England and France, and the Bay of Biscay borders the west coast of France and the north coast of Spain. The Black Sea, on the southern border of Russia and the Ukraine, is connected by water passages to the Aegean Sea. The Caspian Sea, which lies partly in Russia and Kazakhstan, and

Elevation

Meters	Feet
4,000	13,120
2,000	6,560
500	1,640
200	656
Sea level	Sea level
Below sea level	Below sea level

⊛ National capital

• Other city

0 100 200 300 400 500 Km.

0 100 200 300 400 500 Mi.

ATLANTIC

OCEAN

North Sea

NORWAY

Oslo ⊛

SWE

DENMARK

Copenhagen ⊛

SCOTLAND

NORTHERN IRELAND

UNITED KINGDOM

IRELAND

Dublin ⊛

ENGLAND

WALES

London •

Thames

NETHERLANDS

Amsterdam ⊛

Berlin ⊛

GERMANY

Elbe

Prague ⊛

CZ REPU

English Channel

Brussels ⊛

BELGIUM

LUXEMBOURG

Luxembourg ⊛

Seine

Paris ⊛

FRANCE

Loire

Bern ⊛

SWITZERLAND

ALPS

AUSTR

Vi

Po

SLOVEN

Ljubljana ⊛

APENNINES

Adriatic

Bay

of

Biscay

PYRENEES

Ebro

PORTUGAL

SPAIN

Madrid •

Lisbon ⊛

Corsica

Rome ⊛

ITALY

Tyrrhenian

Sea

Sardinia

Balearic Is.

GIBRALTAR
(Gr. Br.)

Algiers •

Sicily

Rabat ⊛

Tunis ⊛

MALTA

MOROCCO

TUNISIA

Tripoli ⊛

ALGERIA

LIBYA

partly in Asia, is the world's largest saltwater lake and is the lowest point in Europe at 92 feet below sea level.

Europe's many rivers have served as transportation routes for thousands of years. Several of the major rivers, including the longest, flow across the Russian plain. The Volga, Europe's longest river (2,194 miles), rises west of Moscow and empties into the Caspian Sea. It is also linked by canals and other river systems to the Arctic Ocean and the Baltic Sea. The Dnieper flows south through the agricultural heartland of the Ukraine into the Black Sea.

Europe's second longest river, the Danube (1,777 miles), is the principal waterway in the southeastern part of the continent. It originates in Germany and flows through Austria, Slovakia, Hungary, the former Yugoslavian republics, Bulgaria, and Romania into the Black Sea. The Rhine winds northward from the Alps through western Germany and the Netherlands into the North Sea, which is also the destination of the Elbe River in eastern Germany. In France, the Rhône flows south into the Mediterranean, and the Seine and Loire flow west to the English Channel and the Bay of Biscay. Other important waterways are the Po in northern Italy, the Vistula in Poland, and the Thames in England.

The proximity of most areas of the European landmass to the coastline or to major river systems is important to understanding the historical development of European civilization. Trading routes and major cities developed along these waterways, and rivers have served as natural boundaries.

LAND REGIONS   Europe, despite its small size, presents a wide range of landforms, from rugged mountains to sweeping plains. These landforms can be separated into four major regions: the Northwest Mountains, the Great European Plain, the Central Uplands, and the Alpine Mountain System. The mountains of the Northwest Region cover most of the region, running through northwestern France, Ireland, northern Great Britain, Norway, Sweden, northern Finland, and the northwest corner of Russia.

The Great European Plain covers almost all of the European part of the former Soviet Union, extending from the Arctic Ocean to the Caucasus Mountains. This belt stretches westward across Poland, Germany, Belgium, the western portion of France, and southeastern England.

The Central Uplands is a belt of high plateaus, hills, and low mountains. It reaches from the central plateau of Portugal, across Spain, the central highlands of France, to the hills and mountains of southern Germany, the Czech Republic, and Slovakia.

The Alpine Mountain System is made up of several mountain chains. Included in this system are the Pyrenees between Spain and France, the Alps in southeastern France, northern Italy, Switzerland, and western Austria, and the Apennine range in Italy. Also included are the mountain ranges of the Balkan Peninsula, the Carpathian Mountains in Slovakia and Romania, and the Caucasus Mountains between the Black and Caspian Seas. These mountain ranges have been formidable barriers and boundaries throughout history, affecting the movement of people and the relationship of people to each other and to the land.

When studying the map of Europe, it is important to notice the proximity of western areas of Asia, especially those at the eastern end of the Mediterranean Sea, to areas of North Africa. The cultures of these areas have not only interacted with those of Europe but have also played a significant role in shaping the history of Western civilization.

Part Three

The Rise of Modernity: From the Renaissance to the Enlightenment

1350–1789

A Street in Haarlem, c. 1680, by G. A. Berckheyde (1638–1698).

	Politics and Society	Thought and Culture
1300	Hundreds Years' War (1337–1453)	Italian Renaissance begins (c. 1350)
1400	War of Roses in England (1455–1485) Rule of Ferdinand and Isabella in Spain (1469–1516) Charles VIII of France (1483–1498) Henry VII, beginning of Tudor dynasty in England (1485–1509) Columbus reaches America (1492)	Early Renaissance artists and architects: Brunelleschi, Masaccio, van Eyck Printing with movable type (c. 1450) Humanists: Valla, Pico della Mirandola Late Renaissance artists: Botticelli, Leonardo da Vinci, Michelangelo, Raphael, Bellini, Giorgione, Titian Renaissance spreads to northern Europe (late 15th and early 16th cent.)
1500	Henry VIII of England (1509–1547) Francis I of France (1515–1547) Charles V, Holy Roman Emperor (1519–1556) Henry VIII of England breaks with Rome (1529–1536) Council of Trent (1545–1563) Peace of Augsburg in Germany (1555) Philip II of Spain (1556–1598) Elizabeth I of England (1558–1603) Religious wars in France (1562–1598) Revolt of the Netherlands from Spain (1566–1609) Defeat of Spanish Armada (1588)	Humanists: Castiglione, Erasmus, Montaigne, Rabelais, More, Cervantes, Shakespeare Machiavelli, *The Prince* (1513) Luther writes his Ninety-Five Theses (1517) Copernicus, *On the Revolution of the Heavenly Spheres* (1543)
1600	Thirty Years' War (1618–1648) English Revolution (1640–1660, 1688–1689) Louis XIV of France (1643–1715) Peter the Great of Russia (1682–1725)	Scientists: Kepler, Galileo, Newton Philosophers: Bacon, Descartes, Hobbes, Locke
1700	War of Spanish Succession (1702–1714) War of Austrian Succession (1740–1748) Frederick the Great of Prussia (1740–1786) Maria Theresa of Austria (1740–1780) Seven Years' War (1756–1763) American Declaration of Independence (1776) American Revolution (1776–1783) Beginning of French Revolution (1789)	Enlightenment thinkers: Voltaire, Montesquieu, Rousseau, Diderot, Hume, Adam Smith, Thomas Jefferson, Kant

Chapter 8

Transition to the Modern Age: Renaissance and Reformation

*F*rom the Italian Renaissance of the fifteenth century through the Age of Enlightenment of the eighteenth century, the outlook and institutions of the Middle Ages disintegrated and distinctly modern forms emerged. The radical change in European civilization affected every level of society. On the economic level, commerce and industry expanded greatly, and capitalism largely replaced medieval forms of economic organization. On the political level, central government grew stronger at the expense of feudalism. On the religious level, the rise of Protestantism fragmented the unity of Christendom. On the social level, middle-class townspeople, increasing in number and wealth, began to play a more important role in economic and cultural life. On the cultural level, the clergy lost its monopoly over learning, and the otherworldly orientation of the Middle Ages gave way to a secular outlook in literature and the arts. Theology, the queen of knowledge in the Middle Ages, surrendered its crown to science, and reason, which had been subordinate to revelation, asserted its independence.

Many of these tendencies manifested themselves dramatically during the Renaissance (1350–1600). The word *renaissance* means "rebirth," and it is used to refer to the attempt by artists and thinkers to recover and apply the ancient learning and standards of Greece and Rome. During the Renaissance, individuals showed an increasing concern for worldly life and self-consciously aspired to shape their destinies, an attitude that is the key to modernity.

To be sure, the Renaissance was not a complete and abrupt break with the Middle Ages. Many medieval ways and attitudes persisted. Nevertheless, the view that the Renaissance represents the birth of modernity has much to recommend it. Renaissance writers and artists themselves were aware of their age's novelty. They looked back on the medieval centuries as a "Dark Age" that followed the grandeur of ancient Greece and Rome, and they believed that they were experiencing a rebirth of cultural greatness. Renaissance artists and writers were fascinated by the cultural forms of Greece and Rome; they sought to imitate classical style and to capture the secular spirit of antiquity. In the process, they broke with medieval artistic

and literary forms. They valued the full development of human talent and expressed a new excitement about the possibilities of life in this world. This outlook represents a break with the Middle Ages and the emergence of modernity.

The Renaissance, then, was an age of transition. It saw the rejection of certain elements of the medieval outlook, the revival of classical cultural forms, and the emergence of distinctly modern attitudes. This rebirth began in Italy during the fourteenth century and gradually spread north and west to Germany, France, England, and Spain during the late fifteenth and sixteenth centuries.

The Renaissance was one avenue to modernity; another was the Reformation. By dividing Europe into Catholic and Protestant, the Reformation ended medieval religious unity. It also accentuated the importance of the individual person, a distinctive feature of the modern outlook. It stressed individual conscience rather than clerical authority, insisted on a personal relationship between each man or woman and God, and called attention to the individual's inner religious capacities. ❖

ITALY: BIRTHPLACE OF THE RENAISSANCE

The city-states of northern Italy that spawned the Renaissance were developed urban centers, where people had the wealth, freedom, and inclination to cultivate the arts and to enjoy the fruits of worldly life. In Italy, moreover, reminders of ancient Rome's grandeur were visible everywhere: Roman roads, monuments, and manuscripts intensified the Italians' links to their Roman past. Northern Italian city-states had developed into flourishing commercial and banking centers and had monopolized trade in the Mediterranean during the twelfth and thirteenth centuries. The predominance of business and commerce within these city-states meant that the feudal nobility, which held the land beyond the city walls, played a much less important part in government than it

Chronology 8.1 ❖ The Renaissance and the Reformation

1304–1374	Petrarch, "father of humanism"
c. 1445	Johann Gutenberg invents movable metal type
1513	Machiavelli writes *The Prince*
1517	Martin Luther writes his Ninety-five Theses and the Reformation begins
1520	Pope Leo X excommunicates Luther
1524–1526	German peasants revolt
1529	English Parliament accepts Henry VIII's Reformation
1534	Henry VIII is declared head of the Church of England; King Francis I of France declares Protestants to be heretics; Ignatius Loyola founds the Society of Jesus; Anabaptists, radical reformers, capture Münster in Westphalia
1535	Sir Thomas More, English humanist and author of *Utopia*, is executed for treason
1536–1564	Calvin leads the Reformation in Geneva
1545–1563	Council of Trent
1555	Peace of Augsburg

did elsewhere in Europe. By the end of the twelfth century, these city-states had adopted a fairly uniform pattern of republican self-government, built around the office of a chief magistrate.

This republicanism proved precarious, however. During the fourteenth and early fifteenth centuries, republican institutions in one city after another toppled, giving way to rule by despots. The city-states had come to rely on mercenary troops, whose leaders, the notorious *condottieri*—unschooled in and owing no loyalty to the republican tradition—simply seized power during emergencies.

Florence, the leading city of the Renaissance, held out against the trend toward despotism for a long time. But by the mid-fifteenth century, even Florentine republicanism was giving way before the intrigues of a rich banking family, the Medici. They had installed themselves in power in the 1430s with the return of Cosimo de' Medici from exile. Cosimo's grandson, Lorenzo the Magnificent, completed the destruction of the republican constitution in 1480, when he managed to set up a government staffed by his supporters.

New ways of life developed within the Italian city-states. Prosperous businesspeople played a leading role in the political and cultural life of the city. With the expansion of commerce and industry, the feudal values of birth, military prowess, and a fixed hierarchy of lords and vassals decayed in favor of ambition and individual achievement, whether at court, in the counting house, or inside the artist's studio.

Art served as a focus of civic pride and patriotism. Members of the urban upper class became patrons of the arts, providing funds to support promising artists and writers. Just as they contended on the battlefield, rulers competed for art and artists to bolster their prestige. The popes, too, heaped wealth on artists to enhance their own flagging prestige. They became the most lavish patrons of all, as the works of Michelangelo and Raphael testify.

Some women of wealthy and noble Italian families were educated in classical languages and literature and served as patrons of the arts. Thus, Isabella d'Este, wife of the ruler of a small state in northern Italy, knew Latin and Greek, collected

The School of Athens by Raphael (1483–1520). The ancient Greek philosophers, with Plato and Aristotle at the center, are depicted here, assembled in classical grandeur. Painted to decorate the Vatican, the papal palace in Rome, the picture exudes the Renaissance reverence for classical antiquity and reflects the widely held view that ancient philosophy represented a foreshadowing of Christianity and was essentially in harmony with it. *(Stanza della segnaturna, Vatican Palace, Vatican State/Art Resource, NY)*

books, and displayed works of artists that she had commissioned.

The result of this new patronage by popes and patricians was an explosion of artistic creativity. The amount, and especially the nature, of this patronage also helped shape both art and the artist. Portraiture became a separate genre for the first time since antiquity and was developed much further than ever before. Patrician rivalry and insecurity of status, fed by the Renaissance ethic of individual achievement and reward, produced a scramble for honor and reputation. This pursuit fostered the desire to be memorialized in a painting, if not in a sculpture. Distinguished portrait painters and sculptors were in great demand.

The great artists emerged as famous men by virtue of their exercise of brush and chisel. In the Middle Ages, artists had been regarded as craftsmen who did lowly (manual) labor and who, as a result, were to be accorded little, if any, status.

Indeed, for the most part they remained anonymous. But the unparalleled Renaissance demand for art brought artists public recognition.

THE RENAISSANCE OUTLOOK

Increasingly, a secular outlook came to dominate Renaissance society. Intrigued by the active life of the city and eager to enjoy the worldly pleasures that their money could obtain, wealthy merchants and bankers moved away from the medieval preoccupation with salvation. Reviving the Greco-Roman view that the complete individual is a political animal who participates actively in civil affairs, many Renaissance figures were critical of monastic withdrawal and asceticism and of the scholastics' purely contemplative life. To be sure, the urban elite were neither nonbelievers nor atheists, but more and more, religion had to compete with worldly concerns. Consequently, members of the urban upper class paid religion less heed, or at least did not allow it to interfere with their quest for the full life. The challenge and pleasure of living well in this world seemed more exciting than the promise of heaven. This outlook found concrete expression in Renaissance art and literature.

Individualism was another hallmark of the Renaissance. In contrast to medieval thinkers, who emphasized the Christian belief in human weakness, sinfulness, and dependency, Renaissance figures revived the classical confidence in human capacities and extolled the infinite possibilities of individual life. The urban elite sought to assert their own personalities, demonstrate their unique talents, and gain recognition for their accomplishments. Traditional feudal values of birth and place in a fixed hierarchy were superseded by the desire for individual achievement. Individual worth was interpreted far more broadly than it had been by feudal lords, who had equated worth with military prowess. Renaissance Italy produced a distinctive human type, the "universal man": a many-sided person, who not only showed mastery of the ancient classics, an appreciation of and even talent for the visual arts, and a concern for the day-to-day affairs of his city, but also aspired to mold his life into a work of art. Disdaining Christian humility, Renaissance individuals took pride in their talents and worldly accomplishments—"I can work miracles," said the great Leonardo da Vinci. Renaissance artists portrayed the individual character of human beings, captured the rich diversity of human personality, produced the first portraits since Roman times, and affixed their signatures to their works. Renaissance writers probed their own feelings and manifested a self-awareness that characterizes the modern outlook. This new outlook, however, applied almost exclusively to an elite—princes, courtiers, court ladies, wealthy urban families, and exceptionally talented artists and writers.

In later centuries, as the secular outlook gathered strength, it focused even more intently on the individual. It led to the conviction that the individual should be freed from domination by otherworldly concerns, theological dogma, and ecclesiastical authority and should concentrate on the full development of human talents and on improving the quality of earthly existence.

During the Renaissance, the secular spirit and the concern with the individual found expression in the intellectual movement called humanism and in a political theory that separated politics from Christian principles.

Humanism

Humanism, the most characteristic intellectual movement of the Renaissance, was an educational and cultural program based on the study of ancient Greek and Roman literature. The humanist attitude toward antiquity differed from that of medieval scholars, who had taken pains to fit classical learning into a Christian world-view. Renaissance humanists did not subordinate the classics to the requirements of Christian doctrines. Rather, they valued ancient literature for its own sake—for its clear and graceful style and for its insights into human nature. From the ancient classics, humanists expected to learn much that could not be provided by medieval writings: for instance, how to live well in this world and how to perform one's civic duties. For the humanists, the classics were a guide to the good life, the active life. To achieve self-cultivation, to write well, to speak well, and to live well, it was necessary to know the classics. In contrast to scholastic philosophers, who used Greek philosophy to prove the truth of Christian doctrines, Italian humanists used classical learning to nourish their new interest in a worldly life. Whereas medieval scholars were familiar with only some ancient Latin writers, Renaissance humanists restored to circulation every Roman work that could be found. Similarly, knowledge of Greek was very rare in Latin Christendom during the Middle Ages, but Renaissance humanists increasingly cultivated the study of Greek in order to read Homer, Demosthenes, Plato, and other ancients in the original.

Although predominantly a secular movement, Italian humanism was not un-Christian. True, humanists often treated moral problems in a purely secular manner. Yet in dealing with religious and theological issues, they did not challenge Christian belief or question the validity of the Bible. They did, however, attack scholastic philosophy for its hairsplitting arguments and preoccupation with trivial matters. They stressed instead a purer form of Christianity, based on the direct study of the Bible and the writings of the church fathers.

One of the early humanists, sometimes called the father of humanism, was Petrarch (1304–1374). Petrarch and his followers carried the recovery of the classics further through their systematic attempt to discover the classical roots of medieval Italian rhetoric. Petrarch's own efforts to learn Greek were largely unsuccessful, but he advanced humanist learning by encouraging his students to master the ancient tongue. Petrarch was particularly drawn to Cicero, the ancient Roman orator. Following Cicero's example, he maintained that education should consist not only of learning and knowing things, but also of learning how to communicate one's knowledge and how to use it for the public good. Therefore, the emphasis in education should be on rhetoric and moral philosophy—wisdom combined with eloquence. This was the key to virtue in the ruler, the citizen, and the republic. Petrarch helped to make Ciceronian values dominant among the humanists. His followers set up schools to inculcate the new Ciceronian educational ideal.

Implicit in the humanist educational ideal was a radical transformation of the Christian idea of human beings. According to the medieval (Augus-

tinian) view, men and women, because of their sinful nature, were incapable of attaining excellence through their own efforts. They were completely subject to divine will. In contrast, the humanists, recalling the classical Greek concept of human beings, made the achievement of excellence through individual striving the end not only of education, but of life itself. Moreover, because individuals were capable of this goal, it was their duty to pursue it as the end of life. The pursuit was not effortless; indeed, it took extraordinary energy and skill.

People, then, were deemed capable of excellence in every sphere and duty-bound to make the effort. This emphasis on human creative powers was one of the most characteristic and influential doctrines of the Renaissance. A classic expression of it is found in the *Oration on the Dignity of Man* (1486) by Giovanni Pico della Mirandola (1463–1494). Man, said Pico, has the freedom to shape his own life. Pico has God say to man: "We have made you a creature" such that "you may, as the free and proud shaper of your own being, fashion yourself in the form you may prefer."[1]

An attack on the medieval scholastics was also implicit in the humanist educational ideal. Humanists accused scholastics of corrupting the Latin style of ancient Rome and of dealing with useless questions. This humanist emphasis on the uses of knowledge offered a stimulus to science and art.

So hostile were the humanists to things scholastic and medieval that they reversed the prevailing view of history. According to the Christian view, history was a simple unfolding of God's will and providence. The humanists, however, stressed the importance of human actions and human will in history—the importance of people as active participants in the shaping of events. They characterized the epoch preceding their own as a period of decline from classical heights—a dark age—and saw their own time as a period of rebirth, representing the recovery of classical wisdom and ideals. Thus, the humanists invented the notion of the Middle Ages as the period separating the ancient world from their own. To the humanists, then, we owe the current periodization of history into ancient, medieval, and modern. The humanists' view also contained an element of today's idea of progress: they dared to think that they, "the moderns," might even surpass the ancient glories of Greece and Rome.

The humanist emphasis on historical scholarship yielded a method of critical inquiry that could help to undermine traditional loyalties and institutions. Medieval thinkers generally did not relate a text to its times but accepted it uncritically as an authoritative work of wisdom. In contrast, Renaissance humanists approached ancient civilization with a critical attitude; they studied texts in a historical context and examined them for authenticity and accuracy. The work of Lorenzo Valla (c. 1407–1457) provides the clearest example of this trend. Educated as a classicist, Valla trained the guns of critical scholarship on the papacy in his most famous work, *Declamation Concerning the False Decretals of Constantine.* The papal claim to temporal authority rested on a document that purported to verify the so-called Donation of Constantine, through which the Emperor Constantine, when he moved the capital of the Roman Empire to Constantinople in the fourth century, had given the pope dominion over the entire Western Empire. But Valla proved that the document was based on an eighth-century forgery because the language at certain points was unknown in Constantine's time and did not come into use until much later.

Also embedded in the humanist reevaluation of individual potential was a new appreciation of the moral significance of work. For the humanist, the honor, fame, and even glory bestowed by one's city or patron for meritorious deeds were the ultimate rewards for effort. The humanist pursuit of praise and reputation became something of a Renaissance cult.

A Revolution in Political Thought

By turning away from the religious orientation of the Middle Ages and discussing the human condition in secular terms, Renaissance humanists opened up new possibilities for thinking about political and moral problems. Niccolò Machiavelli (1469–1527), a keen observer of Italian politics, saw the Italian city-states, ruled by men whose authority rested solely on their cunning and effective use of force, as a new phenomenon. He recognized that traditional political theory,

concerned with ideal Christian ends, could not adequately explain it. Italian princes made no effort to justify their policies on religious grounds; war was endemic, and powerful cities took over weaker ones; diplomacy was riddled with intrigue, betrayal, and bribery. In such a tooth-and-claw world—where political survival depended on alertness, cleverness, and strength—medieval theorists, who expected the earthly realm to accord with standards revealed by God, seemed utterly irrelevant. Machiavelli simply wanted rulers to understand how to prepare and expand the state's power. In his book *The Prince,* he expounded a new political theory—one that had no place for Christian morality but coincided with the emerging modern secular state. He himself was aware that his study of statecraft in the cold light of reason, free of religious and moral illusions, represented a new departure.

For Machiavelli, survival was the state's overriding aim; it transcended any concern with moral or religious values and the interests of individual subjects. Removing questions of good and evil from the political realm, Machiavelli maintained that the prince may use any means to save the state when its survival is at stake. Successful princes, he contended, have always been indifferent to moral and religious considerations—a lesson of history that rulers ignore at their peril. Thus, if the situation warrants it, the prince can violate agreements with other rulers, go back on his word with his subjects, and resort to cruelty and terror.

Machiavelli broke with the distinguishing feature of medieval thought: the division of the universe into the higher world of the heavens and a lower earthly realm. To this extent, he did for politics what Galileo accomplished a century later for physics. Medieval thinkers believed that rulers derived their power from God and had a religious obligation to govern in accordance with God's commands. Rejecting completely this otherworldly, theocentric orientation, Machiavelli ascribed no divine origin or purpose to the state. He saw it as a natural entity; politics had nothing to do with God's intent or with moral precepts originating in a higher world. Machiavelli's significance as a political thinker rests on the fact that he removed political thought from a religious frame of reference and viewed the state and politi-

Niccolo Machiavelli (1469–1527). Marchiavelli looked back to the ancient Roman republic for his ideals and spent his life serving the city-state of Florence, but as the author of *The Prince,* his name became a byword for atheism and deceit. "Machiavellian" is still used to describe an unscrupulous politician. *(Palazzo Vecchio, Florence, Italy/Erich Lessing/Art Resource, NY)*

cal behavior in the detached and dispassionate manner of a scientist. In secularizing and rationalizing political philosophy, he initiated a trend of thought that we recognize as distinctly modern.

RENAISSANCE ART

The essential meaning of the Renaissance is conveyed through its art, particularly architecture, sculpture, and painting. Renaissance examples of all three art forms reflect a style that stressed proportion, balance, and harmony. These artistic values were achieved through a new, revolutionary conceptualization of space and spatial relations. To a considerable extent, Renaissance art also re-

flects the values of Renaissance humanism: a return to classical models in architecture, to the rendering of the nude figure, and to a heroic vision of human beings.

Medieval art served a religious function: the world was a veil merely hinting at the other perfect and eternal world. Renaissance artists continued to utilize religious themes, but they shattered the dominance of religion over art by shifting attention from heaven to the natural world and to the human being. Renaissance artists depicted the human qualities of men and women and celebrated the beauty and grace of the human form. The reference was less to the other world and more to this world, and people were treated as creatures who found their spiritual destiny as they fulfilled their human one. Renaissance artists also developed a new conception of visual space, which resulted in a naturalistic, three-dimensional rendering of the real world. It was a quantitative space in which the artist, employing reason and mathematics, portrayed the essential form of the object in perspective, as it would appear to the human eye. Thus, at its most distinctive, Renaissance art represents a conscious revolt against the art of the Middle Ages. This revolt produced revolutionary discoveries that served as the foundation of Western art up to the twentieth century.

In art, as in philosophy, the Florentines played a leading role in this esthetic transformation. They, more than anyone else, were responsible for the way artists saw and drew for centuries and for the way most Western people still see or want to see. The first major contributor to Renaissance painting was the Florentine painter Giotto (c. 1276–1337). Borrowing from Byzantine painting, he created figures delineated by alterations in light and shade. He also developed several techniques of perspective, representing three-dimensional figures and objects on two-dimensional surfaces so that they appear to stand in space. Giotto's figures look remarkably alive. They are drawn and arranged in space to tell a story, and their expressions and the illusion of movement they convey heighten the dramatic effect. Giotto's best works were *frescoes,* wall paintings painted while the plaster was still wet, or *fresh.* Lionized in his own day, Giotto had no immediate successors, and his ideas were not taken up and developed further for almost a century.

By the early fifteenth century, the revival of classical learning had begun in earnest. In Florence, it had its artistic counterpart among a circle of architects, painters, and sculptors who sought to revive classical art. The leader of this group was an architect, Filippo Brunelleschi (1377–1446). He designed churches reflecting classical models. To him we also owe a scientific discovery of the first importance in the history of art: the rules of perspective. Giotto had revived the ancient technique of foreshortening; Brunelleschi completed the discovery by rendering perspective in mathematical terms. His devotion to ancient models and his new tool of mathematical perspective set the stage for the further development of Renaissance painting. Brunelleschi's young Florentine friend Masaccio (1401–1428) took up the challenge. Faithful to the new rules of perspective, Masaccio was also concerned with painting statuesque figures and endowing his paintings with a grandeur and simplicity whose inspiration was classical. Perspective came with all the force of religious revelation.

In his work *On Painting*, Leon Battista Alberti (1404–1472), a humanist, scholar, and art theoretician, brought the Renaissance trend toward perspectival art to a summation by advancing the first mathematical theory of artistic perspective. By defining visual space and the relationship between the object and the observer in mathematical terms, Renaissance art and artistic theory helped to pave the way for the development of the modern scientific approach to nature, which later found expression in the astronomy of Copernicus and the physics of Galileo.

Renaissance artists were dedicated to representing things as they are, or at least as they are seen to be. Part of the inspiration for this was also classical. The ancient ideal of beauty was the beautiful nude. Renaissance admiration for ancient art meant that for the first time since the fall of Rome, artists studied anatomy; they learned to draw the human form by having models pose for them, a practice fundamental to artistic training to this day. Another member of Brunelleschi's circle, the Florentine sculptor Donatello (1386–

1466), also showed renewed interest in the human form.

The great Renaissance artists included Leonardo da Vinci (1452–1519), Michelangelo Buonarroti (1475–1564), and Raphael Santi (1483–1520). All of them were closely associated with Florence. Leonardo was a scientist and engineer as well as a great artist. He was an expert at fortifications and gunnery, an inventor, an anatomist, and a naturalist. Bringing careful observation of nature to his paintings, he combined it with powerful psychological insight to produce works of unsurpassed genius, though few in number. Among his most important paintings are *The Last Supper* and *La Gioconda*, or the *Mona Lisa*. The *Mona Lisa* is an example of an artistic invention of Leonardo's—what the Italians call *sfumato*. Leonardo left the outlines of the face a little vague and shadowy; this freed it of any wooden quality, which more exact drawing would impart, and thus made it more lifelike and mysterious.

Michelangelo's creation of artistic harmony derived from a mastery of anatomy and drawing. His model in painting came from sculpture: his paintings are sculpted drawings. He was, of course, a sculptor of the highest genius whose approach to his art was poetic and visionary. Instead of trying to impose form on marble, he thought of sculpting as releasing the form from the rock. Among his greatest sculptures are *David, Moses,* and *The Dying Slave*. Michelangelo was also an architect; patronized by the pope, he designed the dome of the new Saint Peter's Basilica in Rome. But perhaps his most stupendous work was the ceiling of the Sistine Chapel in the Vatican, commissioned by Pope Julius II. In four years, working with little assistance, Michelangelo covered the empty space with the most monumental sculpted pictures ever painted, pictures that summarize the Old Testament story. *The Creation of Adam* is the most famous of these superlative frescoes.

Raphael, the last of these three artistic giants, is especially famous for the sweetness of his Madonnas. But he was capable of painting other subjects and conveying other moods, as his portrait of his patron, *Pope Leo X with Two Cardinals*, reveals.

THE SPREAD OF THE RENAISSANCE

Aided by the invention of printing, the Renaissance spread to Germany, France, England, and Spain in the late fifteenth and sixteenth centuries. In its migration northward, Renaissance culture adapted itself to conditions different from those in Italy—particularly the strength of lay piety. For example, the Brethren of the Common Life was a lay movement emphasizing education and practical piety. Intensely Christian and at the same time anticlerical, the people in such lay movements found in Renaissance culture tools for sharpening their wits against the clergy—not to undermine the faith, but rather to restore it to its apostolic purity.

Thus, northern humanists, like those in Italy, were profoundly devoted to ancient learning. But nothing in northern humanism compares with the non-Christian trend of the Italian Renaissance. The northerners were chiefly interested in the question of what constituted original Christianity. They sought a model in the light of which they might reform the corrupted church of their own time.

Humanism outside Italy was less concerned with the revival of classical values than with the reform of Christianity and society through a program of Christian humanism. The Christian humanists cultivated the new arts of rhetoric and history, as well as the classical languages—Latin, Greek, and Hebrew. But the ultimate purpose of these pursuits was more religious than it had been in Italy, where secular interests predominated. Northern humanists used humanist scholarship and language to satirize and vilify medieval scholastic Christianity and to build a purer, more Scriptural Christianity. The discovery of accurate biblical texts, it was hoped, would lead to a great religious awakening. Protestant reformers, including Martin Luther, relied on humanist scholarship.

Erasmian Humanism

To Erasmus (c. 1466–1536) belongs the credit for making Renaissance humanism an international

Giovanni Arnolfini and His Bride by Jan van Eyck (c. 1390–1441). The painting uses the new technique of perspective and draws a careful, and idealized, portrait of a prosperous married couple in their bedroom. It depicts a world that values privacy, sober prosperity, and intimacy of a certain kind: he stares out at us, while she looks deferentially at him. *(Reproduced by courtesy of the Trustees, The National Gallery, London)*

movement. He was educated in the Netherlands by the Brethren of the Common Life, which was one of the most advanced religious movements of the age, combining mystical piety with rigorous humanist pedagogy. Erasmus traveled throughout Europe as a humanist educator and biblical scholar. Like other Christian humanists, he trusted the power of words and used his pen to attack scholastic theology and clerical abuses and promote his philosophy of Christ. His weapon was satire, and his *Praise of Folly* and *Colloquies* won him a reputation for acid wit vented at the expense of conventional religion.

True religion, Erasmus argued, does not depend on dogma, ritual, or clerical power. Rather, it is revealed clearly and simply in the Bible and therefore is directly accessible to all people, from the wise and great to the poor and humble. Erasmian humanism stressed toleration, kindness, and respect for human rationality.

This clear but quiet voice was drowned out by the storms of the Reformation, and the Erasmian emphasis on the individual's natural capacities succumbed to a renewed emphasis on human sinfulness and dogmatic theology. Erasmus was caught in the middle and condemned on all sides; for him, the Reformation was both a personal and a historical tragedy. He had worked for peace and unity, only to experience a spectacle of war and fragmentation. Erasmian humanism, however, survived these horrors as an ideal, and during the next two centuries, whenever thinkers sought toleration and rational religion, they looked back to Erasmus for inspiration.

French and English Humanism

François Rabelais (c. 1494–c. 1553), a former monk, exemplified the humanist spirit in France. In response to religious dogmatism, he asserted the essential goodness of the individual and the right to enjoy the world rather than being bound by the fear of a punishing God. His folk-epic, *Gargantua and Pantagruel,* celebrates earthly life and earthly enjoyments, expresses an appreciation for secular learning and a confidence in human nature, and attacks monastic orders and clerical education for stifling the human spirit.

According to Rabelais, once freed from dogmatic theology, with its irrelevant concerns, and narrow-minded clergy, who deprived them of life's joys, people could, by virtue of their native goodness, build a paradise on earth and disregard the one dreamed up by theologians. In *Gargantua and Pantagruel,* Rabelais imagined a monastery where men and women spend their lives "not in laws, statutes, or rules, but according to their own free will and pleasure." They slept and ate when they desired and learned to "read, write, sing, play upon several musical instruments, and speak five or six . . . languages and compose in them all very quaintly." They observed only one rule: "do what thou wilt."[2]

The most influential humanist of the early English Renaissance was Sir Thomas More (1478–1535), who studied at Oxford. His impact came from both his writing and his career. Trained as a lawyer, he was a successful civil servant and member of Parliament. His most famous book is *Utopia,* the first major utopian treatise to be written in the West since Plato's *Republic* and one of the most original works of the entire Renaissance. Many humanists had attacked private wealth as the principal source of pride, greed, and human cruelty. However, only More carried this insight to its ultimate conclusion: in *Utopia,* he called for the elimination of private property. He had too keen a sense of human weakness to think that people could become perfect, but he used *Utopia* to call attention to contemporary abuses and to suggest radical reforms.

More succeeded Cardinal Wolsey as lord chancellor under Henry VIII. But when the king broke with the Roman Catholic church, More resigned, unable to reconcile his conscience with the king's rejection of papal supremacy. Three years later, in July 1535, More was executed for treason because he refused to swear an oath acknowledging the king's ecclesiastical supremacy.

William Shakespeare (1564–1616), widely considered the greatest playwright the world has ever produced, gave expression to conventional Renaissance values: honor, heroism, and the struggle against fate and fortune. But there is nothing conventional about Shakespeare's treatment of characters possessing these virtues. His greatest plays, the tragedies (*King Lear, Julius Caesar,* and others), explore a common theme: men, even heroic men, despite virtue, are able to overcome their human weaknesses only with the greatest difficulty, if at all. What fascinated Shakespeare was the contradiction between the Renaissance image of nobility, which is often the self-image of Shakespeare's heroes, and humans' capacity for evil and self-destruction. The plays are thus intensely human, but so much so that humanism fades into the background; art transcends doctrine to represent life itself.

THE RENAISSANCE AND THE MODERN AGE

The Renaissance, then, marks the birth of modernity—in art, in the idea of the individual's role in history and nature, and in society, politics, war, and diplomacy. Central to this birth was a bold new view of human nature that departed from the medieval view: individuals in all endeavors are not constrained by a destiny imposed by God from the outside but are free to make their own destiny, guided only by the example of the past, the force of present circumstances, and the drives of their own inner nature. Set free from theology, individuals were seen as the products, and in turn the shapers, of history; their future would be the work of their own free will.

Within the Italian city-states where the Renaissance was born, rich merchants were at least as important as the church hierarchy and the old nobility. Commercial wealth and a new politics produced a new culture that relied heavily on ancient Greece and Rome. This return to antiquity also entailed a rejection of the Middle Ages as dark, barbarous, and rude. The humanists clearly preferred the secular learning of ancient Greece and Rome to the clerical learning of the more recent past. The reason for this was obvious: the ancients had the same worldly concerns as the humanists; the scholastics did not.

The revival of antiquity by the humanists did not mean, however, that they identified completely with it. The revival itself was done too self-consciously for that. In the very act of looking back, the humanists differentiated themselves from the past and recognized that they were different. They were in this sense the first modern historians, because they could study and appreciate the past for its own sake and, to some degree, on its own terms.

In the works of Renaissance artists and thinkers, the world was, to a large extent, depicted and explained without reference to a higher supernatural realm of meaning and authority. This is clearly seen in Machiavelli's analysis of politics. Renaissance humanism exuded a deep confidence in the capacities of able people, instructed in the wisdom of the ancients, to understand and change the world.

This new confidence was closely related to another distinctive feature of the Renaissance: the cult of the individual. Both prince and painter were motivated in part by the desire to display their talents and to satisfy their ambitions. This individual striving was rewarded and encouraged by the larger society of rich patrons and calculating princes, which valued ability. Gone was the medieval Christian emphasis on the virtue of self-denial and the sin of pride. Instead, the Renaissance placed the highest value on self-expression and self-fulfillment—on the realization of individual potential, especially of the gifted few. The Renaissance fostered an atmosphere in which talent, even genius, was allowed to flourish.

To be sure, the Renaissance image of the individual and the world, bold and novel, was the exclusive prerogative of a small, well-educated urban elite and did not reach down to include the masses. Nevertheless, the Renaissance set an example of what people might achieve in art and architecture, taste and refinement, education and urban culture. In many fields, the Renaissance set the cultural standards of the modern age.

BACKGROUND TO THE REFORMATION: THE MEDIEVAL CHURCH IN CRISIS

The Renaissance had revitalized European intellectual life and in the process discarded the medieval preoccupation with theology. Similarly, the Reformation marked the beginning of a new religious outlook. The Protestant Reformation, however, did not originate in the elite circles of humanistic scholars. Rather, it was sparked by Martin Luther (1483–1546), an obscure German monk and brilliant theologian. Luther started a rebellion against the church's authority that in less than one decade shattered the religious unity of Christendom. Begun in 1517, the Reformation dominated European history throughout much of the sixteenth century.

The Roman Catholic church, centered in Rome, was the one European institution that transcended geographic, ethnic, linguistic, and national boundaries. For centuries, it had extended its influence into every aspect of European society and culture. As a result, however, its massive wealth and power appeared to take precedence over its commitment to the search for holiness in this world and salvation in the next. Encumbered by wealth, addicted to international power, and protective of their own interests, the clergy, from the pope down, became the focus of a storm of criticism, starting in the Late Middle Ages.

In the fourteenth century, as kings increased their power and as urban centers with their sophisticated laity grew in size and number, people began to question the authority of the international church and its clergy. Political theorists rejected the pope's claim to supremacy over kings. The central idea of medieval Christendom—a Christian commonwealth led by the papacy—increasingly fell into disrepute. Theorists argued that the church was only a spiritual body, and therefore its power did not extend to the political realm. They said that the pope had no authority over kings, that the state needed no guidance from the papacy, and that the clergy were not above secular law. During the late fourteenth century, Latin Christendom witnessed the first systematic attacks ever launched against the church. Church corruption—such as the selling of indulgences (see the upcoming section on "The Break with Catholicism"), nepotism (the practice of appointing one's relatives to offices), the pursuit of personal wealth by bishops, and the sexual indulgence of the clergy—was nothing new. What was new and startling was the willingness of both educated and uneducated Christians to attack these practices publicly.

Thus, the Englishman John Wycliffe and the Bohemian Jan Hus (see "Fourteenth-Century Heresies" in the preceding chapter), both learned theologians, denounced the wealth of the clergy as a violation of Christ's precepts and attacked the church's authority at its root by arguing that the church did not control an individual's destiny. They maintained that salvation depends not on participating in the church's rituals or receiving its sacraments, but on accepting God's gift of faith.

Wycliffe's and Hus's efforts to initiate reform coincided with a powerful resurgence of religious feeling in the form of mysticism. Late medieval mystics sought an immediate and personal communication with God, and such experiences inspired them to advocate concrete reforms aimed at renewing the church's spirituality. The church hierarchy inevitably regarded mysticism with some suspicion, for if individuals could experience God directly, they would seemingly have little need for the church and its rituals. In the fourteenth century, these mystical movements seldom became heretical. But in the sixteenth and seventeenth centuries, radical reformers often found in Christian mysticism a powerful alternative to institutional control and even to the need for a priesthood.

With the advent of Lutheranism, personal faith, rather than adherence to the practices of the church, became central to the religious life of European Protestants. Renaissance humanists had sought to reinstitute the wisdom of ancient times; Protestant reformers wanted to restore the spirit of early Christianity, in which faith seemed purer, believers more sincere, and clergy uncorrupted by luxury and power. By the 1540s, the Roman Catholic church had initiated its own internal reformation, but it came too late to stop the movement toward Protestantism in northern and Western Europe.

THE LUTHERAN REVOLT

The Protestant Reformation of the sixteenth century ushered in a spiritual revolution that had a great impact on the Western world. This reformation was precipitated and largely defined by the Augustinian monk Martin Luther. Luther had no intention of founding a new church or overthrowing the political and ecclesiastical order of his native Germany. Rather, it was a search to resolve his own spiritual crisis that led to the permanent schism within the church. In his youth, Luther at first fulfilled his father's wish and studied law, but at the age of twenty-one, he suddenly abandoned his legal studies to enter the Augustinian monastery at Erfurt. Luther began his search for spiritual and personal identity, and therefore for salvation, within the strict confinement and discipline of the monastery. He pursued his theological studies there and prepared for ordination.

Portrait of Martin Luther by Lucas Cranach the Elder (1529). Martin Luther was both a dour and thoughtful man with great determination. *(Uffizi, Florence/Erich Lessing/Art Resource, NY)*

The Break with Catholicism

As he studied and prayed, Luther grew increasingly terrified by the possibility of his damnation. As a monk, he sought union with God, and he understood the church's teaching that salvation depended on faith, works (meaning acts of charity, prayer, fasting, and so on), and grace—God's influence and favor, which sanctifies and regenerates human life. He participated in the sacraments of the church, which, according to its teaching, were intended to give grace. Indeed, after his ordination, Luther administered the sacraments. Yet he still felt the weight of his sins,

and nothing the church could offer seemed to relieve that burden. Seeking solace and salvation, Luther increasingly turned to reading the Bible. Two passages seemed to speak directly to him: "For therein is the righteousness of God revealed from faith to faith: as it is written, 'He who through faith is righteous shall live'" (Romans 1:17); and "They are justified by his grace as a gift, through the redemption which is in Christ Jesus" (Romans 3:24). In these two passages, Luther found, for the first time in his adult life, some hope for his own salvation. Faith, freely given by God through Christ, enables the recipient to receive salvation.

The concept of salvation by faith alone provided an answer to Luther's spiritual quest. Practicing such good works as prayer, fasting, pilgrimages, and participation in the Mass and the other sacraments had never brought Luther peace of mind. He concluded that no amount of good works, however necessary for maintaining the Christian community, would bring salvation. Through reading the Bible and through faith alone, the Christian could find the meaning of earthly existence. For Luther, the true Christian was a courageous figure who faced the terrifying quest for salvation armed only with the hope that God had granted the gift of faith. The new Christian served others not to trade good works for salvation, but solely to fulfill the demands of Christian love.

The starting point for the Reformation was Luther's attack in 1517 on the church's practice of selling indulgences. The church taught that some individuals go directly to heaven or hell, while others go to heaven only after spending time in purgatory—a period of expiation necessary for those who have sinned excessively in this life but who have had the good fortune to repent before death. To die in a state of mortal sin meant to writhe in hell eternally. Naturally, people worried about how long they might have to suffer in purgatory. Indulgences were intended to remit portions of that time and were granted to individuals by the church for their prayers, attendance at Mass, and almost any acts of charity—including monetary offerings to the church. This last good work was the most controversial, since it could easily appear that people were buying their way into heaven.

In the autumn of 1517, a Dominican friar named John Tetzel was selling indulgences in the area near Wittenberg. Luther launched his attack on Tetzel and the selling of indulgences by tacking on the door of the Wittenberg castle church his Ninety-five Theses. Luther's theses (propositions) challenged the entire notion of selling indulgences not only as a corrupt practice, but also as a theologically unsound assumption—namely, that salvation can be earned by good works.

At the heart of Luther's argument in the Ninety-five Theses and in his later writings were the beliefs that the individual achieves salvation through inner religious feeling, a sense of contrition for sins, and a trust in God's mercy, and that church attendance, fasting, pilgrimages, charity, and other good works did not earn salvation. The church, in contrast, held that *both* faith and good works were necessary for salvation. Luther further insisted that every individual could discover the meaning of the Bible unaided by the clergy; the church, however, maintained that only the clergy could read and interpret the Bible properly. Luther argued that in matters of faith there was no difference between the clergy and the laity, for each person could receive faith directly and freely from God. But the church held that the clergy were intermediaries between individuals and God and that, in effect, Christians reached eternal salvation through the clergy. For Luther, no priest, no ceremony, and no sacrament could bridge the gulf between the Creator and his creatures. Hope lay only in a personal relationship between the individual and God, as expressed through faith in God's mercy and grace. By declaring that clergy and church rituals do not hold the key to salvation, Luther rejected the church's claim that it alone offered men and women the way to eternal life.

Recognizing that he might be in danger if he continued to preach without a protector, Luther appealed for support to the prince of his district, Frederick, the elector of Saxony. The elector was a powerful man in international politics—one of seven lay and ecclesiastical princes who chose the Holy Roman Emperor. Frederick's support convinced church officials, including the pope, that this monk would have to be dealt with cautiously. When the pope finally acted against Luther in 1520, it was too late; Luther had been given the needed time to promote his views. He proclaimed that the pope was the Antichrist and that the church was the "most lawless den of robbers, the most shameless of all brothels, the very kingdom of sin, death and Hell."[3] When the papal bull excommunicating him was delivered, Luther burned it.

No longer members of the church, Luther and his followers established congregations for the purpose of Christian worship. Christians outside the church needed protection, and in 1520 Luther published the *Address to the Christian Nobility of the German Nation*. In it he appealed to the emperor and the German princes to reform the church and to cast off their allegiance to the pope, who, he argued, had used taxes and political power to exploit them for centuries. His appeal produced some success; the Reformation flourished on the resentment against foreign papal intervention that had long festered in Germany. In this and other treatises, Luther made it clear that he wanted to present no threat to legitimate political authority, that is, to the power of the German princes.

In 1521, Charles V, the Holy Roman Emperor, who was a devout Catholic, summoned Luther to Worms, giving him a pass of safe conduct. There, Luther was to answer to the charge of heresy, both an ecclesiastical and a civil offense. When asked to recant, Luther replied: "Unless I am convinced of error by the testimony of Scripture or by clear reason . . . I cannot and will not recant anything, for it is neither safe nor honest to act against one's conscience. God help me. Amen." Shortly after this confrontation with the emperor, Luther went into hiding to escape arrest. During that one-year period, he translated the New Testament into German. His followers, or Lutherans, were eventually called *Protestants*—those who protested against the established church—and the term became generic for all followers of the Reformation.

The Appeal and Spread of Lutheranism

Rapidly disseminated by the new printing press, the tenets of Protestantism offered the hope of revitalization and renewal to Protestantism's adherents. Lutheranism appealed to the devout, who resented the worldliness and lack of piety of many clergy. But the movement found its greatest following among German townspeople, who objected to money flowing from their country to Rome in the form of church taxes and payment for church offices. In addition, the Reformation provided the nobility with an unprecedented opportunity to confiscate church lands, eliminate church taxes, and gain the support of their subjects by serving as leaders of a popular and dynamic religious movement. The Reformation also gave the nobles a way of resisting the Catholic Holy Roman Emperor, Charles V, who wanted to extend his authority over the German princes. Resenting the Italian domination of the church, many other Germans who supported Martin Luther believed that they were freeing German Christians from foreign control.

Lutheranism drew support from the peasants as well, for they saw Luther as their champion against their oppressors—both lay and ecclesiastical lords and the townspeople. Indeed, in his writings and sermons, Luther often attacked the greed of the princes and bemoaned the plight of the poor. Undoubtedly, Luther's successful confrontation with the authorities served to inspire the peasants. In 1524, these long-suffering people openly rebelled against their lords. The Peasants' Revolt spread to over one-third of Germany; some 300,000 people took up arms against their masters.

Luther, however, had no wish to associate his movement with a peasant uprising and risk alienating the nobility who supported him. As a political conservative, he hesitated to challenge secular authority; to him, the good Christian was an obedient subject. Therefore, he virulently attacked the rebellious peasants, urging the nobility to become "both judge and executioner" and to "knock down, strangle, and stab" the insurgents. By 1525, the peasants had been put down by the sword. The failure of the Peasants' Revolt meant that the German peasantry remained among the most backward and oppressed until well into the nineteenth century.

Initially, the Holy Roman Emperor, who was at war with France over parts of Italy and whose eastern territories were threatened by the Ottoman Turks, hesitated to intervene militarily in the strife between Lutheran and Catholic princes—a delay that proved crucial. Despite years of warfare, Charles V was unable to subdue the Lutheran princes. The religious conflict was settled by the Peace of Augsburg (1555), which decreed that each territorial prince should determine the religion of his subjects. Broadly speaking, northern Germany became largely Protestant, while Bavaria and other southern territories remained in the Roman Catholic church. The Holy Roman Emperor, who had been successfully challenged by the Lutheran princes, saw his power diminished. The decentralization of the empire and its division into Catholic and Protestant regions would block German unity until the last part of the nineteenth century.

THE SPREAD OF THE REFORMATION

Nothing better illustrates people's dissatisfaction with the church in the early sixteenth century than the rapid spread of Protestantism. There was a pattern to this phenomenon. Protestantism grew strong in northern Europe—northern Germany, Scandinavia, the Netherlands, and England. It failed in the Latin countries, although not without a struggle in France. In general, Protestantism was an urban phenomenon, and it prospered where local magistrates supported it and where the distance from Rome was greatest.

Calvinism

The success of the Reformation outside Germany and Scandinavia derived largely from the work of John Calvin (1509–1564), a French scholar and theologian. Sometime in 1533 or 1534, Calvin met French followers of Luther and became convinced of the truth of the new theology. He began to spread its beliefs immediately after his conversion, and within a year he and his friends were in trouble with the civil and ecclesiastical authorities.

Calvin soon abandoned his humanistic and literary studies to become a preacher of the Reformation. Even early in his religious experience, he emphasized the power of God over sinful and

Interior of St. Odulphus, Assendelft, the Netherlands. Early Calvinism was an austere faith that is manifest in the exact and simple construction of Protestant churches in the Dutch Republic, as shown in this painting by Pieter Saenredem. Many of these churches are still standing. *(Rijksmuseum-Stichting, Amsterdam)*

corrupt humanity. Calvin's God thundered and demanded obedience, and the terrible distance between God and the individual was mediated only by Christ. Calvin embraced a stern theology, holding that God's laws must be rigorously obeyed, that social and moral righteousness must be earnestly pursued, that political life must be carefully regulated, and that human emotions must be strictly controlled.

Even more than Luther, Calvin explained salvation in terms of uncertain predestination: that God, who grants grace for his own inscrutable reasons, knows in advance who will be saved and who will be condemned to hell. Calvin argued that although people are predestined to salvation or damnation, they can never know their fate with certainty in advance. This terrible decree could and did lead some people to despair. To others—

in a paradox difficult for the modern mind to grasp—Calvinism gave a sense of self-assurance and righteousness that made the saint—that is, the truly predestined man or woman—into a new kind of European. Most of Calvin's followers seemed to believe that in having understood the fact of predestination, they had received a bold insight into their unique relationship with God.

Calvinists were individuals who assumed that only unfailing dedication to God's law could be seen as a sign of salvation; thus, Calvinism made for stern men and women, active in their congregations and willing to suppress vice in themselves and others. Calvinism could also produce revolutionaries willing to defy any temporal authorities perceived to be in violation of God's laws. For Calvinists, obedience to Christian law became the dominating principle of life. Forced to flee

France, Calvin finally sought safety in Geneva, a small, prosperous Swiss city near the French border. There, he eventually established a Protestant church that closely regulated the citizens' personal and social lives. Elders of the Calvinist church governed the city and imposed strict discipline in dress, sexual mores, church attendance, and business affairs; they severely punished irreligious and sinful behavior. Prosperous merchants, as well as small shopkeepers, saw in Calvinism doctrines that justified the self-discipline they already exercised in their own lives and wished to impose on the unruly masses. They particularly approved of Calvin's economic views, for he saw nothing sinful in commercial activities, unlike many Catholic clergy.

Geneva became the center of international Protestantism. Calvin trained a new generation of Protestant reformers of many nationalities, who carried his message back to their homelands. Calvin's *Institutes of the Christian Religion* (1536), in its many editions, became (after the Bible) the leading textbook of the new theology. In the second half of the sixteenth century, Calvin's theology of predestination spread into France, England, the Netherlands, and parts of the Holy Roman Empire.

Calvin always opposed any recourse to violence and supported the authority of magistrates. Yet when monarchy became their persecutor, his followers felt compelled to resist. Calvinist theologians became the first political theoreticians of modern times to publish cogent arguments for opposition to monarchy, and eventually for political revolution. In France and later in the Netherlands, Calvinism became a revolutionary ideology, complete with an underground organization composed of dedicated followers who challenged monarchical authority. In the seventeenth century, the English version of Calvinism—Puritanism—performed the same function. Thus, in certain circumstances, Calvinism possessed the moral force to undermine the claims of the monarchical state on the individual.

France

Although Protestantism was illegal in France after 1534, the Protestant minority, the Huguenots, grew, becoming a well-organized underground movement. Huguenot churches, often under the protection of powerful nobles, assumed an increasingly political character in response to monarchy-sponsored persecution. French Protestants became sufficiently organized and militant to challenge their persecutors, King Henry II and the Guise, one of the foremost Catholic families in Europe, and in 1562 civil war erupted between Catholics and Protestants. What followed was one of the most brutal religious wars in the history of Europe. In 1572, on Saint Bartholomew's Day, the gruesome slaughter of thousands of Protestant men, women, and children stained the streets with blood. So intense was the religious hatred at the time that the massacre inspired the pope to have a Mass said in thanksgiving for a Catholic "victory."

After nearly thirty years of brutal fighting throughout France, victory went to the Catholic side—but barely. Henry of Navarre, a Protestant leader, became King Henry IV, though only after he agreed to reconvert to Catholicism. Henry established a tentative peace by granting Protestants limited toleration. In 1598, he issued the Edict of Nantes, the first document in any national state that attempted to institutionalize a degree of religious toleration. In the seventeenth century, the successors of Henry IV (who was assassinated in 1610) gradually weakened and then in 1685 revoked the edict. The theoretical foundations of toleration, as well as its practice, remained tenuous in early modern Europe.

England

The king himself rather than religious reformers initiated the Reformation in England. Henry VIII (1509–1547) removed the English church from the jurisdiction of the papacy because the pope refused to grant him an annulment of his marriage to his first wife. The English Reformation thus began as a political act on the part of a self-confident Renaissance monarch. But the Reformation's origins stretched back into the Middle Ages, for England had a long tradition of heresy, as well as anticlericalism, rooted in Wycliffe's actions in the fourteenth century.

When Henry VIII decided that he wanted a divorce from the Spanish princess Catherine of

Black Sea

OTTOMAN EMPIRE

LITHUANIA

PRUSSIA

•Warsaw

POLAND

Baltic Sea

S W E D E N

TRANSYLVANIA

•Pest

Buda•

HUNGARY

NORWAY

•Berlin

BRANDENBURG

•Wittenberg

Prague•

BOHEMIA

MORAVIA

Vienna•

AUSTRIA

Hamburg•

•Leipzig

DENMARK

Münster•

SAXONY

•Nuremberg

•Munich

BAVARIA

Augsburg•

•Trent

Adriatic Sea

HOLY ROMAN EMPIRE

Venice•

•Milan

Zurich•

SWITZERLAND

•Rome

Naples•

ITALY

Corsica

Sardinia

North Sea

NETHERLANDS

Worms•

Basel•

Geneva•

•Avignon

WESTPHALIA

Amsterdam•

Brussels•

Strasbourg•

•Noyon

•Paris

Mediterranean Sea

FRANCE

Edinburgh•

SCOTLAND

•Oxford

•London

ENGLAND

Orléans•

Toulouse•

Nantes•

Bay of Biscay

Bordeaux•

•Loyola

IRELAND

•Dublin

SPAIN

•Madrid

ATLANTIC OCEAN

PORTUGAL

Lisbon•

Lutheran

Calvinist (Reformed)

Church of England

Roman Catholic

Huguenot centers

Spread of Calvinism

400 Mi.

400 Km.

200

200

0

0

Aragon, in 1527–28, the pope ignored his request. As the pope stalled, Henry grew more desperate: he needed a male heir and presumed that the failure to produce one lay with his wife. At the same time, he desired the shrewd and tempting Anne Boleyn. Henry VIII arranged to grant himself a divorce by severing England from the church. In 1534, with Parliament's approval, he had himself declared supreme head of the Church of England. In 1536, he dissolved the monasteries and seized their property, which was distributed or sold to his loyal supporters. In most cases, it went to the lesser nobility and landed gentry. By involving Parliament and the gentry, Henry VIII turned the Reformation into a national movement. Political considerations, not profound theological differences, were at the root of the English Reformation.

Henry VIII was succeeded by his son, Edward VI (1547–1553), a Protestant, who in turn was succeeded by Mary (1553–1558), the daughter of Henry VIII and Catherine of Aragon. A devout Catholic, Mary severely persecuted Protestants. With the succession of Elizabeth I, Henry's second daughter (by Anne Boleyn), in 1558, England again became a Protestant country. Elizabeth's reign, which lasted until 1603, was characterized by a heightened sense of national identity and the persecution of Catholics, who were deemed a threat to national security. Fear of invasion by Spain, which was bent on returning England to the papacy, contributed to English anti-Catholicism.

In its customs and ceremonies, the English, or Anglican, church as it developed in the sixteenth century differed to only a limited degree from the Roman Catholicism it replaced. The exact nature of England's Protestantism became a subject of growing dispute. Was the Anglican church to be truly Protestant? Were its services and churches to be simple, lacking in "popish" rites and rituals and centered on Scripture and sermon? Obviously, the powerful Anglican bishops would accept no form of Protestantism that might limit their privileges, ceremonial functions, and power. These issues contributed to the English Revolution of the seventeenth century (see the following chapter).

◀ Map 8.1 The Protestant and the Catholic Reformations Europe fractured into competing camps, and religious warfare became a way of life.

The Radical Reformation

The leading Protestant reformers generally supported established political authorities, whether they were territorial princes or urban magistrates. For the reformers, human freedom was a spiritual, not a social, concept. Yet the Reformation did help trigger revolts among the artisan and peasant classes of central and then Western Europe. By the 1520s, several radical reformers arose, often from the lower classes of European society. They attempted to channel popular religion and folk beliefs into a new version of reformed Christianity that spoke directly to the temporal and spiritual needs of the oppressed.

Radical reformers proclaimed that God's will was known by his saints—those predestined for salvation. They said that the poor would inherit the earth, which at present was ruled by the Antichrist; the saint's task was to purge this earth of evil and thus make it ready for Christ's Second Coming. For the radicals, the Scriptures, which spoke of God's love for the wretched and lowly, became an inspiration for social revolution. Luther, Calvin, and other reformers vigorously condemned the social doctrines preached by the radical reformers.

The largest group in the Radical Reformation before 1550 has the general name of *Anabaptists*. Having received the inner light—the message of salvation—Anabaptists felt born anew and yearned to be rebaptized. Anabaptists were new Christians, new persons led by the light of conscience to seek reform and renewal of all institutions in preparation for Christ's Second Coming.

In 1534, Anabaptists captured the city of Münster in Westphalia, near the western border of Germany. They seized the property of nonbelievers, burned all books except the Bible, and, in a mood of jubilation and sexual excess, openly practiced polygamy. All the while, the Anabaptists proclaimed that the Day of Judgment was close at hand. Provoked by their actions, Lutheran Prince Philip of Hesse and his army crushed the Anabaptists.

In early modern Europe, *Münster* became a byword for dangerous revolution. Determined to prevent these wild enthusiasts from gaining strength in their own territories, princes attacked them with ferocity. In Münster today, the cages still hang from the church steeple where the Anabaptist leaders were tortured and left to die as a warning to all would-be imitators.

By the late sixteenth century, many radical movements had either gone underground or grown quiet. But a century later, during the English Revolution (1640–1660), the beliefs and political goals of the Radical Reformation surfaced again, threatening to push the revolution in a direction that its gentry leaders desperately feared. Although the radicals failed in England, too, they left a tradition of democratic and antihierarchical thought. The radical assertion that saints, who have received the inner light, are the equal of anyone, regardless of social status, helped shape modern democratic thought.

THE CATHOLIC RESPONSE

The Protestant threat impelled the Roman Catholic church to institute reforms. At first, the energy for reform came from ordinary clergy, as well as laypeople such as Ignatius Loyola (1491–1556). Trained as a soldier, this pious Spanish reformer sought to create a new religious order, fusing the intellectual excellence of humanism with a reformed Catholicism that would appeal to powerful economic and political groups. Founded in 1534, the Society of Jesus, more commonly known as the Jesuits, became the backbone of the Catholic Reformation in southern and Western Europe. The Jesuits combined traditional monastic discipline with a dedication to teaching and an emphasis on the power of preaching. They sought to use both to win converts back to the church.

The Jesuits brought hope: a religious revival based on ceremony, tradition, and the power of the priest to offer forgiveness. In addition, they opened some of the finest schools in Europe. Just as the Lutherans in Germany sought to bring literacy to the masses so that they might read the Bible, the Jesuits sought to bring intellectual enhancement to the laity, especially to the rich and powerful. The Jesuits pursued positions as confessors to princes and urged them to intensify their efforts to strengthen the church in their territories.

By the 1540s, the Counter Reformation was well under way. The leaders of this Catholic movement attacked many of the same abuses that had impelled Luther to speak out, but they avoided a break with the doctrinal and spiritual authority of the clergy. The Counter Reformation also took aggressive and hostile measures against Protestantism. The church tried to counter the popular appeal of Protestantism by emphasizing spiritual renewal through faith, prayer, and religious ceremony. It also resorted to sterner means. The Inquisition—the church court dealing with heretics—expanded its activities, and wherever Catholic jurisdiction prevailed, unrepentant Protestant heretics were subject to death or imprisonment. Catholics did not hold a monopoly on persecution: wherever Protestantism obtained official status—in England, Scotland, and Geneva, for instance—Catholics or religious radicals at times faced persecution.

One of the Catholic church's main tools was censorship. By the 1520s, the impulse to censor and burn dangerous books intensified dramatically as the church tried to prevent the spread of Protestant ideas. In the rush to eliminate heretical literature, the church condemned the works of reforming Catholic humanists as well as those of Protestants. The Index of Prohibited Books became an institutional part of the church's life. Over the centuries, the works of many leading thinkers were placed on the Index, which was not abolished until 1966.

The Counter Reformation policies of education, vigorous preaching, church building, persecution, and censorship did succeed in bringing thousands of people, Germans and Bohemians in particular, back into the church. Furthermore, the church implemented some concrete changes in policy and doctrine. In 1545, the Council of Trent met to reform the church and strengthen it for confronting the Protestant challenge. Over the many years that it was convened (until 1563), the council modified and unified church doctrine; abolished many corrupt practices, such as the selling of indulgences; and vested final authority in the papacy, thereby ending the long and bitter struggle within the church over papal authority. The Council of Trent reaffirmed the church's teaching that both faith and good works were necessary for attaining salvation. It passed a decree that the church shall be the final arbiter of the Bible. All compromise with Protestantism was rejected (not that Protestants were eager for it).

Baroque Catholic Altar From Koden, Poland. To this day many Poles remain intensely Catholic. *(Art Resource, NY)*

The Reformation had split Western Christendom irrevocably.

THE REFORMATION AND THE MODERN AGE

The Renaissance broke with medieval artistic and literary forms and ushered in a vibrant secularism and individualism. Like the Renaissance, the Reformation drew its inspiration from the ancient world. Renaissance humanists and artists sought to imitate and revive classical art and literary forms; Reformation thinkers aspired to restore the spiritual purity of early Christianity, before the growth of a powerful clergy and a dogmatic theology. They used the Gospels in order to undermine the authority of the Church.

At first glance, the Reformation would seem to have renewed the medieval stress on otherworld-liness and reversed the direction toward secularism taken by the Renaissance. Attracted to the ancient Stoic doctrine of the autonomous will, Renaissance humanists had broken with Augustine's stern view of original sin—a corrupt human nature and the person's inability to achieve salvation through his or her own efforts. Both Luther and Calvin, however, saw human beings as essentially depraved and corrupt and rejected completely the notion that individuals can do something for their own salvation; such an assertion of human will, they held, revealed a dangerous self-confidence in human beings. Whereas the humanists fostered freer discussion and criticism, the Reformation, at times, degenerated into narrow-mindedness and intolerance.

Yet in several important ways, the Reformation contributed to the shaping of modernity. By dividing Christendom into Catholic and Protestant, the Reformation destroyed the religious unity of Europe, the distinguishing feature of the Middle Ages, and weakened the church, the chief institution of medieval society. The Reformation promoted religious pluralism, for in addition to Lutheranism and Calvinism, various other Protestant churches, each with its own distinctive traits, emerged.

During the Middle Ages, popes challenged and, at times, dominated kings. By strengthening monarchs at the expense of church bodies, the Reformation furthered the growth of the modern secular and centralized state. Protestant rulers repudiated all papal claims to temporal authority and extended their power over the newly established Protestant churches in their lands. In Catholic lands, the weakened church was reluctant to challenge monarchs, whose support it now needed more than ever. This subordination of clerical authority to the throne permitted kings to build strong centralized states, a characteristic of political life of the modern West.

Although absolute monarchy was the immediate beneficiary of the Reformation, indirectly Protestantism contributed to the growth of political liberty—another feature of the modern West. To be sure, neither Luther nor Calvin championed political freedom. For Luther, a good Christian was an obedient subject. Thus, he declared that subjects should obey their rulers' commands: "It is in no wise proper for anyone who would be a Christian to set himself up against his government, whether it act justly or unjustly."[4] And again, "Those who sit in the office of magistrate sit in the place of God, and their judgment is as if God judged from heaven....If the emperor... calls me, God calls me."[5] Calvinists created a theocracy in Geneva that closely regulated the citizens' private lives, and Calvin strongly condemned resistance to political authority as wicked. He held that rulers were selected by God and that punishment of bad rulers belonged only to God and not to the ruler's subjects.

Nevertheless, the Reformation also provided a basis for challenging monarchs. Some Protestant theorists, mainly Calvinists, supported resistance to political authorities whose edicts, they believed, contravened God's law as expressed in the Bible. This religious justification for revolution against tyrannical rule helped fuel the resistance of English Calvinists, or Puritans, to the English monarchy in the seventeenth century.

The Reformation advanced the idea of equality. Equality is rooted in the Judeo-Christian belief that all people are the creatures of a single God. In two important ways, however, medieval society contravened the principle of equality. First, feudalism stressed hereditary distinctions between nobles and commoners. Medieval society was hierarchical, arranged in an ascending order of legal ranks, or estates: commoners, nobles, and clergy. Second, the medieval church taught that only the clergy could administer the sacraments, which provided people with the means of attaining salvation; for this reason, they were superior to the laity. Luther, in contrast, held that there was no spiritual distinction between the laity and the clergy. There was a spiritual equality of all believers: all were equally Christian; all were equally priests.

The Reformation also contributed to the creation of an individualistic ethic, which characterizes the modern world. Since Protestants, unlike Catholics, had no official interpreter of Scripture, the individual bore the awesome responsibility of interpreting the Bible according to the dictates of his or her conscience. Protestants confronted the prospect of salvation or damnation entirely on their own. No church provided them with security or certainty, and no priesthood interceded between them and God. Piety was not determined by the church, but by the autonomous individual, whose subjective faith or conscience, illuminated by God, was the source of judgment and authority.

For the Protestant, faith was personal and inward. This new arrangement called for a personal relationship between each individual and God and called attention to the individual's inner religious capacities. Certain that God had chosen them for salvation, many Protestants developed the inner self-assurance and assertiveness that marks the modern individual. Thus, the Protestant emphasis on private judgment in religious matters and on an inner personal conviction accentuated the importance of the individual and helped to mold a new and distinctly modern European.

The Reformation's stress on individual conscience may have contributed to the development of the capitalist spirit, which underlies modern economic life. So argued German sociologist Max Weber in *The Protestant Ethic and the Spirit of Capitalism* (1904). Weber acknowledged that capitalism had existed in Europe before the Reformation; merchant bankers in medieval Italian and German towns, for example, engaged in capitalistic activities. But, he contended, Protestantism (particularly Calvinism) made capitalism more dynamic; it produced a new type of individual who confidently set out to master himself and his environment. Protestant businesspeople believed that they had a religious obligation to prosper, and their faith gave them the self-discipline to do so. Convinced that prosperity was God's blessing and poverty his curse, Calvinists had a spiritual inducement to labor industriously and to avoid laziness.

According to Calvin's doctrine of predestination, God had already determined in advance who would be saved; salvation could not be attained through any worldly actions. Although there was no definite way of discovering who had received God's grace, Calvin's followers came to believe that certain activities were signs that God was working through them, that they had indeed been elected. Thus, Calvinists viewed hard work, diligence, dutifulness, efficiency, frugality, and a disdain for pleasurable pursuits—all virtues that contribute to rational and orderly business procedures and to business success—as signs of election. In effect, Weber argued, Protestantism—unlike Catholicism—gave religious approval to moneymaking and the businesspeople's way of life. Moreover, Calvin's followers seemed to believe that they had attained a special insight into their relationship with God; this conviction fostered a sense of self-assurance and righteousness. Protestantism, therefore, produced a highly individualistic attitude that valued inner strength, self-discipline, and methodical and sober behavior—necessary traits for a middle class seeking business success in a highly competitive world.

❖   ❖   ❖

NOTES

1. Giovanni Pico della Mirandola, *Oration on the Dignity of Man,* trans. A. Robert Caponigri (Chicago: Henry Regnery, 1956), p. 7.

2. François Rabelais, *Gargantua and Pantagruel,* trans. Sir Thomas Urquhart (1883), bk. 1, chap. 57.

3. John Dillenberger, ed., *Martin Luther: Selections from His Writings* (Garden City, N.Y.: Doubleday, 1961), p. 46, taken from *The Freedom of a Christian* (1520).

4. Quoted in George H. Sabine, *A History of Political Thought* (New York: Holt, Rinehart & Winston, 1961), p. 361.

5. Quoted in Roland Bainton, *Here I Stand* (New York: Abingdon Press, 1950), p. 238.

SUGGESTED READING

Brucker, Gene A., *Renaissance Florence,* rev. ed. (1983). An excellent analysis of the city's physical character, its economic and social structure, its political and religious life, and its cultural achievements.

Burckhardt, Jacob, *The Civilization of the Renaissance in Italy* (1860), 2 vols. (1958). The first major interpretive synthesis of the Renaissance; still an essential resource.

Burke, Peter, *Popular Culture in Early Modern Europe* (1978). A fascinating account of the social underside from the Renaissance to the French Revolution.

Dillenberger, John, ed., *Martin Luther, Selections from His Writings* (1962). Selected for the general reader.

Dixon, C. Scott, ed., *The German Reformation* (1999). A valuable collection of essays on important aspects of the Reformation.

Grimm, Harold J., *The Reformation Era, 1500–1650,* 2nd ed. (1973). The best and most complete narrative available.

Hale, John, *The Civilization of Europe in the Renaissance* (1994). An informed and entertaining survey.

Kelley, Donald R., *Renaissance Humanism* (1991). A recent synthesis.

King, Margaret L., *Women of the Renaissance* (1991). A useful survey of a burgeoning field of scholarship.

Marius, Richard, *Martin Luther* (1999). A new biography.

Ozment, Steven E., *Protestants* (1992). The rise of Protestantism.

———, *The Reformation in the Cities* (1975). A good survey of the Reformation in Germany.

Pullan, Brian S., *A History of Early Renaissance Italy* (1973). A solid, brief account.

Reardon, Bernard M. G., *Religious Thought in the Reformation* (1981). Doctrinal issues and disputes.

Skinner, Quentin, *The Foundations of Modern Political Thought,* 2 vols. (1978). The first volume covers the Renaissance; highly informed.

Stephens, John, *The Italian Renaissance* (1990). A useful survey.

REVIEW QUESTIONS

1. What is the connection between the Renaissance and the Middle Ages? What special conditions gave rise to the Italian Renaissance?

2. What is humanism, and how did it begin? What did the humanists contribute to education and the writing of history?

3. How can it be said that Machiavelli invented a new politics?

4. What are the general features of Renaissance art?

5. What factors encouraged the spread of the Renaissance into other lands?

6. Why is the Renaissance considered a departure from the Middle Ages and the beginning of modernity?

7. What were the medieval roots of the Reformation?

8. How did Luther's theology mark a break with the church? Why did many Germans become followers of Luther?

9. In what ways did the radical reformers differ from the other Protestants?

10. What role did the Jesuits and the Inquisition play in the Counter Reformation? What did the Counter Reformation accomplish?

11. How did the Reformation contribute to the shaping of the modern world?

Chapter 9

Political and Economic Transformation: National States, Overseas Expansion, Commercial Revolution

*F*rom the thirteenth to the seventeenth century, a new and unique form of political organization emerged in the West: the dynastic, or national, state. It harnessed the material resources of its territory, directed the energies of the nobility into national service, and increasingly centralized political authority. The national state, a product of dynastic consolidation, is the essential political institution of the modern West.

The disintegration of medieval political forms and the emergence of the modern state coincided with the gradual breakdown of the medieval socioeconomic system, which was based on tradition, hierarchy, and orders or estates. In the medieval system, every group—clergy, lords, serfs, guild members—occupied a particular place and performed a specific function. Society functioned best when each person fulfilled the role allotted to him or her by God and tradition. Early modern times saw the growth of a capitalist market economy whose central focus was the self-sufficient individual, striving, assertive, and motivated by self-interest. This nascent market economy, greatly boosted by the voyages of discovery and the conquest and colonization of other parts of the world, subverted the hierarchically arranged and tradition-bound medieval community. Seeking to enrich their treasuries and extend their power, states promoted commercial growth and overseas expansion. The extension of European hegemony over much of the world was well under way by the eighteenth century. ❖

TOWARD THE MODERN STATE

During the Middle Ages, some kings began to forge national states. However, medieval political forms differed considerably from those that developed later, in the early modern period. In the Middle Ages, kings had to share political power with feudal lords, the clergy, free cities, and representative assemblies. Central authority was tempered by overlapping jurisdictions and numerous and competing allegiances. People saw themselves as members of an estate—clergy, aristocracy, or commoners—rather than as subjects or citizens of a state. Church theorists envisioned Christian Europe as a unitary commonwealth, in which spiritual concerns prevailed over secular authority. According to this view, kings, who received their power from God, must never forget their religious obligation to rule in accordance with God's commands as interpreted by the clergy.

In the sixteenth and seventeenth centuries, kings successfully asserted their authority over competing powers, continuing a trend that had begun in the Late Middle Ages. Strong monarchs dominated or crushed the parliaments that had acted as a brake on royal power during the Middle Ages. Increasingly, too, these monarchs subjected lords and ecclesiastical authorities to royal control. They created a bureaucracy to coordinate the activities of the central government. The old medieval political order dissolved. It had been characterized on the one hand by feudal particularism and the strength of local authorities, and on the other by the supranational claims and goals of a universal church. Gradually, the national, territorial state, the hallmark of the modern world, became the essential political unit. Kings were the central figures in the creation of the national state. Strong dynastic states were formed wherever monarchs succeeded in subduing local aristocratic and ecclesiastical power systems. In their struggle to subdue the aristocracy, kings were aided by artillery; the lords' castles quickly became obsolete in the face of royal siege weapons. Where the monarchs failed, as they did in Germany and Italy, no viable states evolved until well into the nineteenth century.

By the early seventeenth century, Europeans had developed the concept of the state: an autonomous political entity to which its subjects owed duties and obligations. The essential prerequisite for the Western concept of the state, as it emerged in the early modern period, was the idea of *sovereignty*. Within its borders, the state was supreme; all other institutions, both secular and religious, had to recognize the state's authority. The art of governing entailed molding the ambitions and strength of the powerful and wealthy so that they could be harnessed to serve the state. Its power growing through war and

Chronology 9.1 ❖ Economic and Political Transformations

1394–1460	Henry the Navigator, prince of Portugal, encourages expansion into Africa for gold and his anti-Muslim crusade
1469	Ferdinand and Isabella begin their rule of Castile and Aragon
1485	Henry VII begins the reign of the Tudor dynasty in England
1488	Bartholomeu Dias reaches the tip of Africa
1492	Christopher Columbus reaches the Caribbean island of Española on his first voyage; the Jews are expelled from Spain; Granada, the last Muslim kingdom in Spain, is conquered, completing the Reconquest
1497	Vasco da Gama sails around the Cape of Good Hope (Africa) to India
1519	Charles V of Spain becomes Hapsburg emperor of the Holy Roman Empire
1519–1521	Hernando Cortés conquers the Aztecs in Mexico
1531–1533	Francisco Pizarro conquers the Incas in Peru
1552	Silver from the New World flows into Europe via Spain, contributing to a price revolution
1556–1598	Philip II of Spain persecutes Jews and Muslims
1562–1598	Religious wars in France

(Continued on p. 200)

taxation, the state had become the basic unit of political authority in the West.

Historically, the modern state has been characterized by a devotion to the nation and by feelings of national pride. A national language is used throughout the land, and the people have a sense of sharing a common culture and history, of being distinct from other peoples. There were some signs of growing national feeling during the sixteenth and seventeenth centuries, but this feature of the modern state did not become a major part of European political life until the nineteenth century. During the early modern period, devotion was largely given to a town, a province, or a noble or to the person of the king rather than to the nation, the people as a whole.

In the sixteenth and seventeenth centuries, the idea of liberty, now so basic to Western political life and thought, was only rarely discussed, and then chiefly by Calvinist opponents of absolutism. Not until the mid-seventeenth century in England was there a body of political thought contending that human liberty was compatible with the new modern state. In general, despite the English (and Dutch) developments, absolutism dominated the political structure of early modern Europe. It was not until the late eighteenth and nineteenth centuries that absolutism was widely challenged by advocates of liberty.

The principle of the balance of power, an integral part of modern international relations, also emerged during early modern times. When one state threatened to dominate Europe, as did Spain under Philip II and France under Louis XIV, other states joined forces and resisted. The fear that one state would upset the balance of power and achieve European domination pervaded international relations in later centuries.

HAPSBURG SPAIN

The Spanish political experience of the sixteenth century was one of the most extraordinary in the history of modern Europe. Spanish kings built a dynastic state that burst through its frontiers and encompassed Portugal, part of Italy, the Netherlands, and enormous areas in the New World.

199

1572	Saint Bartholomew's Day Massacre—Queen Catherine of France orders thousands of Protestants executed
1588	English fleet defeats the Spanish Armada
1598	French Protestants are granted religious toleration by the Edict of Nantes
1624–1642	Cardinal Richelieu, Louis XIII's chief minister, determines royal policies
1640–1660	English Revolution
1648	Treaty of Westphalia ends the Thirty Years' War
1649	Charles I, Stuart king of England, is executed by an act of Parliament
1649–1660	England is co-ruled by Parliament and the army under Oliver Cromwell
1660	Charles II returns from exile and becomes king of England
1685	Louis XIV of France revokes the Edict of Nantes
1688–1689	Revolution in England: end of absolutism
1694	The Bank of England is founded
1701	Louis XIV tries to bring Spain under French control

Spain became an intercontinental empire—the first in the West since Roman times.

In the eighth and ninth centuries, the Muslims controlled all of Spain except some tiny Christian kingdoms in the far north. In the ninth century, these Christian states began a five-hundred-year struggle, the Reconquest, to drive the Muslims from the Iberian Peninsula. By the middle of the thirteenth century, Granada in the south was all that remained of Muslim lands in Spain. This long struggle for Christian hegemony in the Iberian Peninsula left the Spanish fiercely religious and strongly suspicious of foreigners. Despite centuries of intermarriage with non-Christians, by the early sixteenth century purity of blood and orthodoxy of faith became necessary for, and synonymous with, Spanish identity.

Ferdinand and Isabella

In 1469, Ferdinand, heir to the throne of Aragon, married Isabella, heir to the throne of Castile. Although Ferdinand and Isabella did not give Spain a single legal and tax system or a common currency, their policies did contribute decisively to Spanish unity and might. They broke the power of aristocrats, who had operated from their fortified castles like kings, waging their private wars at will; they brought the Spanish church into alliance with the state; and in 1492, they drove the Muslims from Granada, the Muslims' last territory in Spain. The crusade against the Muslim infidels accorded with the aims of the militant Spanish church. With a superior army, with the great aristocrats pacified, and with the church and the Inquisition under monarchical control, the Catholic kings expanded their interests and embarked on an imperialist foreign policy that made Spain dominant in the New World.

The Spanish state and church persecuted both Muslims and Jews, who for centuries had contributed substantially to Spanish cultural and economic life. In 1391, thousands of Jews were massacred when anti-Jewish sentiments, fanned by popular preachers, turned to violence in major cities. Under threat of death, many Jews submitted to baptism. In succeeding years, other attacks on Jews led to more conversions. A number of these *conversos*, or new Christians, continued to practice the religion of their fathers in secret, a situation that appalled clerical authorities and the devout Ferdinand and Isabella.

In 1492, in a move to enforce religious uniformity, the crown expelled from Spain Jews who were unwilling to accept baptism. About 150,000 Jews (some estimates are considerably higher) were driven out, including many conversos, who opted to stay with their people. The thousands of Jews who underwent conversion and the conversos who remained were watched by the Inquisition—the church tribunal that dealt with insincere converts—for signs of backsliding. Death by fire, sometimes in elaborate public ceremonies, was the ultimate penalty for those of the conversos and their descendants who were suspected of practicing Judaism. Muslims also bore the pain of forced conversions and investigations, torture, and executions conducted by the Inquisition. Finally, in 1609–1614, Spain expelled them.

The Reign of Charles V: King of Spain and Holy Roman Emperor

Dynastic marriage constituted another crucial part of Ferdinand and Isabella's foreign policy. They strengthened their ties with the Austrian Hapsburg kings by marrying one of their children, Juana (called "the Mad" for her insanity), to Philip the Fair, son of Maximilian of Austria, the head of the ruling Hapsburg family. Philip and Juana's son Charles inherited the kingdom of Ferdinand and Isabella in 1516 and reigned until 1556. Through his other grandparents, he also inherited the Netherlands, Austria, Sardinia, Sicily, the kingdom of Naples, and Franche Comté. In 1519, he was elected Holy Roman emperor, Charles V. Charles became the most powerful ruler in Europe. But his reign saw the emergence of political, economic, and social problems that eventually led to Spain's decline.

Charles's inheritance was simply too vast to be governed effectively, but that was only dimly perceived at the time. The Lutheran Reformation proved to be the first successful challenge to Hapsburg power. It was the first phase of a religious and political struggle between Catholic Spain and Protestant Europe, a struggle that would dominate the last half of the sixteenth century.

The achievements of Charles V's reign rested on the twin instruments of army and bureaucracy. The Hapsburg Empire in the New World was vastly extended but, on the whole, effectively administered and policed. Out of this sprawling empire, with its exploited native populations, came the greatest flow of gold and silver ever witnessed by Europeans. Constant warfare in Europe, coupled with the immensity of the Spanish administrative network, required a steady intake of capital. In the long run, however, this easy access to capital seems to have hurt the Spanish economy. There was no incentive for the development of domestic industry, bourgeois entrepreneurship, or international commerce.

Moreover, constant war engendered and perpetuated a social order geared to the aggrandizement of a military class rather than the development of a commercial class. Although war expanded Spain's power in the sixteenth century, it sowed the seeds for the financial crises of the 1590s and beyond and for the eventual decline of Spain as a world power.

Philip II

Philip II inherited the throne from his father, Charles V, who abdicated in 1556. Charles left his son with a vast empire in both the Old World and the New. Although this empire had been administered competently enough, it was facing the specters of bankruptcy and heresy. A zeal for Catholicism ruled Philip's private conduct and infused his foreign policy. In the 1560s, Philip sent the largest land army ever assembled in Europe into the Netherlands with the intention of crushing Protestant-inspired opposition to Spanish authority. The ensuing revolt of the Netherlands lasted until 1609, and the Spanish lost their industrial heartland as a result of it.

The Dutch established a republic governed by the prosperous and progressive bourgeoisie. Rich from the fruits of manufacture and trade in everything from tulip bulbs to ships and slaves, the Dutch merchants ruled their cities and provinces with fierce pride. In the early seventeenth century, this new nation of only 1.5 million people already practiced the most innovative commercial and financial techniques in Europe.

Philip's disastrous attempt to invade England was also born of religious zeal. Philip regarded an

Allegory of the Abdication of Charles V by Frans Francken II, 1556. Emperor Charles V, who ruled half of Europe and most of the Americas, abdicated in 1555, giving his German imperial crown to his brother Ferdinand, archduke of Austria, and the kingdoms of Spain and the Netherlands to his son Philip II. The Hapsburg dynasty ruled Spain until the eighteenth century and Austria and Hungary until the early twentieth century. *(Rijksmuseum, Amsterdam)*

assault on England, the main Protestant power, as a holy crusade against the "heretic and bastard," Queen Elizabeth; he particularly resented English assistance to the Protestant Dutch rebels. Sailing from Lisbon in May 1588, the Spanish Armada, carrying twenty-two thousand seamen and soldiers, met with defeat. More than half of the Spanish ships were destroyed or put out of commission. Many ships were wrecked by storms as they tried to return to Spain by rounding the coasts of Scotland and Ireland. The defeat had an enormous psychological effect on the Spanish, who saw it as divine punishment and openly pon-

dered what they had done to incur God's displeasure.

The End of the Spanish Hapsburgs

After the defeat of the Armada, Spain gradually and reluctantly abandoned its imperial ambitions in northern Europe. The administrative structure built by Charles V and Philip II remained strong throughout the seventeenth century; nevertheless, by the first quarter of the century, enormous weaknesses in Spanish economic and social life had surfaced. In 1596, Philip II was bankrupt, his vast wealth depleted by the cost of foreign wars. Bankruptcy reappeared at various times in the seventeenth century, while the agricultural economy, at the heart of any early modern nation, stagnated. The Spanish in their golden age had never paid enough heed to increasing domestic production.

Despite these setbacks, Spain was still capable of taking a very aggressive posture during the Thirty Years' War (1618–1648). The Austrian branch of the Hapsburg family joined forces with their Spanish cousins, and neither the Swedes and Germans nor the Dutch could stop them. Only French participation in the Thirty Years' War on the Protestant side tipped the balance decisively against the Hapsburgs. Spanish aggression brought no victories, and with the Peace of Westphalia (1648), Spain officially recognized the independence of the Netherlands and severed its diplomatic ties with the Austrian branch of the family.

By 1660, the imperial age of the Spanish Hapsburgs had ended. The rule of the Protestant princes had been secured in the Holy Roman Empire; the largely Protestant Dutch Republic flourished; Portugal and its colony of Brazil were independent of Spain; and dominance over European affairs had passed to France. The quality of material life in Spain deteriorated rapidly, and the ever-present gap between the rich and the poor widened even more drastically. The traditional aristocracy and the church retained their land and power but failed to produce effective leadership.

The Spanish experience illustrates two aspects of the history of the European state. First, the state as empire could survive and prosper only if the domestic economic base remained sound. The Spanish reliance on bullion from its colonies and the failure to cultivate industry and reform the taxation system spelled disaster. Second, states with a vital and aggressive bourgeoisie, such as England and Holland, flourished at the expense of the regions where the aristocracy and the church dominated and controlled society and its mores— as in Spain's situation. The latter social groups tended to despise manual labor, profit taking, and technological progress. Even though they had been created by kings and dynastic families, after 1700 the major dynastic states were increasingly nur-

tured by the economic activities of merchants and traders—the bourgeoisie. Yet the bureaucracy of the dynastic states continued to be dominated by men drawn from the lesser aristocracy.

THE GROWTH OF FRENCH POWER

Although both England and France effectively consolidated the power of their central governments, each became a model of a different form of statehood. The English model was a constitutional monarchy, in which the king's power was limited by Parliament and the rights of the English people were protected by law and tradition. The French model emphasized at every turn the glory of the king and, by implication, the sovereignty of the state and its right to stand above the interests of its subjects. France's monarchy became absolute, and French kings claimed that they had been selected by God to rule, a theory known as the divine right of kings. This theory gave monarchy a sanctity that various French kings exploited to enforce their commands on the population, including rebellious feudal lords.

The evolution of the French state was a very gradual process, completed only in the late seventeenth century. In the Middle Ages, the French monarchs recognized the rights of representative assemblies—the Estates—and consulted with them. These assemblies (whether regional or national) were composed of deputies drawn from the various elites: the clergy, the nobility, and, significantly, the leaders of cities and towns in a given region. Early modern French kings increasingly wrested power from the nobility, reduced the significance of the Estates, and eliminated interference from the church.

Religion and the French State

In every emergent state, tension existed between the monarch and the papacy. At issue was control over the church within that territory—over its personnel, its wealth, and, of course, its pulpits, from which an illiterate majority learned what their leaders wanted them to know, not only about religious issues, but also about submission to civil authority. The monarch's power to make church appointments could ensure a complacent church—a church willing to preach obedience to royal authority and to comply on matters of taxes.

For the French monarchs, centuries of tough bargaining with the papacy paid off in 1516, when Francis I (1515–1547) concluded the Concordat of Bologna. Under this agreement, Pope Leo X permitted the French king to nominate, and so in effect appoint, men of his choice to all the highest offices in the French church. The Concordat of Bologna laid the foundation for what became known as the *Gallican church*—a term signifying that the Catholic church in France was sanctioned and overseen by the French kings. Thus, in the early sixteenth century, the central government had been strengthened at the expense of papal authority and of traditional privileges enjoyed by local aristocracy.

The Protestant Reformation, however, challenged royal authority and threatened the very survival of France as a unified state. Fearful that Protestantism would undermine his power, Francis I declared Protestant beliefs and practices illegal and punishable by fines, imprisonment, and even execution. Nevertheless, the Protestant minority (the Huguenots) grew in strength. From 1562 to 1598, France experienced waves of religious wars, which cost the king control over vast areas of the kingdom. The great aristocratic families, the Guise for the Catholics and the Bourbons for the Protestants, drew up armies that scourged the land, killing and maiming their religious opponents and dismantling the authority of the central government.

In 1579, extreme Huguenot theorists published the *Vindiciae contra Tyrannos*. This statement, combined with a call to action, was the first of its kind in early modern times. It justified rebellion against, and even the execution of, an unjust king. European monarchs might claim power and divinely sanctioned authority, but by the late sixteenth century, their subjects had available the moral and theoretical justification for opposing their monarch's will, by force, if necessary, and this justification rested on Scripture and religious conviction. Significantly, this same treatise was translated into English in 1648, a year before Parliament publicly executed Charles I, king of England.

The Valois kings floundered in the face of this kind of political and religious opposition. The era of royal supremacy instituted by Francis I came to an abrupt end during the reign of his successor, Henry II (1547–1559). Wed to Catherine de Medici, a member of the powerful Italian banking family, Henry occupied himself not with the concerns of government, but with the pleasures of the hunt. The sons who succeeded Henry—Francis II (1559–1560), Charles IX (1560–1574), and Henry III (1574–1589)—were uniformly weak. Their mother, Catherine, who was the virtual ruler, ordered the execution of thousands of Protestants by royal troops in Paris—the beginning of the infamous Saint Bartholomew's Day Massacre (1572), which, with the bloodbath that followed, became a symbol of the excesses of religious zeal.

The civil wars begun in 1562 were renewed in the massacre's aftermath. They dragged on until the death of the last Valois king in 1589. The Valois failure to produce a male heir to the throne placed Henry, duke of Bourbon and a Protestant, in line to succeed to the French throne. Realizing that the overwhelmingly Catholic population would not accept a Protestant king, Henry (apparently without much regret) renounced his adopted religion and embraced the church. Henry IV (1589–1610) granted his Protestant subjects and former followers a degree of religious toleration through the Edict of Nantes (1598), but they were never welcomed into the royal bureaucracy in significant numbers. Throughout the seventeenth century, every French king attempted to undermine the Protestants' regional power bases and ultimately to destroy their religious liberties.

The Consolidation of French Monarchical Power

The defeat of Protestantism as a national force set the stage for the final consolidation of the French state in the seventeenth century under the great Bourbon kings, Louis XIII and Louis XIV. Louis XIII (1610–1643) realized that his rule depended on an efficient and trustworthy bureaucracy, a replenishable treasury, and constant vigilance against the localized claims to power by the great aristocracy and Protestant cities and towns. Cardinal Richelieu, who served as Louis XIII's chief minister from 1624 to 1642, became the great architect of French absolutism.

Richelieu's morality rested on one absolute principle, embodied in a phrase he invented: *raison d'état,* reason of state. Richelieu sought to serve the state by bringing under the king's control the disruptive and antimonarchical elements within French society. He increased the power of the central bureaucracy, attacked the power of independent, and often Protestant, towns and cities, and persecuted the Huguenots. Above all, he humbled the great nobles by limiting their effectiveness as councilors to the king and prohibiting their traditional privileges, such as settling grievances through a duel rather than through court action. Reason of state also guided Richelieu's foreign policy. It required that France turn against Catholic Spain and enter the war that was raging at the time in the Holy Roman Empire on the Protestant—and hence anti-Spanish—side. France's entry into the Thirty Years' War produced a decisive victory for French power on the Continent.

Richelieu died in 1642, and Louis XIII the following year. Cardinal Mazarin, who took charge during the minority of Louis XIV (he was five years old when Louis XIII died), continued Richelieu's policies. Mazarin's heavy-handed actions produced a rebellious reaction, the *Fronde,* a series of street riots that lasted from 1648 to 1653 and that eventually cost the government control over Paris. Centered in Paris and supported by the great aristocracy, the courts, and the city's poorer classes, the Fronde threatened to develop into a full-scale uprising. It might have done so, but for one crucial factor: its leadership was divided. Court judges (lesser nobles who had often just risen from the ranks of the bourgeoisie) deeply distrusted the great aristocrats and refused in the end to make common cause with them. And both groups feared disorders among the urban masses.

When Louis XIV finally assumed responsibility for governing in 1661, he vowed that the events he had witnessed as a child during the Fronde would never be repeated. In the course of his reign, he achieved the greatest degree of monarchical power held during the early modern period. No absolute monarch in Western Europe, before or at that time, had so much personal authority or commanded such a vast and effective military and administrative machine. Louis XIV's reign represents the culmination of the process of increasing monarchical authority that had been under way for centuries. Intelligent, cunning, and possessing a unique understanding of the requirements of his office, Louis XIV worked long hours at being king, and he never undertook a venture without an eye to his personal grandeur. The sumptuous royal palace at Versailles was built for that reason; similarly, etiquette and style were cultivated there on a scale never before seen in any European court.

When Mazarin died, Louis XIV did away with the office of first minister; he would rule France alone. The great nobles, "princes of the blood," enjoyed great social prestige but exercised decreasing political influence. Louis XIV treated the aristocrats to elaborate rituals, processions, displays, and banquets; amid all the clamor, however, their political power dwindled.

Louis XIV's domestic policies centered on his incessant search for new revenues. Not only the building of Versailles but also wars cost money, and Louis XIV waged them to excess. To raise capital, he used the services of Jean Baptiste Colbert, a brilliant administrator who improved the methods of tax collecting, promoted new industries, and encouraged international trade. Operating with a total bureaucracy of about a thousand officials and no longer bothering even to consult the parlements or Estates, Louis XIV ruled absolutely in accordance with the principle of divine right—that the monarch is selected to rule by God.

Yet Louis XIV's system was fatally flawed. Without any effective check on his power and on his dreams of international conquest, no limit was imposed on the state's capacity to make war or on the ensuing national debt. Louis XIV coveted vast sections of the Holy Roman Empire; he also sought to curb Dutch commercial prosperity and had designs on the Spanish Netherlands. By the 1680s, his domestic and foreign policies turned violently aggressive. In 1685, he revoked the Edict of Nantes, forcing many of the country's remaining Protestants to flee. In 1689, he embarked on a military campaign to secure territory from the Holy Roman Empire. And in 1701,

The Royal Palace at Versailles. Immense and grand, Versailles was the wonder of the age. Like the person of the king, it said to his subjects: I am grandeur incarnate. Even by today's standards, it is an impressive building, both inside and out. (*C. L. Chrysun/The Image Bank*)

he tried to bring Spain under the control of the Bourbon dynasty. Louis XIV, however, underestimated the power of his northern rivals, England and the Netherlands. Their combined power, in alliance with the Holy Roman Empire and the Austrians, defeated his ambitions.

Louis XIV's participation in these long wars emptied the royal treasury. By the late seventeenth century, taxes had risen intolerably, and they were levied mostly on those least able to pay—the peasants. Absolutism also meant increased surveillance of the population. Royal authorities censored books, spied on suspected heretics, Protestants, and freethinkers, and tortured and executed opponents of state policy.

In the France of Louis XIV, the dynastic state had reached maturity and had begun to display some of its classic characteristics: centralized bureaucracy, royal patronage to enforce allegiance, a system of taxation universally but inequitably applied, and suppression of political opposition either through the use of patronage or, if necessary, through force. Another important feature was the state's cultivation of the arts and sciences as a means of increasing national power and prestige. Together, these policies enabled the French monarchy to achieve political stability, enforce a uniform system of law, and channel the country's wealth and resources into the service of the state as a whole.

Yet at his death in 1715, Louis XIV left his successors a system of bureaucracy and taxation that was vastly in need of overhaul but was still locked into the traditional social privileges of the church and nobility to an extent that made reform virtually impossible. The pattern of war, excessive taxation of the lower classes, and expenditures that surpassed revenues had severely damaged French finances. Failure to reform the system led to the French Revolution of 1789.

THE GROWTH OF LIMITED MONARCHY AND CONSTITUTIONALISM IN ENGLAND

In 1066, William, duke of Normandy and vassal to the French king, had invaded and conquered England, acquiring at a stroke the entire kingdom. In succeeding centuries, English monarchs continued to strengthen central authority and to tighten the bonds of national unity. At the same time, however, certain institutions and traditions evolved—common law, Magna Carta, and Parliament—that checked royal power and protected the rights of the English people.

Central government in England was threatened after the Hundred Years' War (1337–1453), when English aristocrats brought back from France a taste for warfare. In the ensuing civil war—the War of the Roses (1455–1485)—gangs of noblemen with retainers roamed the English countryside, and lawlessness prevailed for a generation. Only in 1485 did the Tudor family emerge triumphant.

The Tudor Achievement

Victory in the civil war allowed Henry VII (1485–1509) to begin the Tudor dynasty. Henry VII's goal was to check the unruly nobility. To this end, he brought commoners into the government. These commoners, unlike the great magnates, could be channeled into royal service because they craved what the king offered: financial rewards and elevated social status. Although they did not fully displace the aristocracy, commoners were brought into Henry VII's inner circle, into the Privy Council, and into the courts. The strength and efficiency of Tudor government were shown during the Reformation, when Henry VIII (1509–1547) made himself head of the English church.

The Protestant Reformation in England was a revolution in royal, as well as ecclesiastical, government. It attacked and defeated the main obstacle to monarchical authority: the power of the papacy. However, no change in religious practice could be instituted by the monarchy alone. Parliament's participation in the Reformation gave it a greater role and sense of importance than it had ever possessed in the past.

At Henry VIII's death, the Tudor bureaucracy and centralized government were strained to the utmost, yet they survived. The government weathered the reign of Henry's sickly son Edward VI (1547–1553) and the extreme Protestantism of some of his advisers; it also survived the brief and deeply troubled reign of Henry's first daughter, Mary (1553–1558), who attempted to return England to Catholicism. At Mary's death, England had come dangerously close to the religious instability and sectarian tension that undermined the French kings during the final decades of the sixteenth century.

Henry's second daughter, Elizabeth I, became queen in 1558 and reigned until her death in 1603. The Elizabethan period was characterized by a heightened sense of national identity. The English Reformation enhanced that sense, as did the increasing fear of foreign invasion by Spain. That fear was abated only by the defeat of the Spanish Armada in 1588. In the seventeenth century, the English would look back on Elizabeth's reign as a golden age. It was the calm before the storm: a time when a new commercial class was formed that, in the seventeenth century, would demand a greater say in government operations.

Religion played a vital role in this realignment of political interests and forces. Many of the old aristocracy clung to the Anglicanism of the Henrician Reformation and in some cases to Catholicism. The newly risen gentry found in the Protestant Reformation of Switzerland and Germany a form of religious worship more suited to their independent and entrepreneurial spirit. Many of them embraced Puritanism, the English version of Calvinism.

The English Revolution, 1640–1660 and 1688–1689

The forces threatening established authority were dealt with ineffectively by the first two Stuart kings, James I (1603–1625) and Charles I (1625–1649). Like their Continental counterparts, both believed in royal absolutism, and both preached, through the established church, the doctrine of the divine right of kings. James I angered Parliament

Henry VIII. Although the ruler of a second-rate power, Henry VIII sought to impress upon his subjects that he was a new and powerful monarch. He sought to compete in style, if not in power, with the French and the Spanish kings. (*Walker Art Gallery, Liverpool*)

king could not collect taxes without Parliament's consent or imprison people without a specific charge. Thus, the monarch had to acknowledge formally the long-established traditions protecting the rights of the English people.

Nevertheless, tensions between the throne and Parliament persisted, and in 1629 Charles I dissolved Parliament, which would not meet again for eleven years. What forced him to reconvene Parliament in 1640 was his need for funds to defend the realm against an invasion from Scotland. The conflict stemmed from Archbishop William Laud's attempt, approved by Charles I, to impose a common prayer book on Scottish Calvinists, or Presbyterians. Infuriated by this effort to impose Anglican liturgy on them, Scottish Presbyterians took up arms. The Long Parliament—so called because it was not disbanded until 1660—abolished the extralegal courts and commissions that had been used by the king to try opponents, provided for regular meetings of Parliament, and strengthened Parliament's control over taxation. When Puritan members pressed to reduce royal authority even more and to strike at the power of the Anglican church, a deep split occurred in Parliament's ranks: Puritans and all-out supporters of parliamentary supremacy were opposed by Anglicans and supporters of the king. The ensuing civil war was directed by Parliament, financed by taxes and the merchants, and fought by the New Model Army led by Oliver Cromwell (1599–1658), a Puritan squire who gradually realized his potential for leadership.

Parliament's rich supporters financed the New Model Army, gentlemen farmers led it, and religious zealots filled its ranks, along with the usual cross section of poor artisans and day laborers. This army brought defeat to the king, his aristocratic followers, and the Anglican church's hierarchy. In January 1649, Charles I was publicly executed by order of Parliament. During the interregnum (time between kings), which lasted eleven years, one Parliament after another joined with the army to govern the country as a republic. In the distribution of power between the army and Parliament, Cromwell proved to be a key element. He had the support of the army's officers and some of its rank and file, and he had been a member of Parliament for many years. His control over the army was secured, however,

by conducting foreign policy without consulting it. The conflict between Parliament and Charles I centered on taxes and religion.

Badly needing funds in order to wage war, Charles I exacted "forced loans" from subjects and imprisoned without a specific charge those who would not pay. Fearing that such arbitrary behavior threatened everyone's property and person, Parliament struck back. In 1628, it refused to grant Charles I tax revenues unless he agreed to the Petition of Right, which stated that the only after its rank and file was purged of radicals, drawn largely from the poor. Some of these radicals wanted to level society, that is, to redistribute property and to give the vote to all male citizens.

Cromwell's death left the country without effective leadership. Parliament, having secured the interests of its constituency (gentry, merchants, and some small landowners), chose to restore court and crown and invited the exiled son of the executed king to return to the kingship. Having learned the lesson his father had spurned, Charles II (1660–1685) never instituted royal absolutism.

But Charles's brother, James II (1685–1688), was a foolishly fearless Catholic and admirer of French absolutism. He gathered at his court a coterie of Catholic advisers and supporters of royal prerogative and attempted to bend Parliament and local government to the royal will. James II's Catholicism was the crucial element in his failure. The Anglican church would not back him, and political forces similar to those that in 1640 had rallied against his father, Charles I, descended on him. The ruling elites, however, had learned their lesson back in the 1650s: civil war would produce social discontent among the masses. The upper classes wanted to avoid open warfare and preserve the monarchy, but as a constitutional authority not as an absolute one. Puritanism, with its sectarian fervor and its dangerous association with republicanism, was allowed to play no part in this second and last phase of the English Revolution.

In early 1688, Anglicans, some aristocrats, and opponents of royal prerogative formed a conspiracy against James II. Their purpose was to invite his son-in-law, William of Orange, stadholder (head) of the Netherlands and husband of James's Protestant daughter Mary, to invade England and rescue its government from James's control. Having lost the loyalty of key men in the army, powerful gentlemen in the counties, and the Anglican church, James II fled the country, and William and Mary were declared king and queen by act of Parliament.

This bloodless revolution—sometimes called the Glorious Revolution—created a new political and constitutional reality. Parliament secured its rights to assemble regularly and to vote on all matters of taxation; the rights of habeas corpus and trial by jury (for men of property and social status) were also secured. These rights were in turn legitimated in a constitutionally binding document, the Bill of Rights (1689). All Protestants, regardless of their sectarian bias, were granted toleration.

The English Revolution, in both its 1640 and its 1688 phases, secured English parliamentary government and the rule of law. Eventually, the monarchical element in that system would yield to the power and authority of parliamentary ministers and state officials. The Revolution of 1688–89 was England's last revolution. In the nineteenth and twentieth centuries, parliamentary institutions would be gradually and peacefully reformed to express a more democratic social reality. The events of 1688–89 have rightly been described as "the year one," for they fashioned a system of government that operated effectively in Britain and could also be transplanted elsewhere with modification. The British system became a model for other forms of representative government, adopted in France and in the former British colonies, beginning with the United States.

THE HOLY ROMAN EMPIRE: THE FAILURE TO UNIFY GERMANY

In contrast to the experience of the French, English, Spanish, and Dutch in the early modern period, the Germans failed to achieve national unity. This failure is tied to the history of the Holy Roman Empire. That union of various distinct central European territories was created in the tenth century when Otto I, in a deliberate attempt to revive Charlemagne's empire, was crowned emperor of the Romans. Later, the title was changed to Holy Roman emperor, with the kingdom consisting mainly of German-speaking principalities.

Most medieval Holy Roman emperors busied themselves not with administering their territories, but with attempting to gain control of the rich Italian peninsula and with challenging the rival authority of various popes. In the meantime, the German nobility extended and consolidated

their rule over their peasants and over various towns and cities. The feudal aristocracy's power remained a constant obstacle to German unity.

In the medieval and early modern periods, the Holy Roman emperors were dependent on their most powerful noble lords—including an archbishop or two—because the office of emperor was elective rather than hereditary. German princes, some of whom were electors—for instance, the archbishops of Cologne and Mainz, the Hohenzollern elector of Brandenburg, the landgrave of Hesse, and the duke of Saxony—were fiercely independent. All belonged to the empire, yet all regarded themselves as autonomous powers. These decentralizing tendencies were highly developed by the fifteenth century. The Hapsburgs had maneuvered themselves into a position from which they could monopolize the imperial elections.

The centralizing efforts of the Hapsburg Holy Roman emperors Maximilian I (1493–1519) and Charles V (1519–1556) were impeded by the Reformation, which bolstered the Germans' already strong propensity for local independence. The German nobility were all too ready to use the Reformation as a vindication of their local power, and indeed Luther made just such an appeal to their interests. War raged in Germany between the Hapsburgs and the Protestant princes, united for mutual protection in the Schmalkaldic League. The Treaty of Augsburg (1555) conferred on every German prince the right to determine the religion of his subjects. The princes retained their power, and a unified German state was never constructed by the Hapsburgs. Religious disunity and the particularism and provinciality of the German nobility prevented its creation.

When an exhausted Emperor Charles V abdicated in 1556, he gave his kingdom to his son Philip and his brother Ferdinand. Philip inherited Spain and its colonies, as well as the Netherlands, and Ferdinand acquired the Austrian territories; two branches of the Hapsburg family were thus formed. Throughout the sixteenth century, the Austrian Hapsburgs barely managed to control the sprawling and deeply divided German territories. However, they never missed an opportunity

◀ **Map 9.1 Europe, 1648** Europe in 1648, exhausted by war.

to further the cause of Catholicism and to strike at the power of the German nobility.

No Hapsburg was ever more fervid in that regard than the Jesuit-trained Archduke Ferdinand II, who ascended the throne in Vienna in 1619. His policies provoked a war within the empire that engulfed the whole of Europe: the Thirty Years' War. It began when the Bohemians, whose anti-Catholic tendencies could be traced back to Jan Hus, tried to put a Protestant king on their throne. The Austrian and Spanish Hapsburgs reacted by sending an army into the kingdom of Bohemia, and suddenly the whole empire was forced to take sides along religious lines. Bohemia suffered an almost unimaginable devastation; the ravaging Hapsburg army sacked and burned three-fourths of the kingdom's towns and practically exterminated its aristocracy.

Until the 1630s, it looked as if the Hapsburgs would be able to use the war to enhance their power and promote centralization. But the intervention of Protestant Sweden, led by Gustavus Adolphus and encouraged by France, wrecked Hapsburg ambitions. The ensuing military conflict devastated vast areas of northern and central Europe. The civilian population suffered untold hardships. Partly because the French finally intervened directly, the Spanish Hapsburgs emerged from the Thirty Years' War with no benefits. The Treaty of Westphalia gave the Austrian Hapsburgs firm control of the eastern states of the kingdom, with Vienna as their capital. Austria took shape as a dynastic state, while the German territories in the empire remained fragmented by the independent interests of the feudal nobility.

EUROPEAN EXPANSION

The emergence of the modern state paralleled the gradual disintegration of traditional medieval socioeconomic forms. Medieval society was divided into three principal groups—clergy, lords, and peasants. It was believed that this hierarchically arranged social order worked best when each social group performed a specific function ordained by God: the clergy led according to God's commands; the aristocracy, guided by the church, defended Christian interests; and the peasants toiled to provide sustenance for themselves and their superiors. The focus was on a social group performing its proper role, the one assigned to it by God and tradition. In early modern times a capitalist market economy arose whose focus was not on the group but on the individual motivated by self-interest. A new European was emerging, striving, assertive, and willing to break with traditional social forms in order to succeed in the market place. The nascent market economy was greatly aided by the expansion of trade and wealth resulting from the voyages of discovery and the conquest and colonization of the New World.

During the period from 1450 to 1750, Western Europe entered an era of overseas exploration and economic expansion that transformed society. European adventurers discovered a new way to reach the rich trading centers of India by sailing around Africa. They also conquered, colonized, and exploited a new world across the Atlantic. These discoveries and conquests brought about an extraordinary increase in business activity and the supply of money, which stimulated the growth of capitalism. People's values changed in ways that were alien and hostile to the medieval outlook. By 1750, the model Christian in northwestern Europe was no longer the selfless saint but the enterprising businessman. The era of secluded manors and walled towns was drawing to a close. A world economy was emerging, in which European economic life depended on the market in Eastern spices, African slaves, and American silver. During this age of exploration and commercial expansion, Europe generated a peculiar dynamism unmatched by any other civilization. A process was initiated that by 1900 would give Europe mastery over most of the globe and wide-ranging influence over other civilizations.

Forces Behind the Expansion

A combination of forces propelled Europeans outward and enabled them to dominate Asians, Africans, and American Indians. European monarchs, merchants, and aristocrats fostered expansion for power and profit. As the numbers of the landed classes exceeded the supply of available land, the sons of the aristocracy looked beyond Europe for the lands and fortunes denied them at home. Nor was it unnatural for them to try to gain these things by plunder and conquest; their ancestors had done the same thing for centuries.

Merchants and shippers also had reason to look abroad. Trade between Europe, Africa, and the Orient had gone on for centuries, but always through intermediaries, who increased the costs and decreased the profits on the European end. Gold from the riverbeds of West Africa had been transported across the Sahara by Arab nomads. Spices had been shipped from India and the East Indies by way of Muslim and Venetian merchants. Western European merchants now sought to break those monopolies by going directly to the source: to West Africa for gold, slaves, and pepper, and to India for pepper, spices, and silks.

The centralizing monarchical state was an important factor in the expansion. Monarchs who had successfully established royal hegemony at home, like Ferdinand and Isabella of Spain, sought opportunities to extend their control overseas. From overseas empires came gold, silver, and commerce, which paid for ever more expensive royal government at home and for war against rival dynasties both at home and abroad.

Religion helped in the expansion because the crusading tradition was well established—especially on the Iberian Peninsula, where a five-hundred-year struggle, known as the Reconquest, to drive out the Muslims had taken place. Cortés, the Spanish conqueror of Mexico, for example, saw himself as following in the footsteps of Paladin Roland, the great medieval military hero who had fought to drive back Muslims and pagans. Prince Henry the Navigator (see below) hoped that the Portuguese expansion into Africa would serve two purposes: the discovery of gold and the extension of Christianity at the expense of Islam.

Not only did the West have the will to expand, but it also possessed the technology needed for successful expansion, the armed sailing vessels. This asset distinguished the West from China and the lands of Islam and helps explain why the West, rather than Eastern civilizations, launched an age of conquest resulting in global mastery. Not only were sailing ships more maneuverable and faster in the open seas than galleys (ships propelled by oars), but the addition of guns below deck that could fire on and cripple or sink distant enemy ships gave them another tactical advantage. The galleys of the Arabs in the Indian Ocean and the junks of the Chinese were not

Portuguese in India. A charming watercolor by a Portuguese traveler in India, this painting mixes what to Western eyes was strange and foreign with the more familiar. The elephant, the clothes, and the elaborate parasols held high by turbaned servants may have seemed exotic, but the hunt, the horse, and the hunting dogs had their counterparts in western European landed society. (*Biblioteca Casanatense, Rome. Photo: Humberto Nicoletti Serra.*)

armed with such guns. In battle, they relied instead on the ancient tactic of coming up alongside the enemy vessel, shearing off its oars, and boarding to fight on deck.

The gunned ship gave the West naval superiority from the beginning. The Portuguese, for example, made short work of the Muslim fleet sent to drive them out of the Indian Ocean in 1509. That victory at Diu, off the western coast of India, indicated that the West not only had found an all-water route to the Orient, but was there to stay.

The Portuguese Empire

In the first half of the fifteenth century, a younger son of the king of Portugal, named Prince Henry the Navigator (1394–1460) by English writers, sponsored voyages of exploration and the nautical studies needed to undertake them. The Portuguese first expanded into islands in the Atlantic Ocean. In 1420, they began to settle Madeira and farm there, and in the 1430s, they pushed into the Canaries and the Azores in search of new farmlands and slaves for their colonies. In the middle decades of the century, they moved down the West African coast to the mouth of the Congo River and beyond, establishing trading posts as they went.

By the end of the fifteenth century, the Portuguese had developed a viable imperial economy among the ports of West Africa, their Atlantic islands, and Western Europe—an economy based on sugar, black slaves, and gold. Africans panned gold in the riverbeds of central and Western Africa, and the Portuguese purchased it at its source.

The Portuguese did not stop in Western Africa. By 1488, Bartholomeu Dias had reached the southern tip of the African continent; a decade later, Vasco da Gama sailed around the Cape of Good Hope and across the Indian Ocean to India. By discovering an all-water route to the Orient, Portugal broke the commercial monopoly on Eastern goods that Genoa and Venice had enjoyed. With this route to India and the East Indies, the Portuguese found the source of the spices needed to make dried and tough meat palatable. As they had done along the African coast, they established fortified trading posts—most notably at Goa on the western coast of India (Malabar) and at Malacca, on the Malay Peninsula.

The Spanish Empire

Spain stumbled onto its overseas empire, and it proved to be the biggest and richest of any until the eighteenth century. Christopher Columbus, who believed that he could reach India by sailing west, won the support of Isabella, queen of Castile. But on his first voyage (1492), he landed on a large Caribbean island, which he named Española (Little Spain). Within decades, two events revealed that Columbus had discovered not a new route to the East, but new continents: Vasco Nuñez de Balboa's discovery of the Pacific Ocean at the Isthmus of Panama in 1513, and the circumnavigation of the globe (1519–1521) by the expedition led by Ferdinand Magellan, which sailed through the strait at the tip of South America that now bears Magellan's name.

Stories of the existence of large quantities of gold and silver to the west lured the Spaniards from their initial settlements in the Caribbean to Mexico. In 1519, Hernando Cortés landed on the Mexican coast with a small army; during two years of campaigning, he managed to defeat the native rulers, the Aztecs, and to conquer Mexico for the Spanish crown. A decade later, Francisco Pizarro achieved a similar victory over the mountain empire of the Incas in Peru.

For good reasons, the Mexican and Peruvian conquests became the centers of the Spanish overseas empire. First, there were the gold hoards accumulated over the centuries by the indigenous rulers for religious and ceremonial purposes. When these supplies were exhausted, the Spanish discovered silver at Potosí in Upper Peru in 1545 and at Zacatecas in Mexico a few years later. From the middle of the century, the annual treasure fleets sailing to Spain became the financial bedrock of Philip II's war against the Muslim Turks and the Protestant Dutch and English.

Not only gold and silver lured Spaniards to the New World. The crusading spirit spurred them on as well. The will to conquer and convert the pagan peoples of the New World stemmed from the crusading tradition developed during the five previous centuries of Spanish history, in campaigns against the Muslims. The rewards were what they had always been: the propagation of the true faith, service to the crown, and handsome land grants. The land was especially attractive in the sixteenth century, for the number of *hidalgos* (lesser nobility) was increasing with the general rise in population; as a result, the amount of land available to them at home was shrinking.

In the New World, power and land gradually became concentrated in fewer and fewer hands. In particular, royal officials, their associates, and the church gained substantially in wealth and privilege. As recurrent depressions ruined smaller landowners, they were forced to sell out to their bigger neighbors. Upon their conversion to Christianity, the Indians were persuaded to give more and more land to the church. Thus, Spanish America became permanently divided between the privileged elite and the impoverished masses.

The effects of conquest were severe in other ways. Between 1500 and 1600, the number of Indians shrank from about twenty million to little

Map 9.2 Portuguese and Spanish Empire Building, 1415–1635 ▶ Not only did Spain and Portugal carve out empires in different parts of the world, but, as the map shows, they built two different kinds of empires. Portugal established small colonies along the seacoast. Spain went in for conquering and governing large territories and large populations in the New World.

ASIA

JAPAN
1542

CHINA
Canton 1513
Macao
1517

PHILIPPINES

NEW
GUINEA

AUSTRALIA

MOLUCCAS ISL.

Malacca 1509

BORNEO

SUMATRA

JAVA

1521

1522

CEYLON
1505

INDIA
Goa
1510
Calicut
1498

PERSIA
Ormuz 1507

ARABIA
Muscat
Aden 1513

MADAGASCAR
1500

1498

Malindi
1498

Mozambique

EUROPE
Amsterdam
Antwerp
Genoa Venice
Constantinople

SPAIN
Seville
Ceuta
1415

PORTUGAL
Lisbon

AFRICA

Timbuktu

GOLD COAST

GUINEA

CAPE
VERDE
1445

1522

1497

Cape of Good Hope

ANTARCTICA

500 Mi.

250 500 Km.

0   250

0

NORTH
AMERICA

NEWFOUNDLAND
1497

AZORES

MADEIRA

CANARY IS.

CAPE
VERDE IS.
1456

1519

St. Augustine 1565

SAN SALVADOR 1492

HISPANIOLA 1492

CUBA
1492

HONDURAS

TRINIDAD 1498

SPANISH
MAIN

1492

Mexico City
1519

Vera Cruz 1519

NEW SPAIN

Panamá

Cartagena

Bogotá

Quito
1534

PERU

Lima
1535

Potosí

Buenos Aires
1535

Santiago

SOUTH
AMERICA

BRAZIL

Rio de Janeiro
1516

Straits of Magellan

Cape Horn

1520

Columbus
Da Gama
Magellan and crew
Spanish holdings
Portuguese holdings

215

more than two million. The major cause of this catastrophe, however, was not forced labor but the diseases introduced from Europe—dysentery, malaria, hookworm, and smallpox—against which the Indians had little or no natural resistance. Beginning in the 1540s, the position of the natives gradually improved as the crown withdrew grants that gave authority over the native population and took increasing responsibility for controlling the Indians.

BLACK SLAVERY AND THE SLAVE TRADE

One group suffered even more than the Indians: the black slaves originally brought over from West Africa. During the long period of their dominance in North Africa and the Middle East (from the seventh to the nineteenth century), the Muslim states relied on slave labor and slave soldiers from black Africa south of the Sahara. Blacks were captured and transported across the Sahara to be sold in the slave markets of North Africa. At its height in the eighteenth century, this trans-Saharan trade may have risen to some ten thousand slaves a year.

But this annual traffic was eventually dwarfed by the slave trade between West Africa and the European colonies in the New World, which began in earnest in the early sixteenth century. As Roland Oliver notes, "By the end of the seventeenth century, stimulated by the growth of plantation agriculture in Brazil and the West Indies, Atlantic shipments had increased to about thirty thousand a year, and by the end of the eighteenth century they were nearly eighty thousand."[1]

Captured in raids by African slavers, the victims were herded into specially built prisons on the West African coast. Those accepted for sale were "marked on the breast with a red-hot iron, imprinting the mark of the French, English or Dutch companies so that each nation may distinguish their own property."[2] Across the centuries, some eleven or twelve million blacks in all were exported to the New World. Of these, some 600,000 ended up in the thirteen colonies of British North America, forming the basis of the

slave population of the new United States at the end of the American Revolution.

The conditions of the voyage from Africa, the so-called middle passage, were brutal. Crammed into the holds of ships, some 13 to 30 percent of blacks died on board. Upon arrival in the New World, slaves were greased with palm oil to improve their appearance and paraded naked into the auction hall for the benefit of prospective buyers, who paid top prices for "the strongest, youthfullest, and most beautiful."[3] The standard workload for slaves everywhere was ten or eleven hours a day six days a week. But some distinction must be made between slavery in the American South and elsewhere in the New World. In Brazil and the West Indies, slaves were worked to exhaustion and death and then replaced. Slaves formed a large majority there and were concentrated on very large plantations. Revolts were frequent but were always crushed and savagely punished. In the American South, by contrast, slaves were a minority dispersed over relatively small holdings; large plantations were few. As a result, revolts and deadly epidemics were rare. After 1808, when the United States abolished the external slave trade, slaveholders could not ruthlessly exploit their slaves if they were to meet the growing need for workers caused by the increasing industrial demand for raw cotton. By 1830, the slave population of the southern states rose through natural increase to more than two million, which represented over one-third of all slaves in the New World.

THE PRICE REVOLUTION

Linked to overseas expansion was another phenomenon: an unprecedented inflation during the sixteenth century, known as the price revolution. For example, cereal prices multiplied by eight times or more in certain regions in the course of that century, and they continued to rise, although more slowly, during the first half of the seventeenth century. Economic historians have generally assumed that the prices of goods other than cereals increased by half as much as grain prices.

The main cause of the price revolution was the population growth during the late fifteenth and sixteenth centuries. The population of Europe almost doubled between 1460 and 1620. Until the middle of the seventeenth century, the number of mouths to feed outran the capacity of agriculture to supply basic foodstuffs, causing the vast majority of people to live close to subsistence. Until food production could catch up with the increasing population, prices, especially those of the staple food, bread, continued to rise.

The other principal cause of the price revolution was probably the silver that flowed into Europe from the New World via Spain, beginning in 1552. At some point, the influx of silver may have exceeded the necessary expansion of the money supply and may have begun contributing to the inflation. A key factor in the price revolution, then, was too many people with too much money chasing too few goods. The effects of the price revolution were momentous.

THE EXPANSION OF AGRICULTURE

The price revolution had its greatest effect on farming. Food prices, which rose roughly twice as much as the prices of other goods, spurred ambitious farmers to take advantage of the situation and to produce for the expanding market. The opportunity for profit drove some farmers to work harder and manage their land better.

All over Europe, landlords held their properties in the form of manors. A particular type of rural society and economy had evolved on these manors in the Late Middle Ages. By the fifteenth century, much manor land was held by peasant tenants according to the terms of a tenure known in England as *copyhold*. The tenants had certain hereditary rights to the land in return for the performance of certain services and the payment of certain fees to the landlord. Principal among these rights was the use of the commons—the pasture, woods, and pond. For the copyholder, access to the commons often made the difference between subsistence and real want because the land tilled on the manor might not produce enough to support a family. Arable land was worked according to ancient custom. The land was divided into strips, and each peasant of the manor was traditionally assigned a certain number of strips. This whole pattern of peasant tillage

Medieval Agriculture. A manuscript page from a book copied about 1500 in what is now Belgium. Agriculture was the foundation of economic life, and because the population was growing rapidly, every effort was being made to increase food production. (*Corbis-Bettmann*)

and rights in the commons was known as the *open-field system*. After changing little for centuries, it was met head-on by the incentives generated by the price revolution.

In England, landlords aggressively pursued the possibilities for profit resulting from the inflation of farm prices. This pursuit required far-reaching changes in ancient manorial agriculture, changes that are called *enclosure*. The open-field system was geared to providing subsistence for the local village and, as such, prevented large-scale farming for a distant market. In the open-field system, the commons could not be diverted to the production of crops for sale. Moreover, the division of the arable land into strips reserved for each peasant made it difficult to engage in profitable commercial agriculture.

English landlords in the sixteenth century launched a two-pronged attack against the open-field system in an effort to transform their holdings into market-oriented, commercial ventures. First they denied their tenant peasantry the use of the commons, depriving poor tenants of critically needed produce; then they changed the conditions of tenure from copyhold to leasehold. Whereas copyhold was heritable and fixed, leasehold was not. When a lease came up for renewal, the landlord could raise the rent beyond the tenant's capacity to pay. Both acts of the landlord forced peasants off the manor or into the landlord's employ as farm laborers. With tenants gone, fields could be incorporated into larger, more productive units. Landlords could hire labor at bargain prices because of the swelling population and the large supply of peasants forced off the land by enclosure. Subsistence farming gave way to commercial agriculture: the growing of a surplus for the marketplace. But rural poverty increased because of the mass evictions of tenant farmers.

In the fifteenth and sixteenth centuries, the Dutch developed a new kind of farming known as *convertible husbandry* that also expanded production. This farming system employed a series of innovations, including the use of soil-restoring legumes, that replaced the old three-field system of crop rotation, which had left one-third of the land unused at any given time. The new techniques used all the land every year and provided a more diversified agriculture.

THE EXPANSION OF TRADE AND INDUSTRY

The conditions of the price revolution also caused trade and industry to expand. Population growth that exceeded the capacity of local food supplies stimulated commerce in basic foodstuffs—for example, the Baltic trade with western Europe. Equally important as a stimulus to trade and industry was the growing income of landlords, merchants, and, in some instances, peasants. This income created a rising demand for consumer goods. Another factor in commercial and industrial expansion was the growth of the state. With increasing amounts of tax revenue to spend, the expanding monarchies of the sixteenth and seventeenth centuries bought more and more supplies—ships, weapons, uniforms, paper—and so spurred economic expansion.

Innovations in Business

Markets tended to shift from local to regional or even to international—a condition that gave rise to the merchant capitalist. The merchant capitalists' operations, unlike those of local producers, extended across local and national boundaries. An essential feature of merchant capitalism was the *putting-out system* of production. The manufacture of woolen textiles is a good example of how the system worked. The merchant capitalist would buy the raw wool from English landlords, who had enclosed their manors to take advantage of the rising price of wool. The merchant's agents collected the wool and took it (put it out) to nearby villages for spinning, dyeing, and weaving. The work was done in the cottages of peasants, many of whom had been evicted from the surrounding manors as a result of enclosure and therefore had to take what work they could get at very low wages. When the wool had been processed into cloth, it was picked up and shipped to market.

A cluster of other innovations in business life accompanied the emergence of the merchant capitalist and the putting-out system. Some of these innovations had roots in the Middle Ages and were important in the evolution of the modern capitalist economy. Banking operations grew more sophisticated, making it possible for depositors to pay their debts by issuing written orders to their banks to make transfers to their creditors' accounts—the origins of the modern check. Accounting methods also improved. The widespread use of double-entry bookkeeping made errors immediately evident and gave a clear picture of the financial position of a commercial enterprise. Very important to overseas expansion was a new form of business enterprise known as the joint-stock company, which allowed small investors to buy shares in a venture. These companies made possible the accumulation of the large amounts of capital needed for large-scale operations, like the building and deployment of merchant fleets, that were quite beyond the resources of one person.

Different Patterns of Commercial Development

England and the Netherlands In both England and the United Provinces (the Netherlands), the favorable conditions led to large-scale commercial expansion. In the 1590s, the Dutch devised a new ship, the *fluit*, or flyboat, to handle bulky grain shipments at the lowest possible cost. This innovation allowed them to capture the Baltic trade, which became a principal source of their phenomenal commercial expansion between 1560 and 1660.

Equally dramatic was their commercial penetration of the Orient. Profits from the European carrying trade built the ships that allowed the Dutch first to challenge and then to displace the Portuguese in the spice trade with the East Indies during the early seventeenth century. The Dutch chartered the United East India Company in 1602 and established trading posts in the islands, which were the beginnings of a Dutch empire that lasted until World War II.

The English traded throughout Europe in the sixteenth and seventeenth centuries, especially with Spain and the Netherlands. The seventeenth century saw the foundation of a British colonial empire along the Atlantic seaboard in North America, from Maine to the Carolinas, and in the West Indies, where the English managed to dislodge the Spanish in some places.

In both England and the Netherlands, government promoted the interests of business. Political power in the Netherlands passed increasingly into the hands of an urban patriciate of merchants and manufacturers, based in cities like Delft, Haarlem, and especially Amsterdam. There, urban interests pursued public policies that served their pocketbooks. In England, because of the revolutionary transfer of power from the king to Parliament, economic policies also reflected the interests of big business, whether agricultural or commercial. Enclosure, for example, was abetted by parliamentary enactment. The Bank of Eng-

land, founded in 1694, expanded credit and increased business confidence. The Navigation Acts, which proved troublesome to American colonists, placed restrictions on colonial trade and manufacturing in order to prevent competition with English merchants and manufacturers.

France and Spain France benefited from commercial and industrial expansion, but not to the same degree as England, mainly because of the aristocratic structure of French society. Family ties and social intercourse between the aristocracy and the merchants, like those that developed in England, were much less in France. Consequently, the French aristocracy remained contemptuous of commerce. Also inhibiting economic expansion were the guilds—remnants of the Middle Ages that restricted competition and production. In France, there was relatively less room than in England for the merchant capitalist operating outside the guild structures.

Spain presents an even clearer example of the failure to grasp the opportunities afforded by the price revolution. By the third quarter of the sixteenth century, Spain possessed the makings of economic expansion: unrivaled amounts of capital in the form of silver, a large and growing population, rising consumer demand, and a vast overseas empire. These factors did not bear fruit because the Spanish value system regarded business as social heresy. The Spanish held in high esteem gentlemen who possessed land gained through military service and crusading ardor, which enabled them to live on rents and privileges. Commerce and industry remained contemptible pursuits.

Numerous wars in the sixteenth century (with France, the Lutheran princes, the Ottoman Turks, the Dutch, and the English) put an increasing strain on the Spanish treasury, despite the annual shipments of silver from the New World. Spain spent its resources on maintaining and extending its imperial power and Catholicism, rather than on investing in economic expansion. In the end, the wars cost more than Spain could handle. The Dutch for a time and the English and the French for a much longer period displaced Spain as the great power. The English and the Dutch had taken advantage of the opportunities presented by the price revolution; the Spanish had not.

View of a Sixteenth-Century Marketplace. Market towns were growing all over Western Europe after 1500. The increasing population made for brisk business in the marketplace. Note the ships in the harbor, the churches, and the variety of products available to those who could afford them. (*Private Collection/Bridgeman Art Library*)

THE FOSTERING OF MERCANTILE CAPITALISM

The changes described—especially in England and the Netherlands—represent a crucial stage in the development of the modern economic system known as *capitalism*. This is a system of *private enterprise*: the main economic decisions (what, how much, where, and at what price to produce, buy, and sell) are made by private individuals in their capacity as owners, workers, or consumers.

From 1450 to 1600, several conditions sustained the incentive to invest and reinvest—a basic factor in the emergence of modern capitalism. One was the price revolution stemming from a supply of basic commodities that could not keep pace with rising demand. Prices continued to climb, creating the most powerful incentive of

all to invest rather than to consume. Why spend now, those with surplus wealth must have asked, when investment in commercial farming, mining, shipping, and publishing (to name a few important outlets) is almost certain to yield greater wealth in the future?

Additional stimuli for investment came from governments. Governments acted as giant consumers, and throughout the early modern period their appetites were expanding. Merchants who supplied governments with everything from guns to frescoes not only prospered, but reinvested as well, because of the constancy and growth of government demand. Governments also sponsored new forms of investment, whether to supply the debauched taste for new luxuries at the king's court or to meet the requirements of the military. Moreover, private investors reaped incalculable advantages from overseas empires.

Colonies supplied cheap raw materials and cheap (slave) labor and served as markets for exports. They greatly stimulated the construction of both ships and harbor *facilities and the sale of insurance.*

State policies, known as mercantilism, were also aimed at augmenting national wealth and power. According to mercantilist theory, wealth from trade was measured in gold and silver, of which there was believed to be a more or less fixed quantity. The state's goal in international trade became to sell more abroad than it bought, that is, to establish a favorable balance of payments. When the amount received for sales abroad was greater than that spent for purchases, the difference would be an influx of precious metal into the state. By this logic, mercantilists were led to argue for the goal of national sufficiency: a country should try to supply most of its own needs to keep imports to a minimum.

To fuel the national economy, governments subsidized new industries, chartered companies to engage in overseas trade, and broke down local trade barriers, such as guild regulations and internal tariffs. The price revolution, the concentration of wealth in private hands, and government activity combined to provide the foundation for sustained investment and for the emergence of mercantile capitalism. This new force in the world should not be confused with industrial capitalism. The latter evolved with the Industrial Revolution in eighteenth-century England, but mercantile capitalism paved the way for it.

TOWARD A GLOBAL ECONOMY

The transformations considered in this chapter were among the most momentous in the world's history. In an unprecedented development, one small part of the world, western Europe, had become the lord of the sea-lanes, the master of many lands throughout the globe, and the banker and profit taker in an emerging world economy. Western Europe's global hegemony was to last well into the twentieth century. In conquering and settling new lands, Europeans exported Western culture around the globe, a process that accelerated in the twentieth century.

The effects of overseas expansion were profound. The native populations of the New World were decimated. As a result of the labor shortage, millions of blacks were imported from Africa to work as slaves on plantations and in mines. Black slavery would produce large-scale effects on culture, politics, and society that have lasted to the present day.

The widespread circulation of plant and animal life also had great consequences. Horses and cattle were introduced into the New World. (So amazed were the Aztecs to see men on horseback that at first they thought horse and rider were one demonic creature.) In return, the Old World acquired such novelties as corn, the tomato, and, most important, the potato, which was to become a staple of the northern European diet. Manioc, from which tapioca is made, was transplanted from the New World to Africa, where it helped sustain the population.

Western Europe was wrenched out of the subsistence economy of the Middle Ages and launched on a course of sustained economic growth. This transformation resulted from the grafting of traditional forms, such as primogeniture and holy war, onto new forces, such as global exploration, price revolution, and convertible husbandry. Out of this change emerged the beginnings of a new economic system, mercantile capitalism. This system, in large measure, paved the way for the Industrial Revolution of the eighteenth and nineteenth centuries and provided the economic thrust for European world predominance.

❖   ❖   ❖

NOTES

1. Roland Oliver, *The African Experience* (New York: HarperCollins, 1991), p. 123.

2. Quoted in Basil Davidson, *Africa in History* (New York: Collier Books, 1991), p. 215.

3. Quoted in Richard S. Dunn, *Sugar and Slaves* (Chapel Hill: University of North Carolina Press, 1972), p. 248.

SUGGESTED READING

Anderson, Perry, *Lineages of the Absolutist State* (1974). A useful survey, written from a Marxist perspective.

Cipolla, Carlo M., *Guns, Sails and Empires* (1965). Connections between technological innovation and overseas expansion, 1400 to 1700.

Davis, David Brion, *The Problem of Slavery in Western Culture* (1966). An authoritative study.

Davis, Ralph, *The Rise of the Atlantic Economies* (1973). A reliable survey of early modern economic history.

Dor Ner, Zvi, *Columbus and the Age of Discovery* (1991). Companion volume to the seven-part PBS series; lavishly illustrated.

Elliott, J. H., *Imperial Spain, 1469–1716* (1963). An excellent survey of the major European power of the early modern period.

Koenigsberger, H. G., *Early Modern Europe, 1500–1789* (1987). A valuable survey of the period.

Kolchin, Peter, *American Slavery: 1619–1877* (1993). An informed synthesis.

Parker, Geoffrey, *The Military Revolution: Military Innovation and The Rise of the West* (1988). Sweeping coverage of an important topic.

Parry, J. H., *The Age of Reconnaissance* (1963). A short survey of exploration.

Plumb, J. H., *The Growth of Political Stability in England, 1675–1725* (1967). A basic book, clear and readable.

Sharpe, J. A., *Early Modern England*, 2nd ed., (1997). A readable overview.

Shennan, J. H., *The Origins of the Modern European State* (1974). An excellent brief introduction.

REVIEW QUESTIONS

1. What are key features of the modern state? In what ways did early modern kings help shape the modern state?

2. What were the strengths and weaknesses of the Spanish state?

3. Why did England move in the direction of parliamentary government, while most countries on the Continent embraced absolutism? Describe the main factors.

4. What were the new forces for expansion operating in early modern Europe?

5. Discuss the connection between the price revolution and overseas expansion. What was the principal cause of the price revolution? Why?

6. What was enclosure? How did the price revolution encourage it?

7. What is mercantile capitalism? What fostered its development?

8. European expansion gave rise to an emerging world economy. Discuss this statement.

Chapter 10

Intellectual Transformation: The Scientific Revolution and the Age of Enlightenment

*T*he movement toward modernity initiated by the Renaissance was greatly advanced by the Scientific Revolution of the seventeenth century. The Scientific Revolution destroyed the medieval view of the universe and established the scientific method—rigorous and systematic observation and experimentation—as the essential means of unlocking nature's secrets. Increasingly, Western thinkers maintained that nature was a mechanical system, governed by laws that could be expressed mathematically. The new discoveries electrified the imagination. Science displaced theology as the queen of knowledge, and reason, which had been subordinate to religion in the Middle Ages, asserted its autonomy. The great confidence in reason inspired by the Scientific Revolution helped give rise to the Enlightenment, which explicitly rejected the ideas and institutions of the medieval past and articulated the essential norms of modernity. ❖

THE MEDIEVAL VIEW
OF THE UNIVERSE*

Medieval thinkers had constructed a coherent picture of the universe that blended the theories of two ancient Greeks, Aristotle and Ptolemy of Alexandria, with Christian teachings. To the medieval mind, the cosmos was a giant ladder, a qualitative order, ascending toward heaven. God was at the summit of this hierarchical universe, and the earth, base and vile, was at the bottom, just above hell. It was also the center of the universe. In the medieval view, the earth's central location meant that the universe centered on human beings, that by God's design, human beings—the only creatures on whom God had bestowed reason and the promise of salvation— were lords of the earth. Around the stationary earth revolved seven transparent spheres, each of which carried one of the "planets"—the moon, Mercury, Venus, the sun, Mars, Jupiter, and Saturn. (Since the earth did not move, it was not considered a planet.) The eighth sphere, in which the stars were embedded, also revolved about the earth. Beyond the stars was a heavenly sphere, the prime mover, that imparted motion to the

*See also the chapter entitled "The Flowering and Dissolution of Medieval Civilization."

planets and the stars, so that in one day the entire celestial system turned around the stationary earth. Enclosing the entire system was another heavenly sphere, the Empyrean, where God sat on his throne, attended by angels.

Medieval thinkers inherited Aristotle's view of a qualitative universe. Earthly objects were composed of earth, water, air, and fire, whereas celestial objects, belonging to a higher world, were composed of ether or quintessence—an element too pure and perfect to be found on earth, which consisted of base matter. In contrast to earthly objects, heavenly bodies were incorruptible; that is, they experienced no change. Since the quintessential heavens differed totally from earth, the paths of planets could not follow the same laws that governed the motion of earthly objects. This two-world orientation blended well with the Christian outlook.

Like Aristotle, Ptolemy held that planets moved around the earth in perfect circular orbits and at uniform speeds. However, in reality the path of planets is not a circle but an ellipse, and planets do not move at uniform speed but accelerate as they approach the sun. Therefore, problems arose that required Ptolemy to incorporate into his system certain ingenious devices that earlier Greek astronomers had employed. For example, to save the appearance of circular orbits, Ptolemy made use of epicycles, small circles attached to the rims of larger circles. A planet revolved uniformly around the small circle, the epicycle, which in turn revolved about the earth in a larger circle. If one ascribed a sufficient number of epicycles to a planet, the planet could seem to move in a perfectly circular orbit.

The Aristotelian-Ptolemaic model of the cosmos did appear to accord with common sense and raw perception: the earth does indeed seem and feel to be at rest. And the validity of this view seemed to be confirmed by evidence, for the model enabled thinkers to predict with considerable accuracy the movement and location of celestial bodies and the passage of time. This geocentric model and the division of the universe into higher and lower worlds also accorded with passages in Scripture. Scholastic philosophers harmonized Aristotelian and Ptolemaic science with Christian theology, producing an intellectually and emotionally satisfying picture of the uni-

1543	Publication of Copernicus's *On the Revolutions of the Heavenly Spheres* marks the beginning of modern astronomy
1605	Publication of Bacon's *Advancement of Learning*
1610	Publication of Galileo's *The Starry Messenger,* asserting the uniformity of nature
1632	Galileo's teachings are condemned by the church, and he is placed under house arrest
1687	Publication of Newton's *Principia Mathematica*
1690	Publication of Locke's *Two Treatises of Government*
1733	Publication of Voltaire's *Letters Concerning the English Nation*
1751–1765	Publication of the *Encyclopedia* edited by Diderot
1776	Declaration of Independence
1789	French Revolution begins

verse in which everything was arranged according to a divine plan.

A NEW VIEW OF NATURE

In several ways, the Renaissance contributed to the Scientific Revolution. The revival of interest in antiquity during the Renaissance led to the rediscovery of some ancient scientific texts, including the works of Archimedes (287–212 B.C.), which fostered new ideas in mechanics, and to improved translations of the medical works of Galen, a contemporary of Ptolemy, which stimulated the study of anatomy. Renaissance art, too, was a factor in the rise of modern science, for it linked an exact representation of the human body to mathematical proportions and demanded accurate observation of natural phenomena. By defining visual space and the relationship between the object and the observer in mathematical terms and by delineating the natural world with unprecedented scientific precision, Renaissance art helped to promote a new view of nature, which later found expression in the astronomy of Copernicus and Kepler and the physics of Galileo.

The Renaissance revival of ancient Pythagorean and Platonic ideas, which stressed mathematics as the key to comprehending reality, also contributed to the Scientific Revolution. Extending the mathematical harmony found in music to the universe at large, Pythagoras (c. 580–507 B.C.) and his followers believed that all things have form, which can be expressed numerically, and that reality consists fundamentally of number relations, which the mind can grasp. Plato maintained that beyond the world of everyday objects made known to us through the senses lies a higher reality, the world of Forms, which contains an inherent mathematical order apprehended only by thought. The great thinkers of the Scientific Revolution were influenced by these ancient ideas of nature as a harmonious mathematical system knowable to the mind.

Nicolaus Copernicus: The Dethronement of the Earth

Modern astronomy begins with Nicolaus Copernicus (1473–1543), a Polish astronomer, mathematician, and church canon. He proclaimed that earth is a planet that orbits a centrally located sun together with the other planets. This heliocentric theory served as the kernel of a new world picture that eventually supplanted the medieval view of the universe. Copernicus did not base his

Copernican System. In his *On the Revolutions of the Heavenly Spheres* Copernicus proposed a heliocentric model in which the planets orbit around the sun. (*The Granger Collection*)

heliocentric theory on new observations and new data. What led him to remove the earth from the center of the universe was the complexity and cumbersomeness of the Ptolemaic system, which offended his sense of mathematical order. To Copernicus, the numerous epicycles (the number had been increased since Ptolemy, making the model even more cumbersome) violated the Platonic vision of the mathematical symmetry of the universe.

Concerned that his theories would spark a controversy, Copernicus refused to publish his work, but, persuaded by his friends, he finally relented. His masterpiece, *On the Revolutions of the Heavenly Spheres,* appeared in 1543. As Copernicus had feared, his views did stir up controversy, but the new astronomy did not become a passionate issue until the early seventeenth century, more than fifty years after the publication of *On the Revolutions.* The Copernican theory

frightened clerical authorities, who controlled the universities as well as the pulpits, for it seemed to conflict with Scripture. For example, Psalm 93 says: "Yea, the world is established, that it cannot be moved." And Psalm 103 says that God "fixed the earth upon its foundation not to be moved forever." In 1616, the church placed *On the Revolutions* and all other works that ascribed motion to the earth on the Index of Prohibited Books.

Galileo: Uniformity of Nature and Experimental Physics

Galileo Galilei (1564–1642) is the principal reason that the seventeenth century has been called "the century of genius." A Pisan by birth, Galileo was a talented musician and artist and a cultivated humanist; he knew and loved the Latin classics and Italian poetry. He was also an astronomer and physicist who helped shatter the medieval conception of the cosmos and shape the modern scientific outlook. Galileo was indebted to the Platonic tradition, which tried to grasp the mathematical harmony of the universe, and to Archimedes, the Hellenistic mathematician-engineer who had sought a geometric understanding of space and motion.

Galileo rejected the medieval division of the universe into higher and lower realms and proclaimed the modern idea of nature's uniformity. Learning that a telescope had been invented in Holland, Galileo built one for himself and used it to investigate the heavens—the first person to do so. From his observations of the moon, Galileo concluded

> *that the surface of the moon is not smooth, uniform, and precisely spherical as a great number of philosophers believe it (and the other heavenly bodies) to be, but is uneven, rough, and full of cavities and prominences, being not unlike the face of the earth, relieved by chains of mountains and deep valleys.*[1]

This discovery of the moon's craters and mountains and of spots on the supposedly unblemished sun led Galileo to break with the Aristotelian notion that celestial bodies were pure, perfect, and unchangeable. For Galileo, there was no difference in quality between celestial and terrestrial bodies. Nature was not a hierarchical order, in which physical entities were ranked according to their inherent quality; rather, it was a homogeneous system, the same throughout.

With his telescope, Galileo discovered the four moons that orbit Jupiter, an observation that overcame a principal objection to the Copernican system. Galileo showed that a celestial body could indeed move around a center other than the earth, that the earth was not the common center for all celestial bodies, and that a celestial body (the earth's moon or Jupiter's moons) could orbit a planet at the same time that the planet revolved around another body (the sun).

Galileo pioneered in experimental physics and advanced the modern idea that knowledge of motion should be derived from direct observation and from mathematics. In dealing with problems

Galileo's Telescope. When Galileo looked through his telescope he saw shadows. But shadows meant depth and contour and that meant real, solid matter. The notion that the planets were ethereal globes of light gave way to their being just matter like the earth. (*The Granger Collection*)

of motion, he insisted on applying mathematics to the study of moving bodies and did in fact study acceleration by performing experiments, which required careful mathematical measurement. For Aristotelian scholastics, a rock fell because it was striving to reach its proper place in the universe, thereby fulfilling its nature; it was acting in accordance with the purpose God had assigned it. Galileo completely rejected the view that motion is due to a quality inherent in an object. Rather, he said, motion is the relationship of bodies to time and distance. By holding that bodies fall according to uniform and quantifiable laws, Galileo posited an entirely different conceptual system. This system requires that we study angles and distances and search for mathematical ratios but avoid inquiring into an object's quality and purpose—the role God assigned it in a hierarchical universe.

For Galileo, the universe was a "grand book which . . . is written in the language of mathematics and its characters are triangles, circles, and other geometric figures without which it is humanly impossible to understand a single word of it."[2] In the tradition of Plato, Galileo sought to grasp the mathematical principles governing reality—reality was physical nature itself, not Plato's higher realm, of which nature was only a poor copy—and ascribed to mathematics absolute authority. Like Copernicus and Kepler (see below), he believed that mathematics expresses the harmony and beauty of God's creation.

Attack on Authority

Insisting that physical truth is arrived at through observation, experimentation, and reason, Galileo strongly denounced reliance on authority. Scholastic thinkers regarded Aristotle as the supreme authority on questions concerning nature, and university education was based on his works. These doctrinaire Aristotelians angered Galileo, who protested that they sought truth not by opening their eyes to nature and new knowledge but by slavishly relying on ancient texts. In *Dialogue Concerning the Two Chief World Systems—Ptolemaic and Copernican* (1632), Galileo upheld the Copernican view and attacked the unquestioning acceptance of Aristotle's teachings.

Galileo also criticized Roman Catholic authorities for attempting to suppress the Copernican theory. He argued that passages from the Bible had no authority in questions involving nature.

A sincere Christian, Galileo never intended to use the new science to undermine faith. What he desired was to separate science from faith so that reason and experience alone would be the deciding factors on questions involving nature. He could not believe that "God who has endowed us with senses, reason and intellect,"[3] did not wish

us to use these faculties in order to acquire knowledge. He was certain that science was compatible with Scripture rightly understood, that is, allowing for the metaphorical language of Scripture and its disinterest in conveying scientific knowledge. For Galileo, the aim of Scripture was to teach people the truths necessary for salvation, not to instruct them in the operations of nature, which is the task of science.

Galileo's support of Copernicus aroused the ire of both scholastic philosophers and the clergy, who feared that the brash scientist threatened a world picture that had the support of venerable ancient authorities, Holy Writ, and scholastic tradition. Already traumatized by the Protestant threat, Catholic officials cringed at ideas that might undermine traditional belief and authority.

In 1616, the Congregation of the Index, the church's censorship organ, condemned the teaching of Copernicanism. In 1633, the aging and infirm Galileo was summoned to Rome. Tried and condemned by the Inquisition, he was ordered to abjure the Copernican theory. Not wishing to bring harm to himself and certain that the truth would eventually prevail, Galileo bowed to the Inquisition. He was sentenced to life imprisonment—mostly house arrest at his own villa near Florence—the *Dialogue* was banned, and he was forbidden to write on Copernicanism. Not until 1820 did the church lift the ban on Copernicanism.

Johannes Kepler: Laws of Planetary Motion

Johannes Kepler (1571–1630), a German mathematician and astronomer, combined the Pythagorean-Platonic quest to comprehend the mathematical harmony within nature with a deep commitment to Lutheran Christianity. He contended that God gave human beings the ability to understand the laws of harmony and proportion.

As a true Pythagorean, Kepler yearned to discover the geometric harmony of the planets—what he called the "music of the spheres." Such knowledge, he believed, would provide supreme insight into God's mind. No doubt this mystical quality sparked the creative potential of his imagination, but to be harnessed for science, it had to be disciplined by the rational faculties.

Kepler discovered the three basic laws of planetary motion, which shattered the Ptolemaic cosmology. In doing so, he utilized the data collected by Tycho Brahe, a Danish astronomer, who for twenty years had systematically observed the planets and stars and recorded their positions with far greater accuracy than had ever been done. Kepler sought to fit Tycho's observations into Copernicus's heliocentric model.

Kepler's first law demonstrated that planets move in elliptical orbits—not circular ones, as Aristotle and Ptolemy (and Copernicus) had believed—and that the sun is one focus of the ellipse. This discovery that a planet's path was one simple oval eliminated all the epicycles that had been used to preserve the appearance of circular motion. Kepler's second law showed that planets do not move at uniform speed, as had been believed, but accelerate as they near the sun, and he provided the rule for deciphering a planet's speed at each point in its orbit. His third law drew a mathematical relationship between the time it takes a planet to complete its orbit of the sun and its average distance from the sun. On the basis of these laws, one could calculate accurately a planet's position and velocity at a particular time—another indication that the planets were linked together in a unified mathematical system.

Derived from carefully observed facts, Kepler's laws of planetary motion buttressed Copernicanism, for they made sense only in a heliocentric universe. But why did the planets move in elliptical orbits? Why did they not fly off into space or crash into the sun? To these questions Kepler had no satisfactory answers. It was Isaac Newton (1642–1727), the great British mathematician-scientist, who arrived at a celestial mechanics that linked the astronomy of Copernicus and Kepler with the physics of Galileo and accounted for the behavior of planets.

THE NEWTONIAN SYNTHESIS

The publication in 1687 of Isaac Newton's *Mathematical Principles of Natural Philosophy* marks the climax of the Scientific Revolution. Newton postulated three laws of motion that joined all celestial and terrestrial objects into a vast mechanical system, whose parts worked in perfect harmony and whose connections could be expressed in mathematical terms, and he invented the calculus, which facilitated the expression of physical laws in mathematical equations. Since Copernican astronomy was essential to his all-encompassing theory of the universe, Newton provided mathematical proof for the heliocentric system, and opposition to it dissipated.

Newton's first law is the principle of inertia: that a body at rest remains at rest unless acted on by a force and that a body in rectilinear motion continues to move in a straight line at the same velocity unless a force acts on it. A moving body does not require a force to keep it in motion, as ancient and medieval thinkers had believed. Once started, bodies continue to move; motion is as natural a condition as rest. Newton's second law states that a given force produces a measurable change in a body's velocity; a body's change of velocity is proportional to the force acting on it. Newton's third law holds that for every action or force there is an equal and opposite reaction or force. The sun pulls the earth with the same force that the earth exercises on the sun. An apple falling to the ground is being pulled by the earth, but the apple is also pulling the earth toward it. (However, since the mass of the apple is so small in comparison with that of the earth, the force that the apple exercises on the earth causes no visible change in the earth's motion.)

Newton asserted that the same laws of motion and gravitation that operate in the celestial world also govern the movement of earthly bodies. Ordinary mechanical laws explain both why apples fall to the ground and why planets orbit the sun. Both the planet and the apple are subject to the same force, and the very same mathematical formula describes the sun's action on a planet and the earth's pull on an apple. Newtonian physics ended the medieval division of the cosmos into higher and lower worlds, with different laws operating in each realm. The universe is an integrated, harmonious mechanical system held together by the force of gravity. By demonstrating that the universe contains an inherent mathematical order, Newton realized the Pythagorean and Platonic visions. To his contemporaries, it seemed that Newton had unraveled all of nature's mysteries: the universe was fully explicable. It was as if Newton had penetrated God's mind.

Deeply committed to Anglican Christianity, Newton retained a central place for God in his world system. God for him was the grand architect whose wisdom and skill accounted for nature's magnificent clockwork design. Newton also believed that God periodically intervened in his creation to restore energy to the cosmic system and that there was no conflict between divine miracles and a mechanical universe. However, in future generations, thinkers called deists (see upcoming section on "Christianity Assailed: The Search for a Natural Religion") came to regard miracles as incompatible with a universe governed by impersonal mechanical principles.

With his discovery of the composition of light, Newton also laid the foundation of the science of optics. He was a cautious experimentalist who valued experimental procedures, including drawing appropriate conclusions from accumulated data. Both Newton's mechanical universe and his championing of the experimental method were foundation blocks of the Age of Enlightenment.

PROPHETS OF MODERN SCIENCE

The accomplishments of the Scientific Revolution extended beyond the creation of a new model of the universe. They also included the formulation of a new method of inquiry into nature and the recognition that science could serve humanity. Two thinkers instrumental in articulating the implications of the Scientific Revolution were Francis Bacon and René Descartes. Both repudiated the authority of Aristotle and other ancients in scientific matters and urged the adoption of new methods for seeking and evaluating truth.

Francis Bacon: The Inductive Method

Sir Francis Bacon (1561–1626), an English statesman and philosopher, vigorously supported the advancement of science and the scientific method. Although he himself had no laboratory and made no discoveries, his advocacy of the scientific method has earned him renown as a prophet of modern science. Bacon attributed the limited progress of science over the ages to the interference of scholastic philosophers, who sought to

bend theories of nature to the requirements of Scripture. Bacon also denounced scholastic thinkers for their slavish attachment to Aristotelian doctrines, which prevented independent thinking and the acquisition of new information about nature. To acquire new knowledge and improve the quality of human life, said Bacon, we should not depend on ancient texts: old authorities must be discarded, and knowledge must be pursued and organized in a new way.

The method that Bacon advocated as the way to truth and useful knowledge was the inductive approach: careful observation of nature and the systematic accumulation of data, drawing general laws from the knowledge of particulars, and testing these laws through constant experimentation. People committed to such a method would never subscribe to inherited fables and myths about nature or invent new ones. Rather, they would investigate nature directly and base their conclusions on observable facts. In his discovery of the circulation of blood, Bacon's contemporary, British physician William Harvey (1578–1657), successfully employed the inductive method championed by Bacon. Grasping the essential approach of modern natural science, Bacon attacked practitioners of astrology, magic, and alchemy for their errors, secretiveness, and enigmatic writings and urged instead the pursuit of cooperative and methodical scientific research that could be publicly criticized.

Bacon was among the first to appreciate the value of the new science for human life. Knowledge, he said, should help us utilize nature for human advantage; it should improve the quality of human life by advancing commerce, industry, and agriculture. Holding that knowledge is power, Bacon urged the state to found scientific institutions and praised progress in technology and the mechanical arts. In Bacon's transvaluation of values, the artisan, mechanic, and engineer advanced knowledge more and contributed more to human betterment than did philosopher-theologians who constructed castles in the air.

René Descartes: The Deductive Method

The scientific method encompasses two approaches to knowledge that usually complement each other:

the empirical (inductive) and the rational (deductive). In the inductive approach, which is employed in such descriptive sciences as biology, anatomy, and geology, general principles are derived from the analysis of data collected through observation and experiment. The essential features of the inductive method, as we have seen, were championed by Bacon, who regarded sense data as the foundation of knowledge. In the deductive approach, which is employed in mathematics and theoretical physics, truths are derived in successive steps from first principles, indubitable axioms. In the seventeenth century, the deductive method was formulated by René Descartes (1596–1650), a French mathematician and philosopher, who is also regarded as the founder of modern philosophy.

In the *Discourse on Method* (1637), Descartes expressed his disenchantment with the learning of his day. Since much of what he had believed on the basis of authority had been shown to be untrue, Descartes resolved to seek no knowledge other than that which he might find within himself or within nature. Rejecting as absolutely false anything about which he could have the least doubt, Descartes searched for an incontrovertible truth that could serve as the first principle of knowledge, the basis of an all-encompassing philosophical system.

Descartes found one truth to be certain and unshakable: that it was he who was doing the doubting and thinking. In his dictum "I think therefore I am," Descartes had his starting point of knowledge. Descartes is viewed as the founder of modern philosophy because he called for the individual to question and if necessary to overthrow all traditional beliefs, and he proclaimed the mind's inviolable autonomy and importance, its ability and right to understand truth. His assertions about the power of thought made people aware of their capacity to comprehend the world through their own mental powers.

Descartes saw the method used in mathematics as the most reliable avenue to certain knowledge. By applying mathematical reasoning to philosophical problems, we can achieve the same certainty and clarity evidenced in geometry. Mathematics is the key to understanding both the truths of nature and the moral order underlying human existence. The mathematical, or deductive, approach favored by Descartes consists of finding a self-

Engraving of René Descartes (1596–1650) Tutoring Queen Christina of Sweden. Descartes was rare among major scientists in that he believed passionately in the intelligence of his female followers and correspondents. Rejecting authority, he asserted confidence in the human mind's ability to arrive at truth through its own capacities. (*Jean-Loup Charmet*)

evident principle, an irrefutable premise, such as a geometric axiom, and then deducing other truths from it through a chain of logical reasoning. The Cartesian deductive method, with its mathematical emphasis, perfectly complements Bacon's inductive approach, which stresses observation and experimentation. The scientific achievements of modern times have stemmed from the skillful synchronization of induction and deduction.

THE MEANING OF THE SCIENTIFIC REVOLUTION

The radical transformation of our conception of the physical universe produced by the Scientific Revolution ultimately transformed our understanding of the individual, society, and the purpose of life. The Scientific Revolution, therefore, was a decisive factor in the shaping of the modern world. It destroyed the medieval worldview, in which the earth occupied the central position, heaven lay just beyond the fixed stars, and every object had its place in a hierarchical and qualitative order. It replaced this view with the modern conception of a homogeneous universe of unbounded space and an infinite number of celestial bodies. Gone were the barriers that separated the heavens and the earth. The glory of the heavens was diminished by the new view that celestial objects were composed of the same stuff and subject to the same laws as all other natural objects. Gone also was the medieval notion that God had assigned an ultimate purpose to all natural objects and to all plant and animal life, that in God's plan everything had an assigned role: we have eyes because God wants us to see and rain because God wants crops to grow. Eschewing ultimate purposes, modern science examines physical nature for mathematical relationships and chemical composition.

In later centuries, further implications of the new cosmology caused great anguish. The conviction that God had created the universe for them, that the earth was fixed beneath their feet, and that God had given the earth the central position in his creation had brought medieval people a profound sense of security. They knew why they were here, and they never doubted that heaven was the final resting place for the faithful. Copernican astronomy dethroned the earth, expelled human beings from their central position, and implied an infinite universe. In the sixteenth and seventeenth centuries, few thinkers grasped the full significance of this displacement. However, in succeeding centuries, this radical cosmological transformation proved as traumatic for the modern mind as did Adam and Eve's expulsion from the Garden of Eden for the medieval mind. Today we know that the earth is one of billions and billions of celestial bodies, a tiny speck in an endless cosmic ocean, and that the universe is some twelve billion years old. Could such a universe have been created just for human beings? Could it contain a heaven that assures eternal life for the faithful and a hell with eternal fires and torments for sinners?

Few people at the time were aware of the full implications of the new cosmology. One who did understand was Blaise Pascal (1623–1662), a French scientist and mathematician. A devout Catholic, Pascal was frightened by what he called "the eternal silence of these infinite spaces" and realized that the new science could stir doubt, uncertainty, and anxiety, which threatened belief.

The conception of reason advanced by Galileo and other thinkers of the period differed fundamentally from that of medieval scholastics. Scholastic thinkers viewed reason as a useful aid for contemplating divine truth; as such, reason always had to serve theology. Influenced by the new scientific spirit, thinkers now saw the investigation of nature as reason's principal concern. What is more, they viewed this activity as autonomous and not subject to theological authority.

The Scientific Revolution fostered a rational and critical spirit among the intellectual elite. Descartes's methodical doubt, rejection of authority, and insistence on the clarity, precision, and accuracy of an idea and Francis Bacon's insistence on verification pervaded the outlook of the eighteenth-century Enlightenment thinkers; they denounced magic, spells, demons, witchcraft, alchemy, and astrology as vulgar superstitions. Phenomena attributed to occult forces, they argued, could be explained by reference to natural forces. A wide breach opened up between the intellectual elite and the massés, who remained steeped in popular superstitions and committed to traditional Christian dogma.

The creators of modern science had seen no essential conflict between traditional Christianity and the new view of the physical universe and made no war on the churches. Indeed, they believed that they were unveiling the laws of nature instituted by God at the Creation—that at last the human mind could comprehend God's magnificent handiwork. But the new cosmology and new scientific outlook ultimately weakened traditional Christianity, for it dispensed with miracles and the need for God's presence.

The new critical spirit led the thinkers of the Enlightenment to doubt the literal truth of the Bible and to dismiss miracles as incompatible with what science teaches about the regularity of nature. So brilliantly had God crafted the universe, they said, so exquisite a mechanism was nature, that its operations did not require God's intervention. In the generations after the Scientific Revolution, theology, long considered the highest form of contemplation, was denounced as a barrier to understanding or even dismissed as irrelevant, and the clergy rapidly lost their position as the arbiters of knowledge. To many intellectuals, theology seemed sterile and profitless in comparison with the new science. Whereas science promised the certitude of mathematics, theologians seemed to quibble endlessly over unfathomable and, even worse, inconsequential issues. That much blood had been spilled over these questions discredited theology still more. In scientific academies, in salons, and in coffee houses, educated men and some women met to discuss the new ideas, and journals published the new knowledge for eager readers. European culture was undergoing a great transformation, marked by the triumph of a scientific and secular spirit among the intellectual elite.

The Scientific Revolution repudiated reliance on Aristotle, Ptolemy, and other ancient authorities in matters concerning nature and substituted in their place knowledge derived from observation, experimentation, and mathematical thinking. Citing an ancient authority was no longer sufficient to prove a point or win an argument. The new standard of knowledge derived from experience with the world, not from ancient texts or inherited views. This new outlook had far-reaching implications for the Age of Enlightenment. If the authority of ancient thinkers regarding the universe could be challenged, could not inherited political beliefs be challenged as well—for example, the divine right of kings to rule? Impressed with the achievements of science, many intellectuals started to urge the application of the scientific method to all fields of knowledge.

The new outlook generated by the Scientific Revolution served as the foundation of the Enlightenment. The Scientific Revolution gave thinkers great confidence in the power of the mind, which had discovered nature's laws, reinforcing the confidence in human abilities expressed by Renaissance humanists. In time, it was believed, the scientific method would unlock all nature's secrets, and humanity, gaining ever greater knowledge and control of nature, would progress rapidly.

THE AGE OF ENLIGHTENMENT: AFFIRMATION OF REASON AND FREEDOM

The Enlightenment of the eighteenth century was the culmination of the movement toward modernity initiated by the Renaissance. The thinkers of the Enlightenment, called *philosophes,* aspired to create a more rational and humane society. To attain this goal, they attacked medieval otherworldliness, rejected theology as an avenue to truth, denounced the Christian idea of people's inherent depravity, and sought to understand nature and society through reason alone, unaided by revelation or priestly authority. Adopting Descartes's method of systematic doubt, they questioned all inherited opinions and traditions. "We think that the greatest service to be done to men," said Denis Diderot, "is to teach them to use their reason, only to hold for truth what they have verified and proved."[4] The philosophes believed that they were inaugurating an enlightened age. Through the power of reason, humanity was at last liberating itself from the fetters of ignorance, superstition, and despotism with which tyrants and priests had bound it in past ages. Paris was the center of the Enlightenment, but there were philosophes and adherents of their views in virtually every leading city in Western Europe and North America.

In many ways, the Enlightenment grew directly out of the Scientific Revolution. The philosophes sought to expand knowledge of nature and to apply the scientific method to the human world in order to uncover society's defects and to achieve appropriate reforms. Newton had discovered universal laws that explained the physical phenomena. Are there not general rules that also apply to human behavior and social institutions? asked the philosophes. Could a "science of man" be created that would correspond to and complement Newton's science of nature—that would provide clear and certain answers to the problems of the social world in the same way that Newtonian science had solved the mysteries of the physical world?

By relying on the same methodology that Newton had employed to establish certain knowledge of the physical universe, the philosophes hoped to arrive at the irrefutable laws that operated in the realm of human society. They aspired to shape religion, government, law, morality, and economics in accordance with these natural laws. They believed that all things should be reevaluated to see if they accorded with nature and promoted human well-being.

In championing the methodology of science, the philosophes affirmed respect for the mind's capacities and for human autonomy. Individuals are self-governing, they insisted. The mind is self-sufficient; rejecting appeals to clerical or princely authority, it relies on its own ability to think, and it trusts the evidence of its own experience. Rejecting the authority of tradition, the philosophes wanted people to have the courage to break with beliefs and institutions that did not meet the test of reason and common sense and to seek new guideposts derived from experience and reason unhindered by passion, superstition, dogma, and authority. The numerous examples of injustice, inhumanity, and superstition in society outraged the philosophes. Behind their devotion to reason and worldly knowledge lay an impassioned moral indignation against institutions and beliefs that degraded human beings.

CHRISTIANITY ASSAILED: THE SEARCH FOR A NATURAL RELIGION

The philosophes waged an unremitting assault on traditional Christianity, denouncing it for harboring superstition, promulgating unreason, and fostering fanaticism and persecution. Relying on the facts of experience, as Bacon had taught, the philosophes dismissed miracles, angels, and devils as violations of nature's laws and figments of the imagination, which could not be substantiated by the norms of evidence. Applying the Cartesian spirit of careful reasoning to the Bible, they pointed out flagrant discrepancies be-

tween various biblical passages and rejected as preposterous the theologians' attempts to resolve these contradictions. David Hume (1711–1776), the Scottish skeptic, wrote in *The Natural History of Religion* (1757):

> *Examine the religious principles, which have, in fact, prevailed in the world. You will scarcely be persuaded, that they are anything but sick men's dreams: Or perhaps will regard them more as the playsome, whimsies of monkies in human shape, than the serious, positive, dogmatical asseverations of a being, who dignifies himself with the name rational. . . . No theological absurdities so glaring that they have not, sometimes, been embraced by men of the greatest and most cultivated understanding.*[5]

With science as an ally, the philosophes challenged Christianity's claim that it possessed infallible truths, and they ridiculed theologians for wrangling over pointless issues and for compelling obedience to doctrines that defied reason.

Moreover, the philosophes assailed Christianity for viewing human nature as evil and human beings as helpless without God's assistance, for focusing on heaven at the expense of human happiness on earth, and for impeding the acquisition of useful knowledge by proclaiming the higher authority of dogma and revelation. Frightened and confused by religion, people have been held in subjection by clergy and tyrants, the philosophes argued. To establish an enlightened society, clerical power must be broken, Christian dogmas repudiated, and the fanaticism that produced tortures, burnings, and massacres purged from the European soul. The philosophes broke with the Christian past, even if they retained the essential elements of Christian morality.

François Marie Arouet (1694–1778), known to the world as Voltaire, was the recognized leader of the French Enlightenment. Few of the philosophes had a better mind, and none had a sharper wit. Living in exile in Britain in the late 1720s, Voltaire acquired a great admiration for English liberty, commerce, science, and religious toleration. Voltaire's angriest words were directed against established Christianity, to which he attributed many of the ills of French society.

He regarded Christianity as "the Christ-worshiping superstition," which someday would be destroyed "by the weapons of reason." Many Christian dogmas are incomprehensible, said Voltaire, yet Christians have slaughtered one another to enforce obedience to these doctrines. Voltaire was appalled by all the crimes committed in the name of Christianity.[6]

While some philosophes were atheists, most were deists, including Voltaire and Thomas Paine (1737–1809), the English-American radical. Deists sought to fashion a natural religion that accorded with reason and science, and they tried to adapt the Christian tradition to the requirements of the new science. They denied that the Bible was God's revelation, rejected clerical authority, and dismissed Christian mysteries, prophecies, and miracles—the virgin birth, Jesus walking on water, the Resurrection, and others—as violations of a lawful natural order. They did consider it reasonable that this magnificently structured universe, operating with clockwork precision, was designed and created at a point in time by an all-wise Creator. But in their view, once God had set the universe in motion, he refrained from interfering with its operations. Thus, deists were at odds with Newton, who allowed for divine intervention in the world.

For deists, the essence of religion was morality—a commitment to justice and humanity—and not adherence to rituals, doctrines, or clerical authority. In *The Age of Reason* (1794–95), Paine declared: "I believe in the equality of man; and I believe that religious duties consist in doing justice, loving mercy, and endeavoring to make our fellow-creatures happy."[7] Deists deemed it entirely reasonable that after death those who had fulfilled God's moral law would be rewarded, while those who had not would be punished.

POLITICAL THOUGHT

Besides established religion, the philosophes identified another source of the evil that beset humanity: despotism. If human beings were to achieve happiness, they had to extirpate revealed religion and check the power of their rulers. "Every age has its dominant idea," wrote Diderot; "that of our age seems to be Liberty."[8] Eighteenth-century

political thought is characterized by a thoroughgoing secularism; an indictment of despotism, the divine right of kings, and the special privileges of the aristocracy and the clergy; a respect for English constitutionalism because it enshrined the rule of law; and an affirmation of John Locke's theory that government had an obligation to protect the natural rights of its citizens. Central to the political outlook of the philosophes was the conviction that political solutions could be found for the ills that afflicted society.

In general, the philosophes favored constitutional government that protected citizens from the abuse of power. With the notable exception of Rousseau, the philosophes' concern for liberty did not lead them to embrace democracy, for they put little trust in the masses. Several philosophes, notably Voltaire, placed their confidence in reforming despots, like Frederick II of Prussia, who were sympathetic to enlightened ideas. However, the philosophes were less concerned with the form of government—monarchy or republic—than with preventing the authorities from abusing their power.

Seventeenth-Century Antecedents: Hobbes and Locke

The political thought of the Enlightenment was greatly affected by the writings of two seventeenth-century philosophers: Thomas Hobbes (1588–1679) and John Locke (1632–1704). Hobbes witnessed the agonies of the English civil war, including the execution of Charles I in 1649. These developments fortified his conviction that absolutism was the most desirable and logical form of government. Only the unlimited power of a sovereign, Hobbes wrote in his major work, *Leviathan* (1651), could contain the human passions that disrupt the social order and threaten civilized life; only absolute rule could provide an environment secure enough for people to pursue their individual interests.

Influenced by the new scientific thought that saw mathematical knowledge as the avenue to truth, Hobbes aimed at constructing political philosophy on a scientific foundation and rejected the authority of tradition and religion as inconsistent with a science of politics. Thus, although Hobbes supported absolutism, he dismissed the idea advanced by other theorists of absolutism that the monarch's power derived from God. He also rejected the idea that the state should not be obeyed when it violated God's law. Like Machiavelli, Hobbes made no attempt to fashion the earthly city in accordance with Christian teachings. *Leviathan* is a rational and secular political statement; its significance lies in its modern approach, rather than in Hobbes's justification of absolutism.

Hobbes had a pessimistic view of human nature. Believing that people are innately selfish and grasping, he maintained that competition and dissension, rather than cooperation, characterize human relations. Without a stringent authority to make and enforce law, life would be miserable, a war of every man against every man, he said. Therefore, he prescribed a state with unlimited power, since only in this way could people be protected from one another and civilized life preserved. Although the philosophes generally rejected Hobbes's gloomy view of human nature, they embraced his secular approach to politics, particularly his denunciation of the theory of the divine right of kings. Hobbes's concern with protecting the social order from human antisocial tendencies is still a central consideration of modern political life.

In contrast to Hobbes, John Locke saw people as essentially good and humane and developed a conception of the state that was fundamentally different from Hobbes's. In the *Two Treatises of Government* (1690), Locke maintained that human beings are born with natural rights to life, liberty, and property, and they establish the state to protect these rights. Consequently, neither executive nor legislature—neither king nor assembly—has the authority to deprive individuals of their natural rights. Whereas Hobbes justified absolute monarchy, Locke explicitly endorsed constitutional government, in which the power to govern derives from the consent of the governed and the state's authority is limited by agreement. Rulers hold their authority under the law; when they act outside the law, they forfeit their right to govern. Thus, if government fails to fulfill the end for which it was established—the preservation of the individual's right to life, liberty, and property—the people have a right to dissolve that government.

Both Hobbes and Locke agreed that the state exists in order to ensure the tranquillity, security, and well-being of its citizens. However, they proposed radically different ways of attaining this end. Unlike Hobbes, Locke believed that social well-being encompassed personal freedom. Rejecting Hobbes's view that absolute power can remedy the defects of the state of nature, Locke stated the case for limited government, the rule of law, the protection of fundamental human rights, and the right of resistance to arbitrary power. Underlying Locke's conception of the state is the conviction that people have the capacity for reason and freedom: "We are born Free as we are born Rational."

The value that Locke gave to reason and freedom and his theories of natural rights, the rule of law, and the right to resist despotic authority had a profound effect on the Enlightenment and the liberal revolutions of the late eighteenth and early nineteenth centuries. Thus, in the Declaration of Independence, Thomas Jefferson restated Locke's principles to justify the American Revolution. Locke's tenets that property is a natural right and that state interference with personal property leads to the destruction of liberty also became core principles of modern liberalism.

Montesquieu

The contribution of Charles Louis de Secondat, baron de la Brède et de Montesquieu (1689–1755), to political theory rests essentially on his *Spirit of the Laws* (1748), a work of immense erudition covering many topics. Montesquieu held that the study of political and social behavior is not an exercise in abstract thought, but must be undertaken in relation to geographic, economic, and historic conditions. To this end, Montesquieu accumulated and classified a wide diversity of facts, from which he tried to draw general rules governing society. He concluded that different climatic and geographic conditions and different national customs, habits, religions, and institutions give each nation a particular character; each society requires constitutional forms and laws that pay heed to the character of its people. Montesquieu's effort to explain social and political behavior empirically—to found a science of society based on the model of natural science—makes him a forerunner of modern sociology.

Montesquieu regarded despotism as a pernicious form of government, corrupt by its very nature. Ruling as he wishes and unchecked by law, the despot knows nothing of moderation and institutionalizes cruelty and violence. The slavelike subjects, wrote Montesquieu, know only servitude, fear, and misery. Driven by predatory instincts, the despotic ruler involves his state in wars of conquest, caring not at all about the suffering this causes his people. In a despotic society, economic activity stagnates, for merchants, fearful that their goods will be confiscated by the state, lose their initiative. Reformers used Montesquieu's characterization of despotism to show the limitations of absolute monarchy.

To safeguard liberty from despotism, Montesquieu advocated the principle of separation of powers. In every government, said Montesquieu, there are three sorts of powers: legislative, executive, and judiciary. When one person or one body exercises all three powers—if the same body both prosecutes and judges, for example—liberty cannot be preserved. Where sovereignty is monopolized by one person or body, power is abused and political liberty is denied. In a good government, one power balances and checks another power, an argument that impressed the framers of the U.S. Constitution.

Several of Montesquieu's ideals were absorbed into the liberal tradition—constitutional government and the rule of law, separation of powers, freedom of thought, religious toleration, and protection of individual liberty. The conservative tradition drew on Montesquieu's respect for traditional ways of life and his opposition to sudden reforms that ignored a people's history and culture.

Voltaire

Unlike Hobbes and Locke, Voltaire was not a systematic political theorist, but a propagandist and polemicist, who hurled pointed barbs at all the abuses of the French society. Nevertheless, Voltaire's writings do contain ideas that form a coherent political theory that in many ways expresses the outlook of the Enlightenment.

Voltaire disdained arbitrary power, since it is based on human whim rather than on established law. He described a prince who imprisons or executes his subjects unjustly and without due process as "nothing but a highway robber who is called 'Your Majesty.'" For Voltaire, freedom consisted in being governed by an established and standard code of law that applies equally to all. Without the rule of law, wrote Voltaire, there is no liberty of person, no freedom of thought or of religion, no protection of personal property, no impartial judiciary, and no protection from arbitrary arrest. Underlying Voltaire's commitment to the rule of law was his conviction that power should be used rationally and beneficially.

Voltaire's respect for the rule of law was strengthened by his stay in England between 1726 and 1729, which led to the publication of *The English Letters* in 1733. In this work, Voltaire presents an idealized and, at times, inaccurate picture of English politics and society. More important, however, is the fact that his experience with English liberty gave him hope that a just and tolerant society was not a utopian dream, thereby strengthening his resolve to attack the abuses of French society.

As noted earlier, Voltaire was no democrat. He had little confidence in the capacities of the common people, whom he saw as prone to superstition and fanaticism. Nor did he advocate revolution. What he did favor was reforming society through the advancement of reason and the promotion of science and technology. Voltaire himself fought to introduce several reforms into France, including freedom of the press, religious toleration, a fair system of criminal justice, proportional taxation, and curtailment of the privileges of the clergy and nobility.

Rousseau

"Man is born free and everywhere he is in chains."[9] With these stirring words, the Geneva-born French thinker Jean Jacques Rousseau (1712–1778) began *The Social Contract* (1762). Rousseau considered the state as it was then constituted to be unjust and corrupt. It was dominated by the rich and the powerful, who used it to further their interests, whereas the weak knew only oppression and misery. In Rousseau's view, the modern state deprived human beings of their

Voltaire and King Frederick. The roundtable was beloved by the aristocracy because it claimed everyone as an equal. Here Voltaire visits with Frederick the Great and perhaps imagined himself as an equal. (*Bildarchiv Preussischer Kulturbesitz/Art Resource, NY*)

natural freedom and fostered a selfish individualism, which undermined feelings of mutuality and concern for the common good.

Rousseau wanted the state to be a genuine democracy, a moral association that bound people together in freedom, equality, and civic devotion. For Rousseau, individuals fulfilled their moral potential not in isolation, but as committed members of the community; human character was ennobled when people cooperated with one another and cared for one another. Rousseau admired the ancient Greek city-state, the polis, for it was an organic community in which citizens set aside private interests in order to attain the common good. In *The Social Contract,* he sought to recreate the community spirit and the political freedom that characterized the Greek city-state.

What Rousseau proposed was that each person surrender unconditionally all his rights to the community as a whole and submit to its authority. To prevent the assertion of private interests over the common good, Rousseau wanted the state to be governed in accordance with the general will—an underlying principle that expressed what was best for the community. He did not conceive of the general will as a majority or even a unanimous vote, both of which could be wrong. Rather, it was a plainly visible truth, easily discerned by common sense and by reason and by listening to our hearts. In Rousseau's view, just and enlightened citizens imbued with public spirit would have the good sense and moral awareness to legislate in accordance with the general will.

Like ancient Athens, the state that Rousseau envisioned was a direct democracy, in which the citizens themselves, not their representatives, constituted the lawmaking body. Consequently, the governed and the government were one and the same. Rousseau condemned arbitrary and despotic monarchy, the divine-right theory of kingship, and the traditional view that people should be governed by their betters, lords and clergy, who were entitled to special privileges. He granted sovereignty to the people as a whole and affirmed the principle of equality.

Rousseau remains a leading theorist of democratic thought. His critics assert that his political thought, whose goal is a body of citizens who think alike, buttresses a dangerous collectivism and even totalitarianism. These critics argue that Rousseau did not place constitutional limitations on sovereignty or erect safeguards to protect individual and minority rights from a potentially tyrannical majority. They note, too, that Rousseau rejected entirely the Lockean principle that citizens possess rights independently of the state, as well as the right to act against the state.

SOCIAL AND ECONOMIC THOUGHT

The philosophes rejected the Christian belief that human beings are endowed with a sinful nature, a consequence of Adam and Eve's disobedience of

God. They knew from experience, of course, that human beings behave wickedly and seem hopelessly attached to nonrational modes of thinking. While they retained a certain pessimism about human nature, however, the philosophes generally believed in individuals' essential goodness and in their capacity for moral improvement. "Nature has not made us evil," wrote Diderot, "it is bad education, bad models, bad legislation that corrupt us."[10] And Voltaire declared that a person is "born neither good nor wicked; education, example, the government into which he is thrown—in short, occasion of every kind—determines him to virtue or vice."[11] The philosophes' conception of human nature rested heavily on John Locke's epistemology, or theory of knowledge. To the philosophes, it seemed that Locke had discovered the fundamental principles governing the human mind, an achievement comparable to Newton's discovery of the laws governing physical bodies.

Epistemology, Psychology, and Education

In his *Essay Concerning Human Understanding* (1690), a work of immense significance in the history of philosophy, Locke argued that human beings are not born with innate ideas (the idea of God, principles of good and evil, and rules of logic, for example) divinely implanted in their minds, as Descartes had maintained. Rather, said Locke, the human mind is a blank slate upon which are imprinted sensations derived from contact with the phenomenal world. Knowledge is derived from experience.

Locke's theory of knowledge had profound implications. If there are no innate ideas, said the philosophes, then human beings, contrary to Christian doctrine, are not born with original sin, are not depraved by nature. All that individuals are derives from their particular experiences. If people are provided with a proper environment and education, they will behave morally; they will become intelligent and productive citizens. By the proper use of their reason, people could bring their beliefs, their conduct, and their institutions into harmony with natural law. This was how the reform-minded philosophes interpreted Locke.

They preferred to believe that evil stemmed from faulty institutions and poor education, both of which could be remedied, rather than from a defective human nature.

The most important work of Enlightenment educational thought was Rousseau's *Émile* (1762), in which he suggested educational reforms that would instill in children self-confidence, self-reliance, and emotional security—necessary qualities if they were to become productive adults and responsible citizens. If the young are taught to think for themselves, said Rousseau, they will learn to cherish personal freedom. A strong faith in the essential goodness of human nature underlay Rousseau's educational philosophy. He also assumed that youngsters have an equal capacity to learn and that differences in intelligence are due largely to environmental factors.

Rousseau understood that children should not be treated like little adults, for children have their own ways of thinking and feeling. He railed against those who robbed children of the joys and innocence of childhood by chaining them to desks, ordering them about, and filling their heads with rote learning. Instead, he urged that children experience direct contact with the environment to develop their bodies and senses and their curiosity, ingenuity, resourcefulness, and imagination. It is the whole child that concerns Rousseau.

Freedom of Conscience and Thought

The philosophes regarded religious persecution—whose long and bloodstained history included the burning of heretics in the Middle Ages, the slaughter of Jews and Muslims during the First Crusade, and the massacres of the wars of the Reformation—as humanity's most depraved offense against reason. While the worst excesses of religious fanaticism had dissipated by the eighteenth century, examples of religious persecution still abounded, particularly in Catholic lands. In his pleas for tolerance, Voltaire spoke for all the philosophes:

> *I shall never cease . . . to preach tolerance from the housetops . . . until persecution is no more. The progress of reason is slow, the*

roots of prejudice lie deep. Doubtless, I shall never see the fruits of my efforts, but they are seeds which may one day germinate.[12]

Censorship was a serious and ever-present problem for the philosophes. After the publication of Voltaire's *English Letters,* his printer was arrested and the book confiscated and publicly burned as irreligious. On another occasion, when Voltaire was harassed by the authorities, he commented that "it is easier for me to write books than to get them published."[13] Denounced by ecclesiastical and ministerial authorities as a threat to religion and constituted authority, *On the Mind* (1758), by Claude-Adrien Helvetius (1715–1771), was burned by the public executioner. Denis Diderot (1713–1784), the principal editor of the thirty-eight-volume *Encyclopedia,* whose 150 or more contributors included the leading Enlightenment thinkers, had to contend with French authorities, who at times suspended publication. After the first two volumes appeared, the authorities condemned the work for containing "maxims that would tend to destroy royal authority, foment a spirit of independence and revolt . . . and lay the foundations for the corruption of morals and religion."[14] In 1759, Pope Clement XIII condemned the *Encyclopedia* for having "scandalous doctrines [and] inducing scorn for religion."[15] It required careful diplomacy and clever ruses to finish the project and still incorporate ideas considered dangerous by religious and governmental authorities. The *Encyclopedia* had been undertaken in Paris during the 1740s as a monumental effort to bring together all human knowledge and to propagate Enlightenment ideas. Its numerous articles on science and technology and its limited coverage of theological questions attest to the new interests of eighteenth-century intellectuals. With the project's completion in 1772, Diderot and Enlightenment opinion triumphed over clerical, royal, and aristocratic censors.

An article in the *Encyclopedia,* "The Press," conveys the philosophes' yearning for freedom of thought and expression. For them, the term *press* designated more than newspapers and journals; it encompassed everything in print, particularly books.

People ask if freedom of the press is advantageous or prejudicial to a state. The answer is not difficult. It is of the greatest importance to conserve this practice in all states founded on liberty. I would even say that the disadvantages of this liberty are so inconsiderable compared to the advantages that this ought to be the common right of the universe, and it is certainly advisable to authorize its practices in all governments.[16]

Humanitarianism

A humanitarian spirit, which no doubt owed something to Christian compassion, pervaded the outlook of the philosophes. It expressed itself in attacks on torture, which was commonly used to obtain confessions in many European lands, on cruel punishments for criminals, on slavery, and on war. The philosophes' humanitarianism rested on the conviction that human nature was essentially virtuous and that human beings were capable of benevolent feelings toward one another.

In *On Crimes and Punishments* (1764), Cesare Beccaria (1738–1794), an Italian economist and criminologist inspired in part by Montesquieu, condemned torture as inhuman, "a criterion fit for a cannibal."[17] He saw it as an irrational way of determining guilt or innocence, for an innocent person unable to withstand the agonies of torture will confess to anything and a criminal with a high threshold for pain will be exonerated. Influenced by Beccaria's work, reform-minded jurists, legislators, and ministers called for the elimination of torture from codes of criminal justice, and several European lands abolished torture in the eighteenth century.

Though not pacifists, the philosophes denounced war as barbaric and an affront to reason. They deemed it to be a scourge promoted by power-hungry monarchs and supported by fanatical clergy, wicked army leaders, and ignorant commoners. In his literary masterpiece, *Candide* (1759), Voltaire ridiculed the rituals of war.

Nothing could be smarter, more splendid, more brilliant, better drawn up than the two armies. Trumpets, fifes, hautboys [oboes], drums, cannons, formed a harmony such as

Engraving, Newgate Prison, Eighteenth Century. Prison conditions during the Age of Enlightenment were appalling. Here, a manacled man struggles with a wheelbarrow, and two others are led off to the gallows. Meanwhile, a guard watches over the dungeon filled with bound prisoners, who were as often debtors as criminals.

has never been heard even in hell. The cannons first of all laid flat about six thousand men on each side; then the musketry removed from the best of worlds some nine or ten thousand blackguards who infested its surface. The bayonet also was the sufficient reason for the death of some thousands of men. The whole might amount to thirty thousand souls.[18]

Voltaire was particularly outraged by the belief that the outcome of this "heroic butchery" was ordained by God. The article "Peace" in the *Encyclopedia* described war as

the fruit of man's depravity; it is a convulsive and violent sickness of the body politic. . . . [It] depopulates the nation, causes the reign of disorder. . . . makes the freedom and property of citizens uncertain . . . disturbs and causes the neglect of commerce; land becomes uncultivated and abandoned. . . . If reason governed men and had the influence over the heads of nations that it deserves, we would never see them inconsiderately surrender themselves to the fury of war; they would not show that ferocity that characterizes wild beasts.[19]

Tortures of the Inquisition. Torture was part of everyday criminal justice in every European country. Only around the middle of the eighteenth century did the practice come under withering attack by enlightened thinkers. (*The Granger Collection.*)

Montesquieu, Voltaire, Hume, Benjamin Franklin, Thomas Paine, and other philosophes condemned slavery and the slave trade. In Book 15 of *The Spirit of the Laws,* Montesquieu scornfully refuted all justifications for slavery. Ultimately, he said, slavery, which violates the fundamental principle of justice underlying the universe, derived from base human desires to dominate and exploit other human beings. Adam Smith (see next section), the Enlightenment's leading economic theorist, demonstrated that slave labor was inefficient and wasteful. In 1780, Paine helped draft the act abolishing slavery in Pennsylvania. An article in the *Encyclopedia,* "The Slave Trade," denounced slavery as a violation of the individual's natural rights:

> *If commerce of this kind can be justified by a moral principle, there is no crime, however atrocious it may be, that cannot be made le-gitimate. . . . Men and their liberty are not objects of commerce; they can be neither sold nor bought. . . . There is not, therefore, a single one of these unfortunate people regarded only as slaves who does not have the right to be declared free.*[20]

The philosophes, although they often enjoyed the company of intelligent and sophisticated women in the famous salons, continued to view women as intellectually and morally inferior to men. Although some philosophes, notably Condorcet (see upcoming section on "The Idea of Progress"), who wrote *Plea for the Citizenship of Women* (1791), did argue for female emancipation, they were the exception. Most retained traditional views, concurring with David Hume, who held that "nature has subjected" women to men and that their "inferiority and infirmities are absolutely incurable."[21] Rousseau, who also believed that nature had granted men power over women, regarded traditional domesticity as a woman's proper role.

> *I would a thousand times rather have a homely girl, simply brought up, than a learned lady and a wit who would make a literary circle of my house and install herself as its president. A female wit is a scourge to her husband, her children, her friends, her servants, to everybody. From the lofty height of her genius, she scorns every womanly duty, and she is always trying to make a man of herself.*[22]

Nevertheless, by clearly articulating the ideals of liberty and equality, the philosophes made a women's movement possible. The growing popularity of these ideals could not escape women, who measured their own position by them. Moreover, by their very nature, these ideals were expansive. Denying them to women would ultimately be seen as an indefensible contradiction.

Thus, Mary Wollstonecraft's *Vindication of the Rights of Woman* (1792), written under the influence of the French Revolution, protested against the prevailing subordination and submissiveness of women and the limited opportunities afforded them to cultivate their minds. If women were also endowed with reason, why should men alone determine the standards and ground rules, she asked pungently. She reminded enlightened thinkers that the same arbitrary power that they objected to when wielded by monarchs and slave owners they condoned when exercised by husbands in domestic life. She considered it an act of tyranny for women "to be excluded from a participation of the natural rights of mankind."[23]

Laissez-Faire Economics

In *An Inquiry into the Nature and Causes of the Wealth of Nations* (1776), Adam Smith (1732–1790), professor of moral philosophy in Scotland, attacked the theory of mercantilism, which held that a state's wealth was determined by the amount of gold and silver it possessed. According to this theory, to build up its reserves of precious metals, the state should promote domestic industries, encourage exports, and discourage imports. Mercantilist theory called for government regulation of the economy so that the state could compete successfully with other nations for a share of the world's scarce resources. Smith argued that the real basis of a country's wealth was measured by the quantity and quality of its goods and services, not by its storehouse of precious metals. Government intervention, he said, retards economic progress; it reduces the real value of the annual produce of the nation's land and labor. On the other hand, when people pursue their own interests—when they seek to better their condition—they foster economic expansion, which benefits the whole society.

Smith limited the state's authority to maintaining law and order, administering justice, and defending the nation. The concept of *laissez faire*—that government should not interfere with the market—became a core principle of nineteenth-century liberal thought.

The Idea of Progress

The philosophes were generally optimistic about humanity's future progress. Two main assumptions contributed to this optimism. First, accepting Locke's theory of knowledge, the philosophes attributed evil to a flawed but remediable environment, not to an inherently wicked human nature. Hopeful that a reformed environment would bring out the best in people, they looked forward to a day when reason would prevail over superstition, prejudice, intolerance, and tyranny. Second, the philosophes' veneration of science led them to believe that the progressive advancement of knowledge would promote material and moral progress.

A work written near the end of the century epitomized the philosophes' vision of the future: *Sketch for a Historical Picture of the Progress of the Human Mind* (1794) by Marie Jean Antoine Nicolas Caritat, marquis de Condorcet (1743–1794). A mathematician and historian of science and a contributor to the *Encyclopedia,* Condorcet campaigned for religious toleration and the abolition of slavery. During the French Revolution, he attracted the enmity of the dominant Jacobin party and in 1793 was forced to go into hiding.

Secluded in Paris, he wrote *Sketch*. Arrested in 1794, Condorcet died during his first night in prison, either from exhaustion or from self-administered poison. In *Sketch,* Condorcet lauded recent advances in knowledge that enabled reason to "lift her chains (and) shake herself free"[24] from superstition and tyranny. Passionately affirming the Enlightenment's confidence in reason and science, Condorcet expounded a theory of continuous and indefinite human improvement. He pointed toward a future golden age, characterized by the triumph of reason and freedom.

> *Our hopes for the future condition of the human race can be subsumed under three important heads: the abolition of inequality between nations, the progress of equality within each nation, and the true perfection of mankind. . . .*
>
> *The time will therefore come when the sun will shine only on free men who know no other master but their reason; when tyrants and slaves, priests and their stupid or hypocritical instruments will exist only in works of history and on the stage; and we shall think of them only to pity their victims and their dupes; to maintain ourselves in a state of vigilance by thinking on their excesses; and to learn how to recognize and so to destroy, by force of reason, the first seeds of tyranny and superstition, should they ever dare to reappear amongst us.*[25]

But the philosophes were not starry-eyed dreamers. They knew that progress was painful, slow, and reversible. Voltaire's *Candide* was a protest against a naive optimism that ignored the granite might of human meanness, ignorance, and irrationality. "Let us weep and wail over the lot of philosophy," wrote Diderot. "We preach wisdom to the deaf and we are still far indeed from the age of reason."[26]

CONFLICTS AND POLITICS

The major conflicts of the eighteenth century were between Britain and France for control of territory in the New World and between Austria and Prussia for dominance in central Europe. Then, in the late 1700s, the American and French Revolutions broke out; they helped shape the liberal-democratic tradition.

Warfare and Revolution

In 1740, Prussia, ruled by the aggressive Frederick the Great, launched a successful war against Austria and was rewarded with Silesia, which increased the Prussian population by 50 percent. Maria Theresa, the Austrian queen, never forgave Frederick and in 1756 formed an alliance with France against Prussia. The ensuing Seven Years' War (1756–1763), which involved every major European power, did not significantly change Europe, but it did reveal Prussia's growing might.

At the same time, the French and the English fought over their claims in the New World. England's victory in the conflict (known in American history as the French and Indian War) deprived France of virtually all of its North American possessions and set in motion a train of events that culminated in the American Revolution. The war drained the British treasury, and now Britain had the additional expense of paying for troops to guard the new North American territories that it had gained in the war. As strapped British taxpayers could not shoulder the whole burden, the members of Parliament thought it quite reasonable that the American colonists should help pay the bill; after all, Britain had protected the colonists from the French and was still protecting them in their conflicts with Indians. New colonial taxes and import duties imposed by Parliament produced vigorous protests from the Americans.

The quarrel turned to bloodshed in April and June 1775, and on July 4, 1776, delegates from the various colonies adopted the Declaration of Independence, written mainly by Thomas Jefferson. Applying Locke's theory of natural rights, this document declared that government derives its power from the consent of the governed, that it is the duty of a government to protect the rights of its citizens, and that people have the right to "alter or abolish" a government that deprives them of their "unalienable rights."

Why were the American colonists so ready to revolt? Each of the thirteen colonies had an elected assembly, which acted like a miniature parliament. In these assemblies, Americans gained political experience and quickly learned to be self-governing.

Familiarity with the thought of the Enlightenment and the republican writers of the English Revolution also contributed to the Americans' awareness of liberty. The ideas of the philosophes traversed the Atlantic and influenced educated Americans, particularly Thomas Jefferson and Benjamin Franklin. Like the philosophes, American thinkers expressed a growing confidence in reason, valued freedom of religion and of thought, and championed the principle of natural rights.

Another source of hostility toward established authority among the American colonists was their religious traditions, particularly those of the Puritans, who believed that the Bible was infallible and its teachings a higher law than the law of the state. Like their counterparts in England, American Puritans challenged political and religious authorities who, in their view, contravened God's law. Thus, Puritans acquired two habits that were crucial to the development of political liberty: dissent and resistance. When transferred to the realm of politics, these Puritan tendencies led Americans to resist authority that they considered unjust.

American victory came about in 1783 as a result of several factors. George Washington proved to be a superior leader, able to organize and retain the loyalty of his troops. France, seeking to avenge its defeat in the Seven Years' War, helped the Americans with money and provisions and then, in 1778, entered the conflict. Britain had difficulty shipping supplies across three thousand miles of ocean, was fighting the French in the West Indies and elsewhere at the same time, and ultimately lacked commitment to the struggle.

Reformers in other lands quickly interpreted the American victory as a successful struggle of liberty against tyranny. During the Revolution, the various American states drew up constitutions based on the principle of popular sovereignty and included bills of rights that protected individual liberty. They also managed, somewhat reluctantly, to forge a nation. Rejecting both monarchy and hereditary aristocracy, the Constitution of the United States created a republic in which power derived from the people. A system of separation of powers and checks and balances set safeguards against the abuse of power, and the Bill of Rights provided for protection of individual rights. To be sure, the ideals of liberty and equality were not extended to all people—slaves knew nothing of the freedom that white Americans cherished, and women were denied the vote and equal opportunity. But to reform-minded Europeans, it seemed that Americans were fulfilling the promise of the Enlightenment; they were creating a freer and better society.

Enlightened Despotism

The philosophes used the term *enlightened despotism* to refer to an ideal shared by many of them: rule by a strong monarch who would implement rational reforms and remove obstacles to freedom. Some eighteenth-century monarchs and their ministers—Frederick the Great in Prussia, Catherine the Great in Russia, Charles III in Spain, Maria Theresa and, to a greater extent, her son Joseph II in Austria, and Louis XV in France—did institute educational, commercial, and religious reforms.

Behind the reforms of enlightened despots lay the realization that the struggle for power in Europe called for efficient government administration and ample funds. Enlightened despots appointed capable officials to oversee the administration of their kingdoms, eliminate costly corruption, and collect taxes properly. Rulers strengthened the economy by encouraging the expansion of commerce through reduced taxes on goods and through agricultural reforms. In central and Eastern Europe, some rulers moved toward abolishing serfdom, or at least improving conditions for serfs. (In western Europe, serfdom had virtually died out.) Provisions were made to care for widows, orphans, and invalids. Censorship was eased, greater religious freedom was granted to minorities, criminal codes were made less harsh, and there were some attempts at prison reform. By these measures, enlightened despots hoped to inspire greater popular support for the state, an important factor in the European power struggle.

THE ENLIGHTENMENT AND
THE MODERN MENTALITY

The philosophes articulated core principles of the modern outlook. Asserting that human beings are capable of thinking independently of authority, they insisted on a thoroughgoing rational and secular interpretation of nature and society. They critically scrutinized authority and tradition and valued science and technology as a means for promoting human betterment. Above all, they sought to emancipate the mind from the bonds of ignorance and superstition and to rescue people from intolerance, cruelty, and oppression. Because of their efforts, torture (which states and Christian churches had endorsed and practiced) was eventually abolished in Western lands, and religious toleration and freedom of speech and of the press became the accepted norms. The arguments that the philosophes marshaled against slavery were utilized by those who fought against the slave trade and called for emancipation. Enlightenment economic thought, particularly Adam Smith's *Wealth of Nations,* gave theoretical support to a market economy based on supply and demand—an outlook that fostered commercial and industrial expansion. The separation of church and state, a basic principle of modern political life, owes much to the philosophes, who frequently cited the dangers of politics inflamed by religious passions. The philosophes' denunciation of despotism and championing of natural rights, equality under the law, and constitutional government are the chief foundations of modern liberal government.

The ideals of the Enlightenment spread from Europe to America and helped shape the political thought of the Founding Fathers. The Declaration of Independence clearly articulated Locke's basic principles: that government derives its authority from the governed; that human beings are born with natural rights, which government has a responsibility to protect; and that citizens have the right to resist a government that deprives them of these rights. The Constitution asserted that the people are sovereign: "We the People of the United States . . . do ordain and establish this Constitution for the United States of America." And it contained several safeguards against despotic power, including Montesquieu's principle of separation of powers, which was also written into several state constitutions. Both the bills of rights drawn up by the various states and the federal Bill of Rights gave recognition to the individual's inherent rights and explicitly barred government from tampering with them—a principal concern of the philosophes.

The philosophes broke with the traditional Christian view of human nature and the purpose of life. In that view, men and women were born in sin; suffering and misery were divinely ordained, and relief could come only from God; social inequality was instituted by God; and for many, eternal damnation was a deserved final consequence. In contrast, the philosophes saw injustice and suffering as man-made problems that could be solved through reason; they expressed confidence in people's ability to attain happiness by improving the conditions of their earthly existence and articulated a theory of human progress that did not require divine assistance.

To be sure, the promise of the Enlightenment has not been achieved. More education for more people and the spread of constitutional government have not eliminated fanaticism and superstition, violence and war, or evil and injustice. In the light of twentieth-century events, it is difficult to subscribe to Condorcet's belief in linear progress. As Peter Gay observes:

> *The world has not turned out the way the philosophes wished and half expected that it would. Old fanaticisms have been more intractable, irrational forces more inventive than the philosophes were ready to conjecture in their darkest moments. Problems of race, of class, of nationalism, of boredom and despair in the midst of plenty have emerged almost in defiance of the philosophes' philosophy. We have known horrors, and may know horrors, that the men of the Enlightenment did not see in their nightmares.*[27]

Nevertheless, the philosophes' achievement should not be diminished. Their ideals became an intrinsic part of the liberal-democratic tradition and inspired nineteenth- and twentieth-century reformers. The spirit of the Enlightenment will always remain indispensable to all those who cherish the traditions of reason and freedom.

❖   ❖   ❖

NOTES

1. Galileo Galilei, *The Starry Messenger, in Discoveries and Opinions of Galileo,* trans. and ed. Stillman Drake (Garden City, N.Y.: Doubleday Anchor Books, 1957), p. 31.

2. Galileo Galilei, *The Assayer, in Discoveries and Opinions,* pp. 237–238.

3. Galileo Galilei, "Letter to the Grand Duchess Christina," in *Discoveries and Opinions,* p. 183.

4. Quoted in Frank E. Manuel, *Age of Reason* (Ithaca, N.Y.: Cornell University Press, 1951), p. 28.

5. David Hume, *The Natural History of Religion,* ed. H. E. Root (London: Adam and Charles Black, 1956), p. 75.

6. Quoted in Ben Ray Redman, ed., *The Portable Voltaire* (New York: Viking Press, 1949), p. 26.

7. Thomas Paine, *The Age of Reason* (New York: Eckler, 1892), p. 5.

8. Quoted in Paul Hazard, *European Thought in the Eighteenth Century* (New Haven: Yale University Press, 1954), p 174.

9. Jean Jacques Rousseau, *The Social Contract,* in *The Social Contract and Discourses,* ed. and trans. G. D. H. Cole (New York: Dutton, 1950), bk. 1, chap. 1, p. 3.

10. Quoted in Peter Gay, *The Enlightenment: An Interpretation,* vol. 2, *The Science of Freedom* (New York: Vintage Books, 1966), p. 170.

11. Quoted in Steven Seidman, *Liberalism and the Origins of European Social Theory* (Berkeley: University of California Press, 1983), p. 30.

12. Voltaire, *"Letter to M. Bertrand,"* in *Candide and Other Writings,* ed. Haskell M. Block (New York: Modern Library, 1956), p. 525.

13. Quoted in Peter Gay, *Voltaire's Politics* (New York: Random House, Vintage Books, 1965), p. 71.

14. Quoted in Stephen J. Gendzier, ed. and trans., *Denis Diderot's The Encyclopedia Selections* (New York: Harper Torchbooks, 1967), p. xxv.

15. Ibid., p. xxvi.

16. Excerpted in Gendzier, *Diderot's Encyclopedia Selections,* p. 199.

17. Cesare Beccaria, *On Crimes and Punishments,* trans. Henry Paolucci (Indianapolis: Library of Liberal Arts, 1963), p. 32.

18. Voltaire, *Candide,* in *The Portable Voltaire,* ed. Ben Ray Redman (New York: Viking, 1949), p. 234.

19. Excerpted in Gendzier, *Diderot's Encyclopedia Selections,* pp. 183–184.

20. Excerpted in ibid., pp. 229–230.

21. Quoted in Bonnie S. Anderson and Judith P. Zinsser, *A History of Their Own* (New York: Harper & Row, 1988), vol 2, p. 113.

22. Jean Jacques Rousseau, *Emile,* trans. Barbara Foxley (London: Dent, Everyman's Library, 1974), p. 370.

23. Mary Wollstonecraft, *Vindication of the Rights of Woman* (London: Dent, 1929), pp. 11–12.

24. Antoine Nicolas de Condorcet, *Sketch for a Historical Picture of the Progress of the Human Mind,* trans. June Barraclough (London: Weidenfeld & Nicholas, 1955), p. 124.

25. Ibid., pp. 173–179.

26. Quoted in Gay, *The Enlightenment,* vol. 1, *The Rise of Modern Paganism,* p. 20.

27. Ibid., vol. 2, p. 567.

SUGGESTED READING

Anchor, Robert, *The Enlightenment Tradition* (1967). A useful survey.

Andrade, da C. E. N., *Sir Isaac Newton* (1954). Brief and clear.

Armitage, Angus, *The World of Copernicus* (1951). Good discussion of the old astronomy and the birth of the new.

Brumfit, J. H., *The French Enlightenment* (1972). A useful survey.

Cohen, I. B., *The Birth of a New Physics* (1960). A classic study.

Commager, Henry Steele, *The Empire of Reason* (1977). The Enlightenment in the United States.

Drake, Stillman, *Galileo* (1980). By a leading authority.

Einaudi, Mario, *The Early Rousseau* (1967). Good discussions of some key works.

Gay, Peter, *The Enlightenment: An Interpretation,* 2 vols. (1966). An exhaustive study.

Hampson, Norman, *The Enlightenment* (1968). A useful survey.

McMullen, Ernan, ed., *Galileo Man of Science* (1967). Contains many thoughtful essays on Galileo's life and achievement.

Oster, Malcolm, ed., *Science in Europe 1500–1800* (2000). An excellent collection of documents.

Outram, Dorinda, *The Enlightenment* (1995). An accessible recent synthesis.

Rosen, Edward, *Copernicus and the Scientific Revolution* (1984). By a recognized authority.

Yolton, John W., ed., *The Blackwell Companion to the Enlightenment* (1991). An excellent reference work for all phases of the Enlightenment.

REVIEW QUESTIONS

1. How did the Scientific Revolution transform the medieval view of the universe?

2. Describe the major achievements of Copernicus, Kepler, Galileo, and Newton.

3. How did the Scientific Revolution contribute to the shaping of the modern mentality?

4. Why is the eighteenth century referred to as the Age of Enlightenment? What are the antecedents of the Enlightenment?

5. Why did the philosophes attack Christianity?

6. How did Voltaire exemplify the philosophes?

7. Compare and contrast the political thought of Hobbes and Locke. Why is Locke considered a forerunner of liberalism?

8. Why is Rousseau considered a theorist of democracy? Why has his political thought come under attack?

9. What was the significance of Locke's theory of knowledge for the Enlightenment?

10. How did the ideals of the Enlightenment contribute to feminism and the movement to abolish slavery?

11. What ideals of the Enlightenment found expression during the period of the American Revolution?

12. How did the Enlightenment contribute to the shaping of the modern mentality?

Part Four

The Modern West: Progress and Breakdown

1789–1914

Formation of the National Assembly by Jacques Louis David (Detail). (Versailles ® Reúnion des Musées Nationaux)

Politics and Society	Thought and Culture

1790 French Revolution begins (1789)
Declaration of the Rights of Man and
   of the Citizen (1789)
Reign of Terror (1793–1794)
Napoleon seizes power (1799)
	Kant, *Critique of Pure Reason* (1781)
	Burke, *Reflections on the Revolution in
	   France* (1790)
	Wollstonecraft, *Vindication of the Rights
	   of Woman* (1792)
	Wordsworth, *The Lyrical Ballads* (1798)
	Beethoven, Fifth Symphony (1807–1808)
	Goya, *The Third of May* (1808)
	Goethe, *Faust* (1808, 1832)

1810 Napoleon invades Russia (1812)
Napoleon defeated at Waterloo (1815)
Congress of Vienna (1814–1815)
Revolutions in Spain, Italy, Russia,
   and Greece (1820–1829)
	Byron, *Childe Harold' Pilgrimage* (1812)
	Shelley, *Prometheus Unbound* (1820)
	Hegel, *The Philosophy of History*
	   (1822–1831)

1830 First railway built in Britain (1830)
Revolutions in France, Belgium, Poland,
   and Italy (1830–1832)
Reform Act of 1832 in Britain
Irish famine (1845–1849)
Revolutions in France, Germany, Austria,
   and Italy (1848)
	Comte, *Course in Positive Philosophy*
	   (1830–1842)
	De Tocqueville, *Democracy in America*
	   (1835–1840)
	Marx, *Communist Manifesto* (1848)

1850 Second Empire in France (1852–1870)
Commodore Perry opens Japan to trade
   (1853)
Unification of Italy (1859–1870)
Civil War in the United States (1861–1865)
Unification of Germany (1866–1871)
Opening of Suez Canal (1869)
	Dickens, *Hard Times* (1854)
	Flaubert, *Madame Bovary* (1856)
	Darwin, *Origin of Species* (1859)
	Mill, *On Liberty* (1859)
	Impressionism in art: Manet, Monet,
	   Pissaro, Degas, Renoir (1860–1886)
	Marx, *Capital* (1867)
	Dostoevski, *The Idiot* (1868)
	Mill, *The Subjection of Women* (1869)

1870 Franco-Prussian War (1870–1871) Third Republic in France (1870–1940) Berlin Conference on Africa (1884) Reform Bill of 1884 in Great Britain	Darwin, *Descent of Man* (1871) Nietzsche, *The Birth of Tragedy* (1872) Ibsen, *A Doll's House* (1879) Zola, *The Experimental Novel* (1880) Nietzsche, *The Anti-Christ* (1888)
1890 Dreyfus affair in France (1894–1899) Sino-Japanese War (1894–1895) Boer War in South Africa (1899–1902)	Chamberlain, *The Foundations of the Nineteenth Century* (1899) Durkheim, *Suicide* (1899)
1900 Russo-Japanese War (1904–1905) Anglo-French Entente Cordiale (1904) Anglo-Russian Entente (1907)	Freud, *The Interpretation of Dreams* (1900) Cubism in art: Picasso, Braque (1909–1914) Planck's quantum theory (1900) Lenin, *What Is to Be Done?* (1902) Einstein's theory of relativity (1905) Sorel, *Reflections on Violence* (1908)

Chapter 11

The Era of the French Revolution: Affirmation of Liberty and Equality

The outbreak of the French Revolution in 1789 stirred the imagination of Europeans. Both participants and observers sensed that they were living in a pivotal age. On the ruins of the Old Order, founded on privilege and despotism, a new era that promised to realize the ideals of the Enlightenment was forming.

These ideals included the emancipation of the human person from superstition and tradition, the triumph of liberty over tyranny, the refashioning of institutions in accordance with reason and justice, and the tearing down of barriers to equality. It seemed that the natural rights of the individual, hitherto a distant ideal, would now reign on earth, ending centuries of oppression and misery. Never before had people shown such confidence in the power of human intelligence to shape the conditions of existence. Never before had the future seemed so full of hope. ❖

THE OLD REGIME

Eighteenth-century French society was divided into three orders, or Estates, which were legally defined groupings. The clergy constituted the First Estate, the nobility the Second Estate, and everyone else the Third Estate. The clergy and nobility, totaling about 500,000 out of a population of 26 million, enjoyed special privileges, receiving pensions and profitable positions from the king. The social structure of the Old Regime, based on privileges and inequalities sanctioned by law, produced tensions that contributed to the Revolution.

The First Estate

The powers and privileges of the French Catholic church made it a state within a state. As it had done for centuries, the church registered births, marriages, and deaths; collected tithes (a tax on products from the soil); censored books considered dangerous to religion and morals; operated schools; and distributed relief to the poor. Although its land brought in an immense revenue, the church paid no taxes. Instead, it made a "free gift" to the state—the church determined the amount—which was always smaller than direct taxes would have been.

The clergy reflected the social divisions in France. The upper clergy shared the attitudes and way of life of the nobility from which they sprang. The parish priests, commoners by birth, resented the haughtiness and luxurious living of the upper clergy. In 1789, when the Revolution began, many priests sympathized with the reform-minded people of the Third Estate.

The Second Estate

Like the clergy, the nobility was a privileged order. Nobles held the highest positions in the church, the army, and the government. They were exempt from most taxes (or used their influence to evade paying taxes), collected manorial dues from peasants, and owned between one-quarter and one-third of the land. In addition to the income that they drew from their estates, nobles were becoming increasingly involved in such nonaristocratic enterprises as banking and finance. Nobles were the leading patrons of the arts. Many key philosophes—Montesquieu, Condorcet, d'Holbach—were nobles. Most nobles, however, were suspicious and intolerant of the liberal ideas advanced by the philosophes.

All nobles were not equal; there were gradations of dignity among the 350,000 members of the nobility. Enjoying the most prestige were *nobles of the sword:* families that could trace their aristocratic status back several centuries. The highest of the ancient nobles were engaged in the social whirl at Versailles and Paris, receiving pensions and sinecures from the king but performing few useful services for the state. Most nobles of the sword, unable to afford the gilded life at court, remained on their provincial estates, the poorest of them barely distinguishable from prosperous peasants.

Alongside this ancient nobility, a new nobility created by the monarchy had arisen. To obtain money, reward favorites, and weaken the old nobility, French kings had sold titles of nobility to members of the bourgeoisie and had conferred noble status on certain government offices bought by wealthy bourgeois. Particularly significant were the *nobles of the robe,* whose ranks included many former bourgeois who had purchased judicial offices in the parlements—the high law courts.

Opinion among the aristocrats was divided. Some nobles, influenced by the liberal ideals of the philosophes, sought to reform France; they wanted to end royal despotism and establish a constitutional government. To this extent, the

Chronology 11.1 ❖ The French Revolution

July 1788	Calling of the Estates General
June 17, 1789	Third Estate declares itself the National Assembly
July 14, 1789	Storming of the Bastille
Late July 1789	The Great Fear
August 4, 1789	Nobles surrender their special privileges
April 20, 1792	Legislative Assembly declares war on Austria
Sept. 21–22, 1792	Abolition of the monarchy
June 1793	Jacobins replace Girondins as the dominant group in the National Convention
July 28, 1794	Robespierre is guillotined

liberal nobility had a great deal in common with the bourgeoisie. These liberal nobles saw the king's difficulties in 1788 as an opportunity to regenerate the nation under enlightened leadership. When they resisted the king's policies, they claimed that they were opposing royal despotism. But, at the same time, many nobles remained hostile to liberal ideals and opposed reforms that threatened their privileges and honorific status.

The Third Estate

The Third Estate comprised the bourgeoisie, the peasants, and the urban workers. Although the bourgeoisie provided the leadership for the Revolution, its success depended on the support given by the rest of the Third Estate.

The Bourgeoisie The bourgeoisie consisted of merchant manufacturers, wholesale merchants, bankers, master craftsmen, doctors, lawyers, intellectuals, and government officials below the top ranks. Although the bourgeoisie had wealth, it lacked social prestige. A merchant, despite his worldly success, felt that his occupation denied him the esteem enjoyed by the nobility.

Influenced by the aristocratic values of the day and envious of the nobility's lifestyle, the bourgeoisie sought to erase the stigma of common birth and to rise socially by becoming landowners. By 1789, the bourgeoisie owned about 20 percent of the land. Traditionally, some of its members

had risen socially either by purchasing a judicial or political office that carried with it a title of nobility or by gaining admission to the upper clergy or the officer ranks of the army. Access to the nobility remained open throughout the eighteenth century. Nevertheless, since the highest and most desired positions in the land were reserved for the nobility, able bourgeois were often excluded for a variety of reasons: the high cost of purchasing an office, the limited number of new offices created, the resistance of nobles to their advancement, or the hostility of the older nobility toward those recently ennobled. No doubt these men felt frustrated and came to resent a social system that valued birth more than talent. For most of the century, however, the bourgeoisie did not challenge the existing social structure, including the special privileges of the nobility.

By 1789, the bourgeois had many grievances. They wanted all positions in the church, army, and state to be open to men of talent regardless of birth. They sought a parliament that would make laws for the nation; a constitution that would limit the king's power and guarantee freedom of thought, a fair trial, and religious toleration; and administrative reforms that would eliminate waste, inefficiency, and interference with business.

The Peasantry The condition of the more than twenty-one million French peasants was a paradox. On the one hand, they were better off than peasants in Austria, Prussia, Poland, and Russia,

"Let's Hope That the Game Finishes Well." This political cartoon shows a laboring-class woman carrying smug representatives of the privileged orders on her back. (*Musée de la Ville de Paris*)

An unjust and corrupt system of taxation weighed heavily on the peasantry. Louis XIV had maintained his grandeur and financed his wars by milking ever more taxes from the peasants, a practice that continued throughout the eighteenth century. An army of tax collectors victimized the peasantry. In addition to royal taxes, peasants paid the tithe to the church and manorial dues to lords.

Although serfdom had ended in most parts of France, lords continued to demand obligations from peasants as they had done in the Middle Ages. Besides performing labor services on the lord's estate, peasants still had to grind their grain in the lord's mill, bake their bread in his oven, press their grapes in his winepress, and give him part of their produce in payment. (These fees were called *banalities*.) In addition, the lord exercised exclusive hunting rights on lands tilled by peasants. Those rights were particularly onerous, for the lord's hunting parties damaged crops. Lords were determined to hold on to these privileges not only because of the income they brought, but because they were symbols of authority and social esteem.

Urban Laborers The urban laboring class in this preindustrial age consisted of journeymen working for master craftsmen, factory workers in small-scale industries, and wage earners such as day laborers, gardeners, handymen, and deliverymen, who were paid by those whom they served. Conditions for the urban poor, like those for the peasant wage earners, worsened in the late eighteenth century. From 1785 to 1789, the cost of living increased by 62 percent, while wages rose only by 22 percent. For virtually the entire decade of the Revolution, urban workers struggled to keep body and soul together in the face of food shortages and rising prices, particularly the price of their staple food, bread. Material want drove the urban poor to acts of violence that affected the course of the Revolution.

Inefficient Administration and Financial Disorder

The administration of France was complex, confusing, and ineffective. The practice of buying

where serfdom still predominated. In France, serfdom had largely disappeared; many peasants owned their land, and some were even prosperous. On the other hand, most French peasants lived in poverty, which worsened in the closing years of the Old Regime.

The typical peasant holding was barely large enough to eke out a living. The rising birthrate (between 1715 and 1789, the population may have increased from eighteen million to twenty-six million) led to the continual subdivision of farms among heirs. Moreover, many peasants did not own land but rented it from a nobleman or a prosperous neighbor. Others worked as sharecroppers, turning over a considerable portion of the harvest to their creditors.

state offices from the king, introduced as a means of raising money, resulted in many incompetent officeholders. Tariffs on goods shipped from one province to another and differing systems of weights and measures hampered trade. No single law code applied to all the provinces; instead, there were overlapping and conflicting law systems based on old Roman law or customary feudal law, which made the administration of justice slow, arbitrary, and unfair. To admirers of the philosophes, the administrative system was an insult to reason. The Revolution would sweep the system away.

Financial disorders also contributed to the weakness of the Old Regime. In the regime's last years, the government could not raise sufficient funds to cover expenses. By 1787, it still had not paid off the enormous debt incurred during the wars of Louis XIV, let alone the costs of succeeding wars during the eighteenth century, particularly France's aid to the colonists in the American Revolution. The king's gifts and pensions to court nobles and the extravagant court life further drained the treasury.

Finances were in a shambles not because France was impoverished, but because of an inefficient and unjust tax system. Although serious, the financial crisis could have been solved if the clergy, nobility, and bourgeoisie had paid their fair share of taxes. With France on the brink of bankruptcy, some of the king's ministers proposed that the nobility and church surrender some of their tax exemptions, but the privileged orders resisted. Some nobles resisted because they were steadfast defenders of noble prerogatives; the more liberal nobles resisted because they saw an opportunity to check absolutism and introduce fundamental reforms that would regenerate the nation.

The resistance of the nobility forced the government, in July 1788, to call for a meeting of the Estates General—a medieval representative assembly that had last met in 1614—to deal with the financial crisis. The body was to convene in May 1789. Certain that they would dominate the Estates General, the nobles intended to weaken the power of the throne. Once in control of the government, they would introduce financial reforms. But the revolt of the nobility against the crown had unexpected consequences. It opened the way for a revolution by the Third Estate that destroyed the Old Regime and with it the aristocracy and its privileges.

The Roles of the Enlightenment and the American Revolution

Revolutions are born in the realm of the spirit. Revolutionary movements, says George Rudé, a historian of the French Revolution, require "some unifying body of ideas, a common vocabulary of hope and protest, something, in short, like a common 'revolutionary psychology.'"[1] For this reason, many historians see a relationship between the Enlightenment and the French Revolution. The philosophes were not revolutionaries themselves, but their attacks on the pillars of the established order helped to create revolutionary psychology. As Henri Peyre observes,

> Eighteenth-century philosophy taught the Frenchman to find his condition wretched, or in any case, unjust and illogical and made him disinclined to the patient resignation to his troubles that had long characterized his ancestors. . . . The propaganda of the "Philosophes" perhaps more than any other factor accounted for the fulfillment of the preliminary condition of the French Revolution, namely discontent with the existing state of things.[2]

As the Revolution progressed, its leaders utilized the philosophes' ideas and language to justify their own reform program.

The American Revolution, which gave practical expression to the liberal philosophy of the philosophes, also helped to pave the way for the French Revolution. The Declaration of Independence (1776), which proclaimed the natural rights of man and sanctioned resistance against a government that deprived men of these rights, influenced the framers of the Declaration of the Rights of Man and of the Citizen (1789) (see the upcoming section on "Reforms of the National Assembly"). The United States showed that a nation could be established on the principle that sovereign power derived from the people. The Americans set an example of social equality unparalleled in Europe. In the United States, there was no hereditary aristocracy, no serfdom, and no state church. Liberal

French aristocrats, such as the Marquis de Lafayette, who had fought in the American Revolution, returned to France more optimistic about the possibilities of reforming French society.

A Bourgeois Revolution?

Because the bourgeois were the principal leaders and chief beneficiaries of the French Revolution, many historians have viewed it, along with the English revolutions of the seventeenth century and the growth of capitalism, as "an episode in the general rise of the bourgeoisie."[3] Those who regard the Revolution as a "bourgeois revolution" argue that in the last part of the eighteenth century, it became increasingly difficult for the bourgeoisie to gain the most honored offices in the land. According to this view, in the eighteenth century, a decadent and reactionary aristocracy sought to regain the powers that it had lost under Louis XIV. Through parlements, aristocrats blocked reforms proposed by the king that threatened their privileges, and they united to prevent commoners from entering their ranks.

The nobility's determination to safeguard its power and social exclusiveness collided head-on with the aspirations of a wealthy, talented, and progressive bourgeoisie. Finding the path to upward mobility and social dignity barred, the bourgeoisie, imbued with the rational outlook of the Enlightenment, came to perceive nobles as an obstacle to its advancement and the nation's progress. "The essential cause of the Revolution," concludes French historian Albert Soboul, "was the power of a bourgeoisie arrived at its maturity and confronted by a decadent aristocracy holding tenaciously to its privileges."[4] Thus, when the bourgeois found the opportunity during the Revolution, they ended the legal division of France into separate orders.

In recent decades, some historians have challenged this interpretation. These revisionists argue that before 1789 France did not have a self-conscious bourgeois class aspiring to take control of the state in order to promote a capitalist economy, that the nobles and the bourgeoisie did not represent antagonistic classes divided by sharp differences. On the contrary, they were not clearly distinguishable from each other. The bourgeois aspired to noble status, and many nobles were involved in business enterprises—mining, metallurgy, textiles, and overseas trading companies—traditionally considered the province of the bourgeoisie. Abandoning a traditional aristocratic disdain for business, many nobles had acquired the capitalist mentality associated with the middle class. Some nobles also shared with the bourgeois the liberal values of the philosophes and a desire to do away with monarchical despotism and reform France according to rational standards. Thus, French nobles, particularly those who lived in urban centers or had traveled to Britain and the American colonies, were receptive both to new means of livelihood and to progressive ideas.

Moreover, the French nobility was constantly infused with new blood from below. During the eighteenth century, thousands of bourgeois, through marriage, the purchase of an office, or service as local officials—mayors, for example—had some entitlement of nobility. As British historian William Doyle puts it, "the nobility was an open elite, not a hereditary class apart. Nor is it now possible to maintain that this elite grew less open as the eighteenth century went on thanks to some exclusive 'aristocratic reaction.'"[5]

Just prior to 1789, revisionists contend, nobles and prosperous bourgeois were no longer clearly differentiated; the traditional distinctions that had set them apart were now obsolete. France's social elite actually consisted not of a hereditary nobility, but of *notables*—both nobles and bourgeois—distinguished more by wealth than by birth. Bourgeois notables were essentially moderate; they did not seek the destruction of the aristocracy that was accomplished in the opening stage of the Revolution. The elimination of aristocratic privileges was not part of a preconceived bourgeois program, revisionists maintain, but an improvised response to the violent upheavals in the countryside in July and August 1789. Moreover, not until early 1789, when a struggle erupted over the composition of the Estates General (see the next section), did the bourgeoisie start to become conscious of itself as a class with interests that clashed with those of the aristocracy. Until then, both the bourgeoisie and many aristocrats were united around a common and moderate reform program.

Finally, revisionists argue that the feudal nobility was not as decadent or reactionary as traditional accounts would have it. The nobles resisted the king's reforming ministers because they doubted the ability of a despotic and incompetent state to solve the financial crisis. To be sure, there were aristocrats who selfishly wanted to cling to their privileges, but many also aspired to serve the public good by instituting structural changes that would liberate the nation from despotic and inefficient rule and reform its financial and administrative system. It was this desire to institute crucial changes in French political life, say revisionists, that led nobles to press for the convening of the Estates General.

THE MODERATE STAGE, 1789–1791

Since a significant number of nobles were sympathetic to reform, there was no insuperable gulf between the Second and Third Estates as the Estates General prepared to meet. However, it soon became clear that the hopes of reformers clashed with the intentions of many aristocrats.

What had started as a struggle between the crown and the aristocracy was turning into something far more significant: a conflict between the two privileged orders on one side and the Third Estate on the other. One pamphleteer, Abbé Sieyès (1748–1836), expressed the hatred that members of the bourgeoisie felt for the aristocracy. "The privileged order has said to the Third Estate: 'Whatever be your services, whatever be your talents, you shall go thus far and no farther. It is not fitting that you be honored.'" The higher positions in the land, said Sieyès, should be the "reward for talents," not the prerogative of birth. Without the Third Estate, "nothing can progress"; without the nobility, "everything would proceed infinitely better."[6]

Formation of the National Assembly

The Estates General convened at Versailles on May 5, 1789, but was stalemated by the question of procedure. Seeking to control the assembly, the nobility insisted that the three Estates follow the traditional practice of meeting separately and voting as individual bodies. Since the two privileged orders were likely to stand together, the Third Estate would always be outvoted, two to one. But the delegates from the Third Estate, unwilling to allow the nobility and the higher clergy to dominate the Estates General, proposed instead that the three Estates meet as one body and vote by head. There were some 610 delegates from the Third Estate; the nobility and clergy together had an equivalent number. Since the Third Estate could rely on the support of sympathetic parish priests and liberal nobles, it would be assured a majority if all the orders met together. As aristocrats and bourgeois became more polarized, anti-noble rhetoric gained a growing audience among all segments of the Third Estate. Many commoners now saw the aristocracy as the chief obstacle to reform.

On June 17, the Third Estate made a revolutionary move. It declared itself the National Assembly. On June 20, locked out of their customary meeting hall (apparently by accident), the Third Estate delegates moved to a nearby tennis court and took a solemn oath not to disband until a constitution had been drawn up for France. Louis XVI commanded the National Assembly to separate into orders, but the Third Estate held firm. The steadfastness of the delegates and the menacing actions of Parisians who supported the National Assembly forced Louis XVI to yield. On June 27, he ordered the nobility (some had already done so) and the clergy (a majority had already done so) to join with the Third Estate in the National Assembly.

But the victory of the bourgeoisie was not yet secure, for most nobles had not resigned themselves to a bourgeois-dominated National Assembly. It appeared that Louis XVI, influenced by court aristocrats, had resolved to use force against the National Assembly and stop the incipient revolution. At this point, uprisings by the common people of Paris and peasants in the countryside saved the National Assembly, exacerbated hostilities between the Third Estate and the nobility, and ensured the victory of the forces of reform.

Storming of the Bastille

In July 1789, the level of tension in Paris was high for three reasons. First, the calling of the Estates General had aroused hopes for reform. Sec-

Storming of the Bastille, July 14, 1789. A Parisian crowd stormed the dreaded fortress of the Bastille, long identified with the abuses of the Old Regime. (*AKG London*)

ond, the price of bread was soaring: in August 1788, a Parisian laborer had spent 50 percent of his income on bread; by July 1789, he was spending 80 percent. A third element in the tension was the fear of an aristocratic plot to crush the National Assembly. Afraid that royal troops would bombard and pillage the city, Parisians searched for weapons.

On July 14, eight hundred to nine hundred Parisians gathered in front of the Bastille, a fortress used as a prison and a scorned symbol of royal despotism. They gathered primarily to obtain gunpowder and to remove the cannon that threatened a heavily populated working-class district. As the tension mounted, the Parisians stormed and captured the Bastille. The fall of the Bastille had far-reaching consequences: a symbol of the Old Regime had fallen; some court nobles hostile to the Revolution decided to flee the country; the frightened king told the National Assembly that he would withdraw the troops ringing Paris. The revolutionary act of the Parisians had indirectly saved the National Assembly and its bourgeois leadership.

The Great Fear

Revolution in the countryside also served the interests of the reformers. Inflamed by economic misery and stirred by the uprisings of the Parisians, peasants began to burn manor houses and destroy the registers on which their obligations to the lords were inscribed. The flames of the peasants' insurrection were fanned by rumors that aristocrats were organizing bands of brigands to attack the peasants. The mythical army of brigands never materialized, but the Great Fear, as this episode is called, led more peasants to take up arms. Suspicious of an aristocratic plot to thwart efforts at reform and releasing years of stored-up hatred for the nobles, the peasants attacked the lords' chateaux with great fury.

Like the insurrection in Paris, the peasant upheavals in late July and early August worked to the advantage of the reformers. The attacks provided the National Assembly with an opportunity to strike at noble privileges by putting into law what the peasants had accomplished with the torch—the destruction of feudal remnants. On the night of August 4, 1789, aristocrats seeking to restore calm in the countryside surrendered their special privileges: exclusive hunting rights, tax exemptions, monopoly of highest offices, manorial courts, and the right to demand labor services from peasants.

In the decrees of August 5 and 11, the National Assembly implemented the resolutions of August 4. The Assembly also declared that the planned constitution should be prefaced by a declaration of rights. On August 26, it adopted the Declaration of the Rights of Man and of the Citizen.

October Days

Louis XVI, cool to these reforms, postponed his approval of the August Decrees and the Declaration of Rights. It would require a second uprising by the Parisians to force the king to agree to the reforms and to nail down the victory of the reformers.

On October 5, 1789, Parisian women and men marched twelve miles to Versailles to protest the lack of bread to the National Assembly and the king. A few hours later, twenty thousand Paris Guards, a citizen militia sympathetic to the Revolution, also set out for Versailles in support of the protesters. The king had no choice but to promise bread and to return with the demonstrators to Paris. Aware that he had no control over the Parisians and fearful of further violence, Louis XVI approved the August Decrees and the Declaration of Rights. Nobles who had urged the king to use force against the Assembly and had tried to block reforms fled the country in large numbers.

Reforms of the National Assembly

With resistance weakened, the National Assembly continued the work of reform begun in the summer of 1789. Its reforms, which are summarized below, destroyed the Old Regime.

1. *Abolition of special privileges.* By ending the special privileges of the nobility and the clergy in the August Decrees, the National Assembly legalized the equality that the bourgeoisie had demanded. The aristocratic structure of the Old Regime, a remnant of the Middle Ages that had hindered the progressive bourgeoisie, was eliminated.

2. *Statement of human rights.* The Declaration of the Rights of Man and of the Citizen expressed the liberal and universal goals of the philosophes. In proclaiming the inalienable right to liberty of person, freedom of religion and thought, and equal treatment under the law, the declaration affirmed the dignity of the individual. It asserted that government belonged not to any ruler, but to the people as a whole, and that its aim was the preservation of the natural rights of the individual. Because the declaration contrasted sharply with the principles espoused by an intolerant clergy, a privileged aristocracy, and a despotic monarch, it has been called the death warrant of the Old Regime. A significant example of the new leadership's commitment to equality and religious toleration was the law passed in 1791 granting civil rights to Jews. Jews were now free to leave the ghetto, to which they had been forcibly confined for centuries to keep them apart from Gentiles, and, in theory, to participate in French society as equal citizens.

3. *Subordination of church to state.* The National Assembly also struck at the privileges of the Roman Catholic church. The August Decrees declared the end of tithes. To obtain badly needed funds, the Assembly in November 1789 confiscated church lands and put them up for sale. In 1790, the Assembly passed the Civil Constitution of the Clergy, which altered the boundaries of the dioceses, reducing the number of

bishops and priests, and transformed the clergy into government officials elected by the people and paid by the state.

Almost all bishops and many priests opposed the Civil Constitution. It divided the French and gave opponents of the Revolution an emotional issue around which to rally supporters.

4. *A constitution for France.* In September 1791, the National Assembly issued a constitution limiting the power of the king and guaranteeing all French citizens equal treatment under the law. Citizens paying less than a specified amount in taxes could not vote. Probably about 30 percent of the males over the age of twenty-five were excluded by this stipulation, and only the more well-to-do citizens qualified to sit in the Legislative Assembly, a unicameral parliament created to succeed the National Assembly. The drafters of the constitution did not trust illiterate and propertyless men to vote and enact legislation. Nevertheless, the suffrage requirements under the constitution of 1791 were far more generous than those in Britain.

5. *Administrative and judicial reforms.* The National Assembly replaced the patchwork of provincial units with eighty-three new administrative units, or departments, approximately equal in size. Judicial reforms complemented the administrative changes. A standardized system of courts replaced the innumerable jurisdictions of the Old Regime, and the sale of judicial offices was ended. The penal code completed by the National Assembly abolished torture and barbarous punishments.

6. *Aid for business.* The National Assembly abolished all tolls and duties on goods transported within the country, established a uniform system of weights and measures, eliminated the guilds (medieval survivals, which blocked business expansion), and forbade workers to form unions or to strike.

By ending absolutism, striking at the privileges of the nobility, and preventing the mass of people from gaining control over the government, the National Assembly consolidated the rule of the bourgeoisie. With one arm, it broke the power of aristocracy and throne; with the other, it held back the common people. Although the reforms benefited the bourgeoisie, it would be a mistake to view them merely as a selfish expression of bourgeois interests. The Declaration of the Rights of Man and of the Citizen was addressed to all; it proclaimed liberty and equality as the right of all and called on citizens to treat one another with respect.

THE RADICAL STAGE, 1792–1794

Pleased with their accomplishments—equality before the law, careers open to talent, a written constitution, parliamentary government—the men of 1789 wished the Revolution to go no further. But revolutionary times are unpredictable. Soon the Revolution moved in a direction neither anticipated nor desired by the reformers. A counterrevolution, led by irreconcilable nobles and alienated churchmen, gained the support of the strongly Catholic peasants. It threatened the Revolution, forcing the revolutionary leadership to resort to extreme measures.

The Sans-Culottes

The discontent of the *sans-culottes**—small shopkeepers, artisans, and wage earners—also propelled the Revolution toward radicalism. Although they had played a significant role in the Revolution, particularly in the storming of the Bastille and in the October Days, they had gained little. The sans-culottes, says French historian Albert Soboul, "began to realize that a privilege of wealth was taking the place of a privilege of birth. They foresaw that the bourgeoisie would succeed the fallen aristocracy as the ruling class."[7] Inflamed by poverty and their hatred of the rich, the sans-culottes insisted that it was the government's duty to guarantee them the "right of existence"—a policy that ran counter to the economic individualism of the bourgeoisie.

*Literally, *sans-culottes* means "without culottes" and refers to the people who wore the simple trousers of a laborer and not the knee breeches that aristocrats wore before the Revolution.

The sans-culottes demanded that the government increase wages, set price controls on food supplies, end food shortages, and pass laws to prevent extremes of wealth and poverty. Whereas the men of 1789 sought equality of rights, liberties, and opportunities, the sans-culottes expanded the principle of equality to include narrowing the gap between the rich and the poor. To reduce economic inequality, they called for higher taxes for the wealthy and the redistribution of land. Politically, they favored a democratic republic in which the common man had a voice.

In 1789, the bourgeoisie had demanded equality with the aristocrats: the right to hold the most honored positions in the nation and an end to the special privileges of the nobility. By the close of 1792, the sans-culottes were demanding equality with the bourgeois. They wanted political reforms that would give the poor a voice in the government and social reforms that would improve their lot.

Despite the pressures exerted by reactionary nobles and clergy on the one hand and discontented sans-culottes on the other, the Revolution might not have taken a radical turn if France had remained at peace. The war that broke out with Austria and Prussia in April 1792 exacerbated internal dissensions, worsened economic conditions, and threatened to undo the reforms of the Revolution. It was in these circumstances that the Revolution moved from its moderate stage to a radical one, which historians refer to as the Second French Revolution.

Foreign Invasion

In June 1791, Louis XVI and the royal family, traveling in disguise, fled Paris for northeastern France to join with *émigrés* (nobles who had left revolutionary France and were organizing a counterrevolutionary army) and to rally foreign support against the Revolution. Discovered at Varennes by a village postmaster, they were brought back to Paris as virtual prisoners. The flight of the king turned many French people against the monarchy, strengthening the position of the radicals who wanted to do away with kingship altogether and establish a republic. But it was foreign invasion that ultimately led to the destruction of the monarchy.

On April 20, 1792, fearful that Austria intended to overthrow the Revolution and eager to spread revolutionary ideals, France declared war on Austria. A combined Austrian and Prussian army commanded by the duke of Brunswick crossed into France. In an atmosphere already charged with tension, the duke of Brunswick issued a manifesto declaring that if the royal family were harmed, he would exact a terrible vengeance on the Parisians. On August 10, enraged Parisians and militia from other cities attacked the king's palace, killing several hundred Swiss guards.

In early September, as foreign troops advanced deeper into France, rumors spread that jailed priests and aristocrats were planning to break out of their cells to support the duke of Brunswick. The Parisians panicked. Driven by fear, patriotism, and murderous impulses, they raided the prisons and massacred eleven hundred to twelve hundred prisoners. Most of the victims were not political prisoners but ordinary criminals.

On September 21 and 22, the National Convention (the new lawmaking body) abolished the monarchy and established a republic. In December, Louis XVI was placed on trial, and in January 1793 he was executed for conspiring against the liberty of the French people. The uprising of August 10, the September massacres, the creation of a republic, and the execution of Louis XVI all confirmed that the Revolution was taking a radical turn.

Meanwhile, the war continued. Short of supplies, hampered by bad weather, and lacking sufficient manpower, the duke of Brunswick never did reach Paris. Outmaneuvered at Valmy on September 20, 1792, the foreign forces retreated to the frontier, and the armies of the republic took the offensive. By the beginning of 1793, French forces had overrun Belgium (then a part of the Austrian Empire), the German Rhineland, and the Sardinian provinces of Nice and Savoy. To the peoples of Europe, the National Convention had solemnly announced that it was waging a popular crusade against privilege and tyranny, against aristocrats and princes.

These revolutionary social ideas, the execution of Louis XVI, and, most important, French expansion, which threatened the balance of power, centralized government in Paris. The republic was unable to exercise control over much of the country.

The Jacobins

As the republic tottered under the weight of foreign invasion, internal insurrection, and economic crisis, the revolutionary leadership grew still more radical. In June 1793, the Jacobins replaced the Girondins as the dominant group in the National Convention. The Girondins favored a government in which the departments would exercise control over their own affairs. The Jacobins, on the other hand, wanted a strong central government, with Paris as the seat of power. Both Girondins and Jacobins came from the bourgeoisie, but the Girondins opposed government interference in business, whereas the Jacobins supported temporary government controls to deal with the needs of war and economic crisis. This last point was crucial; it won the Jacobins the support of the sans-culottes. On June 2, 1793, some eighty thousand armed sans-culottes surrounded the Convention and demanded the arrest of Girondin delegates—an act that enabled the Jacobins to gain control of the government.

The problems confronting the Jacobins were staggering. They had to cope with civil war, particularly in the Vendée, economic distress, blockaded ports, and foreign invasion. They lived with the terrible dread that if they failed, the Revolution for liberty and equality would perish. Only strong leadership could save the republic. It was provided by the Committee of Public Safety, which organized the nation's defenses, supervised ministers, ordered arrests, and imposed the central government's authority throughout the nation.

The Jacobins continued the work of reform. In 1793, a new constitution expressed Jacobin enthusiasm for political democracy. It contained a new Declaration of Rights, which affirmed and amplified the principles of 1789. By giving all adult males the right to vote, it overcame sans-culotte objections to the constitution of 1791. However, the threat of invasion and the revolts caused the implementation of the new constitution to be postponed, and it was never put into

The Execution of Louis XVI. The king died with dignity. His last words were, "I forgive my enemies; I trust that my death will be for the happiness of my people, but I grieve for France, and I fear that she may suffer the anger of the Lord." (*Giraudon/Art Resource, NY*)

frightened the rulers of Europe. Urged on by Britain, by the spring of 1793 they formed an anti-French alliance. The allies' forces pressed toward the French borders, endangering the republic.

Counterrevolutionary insurrections further undermined the fledgling republic. In the Vendée, in western France, peasants who were protesting against taxation and conscription and were still loyal to their priests and Catholic tradition, which the Revolution had attacked, took up arms against the republic. Led by local nobles, the peasants of the Vendée waged a guerrilla war for religion, royalism, and their traditional way of life. In other quarters, federalists revolted in the provinces, objecting to the power wielded by the effect. By abolishing both slavery in the French colonies and imprisonment for debt and by making plans for free public education, the Jacobins revealed their humanitarianism and their debt to the philosophes. To halt inflation and gain the support of the poor—both necessary for the war effort—the Jacobins decreed the *law of the maximum*, which fixed prices on bread and other essential goods and raised wages.

The Nation in Arms

To fight the war against foreign invaders, the Jacobins, in an act that anticipated modern conscription, drafted unmarried men between eighteen and twenty-five years of age. They mobilized all the resources of the country, infused the army with a love for *la patrie* (the nation), and, in a remarkable demonstration of administrative skill, equipped an army of more than 800,000 men. In creating the nation in arms, the Jacobins heralded the emergence of modern warfare. Inspired by the ideals of liberty, equality, and fraternity and commanded by officers who had proved their skill on the battlefield, the citizen soldiers of the republic won decisive victories. In May and June 1794, the French routed the allied forces on the vital northern frontier, and by the end of July, France had become the triumphant master of Belgium.

By demanding complete devotion to the nation, the Jacobin phase of the Revolution also heralded the rise of modern nationalism. In the schools, in newspapers, speeches, and poems, on the stage, and at rallies and meetings of patriotic societies, the French people were told of the glory won by republican soldiers on the battlefield and were reminded of their duties to *la patrie*. "The citizen is born, lives, and dies for the fatherland"—these words were written in public places for all citizens to read and ponder. The soldiers of the Revolution fought not for money or for a king, but for the nation. Could this heightened sense of nationality, which concentrated on the special interests of the French people, be reconciled with the Declaration of the Rights of Man, whose principles were addressed to all humanity? The revolutionaries themselves did not understand the implications of the new force that they had unleashed.

The Republic of Virtue and the Reign of Terror

While forging a revolutionary army to deal with external enemies, the Jacobins were also waging war against internal opposition. The pivotal personality in this struggle was Maximilién Robespierre (1758–1794), who had a fervent faith in the rightness of his beliefs and a total commitment to republican democracy. In the early stage of Revolution, Robespierre had strongly supported liberal reforms. He attacked, at times with great fervor, slavery, capital punishment, and censorship; he favored civil rights for Jews; and, in what was considered a radical measure, he supported giving all men the vote regardless of how much property they owned. Robespierre wanted to create a better society founded on reason, good citizenship; and patriotism. In his Republic of Virtue, there would be no kings or nobles, men would be free, equal, and educated, and reason would be glorified and superstition ridiculed. There would be no extremes of wealth or poverty; people's natural goodness would prevail over vice and greed; and laws would preserve, not violate, inalienable rights. In this utopian vision, an individual's duties would be "to detest bad faith and despotism, to punish tyrants and traitors, to assist the unfortunate, to respect the weak, to defend the oppressed, to do all the good one can to one's neighbor, and to behave with justice towards all men."[8] Robespierre pursued his ideal society with religious zeal. Knowing that the Republic of Virtue could not be established while France was threatened by foreign and civil war, Robespierre urged harsh treatment for enemies of the republic, who "must be prosecuted by all not as ordinary enemies, but as rebels, brigands, and assassins."[9]

With Robespierre playing a key role, the Jacobin leadership attacked those they considered enemies of the republic: Girondins who challenged Jacobin authority; federalists who opposed a strong central government emanating from Paris; counterrevolutionary priests and no-

The Reign of Terror. During the Terror thousands of men and women were condemned to death by the guillotine, often in front of cheering crowds. In this painting a court official reads the names of those sentenced for execution. (*Hulton/Getty Images*)

bles and their peasant supporters; and profiteers who hoarded food. The Jacobins even sought to discipline the ardor of the sans-culottes, who had given them power. Fearful that sans-culotte spontaneity would undermine central authority and promote anarchy, Robespierrists brought about the dissolution of sans-culotte societies. They also executed sans-culotte leaders known as the *enragés* (literally, madmen), who threatened insurrection against Jacobin rule and pushed for more social reforms than the Jacobins would allow. The enragés wanted to set limits on income and on the size of farms and businesses—policies considered far too extreme by the supporters of Robespierre.

Robespierre and his fellow Jacobins did not make terror a deliberate government policy because they were bloodthirsty or power mad. Instead, they sought to establish a temporary dictatorship in a desperate attempt to save the republic and the Revolution. Deeply devoted to republican democracy, the Jacobins viewed themselves as bearers of a higher faith. Like all visionaries, Robespierre was convinced that he knew the right way and that the new society he envisaged would benefit all humanity. He saw those who impeded its implementation not just as opponents, but as sinners who had to be liquidated for the general good.

Special courts were established in Paris and other cities to try suspects. The proceedings were carried on in haste, and most judgments called for either acquittal or execution. In the Vendée, where civil war raged, many of the arrested were executed by firing squads, without trial; some five thousand were loaded onto barges, which were then sunk in the middle of the Loire River. Ironically, most of the executions took place after the frontiers had been secured and the civil war crushed. In many respects, the Terror was less a means of saving the beleaguered republic and more a way of shaping the new republican society and the new individual in accordance with the radical Jacobin ideology. Of the 500,000 people imprisoned for crimes against the republic, some 16,000 were sentenced to death by guillotine and another 20,000 perished in prison before they could be tried. More than 200,000 died in the civil war in the provinces, and 40,000 were summarily executed by firing squad, guillotine, and mass drownings ordered by military courts authorized by the Convention.

The Jacobins did save the republic. Their regime expelled foreign armies, crushed the federalist uprisings, contained the counterrevolutionaries in the Vendée, and prevented anarchy. Without the discipline, order, and unity imposed on France by the Jacobins, it is likely that the republic would have collapsed under the twin blows of foreign invasion and domestic anarchy.

Nonetheless, the Reign of Terror poses fundamental questions about the meaning of the French Revolution and the validity of the Enlightenment conception of the individual. To what extent was the Terror a reversal of the ideals of the Revolution as formulated in the Declaration of the Rights of Man? To what extent did the feverish passions and fascination with violence demonstrated in the mass executions in the provinces and in the public spectacles in Paris indicate a darker side of human nature, beyond the control of reason? Did Robespierre's religion of humanity revive the fanaticism and cruelty of the wars of religion, which had so disgusted the philosophes? Did the Robespierrists, who considered themselves the staunchest defenders of the Revolution's ideals, soil and subvert these ideals by their zeal? The Jacobins mobilized the might of the nation, created the mystique of *la patrie*, imposed dictatorial rule in defense of liberty and equality, and legalized and justified terror committed in the people's name. In so doing, were they unwittingly unleashing new forces—total commitment to a political ideology that promised to regenerate the nation and mass executions carried out in good conscience—that would be harnessed by totalitarian ideologies that were consciously resolved to stamp out the liberal heritage of the Revolution? Did 1793 mark a change in the direction of Western civilization: a movement away from the ideals of the philosophes and the opening of an age of political coercion and ideological fanaticism that would culminate in the cataclysms of the twentieth century?

The Fall of Robespierre

Feeling the chill of the guillotine blade on their own necks, Robespierre's opponents in the Convention ordered his arrest and the arrest of some of his supporters. On July 28, 1794, the tenth of Thermidor according to the new republican calendar, Robespierre was guillotined. After the fall of Robespierre, the machinery of the Jacobin republic was dismantled.

Leadership passed to the property-owning bourgeois who had endorsed the constitutional ideas of 1789–91, the moderate stage of the Revolution. The new leadership, known as Thermidoreans until the end of 1795, wanted no more of the Jacobins or of Robespierre's society. They had viewed Robespierre as a threat to their political power because he would have allowed the common people a considerable voice in the government. They had also deemed him a threat to their property because he would have introduced some state regulation of the economy to aid the poor.

The Thermidorean reaction was a counterrevolution. The new government purged the army of officers who were suspected of Jacobin leanings, abolished the law of the maximum, and declared void the constitution of 1793. A new constitution, approved in 1795, reestablished property requirements for voting. The counterrevolution also produced a counterterror, as royalists and Catholics massacred Jacobins in the provinces.

Chronology 11.2 ❖ Napoleon's Career

1796	Napoleon gets command of the French Army of Italy
November 10, 1799	He helps to overthrow the Directory's rule, establishing a strong executive in France
December 2, 1804	He crowns himself emperor of the French
October 21, 1805	Battle of Trafalgar—French and Spanish fleets are defeated by the British
October 1806	Napoleon defeats the Prussians at Jena, and French forces occupy Berlin
1808–1813	Peninsular War—Spaniards, aided by the British, fight against French occupation
October–December 1812	Grand Army retreats from Russia
October 1813	Allied forces defeat Napoleon at Leipzig
1814	Paris is captured and Napoleon is exiled to Elba
March 20, 1815	Escaping, he enters Paris and begins "hundred days" rule
June 1815	Defeated at Waterloo, Napoleon is exiled to St. Helena

At the end of 1795, the new republican government, the Directory, was burdened by war, a sagging economy, and internal unrest. The Directory crushed insurrections by Parisian sans-culottes, maddened by hunger and hatred of the rich (1795, 1796), and by royalists seeking to restore the monarchy (1797). As military and domestic pressures increased, power began to pass into the hands of generals. One of them, Napoleon Bonaparte, seized control of the government in November 1799, pushing the Revolution into yet another stage.

NAPOLEON AND FRANCE: RETURN TO AUTOCRATIC RULE

Napoleon was born on August 15, 1769, on the island of Corsica, the son of a petty noble. After finishing military school in France, he became an artillery officer. The wars of the French Revolution afforded him an opportunity to advance his career; in 1796, he was given command of the French Army of Italy. In Italy, against the Austrians, Napoleon demonstrated a dazzling talent for military planning and leadership, which earned him an instant reputation. Having tasted glory, he could never do without it. Since he had experienced only success, nothing seemed impossible; he sensed that he was headed for greatness.

In 1799, Napoleon was leading a French army in Egypt when he decided to return to France and make his bid for power. He joined a conspiracy that overthrew the Directory and created an executive office of three consuls. As first consul, Napoleon monopolized power. In 1802, he was made first consul for life, with the right to name his successor. And on December 2, 1804, in a magnificent ceremony at the Cathedral of Notre Dame in Paris, Napoleon crowned himself emperor of the French. General, first consul, and then emperor—it was a breathless climb to the heights of power. Napoleon, who once said that he loved "power as a musician loves his violin," was determined never to lose it.

An Enlightened Despot

Napoleon did not identify with the republicanism and democracy of the Jacobins; rather, he belonged to the tradition of eighteenth-century enlightened despotism. Like the reforming despots,

Coronation of Napoleon and Josephine by Jacques Louis David.   Napoleon crowned himself emperor in a magnificent ceremony. To French émigrés and nobles throughout Europe, he was the "crowned Jacobin" who threatened aristocratic privileges and European stability. (*Louvre © R.M.N.*)

he admired administrative uniformity and efficiency; disliked feudalism, religious persecution, and civil inequality; and favored government regulation of trade and industry. He saw in enlightened despotism a means of ensuring political stability and strengthening the state. Napoleon did preserve several gains of the Revolution: equality under the law, careers open to men of talent, promotion of secular education, and the weakening of clerical power. But he suppressed political liberty.

Napoleon succeeded in giving France a strong central government and administrative uniformity. An army of officials, subject to the emperor's will, reached into every village, linking together the entire nation. This centralized state suited Napoleon's desire for orderly government and rational administration, enabled him to concentrate power in his own hands, and provided him with the taxes and soldiers needed to fight his wars. To suppress irreconcilable opponents,

primarily diehard royalists and republicans, Napoleon used the instruments of the police state—secret agents, arbitrary arrest, summary trials, and executions.

To prevent hostile criticism of his rule and to promote popular support for his policies and person, Napoleon also shaped public opinion. He was thus a precursor of twentieth-century dictators. Liberty of the press came to an end. Printers swore an oath of obedience to the emperor, and newspapers were converted into government mouthpieces.

Napoleon tried to close the breach between the state and the Catholic church that had opened during the Revolution. Such a reconciliation would gain the approval of the mass of the French people, who still remained devoted to their faith, and would also reassure the peasants and bourgeois who had bought confiscated church lands. For these reasons, Napoleon negotiated an agreement with the pope. The Concordat of 1801 recognized Catholicism as the religion of the great majority of the French, rather than as the official state religion (the proposal that the pope desired). Napoleon had achieved his aim. The Concordat made his regime acceptable to Catholics and to owners of former church lands.

Legal, Educational, and Financial Policies

Under the Old Regime, France was plagued by numerous and conflicting law codes. Reflecting local interests and feudal traditions, these codes obstructed national unity and administrative efficiency. Efforts by the revolutionaries to draw up a unified code of laws bogged down. Recognizing the value of such a code in promoting effective administration throughout France, Napoleon pressed for the completion of the project. The Code Napoléon incorporated many principles of the Revolution: equality before the law, the right to choose one's profession, freedom of conscience, protection of property rights, the abolition of serfdom, and the secular character of the state.

The code also had its less liberal side, denying equal treatment to workers in their dealings with employers, to women in their relations with their husbands, and to children in their relations with their fathers. In making wives inferior to their husbands in matters of property, adultery, and divorce, the code reflected both Napoleon's personal attitude and the general view of the times toward women and family stability. The restoration of slavery in the French colonies—which the Jacobins had abolished—was another violation of equality.

Napoleon's educational policy was in many ways an elaboration of the school reforms initiated during the Revolution. Like the revolutionaries, Napoleon favored a system of public education with a secular curriculum and a minimum of church involvement. For Napoleon, education served a dual purpose: it would provide him with capable officials to administer his laws and trained officers to lead his armies, and it would indoctrinate the young in obedience and loyalty. He established the University of France, a giant board of education that placed education under state control. To this day, the French school system, unlike that in the United States, is strictly centralized, with curriculum and standards set for the entire country.

Napoleon's financial and economic policies were designed to strengthen France and enhance his popularity. To stimulate the economy and to retain the favor of the bourgeois who supported his seizure of power, Napoleon aided industry through tariffs and loans, and he fostered commerce (while also speeding up troop movements) by building or repairing roads, bridges, and canals. To protect the currency from inflation, he established the Bank of France, which was controlled by the nation's leading financiers. By keeping careers open to talent, he endorsed one of the key demands of the bourgeoisie during the Revolution. Fearing a revolution based on lack of bread, he provided food at low prices and stimulated employment for the laboring poor. He endeared himself to the peasants by not restoring feudal privileges and by allowing them to keep the land they had obtained during the Revolution.

NAPOLEON AND EUROPE: DIFFUSION OF REVOLUTIONARY INSTITUTIONS

Napoleon, the Corsican adventurer, realized Louis XIV's dream of French mastery of Europe. Between 1805 and 1807, he decisively defeated Austria, Prussia, and Russia, becoming the virtual ruler of Europe. In these campaigns, as in his earlier successes in Italy, Napoleon demonstrated his greatness as a military commander.

By 1810, Napoleon dominated the Continent, except for the Balkan Peninsula. The Grand Empire comprised lands annexed to France, vassal states, and cowed allies.

With varying degrees of determination and success, Napoleon extended the reforms of the Revolution to other lands. His officials instituted the Code Napoléon, organized an effective civil service, opened careers to talent, and equalized the tax burden. Besides abolishing serfdom, manorial payments, and the courts of the nobility, they

Moscow
⚔ Borodino (1812)
• Smolensk

RUSSIAN EMPIRE

• Kiev

Black Sea

OTTOMAN EMPIRE

• St. Petersburg

Neman R.

⚔ Friedland (1807)
Tilsit

GRAND DUCHY OF WARSAW

⚔ Austerlitz (1805)

Danube R.

ILLYRIAN PROVINCES

Stockholm

SWEDEN

Baltic Sea

Königsberg
• Danzig

PRUSSIA

SWEDISH POMERANIA

KINGDOM OF SWEDEN

Copenhagen

Pressburg
Vienna

AUSTRIAN EMPIRE

KINGDOM OF NAPLES

• Naples
Palermo

KINGDOM OF SICILY

NORWAY

KINGDOM OF NORWAY AND DENMARK

DENMARK

Elbe R.

Berlin
SAXONY
⚔ Leipzig (1813)
WESTPHALIA

⚔ Jena (1806)

CONFEDERATION OF THE RHINE

⚔ Ulm (1805)
BAVARIA

• Rome

Elba

North Sea

Rhine R.

⚔ Waterloo (1815)
Brussels •

WÜRTTEMBERG
BADEN
Zürich
SWITZERLAND

KINGDOM OF ITALY

Milan •

Genoa •

Corsica

Sardinia

Mediterranean Sea

GREAT BRITAIN

London •

• Paris

FRANCE

• Marseilles

SPAIN

Madrid •

ATLANTIC OCEAN

PORTUGAL

Trafalgar ⚔
(1805)

Lisbon •

400 Mi.
400 Km.
200
200
0
0

French empire
Dependent states
Allied with Napoleon
At war with Napoleon
⚔ Major battle

270

did away with clerical courts, promoted freedom of religion, permitted civil marriage, pressed for civil rights for Jews, and fought clerical interference with secular authority. They also abolished guilds, introduced a uniform system of weights and measures, eliminated internal tolls, and built roads, bridges, and canals. They promoted secular education and improved public health. Napoleon had launched a European-wide social revolution that attacked the privileges of the aristocracy and the clergy—who regarded him as that "crowned Jacobin"—and worked to the advantage of the bourgeoisie. This diffusion of revolutionary institutions weakened the Old Regime irreparably in much of Europe and speeded up the modernization of nineteenth-century Europe.

Pleased by the overhaul of feudal practices and the reduction of clerical power, many Europeans, particularly the progressive bourgeoisie, welcomed Napoleon as a liberator. But there was another side to Napoleon's rule. Napoleon, the tyrant of Europe, turned conquered lands into satellite kingdoms and exploited them for the benefit of France—a policy that gained him the enmity of many Europeans.

THE FALL OF NAPOLEON

As well as the hostility of subject nationals, Napoleon had to cope with the determined opposition of Great Britain. Its subsidies and encouragement kept resistance to the emperor alive. But perhaps Napoleon's greatest obstacle was his own boundless ambition, which warped his judgment. From its peak, the emperor's career soon slid downhill to defeat, dethronement, and deportation.

Failure to Subdue England

Britain was Napoleon's most resolute opponent. It could not be otherwise, for any power that domi-

◀ Map 11.1 Napoleon's Europe, 1810 By 1810, Napoleon dominated much of the Continent. His Grand Empire comprised lands annexed to France, vassal states, and cowed allies.

nated the Continent could organize sufficient naval might to threaten British commerce, challenge its sea power, and invade the island kingdom. Britain would not make peace with any state that sought European hegemony, and Napoleon's ambition would settle for nothing less.

Unable to invade Britain while British warships commanded the English Channel, Napoleon decided to bring what he called "the nation of shopkeepers" to its knees by damaging the British economy. His plan, called the *Continental System,* was to bar all countries under France's control from buying British goods. However, by smuggling goods onto the Continent and increasing trade with the New World, Britain, although hurt, escaped economic ruin. Besides, the Continental System also punished European lands that were dependent on British imports; the bourgeoisie, generally supportive of Napoleon's social and administrative reforms, turned against him because of the economic distress it caused. Furthermore, Napoleon's efforts to enforce the system enmeshed him in two catastrophic blunders: the occupation of Spain and the invasion of Russia.

The Spanish Ulcer

An ally of France since 1796, Spain proved a disappointment to Napoleon. It failed to prevent the Portuguese from trading with Britain, and it contributed little military or financial aid to France's war effort. Napoleon decided to incorporate Spain into his empire; in 1808, he deposed the Spanish ruler and designated his own brother Joseph as king of Spain.

Napoleon believed that the Spanish would rally round the gentle Joseph and welcome his liberal reforms. This confidence was a fatal illusion. Spanish nobles and clergy feared French liberalism; the overwhelmingly peasant population, illiterate and credulous, intensely proud, fanatically religious, and easily aroused by the clergy, viewed Napoleon as the Devil's agent. Loyal to the Spanish monarchy and faithful to the church, the Spanish fought a "War to the Knife" against the invaders.

Seeking to keep the struggle against Napoleon alive, Britain came to the aid of the Spanish insurgents. The intervention of British troops, commanded by Sir Arthur Wellesley, the future duke of Wellington, led to the ultimate defeat of Joseph in 1813. The "Spanish ulcer" drained Napoleon's treasury, tied down hundreds of thousands of French troops, enabled Britain to gain a foothold on the Continent from which to invade southern France, and inspired patriots in other lands to resist the French emperor.

The German War of Liberation

Anti-French feeling also broke out in the German states. Hatred of the French invaders evoked a feeling of national outrage among some Germans, who up to this time had thought only in terms of their own particular state and prince. Some German intellectuals, using the emotional language of nationalism, called for a war of liberation against Napoleon and, in some instances, for the creation of a unified Germany.

Besides kindling a desire for national independence and unity, the disastrous defeat of the Prussians at Jena (1806) and French domination of Germany stimulated a movement for reform among members of the Prussian high bureaucracy and officer corps. To survive in a world altered by the French Revolution, Prussia would have to learn the principal lessons of the Revolution: that aroused citizens fighting for a cause make better soldiers than mercenaries and oppressed serfs, and that officers selected for daring and intelligence command better than nobles possessing only a gilded birthright. The reformers believed that the elimination of social abuses would overcome defeatism and apathy and encourage Prussians to serve the state willingly and to fight bravely for national honor. A revitalized Prussia could then deal with the French.

Among the important reforms introduced in Prussia between 1807 and 1813 were the abolition of serfdom, the granting to towns of a large measure of self-administration, the awarding of army commissions on the basis of merit instead of birth, the elimination of cruel punishment in the ranks, and the establishment of national conscription. In 1813, the reform party forced King Frederick William III to declare war on France. The military reforms did improve the quality of the Prussian army. In the War of Liberation (1813), Prussian soldiers demonstrated far more enthusiasm and patriotism than they had at Jena in 1806, and the French were driven from Germany. The German War of Liberation came on the heels of Napoleon's disastrous Russian campaign.

Disaster in Russia

Deteriorating relations between Russia and France led Napoleon to his fatal decision to attack the Eastern giant. His creation of the Grand Duchy of Warsaw irritated the tsar, who feared a revival of Polish power and resented French influence on Russia's border. Another source of friction between the tsar and Napoleon was Russia's illicit trade with Britain, in violation of the Continental System. No doubt Napoleon's inexhaustible craving for glory and power also compelled him to strike at Russia.

In June 1812, the Grand Army, 614,000 men strong, crossed the Neman River into Russia. Fighting mainly rear-guard battles and retreating according to plan, the tsar's forces lured the invaders into the vastness of Russia, far from their lines of supply. On September 14, the Grand Army, its numbers greatly reduced by disease, hunger, exhaustion, desertion, and battle, entered Moscow, which the Russians had virtually evacuated. To show their contempt for the French conquerors and to deny the French shelter, the Russians set fire to the city, which burned for five days. Taking up headquarters in Moscow, Napoleon waited for Alexander I to admit defeat and come to terms. But the tsar remained intransigent.

Napoleon was in a dilemma: to penetrate deeper into Russia was certain death; to stay in Moscow with winter approaching meant possible starvation. Faced with these alternatives, Napoleon decided to retreat westward. On October 19, 1812, ninety-five thousand troops and thousands of wagons loaded with loot left Moscow for the long trek back. In early November came the first snow and frost. Army stragglers were slaughtered by Russian Cossacks and peasant partisans. In the middle of December, with the Russians in pursuit, the remnants of the Grand Army staggered across the Neman River into East Prussia.

Disaster in Russia. Lacking winter provisions, Napoleon's Grand Army abandoned Moscow in October 1812. The retreating French were decimated by hunger, winter, and Russian attacks. (*Musée de l'Armee*)

Final Defeat

After the destruction of the Grand Army, the empire crumbled. Although Napoleon raised a new army, he could not replace the equipment, cavalry horses, and experienced soldiers squandered in Russia. Now he had to rely on schoolboys and overage veterans. Most of Europe joined in a final coalition against France. In October 1813, allied forces from Austria, Prussia, Russia, and Sweden defeated Napoleon at Leipzig; in November, Anglo-Spanish forces crossed the Pyrenees into France. Finally, in the spring of 1814, the allies captured Paris. Napoleon abdicated and was exiled to the tiny island of Elba, off the coast of Italy. The Bourbon dynasty was restored to the throne of France in the person of Louis XVIII, younger brother of the executed Louis XVI and the acknowledged leader of the émigrés.

Only forty-four years of age, Napoleon did not believe that it was his destiny to die on Elba. On March 1, 1815, he landed on the French coast with a thousand soldiers, and three weeks later he entered Paris to a hero's welcome. Raising a new army, Napoleon moved against the allied forces in Belgium. There, the Prussians, led by Field Marshal Gebhard von Blücher, and the British, led by the duke of Wellington, defeated Napoleon at Waterloo in June 1815. Napoleon's desperate gamble to regain power—the famous "hundred days"—had failed. This time the allies sent Napoleon to Saint Helena, a lonely island in the South Atlantic a thousand miles off the coast of southern Africa. On this gloomy and rugged rock, Napoleon Bonaparte, emperor of France and would-be conqueror of Europe, spent the last six years of his life.

THE MEANING OF THE FRENCH REVOLUTION

The French Revolution was a decisive period in the shaping of the modern West. It implemented the thought of the philosophes, destroyed the hierarchical and corporate society of the Old Regime, which was a legacy of the Middle Ages, promoted the interests of the bourgeoisie, and quickened the growth of the modern state.

The French Revolution weakened the aristocracy. With their feudal rights and privileges eliminated, the nobles became simply ordinary citizens. Throughout the nineteenth century, France would be governed by both the aristocracy and the bourgeoisie; property, not noble birth, determined the composition of the new ruling elite.

The principle of careers being open to talent gave the bourgeois access to the highest positions in the state. Having wealth, talent, ambition, and now opportunity, the bourgeois would play an ever more important role in French political life. Throughout Continental Europe, the reforms of the French Revolution served as a model for progressive bourgeois, who sooner or later would challenge the Old Regime in their own lands.

The French Revolution transformed the dynastic state, on which the Old Regime was based, into the modern state: national, liberal, secular, and rational. When the Declaration of the Rights of Man and of the Citizen stated that "the source of all sovereignty resides essentially in the nation," the concept of the state took on a new meaning. The state was no longer merely a territory or a federation of provinces, nor was it the private possession of a king who claimed to be God's lieutenant on earth. In the new conception, the state belonged to the people as a whole, and the individual, formerly a subject, was now a citizen with both rights and duties and was governed by laws that drew no distinction on the basis of birth.

The liberal thought of the Enlightenment found practical expression in the reforms of the Revolution. Absolutism and divine right of monarchy, repudiated in theory by the philosophes, were invalidated by constitutions affirming that sovereignty resides with the people, not with a monarch, and setting limits to the powers of government and by elected parliaments that represented the governed. By providing for equality before the law and the protection of human rights—habeas corpus, trial by jury, and freedom of religion, speech, and the press—the Revolution struck at the abuses of the Old Regime. Because of violations and interruptions, these gains seemed at times more theoretical than actual. Nevertheless, these liberal ideals reverberated

throughout the Continent. In the early nineteenth century, revolutionaries in France and other lands, aspiring for political and social change, took the French Revolution as their inspiration, and the pace of reform quickened.

By disavowing any divine justification for the monarch's power and by depriving the church of its special position, the Revolution accelerated the secularization of European political life. Sweeping aside the administrative chaos of the Old Regime, the Revolution attempted to impose rational norms on the state. The sale of public offices, which had produced ineffective and corrupt administrators, was eliminated, and the highest positions in the land were opened to men of talent, regardless of birth. The Revolution abolished the peasantry's manorial obligations, which had hampered agriculture, and swept away barriers to economic expansion. It based taxes on income and streamlined their collection. The destruction of feudal remnants, internal tolls, and the guilds speeded up the expansion of a competitive market economy. In the nineteenth century, reformers in the rest of Europe would follow the lead set by France.

By spreading revolutionary ideals and institutions, Napoleon made it impossible for the traditional rulers to restore the Old Regime intact after his downfall. The secularization of society, the transformation of the dynastic state into the modern national state, and the prominence of the bourgeoisie were ensured.

By showing that a decadent old order could be toppled and supplanted by a new one, the French Revolution inspired generations of revolutionaries aspiring to end long-standing abuses and to remodel society. In the process, it unleashed three potentially destructive forces identified with the modern state: total war, nationalism, and a fanatic utopian mentality. All of these forces contradicted the rational and universal aims of the reformers as stated in the Declaration of the Rights of Man and of the Citizen. Whereas eighteenth-century wars were fought by professional soldiers for limited aims, the French Revolution brought conscription and the mobilization of all the state's resources for armed conflict. The world wars of the twentieth century were the terrible fulfillment of this new development in warfare.

The French Revolution also gave birth to modern nationalism. During the Revolution, loyalty was directed to the entire nation, not to a village or province or to the person of the king. The whole of France became the fatherland. Under the Jacobins, the French became converts to a secular faith preaching total reverence for the nation. "In 1794 we believed in no supernatural religion; our serious interior sentiments were all summed up in the one idea, how to be useful to the fatherland. Everything else . . . was, in our eyes, only trivial. . . . It was our only religion."[10] Few suspected that the new religion of nationalism was fraught with danger. Louis-Antoine de Saint-Just, a young, ardent Robespierrist, was gazing into the future when he declared: "There is something terrible in the sacred love of the fatherland. This love is so exclusive that it sacrifices everything to the public interest, without pity, without fear, with no respect for the human individual."[11] The philosophes would have deemed nationalism, which demanded total dedication of body and soul to the nation and eclipsed thought, to be a repudiation of their universalism and hopes for rational solutions to political conflicts. It was a new dogma capable of evoking wild and dangerous passions and a setback for the progress of reason.

The French Revolution gave rise to still another potentially destructive force: a revolutionary mentality that sought to demolish an unjust traditional society and create a new social order that would restore individuals to their natural goodness. The negative side of this lofty vision was its power to whip up an extremism that justified mass murder in the name of a higher good.

Such was the case with Robespierre and other Jacobins. In the twentieth century, Nazis in Germany and radical socialists in Russia, China, and Cambodia, seeing themselves as idealists striving for a social regeneration of humanity, oppressed, terrorized, and murdered with intense dedication—and a clear conscience.

The Revolution attempted to reconstruct society on the basis of Enlightenment thought. The Declaration of the Rights of Man and of the Citizen, whose spirit permeated the reforms of the Revolution, upheld the dignity of the individual, demanded respect for the individual, attributed to each person natural rights, and barred the state from denying these rights. It insisted that society and the state have no higher duty than to promote the freedom and autonomy of the individual. "It is not enough to have overturned the throne," said Robespierre; "our concern is to erect upon its remains holy Equality and the sacred Rights of Man."[12] The tragedy of the Western experience is that this humanist vision, brilliantly expressed by the Enlightenment and given recognition in the reforms of the French Revolution, would be undermined in later generations. And, ironically, by its fanatical commitment to a seductive ideology that promised worldly salvation—the creation of a republic of virtue and truth—the French Revolution itself contributed to the shattering of this vision. It had spawned total war, aggressive nationalism, terror as government policy, and a revolutionary mentality that sought to change the world through coercion and violence. In the twentieth century, these dangerous forces almost succeeded in crushing the liberty and equality so valued by the French reformers.

❖   ❖   ❖

NOTES

1. George Rudé, *Revolutionary Europe, 1783–1815* (New York: Harper Torchbooks, 1966), p. 74.

2. Henri Peyre, "The Influence of Eighteenth-Century Ideas on the French Revolution," *Journal of the History of Ideas,* 10 (1949):73.

3. George Lefebvre, *The French Revolution from 1793 to 1799,* trans. John Hall Stewart and James Friguglietti (New York: Columbia University Press, 1964) vol. 2, p. 360.

4. Quoted in T. C. W. Blanning, *The French Revolution: Aristocrats Versus Bourgeois?* (Atlantic Highlands, N.J.: Humanities Press, 1987), p. 9.

5. William Doyle, *Origins of the French Revolution* (London: Oxford University Press, 1980), p. 21.

6. Excerpted in John Hall Stewart, ed., *A Documentary Survey of the French Revolution* (New York: Macmillan, 1951), pp. 43–44.

7. Albert Soboul, *The Parisian Sans-Culottes and the French Revolution, 1793–94,* trans. Gwynne Lewis (London: Oxford University Press, 1964), pp. 28–29.

8. Excerpted in George Rudé, ed., *Robespierre* (Englewood Cliffs, N.J.: Prentice-Hall, 1976), p. 72.

9. Ibid., p. 57.

10. Quoted in Carlton J. H. Hayes, *The Historical Evolution of Modern Nationalism* (New York: Richard R. Smith, 1931), p. 55.

11. Quoted in Hans Kohn, *Making of the Modern French Mind* (New York: D. Van Nostrand, 1955), p. 17.

12. Quoted in Christopher Dawson, *The Gods of Revolution* (New York: New York University Press, 1972), p. 83.

Suggested Reading

Blanning, T. C. W., *The French Revolution: Aristocrats Versus Bourgeois?* (1987). Summarizes recent scholarship on the question; a volume in Studies of European History series.

Campbell, Peter Robert, *The Ancien Régime in France* (1988). An incisive essay on French society prior to the Revolution.

Carr, John L., *Robespierre* (1972). A biography of the revolutionary leader.

Chandler, David, *The Campaigns of Napoleon* (1966). An exhaustive analysis of Napoleon's art of war.

Connelley, Owen, *Napoleon's Satellite Kingdoms* (1965). Focuses on the kingdoms in Naples, Italy, Holland, Spain, and Westphalia, which were created by Napoleon and ruled by his relatives.

Cronin, Vincent, *Napoleon Bonaparte* (1972). A highly acclaimed biography.

Doyle, William, *Origins of the French Revolution* (1980). In recent decades, several historians have challenged the traditional view that the French Revolution was an attempt by the bourgeoisie to overthrow the remnants of aristocratic power and privilege and that it was a victory of a capitalist bourgeois order over feudalism. This book summarizes the new scholarship and argues that the nobility and bourgeoisie had much in common before the Revolution.

Forrest, Alan, *The French Revolution* (1995). Social, political, and ideological changes wrought by the Revolution.

Furet, François, and Mona Ozouf, eds., *A Critical Dictionary of the French Revolution* (1989). Articles on many topics; highly recommended.

Gershoy, Leo, *The Era of the French Revolution* (1957). A brief survey, with useful documents.

Gottschalk, Louis, and Donald Lach, *Toward the French Revolution* (1973). A survey of the eighteenth-century background of the French Revolution.

Herold, J. Christopher, ed., *The Mind of Napoleon* (1955). A valuable selection from the written and spoken words of Napoleon.

———, *The Horizon Book of the Age of Napoleon* (1965). Napoleon and his time.

Higgins, E. L., ed., *The French Revolution* (1938). Excerpts from contemporaries.

Holtman, Robert B., *The Napoleonic Revolution* (1967). A portrait of Napoleon as revolutionary innovator who influenced every aspect of European life; particularly good on Napoleon the propagandist.

Lefebvre, Georges, *The French Revolution,* 2 vols. (1962, 1964). A detailed analysis by a master historian.

———, *The Coming of the French Revolution* (1967). A brilliant analysis of the social structure of the Old Regime and the opening phase of the Revolution.

Markham, Felix, *Napoleon* (1963). A first-rate short biography.

———, *Napoleon and the Awakening of Europe* (1965). An exploration of Napoleon's influence on other lands.

McPhee, Peter, *The French Revolution 1789–1799* (2002). Recent, readable, and reliable.

Palmer, R. R., *The Age of the Democratic Revolution,* 2 vols. (1959, 1964). The French Revolution as part of a revolutionary movement that spread on both sides of the Atlantic.

———, *Twelve Who Ruled* (1965). An admirable treatment of the Terror.

Rudé, George, *The Crowd in the French Revolution* (1959). An analysis of the composition of the crowds that stormed the Bastille, marched to Versailles, and attacked the king's palace.

———, *Robespierre: Portrait of a Revolutionary Democrat* (1976). A biography of the revolutionary leader.

Stewart, J. H., ed. *A Documentary Survey of the French Revolution* (1951). A valuable collection of documents.

Sutherland, D. M. G., *France 1789–1815* (1986). Like Doyle, Sutherland departs from the classic theory of the bourgeois revolution.

REVIEW QUESTIONS

1. Analyze the causes of the French Revolution.

2. Identify and explain the significance of the following: the formation of the National Assembly, the storming of the Bastille, the Great Fear, and the October Days.

3. Analyze the nature and significance of the reforms of the National Assembly.

4. What were the grievances of the sans-culottes?

5. What were the accomplishments of the Jacobins?

6. Describe Robespierre's basic philosophy.

7. Napoleon both preserved and destroyed the ideals of the French Revolution. Discuss this statement.

8. Account for Napoleon's downfall. What were Napoleon's greatest achievements? What were his greatest failures?

9. Why was the era of the French Revolution a decisive period in the shaping of the West?

Chapter 12

The Industrial Revolution: The Transformation of Society

- **Britain First**
- **Society Transformed**
- **The Rise of Reform in Britain**
- **Responses to Industrialization**
- **Industrialism in Perspective**

*I*n the last part of the eighteenth century, as a revolution for liberty and equality swept across France and sent shock waves through Europe, a different kind of revolution, a revolution in industry, was transforming life in Great Britain. In the nineteenth century, the Industrial Revolution spread to the United States and to the European continent. Today, it encompasses virtually the entire world; everywhere the drive to substitute machines for human labor continues at a rapid pace.

After 1760, dramatic changes occurred in Britain in the way goods were produced and labor organized. New forms of power, particularly steam, replaced animal strength and human muscle. Better ways of obtaining and using raw materials were discovered, and a new way of organizing production and workers—the factory—came into use. In the nineteenth century, technology moved from triumph to triumph with a momentum unprecedented in human history. The resulting explosion in economic production and productivity transformed society with breathtaking speed. ❖

BRITAIN FIRST

Britain possessed several advantages that enabled it to take the lead in industrialization. Large and easily developed supplies of coal and iron had given the British a long tradition of metallurgy and mining. In the early stages of industrialization, Britain's river transportation system was supplemented by canals and toll roads (turnpikes), which private entrepreneurs financed and built for profit. In addition, the enclosure movement provided factories with a labor pool. During the eighteenth century great landlords enclosed, or fenced off and claimed as their own, land formerly used in common by villagers for grazing farm animals. Once the peasants were gone, lords could bring this land under cultivation for their own private gain. No longer able to earn a living from the land, these dispossessed farmers sought work in emerging factories.

Britain also had capital available for investment in new industries. These funds came from wealthy landowners and merchants who had grown rich through commerce, including the slave trade. Interest rates on loans fell in the eighteenth century, stimulating investment. Britain's expanding middle class provided a home market for emerging industries. So, too, did its overseas colonies, which also supplied raw materials—particularly cotton, needed for the developing textile industry. A vigorous spirit of enterprise and the opportunity for men of ability to rise

from common origins to riches and fame also help explain the growth of industrialization.

Finally, two European cultural traditions in which Britain shared played crucial roles in the rise of industrialism. One was individualism, which had its roots in both the Renaissance and the Reformation; during the era of the commercial revolution, it manifested itself in hard-driving, ambitious merchants and bankers. This spirit of individualism, combined with the wide latitude states gave to private economic activity, fostered the development of dynamic capitalist entrepreneurs. The second cultural tradition promoting industrialization was the high value westerners placed on the rational understanding and control of nature. Both individualism and the tradition of reason, concludes historian David S. Landes, "gave Europe a tremendous advantage in the invention and adoption of new technology. The will to mastery, the rational approach to problems that we call scientific method, the competition for wealth and power—together these broke down the resistance of inherited ways and made change a positive good."[1]

Changes in Technology

The Cotton Industry Long the home of an important wool trade, Britain in the eighteenth century jumped ahead in the production of cotton, the industry that first showed the possibility of unprecedented growth rates. British cotton production expanded tenfold between 1760 and 1785, and another tenfold between 1785 and 1825. A series of inventions revolutionized the industry and drastically altered the social conditions of the work.

In 1733, long before the expansion started, a simple invention—John Kay's flying shuttle—made it possible for weavers to double their output. The flying shuttle enabled weavers to produce faster than spinners could spin—until James Hargreaves's spinning jenny, perfected by 1768, allowed an operator to work several spindles at once, powered only by human energy. Within five years, Richard Arkwright's water frame spinning machine could be powered by water or animals, and Samuel Crompton's spinning mule (1779) powered many spindles, first by

Chronology 12.1 ❖ The Industrial Revolution

1764–1767	Hargreaves invents the spinning jenny
1769	Watt invents the modern steam engine
1785	Cartwright develops power loom
1825	Workers are allowed to unionize but not to strike
1830	First railway line is built in England
1832	Reform Bill of 1832 expands British voting rights

human and later by animal and water energy. These changes improved spinning productivity so much that it caused bottlenecks in weaving until Edmund Cartwright developed a power loom in 1785.* To the end of the century, there was a race to speed up the spinning part of the process and then the weaving part by applying water power to looms or new, larger devices to the jenny.

Arkwright's water frame made it more efficient to bring many workers together, rather than sending work out to individuals in their own homes. This development was the beginning of the factory system, which within a generation would revolutionize the conditions of labor. Because water power drove these early machines, mills were located near rivers and streams. Towns thus grew up where machinery could be powered by water; the factory system concentrated laborers and their families near the factories.

The Steam Engine   James Watt, a Scottish engineer, developed the steam engine in the 1760s. Because steam engines ran on coal or wood, not water power, they allowed greater flexibility in locating textile mills. Factories were no longer restricted to the power supplied by a river or a stream or to the space available beside flowing water; they could be built anywhere. With steam,

*Technological developments in America helped to meet the growing demand for raw cotton. Eli Whitney's cotton gin (1793) removed the seeds from raw cotton quickly and cheaply, leading farmers and plantation owners to devote more land to cotton. Within a generation, more laborers were required for the fields and fewer to process the cotton. The increased demand for slave labor had far-reaching repercussions.

the whole pattern of work changed because weaker, younger, and less skilled workers could be taught the few simple tasks necessary to tend the machine. The shift from male to female and child labor was a major social change.

The Iron Industry   Although steam power allowed employers to hire weaker people to operate machinery, it required machines made of stronger metal to withstand the forces generated by the stronger power source. By the 1780s, trial and error had perfected the production of wrought iron, which became the most widely used metal until steel began to be cheaply produced in the 1860s.

The iron industry made great demands on the coal mines to fuel its furnaces. Because steam engines enabled miners to pump water from the mines more efficiently and at a much deeper level, rich veins in existing mines became accessible for the first time. The greater productivity in coal allowed the continued improvement of iron smelting. Then, in 1856, Henry Bessemer developed a process for converting pig iron into steel by speedily removing the impurities in the iron. In the 1860s, William Siemens and the brothers Pierre and Émile Martin developed the open-hearth process, which could handle much greater amounts of metal than Bessemer's converter. Steel became so cheap to produce that it quickly replaced iron in industry because of its greater tensile strength and durability.

Transportation   The steam engine and iron and steel brought a new era in transport. As machines speeded up factory production, methods of transportation also improved. In 1830, the first railway

Machine-produced Textile Printing. European machine-produced textile printing copied traditional Indian textile designs. Indian weavers, spinners, printers—an entire cast of craftsmen—were driven to despair and destitution trying to compete with the European women and children who toiled long hours to manufacture the cheap calicos. *(Lewis Hine/Hulton Archive/Getty Images)*

line was built in England, connecting Manchester and Liverpool; this sparked an age of railway building throughout much of the world. Shipping changed radically with the use of vessels without sails, which had greater tonnage capacity.

SOCIETY TRANSFORMED

The innovations in agricultural production, business organization, and technology had revolutionary consequences for society, economics, and politics. People were drawn from the countryside into cities, and traditional ways of life changed. Much of the old life persisted, however, particularly during the first half of the nineteenth cen-

tury. Landed property was still the principal form of wealth, and large landowners continued to exercise political power. From England to Russia, families of landed wealth (often the old noble families) still constituted the social elite. European society remained overwhelmingly rural; as late as the midcentury, only England was half urban. Nevertheless, contemporaries were so overwhelmed by industrialization that they saw it as a sudden and complete break with the past: the shattering of traditional moral and social patterns.

Cities grew in number, size, and population as a result of industrialization. For example, between 1801 and 1851, the population of Birmingham rose from 73,000 to 250,000 and that of

London Row Houses. This painting by the French artist Gustave Dore depicts the overcrowded and unsanitary conditions in industrial London. Workers and their families lived in row houses, each just one room wide with a tiny yard in back. (*Prints/Division, New York Public Library, Astor, Lenox, and Tilden Foundations*)

Liverpool from 77,000 to 400,000. Industrial cities expanded rapidly, without planning or much regulation by local or national government. So much growth with so little planning or control led to cities with little sanitation, no lighting, wretched housing, poor transportation, and little security.

Rich and poor alike suffered in this environment of disease, crime, and ugliness, although the poor obviously bore the brunt of these evils. They lived in houses located as close to the factories as possible. The houses were several stories high and built so close to each other that only courtyards separated them. Sometimes a whole family huddled together in one room or even shared a room with another family. Open sewers, polluted rivers, factory smoke, and filthy streets allowed disease to spread. In Britain, about twenty-six out

of every one hundred children died before the age of five. Almost universally, those who wrote about industrial cities—England's Manchester, Leeds, and Liverpool and France's Lyons—described the stench, the filth, the inhumane crowding, the poverty, and the immorality.

Changes in Social Structure

The Industrial Revolution destroyed forever the old division of society into clergy, nobility, and commoners. The development of industry and commerce caused a corresponding development of a bourgeoisie: a middle class, comprising people of common birth who engaged in trade and other capitalist ventures. The wealthiest bourgeois were bankers, factory and mine owners, and merchants, but the middle class also included shopkeepers, managers, lawyers, and doctors. The virtues of work, thrift, ambition, and prudence characterized the middle class as a whole, as did the perversion of these virtues into materialism, selfishness, callousness, harsh individualism, and smugness.

From the eighteenth century on, as industry and commerce developed, the middle class grew in size, first in England and then throughout Western Europe. During the eighteenth and nineteenth centuries, the middle class struggled against the entrenched aristocracy to end political, economic, and social discrimination. By the end of the nineteenth century, bourgeois politicians held the highest offices in much of western Europe and shared authority with aristocrats, whose birth no longer guaranteed them the only political and social power in the nation. As industrial wealth grew more important, the middle class became more influential. Its wealthy members also tended to imitate the aristocracy: it was common throughout Europe for rich bourgeois to spend fortunes buying great estates and emulating aristocratic manners and pleasures.

Industrialization may have reduced some barriers between the landed elites and the middle class, but it sharpened the distinctions between the middle class and the laboring class. Like the middle class, the proletariat encompassed different economic levels: rural laborers, miners, and city workers. Many gradations existed among city workers, from artisans to factory workers and servants. Factory workers were the newest and most rapidly growing social group; at mid-century, however, they did not constitute most of the laboring people in any major city. For example, as late as 1890, they made up only one-sixth of London's population.

The artisans were the largest group of workers in the cities for the first half of the nineteenth century, and in some places for much longer than that. They worked in construction, printing, small tailoring or dressmaking establishments, food preparation and processing, and crafts producing such luxury items as furniture, jewelry, lace, and velvet. Artisans were distinct from factory workers; their technical skills were difficult to learn, and traditionally their crafts were acquired in guilds, which still functioned as both social and economic organizations. Artisans were usually educated (they could read and write), lived in one city or village for generations, and maintained stable families, often securing places for their children in their craft. As the Industrial Revolution progressed, however, they found it hard to compete with cheap, factory-produced goods, and their livelihoods were threatened.

Servants were especially numerous in capital cities. In the first half of the nineteenth century, in cities like Paris and London, where the number of factories was not great, there were more servants than factory workers. Servants usually had some education. If they married and had a family, they taught their children to read and write and sometimes to observe the manners and values of the household in which the parent had worked. Many historians believe that these servants passed on to their children their own deference to authority and their aspirations to bourgeois status, which may have limited social discontent and radical political activity.

Working-Class Life

Life was not easy for those whose labor contributed to the industrializing process. Usually, factory workers were recent arrivals from agricultural areas, where they had been driven off the land. They frequently moved to the city without their families, leaving them behind until they could afford to support them in town. These people entered rapidly growing industries, where long hours—sometimes fifteen a day—were not unusual. Farming had meant long hours, too, as had the various forms of labor for piecework rates in the home, but the pace of the machine, the dull routine, and dangerous conditions in factories and mines made work even more oppressive. Miners, for example, labored under the hazards of cave-ins, explosions, and deadly gas fumes. Deep beneath the earth's surface, life was dark, cold, wet, and tenuous. Their bodies stunted and twisted, their lungs wrecked, miners toiled their lives away in "the pits."

Sometimes, compared with their lives in the country, the workers' standard of living rose, particularly if the whole family found work; the pay for a family might be better than they could have

Engraving from the *Illustrated Times*, 1859. As unemployed workers flooded into the great cities of Europe, homelessness became a pressing social problem. To keep dry and warm, homeless men sometimes slept in coffins made for the living and lined up in a factory or prisonlike building. These facilities were charitable institutions—not the poor-law workhouses—but they too reflected the common belief of the day that poverty was the fault of the poor, who should learn to help themselves. (*Mansell Collection*)

earned for agricultural labor. But working conditions were terrible, as were living conditions. The factories were dirty, hot, unventilated, and frequently dangerous. Workers toiled long hours, were fined for mistakes and even for accidents, were fired at the will of the employer or foreman, and were laid off during slowdowns. They often lived in overcrowded and dirty housing. If they were unmarried or had left their family in the country, they often lived in barracks with other members of their sex. If they lost their jobs, they also lost their shelter.

In the villages they had left, they had been poor, but they were socially connected to family, church, and even local landlords. But in the cities, factory workers labored in plants with twenty to a hundred workers and had little contact with their employers. Instead, they were pushed by foremen to work hard and efficiently for long hours to keep up with the machines. Workers had

little time on the job to socialize with others; they were fined for talking to one another, for lateness, and for many petty infringements. They often became competitors in order to keep their jobs. Lacking organization, a sense of comradeship, education, and experience of city life, factory workers found little comfort when times were bad.

Workers often developed a life around the pub, the café, or some similar gathering place, where there were drinks and games and the gossip and news of the day. On Sundays, their one day off, workers drank and danced; absenteeism was so great on Monday that the day was called "holy Monday." Gin drinking was denounced on all sides; workers and reformers alike urged temperance. Many workers played sports, and some social organizations grew up around their sporting games. In these and other ways, workers developed a culture of their own—a culture that was misunderstood and often deplored by middle-class reformers.

Many contemporaries felt that the poor—those who were so unfortunate that they needed the assistance of others—were growing in numbers, that their condition was woeful, and that it had actually deteriorated in the midst of increased wealth. If machines could produce so much wealth and so many products, then why, social observers wondered, were there so many poor people? Parliamentary reports and investigations of civic-minded citizens documented the suffering for all to read.

Historians still debate how bad workers' conditions were in the early stages of industrialization. Most workers experienced periods of acute distress, but historians generally conclude that the standard of living slowly improved during the eighteenth and nineteenth centuries. Although historians take an optimistic view of the long-range effects of industrialization, the rapidity of change also wreaked great hardships on the workers of all countries, who endured cruel conditions in factories and slums.

THE RISE OF REFORM IN BRITAIN

Although it was the freest state in Europe in the early decades of the nineteenth century, Britain was far from democratic. A constitutional monarchy, with many limits on the powers of king and state, Britain was nonetheless dominated by aristocrats. Landed aristocrats controlled both the House of Lords and the House of Commons—the House of Lords because they constituted its membership and the House of Commons because they patronized or sponsored men favorable to their interests. The vast majority of people, from the middle class as well as from the working class, could not vote. Many towns continued to be governed by corrupt groups. New industrial towns were not allowed to elect representatives to Parliament; often they lacked a town organization and could not even govern themselves effectively.

The social separation of noble and commoner was not as rigid in Britain as on the Continent. Younger sons of aristocrats did not inherit titles and were therefore obliged to make careers in law, business, the military, and the church. The upper and middle classes mingled much more freely than on the Continent, and the wealthiest merchants tended to buy lands, titles, and husbands for their daughters. However, Parliament, the courts, local government, the established Anglican church, and the monarchy were all part of a social and political system dominated by aristocratic interests and values. This domination persisted despite the vast changes in social and economic structure that had taken place in the process of industrialization during the second half of the eighteenth century.

Some members of Parliament urged timely reforms. In 1828, Parliament repealed a seventeenth-century act that in effect barred Nonconformists (non-Anglican Protestants) from government positions and from universities; the following year, Catholics gained the right to sit in Parliament. In 1833, slavery was abolished within the British Empire. (The British slave trade had been abolished earlier.) The Municipal Corporations Act (1835) granted towns and cities greater authority over their affairs. This measure created town and city governments that could, if they wished, begin to solve some of the problems of urbanization and industrialization. These municipal corporations could institute reforms such as sanitation, which Parliament encouraged by passing the first Public Health Act in 1848.

Increasingly, reform centered on extending suffrage and enfranchising the new industrial towns. Middle-class men, and even workers, hoped to gain the right to vote. Because of population shifts, some sparsely populated regions—called rotten boroughs—sent representatives to the House of Commons, while many densely populated factory towns had little or no representation. Often a single important landowner controlled many seats in the Commons. Voting was public, which allowed intimidation, and candidates frequently tried to influence voters with drinks, food, and even money.

Intense and bitter feelings built up during the campaign for the Reform Bill of 1832. The House of Commons passed the bill to extend the suffrage by some 200,000, almost double the number who were then entitled to vote. The House of Lords, however, refused to pass the bill. There were riots and strikes in many cities, and mass meetings, both of workers and of middle-class people, took place all over the country. King William IV (1830–1837) became convinced, along with many politicians, that the situation was potentially revolutionary. To defuse it, he threatened to increase the number of the bill's supporters in the House of Lords by creating new peers. This threat brought reluctant peers into line, and the bill was passed. The Reform Act of 1832 extended the suffrage to the middle class and made the House of Commons more representative. The rotten boroughs lost their seats, which were granted to towns. However, because there were high property qualifications, workers did not gain the right to vote.

Workers did obtain some relief when humanitarians pressured Parliament to pass the Factory Act (1833), which legislated that no child under thirteen could work more than nine hours a day and that no one aged thirteen to eighteen could work more than sixty-nine hours a week. The act also provided some inspectors to investigate infractions and punish offenders. That same year, Parliament also banned children under ten from the mines. The Factory Act of 1847 stipulated that boys under eighteen and women could work no more than ten hours a day in factories. At first, workers resented the prohibition of child labor, since their family income would be greatly reduced if their children could not work, but they gradually came to approve of this law. The ten-hour day for adult male workers was not enacted until 1874.

The Chartist reform movement, whose adherents came from the ranks of both intellectual radicals and workers, pressed for political, not economic, reforms. During the 1830s and 1840s, the Chartists agitated for democratic measures, such as universal manhood suffrage, the secret ballot, salaries and the abolition of property qualifications for members of Parliament, and annual meetings of Parliament.

The last political effort by the Chartists was led by Feargus O'Connor, a charismatic Irishman who organized a mass demonstration to present a huge petition of demands to Parliament in 1848. The cabinet ignored the great "People's Charter," which had signatures of at least two million names, and the movement died out. But the Chartist platform remained the democratic reform program for the rest of the century, long after the death of Chartism itself at midcentury. All of the Chartists' demands, except for annual elections for members of Parliament, were eventually realized.

At the beginning of the nineteenth century, elementary education in Britain was managed by private individuals and church organizations. Schools were financed by contributions, grants, and fees paid by students. The government neither financed nor promoted education. As a result, very few poor children attended school. Indeed, many government officials feared that educating the poor would incite unrest. If the lower classes read publications attacking Christianity and challenging authority, they would become insolent to their superiors. One member of Parliament declared that schooling would teach the poor "to despise their lot in life, instead of making them good servants in agriculture and other laborious employments to which their rank in society had destined them." However, many Britons, inheriting the Enlightenment's confidence in education, favored schooling for the poor. In 1833, Parliament began to allocate small sums for elementary education. These funds were inadequate; in 1869, only about half of all children of school age attended school. The Education Act of 1870 gave local governments the power to establish elementary schools. By 1891, these schools were free and attendance was required.

Many workers and radicals believed that the only hope for their class lay in unified action through trade unions. At first, Parliament fought the unions, passing the Combination Acts (1799–1800), which made unions illegal. In 1825, Parliament allowed workers to unionize but forbade them to strike. Unions made some headway in protecting their members from unemployment and dangerous working conditions, but strikes (which remained officially illegal until 1875) were rarely successful and were often suppressed by force.

Unlike the Continental states, England avoided revolution. British politicians thought that it was because they had made timely reforms in the 1830s and 1840s. The political experience of the first half of the nineteenth century laid the foundation for British parliamentary practices, which came to be the model of liberal, progressive, and

The Great Exhibition of 1851, by Dickinson. The Crystal Palace exhibition drew enormous crowds from all over Europe to see the products and processes of machine and craft industries. The building itself was a glass structure supported by a cast-iron frame, a construction imitated in many grand railroad terminals, department stores, and auditoriums throughout Europe and the United States. (*By permission of the Houghton Library, Harvard University*)

stable politics. Britain was the symbol for all those who argued for reform rather than revolution.

RESPONSES TO INDUSTRIALIZATION

The problems created by rapid industrialization profoundly influenced political and social thought. Liberalism, which began as an attempt to safeguard individual rights from oppressive state authority, now had to confront an unanticipated problem: the distress caused by rapid in-

dustrialization and urbanization. Also responding to this ordeal was a new group of thinkers, called socialists.

Liberalism*

Adopting the laissez-faire theory of Adam Smith, liberals maintained that a free economy, in which private enterprise would be unimpeded by government regulations, was as important as political freedom to the well-being of the individual and

*See also the following chapter.

the community. When people acted from self-interest, liberals said, they worked harder and achieved more; self-interest and natural competitive impulses spurred economic activity and ensured the production of more and better goods at the lowest possible price, benefiting the entire nation. For this reason, the government must neither block free competition nor deprive individuals of their property, which was their incentive to work hard and efficiently.

Convinced that individuals were responsible for their own misfortunes, liberals were often unmoved by the misery of the poor. Indeed, they used the principle of laissez faire—that government should not interfere with the natural laws of supply and demand—to justify their opposition to humanitarian legislation intended to alleviate the suffering of the factory workers. Liberals regarded such social reforms as unwarranted and dangerous meddling with the natural law of supply and demand.

They drew comfort from the theory advanced by Thomas Malthus (1766–1834) in his *Essay on the Principle of Population* (1798), which supported laissez-faire economics. Malthus asserted that population always grows at a faster rate than the food supply; consequently, government programs to aid the poor and provide higher wages would only encourage larger families and thus perpetuate poverty. Malthus seemed to supply "scientific" justification for opposing state action to help the poor. Poverty, argued Malthusians, was not the fault of factory owners. It was an iron law of nature—the result of population pressure on resources—and could not be eliminated by state policies. According to Malthus, the state could not ameliorate the poor's misery; "the means of redress," he said, "are in their own hands, and in the hands of no other persons whatever."[2] This "means of redress" would be a lowering of the birthrate through late marriages and chastity, but Malthus believed that the poor lacked the self-discipline to refrain from sexual activity. When they received higher wages, they had more children, thereby upsetting the population-resource balance and bringing misery to themselves and others.

A fellow economist, David Ricardo (1772–1823), gave support to Malthus's gloomy outlook. Wages, he said, tended to remain at the minimum needed to maintain workers. Higher wages encouraged workers to have more children, causing an increase in the labor supply, and greater competition for jobs would then force down wages. Ricardo's disciples made his law inflexible. This "iron law of wages" meant bleak prospects for the working poor. Many workers felt that the new science of economics offered them little hope. They argued that the liberals were concerned only with their class and national interests and that they were callous and apathetic toward the sufferings of the poor.

Liberals of the early nineteenth century saw poverty and suffering as part of the natural order and beyond the scope of government. They feared that state intervention in the economy to redress social ills would disrupt the free market, threatening personal liberty and hindering social well-being. In time, however, the liberals modified their position, allowing for government action to protect the poor and the powerless against the economy's ravages.

Early Socialism

The socialists went further than the liberals. They argued that the liberals' concern for individual freedom and equality had little impact on the poverty, oppression, and gross inequality of wealth that plagued modern society. Liberal ideals, socialists claimed, protected the person and property of the wealthy, while the majority were mired in poverty and helplessness. Asserting that the liberals' doctrine of individualism degenerated into selfish egoism, which harmed community life, socialists demanded the creation of a new society based on cooperation rather than competition. Reflecting the spirit of the Enlightenment and the French Revolution, socialists, like liberals, denounced the status quo for perpetuating injustice and held that people could create a better world. Like liberals, too, they placed the highest value on a rational analysis of society and on transforming society in line with scientifically valid premises, whose truth rational people could grasp. Socialists believed that they had discerned a pattern in human society that, if properly understood and acted upon, would lead men and women to an earthly salvation. Thus, socialists

Saint-Simonian Community at Ménilmontant. Followers of Saint-Simon established this community in a suburb of Paris. It was headed by Father Enfantin, whose iconoclastic theories of love and marriage outraged many people. (*Bibliothèque Nationale, Paris*)

were also romantics, for they dreamed of a new social order, a future utopia, where each individual could find happiness and fulfillment. Although they sought to replace the existing social order with a more just arrangement, these early socialists, unlike Marx, did not advocate class warfare. Rather, they aspired to create a new harmonious social order that would reconcile different classes.

Saint-Simon Henri Comte de Saint-Simon (1760–1825) renounced his title during the French Revolution and enthusiastically preached the opportunity to create a new society. His mission, he believed, was to set society right by instilling an understanding of the new age that science and industry were shaping. He argued that just as Christianity had provided social unity and stability during the Middle Ages, so scientific knowledge would bind the society of his time. The scientists, industrialists, bankers, artists, and writers would replace the clergy and the aristocracy as the social elite and would harness technology for the betterment of humanity. Saint-Simon's disciples championed efforts to build great railway and canal systems, including the Suez and Panama Canals. His vision of a scientifically organized society led by trained experts was a powerful force among in-

tellectuals in the nineteenth century and is very much alive today among those who believe in a technocratic society.

Fourier Another early French socialist, Charles Fourier (1772–1837), believed—like the romantics—that society conflicted with the natural needs of human beings and that this tension was responsible for human misery. Only the reorganization of society so that it would satisfy people's desire for pleasure and contentment would end that misery. Whereas Saint-Simon and his followers had elaborate plans to reorganize society on the grand scale of large industries and giant railway and canal systems, Fourier sought to create small communities that would let men and women enjoy life's simple pleasures.

These communities of about sixteen hundred people, called *phalansteries,* would be organized according to the unchanging needs of human nature. All the people would work at tasks that interested them and would produce things that brought them and others pleasure. Like Adam Smith, Fourier understood that specialization bred boredom and alienation from work and life. Unlike Smith, he did not believe that vastly increased productivity compensated for the evils of specialization. In the phalansteries, money and goods would not be equally distributed; those with special skills and responsibilities would be rewarded accordingly. This system of rewards conformed to nature because people have a natural desire to be rewarded.

Fourier thought that marriage distorted the natures of both men and women, since monogamy restricted their sexual needs and narrowed the scope of their lives to just the family. Instead, people should think of themselves as part of the family of all humanity. Because married women had to devote all their strength and time to household and children, they had no time or energy left to enjoy life's pleasures. Fourier did not call for the abolition of the family, but he did hope that it would disappear of its own accord as society adjusted to his theories. Men and women would find new ways of fulfilling themselves sexually, and the community would be organized so that it could care for the children. Fourier's ideas found some acceptance in the United States, where in the 1840s at least twenty-nine communities were founded on Fourierist principles. None, however, lasted more than five or six years.

Owen   In 1799, Robert Owen (1771–1858) became part owner and manager of the New Lanark cotton mills in Scotland. Distressed by the widespread mistreatment of workers, Owen resolved to improve the lives of his employees and show that it was possible to do so without destroying profits. He raised wages, upgraded working conditions, refused to hire children under ten, and provided workers with neat homes, food, and clothing, all at reasonable prices. He set up schools for children and for adults. In every way, he demonstrated his belief that healthier, happier workers produced more than the less fortunate ones. Like Saint-Simon, Owen believed that industry and technology could and would enrich humankind if they were organized according to the proper principles. Visitors came from all over Europe to see Owen's factories.

Just like many philosophes, Owen was convinced that the environment was the principal shaper of character—that the ignorance, alcoholism, and crime of the poor derived from bad living conditions. Public education and factory reform, said Owen, would make better citizens of the poor. Owen came to believe that the entire social and economic order must be replaced by a new system based on harmonious group living rather than on competition. He established a model community at New Harmony, Indiana, but it was short-lived.

INDUSTRIALISM IN PERSPECTIVE

Like the French Revolution, the Industrial Revolution helped to modernize Europe. Eventually, it transformed every facet of society. In preindustrial society—Europe in the mid-eighteenth century—agriculture was the dominant economic activity and peasants were the most numerous class. Peasant life centered on the family and the village, which country folk rarely left. The new rational and critical spirit associated with the Enlightenment hardly penetrated rural Europe; there, religious faith, clerical authority, and ancient superstition remained firmly entrenched.

Traditional society was predominantly rural. By the start of the nineteenth century, 20 percent of the population of Britain, France, and Holland lived in cities; in Russia, the figure was only 5 percent. Artisan manufacturing in small shops and trade for local markets were the foundations of the urban economy, although some cities did produce luxury goods for wider markets. Textile manufacturing was conducted through the putting-out system, in which wool was turned into cloth in private dwellings, usually the homes of peasants.

The richest and most powerful class was the aristocracy, whose wealth stemmed from land. Nobles dominated the countryside and enjoyed privileges protected by custom and law. Eighteenth-century aristocrats, like their medieval forebears, viewed society as a hierarchy, in which a person's position in life was determined by his or her inherited status. By championing the ideals of liberty and equality, the French Revolution undermined the traditional power structure of king, aristocracy, and clergy. French reformers further dismantled the religious and political pillars of traditional rural society by advocating the rational and secular outlook of the Enlightenment.

The Industrial Revolution transformed all areas of society. Eventually, agricultural villages and handicraft manufacturing were eclipsed in importance by cities and factories. In the society fashioned by industrialization and urbanization, aristocratic power and values declined; at the same time, the bourgeoisie increased in number, wealth, importance, and power. More and more, a person was judged by talent rather than by birth, and opportunities for upward social mobility expanded. The Industrial Revolution became a great force for democratization: during the nineteenth century, first the middle class and then the working class gained the vote. The Industrial Revolution also hastened the secularization of European life. In the cities, former villagers, separated from traditional communal ties, drifted away from their ancestral religion. In a world being reshaped by technology, industry, and science, Christian mysteries lost their force, and for many, salvation became a remote concern. Modernization did not proceed everywhere at the same pace and with the same thoroughness. Generally, premodern social and institutional forms remained deeply entrenched in eastern and southern Europe, persisting well into the twentieth century.

Although the Industrial Revolution created many problems, some of which still endure, it was a great triumph. Ultimately, it made possible the highest standard of living in human history and created new opportunities for social advancement, political participation, and educational and cultural development. It also widened the gap between the West and the rest of the world in terms of science and technology. By 1900, Western states, aided by superior technology, extended their power over virtually the entire globe, completing the trend that had begun with the Age of Exploration.

❖ ❖ ❖

NOTES

1. David S. Landes, *The Unbound Prometheus: Technological Change and Industrial Development in Western Europe from 1750 to the Present* (Cambridge, Mass.: Harvard University Press, 1969), p. 33.

2. Thomas Robert Malthus, *First Essay on Population,* reprinted for the Royal Economic Society (London: Macmillan, 1926), p. 17.

SUGGESTED READING

Ashton, T. S., *The Industrial Revolution, 1700–1830* (1962). A still useful account.

Deane, Phyllis, *The First Industrial Revolution, 1750–1850* (1965). An excellent introduction.

Fisher, Douglas, *Industrial Revolution* (1992). Incorporates the latest scholarship on British industrialization.

Heilbroner, Robert, *The Worldly Philosophers* (1953). Good discussions of early economic thinkers.

Himmelfarb, Gertrude, *The Idea of Poverty: England in the Early Industrial Age* (1983). A brilliant history of English social thought, focused on the condition of the poor.

Hobsbawm, Eric, *The Age of Revolution: 1789–1848* (1964). A survey of this tumultuous period, stressing the connections between economic, social, and political revolution.

Jones, E. L., *Growth Recurring* (1988). Concentrates on why industrialization took place in Europe.

Landes, David S., *The Unbound Prometheus: Technological Change and Industrial Development in Western Europe from 1750 to the Present* (1969). A classic treatment of a complex subject.

Langer, William L., *Political and Social Upheaval: 1832–1852* (1969). An excellent source, with good references and bibliography.

Milward, A. S., *Economic Development of Continental Europe, 1780–1870* (1973). A helpful survey.

Stearns, Peter. *The Industrial Revolution in World History* (1993). The spread of industrialization.

Thompson, E. P., *The Making of the English Working Class* (1966). A very readable, dramatic, enormously influential, and controversial book.

Webb, R. K., *Modern England from the Eighteenth Century* (1967 and 1980). A balanced, well-writ-

ten, and well-informed text, up-to-date on historical controversies.

REVIEW QUESTIONS

1. What were the causes of the Industrial Revolution? Why did it begin in Britain?

2. How did the Industrial Revolution transform
the social structure?

3. What problems did the Industrial Revolution
create for the working class?

4. How did Parliament respond to demands for
reform from 1815 to 1848?

5. Why are Saint-Simon, Fourier, and Owen regarded as early socialists?

6. The Industrial Revolution was a principal force
in the shaping of the modern world. Discuss
this statement.

Chapter 13

Thought and Culture in the Early Nineteenth Century

■ **Romanticism: A New Cultural Orientation**

■ **German Idealism**

■ **Conservatism: The Value of Tradition**

■ **Liberalism: The Value of the Individual**

■ **Nationalism: The Sacredness of the Nation**

*A*fter the defeat of Napoleon, the traditional rulers of Europe, some of them just restored to power, were determined to protect themselves and society from future revolutions. As defenders of the status quo, they attacked the reformist spirit of the philosophes, which had produced the French Revolution. In conservatism, which championed tradition over reason, hierarchy over equality, and the community over the individual, they found a philosophy to justify their assault on the Enlightenment and the Revolution.

But the forces unleashed by the Revolution had penetrated European consciousness too deeply to be eradicated. One of them was liberalism, which aimed to secure the liberty and equality proclaimed by the Revolution. Another was nationalism, which sought to free subject peoples and unify fragmented nations.

The postrevolutionary period also witnessed the flowering of a new cultural orientation. *Romanticism,* with its plea for the liberation of human emotions and the free expression of personality, challenged the Enlightenment stress on rationalism. Although primarily a literary and artistic movement, romanticism also permeated philosophy and political thought, particularly conservatism and nationalism. ❖

ROMANTICISM: A NEW CULTURAL ORIENTATION

The Romantic Movement, which began in the closing decades of the eighteenth century, dominated European cultural life in the first half of the nineteenth century. Most of Europe's leading cultural figures came under its influence. Among the exponents of romanticism were the poets Shelley, Wordsworth, Keats, and Byron in England; the novelist Victor Hugo and the Catholic novelist and essayist Chateaubriand in France; and the writers A. W. and Friedrich Schlegel, the dramatist and poet Schiller, and the philosopher Schelling in Germany. Caspar David Friedrich in Germany and John Constable in England expressed the romantic mood in art, and Beethoven, Schubert, Chopin, and Wagner expressed it in music.

Exalting Imagination and Feelings

Perhaps the central message of the romantics was that the imagination of the individual should determine the form and content of an artistic creation. This outlook ran counter to the rationalism of the Enlightenment, which itself had been a reaction against the otherworldly Christian orientation of the Middle Ages. The philosophes had attacked faith because it thwarted and distorted reason; romantic poets, philosophers, and artists now denounced the rationalism of the philosophes because it crushed the emotions and impeded creativity.

The philosophes, said the romantics, had turned flesh-and-blood human beings into soulless thinking machines. For human beings to be restored to their true nature, to become whole again, they must be emancipated from the tyranny of excessive intellectualizing; the feelings must be nurtured and expressed. Taking up one of Rousseau's ideas, romantics yearned to rediscover in the human soul the pristine freedom and creativity that had been squashed by habits, values, rules, and standards imposed by civilization.

Abstract reason and scientific knowledge, said the romantics, are insufficient guides to knowledge. They provide only general principles about nature and people; they cannot penetrate to what really matters—the uniqueness of each person, of each robin, of each tree, cloud, and lake. The philosophes had concentrated on people in general, focusing on the elements of human nature shared by all people. Romantics, on the other hand, emphasized human diversity and uniqueness—those traits that set one human being apart from others. Discover and express your true self, the romantics urged: play your own music; write your own poetry; paint your own vision of nature; live, love, and suffer in your own way.

Whereas the philosophes had asserted the mind's autonomy—its capacity to think for itself and not depend on authority—romantics gave primary importance to the autonomy of the personality—the individual's need and right to find and fulfill an inner self. To the philosophes, feelings were an obstacle to clear thinking, but to the romantics they were the essence of being human. People could not live by reason alone, said the romantics. They agreed with Rousseau, who wrote: "For us, to exist is to feel and our sensibility is incontestably prior to our reason."[1] For the romantics, reason was cold and dreary, and its understanding of people and life meager and inadequate. Reason could not grasp or express the complexities of human nature or the richness of human experience. By always dissecting and analyzing, by imposing deadening structure and form, and by demanding adherence to strict rules, reason crushed inspiration and creativity and barred true understanding. "The Reasoning Power

Dante's Inferno: The Whirlwind of Lovers by William Blake (1757–1827). A radical romantic painter and poet, Blake totally rejected the artistic conventions of the past. His religious and political beliefs were as unique as his art; he spent his life trying to convey tormented inward visions. A prolific illustrator, his imaginative genius was stimulated by great literature such as Dante's *Divine Comedy*. (*National Gallery of Art, Washington, D.C. Gift of W. G. Allen*)

in Man," wrote William Blake (1757–1827), the British poet, artist, and mystic, is "an Incrustation [scab] over my Immortal / Spirit."[2]

The romantics saw spontaneous, unbounded feelings, rather than the constricted intellect, as the avenue to truth. By cultivating emotions, intuition, and the imagination, individuals could experience reality and discover their authentic selves. The romantics wanted people to feel and to experience—"To bathe in the Waters of Life," said Blake.[3] Consequently, they insisted that imaginative poets had a greater insight into life than analytical philosophers. "I am certain of nothing but of the holiness of the Heart's affec-

tions and the truth of Imagination," wrote John Keats (1795–1821). "O for a Life of Sensations rather than of Thoughts."[4]

The Enlightenment mind had been clear, critical, and controlled. It had adhered to standards of esthetics, thought to be universal, that had dominated European cultural life since the Renaissance. Romantic poets, artists, and musicians broke with these traditional styles and uniform rules—essentially those inherited from the classical tradition—and created new cultural forms and techniques. "We do not want either Greek or Roman Models," Blake declared, "but [should be] just & true to our own Imaginations."[5] Victor

Hugo (1802–1885), the dominant figure among French romantics, urged in the Preface to his play *Cromwell:* "Freedom in art! . . . Let us take the hammer to the theories, the poetics [the analysis of poetry] and the systems."[6] The romantics felt deeply that one did not learn how to write poetry or paint pictures by following textbook rules, nor could one grasp the poet's or artist's intent by judging works according to fixed standards.

Only by trusting their own feelings could individuals attain their creative potential and achieve self-realization. Hence, the most beautiful works of art were not photographic imitations of nature but authentic and spontaneous expressions of the artist's feelings, fantasies, and dreams. It was the artist's inner voice that gave a work of art its supreme value. The romantics also explored the inner life of the mind, which Freud would later call *the unconscious.* It was this layer of the mind—the wellspring of creativity, mysterious, primitive, more elemental and more powerful than reason—that the romantics yearned to revitalize and release. Like Freud, some romantics had an intuitive awareness of the dark side of the unconscious. Buried there, they sensed, were our worst fears and most hideous desires.

Nature, God, History

The philosophes had viewed nature as a lifeless machine: a giant clock, all of whose parts worked together with precision and in perfect harmony. Nature's laws, operating with mathematical certainty, were uncovered by the methodology of science. To the romantics, nature was alive and suffused with God's presence. Nature stimulated the creative energies of the imagination; it taught human beings a higher form of knowledge. As William Wordsworth (1770–1850) wrote in his poem "The Tables Turned,"

> *One impulse from a vernal wood [spring*
> * greenery]*
> *May teach you more of man,*
> *Of moral evil and of good,*
> *Than all the sages can.*[7]

Regarding God as a great watchmaker—a detached observer of a self-operating mechanical universe—the philosophes tried to reduce religion to a series of scientific propositions. Many romantics, on the contrary, viewed God as an inspiring spiritual force and condemned the philosophes for weakening Christianity by submitting its dogmas to the test of reason. For the romantics, religion was not science and syllogism, but a passionate and authentic expression of human nature. They called for acknowledgment of the individual as a spiritual being and for cultivation of the religious side of human nature. This appeal accorded with their goal of restoring the whole personality, which, they were convinced, had been fragmented and distorted by the philosophes' excessive emphasis on the intellect.

The philosophes and the romantics viewed the Middle Ages very differently as well. To the former, that period was a time of darkness, superstition, and fanaticism; surviving medieval institutions and traditions only barred progress. The romantics, on the other hand, revered the Middle Ages. To the romantic imagination, the Middle Ages abounded with Christian mysteries, heroic deeds, and social harmony.

The romantics also disagreed with the philosophes on their conception of history. For the philosophes, history served a didactic purpose by providing examples of human folly. Such knowledge helped people to prepare for a better future, and for that reason alone history was worth studying. To the romantics, a historical period, like an individual, was a unique entity with its own soul. They wanted the historian to portray and analyze the variety of nations, traditions, and institutions that constituted the historical experience, always recognizing what is particular and unique to a given time and place. The romantics' insistence on comprehending the specific details of history and culture within the context of the times is the foundation of modern historical scholarship.

Searching for universal principles, the philosophes had dismissed folk traditions as peasant superstitions and impediments to progress. The romantics, on the other hand, rebelling against the standardization of culture, saw native languages, songs, and legends as the unique creations of a people and the deepest expression of national feeling. The romantics regarded the legends, myths, and folk traditions of a people as the fount of poetry and art and the spiritual source of a people's cultural vitality, creativity, and identity. Consequently, they examined these earliest cultural expressions with awe and reverence. In this way, romanticism played a part in shaping modern nationalism.

The Impact of the Romantic Movement

The romantic revolt against the Enlightenment had an important and enduring impact on European history. By focusing on the creative capacities inherent in the emotions—intuition, instinct, passion, will, empathy—the romantics shed light on a side of human nature that the philosophes had often overlooked or undervalued. By encouraging personal freedom and diversity in art, music, and literature, they greatly enriched European cultural life. Future artists, writers, and musicians would proceed along the path opened by the romantics. Modern art, for example, owes much to the Romantic Movement's emphasis on the legitimacy of human feeling and its exploration of the hidden world of dreams and fantasies. Romantics were among the first to attack the emerging industrial capitalism for subordinating individuals to the requirements of the industrial process and treating them as mere things. Furthermore, by recognizing the distinctive qualities of historical periods, peoples, and cultures, they helped create the modern historical outlook. Because it valued a nation's past, romanticism also contributed to modern nationalism and conservatism.

However, the Romantic Movement had a potentially dangerous side: it served as background to the extreme nationalism of the twentieth century. As Ernst Cassirer has pointed out, the romantics "never meant to politicize but to 'poeticize' the world," and their deep respect for human individuality and national diversity was not compatible with Hitler's racial nationalism. Yet by waging their attack on reason with excessive zeal, the romantics undermined respect for the rational tradition of the Enlightenment and thus set up a precondition for the rise and triumph of fascist movements. Although their intention was cultural and not political, by idealizing the past and glorifying ancient folkways, legends, native soil, and native language, the romantics introduced a highly charged nonrational component into political life. In later generations, romanticism, particularly in Germany, fused with political nationalism to produce, says Horst von Maltitz, "a general climate of inexact thinking, an intellectual . . . dream world and an emotional approach to problems of political action to which sober reasoning should have been applied."[8]

The romantics' veneration of a people's history and traditions and their search for a nation's soul in an archaic culture would have struck the philosophes as barbarous—a regression to superstition and a triumph of myth over reason. Indeed, when transferred to the realm of politics, the romantics' idealization of the past and fascination with inherited national myths as the source of wisdom did reawaken a way of thinking about the world that rested more on feeling than on reason. In the process, people became committed to nationalist and political ideas that were fraught with danger. The glorification of myth and the folk community constitutes a link, however unintended, between romanticism and extreme nationalism, which culminated in the world wars of the twentieth century.

GERMAN IDEALISM

The romantics' stress on the inner person also found expression in the school of German philosophy called *idealism*. Idealists held that the world is not something objective that exists independently of individual consciousness. Rather, it is human consciousness, the knowing subject, that builds the world and determines its form. German idealism was partly a response to the challenge posed by David Hume, the great Scottish empiricist and skeptic.

The Challenge Posed by Hume's Empiricism

In his *Treatise of Human Nature* (1739–40) and *Enquiry Concerning Human Understanding* (1748), Hume cast doubt on the view that scientific certainty was possible. Science rests on the conviction that regularities observed in the past and the present will be repeated in the future: that there does exist an objective reality, which rational creatures can comprehend. Hume, however, argued that science cannot demonstrate a *necessary connection* between cause and effect. Because we repeatedly experience a burning sensation when our fingers have contact with a flame, we assume a cause-and-effect relationship. This is unwarranted, said Hume. All we can acknowledge is that there is a constant conjunction between the flame and the burning sensation.

According to Hume, we cannot prove that there is a law at work in nature guaranteeing that a specific cause will produce a specific effect. What we mean by cause and effect is simply something that the mind, through habit, imposes on our sense perceptions. For practical purposes, we can say that two events are in association with each other, but we cannot conclude with certainty that the second was caused by the first—that natural law is operating within the physical universe. Such a radical empiricism undermines the very foundations of science, so revered by progressive thinkers.

Immanuel Kant

In the *Critique of Pure Reason* (1781), Immanuel Kant (1724–1804), the great German philosopher and proponent of Newtonianism and the scientific method, undertook the challenge of rescuing reason and science from Hume's empiricism. The mind—the knowing subject—said Kant, is not a *tabula rasa*, a blank slate that passively receives sense impressions, but an active instrument that structures, organizes, and interprets the multiplicity of sensations coming to it. The mind can coordinate a chaotic stream of sensations because it contains its own inherent logic; it is equipped with several categories of understanding, including cause and effect.

Because of the way our mind is constituted, we presuppose a relationship of cause and effect in all our experiences with the objects of this world. The mind imposes structure and order on our sense experiences. Cause and effect and the other categories of the mind permit us to attribute certainty to scientific knowledge. The physical world

must possess certain definite characteristics because these characteristics conform to the categories of the mind. The object, said Kant, must "accommodate itself to the subject."

Kant rescued science from Hume's assault: The laws of science are universally valid. But in the process, Kant made scientific law dependent on the mind and its a priori categories. We see nature in a certain way because of the mental apparatus that we bring to it. The mind imposes its own laws on nature—on the raw impressions received by the senses—giving the physical world form, structure, and order. By holding that objects must conform to the rules of the human mind, that it is the knowing subject that creates order within nature, Kant gave primacy to the knower rather than to the objects of knowledge. He saw the mind as an active agent, not a passive recipient of sensations. This "turn in philosophy," which Kant considered as revolutionary as the Copernican theory had been for astronomy, gave unprecedented importance to the power of the mind—to the active and creative knower.

It is a fundamental principle of Kant's thought that we cannot know ultimate reality. Our knowledge is limited to the phenomenal world, the realm of natural occurrences. We can know only things that we experience, that is, things that we grasp through the active intervention of the mind's categories. We can have no knowledge of a thing-in-itself, that is, of an object's ultimate or real nature—its nature as it is independently of the way we experience it, apart from the way our senses receive it. The human mind can acquire knowledge of only that portion of reality that is revealed through sense experience. We can say nothing about the sun's true nature but only describe the way the sun appears to us—that is, our impression of the sun formed by the mind's ordering of our sense experiences of it. Thus, at the same time that Kant reaffirmed the validity of scientific law, he also limited the range of science and reason.

G.W. F. Hegel

Kant had insisted that knowledge of what lies beyond phenomena—knowledge of ultimate or absolute reality itself—is forever denied us. Georg

Hegel in His Study. Georg Wilhelm Friedrich Hegel (1770–1831) constructed a comprehensive philosophical system that sought to explain all reality. His philosophy of history, particularly the theories of dialectical conflict and of progression toward an ultimate end, greatly influenced Karl Marx. (*Bildarchiv Preussischer Kulturbesitz/Art Resource, NY*)

Wilhelm Friedrich Hegel (1770–1831), another German philosopher, could not accept this. He constructed an all-embracing metaphysical system that attempted to explain all reality and uncover the fundamental nature and meaning of the universe and human history—to grasp the wholeness of life.

Adopting Kant's notion that the mind imposes its categories on the world, Hegel emphasized the importance of the thinking subject in the quest for truth. However, Kant held that we can have knowledge only of how a thing appears to us, not of the thing-in-itself. Hegel, in contrast, maintained that ultimate reality, total truth, is knowable to the human mind: The mind can comprehend the truths underlying all existence and can grasp the essential meaning of human experience.

Kant had asserted the essential idealist position that the knowing subject organizes our experiences of the phenomenal world. Hegel took a giant step beyond that view by contending that there exists a universal Mind—Absolute Spirit, the thing-in-itself—whose nature can be apprehended through thought.

Because Hegel viewed Absolute Spirit not as fixed and static, but as evolving and developing, history plays a central role in his philosophical system. History is the development of Spirit in time. In the arena of world history, truth unfolds and makes itself known to the human mind. Like the Romantics, Hegel said that each historical period has a distinctive character that separates it from every preceding age. The art, science, philosophy, religion, politics, and leading events are so interconnected that the period may be seen to possess an organic unity, a historical coherence.

Hegel believed that world history reveals a rational process; an internal principle of order underlies historical change. There is a purpose and an end to history: the unfolding of Absolute Spirit. In the course of history, an immanent Spirit manifests itself. Gradually, progressively, and nonrepetitively, it actualizes itself, becoming itself fully. Nations and exceptional human beings, "World Historical" individuals—Alexander the Great, Caesar, Napoleon—are the mediums through which Spirit realizes its potentialities and achieves self-consciousness. Hegel's philosophy of history gives meaning, purpose, and direction to historical events. Where is history taking us? What is its ultimate meaning? For Hegel, history is humanity's progress from lesser to greater freedom: "The History of the World is none other than the progress of the consciousness of Freedom . . . [It is] the absolute goal of history."[9]

According to Hegel, Spirit manifests itself in history through a dialectical confrontation between opposing ideas or forces; the struggle between one idea (thesis) and its adversary (antithesis) is evident in all spheres of human activity. This clash of opposites gains in intensity, eventually ending in a resolution (synthesis) that unifies both opposing views. Thought and history thus enter a new and higher stage, that of synthesis, which, by absorbing the truths within both the thesis and the antithesis, achieves a higher level of truth and a higher stage of history. Soon this synthesis itself becomes a thesis that enters into another conflict with another opposing force; this conflict, too, is resolved by a still higher synthesis. Thus, the dynamic struggle between thesis and antithesis—sometimes expressed in revolutions and war, sometimes in art, religion, and philosophy—and its resolution into a synthesis accounts for movement in history. Or, in Hegelian language, Spirit is closer to realization: its rational essence is progressing from potentiality to actuality. The dialectic is the march of Spirit through human affairs. Historical change is often instituted by world-historical individuals who, unknown to themselves, are agents of Spirit in its progress through history. Since Hegel held that freedom is the essence of Spirit, it is through history that human beings progress toward consciousness of their own freedom. They become self-consciously aware of their own self-determination—their ability to regulate their lives rationally according to their own consciousness.

But for individual freedom to be realized, said Hegel, social and political institutions must be rationally determined and organized: that is, the will of the individual must be harmonized with the needs of the community. For Hegel, freedom is not a matter of securing abstract natural rights for the individual, the goal of the French Revolution. Rather, true freedom is attained only within the social group. Thus, in Hegel's view, human beings discover their essential character—their moral and spiritual potential—only as citizens of a cohesive political community. This view goes back to the city-states of ancient Greece, which Hegel admired. In the state's laws and institutions, which are manifestations of reason and the objectivization of Spirit, individuals find a basis for rationally determining their own lives. In this way, the private interests of citizens become one with the interests of the community.

For Hegel, Absolute Spirit, which is also Ultimate Reason, realizes itself in the state, the highest form of human association. The state joins fragmented individuals together into a community

and substitutes a rule of justice for the rule of instincts. It permits individuals to live the ethical life and to develop their human potential. An individual cannot achieve these goals in isolation. Hegel's thought reveals a powerful undercurrent of statism: the exaltation of the state and the subordination of the individual to it. For Hegel, the national state was the embodiment of Universal Reason and the supreme achievement of Absolute Spirit.

German conservatives used Hegel's idea that existing institutions have a rational legitimacy to support their opposition to rapid change. Existing reality, even if it appears cruel and hateful, is the actualization of Absolute Spirit. Therefore, it is inherently necessary and rational and should not be altered.

Some of Hegel's followers, known as Young Hegelians, interpreted Hegel in a radical sense. They rejected his view that the Prussian state, or any German state, was the goal of world history, the realization of freedom. The Germany of their day, held the Young Hegelians, had not attained a harmony between the individual and society; it was not rationally organized and did not foster freedom. These Young Hegelians saw Hegel's philosophy as a means of radically altering the world to make existing society truly rational. The most important of the radical Young Hegelians was Karl Marx. Marx retained Hegel's overarching principle that history contains an inner logic, that it is an intelligible process, and that a dialectical struggle propels history from a lower to a higher stage (see the chapter entitled "Thought and Culture in the Mid-Nineteenth Century: Realism and Social Criticism).

CONSERVATISM: THE VALUE OF TRADITION

To the traditional rulers of Europe—kings, aristocrats, and clergy—the French Revolution was a great evil that had inflicted a near-fatal wound on civilization. Disgusted and frightened by the revolutionary violence, terror, and warfare, the traditional rulers sought to refute the philosophes' world-view, which had spawned the Revolution. To them, natural rights, equality, the goodness of man, and perpetual progress were perverse doctrines that had produced the Jacobin "assassins." In conservatism, they found a political philosophy to counter the Enlightenment ideology.

Edmund Burke's *Reflections on the Revolution in France* (1790) was instrumental in shaping conservative thought. Burke (1729–1797), an Anglo-Irish statesman and political theorist, wanted to warn his countrymen of the dangers inherent in the ideology of the revolutionaries. Although writing in 1790, he astutely predicted that the Revolution would lead to terror and military dictatorship. To Burke, fanatics armed with pernicious principles—abstract ideas divorced from historical experience—had dragged France through the mire of revolution. Burke developed a coherent political philosophy that served as a counterweight to the ideology of the Enlightenment and the Revolution.

Hostility to the French Revolution

Entranced by the great discoveries in science, the philosophes and French reformers had believed that the human mind could also transform social institutions and ancient traditions according to rational models. Progress through reason became their faith. Dedicated to creating a new future, the revolutionaries abruptly dispensed with old habits, traditional authority, and familiar ways of thought.

To conservatives, who, like the romantics, venerated the past, this was supreme arrogance and wickedness. They regarded the revolutionaries as presumptuous men who recklessly severed society's links with ancient institutions and traditions and condemned venerable religious and moral beliefs as ignorance. By attacking time-honored ways, the revolutionaries had deprived French society of moral leadership and had opened the door to anarchy and terror. "You began ill," wrote Burke of the revolutionaries, "because you began by despising everything that belonged to you. . . . When ancient opinions and rules of life are taken away, the loss cannot possibly be estimated. From that moment we have no compass to govern us; nor can we know distinctly to what port we steer."[10]

The philosophes and French reformers had expressed unlimited confidence in the power of human reason to understand and to improve society. While appreciating human rational capacities, conservatives also recognized the limitations of reason. They saw the Revolution as a natural outgrowth of an arrogant Enlightenment philosophy that overvalued reason and sought to reshape society according to abstract principles.

Conservatives did not view human beings as good by nature. Human wickedness was not caused by a faulty environment, as the philosophes had proclaimed, but lay at the core of human nature, as Christianity taught. Evil was held in check not by reason, but by tried and tested institutions, traditions, and beliefs. Without these habits inherited from ancestors, said conservatives, sinful human nature threatened the social order.

Because monarchy, aristocracy, and the church had endured for centuries, argued the conservatives, they had worth. By despising and uprooting these ancient institutions, revolutionaries had hardened the people's hearts, perverted their morals, and caused them to commit terrible outrages upon one another and upon society. As conservatives saw it, revolutionaries had divorced people and society from their historical settings and reduced them to abstractions; they had drawn up constitutions based on the unacceptable principle that government derives its power from the consent of the governed.

For conservatives, God and history were the only legitimate sources of political authority. States were not made; rather, they were an expression of the nation's moral, religious, and historical experience. No legitimate or sound constitution could be drawn up by a group assembled for that purpose. Scraps of paper with legal terminology and philosophical visions could not produce an effective government. Instead, a sound political system evolved gradually and inexplicably in response to circumstances.

The Quest for Social Stability

The liberal philosophy of the Enlightenment and the French Revolution started with the individual. The philosophes and the revolutionaries envisioned a society in which the individual was free and autonomous. Conservatives, on the other hand, began with the community. They believed that society was not a mechanical arrangement of disconnected individuals but a living organism, held together by centuries-old bonds. Individualism would imperil social stability, destroy obedience to law, and fragment society into self-seeking isolated atoms. Conservatives held that the community was more important than the individual. Whereas the philosophes had attacked Christianity for promoting superstition and fanaticism, conservatives saw religion as the basis of civil society. Catholic conservatives, in particular, held that God had constituted the church and monarchy to check sinful human nature.

Conservatives viewed equality as another pernicious abstraction that contradicted all historical experience. For conservatives, society was naturally hierarchical, and they believed that some men, by virtue of their intelligence, education, wealth, and birth, were best qualified to rule and instruct the less able. They said that by denying the existence of a natural elite and uprooting the long-established ruling elite, which had learned its art through experience, the revolutionaries had deprived society of effective leaders, brought internal disorder, and prepared the way for Napoleon's dictatorship.

Conservatism pointed to a limitation of the Enlightenment. It showed that human beings and social relationships are far more complex than the philosophes had imagined. People do not always accept the rigorous logic of the philosopher and are not eager to break with ancient ways, however illogical those ways appear. They often find familiar customs and ancestral religions more satisfying guides to life than the blueprints of philosophers. The granite might of tradition remains an obstacle to all the visions of reformers. Conservative theorists warned that revolutionary violence in the pursuit of utopian dreams transforms politics into an ideological crusade that ends in terror and despotism. These warnings bore bitter fruit in the twentieth century.

LIBERALISM: THE VALUE
OF THE INDIVIDUAL

The decades after 1815 saw a spectacular rise of the bourgeoisie. Talented and ambitious bankers, merchants, manufacturers, professionals, and officeholders wanted to break the stranglehold of the landed nobility—the traditional elite—on political power and social prestige. They also wanted to eliminate restrictions on the free pursuit of profits. The political philosophy of the bourgeoisie was most commonly liberalism. While conservatives sought to strengthen the foundations of traditional society, which had been severely shaken in the period of the French Revolution and Napoleon, liberals strove to alter the status quo and to realize the promise of the Enlightenment and the French Revolution.

The Sources of Liberalism

In the long view of Western civilization, liberalism is an extension and development of the democratic practices and rational outlook that originated in ancient Greece. Also flowing into the liberal tradition is Judeo-Christian respect for the worth and dignity of the individual endowed by God with freedom to make moral choices. But nineteenth-century liberalism had its immediate historical roots in seventeenth-century England. At that time, the struggle for religious toleration by English Protestant dissenters established the principle of freedom of conscience, which is easily translated into freedom of opinion and expression in all matters. The Glorious Revolution of 1688 set limits on the power of the English monarchy. At the same time, John Locke's natural rights philosophy declared that the individual was by nature entitled to freedom, and it justified revolutions against rulers who deprived citizens of their lives, liberty, or property.

The French philosophes helped to shape liberalism. From Montesquieu, liberals derived the theory of the separation of powers and of checks and balances—principles intended to guard against despotic government. The philosophes supported religious toleration and freedom of thought, expressed confidence in the capacity of the human mind to reform society, maintained that human beings are essentially good, and believed in the future progress of humanity—all fundamental principles of liberalism.

The American and French Revolutions were crucial phases in the history of liberalism. The Declaration of Independence gave expression to

Locke's theory of natural rights, the Constitution of the United States incorporated Montesquieu's principles and demonstrated that people could create an effective government, and the Bill of Rights protected the person and rights of the individual. In destroying the special privileges of the aristocracy and opening careers to talent, the French National Assembly of 1789 had implemented the liberal ideal of equality under the law. It also drew up the Declaration of the Rights of Man and of the Citizen, which affirmed the dignity and rights of the individual, and a constitution that limited the king's power. Both revolutions explicitly called for the protection of property rights, another basic premise of liberalism.

Individual Liberty

The liberals' primary concern was the enhancement of individual liberty. They agreed with Kant that every person exists as an end in himself or herself and not as an object to be used arbitrarily by others. If uncoerced by government and churches and properly educated, a person can develop into a good, productive, and self-directed human being.

Liberals rejected a legacy of the Middle Ages, the classification of an individual as a commoner or aristocrat on the basis of birth. They held that a man was not born into a certain station in life but made his way through his own efforts. Taking their cue from the French Revolution, liberals called for an end to all privileges of the aristocracy.

In the tradition of the philosophes, liberals stressed the preeminence of reason as the basis of political life. Unfettered by ignorance and tyranny, the mind could eradicate evils that had burdened people for centuries and begin an age of free institutions and responsible citizens. For this reason, liberals supported the advancement of education.

Liberals attacked the state and other authorities that prevented the individual from exercising the right of free choice, interfered with the right of free expression, and blocked the individual's self-determination and self-development. They agreed with John Stuart Mill (1806–1873), the British

philosopher, who declared that "over his own body and mind, the individual is sovereign. . . . that the only purpose for which power can be rightfully exercised over any member of a civilized community, against his will, is to prevent harm to others."[11]

To guard against the absolute and arbitrary authority of kings, liberals demanded written constitutions that granted freedom of speech, the press, and religion; freedom from arbitrary arrest; and the protection of property rights. To prevent the abuse of political authority, they called for a freely elected parliament and the distribution of power among the various branches of government. Liberals held that a government that derived its authority from the consent of the governed, as given in free elections, was least likely to violate individual freedom. A corollary of this principle was that the best government is one that governs least—that is, one that interferes as little as possible with the economic activities of its citizens and does not involve itself in their private lives or their beliefs.

Liberalism and Democracy

Many bourgeois liberals viewed with horror the democratic creed that all people should share in political power. To them, the participation of commoners in politics meant a vulgar form of despotism and the end of individual liberty. They saw the masses—uneducated, unpropertied, inexperienced, and impatient—as lacking both the ability and the temperament to maintain liberty and protect property.

Because bourgeois liberals feared that democracy could crush personal freedom as ruthlessly as any absolute monarch, they called for property requirements for voting and officeholding. They wanted political power to be concentrated in the hands of a safe and reliable—that is, a propertied and educated—middle class. Such a government would prevent revolution from below, a prospect that caused anxiety among bourgeois liberals.

To be sure, early-nineteenth-century liberals engaged in revolutions, but their aims were always limited. Once they had destroyed absolute monarchy and gained a constitution and a parliament or a change of government, they quickly tried to end the revolution. When the fever of revolution spread to the masses, liberals either withdrew or turned counterrevolutionary, for they feared the stirrings of the multitude.

Although liberalism was the political philosophy of a middle class that was generally hostile to democracy, the essential ideals of democracy flowed logically from liberalism. Eventually, democracy became a later stage in the evolution of liberalism because the masses, their political power enhanced by the Industrial Revolution, pressed for greater social, political, and economic equality. Thus, by the early twentieth century, many European states had introduced universal suffrage, abandoned property requirements for officeholding, and improved conditions for workers.

But the fears of nineteenth-century liberals were not unfounded. In the twentieth century, the participation of common people in politics did, at times, threaten freedom. Impatient with parliamentary procedures, the masses, particularly when troubled by economic problems, at times gave their support to demagogues who promised swift and decisive action. The granting of political participation to the masses has not always made people freer. The confidence of democrats was shaken in the twentieth century by the seeming willingness of the masses to trade freedom for authority, order, economic security, and national power. Liberalism is based on the assumption that human beings can and do respond to rational argument and that reason will prevail over base human feelings. Recent history shows that this may be an overly optimistic assessment of human nature.

NATIONALISM: THE SACREDNESS OF THE NATION

Nationalism is a conscious bond shared by a group of people who feel strongly attached to a particular land and who possess a common language, culture, and history, marked by shared glories and sufferings. Nationalists contend that one's highest loyalty and devotion should be given to the nation. They exhibit great pride in their people's history and traditions and often feel that their nation has been specially chosen by God or history. They assert that the nation—its culture and history—gives meaning to an individual's life and actions. Like a religion, nationalism provides the individual with a sense of community and with a cause worthy of self-sacrifice. Identifying with the nation's collective achievements enhances feelings of self-worth.

In an age when Christianity was in retreat, nationalism became the dominant spiritual force in nineteenth-century European life. Nationalism provided new beliefs, martyrs, and "holy" days that stimulated reverence; it offered membership in a community, which satisfied the overwhelming psychological need of human beings for fellowship and identity. And nationalism gave a mission—the advancement of the nation—to which people could dedicate themselves.

The Emergence of Modern Nationalism

The essential components of modern nationalism emerged at the time of the French Revolution. The Revolution asserted the principle that sovereignty derived from the nation, from the people as a whole: the state was not the private possession of the ruler but the embodiment of the people's will. The nation-state was above king, church, estate, guild, or province; it superseded all other loyalties. The French people must view themselves not as subjects of the king, not as Bretons or Normans, not as nobles or bourgeois, but as citizens of a united fatherland, *la patrie*. These two ideas—that the people possess unlimited sovereignty and that they are united in a nation—were crucial in fashioning a nationalist outlook.

As the Revolution moved from the moderate to the radical stage, French nationalism intensified. In 1793–94, when foreign invasion threatened the republic, the Jacobins created a national army, demanded ever greater allegiance to and sacrifice for the nation, and called for the expansion of France's borders to the Alps and the Rhine. With unprecedented success, the Jacobins used every means—press, schoolroom, and rostrum—to instill a love of country.

The Romantic Movement also awakened nationalist feelings. By examining the language, literature, and folkways of their people, romantic thinkers instilled a sense of national pride in their compatriots. Johann Gottfried Herder (1744–1803), a prominent German writer, conceived the idea of the *Volksgeist*—the soul of the people. For Herder, each people was unique and creative; each expressed its peculiar genius in language, literature, monuments, and folk traditions. Herder did not make the theoretical jump from a spiritual or cultural nationalism to political nationalism; he did not call for the formation of states based on nationality. But his emphasis on the unique culture of a people stimulated a national consciousness among Germans and the various Slavic peoples who lived under foreign rule. Fascination with the Volksgeist prompted intellectuals to investigate the past of their own people, to rediscover their ancient traditions, and to extol their historic language and culture. From this cultural nationalism, it was only a short step to a political nationalism that called for national liberation, unification, and statehood.

The romantics were the earliest apostles of German nationalism. Resisting the French philosophes, who sought to impose universal norms on all peoples, German romantics stressed the uniqueness of the German nation and its history. They restored to consciousness memories of the German past, and they emphasized the peculiar qualities of the German folk and the special destiny of the German nation. The romantics glorified medieval Germany and valued hereditary monarchy and aristocracy as vital links to the nation's past. They saw the existence of each individual as inextricably bound up with folk and fatherland, and they found the self-realization for which they yearned in the uniting of their own egos with the national soul. To these romantics, the national community was the source of artistic and spiritual creativity and the vital force, giving the individual both an identity and a purpose in life. The nation stood above the individual; the national spirit linked isolated souls into a community of brethren.

To the philosophes, the state was a human institution, a rational arrangement between individuals that safeguarded their rights and permitted them to realize their individual goals. To German romantics, such a state was an artificial and lifeless construction. The true German state was something holy, the expression of the divine spirit of the German people; it could not be manufactured to order by the intellect. The state's purpose was neither the protection of natural rights nor the promotion of economic well-being; rather, the state was a living organism that linked each person to a sacred past and reconciled and united heterogeneous wills, imbuing them with a profound sense of community, with which one entered into mystical communion. "This 'Romantic' image of a state founded not on any rational idea of the functions and purposes of a state but on love and perfect communion, is of course a formula for totalitarianism," observes R. J. Hollingdale, "and it was towards a state modeled on this formula that German nationalism continually moved."[12] Building on the romantics' views, radical German nationalists came to propound the dangerous racist idea that national identity was an inherited characteristic—that being and feeling German depended on birth rather than acculturation. Holding this belief, some German nationalists maintained that Jews, no matter how many generations they had resided in Germany, could never be truly German.

Nationalism and Liberalism

In the early 1800s, liberals were the principal leaders and supporters of nationalist movements. They viewed the struggle for national rights—the freedom of a people from foreign rule—as an extension of the struggle for the rights of the individual. There could be no liberty, said liberal nationalists, if people were not free to rule themselves in their own land.

Liberals called for the unification of Germany and Italy, the rebirth of Poland, the liberation of Greece from Turkish rule, and the granting of autonomy to the Hungarians of the Austrian Empire. Liberal nationalists envisioned a Europe of independent states based on nationality and popular sovereignty. Free of foreign domination and tyrant princes, these newly risen states would protect the rights of the individual and strive to create a brotherhood of nationalities in Europe.

In the first half of the nineteenth century, few intellectuals recognized the dangers inherent in nationalism or understood the fundamental contradiction between liberalism and nationalism.

Massacre at Chios. In the Greek War of Independence, 1821–1830, the Turks took the island of Chios and either massacred or sold into slavery most of the Greek inhabitants. French artist Eugene Delacroix depicted the atrocity in this famous painting. *(Louvre, Paris Reunion des Musées Nationaux/Art Resource, NY)*

For the liberal, the idea of universal natural rights transcended all national boundaries. Inheriting the cosmopolitanism of the Enlightenment, liberalism emphasized what all people had in common, demanded that all individuals be treated equally under the law, and preached toleration. Nationalists, manifesting the particularist attitude of the in-group and the tribe, regarded the nation as the essential fact of existence. Consequently, they often willingly subverted individual liberty for the sake of national grandeur. Whereas the liberal sought to protect the rights of all within the state, the nationalist often ignored or trampled on the rights of individuals and national minorities.

Liberalism grew out of the rational tradition of the West, but nationalism derived from an emotional attachment to ancient customs and bonds. Because it fulfilled an elemental yearning for community and kinship, nationalism exerted a powerful hold over human hearts, often driving people to political extremism. Liberalism demanded objectivity in analyzing tradition, society, and history; nationalism, however, evoked a mythic and romantic past that often distorted history.

"Nationalism requires . . . much belief in what is patently not so," wryly observes British historian E. J. Hobsbawm.[13] Thus nationalists inflated their people's past achievements and attributed to the nation a peculiar inner spirit that set it apart from others and accounted for its superiority. While constantly declaiming the wrongs that others had inflicted on them, they turned a blind eye to their own mistreatment of others. Nationalists interpreted history to serve political ends: the unity of their people and the creation of an independent nation-state.

In the last part of the nineteenth century, the irrational and mythic quality of nationalism intensified. By stressing the unique qualities and history of a particular people, nationalism promoted hatred between nationalities. By kindling deep love for the past, including a longing for ancient borders, glories, and power, nationalism led to wars of expansion. When it roused the emotions to fever pitch, nationalism shattered rational thinking, dragged the mind into a world of fantasy and myth, and introduced extremism into politics. Love of nation became an overriding passion, threatening to extinguish the liberal ideals of reason, freedom, and equality.

❖   ❖   ❖

NOTES

1. Quoted in H. G. Schenk, *The Mind of the European Romantics* (Garden City, N.Y.: Doubleday, 1969), p. 4.

2. William Blake, "Milton," in *The Poetry and Prose of William Blake,* ed. David V. Erdman (Garden City, N.Y.: Doubleday, 1965), plate 40, lines 34–36.

3. Ibid., plate 41, line 1.

4. Letter of John Keats, November 22, 1817, in *The Letters of John Keats,* ed. Hyder E. Rollins (Cambridge, Mass.: Harvard University Press, 1958), vol. 1, pp.184–185.

5. Blake, "Milton," Preface.

6. Quoted in Robert T. Denommé, *Nineteenth-Century French Romantic Poets* (Carbondale: Southern Illinois University Press, 1969), p. 28.

7. From "The Tables Turned," in *The Complete Poetical Works of Wordsworth,* ed. Andrew J. George (Boston: Houghton Mifflin, 1904, rev. ed., 1982), p. 83.

8. Horst von Maltitz, *The Evolution of Hitler's Germany* (New York: McGraw-Hill, 1973), p. 217.

9. G. W. F. Hegel, *The Philosophy of History,* trans. J. Sibree (New York: Dover, 1956), pp. 19, 23.

10. Edmund Burke, *Reflections on the Revolution in France* (New York: Liberal Arts Press, 1955), pp. 40, 89.

11. John Stuart Mill, *On Liberty,* ed. Currin V. Shields (Indianapolis: Bobbs-Merrill, 1956), chap. 1.

12. R. J. Hollingdale, *Nietzsche* (London: Routledge & Kegan Paul, 1973), p. 25.

13. E. J. Hobsbawm, *Nations and Nationalism Since 1780* (Cambridge, England: Cambridge University Press), p. 12.

Suggested Reading

Arblaster, Anthony, *The Rise and Decline of Western Liberalism* (1984). A critical analysis of liberalism, its evolution and characteristics.

Bullock, Alan, and Maurice Shock, eds., *The Liberal Tradition from Fox to Keynes* (1956). Selections from the works of British liberals, preceded by an essay on the liberal tradition.

Denommé, Robert T., *Nineteenth-Century French Romantic Poets* (1969). The genesis of romanticism in France; an analysis of several French romantic poets.

de Ruggiero, Guido, *The History of European Liberalism* (1927). A classic study.

Epstein, Klaus, *The Genesis of German Conservatism* (1966). An analysis of German conservative thought as a response to the Enlightenment and the French Revolution.

Fried, Albert, and Ronald Sanders, eds., *Socialist Thought* (1964). Selections from the writings of socialist theorists.

Harris, R. W., *Romanticism and the Social Order, 1780–1830* (1969). Involvement of English romantics in social and political questions.

Hayes, Carlton J. H., *Historical Evolution of Modern Nationalism* (1931). A pioneering work in the study of nationalism.

Honour, Hugh, *Romanticism* (1979). A study of the influence of romanticism on the visual arts.

Kohn, Hans, *The Idea of Nationalism* (1961). A comprehensive study of nationalism from the ancient world through the eighteenth century by a leading student of the subject.

————, *Prelude to Nation-States* (1967). The emergence of nationalism in France and Germany.

Manuel, Frank, *The Prophets of Paris* (1962). Good discussions of Saint-Simon and Fourier.

Schapiro, J. S., *Liberalism: Its Meaning and History* (1958). A useful survey with readings.

Schenk, H. G., *The Mind of the European Romantics* (1966). A comprehensive analysis of the Romantic Movement.

Shafer, B. C., *Faces of Nationalism* (1972). The evolution of modern nationalism in Europe and the non-European world; contains a good bibliography.

Smith, A. D., *Theories of Nationalism* (1972). The relationship between nationalism and modernization.

Weiss, John, *Conservatism in Europe, 1770–1945* (1977). Conservatism as a reaction to social modernization.

Review Questions

1. The Romantic Movement was a reaction against the dominant ideas of the Enlightenment. Discuss this statement.

2. What was the significance of the Romantic Movement?

3. How did Kant try to resolve the problem posed by Hume's empiricism? What was the significance of his thought?

4. What was Hegel's view of history? What influence did it have?

5. What were the attitudes of the conservatives toward the philosophes and the French Revolution?

6. What were the sources of liberalism?

7. The central concern of liberals was the enhancement of individual liberty. Discuss this statement.

8. How did the French Revolution and romanticism contribute to the rise of modern nationalism?

9. What is the relationship between nationalism and liberalism?

10. Account for the great appeal of nationalism.

Chapter 14

Surge of Liberalism and Nationalism: Revolution, Counterrevolution, and Unification

- **The Congress of Vienna**
- **Revolutions, 1820–1829**
- **Revolutions, 1830–1832**
- **The Revolutions of 1848: France**
- **The Revolutions of 1848: Germany, Austria, and Italy**
- **The Revolutions of 1848: an Assessment**
- **The Unification of Italy**
- **The Unification of Germany**
- **Nationality Problems in the Hapsburg Empire**

*D*uring the years 1815 through 1848, the forces unleashed by the French Revolution clashed with the traditional outlook of the Old Regime. The period opened with the Congress of Vienna, which drew up a peace settlement after the defeat of Napoleon, and closed with the revolutions that swept across most of Europe in 1848. Outside France, much of the Old Regime had survived the stormy decades of the French Revolution and Napoleon. Monarchs still held the reins of political power. Aristocrats, particularly in central and Eastern Europe, retained their traditional hold on the army and administration, controlled the peasantry and local government, and enjoyed tax exemptions. Determined to enforce respect for traditional authority and to smother liberal ideals, the conservative ruling elites resorted to censorship, secret police, and armed force. But the liberals and nationalists, inspired by the revolutionary principles of liberty, equality, and fraternity, continued to engage in revolutionary action. ❖

THE CONGRESS OF VIENNA

After the defeat of Napoleon, a congress of European powers met at Vienna (1814–1815) to draw up a peace settlement. The delegates wanted to restore stability to a continent torn by revolution and war and to reestablish the balance of power shattered by Napoleonic France.

Statesmen and Issues

The pivotal figure at the Congress of Vienna was Prince Klemens von Metternich (1773–1859) of Austria. A man of the Old Order, Metternich believed that both domestic and international stability depended on rule by monarchs and respect for the aristocracy. The misguided liberal belief that society could be reshaped according to the ideals of liberty and equality, said Metternich, had led to twenty-five years of revolution, terror, and war. To restore stability and peace, the old Europe must suppress liberal ideas and quash the first signs of revolution.

Metternich also feared the new spirit of nationalism. As a multinational empire, Austria was particularly vulnerable to nationalist unrest. If its ethnic groups—Poles, Czechs, Magyars, Italians,

South Slavs, and Romanians—became infected with the nationalist virus, they would destroy the Hapsburg Empire. Moreover, by arousing the masses and setting people against people, nationalism could undermine the foundations of the European civilization that he cherished.

Determined to end the chaos of the Napoleonic period and restore stability to Europe, Metternich wanted to return to power the ruling families deposed by more than two decades of revolutionary warfare. He also sought to reestablish the balance of power in Europe so that no one country could be in a position to dominate the Continent as Napoleon had done. There must be no more Napoleons who obliterate states, topple kings, and dream of European hegemony.

Other nations at the Congress of Vienna included Britain, Russia, France, and Prussia. Representing Britain was Robert Stewart, Viscount Castlereagh (1769–1822), the British foreign secretary, who was realistic and empirically minded. Although an implacable enemy of Napoleon, Castlereagh demonstrated mature statesmanship by not seeking to punish France severely. Tsar Alexander I (1777–1825) attended the congress himself. Steeped in Christian mysticism, the tsar wanted to create a European community based on Christian teachings. Alexander regarded himself as the savior of Europe, an attitude that caused other diplomats to view him with distrust. Representing France was Prince Charles Maurice de Talleyrand-Périgord (1754–1838). A devoted patriot, Talleyrand sought to remove from France the stigma of the Revolution and Napoleon. Prince Karl von Hardenberg (1750–1822) represented Prussia. Like Metternich, Castlereagh, and Talleyrand, the Prussian statesman believed that the various European states, besides pursuing their own national interests, should concern themselves with the well-being of the European community as a whole.

Two interrelated issues threatened to disrupt the conference and enmesh the Great Powers in another war. One was Prussia's intention to annex the German kingdom of Saxony; the other was Russia's demand for Polish territories. The tsar wanted to combine the Polish holdings of Russia, Austria, and Prussia into a new Polish kingdom under Russian control. Both Britain and Austria regarded such an extension of Russian

Chronology 14.1 ❖ The Surge of Nationalism

1821	Austria crushes revolts in Italy
1823	French troops crush revolt in Spain
1825	Uprising in Russia crushed by Nicholas I
1829	Greece gains its independence from Ottoman Empire
1830	The July Ordinances in France are followed by a revolution, which forces Charles X to abdicate
1831	The Polish revolution fails
1831–1832	Austrian forces crush a revolution in Italy
1848	The year of revolution
1862	Bismarck becomes chancellor of Prussia
1864	Austria and Prussia defeat Denmark in a war over Schleswig-Holstein
1866	Seven Weeks' War between Austria and Prussia: Prussia emerges as the dominant power in Germany
1870–1871	Franco-Prussian War: German unification completed
January 18, 1871	William I becomes German Kaiser

domination into central Europe as a threat to the balance of power.

Talleyrand suggested that Britain, Austria, and France join in an alliance to oppose Prussia and Russia. This clever move restored France to the family of nations. Now France was no longer the hated enemy but a necessary counterweight to Russia and Prussia. Threatened with war, Russia and Prussia moderated their demands and the crisis ended.

The Settlement

After months of discussion, quarrels, and threats, the delegates to the Congress of Vienna finished their work. Resisting Prussia's demands for a punitive peace, the allies did not punish France severely. They feared that a humiliated France would only prepare for a war of revenge. Besides, Metternich continued to need France to balance the power of both Prussia and Russia. France had to pay a large indemnity over a five-year period and submit to allied occupation until the obligation was met.

Although it lost most of its conquests, France emerged with somewhat more land than it had possessed before the Revolution. To guard against a resurgent France, both Prussia and Holland received territories on the French border. Holland obtained the southern Netherlands (Belgium); Prussia gained the Rhineland and part of Saxony, but not as much as the Prussians had desired. Nevertheless, Prussia emerged from the settlement significantly larger and stronger. Russia obtained Finland and a considerable part of the Polish territories, but not as much as the tsar had anticipated; the congress prevented further Russian expansion into central Europe. The northern Italian province of Lombardy was restored to Austria, which also received adjacent Venetia. England obtained strategic naval bases: Helgoland in the North Sea, Malta and the Ionian Islands in the Mediterranean, the Cape Colony in South Africa, and Ceylon in the Indian Ocean. Germany was organized into a confederation of thirty-eight (later thirty-nine) states. Norway was given to Sweden. The legitimate rulers, who had been displaced by the Revolution and the wars of Napoleon, were restored to their thrones in France, Spain, Portugal, the Kingdom of the Two Sicilies, the Papal States, and many German states.

311

Congress of Vienna, 1815, by Jean Baptiste Isabey (1767–1855). The delegates to the Congress of Vienna sought to reestablish many features of Europe that had existed before the French Revolution and Napoleon. They can be accused of shortsightedness; nevertheless, the balance of power that they formulated preserved international peace. Metternich is standing before a chair at the left. (*Print Collection, Miriam and Ira D. Wallach Division of Art, Prints and Photographs, The New York Public Library. Astor, Lenox, and Tilden Foundations*)

The conservative delegates at the Congress of Vienna have often been criticized for ignoring the liberal and nationalist aspirations of the different peoples and turning the clock back to the Old Regime. Critics have castigated the congress for dealing only with the rights of thrones and not the rights of peoples. But after the experience of two world wars in the twentieth century, some historians today are impressed by the peacemakers' success in restoring a balance of power that effectively stabilized international relations. No one country was strong enough to dominate the Continent, and no Great Power was so unhappy that it resorted to war to undo the settlement. Not until the unification of Germany in 1870–71 was the balance of power upset; not until World War I in 1914 did Europe have another general war of the magnitude of the Napoleonic wars.

REVOLUTIONS, 1820–1829

Russia, Austria, Prussia, and Great Britain agreed to act together to preserve the territorial settlement of the Congress of Vienna and the balance of power. After paying its indemnity, France was admitted into this Quadruple Alliance, also known as the Concert of Europe. Metternich intended to use the Concert of Europe to maintain harmony between nations and internal stability within nations. Toward this end, conservatives in their respective countries censored books and newspapers and imprisoned liberal and nationalist activists.

But repression could not contain the liberal and nationalist ideals unleashed by the French Revolution. The first revolution after the restorations of legitimate rulers occurred in Spain in 1820. Fearing that the Spanish uprising, with its quasi-liberal overtones, would inspire revolutions in other lands, the Concert of Europe empowered France to intervene. In 1823, a hundred thousand French troops crushed the revolution.

Revolutionary activity in Italy also frightened the Concert of Europe. In 1815, Italy consisted of several separate states. In the south, a Bourbon king ruled the Kingdom of the Two Sicilies; the pope governed the Papal States in central Italy; and Hapsburg Austria ruled Lombardy and Venetia in the north. Hapsburg princes subservient to Austria ruled the duchies of Tuscany, Parma, and Modena. Piedmont in the northwest and the island of Sardinia were governed by an Italian dynasty, the House of Savoy.

Besides all these political divisions, Italy was split economically and culturally. Throughout the peninsula, attachment to the local region was stronger than devotion to national unity. Economic ties between north and south were weak; inhabitants of the northern Italian cities felt little closeness to Sicilian peasants. Except for the middle class, most Italians clung to the values of the Old Regime.

Through novels, poetry, and works of history, an expanding intellectual elite awakened interest in Italy's glorious past. They insisted that a people who had built the Roman Empire and produced the Renaissance must not remain weak and divided, their land occupied by Austrians. These sentiments appealed particularly to university students and the middle class. But the rural masses, illiterate and preoccupied with the hardships of daily life, showed little interest in this struggle for national revival.

Secret societies kept alive the hopes for liberty and independence from foreign rule in the period after 1815. The most important of these societies was the Carbonari, which had clubs in every state in Italy and a membership drawn largely from the middle class and the army. In 1820, the Carbonari enjoyed a few months of triumph in the Kingdom of the Two Sicilies. Supported by the army and militia, they forced King Ferdinand I to grant a constitution and a parliamentary government. But Metternich feared that the germ of revolution would spread to other countries. Supported by Prussia and Russia, Austria suppressed the constitutional government in Naples and another revolution that broke out in Piedmont. In both cases, Austria firmly fixed an absolute ruler on the throne.

A revolution also failed in Russia. During the Napoleonic wars and the occupation of France, Russian officers were introduced to French ideas. Contrasting French liberal attitudes with Russian autocracy, some officers resolved to change conditions in Russia. Like their Western counterparts, they organized secret societies and disseminated liberal ideas within Russia. When Alexander I died, these liberal officers struck. Their uprising in December 1825 was easily smashed by the new tsar, Nicholas I, and the leaders were severely punished.

The revolutions in Spain, Italy, and Russia were suppressed, but the Concert of Europe also suffered setbacks. Stimulated by the ideals of the French Revolution, the Greeks revolted against their Turkish rulers in 1821. Although the Turkish sultan was the legitimate ruler, Russia, France, and Britain aided the Greek revolutionaries, for they were Christians, whereas the Turks were Muslims; moreover, pro-Greek sentiments were very strong among educated Western Europeans, who had studied the literature and history of ancient Greece. To them, the Greeks were struggling to regain the freedom of their ancient forebears. Not only the pressure of public opinion but also fear of Russian motives led Britain to join in intervention. If Russia carried out its intention of aiding the Greeks on its own, no doubt it would never surrender control. Britain could not permit this extension of Russian power in the eastern Mediterranean. Despite Metternich's objections, Britain, France, and Russia took joint action against the Turks, and in 1829 Greece gained its independence.

REVOLUTIONS, 1830–1832

After Napoleon's defeat, a Bourbon king, Louis XVIII (1814–1824), ascended the throne of France. Recognizing that the French people would not accept a return to the Old Order, Louis pursued a moderate course. Although his pseudoconstitution, the Charter, declared that the king's power rested on divine right, it acknowledged that citizens possessed fundamental rights: freedom of thought and religion and equal treatment under the law. It also set up a two-house parliament. But peasants, urban workers, and most bourgeois could not meet the property requirements for voting. Louis XVIII was resisted by diehard aristocrats, called *ultras*, who wanted to erase the past twenty-five years of French history and restore the power and privileges of church and aristocracy. Their leader was the king's younger brother, the comte d'Artois, who after Louis's death in 1824 ascended the throne as Charles X (1824–1830).

The new government aroused the hostility of the bourgeoisie by indemnifying the émigrés for the property they had lost during the Revolution, censoring the press, and giving the church greater control over education. In the election of 1830, the liberal opposition to Charles X won a decisive victory. Charles responded with the July Ordinances, which dissolved the newly elected chamber; the Ordinances also deprived the upper bourgeois of the vote and severely curbed the press.

The bourgeois, students, and workers rebelled. They hoped to establish a republic, but the wealthy bourgeois who took control of the revolution feared republican radicalism. They offered the throne to the duc d'Orléans; Charles X abdicated and went into exile in Britain. The new king, Louis Philippe (1830–1848), never forgot that he owed his throne to the rich bourgeois. And the Parisian workers who had fought for a republic and economic reforms to alleviate poverty felt betrayed by the outcome, as did the still disenfranchised petty bourgeois.

The Revolution of 1830 in France set off shock waves in Belgium, Poland, and Italy. The Congress of Vienna had assigned Catholic Belgium to Protestant Holland; from the outset, the Belgians had protested. Stirred by the events in Paris, Belgian patriots proclaimed their independence from Holland and established a liberal government. Inspired by the uprisings in France and Belgium, Polish students, intellectuals, and army officers took up arms against their Russian overlords. The revolutionaries wanted to restore Polish independence, a dream that poets, musicians, and intellectuals had kept alive. Polish courage, however, was no match for Russian might, and Warsaw fell in 1831. The tsar took savage revenge on the revolutionaries. In 1831–32, the Austrians suppressed another insurrection by the Carbonari in the Papal States. During these uprisings, the peasants gave the Carbonari little support; indeed, they seemed to side with the traditional rulers.

THE REVOLUTIONS OF 1848:

FRANCE

In 1848, often called "the year of revolution," uprisings for political liberty and nationhood erupted throughout Europe. The economic crisis of the previous two years had aggravated discontent with the existing regimes, but "it was the absence of liberty," concludes historian Jacques Droz, "which . . . was most deeply resented by the peoples of Europe and led them to take up arms."[1]

The February Revolution

An uprising in Paris set in motion the revolutionary tidal wave that was to engulf much of Europe in 1848. The Revolution of 1830 had broken the back of the ultras in France. There would be no going back to the Old Regime. But King Louis Philippe and his ministers, moderates by temperament and philosophy, had no intention of going forward to democracy.

The government of Louis Philippe was run by a small elite consisting of bourgeois bankers, merchants, and lawyers, as well as aristocrats who had abandoned the hope of restoring the Old Regime. This ruling elite championed the revolutionary ideas of equal treatment under the law and of careers open to talent but feared democracy and blocked efforts to broaden the franchise.

Liberty Leading the People, 1830, by Eugene Delacroix (1799–1863). Early-nineteenth-century reformers found their rallying cry in liberty, a legacy of the French Revolution. In this painting, Delacroix, the leader of French romantic artists, glorifies liberty. (*Louvre/Cliche des Musées Nationaux*)

(Only about 3 percent of adult French males were qualified to vote.) The opposition—radical republicans, or democrats—wanted to abolish the monarchy and grant all men the vote. The situation reached a climax in February 1848, when the bourgeoisie, as well as students and workers, took to the streets to demand reforms; this led to a violent confrontation with soldiers. Unable to pacify the enraged Parisians, Louis Philippe abdicated, and France became a republic.

The June Days: Revolution of the Oppressed

The new bourgeois leaders were committed to political democracy, but only a few favored the social reforms demanded by the laboring poor. A meager harvest in 1846 and an international financial crisis in 1847 that drastically curtailed French factory production aggravated the misery of the working class. Workers who could find jobs labored twelve to fourteen hours a day under brutalizing conditions. In some districts, one out of three children died before the age of five, and everywhere in France, beggars, paupers, prostitutes, and criminals were evidence of the struggle to survive. Prevented by law from striking, unable to meet the financial requirements for voting, and afflicted with unemployment, the urban workers wanted relief.

The middle-class leaders of the new republic, however, had little understanding of the workers' plight and little sympathy for it. By reason of occupation and wealth, the middle class saw itself as separate from the working class. To the bourgeoisie, the workers were dangerous creatures, "the wild ones," "the vile mob." But the inhabitants of the urban slums could no longer be ignored. They felt, as Alexis de Tocqueville, the astute statesman and political theorist, stated, "that all that is above them is incapable and unworthy of governing them; that the present distribution of goods [prevalent until now] . . . is unjust; that property rests on a foundation which is not an equitable foundation."[2]

Although the new leaders gave all adult males the vote and abolished censorship, they made only insincere and halfhearted attempts to ease the distress of the urban poor. The government limited the workday to ten hours, legalized labor unions, and established national workshops, which provided food, medical benefits, and employment on public works projects. But to the workers, this was a feeble effort to deal with their monumental hardships. To the property-owning peasantry and bourgeoisie, the national workshops were a hateful concession to socialist radicalism and a waste of government funds. When the government closed the workshops, working-class hostility and despair turned to open rebellion. Again barricades went up in the streets of Paris.

The June revolution in Paris was a revolt against poverty and a cry for the redistribution of property. The workers stood alone. To the rest of the nation, they were barbarians attacking civilized society. Aristocrats, bourgeois, and peasants feared that no one's property would be safe if the revolution succeeded. From hundreds of miles away, Frenchmen flocked to Paris to crush what they considered to be the madness within their midst. After three days of vicious street fighting and atrocities on both sides, the army extinguished the revolt. Some 1,460 lives had been lost, including four generals. The June Days left deep scars on French society. For many years, workers would never forget that the rest of France had united against them; the rest of France would remain terrified of working-class radicalism.

In December 1848, the French people, in overwhelming numbers, elected Louis Napoleon—nephew of the great emperor—president of the Second Republic. They were attracted by the magic of Louis Napoleon's name, and they expected him to prevent future working-class disorders. The election, in which all adult males could vote, demonstrated that most Frenchmen were socially conservative; they were unsympathetic to working-class poverty and deeply suspicious of socialist programs.

THE REVOLUTIONS OF 1848: GERMANY, AUSTRIA, AND ITALY

Like an epidemic, the fever of revolution that broke out in Paris in February raced across the Continent. Liberals, excluded from participation in political life, fought for parliaments and constitutions; many liberals were also nationalists who wanted unity or independence for their nations.

The German States: Liberalism Discredited

After the Congress of Vienna, Germany consisted of a loose confederation of thirty-nine independent states, of which Austria and Prussia were the most powerful. Jealous of the states' independence and determined to preserve their own absolute authority, the ruling princes detested liberal and nationalist ideals.

The German nationalism that had emerged during the French occupation intensified during the restoration (the post-Napoleonic period). Inspired in part by the ideas of the romantics, intellectuals insisted that Germans, who shared a common language and culture, should also be united politically. During the restoration, the struggle for German unity and liberal reforms continued to be waged primarily by students, professors, writers, lawyers, and other educated people. The great mass of people, knowing only loyalty to their local prince, remained unmoved by appeals for national unity.

The successful revolt against Louis Philippe, hostility against absolute princes, and the general economic crisis combined to produce uprisings in the capital cities of the German states in March 1848. Throughout Germany, liberals clamored for constitutions, parliamentary government, freedom of thought, and an end to police intimidation. Some called for the creation of a unified Germany governed by a national parliament and headed by a constitutional monarch. The poor of

Map 14.1 Europe's Age of Revolutions In ▶ the decades after the Vienna settlement, Europe experienced a wave of revolution based chiefly on liberalism and nationalism.

Boundaries after Congress of Vienna, 1815

Boundary of German Confederation

▲ Centers of revolution, 1820s

✪ Centers of revolution, 1830s

• Centers of popular unrest in Britain, 1815–1848

▨ Principal states affected by revolution, 1848

✪ Centers of revolution, 1848

400 Mi.

200

400 Km.

200

0

ATLANTIC OCEAN

North Sea

Baltic Sea

Mediterranean Sea

Black Sea

SWEDEN AND NORWAY

DENMARK

RUSSIAN EMPIRE

St. Petersburg

GREAT BRITAIN

IRELAND

Glasgow

Manchester

Birmingham

Bristol

London

HANOVER

PRUSSIA

PRUSSIA

KINGDOM OF THE NETHERLANDS

BEL.

Brussels

FRANCE

Paris

Lyons

SPAIN

PORTUGAL

La Coruña

Oviedo

Pamplona

Madrid

Saragossa

Valencia

Barcelona

Cadiz

Lisbon

Berlin

Dresden

Frankfurt

BAVARIA

Munich

BOHEMIA

Prague

Brno

Vienna

Salzburg

SWITZ.

Turin

Genoa

Milan

Venice

Modena

Florence

Macerata

PAPAL STATES

Rome

KINGDOM OF PIEDMONT SARDINIA

KINGDOM OF THE TWO SICILIES

Bari

Naples

Salerno

Reggio

Palermo

Sicily

Posen

Warsaw

POLAND

Cracow

Lemberg

AUSTRIAN EMPIRE

Pressburg

Budapest

HUNGARY

Agram

Debrecen

Kolozsvar

Blaj

Jassy

Bucharest

OTTOMAN EMPIRE

GREECE (Independence, 1829)

Morea

317

town and countryside, their plight worsened by the great depression of the 1840s, joined the struggle.

Terrified that these disturbances would lead to anarchy, the princes made concessions to the liberals, whom they had previously censored, jailed, and exiled. During March and April 1848, the traditional rulers in Prussia and other German states replaced reactionary ministers with liberals, eased censorship, established jury systems, framed constitutions, formed parliaments, and ended peasant obligations to lords.

Liberals took advantage of their successes to form a national assembly charged with the task of creating a unified and liberal Germany. Representatives from all the German states attended the assembly, which met at Frankfurt. After many long debates, the Frankfurt Assembly approved a federation of German states. The German union would have a parliament and would be headed by the Prussian king. Austria, with its many non-German nationalities, would be excluded from the federal union. The deputies selected Frederick William IV as emperor of the new Germany, but the Prussian king refused; he would never wear a crown given to him by common people during a period of revolutionary agitation. While the delegates debated, the ruling princes recovered from the first shock of revolution and ordered their armies to crush the revolutionaries. One by one the liberal governments fell.

German liberalism had failed to unite Germany or to create a constitutional government dominated by the middle class. Liberalism, never securely rooted in Germany, was discredited. In the following decades, many Germans, identifying liberalism with failure, abandoned liberal values and turned to authoritarian Prussia for leadership in the struggle for unification. The fact that authoritarians hostile to the spirit of parliamentary government eventually united Germany had deep implications for future German and European history.

Austria: Hapsburg Dominance

The Hapsburg (Austrian) Empire, the product of dynastic marriage and inheritance, had no common nationality or language; it was held together only by the reigning Hapsburg dynasty, its army, and its bureaucracy. The ethnic composition of the empire was enormously complex. The Germans dominated; concentrated principally in Austria, they constituted about 25 percent of the empire's population. The Magyars predominated in the Hungarian lands of the empire. The great bulk of the population consisted of Slavs: Czechs, Poles, Slovaks, Slovenes, Croats, Serbs, and Ruthenians. In addition, there were Italians in northern Italy and Romanians in Transylvania. The Hapsburg dynasty, aided by the army and the German-dominated civil service, prevented the multinational empire from collapsing into anarchy.

Metternich, it is often said, suffered from a "dissolution complex": he understood that the new forces of nationalism and liberalism could break up the Austrian Empire. Liberal ideas could lead Hapsburg subjects to challenge the authority of the emperor, and nationalist feelings could cause the different peoples of the empire to rebel against German domination and Hapsburg rule. To keep these ideas from infecting Austrian subjects, Metternich's police imposed strict censorship, spied on professors, and expelled from the universities students caught reading forbidden books. Despite Metternich's political police, the universities still remained hotbeds of liberalism.

In 1848, revolutions spread throughout the Austrian Empire, starting in Vienna. Aroused by the abdication of Louis Philippe, Viennese liberals denounced Hapsburg absolutism and demanded a constitution, relaxation of censorship, and restrictions on the police. Intimidated by the revolutionaries, the government allowed freedom of the press, accepted Metternich's resignation, and promised a constitution. The Constitutional Assembly was convened and in August voted the abolition of serfdom. At the same time that the Viennese insurgents were tasting the heady wine of reform, revolts in other parts of the empire—Bohemia, Hungary, and northern Italy—added to the distress of the monarchy.

But the revolutionaries' victory was only temporary, and the defeat of the Old Order only illusory. The Hapsburg government soon began to recover its balance. The first government victory came with the crushing of the Czechs in Bohemia. In 1848, Czech nationalists wanted the Austrian

Empire reconstructed along federal lines that would give the Czechs equal standing with Germans. General Alfred zu Windischgrätz bombarded Prague, the capital of Bohemia, into submission and reestablished Hapsburg control.

In October 1848, the Hapsburg authorities ordered the army to attack Vienna. Against the regular army, the courageous but disorganized and divided students and workers had little hope. In March 1849, the Hapsburg rulers replaced the liberal constitution drafted by the popularly elected Constitutional Assembly with a more conservative one drawn up by their own ministers.

The most serious threat to the Hapsburg realm came from the Magyars in Hungary. Some twelve million people lived in Hungary, five million of whom were Magyars. The other nationalities consisted of South Slavs (Croats and Serbs) and Romanians. Louis Kossuth (1802–1894), a member of the lower nobility, called for both social reform and a deepening of national consciousness in Hungary. Led by Kossuth, the Magyars demanded local autonomy. Hungary would remain within the Hapsburg Empire but have its own constitution and national army and control its own finances. The Hungarian leadership introduced liberal reforms: suffrage for all males who could speak Magyar and owned some property, freedom of religion, freedom of the press, the abolition of serfdom, and the end of the privileges of the nobles and the church. Within a few weeks, the Hungarian parliament changed Hungary from a feudal to a modern liberal state.

But the Hungarian leaders' nationalist dreams towered above their liberal ideals. The Magyars intended to incorporate lands inhabited by Croats, Slovaks, and Romanians into their state (Magyars considered these lands an integral part of historic Hungary) and to transform these peoples into Hungarians. In the spring of 1849, the Hungarians renounced their allegiance to the Hapsburgs and proclaimed Hungary an independent state, with Kossuth as president.

The Hapsburg rulers took advantage of the ethnic animosities inside and outside Hungary. They encouraged Romanians and Croats to resist the new Hungarian government. When Hapsburg forces moved against the Magyars, they were joined by an army of Croats, whose nationalist aspirations had been flouted by the Magyars. The

Emperor Francis Joseph, who had recently ascended the Hapsburg throne, also appealed to Tsar Nicholas I for help. The tsar complied, fearing that a successful revolt by the Hungarians might lead the Poles to rise up against their Russian overlords. The Hungarians fought with extraordinary courage but were overcome by superior might.

Italy: Continued Fragmentation

Eager to end the humiliating Hapsburg occupation and domination and to link the disparate states into a unified and liberal nation, Italian nationalists, too, rose in rebellion in 1848. Revolution broke out in Sicily six weeks before the February revolution in Paris. Bowing to the revolutionaries' demands, King Ferdinand II of Naples granted a liberal constitution. The grand duke of Tuscany, King Charles Albert of Piedmont-Sardinia, and Pope Pius IX, ruler of the Papal States, also felt compelled to introduce liberal reforms.

Then the revolution spread to the Hapsburg lands in the north. After "Five Glorious Days" (March 18–22) of street fighting, the citizens of Milan forced the Austrians to withdraw. The people had liberated their city. On March 22, the citizens of Venice declared their city free from Austrian rule and set up a republic. King Charles Albert, who hoped to acquire Lombardy and Venetia, declared war on Austria. Intimidated by the insurrections, the ruling princes of the Italian states and Hapsburg Austria had lost the first round.

But soon everywhere in Italy the forces of reaction recovered and reasserted their authority. The Austrians defeated the Sardinians and reoccupied Milan, and Ferdinand II crushed the revolutionaries in the south. Revolutionary disorders in Rome had forced Pope Pius IX to flee in November 1848; in February 1849, the revolutionaries proclaimed Rome "a pure democracy with the glorious title of the Roman Republic." Heeding the pope's call for assistance, Louis Napoleon, the newly elected French president, attacked Rome, destroyed the infant republic, and allowed Pope Pius to return. The last city to fall to the reactionaries was Venice, which the Austrians subjected to a merciless bombardment. Italy was still a fragmented nation.

THE REVOLUTIONS OF 1848:
AN ASSESSMENT

The revolutions of 1848 began with much promise, but they all ended in defeat. The revolutionaries' initial success was due less to their strength than to the governments' hesitancy to use their superior force. However, the reactionary leaders of Europe overcame their paralysis and moved decisively to smash the revolutions. The courage of the revolutionaries was no match for the sheer power of regular armies. Thousands were killed and imprisoned; many fled to America.

Class divisions weakened the revolutionaries. The union between middle-class liberals and workers, which brought success in the opening stages of the revolutions, was only temporary. Bourgeois liberals favoring political reforms—constitution, parliament, and protection of basic rights—grew fearful of the laboring poor, who demanded social reforms, that is, jobs and bread. To the bourgeois, the workers were radical Jacobins, a mob driven by dark instincts. When the working class engaged in revolutionary action, a terrified middle class deserted the cause of revolution or joined the old elites in subduing the workers. These class divisions showed that the liberals' concern for political reforms—the extension of suffrage and parliamentary government—did not satisfy workers who were mired in poverty. The events of 1848 also showed that social issues—the demands of the working class for an alleviation of their misery—would become a prime consideration of European political life in the generations to come.

Intractable nationalist animosities helped to destroy all the revolutionary movements against absolutism in central Europe. In many cases, the different nationalities hated one another more than they hated the reactionary rulers. Hungarian revolutionaries dismissed the nationalist yearnings of the Croats and Romanians living in Hungary, who in turn helped the Hapsburg dynasty extinguish the nascent Hungarian state. The Germans of Bohemia resisted Czech demands for self-government and the equality of the Czech language with German. When German liberals at the Frankfurt Assembly debated the boundary lines of a united Germany, the problem of Prussia's Polish territories emerged. In 1848, Polish patriots wanted to recreate the Polish nation, but German delegates at the convention, by an overwhelming majority, opposed returning the Polish lands seized by Prussia in the late eighteenth century.

Before 1848, democratic idealists envisioned the birth of a new Europe of free people and liberated nations. The revolutions in central Europe showed that nationalism and liberalism were not natural allies and that nationalists were often indifferent to the rights of other peoples. Disheartened by these nationalist antagonisms, John Stuart Mill, the English liberal statesman and philosopher, lamented that "the sentiment of nationality so far outweighs the love of liberty that the people are willing to abet their rulers in crushing the liberty and independence of any people not of their race or language."[3] In the revolutions of 1848, concludes the British historian Lewis Namier, "'nationality,' the passionate creed of the intellectuals, invades the politics of central and east-central Europe, and with 1848 starts the Great European War of every nation against its neighbors."[4]

Even though the liberal and nationalist aims of the revolutionaries were not realized, liberal gains were not insignificant. All Frenchmen obtained the right to vote; serfdom was abolished in Austria; and parliaments were established in Prussia and other German states.

For German liberalism, however, 1848 was a crucial defeat. Controlled by monarchs and aristocrats hostile to the democratic principles of 1848, the postrevolutionary governments, using the methods of a police state, intimidated and persecuted liberals, large numbers of whom were forced to emigrate. The failure of the revolution and the reactionary policies of the postrevolutionary governments thwarted the growth of a democratic parliamentary system in Germany. Discredited by the failure of 1848, weakened by government intimidation and the loss of many liberals to emigration, and less committed to liberal ideals—which brought no gains in 1848—the German middle class in the period immediately after 1848 became apolitical or willing to sacri-

Erstürmung der Barrikade in der Döngesgasse zu Frankfurt a. M. durch die Oestreicher am 18. Sept.
Nach einer Originalzeichnung von W. Hössler.

Barricades in the Streets of Frankfurt, 1848. In 1848 revolutionary fever spread from France to Germany. In several German states, liberals fought for written constitutions that protected basic rights and parliamentary government that represented the people. At first the ruling princes made concessions but quickly regained their nerve and ordered their professional soldiers to crush the revolutionaries. (*The Granger Collection, New York*)

fice liberal principles to achieve a united and powerful Germany. Nationalism would supersede liberalism as the principal concern of the German middle class. The failure of liberalism to take strong root in Germany would have dire consequences in the early twentieth century.

In later decades, liberal reforms, including legal guarantees of basic rights, would be introduced peacefully in several European countries—in Germany too, but there power still remained in the hands of preindustrial semifeudal elites, not with the middle class—for the failure of the revolutions of 1848 convinced many people, including liberals, that popular uprisings were ineffective ways of changing society. The Age of Revolution, initiated by the French Revolution of 1789, had ended.

THE UNIFICATION OF ITALY

In 1848, liberals had failed to drive the Austrians out of Italy and unite the Italian nation. By 1870, however, Italian unification had been achieved, mainly through the efforts of three men: Mazzini, Cavour, and Garibaldi.

Mazzini: The Soul of the Risorgimento

Giuseppe Mazzini (1805–1872) dedicated his life to the creation of a united and republican Italy—a goal he pursued with extraordinary moral intensity and determination. Mazzini was both a romantic and a liberal. As a liberal, he fought for republican and constitutional government and held that national unity would enhance individual liberty. As a romantic, he believed that an awakened Italy would lead to the regeneration of humanity. Mazzini was convinced that just as Rome had provided law and unity in the ancient world and the Roman pope had led Latin Christendom during the Middle Ages, so a third Rome, a newly united Italy, would usher in a new age of free nations, personal liberty, and equality.

Mazzini had great charisma, determination, courage, and eloquence; he was also a prolific writer. His idealism attracted the intelligentsia and youth and kept alive the spirit of national unity. He infused the *Risorgimento,* the movement for Italian unity, with spiritual intensity. After his release from prison for participating in the insurrection of 1831, Mazzini went into exile and founded a new organization: Young Italy. Consisting of dedicated revolutionaries, many of them students, Young Italy was intended to serve as the instrument for the awakening of Italy and the transformation of Europe into a brotherhood of free peoples. Mazzini believed that a successful revolution must come from below—from the people, moved by a profound love for their nation. They must overthrow the Hapsburg princes and create a democratic republic.

Cavour and Victory over Austria

The failure of the revolutions of 1848 contained an obvious lesson: that Mazzini's approach, an armed uprising by aroused masses, did not work. The masses were not deeply committed to the nationalist cause, and the revolutionaries were no match for the Austrian army. Italian nationalists now hoped that the kingdom of Piedmont-Sardinia, ruled by an Italian dynasty, would expel the Austrians and lead the drive for unity. Count Camillo Benso di Cavour (1810–1861), the chief minister of Piedmont-Sardinia, became the architect of Italian unity.

Unlike Mazzini, Cavour was neither a dreamer nor a speechmaker but a tough-minded practitioner of *realpolitik,* "the politics of reality." Focusing on the world as it actually was, he dismissed ideals as illusions. A cautious and practical statesman, Cavour realized that mass uprisings could not succeed against Austrian might. Moreover, mistrusting the common people, he did not favor Mazzini's goal of a democratic republic. Cavour had no precise blueprint for unifying Italy. His immediate aim was to increase the territory of Piedmont by driving the Austrians from northern Italy and incorporating Lombardy and Venetia into Piedmont-Sardinia.

To improve Piedmont's image in foreign affairs, Cavour launched a reform program to strengthen the economy. He reorganized the currency, taxes, and the national debt; in addition, he had railways and steamships built, fostered improved agricultural methods, and encouraged new businesses. Within a few years, Piedmont had become a progressive modern state.

In 1855, Piedmont joined England and France in the Crimean War against Russia. Cavour had no quarrel with Russia but sought the friendship of Britain and France and a chance to be heard in world affairs. At the peace conference, Cavour was granted an opportunity to denounce Austria for occupying Italian lands. He soon found a supporter in Napoleon III (the former Louis Napoleon), the French emperor, who hoped that a unified northern Italy would become an ally and client of France.

In 1858, Cavour and Napoleon III reached a secret agreement. If Austria attacked Piedmont, France would aid the Italian state. Piedmont would annex Lombardy and Venetia and parts of the Papal States. For its assistance, France would obtain Nice and Savoy from Piedmont. With this agreement in his pocket, Cavour cleverly maneuvered Austria into declaring war, for it had to appear that Austria was the aggressor. He did so by strengthening Piedmont's army and encouraging volunteers from Austrian-controlled Lombardy to join it.

Supported by French forces and taking advantage of poor Austrian planning, Piedmont conquered Lombardy and occupied Milan. But Napoleon III quickly had second thoughts. If Piedmont took any of the pope's territory, French Catholics would blame their own leader. Even more serious was the fear that Prussia, suspicious of French aims, would aid Austria. For these reasons, Napoleon III, without consulting Cavour, signed an armistice with Austria. Piedmont would acquire Lombardy, but no more. An outraged Cavour demanded that his state continue the war until all northern Italy was liberated, but King Victor Emmanuel of Piedmont accepted the Austrian peace terms. The victory of Piedmont-Sardinia, however, proved greater than Cavour had anticipated. During the conflict, patriots in Parma, Modena, Tuscany, and Romagna (one of the Papal States) had seized power. These new revolutionary governments voted to join with Piedmont.

Garibaldi and Victory in the South

Piedmont's success spurred revolutionary activity in the Kingdom of the Two Sicilies. In the spring of 1860, some one thousand red-shirted adventurers and patriots, led by Giuseppe Garibaldi (1807–1882), landed in Sicily, determined to liberate the land from its Bourbon ruler. Garibaldi held progressive views for his day. He supported the liberation of all subject nationalities, female equality, the right of workers to organize, racial equality, and the abolition of capital punishment. But the cause of Italian national unity was his true religion. After the liberation, Garibaldi that same year invaded the mainland. He occupied Naples without a fight and prepared to advance on Rome.

Cavour, however, feared that an assault on Rome by Garibaldi would lead to French intervention. Napoleon III had pledged to defend the pope's lands, and a French garrison had been stationed in Rome since 1849. Besides, Cavour considered Garibaldi too impulsive and rash, too attracted to republican ideals, and too popular to lead the struggle for unification.

To head off Garibaldi, Cavour persuaded Napoleon III to approve an invasion of the Papal States by Piedmont. A papal force offered only token opposition, and the Papal States of Umbria and the Marches soon voted for union with Piedmont, as did Naples and Sicily. Refusing to trade on his prestige with the masses to fulfill personal ambition, Garibaldi turned over his conquests to Piedmont's King Victor Emmanuel, who was declared king of Italy in 1861.

Italian Unification Completed

Two regions still remained outside the control of the new Italy: the city of Rome, ruled by the pope and protected by French troops; and Venetia, occupied by Austria. Cavour died in 1861, but the march toward unification continued. During the conflict between Prussia and Austria in 1866, Italy sided with the victorious Prussians and was rewarded with Venetia. During the Franco-Prussian War of 1870, France withdrew its garrisons from Rome; much to the anger of the pope, Italian troops marched in, and Rome was declared the capital of Italy.

THE UNIFICATION OF GERMANY

In 1848, German liberals and nationalists, believing in the strength of their ideals, had naively underestimated the power of the conservative Old Order. After the failed revolution, some disenchanted revolutionaries retained only a half-hearted commitment to liberalism or embraced conservatism. Others fled the country, weakening the liberal leadership. All liberals came to doubt the effectiveness of revolution as a way to transform Germany into a unified state; all gained a new respect for the realities of power. Abandoning idealism for realism, liberals now thought that German unity would be achieved through Prussian arms, not liberal ideals.

Prussia, Agent of Unification

During the late seventeenth and eighteenth centuries, Prussian kings had fashioned a rigorously trained and disciplined army. The state bureaucracy, often staffed by ex-soldiers, perpetuated the military mentality. As the chief organizations in the state, the army and the bureaucracy drilled into the Prussian people a respect for discipline and authority.

The Prussian throne was supported by the Junkers. These powerful aristocrats, who owned vast estates farmed by serfs, were exempt from most taxes and dominated local government in their territories. The Junkers' commanding position made them officers in the royal army, diplomats, and leading officials in the state bureaucracy. The Junkers knew that a weakening of the king's power would lead to the loss of their own aristocratic prerogatives.

In France in the late 1700s, a powerful and politically conscious middle class had challenged aristocratic privileges. The Prussian monarchy and the Junkers had faced no such challenge, for the Prussian middle class at that time was small and without influence. The idea of the rights of the individual did not deeply penetrate Prussian consciousness or undermine the Prussian tradition of obedience to military and state authority. Liberalism did not take firm root in Germany.

In 1834, under Prussian leadership, the German states, with the notable exception of Austria, established the *Zollverein,* a customs union that abolished tariffs between the states. The customs union stimulated economic activity and promoted a desire for greater unity. The Zollverein led many Germans to view Prussia, not Austria, as the leader of the unification movement.

Bismarck and the Road to Unity

Austria was the chief barrier to the extension of Prussian power in Germany. This was one reason why William I (1861–1888) called for a drastic reorganization of the Prussian army. But the liberals in the lower chamber of the Prussian parliament blocked passage of the army reforms, for they feared that the reforms would greatly increase the power of the monarchy and the military establishment. Unable to secure passage, William withdrew the reform bill and asked the lower chamber for additional funds to cover government expenses. When parliament granted these funds, he used the money to institute the army reforms. Learning from its mistake, the lower chamber would not approve the new budget in 1862 without an itemized breakdown. If the liberals won this conflict between the liberal majority in the lower chamber and the crown, they would, in effect, establish parliamentary control over the king and the army.

At this critical hour, King William asked Otto von Bismarck (1815–1898) to lead the battle against parliament. Descended on his father's side from an old aristocratic family, Bismarck was a staunch supporter of the Prussian monarchy and the Junker class and a devout patriot. He yearned to increase the territory and prestige of his beloved Prussia and to protect the authority of the Prussian king, who, Bismarck believed, ruled by the grace of God. Like Cavour, Bismarck was a shrewd and calculating practitioner of realpolitik.

Liberals were outraged by Bismarck's domineering and authoritarian manner and his determination to preserve monarchical power and the aristocratic order. Set on continuing the reorganization of the army and not bowing to parliamentary pressure, Bismarck ordered the collection of taxes without parliament's approval—an action that would have been unthinkable in Britain or the United States. He dismissed the lower chamber, imposed strict censorship on the press, arrested outspoken liberals, and fired liberals from the civil service. The liberals protested against these arbitrary and unconstitutional moves. What led to a resolution of the conflict was Bismarck's extraordinary success in foreign affairs.

Wars with Denmark and Austria To Bismarck, a war between Austria and Prussia seemed inevitable, for only by removing Austria from German affairs could Prussia extend its dominion over the other German states. Bismarck's first move, however, was not against Austria but against Denmark—in 1864, over the disputed duchies of Schleswig and Holstein. Austria joined as Prussia's ally because it hoped to prevent Prussia from annexing the territories. After Denmark's defeat, Austria and Prussia quarreled over the ultimate disposition of these lands. Bismarck used the dispute to goad Austria into war. The Austrians, on their side, were convinced that Prussia must be defeated if Austria wanted to retain its influence over German affairs.

In the Austro-Prussian war of 1866, Prussia, with astonishing speed, assembled its forces and overran Austrian territory. At the battle of Sadowa (or Königgrätz), Prussia decisively defeated the main Austrian forces, and the Seven Weeks' War ended. Prussia took no territory from Austria, but the latter agreed to Prussia's annexation of Schleswig and Holstein and a number of small German states. Prussia, moreover, organized a

Otto von Bismarck. Bismarck (1815–1898), the Iron Chancellor, was instrumental in unifying Germany. A conservative, he resisted parliament's efforts to weaken the monarch's power. Here he is portrayed in his youth, before becoming chancellor. (*AKG London*)

confederation of North German states, from which Austria was excluded. In effect, Austria was removed from German affairs, and Prussia became the dominant power in Germany.

The Triumph of Nationalism and Conservatism over Liberalism The Prussian victory had a profound impact on political life within Prussia. Bismarck was the man of the hour, the great hero who had extended Prussia's power. Most liberals forgave Bismarck for his authoritarian handling of parliament. The liberal press, which had previously denounced Bismarck for running roughshod over the constitution, embraced him as a hero. Prussians were urged to concentrate on the glorious tasks ahead and to put aside the constitutional struggle, which seemed petty by contrast.

Bismarck recognized the great appeal of nationalism and used it to expand Prussia's power over other German states and strengthen Prussia's voice in European affairs. By heralding his state as the champion of unification, he gained the support of nationalists throughout Germany. In the past, the nationalist cause had belonged to the liberals, but Bismarck appropriated it to promote Prussian expansion and conservative rule.

Prussia's victory over Austria, therefore, was a triumph for conservatism and nationalism and a defeat for liberalism. The liberal struggle for constitutional government in Prussia collapsed. The Prussian monarch retained the right to override parliamentary opposition and act on his own initiative. In 1848, Prussian might had suppressed a liberal revolution; in 1866, many liberals, beguiled by Bismarck's military triumphs, gave up the struggle for responsible parliamentary government. They had traded political freedom for Prussian military glory and power.

The capitulation of Prussian liberals demonstrated the essential weakness of the German liberal tradition. German liberals displayed a diminishing commitment to the principles of parliamentary government and a growing fascination with force, military triumph, and territorial expansion. Enthralled by Bismarck's achievement, many liberals abandoned liberalism and threw their support behind the authoritarian Prussian state. Germans of all classes acquired an adoration for Prussian militarism and for the power state, with its Machiavellian guideline that all means are justified if they result in the expansion of German power. In 1848, German liberals had called for "Unity and Freedom." What Bismarck gave them was unity and authoritarianism.

War with France Prussia emerged from the war with Austria as the leading power in the North German Confederation; the Prussian king controlled the armies and foreign affairs of the states within the confederation. To complete the unification of Germany, Bismarck would have to draw the South German states into the new German confederation. But the South German states, Catholic and hostile to Prussian authoritarianism, feared being absorbed by Prussia.

Map 14.2 Unification of Germany, 1866–1871 Between 1866 and 1871, Prussia fought wars against Denmark, Austria, and France, which resulted in the unification of Germany under Prussian leadership. Otto von Bismarck was the principal architect of German unification.

Bismarck hoped that a war between Prussia and France would ignite the nationalist feelings of the South Germans, causing them to overlook the differences that separated them from Prussia. If war with France would serve Bismarck's purpose, it was also not unthinkable to Napoleon III, the emperor of France. The creation of a powerful

North German Confederation had frightened the French, and the prospect that the South German states might one day add their strength to the new Germany was terrifying. Both France and Prussia had parties that advocated war.

A cause for war arose over the succession to the vacated Spanish throne. King William of

Prussia discussed the issue with the French ambassador and sent Bismarck a telegram informing him of what had ensued. With the support of high military leaders, Bismarck edited the telegram. The revised version gave the impression that the Prussian king and the French ambassador had insulted each other. Bismarck wanted to inflame French feeling against Prussia and arouse German opinion against France. He succeeded. In both Paris and Berlin, crowds of people, gripped by war fever, demanded satisfaction. When France declared a general mobilization, Prussia followed suit; Bismarck had his war.

As Bismarck had anticipated, the South German states came to the aid of Prussia. Quickly and decisively routing the French forces and capturing Napoleon III, the Prussians went on to besiege Paris. Faced with starvation, Paris surrendered in January 1871. France was compelled to pay a large indemnity and to cede to Germany the border provinces of Alsace and Lorraine—a loss that French patriots could never accept.

The Franco-Prussian War completed the unification of Germany. On January 18, 1871, at Versailles, the German princes granted the title of German kaiser (emperor) to William I. A powerful nation had arisen in central Europe. Its people were educated, disciplined, and efficient; its industries and commerce were rapidly expanding; its army was the finest in Europe. Vigorous, confident, and intensely nationalistic, the new German Empire was eager to play a greater role in world affairs. No nation in Europe was a match for the new Germany. Metternich's fears had been realized: a Germany dominated by Prussia had upset the balance of power. The unification of Germany created fears, tensions, and rivalries that would culminate in world wars.

NATIONALITY PROBLEMS IN THE HAPSBURG EMPIRE

In Italy and Germany, nationalism had led to the creation of unified states; in Austria, nationalism eventually caused the destruction of the centuries-old Hapsburg dynasty. A mosaic of different peoples, each with its own history and traditions, the Austrian Empire could not weld together and reconcile antagonistic nationalities when nationalistic consciousness was high. The empire's collapse in the final stages of World War I marked the end of years of hostility among its various subjects.

In the first half of the nineteenth century, the Germans, who constituted less than one-quarter of the population, were the dominant national group in the empire. But Magyars, Poles, Czechs, Slovaks, Croats, Romanians, Ruthenians, and Italians were experiencing national self-awareness. Poets and writers who had been educated in Latin, French, and German began to write in their mother tongue and extol its splendor. By searching their past for glorious ancestors and glorious deeds, writers kindled pride in their native history and folklore and aroused anger against past and present injustices.

In 1848–49, the Hapsburg monarchy had extinguished the Magyar bid for independence, the Czech revolution in Prague, and the uprisings in the Italian provinces of Lombardy and Venetia. Greatly alarmed by these revolutions, the Austrian power structure resolved to resist pressures for political rights by strengthening autocracy and tightening the central bureaucracy. German and Germanized officials took over administrative and judicial duties formerly handled on a local level. An expanded secret police stifled liberal and nationalist expressions. The various nationalities, of course, resented these efforts at centralization and repression.

The defeats by France and Piedmont in 1859 and by Prussia in 1866 cost Austria its two Italian provinces. The defeat by Prussia also forced the Hapsburg monarchy to make concessions to the Magyars, the strongest of the non-German nationalities: without a loyal Hungary, the Hapsburg monarchy could suffer other humiliations. The Settlement of 1867 split the Hapsburg territories into Austria and Hungary. The two countries retained a common ruler, Francis Joseph (1848–1916), who was emperor of Austria and king of Hungary. Hungary gained complete control over its internal affairs: the administration of justice and education. A ministry composed of delegates from both lands conducted foreign and military affairs and dealt with common financial concerns.

With the Settlement of 1867, Magyars and Germans became the dominant nationalities in

The Young Czech Party Demonstrating in the Austrian Parliament, 1900. The Hapsburg Empire was burdened by conflicts between its different nationalities. In Bohemia, Czechs and Germans often engaged in violent confrontations as Czechs pressed for recognition of their language and rights. (*Osterreichische Nationalbibliothek*)

the empire. The other nationalities felt that the German-Magyar political, economic, and cultural domination blocked their own national aspirations. Nationality struggles in the half-century following the Settlement of 1867 consumed the energies of the Austrians and Hungarians. In both lands, however, the leaders failed to solve the problem of minorities—a failure that helped to precipitate World War I and that ultimately led to the dissolution of the empire during the last weeks of the war.

❖   ❖   ❖

NOTES

1. Jacques Droz, *Europe Between Revolutions, 1815–1848* (New York: Harper Torchbooks, 1967), p. 248.

2. *The Recollections of Alexis de Tocqueville,* trans. Alexander Teixeira de Mattos (Cleveland, Ohio: Meridian Books, 1969), pp. 11–12.

3. Quoted in Hans Kohn, *Nationalism: Its Meaning and History* (Princeton, N.J.: Van Nostrand, 1965), pp. 51–52.

4. Lewis Namier, *1848: The Revolution of the Intellectuals* (Garden City, N.Y.: Doubleday, Anchor, 1964), p. 38.

SUGGESTED READING

Beales, Derek, *The Risorgimento and the Unifica-tion of Italy* (1971). A comprehensive overview, followed by documents.

Droz, Jacques, *Europe Between Revolutions, 1815–1848* (1967). A fine survey of the period.

Fasel, George, *Europe in Upheaval: The Revolutions of 1848* (1970). A good introduction.

Fejtö, François, ed., *The Opening of an Era: 1848* (1973). Contributions by nineteen eminent European historians.

Hamerow, T. S., *Restoration, Revolution, Reaction* (1958). An examination of economics and politics in Germany, 1815–1871, stressing the problems caused by the transition from agrarianism to industrialism.

———, ed., *Otto von Bismarck* (1962). A collection of readings from leading historians.

Hibbert, Christopher, *Garibaldi and His Enemies* (1965). A vivid portrait of the Italian hero.

Holborn, Hajo, *A History of Modern Germany, 1840–1945* (1969). A standard reference work.

Kohn, Hans, *Nationalism: Its Meaning and History* (1965). A concise history of modern nationalism by a leading student of the subject.

Langer, W. L., *Political and Social Upheaval, 1832–1852* (1969). Another volume in The Rise of Modern Europe series, by its editor. Rich in data and interpretation; contains a valuable bibliographical essay.

Pauley, B. F., *The Habsburg Legacy, 1867–1939* (1972). A good brief work on a complex subject.

Robertson, Priscilla, *Revolutions of 1848* (1960). Vividly portrays the events and the personalities involved.

Rodes, John E., *The Quest for Unity: Modern Germany, 1848–1970* (1971). A good survey of German history.

Sigmann, Jonathan, *1848: The Romantic and Democratic Revolutions in Europe* (1870). A useful survey.

Sperber, Jonathan, *The European Revolution, 1848–1851* (1994). A recent comprehensive overview.

Stearns, Peter N., *1848: The Revolutionary Tide in Europe* (1974). Strong on social factors.

Talmon, J. L., *Romanticism and Revolt* (1967). The forces shaping European history from 1815 to 1848.

REVIEW QUESTIONS

1. How did the Congress of Vienna violate the principle of nationalism? What was the chief accomplishment of the congress?

2. Between 1820 and 1832, where were revolutions suppressed, and how? Where were revolutions successful, and why?

3. What were the complaints of the urban poor to the new French government after the February revolution in 1848? What was the significance of the June Days in French history?

4. Why did the revolutions of 1848 fail in the German states, the Austrian Empire, and Italy?

5. What were the liberal gains of the revolutions of 1848? Why were liberals and nationalists disappointed with the results of these revolutions?

6. Mazzini was the soul, Cavour the brains, and Garibaldi the sword in the struggle for the unification of Italy. Discuss their participation in and contributions to the struggle.

7. Prussia's victory over Austria was a triumph for conservatism and a defeat for liberalism. Discuss this statement.

8. What was the significance of the Franco-Prussian War for European history?

9. In the Hapsburg Empire, nationalism was a force for disunity. Discuss this statement.

Chapter 15

Thought and Culture in the Mid-Nineteenth Century: Realism and Social Criticism

- **Realism and Naturalism**
- **Positivism**
- **Darwinism**
- **Marxism**
- **Liberalism in Transition**
- **Feminism: Extending the Principle of Equality**

*T*he second half of the nineteenth century was marked by great progress in science, a surge in industrialism, and a continuing secularization of life and thought. The main intellectual currents of the century's middle decades reflected these trends. Realism, positivism, Darwinism, Marxism, and liberalism all reacted against romantic, religious, and metaphysical interpretations of nature and society, focusing instead on the empirical world. Adherents of these movements relied on careful observation and strove for scientific accuracy. This emphasis on objective reality helped to stimulate a growing criticism of social ills; for despite unprecedented material progress, reality was often sordid, somber, and dehumanizing. ❖

REALISM AND NATURALISM

Realism, the dominant movement in art and literature in the mid-nineteenth century, opposed the romantic veneration of the inner life and romantic sentimentality. The romantics exalted passion and intuition, let their imaginations transport them to a presumed idyllic medieval past, and sought inner solitude amid nature's wonders. Realists, on the other hand, concentrated on the actual world: social conditions, contemporary manners, and the familiar details of everyday life. With clinical detachment and meticulous care, they analyzed how people looked, worked, and behaved.

Like scientists, realist writers and artists carefully investigated the empirical world. For example, Gustave Courbet (1819–1877), who exemplified realism in painting, sought to practice what he called a "living art." He painted common people and commonplace scenes: laborers breaking stones, peasants tilling the soil or returning from a fair, a country burial, wrestlers, bathers, family groups. In a matter-of-fact style that sought to reproduce the environment just as it is, without any attempt at glorification or deviation, realist artists also depicted floor scrapers, rag pickers, prostitutes, and beggars.

Seeking to portray life as it is, realist writers frequently dealt with social abuses and the sordid aspects of human behavior and social life. In his novels, Honoré de Balzac (1799–1850) described how social and economic forces affected people's behavior. Ivan Turgenev's *Sketches* (1852) portrayed rural conditions in Russia and expressed compassion for the brutally difficult life of serfs. In *War and Peace* (1863–1869), Leo Tolstoy vividly described the manners and outlook of the Russian nobility and the tragedies that attended Napoleon's invasion of Russia. In *Anna Karenina* (1873–1877), he treated the reality of class divisions and the complexities of marital relationships. The novels of Charles Dickens—*Bleak House* (1853), *Hard Times* (1854), and several others—depicted the squalor of life, the hypocrisy of society, and the drudgery of labor in British industrial cities.

Many regard Gustave Flaubert's *Madame Bovary* (1857) as the quintessential realistic novel; it tells the story of a self-centered wife who shows her hatred for her devoted, hardworking, but dull husband by committing adultery. Commenting on the realism of *Madame Bovary,* one critic noted that it "represents an obsession with description. Details are counted one by one, all are given equal value, every street, every house, every book, every blade of grass is described in full."[1]

Literary realism evolved into naturalism when writers tried to demonstrate a causal relationship between human character and the social environment: that certain conditions of life produced predictable character traits in human beings. The belief that the law of cause and effect governed human behavior reflected the immense prestige attached to science in the closing decades of the nineteenth century. The leading naturalist novelist, Émile Zola (1840–1902), probed the slums, brothels, mining villages, and cabarets of France, examining how people were conditioned by the squalor of their environment. Henrik Ibsen (1828–1906), a Norwegian and the leading naturalist playwright, examined with clinical precision the commercial and professional classes, their personal ambitions and family relationships. His *Pillars of Society* (1877) scrutinized bourgeois social pretensions and hypocrisy. In *A Doll's House* (1879), he took up a theme that shocked the late-nineteenth-century bourgeois audience: a woman leaving her husband to seek a more fulfilling life.

In striving for a true-to-life portrayal of human behavior and the social environment, realism and naturalism reflected attitudes shaped by science, industrialism, and secularism, which stressed the importance of the external world. The same outlook also gave rise to positivism in philosophy.

Interior by Edgar Degas, 1868–1869. Set in a world of poor shopkeepers and clerks, *Thérèse Raquin* (1867) was Émile Zola's first great success as a naturalist novelist. This Degas painting depicts the sexual tension and violent emotions that Zola sought to uncover in his work. (*Philadelphia Museum of Art, The Henry P. McIlhenny Collection in Memory of Francis P. McIlhenny*)

POSITIVISM

Positivists viewed science as the highest achievement of the mind and sought to apply a strict empirical approach to the study of society. They believed that the philosopher must proceed like a scientist, carefully assembling and classifying data and formulating general rules that demonstrate regularities in the social experience. Such knowledge, based on concrete facts, would provide the social planner with useful insights. Positivists rejected metaphysics, which, in the tradition of Plato, tried to discover ultimate principles through reason alone, rather than through observation of the empirical world. For positivists, any effort to go beyond the realm of experience to a deeper reality would be a mistaken and fruitless endeavor.

Auguste Comte (1798–1857), the father of positivism, called for a purely scientific approach to history and society: only through a proper understanding of the laws governing human affairs could society, which was in a state of intellectual anarchy, be rationally reorganized. Comte named his system *positivism* because he believed that it rested on sure knowledge derived from observed facts and was therefore empirically verifiable. Like others of his generation, Comte believed that scientific laws underlay human affairs and could be discovered through the methods of the empirical scientist—that is, through recording and systematizing observable data. "I shall bring factual proof," he said, "that there are just as definite laws for the development of the human race as there are for the fall of a stone."[2]

One of the laws that Comte believed he had discovered was the "law of the three stages." The human mind, he asserted, had progressed through three broad historical stages: the theological, the metaphysical, and the scientific. In the theological stage, the most primitive of the three, the mind found a supernatural explanation for the origins and purpose of things, and society was ruled by priests. In the metaphysical stage, which included the Enlightenment, the mind tried to explain things through abstractions—such as "nature," "equality," "natural rights," or "popular sovereignty"—that rested on hope and belief rather than on empirical investigation. The metaphysical stage was a transitional period between the infantile theological stage and the highest stage of society, the scientific, or positive, stage. In this culminating stage, the mind breaks with all illusions inherited from the past, formulates laws based on careful observation of the empirical world, and reconstructs society in accordance with these laws. People remove all mystery from nature and base their social legislation on laws of society similar to the laws of nature discovered by Newton.

DARWINISM

In a century distinguished by scientific discoveries, perhaps the most important scientific advance was the theory of evolution formulated by Charles Darwin (1809–1882), an English naturalist. Darwin did for his discipline what Newton had done for physics: he made biology an objective science based on general principles. The Scientific Revolution of the seventeenth century had given people a new conception of space; Darwin radically altered our conception of time and biological life, including human origins.

Natural Selection

During the eighteenth century, almost all people had adhered to the biblical account of creation contained in Genesis: God had instantaneously created every river and mountain and the various species of animal and plant life, giving each species a finished and permanent form distinct from that of every other species. God had designed the bird's wings so that it could fly, the fish's eyes so that it could see under water, and the human's legs so that people could walk. All this, it was believed, had occurred some five or six thousand years ago.

Gradually, this view was questioned. In 1794, Erasmus Darwin, the grandfather of Charles Darwin, published *Zoonomia, or the Laws of Organic Life,* which offered evidence that the earth had existed for millions of years before the appearance of people and that animals experienced modifications, which they passed on to their offspring. Nearly forty years later, Sir Charles Lyell published his three-volume *Principles of Geology* (1830–1833), which showed that the planet had evolved slowly over many ages.

In December 1831, Charles Darwin sailed as a naturalist on the H.M.S. *Beagle,* which surveyed the shores of South America and some Pacific islands. During the five-year expedition, Darwin collected and examined specimens of plant and animal life; he concluded that many animal species had perished, that new species had emerged, and that there were links between extinct and living species. In the *Origin of Species* (1859) and the *Descent of Man* (1871), Darwin used empirical evidence to show that the wide variety of animal species was due to a process of development over many millennia, and he supplied a convincing theory that explained how evolution operates.

Darwin adopted the Malthusian idea (see "Responses to Industrialization" in the chapter entitled "The Industrial Revolution: The Transformation of Society") that the population reproduces faster than the food supply, causing a struggle for existence. Not all infant organisms grow to adulthood; not all adult organisms live to old age. The principle of *natural selection* determines which members of the species have a better chance of survival. The offspring of lions, giraffes, or insects are not exact duplications of their parents. A baby lion might have the potential for being slightly faster or stronger than its parents; a baby giraffe might grow up to have a longer neck than its parents; an insect might have a slightly different color.

These small and random variations give the organism a crucial advantage in the struggle for food and against natural enemies. The organism favored by nature is more likely to reach maturity, to mate, and to pass on its superior qualities to its offspring, some of which will acquire the advantageous trait to an even greater degree than the parent. Over many generations, the favorable characteristic becomes more pronounced and more widespread within the species. Over millennia, natural selection causes the death of old, less adaptable species and the creation of new ones. Very few of the species that dwelt on earth ten million years ago still survive, and many new ones, including human beings, have emerged. People themselves are products of natural selection, evolving from earlier, lower, nonhuman forms of life.

Darwinism and Christianity

Like Newton's law of universal gravitation, Darwin's theory of evolution had revolutionary consequences in areas other than science. Evolution challenged traditional Christian belief. To some, it undermined the infallibility of Scripture and the conviction that the Bible was indeed the Word of God.

Darwin's theory touched off a great religious controversy between fundamentalists, who defended a literal interpretation of Genesis, and advocates of the new biology. A Methodist publication contended: "We regard this theory, which seeks to eliminate from the universe the immediate, ever-present, all pervasive action of a living and personal God, which excludes the possibility of the supernatural and the miraculous . . . as practically destructive of the authority of divine revelation, and subversive of the foundation of religion and morality."[3] In time, most religious thinkers tried to reconcile evolution with the Christian view that there was a creation and that it had a purpose. These Christian thinkers held that modifications within a species were made by an intelligent creator—that God created and then directed the evolutionary process, that he steered evolution so that it would culminate in the human being.

Darwinism ultimately helped end the practice of relying on the Bible as an authority in questions of science, completing a trend initiated earlier by Galileo. Darwinism contributed to the waning of religious belief and to a growing secular attitude that dismissed or paid scant attention to the Christian view of a universe designed by God and a soul that rises to heaven.

For many, the conclusion seemed inescapable: nature contained no divine design or purpose,

and the human species itself was a chance product of impersonal forces. The core idea of Christianity—that people were children of God participating in a drama of salvation—rested more than ever on faith rather than reason. Some even talked openly about the death of God. The notion that people are sheer accidents of nature was shocking. Copernicanism had deprived people of the comforting belief that the earth had been placed in the center of the universe just for them; Darwinism deprived people of the privilege of being God's special creation, thereby contributing to the feeling of anxiety that characterized the twentieth century.

Social Darwinism

Darwin's theories were extended by others beyond the realm in which he had worked. Social thinkers recklessly applied Darwin's conclusions to the social order and produced theories that had dangerous consequences for society. (Occasionally Darwin himself departed from his rigorous empiricism and drew murky conclusions about the mentally and physically handicapped and what he termed the "savage races.") Social Darwinists—those who transferred Darwin's scientific theories to social and economic issues—used the terms "struggle for existence" and "survival of the fittest" to buttress an often brutal economic individualism and political conservatism. Successful businessmen, they said, had demonstrated their fitness to prevail in the competitive world of business. Their success accorded with nature's laws and therefore was beneficial to society; those who lost out in the socioeconomic struggle demonstrated their unfitness. Traditionally, failure had been ascribed to human wickedness or to God's plan. Now it was being attributed to an inferior hereditary endowment.

Using Darwin's model of organisms evolving and changing slowly over tens of thousands of years, conservatives insisted that society, too, should experience change at an unhurried pace. Instant reforms conflicted with nature's laws and wisdom and resulted in a deterioration of the social body.

The application of Darwin's biological concepts to the social world, where they did not

A Caricature of Darwin. Darwin's theory of evolution created much controversy and aroused considerable bitterness. In this caricature, the apelike Darwin, holding a mirror, is explaining his theory of evolution to a fellow ape. (*Corbis/Bettman/Hulton Picture Company*)

apply, also buttressed imperialism, racism, nationalism, and militarism—doctrines that preached relentless conflict. Social Darwinists insisted that nations and races were engaged in a struggle for survival in which only the fittest survive and deserve to survive. In their view, war was nature's way of eliminating the unfit. Karl Pearson, a British professor of mathematics, wrote in *National Life from the Standpoint of Science* (1900): "History shows me only one way, and one way only in which a higher state of civilization has been produced, namely the struggle of race with race, and the survival of the physically and mentally fitter race."[4] "We are a conquering race," said U.S. Senator Albert J. Beveridge. "We must obey our blood and occupy new markets, and if necessary, new lands."[5] "War is a biological necessity of the first importance,"[6] asserted the Prussian general Friedrich von Bernhardi in *Germany and the Next War* (1911).

Darwinian biology was used to promote the belief in Anglo-Saxon (British and American) and Teutonic (German) racial superiority. Social Darwinists attributed to racial qualities the growth of the British Empire, the expansion of the United States to the Pacific, and the extension of German power. The domination of other peoples—American Indians, Africans, Asians, Poles—was regarded as the natural right of the superior race.

Social Darwinism also affected racial attitudes in the United States. Too willingly, scholars, joining antiblack polemicists, attributed an inferior biological inheritance to blacks, and some predicted their extinction, seeing them as losers in the Darwinian struggle for existence. Thus, in 1905, William B. Smith, a Tulane University professor, wrote: "The vision . . . of a race vanishing before its superior is not at all dispiriting, but inspiring. . . . The doom that awaits the Negro has been prepared in like measures for all inferior races."[7]

The theory of evolution was a great achievement of the rational mind, but in the hands of the Social Darwinists it served to undermine the Enlightenment tradition. Whereas the philosophes emphasized human equality, Social Darwinists divided humanity into racial superiors and inferiors. The philosophes believed that states would increasingly submit to the rule of law to reduce violent conflicts; Social Darwinists, on the other hand, regarded racial and national conflict as a biological necessity, a law of history, and a means to progress. In propagating a tooth-and-claw version of human and international relations, Social Darwinists dispensed with the humanitarian and cosmopolitan sentiments of the philosophes and distorted the image of progress. Their views promoted territorial aggrandizement and military buildup and led many to welcome World War I. The Social Darwinist notion of the struggle of races for survival became a core doctrine of the

Nazi party after World War I and helped to provide the "scientific" and "ethical" justification for genocide.

MARXISM

The failure of the revolutions of 1848 and a growing fear of working-class violence led liberals to abandon revolution and to press for reforms through the political process. In the last part of the nineteenth century, socialists and anarchists became the chief proponents of revolution. Both liberalism and Marxism shared common principles derived from the Enlightenment. Their adherents believed in the essential goodness and perfectibility of human nature and claimed that their doctrines rested on rational foundations. They wanted to free individuals from the accumulated superstition, ignorance, and prejudices of the past and to fashion a more harmonious and rational society. Both liberals and Marxists believed in social progress and valued the full realization of human talents.

Despite these similarities, liberalism and Marxism differed profoundly. The goal of Marxism—the seizure of power by the working class and the destruction of capitalism—was inimical to bourgeois liberals. So, too, was the Marxist belief that violence and struggle were the essence of history, the instruments of progress, and the vehicle to a higher stage of humanity. Liberals, who placed the highest value on the individual, held that through education and self-discipline people could overcome inequality and poverty. Marxists, however, insisted that without a transformation of the economic system, individual effort by the downtrodden would amount to very little.

Karl Marx (1818–1883) was born of German-Jewish parents (both descendants of prominent rabbis). To save his job as a lawyer, Marx's father converted to Protestantism. Enrolled at a university to study law, Marx switched to philosophy. In 1842, he was editing a newspaper, which was soon suppressed by the Prussian authorities for its outspoken ideas. Leaving his native Rhineland, Marx went to Paris, where he met another German, Friedrich Engels (1820–1895), who was the son of a prosperous textile manufacturer. Marx and Engels entered into a lifelong collaboration and became members of socialist groups. In February 1848, they published the *Communist Manifesto,* which called for a working-class revolution to overthrow the capitalist system. Forced to leave France in 1849 because of his political views, Marx moved to London, where he remained to the end of his life. There he spent years writing *Capital*—a study and critique of the modern capitalistic economic system, which, he predicted, would be destroyed by a socialist revolution.

A Science of History

As did other thinkers influenced by the Enlightenment, Marx believed that human history, like the operations of nature, was governed by scientific law. Marx was a strict materialist: rejecting all religious and metaphysical interpretations of both nature and history, he sought to fashion an empirical science of society. He viewed religion as a human creation—a product of people's imagination and feelings, a consolation for the oppressed—and the happiness it brought as an illusion. Real happiness would come, said Marx, not by transcending the natural world but by improving it. Rather than deluding oneself by seeking refuge from life's misfortunes in an imaginary world, one must confront the ills of society and reform them. This last point was crucial: "The philosophers have only *interpreted* the world in different ways; the point is to *change* it."[8]

The world could be rationally understood and changed, said Marx. People were free to make their own history, but to do so effectively, they must grasp the inner meaning of history: the laws governing human affairs in the past and operating in the present. Marx adopted Hegel's view that history was not an assortment of unrelated and disconnected events, but a progressive development, which, like the growth of a plant, proceeded ineluctably according to its own inner laws (see the section on Hegel in the chapter on "Thought and Culture in the Early Nineteenth Century). For both Hegel and Marx, the historical process was governed by objective and rational principles. Marx also adopted Hegel's view that history advanced dialectically—that the clash of opposing forces propelled history into higher stages.

Karl Marx. Interpreting history in economic terms, Marx predicted that socialism would replace capitalism. He called for the proletariat to overthrow capitalism and to establish a classless society. (*Corbis/Bettmann*)

which cried out for understanding and solution; it was a negation of life.

For Marx, history was explainable solely in terms of natural processes—empirically verifiable developments. Marx valued Hegel's insight that history is a progressive and purposeful process, but he criticized Hegel for embedding his insights in metaphysical theological fantasy. Hegel, said Marx, had made a mystical principle the real subject of history and thought. But, in truth, it is the real human being, the person living in and conditioned by the objective world—the only true reality—who is the center of history. History is not Spirit aspiring to self-actualization but people becoming fully human, fulfilling their human potential.

For Marx, the moving forces in history were economic and technological factors: the ways in which goods are produced and wealth distributed. They accounted for historical change and were the basis of all culture—politics, law, religion, morals, and philosophy. "The history of humanity," he concluded, "must therefore always be studied and treated in relation to the history of industry and exchange."[9] Marx said that material technology—the methods of cultivating land and the tools for manufacturing goods—determined society's social and political arrangements and its intellectual outlook. For example, the hand mill, the loose yoke, and the wooden plow had given rise to feudal lords, whereas power-driven machines had spawned the industrial capitalists.

However, Marx also broke with Hegel in crucial ways. For Hegel, it was the dialectical clash of opposing ideas that moved history into the next stage; for Marx, it was the clash of classes representing conflicting economic interests—what is called dialectical materialism—that accounted for historical change and progress. In Hegel's view, history was the unfolding of the metaphysical Spirit, and a higher stage of development was produced by the synthesis of opposing ideas. According to Marx, Hegel's system suffered from mystification. It transcended the realities of the known world; it downgraded the real world, which became a mere attribute of Spirit. Marx saw Hegel's abstract philosophy as diverting attention from the real world and its problems,

Class Conflict

Throughout history, said Marx, there has been a class struggle between those who own the means of production and those whose labor has been exploited to provide wealth for this upper class. The opposing tension between classes has pushed history forward into higher stages. In the ancient world, when wealth was based on land, the struggle was between master and slave, patrician and plebeian; during the Middle Ages, when land was still the predominant mode of production, the struggle was between lord and serf. In the modern industrial world, two sharply opposed classes were confronting each other: the capitalists who owned the factories, mines, banks, and transportation systems, and the exploited wage earners (the proletariat).

According to Marx and Engels, the class with economic power also controlled the state. That class used political power to protect and increase its property and to hold down the laboring class. "Thus the ancient State was above all the slave-owners' state for holding down the slaves," said Engels, "as a feudal State was the organ of the nobles for holding down the . . . serfs, and the modern representative State is the instrument of the exploitation of wage-labor by capital."[10]

Furthermore, Marx and Engels asserted, the class that controlled material production also controlled mental production: that is, the ideas held by the ruling class became the dominant ideas of society. These ideas, presented as laws of nature or moral and religious standards, were regarded as the truth by oppressor and oppressed alike. In reality, however, these ideas merely reflected the special economic interests of the ruling class. Thus, said Marx, bourgeois ideologists would insist that natural rights and laissez-faire economics were laws of nature having universal validity. But these "laws" were born of the needs of the bourgeoisie in its struggle to wrest power from an obsolete feudal regime and to protect its property from the state. Similarly, nineteenth-century slave owners convinced themselves that slavery was morally right—that it had God's approval and was good for the slave. Slave owners and capitalist employers alike may have defended their labor systems by citing universal principles that they thought were true, but in reality their systems rested on a simple economic consideration: slave labor was good for the pocketbook of the slave owner, and wage labor was good in the same way for the capitalist. They were unaware of the real forces motivating their thinking.

The Destruction of Capitalism

Under capitalism, said Marx, workers knew only poverty. They worked long hours for low wages, suffered from periodic unemployment, and lived in squalid, overcrowded dwellings. Most monstrous of all, they were forced to send their young children into the factories.

Capitalism, as Marx saw it, also produced another kind of poverty: poverty of the human spirit. Under capitalism, the factory worker was reduced to a laboring beast, performing tedious and repetitive tasks in a dark, dreary, dirty cave—an altogether inhuman environment that deprived people of their human sensibilities. Unlike the artisans in their own shops, factory workers found no pleasure and took no pride in their work; they did not have the satisfaction of creating a finished product that expressed their skills. Work, said Marx, should be a source of fulfillment for people. It should enable people to affirm their personalities and develop their potential. By treating people not as human beings but as cogs in the production process, capitalism alienated people from their work, themselves, and one another.

Marx believed that capitalist control of the economy and the government would not endure forever; capitalist society produced its own gravediggers—the working class. The capitalist system would perish just as the feudal society of the Middle Ages and the slave society of the ancient world had perished. From the ruins of a dead capitalist society, a new socioeconomic system, socialism, would emerge.

Marx predicted how capitalism would be destroyed. Periodic unemployment would increase the misery of the workers and intensify their hatred of capitalists. Owners of small businesses and shopkeepers, unable to compete with the great capitalists, would sink into the ranks of the working class, greatly expanding its numbers. Society would become polarized into a small group of immensely wealthy capitalists and a vast proletariat, poor, embittered, and desperate. This monopoly of capital by the few would become a brake on the productive process.

Growing increasingly conscious of their misery, the workers—aroused, educated, and organized by Communist intellectuals—would revolt. "Revolution is necessary," said Marx, "not only because the *ruling class* cannot be overthrown in any other way, but also because only in a revolution *can the class which overthrows it* rid itself of the accumulated rubbish of the past and become capable of reconstructing society."[11] The working-class revolutionaries would smash the government that helped the capitalists maintain their dominance. Then they would confiscate the property of the capitalists, abolish private property, place the means of production in the workers' hands, and organize a new society. The *Communist Manifesto* ends with a ringing call for revolution: "The Communists . . . openly declare that their ends can be attained only by the forcible overthrow of all existing social conditions. Let the ruling classes tremble at a Communist revolution. The proletarians have nothing to lose but their chains. They have a world to win. Workingmen of all countries, unite!"[12]

Marx did not say a great deal about the new society that would be ushered in by the socialist revolution. With the destruction of capitalism, the distinction between capitalist and worker would cease, and with it the class conflict. No longer would society be divided into haves and have-nots, oppressor and oppressed. Since this classless society would contain no exploiters, there would be no need for a state, which was merely an instrument for maintaining and protecting the power of the exploiting class. Thus, the state would eventually wither away. The production and distribution of goods would be carried out through community planning and communal sharing, which would replace the capitalist system of competition. People would work at varied tasks, just as Fourier (see "Responses to Industrialization" in the chapter entitled "The Industrial Revolution: The Transformation of Society") had advocated, rather than being confined to one form of employment. No longer factory slaves, people would be free to fulfill their human potential, to improve their relationships on a basis of equality with others, and to work together for the common good.

Marxism had immense appeal both for the downtrodden and for intellectuals. It promised to end the injustices of industrial society; it claimed the certainty of science; and it assured adherents that the triumph of their cause was guaranteed by history. In many ways, Marxism was a secular religion: the proletariat became a chosen class, endowed with a mission to achieve worldly salvation for humanity.

Marx's influence grew during the second wave of industrialization, in the closing decades of the nineteenth century, when class bitterness between the proletariat and the bourgeoisie seemed to worsen. Many workers thought that liberals and conservatives had no sympathy for their plight and that the only way to improve their lot was through socialist parties.

Critics of Marx

Critics point out serious weaknesses in Marxism. The rigid Marxist who tries to squeeze all historical events into an economic framework is at a disadvantage. Economic forces alone will not explain the triumph of Christianity in the Roman Empire, the fall of Rome, the Crusades, the French Revolution, modern imperialism, World War I, or the rise of Hitler. Economic explanations fall particularly flat in trying to account for the emergence of modern nationalism, whose appeal, resting on deeply ingrained emotional needs, crosses class lines. The greatest struggles of the twentieth century have been not between classes but between nations.

Many of Marx's predictions or expectations failed to materialize. Workers in Western lands did not become the oppressed and impoverished working class that Marx had described in the mid-nineteenth century. Because of increased productivity and the efforts of labor unions and reform-minded governments, Western workers improved their lives considerably, so that they now enjoy the highest standard of living in history. The tremendous growth of a middle class of professionals, civil service employees, and small-business people belies Marx's prediction that capitalist society would be polarized into a small group of very rich capitalists and a great mass of destitute workers.

Marx believed that socialist revolutions would break out in the advanced industrialized lands. But the socialist revolutions of the twentieth century have occurred in underdeveloped, predominantly agricultural countries. The state in Communist lands, far from withering away, grew more centralized, powerful, and oppressive. In no country where Communist revolutionaries have seized power have people achieved the liberty that Marx desired. Nor, indeed, have Communists been able to sustain a viable economic system. The phenomenal collapse of Communist regimes in the former Soviet Union and Eastern Europe in recent years testifies to Marxism's failure. All these failed predictions and expectations seem to contradict Marx's claim that his theories rested on an unassailable scientific foundation.

LIBERALISM IN TRANSITION

In the early part of the nineteenth century, European liberals were preoccupied with protecting the rights of the individual against the demands of the state. They championed laissez faire because they feared that state interference in the economy to redress social evils would threaten individual rights and the free market, which they thought were essential to personal liberty. They favored property requirements for voting and officeholding because they were certain that the unpropertied and uneducated masses lacked the wisdom and experience to exercise political responsibility.

In the last part of the century, liberals began to support—though not without reservation and qualification—both extended suffrage and government action to remedy the abuses of unregulated industrialization. This growing concern for the welfare of the laboring poor coincided with and was influenced by an unprecedented proliferation of humanitarian movements on both sides of the Atlantic. Nurtured by both the Enlightenment and Christian teachings, reform movements called for the prohibition of child labor, schooling for the masses, humane treatment for prisoners and the mentally ill, equality for women, the abolition of slavery, and an end to war. By the beginning of the twentieth century, liberalism had evolved into liberal democracy, and laissez faire had been superseded by a reluctant acceptance of social legislation and government regulation. But from beginning to end, the central concern of liberals remained the protection of individual rights.

ment of individual freedom and minority rights: that the government and the majority may not interfere with the liberty of another human being whose actions do no injury to others.

Mill regarded freedom of thought and expression and the toleration of opposing and unpopular viewpoints as necessary preconditions for the shaping of a rational, moral, and civilized citizen. Political or social coercion, said Mill, is also a barrier to the full development of the individual. Liberty is a supreme good that benefits both the individual and the community. When we silence an opinion, said Mill, we hurt present and future generations. If the opinion is correct, "we are deprived of the opportunity of exchanging error for truth." If the opinion is wrong—and of this we can never be entirely certain—we "lose the clearer perception and livelier impression of truth produced by its collision with error."[13] Therefore, government has no right to force an individual to hold a view "because it will be better for him to do so, or because it will make him happier, or because in the opinions of others, to do so would be wise, or even right. These are good reasons for remonstrating with him, or reasoning with him, or persuading him, or entreating him, but not for compelling him or visiting him with any evil in case he do otherwise."[14]

Mill would place limits on the power of government, for in an authoritarian state citizens cannot develop their moral and intellectual potential. Although he feared the state as a threat to individual liberty, Mill also recognized the necessity for state intervention to promote individual self-development: the expansion of individual moral, intellectual, and esthetic capacities. For example, he maintained that it was permissible for the state to require children to attend school against the wishes of their parents, to regulate hours of labor, to promote health, and to provide workers' compensation and old-age insurance.

John Stuart Mill

The transition from laissez-faire liberalism to a more socially conscious and democratic liberalism is seen in the thought of John Stuart Mill (1806–1873), a British philosopher and statesman. Mill's *On Liberty* (1859) is the classic state-

Thomas Hill Green

Four thinkers stood out in the late 1800s as the leading figures in the shaping of a new liberal position in Britain: Thomas Hill Green (1836–1882), an Oxford University professor; D. G. Ritchie (1853–1903), who taught philosophy at

Oxford and Saint Andrews; J. A. Hobson (1858–1940), a social theorist; and L. T. Hobhouse (1864–1929), an academic who also wrote for the *Manchester Guardian*. In general, they argued that laissez faire protected the interests of the economically powerful class and ignored the welfare of the nation. For example, Green valued private property but could not see how this principle helped the poor. "A man who possesses nothing but his powers of labor and who has to sell these to a capitalist for bare daily maintenance, might as well . . . be denied rights of property altogether."[15]

Green argued that the do-nothing state advocated by traditional laissez-faire liberalism condemned many citizens to destitution, ignorance, and despair. The state must preserve individual liberty and at the same time secure the common good by promoting conditions favorable for the self-development of the majority of the population.

Liberalism, for Green, encompassed more than the protection of individual rights from an oppressive government. A truly liberal society, he said, gives people the opportunity to fulfill their moral potential and human capacities. And social reforms initiated by the state assisted in the realization of this broader conception of liberty. Green and other advocates of state intervention contended that the government has a moral obligation to create social conditions that permit individuals to make the best of themselves. Toward that end, the state should promote public health, ensure decent housing, and provide for education. The uneducated and destitute person cannot be morally self-sufficient or a good citizen, Green and other progressives argued.

Green and his colleagues remained advocates of capitalism but rejected strict laissez faire, which, they said, benefited only a particular class at the expense of the common good. Overcoming a traditional liberal mistrust of state power, they viewed the state as an ethical institution, assigned it a positive role in improving social conditions, and insisted that state actions need not threaten individual freedom.

In general, by the beginning of the twentieth century, liberals in Britain increasingly acknowledged the need for social legislation; the foundations for the British welfare state were being laid. On the Continent, too, social welfare laws were enacted. To be sure, the motives behind such legislation were quite diverse and often had little to do with liberal sentiments. Nevertheless, in several countries, liberalism was expanding into political and social democracy, a trend that would continue in the twentieth century.

FEMINISM: EXTENDING THE PRINCIPLE OF EQUALITY

Another example of the expansion of liberalism was the emergence of feminist movements in Western Europe and the United States. Feminists insisted that the principles of liberty and equality expressed by the philosophes and embodied in the French Declaration of the Rights of Man and of the Citizen and the American Declaration of Independence be applied to women. Thus, Olympe de Gouges's *Declaration of the Rights of Women* (1791), modeled after the Declaration of the Rights of Man and of the Citizen, the French Revolution's tribute to Enlightenment ideals, stated: "Woman is born free and remains equal to man in rights. . . . The aim of every political association is the preservation of the natural . . . rights of man and woman."[16] And in 1837, English novelist and economist Harriet Martineau observed: "One of the fundamental principles announced in the Declaration of Independence is that governments derive their just power from the consent of the governed. How can the political condition of women be reconciled with this?"[17]

In the United States, in the 1830s, Angelina and Sarah Grimké spoke in public—something women rarely did—against slavery and for women's rights. In 1838, Sarah Grimké published *Letters on the Equality of the Sexes and the Condition of Women*, in which she stated emphatically: "Men and women were Created Equal: they are both moral and accountable beings, and whatever is *right* for man to do is *right* for women. . . . How monstrous, how anti-Christian, is the doctrine that woman is to be dependent on man!"[18] The Woman's Suffrage Movement, holding its first convention in 1848 in Seneca Falls, New York, drew up a Declaration of Statements and Principles that broadened the Declaration of Independence: "We hold these truths to be

Elizabeth Cady Stanton and Women's Rights

An American Feminist. Elizabeth Cady Stanton, who participated in the antislavery movement, was a principal founder of the American Woman's suffragist Movement, which held its first convention in 1848 in Seneca Falls, New York. (*Bettmann/Corbis*)

self-evident: that all men and women are created equal." The document protested "that woman has too long rested satisfied in the circumscribed limits which corrupt customs and a perverted application of the Scriptures have marked out for her" and called for the untiring effort of both men and women to secure for women "an equal participation with men in the various trades, professions, and commerce."[19]

In their struggle for equality, feminists had to overcome deeply ingrained premises about female inferiority and deficiencies. Opponents of women's rights argued that feminist demands would threaten society by undermining marriage and the family. An article in the *Saturday Review,* an English periodical, declared that "it is not the interest of States . . . to encourage the existence of women who are other than entirely dependent on man as well for subsistence as for protection and love. . . . Married life is a woman's profession."[20] In 1870, a member of the House of Commons wondered "what would become, not merely of woman's influence, but of her duties at home, her care of the household, her supervision of all those duties and surroundings which make a happy home . . . if we are to see women coming forward and taking part in the government of the country."[21] This concern for the family combined with the traditional, biased view of woman's nature, as one writer for the *Saturday Review* revealed:

> *The power of reasoning is so small in women that they need adventitious help, and if they have not the guidance and check of a religious conscience, it is useless to expect from them self-control on abstract principles. They do not calculate consequences, and they are reckless when they once give way, hence they are to be kept straight only through their affections, the religious sentiment and a well-educated moral sense.*[22]

In contrast to most of their contemporaries, some prominent men did support equal rights for women. "Can man be free if woman be slave?"[23] asked the poet Shelley, who favored female suffrage. So, too, did social theorist Jeremy Bentham and political economist William Thompson, who wrote *Appeal of One Half of the Human Race* (1825). John Stuart Mill thought that differences between the sexes (and between the classes) were due far more to education than to inherited inequalities. Believing that all people—women as well as men—should be able to develop their talents and intellects as fully as possible, Mill was an early champion of female equality, including women's suffrage. In 1867, Mill, as a member of Parliament, proposed that the suffrage be extended to women (the proposal was rejected by a vote of 194 to 74).

In 1851, Mill had married Harriet Taylor, a long-time friend and a recent widow. An ardent feminist, Harriet Mill influenced her husband's thought. In *The Subjection of Women* (1869),

Mill argued that male dominance of women constituted a flagrant abuse of power. He described female inequality as a single relic of an old outlook that had been exploded in everything else. It violated the principle of individual rights and hindered the progress of humanity:

> . . . the principle which regulates the existing social relations between the two sexes—the legal subordination of one sex to the other—is wrong in itself, and now one of the chief hin-

> drances to human improvement . . . it ought to be replaced by a principle of perfect equality, admitting no power or privilege on the one side, nor disability on the other.[24]

Mill considered it only just that women be free to take on all the functions and enter all the occupations until then reserved for men. The struggle for female rights became a major issue in several lands at the end of the nineteenth century and the beginning of the twentieth.

❖   ❖   ❖

NOTES

1. Quoted in Leonard J. Davis, "Gustave Flaubert," in The Romantic Century, vol. 7 of European Writers, ed. Jacques Barzun and George Stade (New York: Charles Scribner's Sons, 1985), p. 1382.

2. Quoted in Ernst Cassirer, The Problem of Knowledge, trans. William H. Woglom and Charles W. Hendel (New Haven, Conn.: Yale University Press, 1950), p. 244.

3. Excerpted in Richard Olson, ed., Science as Metaphor (Belmont, Calif.: Wadsworth, 1971), p. 124.

4. Karl Pearson, National Life from the Standpoint of Science (London: Adam & Charles Black, 1905), p. 21.

5. Quoted in H. W. Koch, "Social Darwinism in the 'New Imperialism,'" in The Origins of the First World War, ed. H. W. Koch (New York: Taplinger, 1972), p. 345.

6. Friedrich von Bernhardi, Germany and the Next War, trans. Allen H. Powles (New York: Longman, Green, 1914), p. 18.

7. Quoted in George M. Fredrickson, The Black Image in the White Mind (New York: Harper Torchbooks, 1972), pp. 26–27.

8. Karl Marx, Theses on Feuerbach, excerpted in Karl Marx: Selected Writings in Sociology and Social Philosophy, ed. T. B. Bottomore and Maximilien Rubel (London: Watts, 1956), p. 69.

9. Karl Marx, The German Ideology (New York: International Publishers, 1939), p. 18.

10. Friedrich Engels, The Origin of the Family, Private Property & the State, in A Handbook of Marxism, ed. Emile Burns (New York: Random House, 1935), p. 330.

11. Marx, German Ideology, p. 69.

12. Karl Marx, Communist Manifesto, trans. Samuel Moore (Chicago: Henry Regnery, 1954), pp. 81–82.

13. John Stuart Mill, On Liberty (Boston: Ticknor & Fields, 1863), p. 36.

14. Ibid., p. 22.

15. Thomas Hill Green, Lectures on the Principles of Political Obligation (Ann Arbor: University of Michigan Press, 1967), p. 219.

16. Excerpted in Eleanor S. Riemer and John C. Fout, eds., European Women: A Documentary History, 1789–1945 (New York: Schocken Books, 1980), pp. 63–64.

17. Excerpted in Gayle Graham Yates, ed., Harriet Martineau on Women (New Brunswick, N.J.: Rutgers University Press, 1985), p. 134.

18. Excerpted in Miriam Schneir, ed., Feminism: The Essential Historical Writings (New York: Vintage Books, 1972), pp. 40–41.

19. Ibid., pp. 76, 82.

20. Quoted in J. A. and Olive Banks, *Feminism and Family Planning in Victorian England* (Liverpool: Liverpool University Press, 1965), p. 43.

21. Ibid., p. 46.

22. Ibid., p. 47.

23. Percy Bysshe Shelley, "The Revolt of Islam," canto 2, stanza 43, in *The Complete Poetical Works of Percy Bysshe Shelley*, ed. Thomas Hutchinson (London: Oxford University Press, 1929), p. 63.

24. John Stuart Mill, *The Subjection of Women, in On Liberty, Etc.* (London: Oxford University Press, 1924), p. 427.

SUGGESTED READING

Andreski, Stanislav, ed., *The Essential Comte* (1974). An excellent collection of excerpts from Comte's works.

Becker, George J., *Master European Realists of the Nineteenth Century* (1982). Discussions of Flaubert, Zola, Chekhov, and other realists.

Bullock, Alan, and Maurice Shock, eds., *The Liberal Tradition* (1956). Well-chosen selections from the writings of British liberals; the introduction is an excellent survey of liberal thought.

Farrington, Benjamin, *What Darwin Really Said* (1966). A brief study of Darwin's work.

Grant, Damian, *Realism* (1970). A very good short survey.

Greene, J. C., *The Death of Adam* (1961). The impact of evolution on Western thought.

Hemmings, F. W. J., ed., *The Age of Realism* (1978). A series of essays exploring realism in various countries.

Hofstadter, Richard, *Social Darwinism in American Thought* (1955). A classic treatment of the impact of evolution on American conservatism, imperialism, and racism.

McLellan, David, *Karl Marx: His Life and Thought* (1977). A highly regarded biography.

———, ed., *Karl Marx: Selected Writings* (1977). A balanced selection of Marx's writings.

Manuel, Frank E., *The Prophets of Paris* (1965). Contains a valuable chapter on Comte.

Nochlin, Linda, *Realism* (1971). The nature of realism; realism in art.

Tucker, Robert, *The Marxian Revolutionary Idea* (1969). Marxism as a radical social philosophy.

———, *Philosophy and Myth in Karl Marx* (1972). Relationship of Marxist thought to German philosophy; good treatment of Marx's early writings.

———, ed., *The Marx-Engels Reader* (1972). An anthology of Marx's essential writings.

REVIEW QUESTIONS

1. How did realism differ from romanticism?

2. Realism and naturalism reflected attitudes shaped by science, industrialism, and secularism. Discuss this statement.

3. What was the relationship between positivism and science?

4. What was Comte's "law of the three stages"?

5. The theory of evolution had revolutionary consequences in areas other than science. Discuss this statement.

6. Why were Social Darwinist theories so popular?

7. What did Marx have in common with the philosophes of the Enlightenment?

8. What did Marx's philosophy of history owe to Hegel? How did it diverge from Hegel?

9. What relationship did Marx see between economics and politics?

10. What relationship did Marx see between economics and ideas?

11. Why did Marxism attract followers?

12. Why was Marx convinced that capitalism was doomed? How would its destruction come about?

13. How did the thoughts of Mill and Green represent an expansion of traditional liberalism?

14. The feminist movement was an outgrowth of certain ideals that emerged during the course of Western history. Discuss this statement.

15. What arguments were used by opponents of equal rights for women?

Chapter 16

Europe in the Late Nineteenth Century: Modernization, Nationalism, Imperialism

- The Advance of Industry
- Great Britain: Reform and Unrest
- France: A Troubled Nation
- Germany: The Power State
- Italy: Unfulfilled Expectations
- Russia: Tsarist Autocracy
- The Rise of Racial Nationalism
- The Emergence of the New Imperialism
- European Domination of Asia
- The Scramble for Africa
- The Legacy of Imperialism

In the last part of the nineteenth century, the accelerated pace of industrialization and urbanization continued the process of modernization that had begun earlier with the Industrial Revolution and transformed European and American societies. Simultaneously, Western nations built governmental machinery for including and controlling great numbers of citizens. This strengthening and centralizing process—*state building*, in modern terminology—became the major activity of Western governments. State building meant not only strengthening central authority, but also absorbing previously excluded classes into the community, primarily through the power of nationalism, which governments fostered. A state's power grew enormously as its government affected the lives of ordinary citizens through military conscription, public education, and broad taxation.

Industrialization facilitated the trends toward centralization by concentrating factory workers in cities and loosening traditional rural ties. It greatly affected international relations as well. The amount of coal and iron produced, the mileage and tonnage of railways and navies, the mechanization of industry, and the skill of the populace became important components of national power.

Nationalism, which intensified during the last part of the nineteenth century, was to turn into the dominant spiritual force of European life. It grew increasingly belligerent, intolerant, and irrational, threatening both the peace of Europe and the liberal humanist tradition of the Enlightenment. Nationalism and industrialization were the principal forces behind imperialism, leading European nations and the United States to extend their power over Asian, African, and Latin American lands. ❖

THE ADVANCE OF INDUSTRY

Historians call the second half of the nineteenth century the Second Industrial Revolution because of the great increase in the speed and scale of economic and social transformation. This changed world was defined by technological advances and new forms of business and labor organization. It was also characterized by the rise of the middle class to political and social power corresponding to its economic power; the decline of traditional groups, or classes; and dramatic changes in the role of women and children in the family.

At the midcentury, farming was still the main occupation of people everywhere—even in Britain, where industrialization was most advanced. Even Britain had more domestic servants than factory workers and twice as many agricultural laborers as textile and clothing workers. Large factories were few, and handicrafts still flourished. Sailing ships still outnumbered steamships, and horses carried more freight than trains. This situation, however, changed radically in two spurts: the first between 1850 and 1870, and the second from the 1890s until World War I.

During the first spurt, in Europe and America the shift from hand to machine production accelerated, leading to the concentration of factory workers in industrial cities and to the growth of unions. The standard of living for most workers rose. New machines and processes, legislation, and trade union bargaining relieved the worst conditions of early industrialization. At the same time, the first regulations of urban development and sanitation began to improve living conditions. In the more advanced industrial areas, the social organization of the workplace changed: the introduction of heavy equipment resulted in men replacing women and children in the factories. However, women forced out of factories (they would return during World War I) were not freed for a life of leisure. They took on jobs as domestics, pieceworkers, seamstresses, or laundresses. Children became students as the state and the economy demanded that they acquire at least a minimal education.

The scale of development changed markedly during the second spurt. Giant firms run by boards of directors, including financiers, operated far-flung enterprises of enormous, mechanized factories, which were manned by unskilled, low-paid, and often seasonal workers. These industrial giants were able to control the output, price,

Chronology 16.1 ❖ Expansion of Western Power

1839–1842	Opium War: the British defeat the Chinese, annexing treaty ports in China and opening them to Western trade
1851–1852	Louis Napoleon Bonaparte overthrows Second Republic, becoming Emperor Napoleon III
1853	Commodore Perry, with U.S. naval forces, opens Japan to trade
1857–1858	Sepoy Mutiny; Britain replaces the East India Company and begins ruling India through a viceroy
1867	Second Reform Bill doubles the English electorate
1869	Opening of the Suez Canal
1870	Third French Republic is established
1870–1871	Franco-Prussian War; Paris Commune; creation of German Empire, with William I as Kaiser and Bismarck as chancellor
1876	Stanley sets up posts in the Congo for Leopold II of Belgium
1882	Britain occupies Egypt
1884	Berlin Conference on Africa; Reform Bill grants suffrage to most English men
1894–1906	Dreyfus affair in France
1898	Spanish-American War: United States acquires the Philippines and Puerto Rico and occupies Cuba; battle of Omdurman
1899–1902	Boer War between the British and the Afrikaners
1900	Boxers rebel against foreign presence in China
1904–1905	Russo-Japanese War: the Japanese defeat the Russians
1911	Parliament Act limits power of the House of Lords
1919	Britain grants a legislative assembly in India; Gandhi's passive resistance movement broadens with the Amritsar Massacre

and distribution of commodities. They dominated smaller firms, financed and controlled research and development, and expanded far beyond their national frontiers. The "captains of industry"—the owners or managers of these large firms—possessed such extraordinary economic power that they often commanded political power as well. The emergence and concentration of heavy industry in large firms, capitalized by specialist banks, characterized the post-1890 period all over Europe. Such rapid growth caught the imagination of businessmen, as well as of socialist critics.

Revolutionary technological changes furthered the growth of industry. At the midcentury, all of Europe caught the railroad mania that had seized Britain in the 1840s. This epic expansion of railroads was paralleled in shipping. In 1850, steam-powered ships constituted only 5 percent of the world's tonnage; by 1893, the figure had risen to half of all tonnage. At the turn of the century, two German engineers, Gottlieb Daimler and Karl Benz, joined to perfect the internal combustion engine. Then an American, Henry Ford, using mass-production assembly-line techniques, brought out his Model T for "the ordinary man," and the automobile age was born. The invention of the diesel engine by another German in 1897 meant that cheaper, more efficient fuel could be used. Diesel engines soon replaced steam engines on giant cargo ships, warships, and luxury liners. In communications, the advent of the telegraph, telephone, and later radio also revolutionized people's lives.

However, economic development was extremely uneven. Central, southern, and eastern Europe remained backward in many respects and stayed so until World War I and after. In these overwhelmingly agricultural societies, manufacturing consisted for the most part of consumer-oriented, small-scale operations in textiles and food processing, in which artisans maintained their place.

Accelerated Urbanization

More rapid industrialization increased the numbers of northwestern Europeans and Americans who lived in cities, which became more numerous, larger, and more densely populated. Although not an industrial city, London had become a megalopolis of five million people by 1880 and was home to seven million by 1914. Paris increased from two million to three million between 1850 and World War I. Berlin, a city of only half a million in 1866, reached two million by World War I. There were only three German cities of more than a hundred thousand on the eve of unification, but by 1903 there were fifteen.

In the cities, the middle class rose to political, economic, and social prominence, often expressing its newfound importance and prosperity through civic activity. As machinery replaced handicraft, the artisan working class experienced a sharp decline. Factory workers, their ranks swelled by peasants and displaced artisans, emerged as an important social group in cities. Cut off from the regions of their birth, the peasants and artisans who worked in factories shed their old loyalties; in the cities, some found a place for themselves in their neighborhoods, some in union and party activities, and some none at all. Industrialization also created a new, "white-collar" group of clerks, who tried to differentiate themselves from factory workers.

The Rise of Socialist Parties

Between 1850 and 1914, workers' lives improved because of trade union organization, government intervention in the economy, and the general increase in productivity brought about by industrialization. Still, members of the working class faced problems and inequities that drew them to socialist parties, which strove for government control of industry and worker control of government and the workplace. Most workers and their families lived in bleak, overcrowded tenements, without central heating or running water. They worked long hours—as much as fifty-five per week in the trades where governments restricted the length of the workweek, and from seventy to seventy-five in unregulated trades. Their jobs were exhausting and monotonous. They also suffered from malnutrition. The English men and boys who appeared for medical exams to serve in the Boer War were found to be so physically unfit that their condition prompted reforms to improve the health and education of the laboring class. The working class as a whole suffered from diseases, particularly tuberculosis, and from lack of medical care. Women often died in childbirth owing to inadequate treatment, and men, particularly miners and dockworkers, commonly experienced job accidents that maimed and killed. Socialists argued that these conditions were due to the capitalist profit system, which exploited and impoverished workers and enriched the owners.

Socialist parties grew phenomenally in Germany and rapidly in much of the rest of Europe. Even Russia, which was scarcely industrial, had a Marxist socialist party. The growth of socialism reflected the workers' increased consciousness that they had special needs, which other political parties did not fulfill. However, socialists were divided about tactics. "Orthodox" Marxists believed that socialist-led revolution was the necessary first step for change; this group included Wilhelm Liebknecht and August Bebel of Germany and Jules Guesde of France. Others—"revisionist" Marxists—who were influenced by the German theoretician Eduard Bernstein, urged socialists to forgo revolution and use the existing political and economic systems to build a socialist society.

Painting of the Bowery by Louis Sonntag, Jr., 1895. New York City street scene bursting with commercial energies and activity as the night is lighted by blazing electricity. The painting puts pushcarts, trolleys, horse-drawn cabs, and trains side by side, as it does the classic architecture of the theater and the four-story buildings housing shops and families on the Bowery. The life of the city throbs with the energy of modern technology. (*Museum of the City of New York #32.275.2. Gift of William B. Miles*)

GREAT BRITAIN: REFORM AND UNREST

The process of reform, begun with the Reform Bill of 1832 and the Factory Acts, continued in the era of the Second Industrial Revolution. The Reform Bill of 1867, skillfully maneuvered through Parliament by Benjamin Disraeli (1804–1881), gave the vote to urban workers, doubling the electorate. Some of Disraeli's fellow members in the Conservative party feared that extending the vote to the largely uneducated masses would ruin the nation, but Disraeli maintained that this democratic advance would strengthen the bonds between the people and the state. Moreover, he believed that the Conservatives' social program and imperialist foreign policy would win the newly enfranchised poor to the party.

The work of electoral reform was continued by the Liberal party under the leadership of William Gladstone (1809–1898), who served four terms as prime minister. The Ballot Act (1872) provided for the secret ballot, which enabled working-class voters to avoid intimidation by their employers. Next, the Reform Bill of 1884 enfranchised rural laborers; now almost all English males could vote.

Social Reform

Unlike their Continental brothers, British workers on the whole had never been attracted to socialism, and particularly not to Marxism. In the 1880s, however, widespread poverty and new trends in industry—especially monopolies, cartels, and foreign competition—led some labor leaders to urge greater militancy. These conditions brought about the creation of the Labour party.

The growth of the Labour party was spurred by the adverse Taff Vale decision (1901), which awarded damages to an employer picketed by a union. If workers could be fined for picketing or other actions restraining trade, their unions could be broken and they would lose the economic gains of half a century. Galvanized by the Taff Vale decision and eager to win reforms for the working class, labor took to politics. In the elections of 1906, the new Labour party gained twenty-nine members in the House of Commons; it would become an important faction in British politics.

Between 1906 and 1911, the Liberals, led by David Lloyd George (1863–1945) and the then Liberal Winston Churchill (1874–1965), introduced a series of important social measures. Aided by the Labour party, they enacted a program of old-age pensions, labor exchanges to help the unemployed find work, unemployment and health insurance (a program deeply influenced by Bismarckian social legislation, see the upcoming section on "Germany: the Power State"), and minimum wages for certain industries. Parliament also repealed the Taff Vale decision. In the process, however, a constitutional crisis developed between the Liberals, who had Labour support, and the Conservatives, who dominated the House of Lords. The crisis ended with the Parliament Act of 1911, which decreed that the House of Lords could only delay, not prevent, the passage of a bill that the House of Commons had approved.

Feminist Agitation

On the issue of women's suffrage, British democracy was lagging. Influenced by the ideals of the American and French revolutions, women had begun to protest their unequal status. In 1867, John Stuart Mill proposed extending the vote to women, but his colleagues in Parliament rejected the proposal. The following year, Lydia Becker became the first Englishwoman to speak in public for women's suffrage. Many people, both men and women, viewed female suffrage as too radical a break with tradition. Some asserted that women were represented by their husbands or male relatives and therefore did not need the right to vote. Others protested that women lacked the ability to participate responsibly in political life. Queen Victoria, who supported other reforms, called women's suffrage "that mad, wicked folly."

Although many Liberals and some Labourites favored women's suffrage, women were advised by the leader of the Liberals "to keep on pestering . . . but exercise the virtue of patience." For the women who deemed this advice patronizing and whose patience was running out, a family of feminists advocated a more militant course of action. Emmeline Pankhurst and her daughters Sylvia and Christabel urged demonstrations, invasions of the House of Commons, destruction of property, and hunger strikes. They did not urge these dramatic actions all at once, but when their petitions and demands were ignored, they moved to more and more shocking deeds. Suffragettes began a campaign of breaking windows, starting fires in mailboxes, and chaining themselves to the gates at Parliament. As a gesture of protest, in 1913 one militant threw herself to her death under King Edward VII's horse at the races.

When feminists were arrested for violating the law, they staged hunger strikes. Ugly situations resulted, with the police force feeding the demonstrators and subjecting them to ridicule and rough treatment. Often the police would release half-starved feminists and, when they had recovered their health, would reimprison them. Ridiculed, humiliated, and punished—but above all legally ignored—the feminists refused to accept the passive role that a male-dominated society had assigned them. When women played a major part on the home front in World War I,

Carson Reviewing Troops of Ulster Volunteers Before WWI. For almost a century the Irish demand for representation, then for home rule (or self-government), had met with political opposition in the British parliament. With Parliament split, Irish nationalists and their opponents, Irish Protestants, armed for civil war. Here a leading member of parliament supports the Irish Protestants who have volunteered for the civil war to keep Ireland in the British empire. The start of the first World War put this treasonous and revolutionary situation out of the public mind only for a couple years. (*Hulton Archive/Getty Images*)

many of the elite changed their minds, and in 1918, British women over the age of thirty gained the vote. In 1928, Parliament lowered the voting age for women to twenty-one, the same qualifying age as that for male voters.

The Irish Question

Feminist agitation was one explosive issue confronting prewar Britain. Another was the Irish question. While moderate Irish nationalists called for *home rule* (self-government within the British Empire), something favored by many members of Parliament, Irish Catholic extremists, such as the Irish Republican Brotherhood and the Gaelic League, pressed for full independence. Fearing Catholic domination, the Protestant Irish (Ulstermen) in the northern counties of Ulster strongly opposed independence for Ireland. The Ulster Volunteers recruited a large private army and openly trained it for revolution in the event that home rule was enacted. Gangs smuggled guns, soldiers fired on demonstrators, violence bred violence, and civil war seemed close.

In 1916, the Easter Rebellion, an Irish insurrection, was suppressed and its leaders executed. But the English cabinet was moved to proceed with home rule at once. The Irish revolt of 1919–20 brought matters to a head: Ireland was divided, the overwhelmingly Catholic south gaining independence and the six predominantly Protestant counties of Ulster remaining part of the United Kingdom.

At the beginning of the twentieth century, labor, Irish, and female militancy marred Britain's image of a stable, liberal, constitutional regime. Nevertheless, British parliamentary government survived every crisis and proved itself able to carry the nation successfully through a grueling world war.

FRANCE: A TROUBLED NATION

In 1852, Louis Napoleon Bonaparte (1808–1873), who had been elected president of the Second French Republic in 1848, took the title of emperor in the tradition of his illustrious uncle. Napoleon III ruled in an authoritarian manner, permitting no opposition, censoring the press, and allowing the legislature little power. But in the 1860s, in a drastic shift, he introduced liberal reforms, pardoning political prisoners, removing press censorship, allowing workers the right to form unions, and approving a new constitution with safeguards for individual liberty. His reforms have perplexed historians. Was Napoleon III a sincere believer in liberal ideals who waited until his power was firmly established before implementing these ideals, or did he introduce reforms only because he feared unrest?

Defeat in the Franco-Prussian War (1870–1871) brought down the empire of Napoleon III. Bitter frustration with defeat and hatred of the Prussian invaders led the people of Paris to rise against the armistice signed by the provisional government—the politicians who had replaced Napoleon III. The Paris Commune (1871) began as a patriotic refusal to accept defeat and as a rejection of Napoleon's rule, but it became a rejection of the provisional government as well. Ultimately, the Communards (as those who resisted the Prussians and the provisional government were called) also challenged property owners.

The Communards included followers of the anarchist Joseph Proudhon and groups of republican and socialist veterans of the revolution of 1848, gathered from prisons, from hiding, and from exile. For two months in the spring of 1871, these revolutionaries ruled Paris. Then Adolphe Thiers, head of the provisional government that still governed the rest of France, ordered an attack on Paris. The fighting was bitter and desperate, with many acts of terrorism and violence. Both sides in this civil war set fires that destroyed large parts of the city they loved. The Communards were defeated and treated as traitors: twenty thousand of them were executed without trial, and those who were tried received harsh sentences (death, life imprisonment, and deportation to prison colonies). Governing classes across Europe viewed the Paris Commune as a sign that the people should be ruled with an iron fist.

At first it seemed that a monarchy would succeed the empire of Napoleon III. But disunity among the monarchists enabled France to become a republic by default. Unlike Britain with its two-party system, the Third French Republic had many political parties, which contributed to instability. No one party had sufficient weight in parliament to provide strong leadership. Prime ministers resigned in rapid succession; cabinets rose and fell frequently, giving the impression of a state without direction. Political life seemed to consist of wheeling and dealing. Yet in the process, legislation was enacted that made elementary education free and compulsory and legalized trade unions. The Third Republic survived, though not without major crises; the principal one was the Dreyfus affair, which left France deeply divided.

In 1894, Captain Alfred Dreyfus, an Alsatian-Jewish artillery officer, was wrongly accused of having sold secrets to the Germans. After a court martial, he was condemned to life imprisonment on Devil's Island. Anti-Semitic elements joined with the Republic's opponents—monarchists, army leaders, clerics, and nationalists—to denounce and block every attempt to clear Dreyfus of the charges against him. In the beginning, few people defended Dreyfus; the vast majority felt that the honor of France and the army was at stake. Then individuals, mainly radical republicans, came to his defense, including the writers Anatole France and Émile Zola and the future republican leader Georges Clemenceau, along with university students. They protested and demonstrated, insisting on a retrial and a revision of the verdict. After many humiliations, Dreyfus was finally cleared in 1906.

The result of the victory of the radical republicans, however, was a fierce campaign to root out those opposing the Republic. The radicals attacked the church, expelled religious orders, confiscated their property, and waged a vigorous campaign to replace the influence of the parish priest with that of the district schoolmaster. Complete separation of church and state was ordered; taxes no longer supported the parishes and religious schools.

Despite progress in the middle of the nineteenth century, French economic development lagged. France had fewer and smaller industries than Britain or Germany, and more French people lived in rural areas and small communities. In the 1880s, both trade unionism and political parties with a socialist program began to make headway and to press for social reform through the democratic parliamentary institutions of the Republic. However, France was very slow to enact social measures such as pensions and regulations governing working conditions, wages, and hours. These measures, which might have improved the lives of ordinary people, were regarded by the ruling elite as hateful socialism; socialists, on the other hand, viewed them as token offerings to buy off workers.

France was a troubled country, and the Third Republic was not a popular regime. The church, the army, socialism, and even memories of the monarchy and the empire inspired deeper passions than did the Republic, which survived only because the dissension among its enemies allowed it to survive. France approached World War I as a deeply divided country. Yet when World War I broke out, the French people rallied to defend the nation.

GERMANY: THE POWER STATE

Prussia's victory over France in the Franco-Prussian War of 1870–71 completed the struggle for German unification. The new government, the German Reich (empire), was headed by the king of Prussia. Though the Reichstag (lower house) was elected by universal suffrage, the real power lay in the hands of the emperor and Bismarck, the "Iron Chancellor," who was responsible only to the emperor. The German kaiser (emperor), unlike the British monarch, had considerable control over lawmaking and foreign affairs and commanded the army and navy. The emperor alone could remove the chancellor or the cabinet members from office. The sole control over Bismarck was the Reichstag's refusal to pass the budget, an extreme measure that politicians were usually unwilling to take.

Bismarck's political practices weakened liberal and democratic elements. Nor did German liberals vigorously struggle for basic political and civil liberties; they tolerated evasions of principles and practices that British politicians would never have allowed. While Britain, France, the United States, and other Western states were becoming more democratic, Germany remained a semiautocratic state. The failure of democratic attitudes and procedures to take root in Germany was to have dangerous consequences for the future.

Bismarck regarded parties as incapable of making policy for the country. In Bismarck's mind, the Catholics and the socialists were internationalists who did not place the interests of Germany first. He began to persecute Catholics, who made up about 40 percent of the population. The *Kulturkampf* (struggle for culture) was a series of laws passed in 1873 to subject the church to the state. The laws discriminated against the Jesuits and required state supervision of the church and training of priests in state schools. Catholics had to be married by the state. Churchmen who refused to accept these laws were imprisoned or exiled. German liberals did not defend the civil liberties of the Catholics against these laws. Persecution only strengthened the German Catholics' loyalty to their church, however, and the Catholic Center party gained support. Prussian conservatives, though Protestant, resented Bismarck's anticlerical policy, which could hurt Lutherans as well as Catholics. With the succession of Leo XIII to the papacy in 1878, Bismarck quietly opened negotiations for peace with the church.

When two attempts were made on William I's life in 1878, Bismarck demanded that the socialists be suppressed. In reality, the socialists, few in number, were not a threat; their immediate practical program was a demand for civil liberties and democracy in Germany. Only the narrowest of conservative views would have labeled the socialists as dangerous, but many in Germany, particularly the Prussian Junker class, held such a narrow view. The liberals once again did not oppose Bismarck's special legislation outlawing subversive organizations and authorizing the police to ban meetings and newspapers. The Social Democratic party, like the Catholic Center party before, survived the persecution. It grew stronger and better disciplined as the liberals grew weaker, discredited by their unwillingness to act.

Bismarck's policy was not merely repressive. He tried to win the workers by paternalistic social legislation. Like many conservatives, he was disturbed by the effects of industrialization, which had developed at a rapid pace in the 1850s and 1860s. Germany was the first state to enact a program of social legislation for the proletariat; it included insurance against sickness, disability, accidents, and old age. The employer, the state, and the worker each contributed small amounts to an insurance fund.

Despite Bismarck's attempts to woo the workers away from socialism, the German working class continued to support the Social Democratic party in elections. On the eve of World War I, union membership was roughly three million, and the Social Democratic party was the largest single party in Germany. The socialists talked revolution, but the unions—the largest and most powerful in Europe—and many party members favored policies of gradual reform. Great numbers of German workers were patriotic, even imperialistic, and thought that their government deserved their loyalty.

By 1900, Germany had caught up with, and in some areas surpassed, Britain in economic growth. Aided by the skill of its scientists and inventors, Germany became a leader in the chemical and electrical industries. It possessed the most extensive sector of large-scale, concentrated industrial and corporate capitalism of any Great Power. Within a short period, Germany had become a strong, industrialized state, ready and eager to play an important role in world affairs. Its growing industrial and military might, linked with an aggressive nationalism, alarmed other countries. This combination of German vitality, aggressiveness, and the fears of its rivals helped lead to World War I.

ITALY: UNFULFILLED EXPECTATIONS

Italian nationalists expected greatness from the unification of their country, so long conquered, plundered, divided, and ruled by absolute princes. But the newly unified Italy faced serious problems. An overwhelmingly Roman Catholic country, it was split by religious controversy. Liberals and republicans wanted a secular state, with civil marriage and public education, which was anathema to the church. Furthermore, few Italians could participate in the constitutional monarchy. Of the twenty-seven million citizens, only about two million could vote—even after the reforms of 1881, which tripled the electorate. Liberals could point out that almost every literate male could vote, but this achievement was small consolation to those who had fought for unification but now were denied voting privileges because they did not pass a literacy test.

Among Italian workers, cynicism about the government was so deep that many turned to radical movements, which advocated the rejection of authority and the tactics of terrorism, assassination, and general strikes. Disgust with parliamentary government led the workers to believe that direct action would gain more than elections and parties. Peasants in some rural areas, particularly in the south, were strongly Catholic, loyal to their landlord, and bitterly unhappy with their economic situation; they saw few signs of the new state other than hateful taxation and conscription.

The ruling elite brushed aside Italy's difficult social and economic problems, concentrating instead on military glory and imperial expansion. The politicians trumpeted Italy's ambitions for Great Power status to justify military expenditures beyond the means of such a poor state. They presented Italy's scramble for African and Mediterranean territories as the solution to all its social ills. The profits from exploiting others would pay for badly needed social reforms, and the raw materials gained would fuel industrialization. None of these promises came true, which deepened the cynicism of a disillusioned people. As a foreign and as a domestic policy, this pursuit of glory was too costly for the fragile nation.

Before World War I, Italy was deeply divided politically. A wave of strikes and rural discontent gave sufficient warning to political leaders so that they declared neutrality, deciding, unlike Russia, not to risk the shaky regime by entering the war. But the appeals of expansionism were too great for them to maintain this policy.

RUSSIA: TSARIST AUTOCRACY

In the middle of the nineteenth century, Russia differed fundamentally from western Europe. The great movements that had shaped the outlook of the modern West—Renaissance, Reformation, Scientific Revolution, Enlightenment, and Industrial Revolution—had barely penetrated Russia. Autocracy, buttressed by the Orthodox church, reigned supreme; the small and insignificant middle class did not possess the dynamic, critical, and individualistic spirit that characterized the Western bourgeoisie, and the vast majority of the people were illiterate serfs.

After Napoleon's defeat in 1814, some returning Russian officers, asking why Russia could not share the civilized life they had seen in western Europe, turned revolutionary. The unsuccessful Decembrist uprising in 1825, during the brief interlude between the death of Alexander I (1801–1825) and the accession of Nicholas I (1825–1855), was the effort of a small group of conspirators demanding a constitution. Fear of revolution determined the character of the reign of Nicholas I and of tsarist governments thereafter.

Aware of the subversive influence of foreign ideas, Nicholas decreed an ideology of Russian superiority, called *official nationality*. The Russian people were taught to believe that the Orthodox creed of the Russian church, the autocratic rule of the tsar, and Russia's Slavic culture made the Russian Empire superior to the West. To enforce this contrived invincibility, Nicholas I created the Third Section, a secret agency of police spies, and controlled access to his country from

Europe. Indeed, toward the end of his reign, he drew a virtual iron curtain to keep out dangerous influences. His ideal was a monolithic country, run like an army by a vigorous administration centered on the monarch; all Russians were to obey his wise and fatherly commands. Nicholas's successor, Alexander II (1855–1881), was determined to preserve autocratic rule. However, he wanted Russia to achieve what had made western Europe strong: the energetic support and free enterprise of its citizens. Whether stimulating popular initiative was possible without undermining autocracy was the key puzzle for him and for his successors to the end of the tsarist regime.

Alexander's boldest reforms included the emancipation of the serfs in 1861. They were liberated from bondage to the nobility and given land of their own, but not individual freedom. They remained tied to their village and to their households, which owned the land collectively. Emancipation did not transform the peasants into enterprising and loyal citizens. For the non-peasant minority, a package of other reforms brought new opportunities: limited self-government for selected rural areas and urban settlements, an independent judiciary, trial by jury, and the introduction of a profession novel to Russians: the practice of law.

Meanwhile, Alexander reopened the borders, allowing closer ties with Europe and westernizing Russian society. The rising class of businesspeople and professional experts looked west and conformed to Western middle-class standards. There was some relaxation in the repression of non-Russian minorities. Railroads were constructed, which facilitated agricultural exports and permitted the import of Western goods and capital. For some years, the economy boomed.

More significant in the long run was the flowering of Russian thought and literature among the intelligentsia. These were educated Russians whose minds were shaped by Western schooling and travel, yet who still were prompted by the "Russian soul." They quarreled with fierce sincerity over whether Russia should pursue superiority by imitating the West or by cultivating its own Slavic genius, possibly through a Pan-Slavic movement. Pan-Slavism, which glorified the solidarity of Russians with other Slavic peoples of eastern Europe, was a popular cause. Even more than the tsars, the intelligentsia hoped for a glorious Russia that would outshine the West.

Yet tsarist autocracy undercut their hopes. The tsar would not permit open discussion likely to provoke rebellion. Liberals advocating gradual change were thwarted by censorship and the police. The 1860s saw the rise of self-righteous fanatics who were ready to match the chicanery of the police and foment social revolution. By the late 1870s, they organized themselves into a secret terrorist organization. In 1881, they assassinated the tsar. The era of reforms ended.

The next tsar, Alexander III (1881–1894), a firm if unimaginative ruler, returned to the repressive policies of Nicholas I. In defense against the revolutionaries, he perfected the police state, even enlisting anti-Semitism in its cause. He updated autocracy and stifled dissent but also promoted economic development. Russia had relied too heavily on foreign loans and goods; it had to build up its own resources. It also needed more railroads to bind its huge empire together. So in 1891 the tsar ordered the construction of the Trans-Siberian Railroad. Soon afterward, Minister of Finance Sergei Witte used railroad expansion to boost heavy industry and industrialization generally.

Yet forced industrialization also brought perils. It propelled the country into alien and often hated ways of life and created a discontented new class of workers. In addition, it promoted literacy and contact with western Europe and thus helped to increase political agitation among the professional classes, intelligentsia, workers, peasants, and subject nationalities. Indispensable for national self-assertion and survival, industrialization strained the country's fragile unity.

The first jolt, the revolution of 1905, followed Russia's defeat by Japan in the Russo-Japanese War. Fortunately for Nicholas II (1894–1917), his soldiers stayed loyal. The autocracy survived, although, as a concession to the revolution, it was now saddled with a parliament, called the Imperial Duma. The new regime, inwardly rejected by Nicholas II, started auspiciously. Under its freedoms, Russian art and literature flourished and the economy progressed. Agrarian reforms introduced the incentives of private property and individual enterprise in the villages. The supporters of the new constitutional experiment hoped for a liberal Russia at last, but in vain.

THE RISE OF RACIAL NATIONALISM

In the first half of the nineteenth century, European nationalism and liberalism went hand in hand. Liberals sought both the rights of the individual and national independence and unification. Liberal nationalists believed that a unified state free of foreign subjugation was in harmony with the principle of natural rights, and they insisted that love of country led to love of humanity. As nationalism grew more extreme, however, its profound difference from liberalism became more apparent. The extreme nationalism of the late nineteenth and early twentieth centuries contributed to World War I and to the rise of fascism after the war; it was the seedbed of totalitarian nationalism.

Concerned exclusively with the greatness of the nation, extreme nationalists rejected the liberal emphasis on political liberty. Liberals regarded the state as a community of individuals voluntarily bonded by law and citizenship and entitled to the same rights. To extreme nationalists, however, the state was the highest development of a folkish-racial spirit inherited from their ancestors. In their eyes, profound and irreconcilable differences separated "their people" from those who did not share this ancestry. Even if others had dwelled in the land for centuries, such people were seen as dangerous aliens. Increasingly, nationalists attacked parliamentary government as an obstacle to national power and greatness and maintained that authoritarian leadership was needed to meet national emergencies. The needs of the nation, they said, transcended the rights of the individual.

Extreme nationalists also rejected the liberal ideal of equality. Placing the nation above everything, nationalists accused national minorities of corrupting the nation's spirit, and they glorified war as a symbol of the nation's resolve and will. In the name of national power and unity, they persecuted minorities at home and stirred up hatred against other nations. Increasingly, they embraced militaristic, imperialistic, and racist doctrines. At the founding of the Nationalist Association in Italy in 1910, one leader declared: "Just as socialism teaches the proletariat the

Celebration of the Unveiling of the Statue of Hermann (Arminius) at the Site of Teutoberger Wald. The Franco-Prussian War (1870–1871) brought German unity and intensified nationalist feelings. German nationalists glorified the traditions and deeds of their ancient ancestors who overran the Roman Empire. Depicted here is the unveiling of the statue erected in 1875 for Arminius, a tribal chieftain who had defeated a Roman force in A.D. 9. German nationalism, which grew more extreme in succeeding decades, helped give rise to the world wars of the twentieth century. (*Bildarchiv Preussischer Kulturbesitz/Art Resource, NY*)

value of class struggle, so we must teach Italy the value of international struggle. But international struggle is war? Well, then, let there be war! And nationalism will arouse the will for a victorious war . . . the only way to national redemption."[1]

Interpreting politics with the logic of emotions, extreme nationalists insisted that they had a sacred mission to regain lands once held in the Middle Ages, to unite with their kinfolk in other lands, or to rule over peoples considered inferior. Loyalty to the nation-state was elevated above all other allegiances. The ethnic state became an object of religious reverence; the spiritual energies that formerly had been dedicated to Christianity were now channeled into the worship of the nation-state, igniting primitive, dark, cruel feelings.

By the beginning of the twentieth century, conservatives had become the staunchest advocates of nationalism, and the nationalism preached by conservative extremists was stripped of Mazzini's humanitarian ideals of liberty, equality, and the fellowship of nations. Landholding aristocrats, generals, and clergy, often joined by big industrialists, saw nationalism as a convenient instrument for gaining a mass following in their struggle against democracy, social reform, and socialism.

Championing popular nationalist myths and dreams and citing Social Darwinist doctrines, a newly radicalized right, dominated by the elite of German society, hoped to harness the instinctual energies of the masses, particularly the peasants and the lower middle class—shopkeepers, civil servants, and white-collar workers—to conservative causes. Peasants viewed liberalism and a godless Marxism as threats to traditional values, while the lower bourgeoisie feared the power of an organized proletariat. These people were receptive to the rhetoric of ultranationalists, who denounced democracy and Marxism as threats to national unity and Jews as aliens endangering the nation. Nationalism was presented as a victory of idealism over materialism and as the subordination of class and personal interests to the general good of the nation.

Volkish Thought

Extreme nationalism was a general European phenomenon, but it proved especially dangerous in Germany. Bismarck's triumphs lured Germans into a dream world. Many started to yearn for the extension of German power throughout the globe. The past, they said, belonged to France and Britain; the future, to Germany.

The most ominous expression of German nationalism (and a clear example of mythical thinking) was *Volkish* thought. (*Volk* means "folk" or "people.") German Volkish thinkers sought to bind the German people together through a deep love of their language, traditions, and fatherland. These thinkers felt that Germans were animated by a higher spirit than that found in other peoples. To Volkish thinkers, the Enlightenment and parliamentary democracy were foreign ideas that corrupted the pure German spirit. With fanatical devotion, Volkish thinkers embraced all things German—the medieval past, the German landscape, the simple peasant, the village—and denounced the liberal humanist tradition of the West as alien to the German soul.

Volkish thought attracted Germans frightened by all the complexities of the modern age—industrialization, urbanization, materialism, class conflicts, and alienation. Seeing their beloved Germany transformed by these forces of modernity,

Volkish thinkers yearned to restore the sense of community, the spiritual unity, that they attributed to the preindustrial age. Only by identifying with their sacred soil and sacred traditions could modern Germans escape from the evils of industrial society. Only then could the different classes band together in an organic unity.

The Volkish movement had little support from the working class, which was concerned chiefly with improving its standard of living. The movement appealed mainly to farmers and villagers, who regarded the industrial city as a threat to native values and a vehicle for spreading foreign ideas; to artisans and small shopkeepers, threatened by big business; and to scholars, writers, teachers, and students, who saw in Volkish nationalism a cause worthy of their idealism. The schools were leading agents for the dissemination of Volkish ideas.

Volkish thinkers glorified the ancient Germanic tribes that had overrun the Roman Empire; they contrasted their courageous and vigorous German ancestors with the effete and degenerate Romans. A few tried to harmonize ancient Germanic religious traditions with Christianity. Such attitudes led Germans to see themselves as a heroic people fundamentally different from and better than the English and the French. It also led them to regard German culture as unique—innately superior and opposed to the humanist outlook of the Enlightenment. Like their romantic predecessors, Volkish thinkers held that the German people and culture had a special destiny and a unique mission. They pitted the German soul against the Western intellect—feeling, intuition, spirit, and idealism against a drab rationalism. To be sure, the Western humanist tradition had many supporters in Germany, but the counterideology of Volkish thought was becoming increasingly widespread. This murky, irrational, radically nationalist, and antiliberal outlook shaped by these Volkish thinkers in the late nineteenth century would later undermine support for the democratic Weimar Republic established in Germany after World War I and provide Hitler with receptive listeners. Many of Hitler's supporters hoped that he would transform these Volkish longings into political realities.

Racist doctrines had an especially strong appeal for Volkish thinkers. According to these doctrines, race was the key to history; not only physical features, but also moral, esthetic, and intellectual qualities distinguished one race from another. For racist thinkers, a race demonstrated its vigor and achieved greatness when it preserved its purity; intermarriage between races was contamination that would result in genetic, cultural, and military decline. Unlike liberals, who held that anyone who accepted German law was a member of the German nation, racists argued that a person's nationality was a function of his or her "racial soul" or "blood." Like their Nazi successors, Volkish thinkers claimed that the German race was purer than, and therefore superior to, all other races. Its superiority was revealed in such physical characteristics as blond hair, blue eyes, and fair skin—all signs of inner qualities lacking in other races.

German racial nationalists insisted that Germany had a unique mission; as a superior race, Germans had a national right to dominate other peoples, particularly the "racially inferior" Slavs of the East. The Pan-German Association, whose membership included professors, schoolteachers, journalists, lawyers, and aristocrats, spread racial and nationalist theories and glorified war as an expression of national vitality. A statement from the association's journal sums up its philosophy: "The racial biological ideology tells us that there are races that lead and races that follow. Political history is nothing but the history of struggles among the leading races. Conquests, above all, are always the work of the leading races. Such men can conquer, may conquer, and shall conquer."[2]

Anti-Semitism

German racial nationalists singled out Jews as a wicked race and a deadly enemy of the German people. Anti-Semitism, which was widespread in late-nineteenth-century Europe, provides a striking example of the perennial appeal, power, and danger of mythical thinking—of elevating to the level of objective truth ideas that have no basis in fact but provide all-encompassing, emotionally satisfying explanations of life and history. By manufacturing the myth of the wicked Jew, the radical right confirmed the insight reached by the political theorist Georges Sorel (see the section on

Sorel under "Irrationalism" in the following chapter): that people are moved and united by myths that offer simple, clear, and emotionally gratifying resolutions to the complexities of the modern world.

Anti-Semitic organizations and political parties sought to deprive Jews of their civil rights, and anti-Semitic publications proliferated. Edouard Drumont, a French journalist, argued that the Jews, racially inferior and believers in a primitive religion, had gained control of France. Like medieval Christian anti-Semites, Drumont accused Jews of deicide and of using Christian blood for ritual purposes. Drumont's newspaper (established with Jesuit funds) blamed all the ills of France on the Jews, called for their expulsion from the country, and predicted that they would be massacred.

Romania barred most Jews from holding office and from voting, imposed various economic restrictions on them, and limited their admission into secondary schools and universities. The Romanian government even financed an international congress of anti-Semites, which met in Bucharest in 1886. In German-speaking Austria, Karl Lueger, a leader of the Christian Social party, founded by conservative German nationalists, exploited anti-Semitism to win elections in overwhelmingly Catholic Vienna. Georg von Schönerer, founder of the German National party in Austria, wanted to eliminate Jews from all areas of public life.

Russia placed a quota on the number of Jewish students admitted to secondary schools and higher educational institutions, confined Jews to certain regions of the country, and, "to purify the sacred historic capital," expelled about twenty thousand Jews from Moscow. Some government officials encouraged and even organized *pogroms* (mob violence) against Jews. Between 1903 and 1906, pogroms broke out in 690 towns and villages, most of them in the Ukraine, traditionally a hotbed of anti-Semitism. (Ukrainian folksongs and legends glorified centuries-old massacres of Jews.) The attackers looted, burned, raped, and murdered, generally with impunity. In Russia and several other lands, Jews were put on trial for slaughtering Christian children as part of a Passover ritual—a deranged accusation that survived from the Middle Ages.

The Protocols of the Elders of Zion. This infamous forgery, commissioned by the Russian secret police, became an international bestseller and contributed to outrages against Jews. Anti-Semitic organizations continue to publish and circulate it today. The picture is the actual cover of a French edition of the *Protocols*, c. 1934. (*Institute of Contemporary History and The Wiener Library*)

Anti-Semitism had a long and bloodstained history in Europe, stemming both from an irrational fear and hatred of outsiders with noticeably different ways and from the commonly accepted myth that the Jews as a people were collectively and eternally cursed for rejecting Christ. Christians saw Jews as the murderers of Christ—an image that promoted terrible anger and hatred. In the Middle Ages, mobs periodically humiliated, tortured, and massacred Jews, and rulers expelled them from their kingdoms. Often barred from owning land and excluded from the craft guilds, medieval Jews concentrated in trade and moneylending—occupations that frequently earned them greater hostility. By the sixteenth century, Jews in a number of lands were forced by law to live in separate quarters of the town, called *ghettos*. Medieval Christian anti-Semitism, which depicted the Jew as vile and Judaism as repulsive, fertilized the soil for modern anti-Semitism.

In the nineteenth century, under the aegis of the liberal ideals of the Enlightenment and the French Revolution, Jews gained legal equality in most European lands. They could leave the ghetto, vote, hold office, and participate in many activities that had been closed to them. Jews took advantage of this new freedom and opportunity.

Motivated by the fierce desire of outsiders to prove their worth and aided by deeply embedded traditions that valued education and family life, many Jews achieved striking success as entrepreneurs, bankers, lawyers, journalists, doctors, scientists, scholars, and performers. For example, in 1880, Jews, who constituted about 10 percent of the Viennese population, accounted for 38.6 percent of the medical students and 23.3 percent of the law students in Vienna. Viennese cultural life before World War I was to a large extent shaped by Jewish writers, artists, musicians, critics, and patrons. All but one of the major banking houses were Jewish. However, most European Jews—peasants, peddlers, and laborers—were quite poor. Perhaps five thousand to six thousand Jews of Galicia in Austria-Hungary died of starvation annually, and many Russian Jews fled to the United States to escape from desperate poverty.

Like other bourgeois, the Jews who were members of the commercial and professional classes gravitated toward liberalism. Moreover, as victims of persecution, they naturally favored societies that were committed to the liberal ideals of legal equality, toleration, the rule of law, and equality of opportunity. Because they strongly supported parliamentary government and the entire system of values associated with the Enlightenment, the Jews became targets for conservatives and Volkish thinkers, who repudiated the humanist and cosmopolitan outlook of liberalism and professed a militant nationalism. To Volkish thinkers, the West represented an alien culture hostile to German racial-national identity; and the Jews, an alien race, symbolized the West.

Anti-Semites invented a mythical evil, the Jew, whom they blamed for all the social and economic ills caused by the rapid growth of industries and cities and for all the new ideas that were undermining the Old Order. Their anxieties and fears concentrated on the Jews, to whom they attributed everything they considered to be wrong in the modern age, all that threatened the German Volk. In the mythical world of Volkish thinkers, the Jews were regarded as foreign intruders who could never be loyal to the fatherland; as racial inferiors whose genes could infect and weaken the German race and debase its culture; and as international conspirators who were plotting to dominate Germany and the world. This latter accusation was a secularized and updated version of the medieval myth that Jews were plotting to destroy Christendom. In an extraordinary display of irrationality, Volkish thinkers held that Jews throughout the world were gaining control over political parties, the press, and the economy in order to dominate the planet.

The myth of a Jewish world conspiracy found its culminating expression in a notorious forgery, the *Protocols of the Elders of Zion*. The *Protocols* was written in France in the 1890s by an unknown author in the service of the Russian secret police, which sought to justify the tsarist regime's anti-Semitic policies. The forger concocted a tale of a meeting of Jewish elders in the Jewish cemetery of Prague. In these eerie surroundings, the elders plot to take over the world. First published in Russia in 1903, the *Protocols* was widely distributed after World War I and widely believed.

German anti-Semites viewed the *Protocols* as convincing evidence that the Jews were responsible for starting World War I, for Germany's defeat, and for the revolution that toppled the monarchy at the war's end. Nazi propagandists exploited the *Protocols* to justify their quest for power. Even after the *Protocols* was exposed as a blatant forgery, it continued to be translated and distributed. For anti-Semites, the myth of a Jewish world conspiracy had become an integrating principle; it provided satisfying answers to the crucial questions of existence.

In the Middle Ages, Jews had been persecuted and humiliated primarily for religious reasons. In the nineteenth century, national-racial considerations supplemented the traditional, biased Christian perception of Jews and Judaism. But whereas Christian anti-Semites believed that Jews could escape the curse of their religion through conversion, racial anti-Semites, who used the language of Social Darwinism, said that Germans and Jews belonged to different species of the human race, that Jews were indelibly stained and eternally condemned by their biological makeup. Their evil and worthlessness derived from inherited racial characteristics, which could not be altered by conversion. As one anti-Semitic deputy stated in a speech before the German Reichstag in 1895,

> *If one designates the whole of Jewry, one does so in the knowledge that the racial qualities of this people are such that in the long run they cannot harmonize with the racial qualities of the Germanic peoples and that every Jew who at this moment has not done anything bad may nevertheless under the proper conditions do precisely that, because his racial qualities drive him to do it. . . . [T]he Jews . . . operate like parasites . . . the Jews are cholera germs.*[3]

The Jewish population of Germany was quite small: in 1900, it was only about 497,000, or 0.95 percent, of the total population of 50,626,000. Jews were proud of their many contributions to German economic and cultural life (by the 1930s, 30 percent of the Nobel Prize winners in Germany were Jews). They considered themselves patriotic Germans, relished German literature and music, and regarded Germany as an altogether desirable place to live—a place of refuge in comparison to Russia, where Jews lived in terrible poverty and suffered violent attacks.

German anti-Semitic organizations and political parties failed to get the state to pass anti-Semitic laws, and by the early 1900s, these groups had declined in political power and importance. But the mischief had been done. In the minds of many Germans, even in respectable circles, the image of the Jew as an evil and dangerous creature had been firmly planted. It was perpetuated by schools, youth groups, the Pan-German

Association, and an array of racist pamphlets and books. Late-nineteenth-century racial anti-Semites had constructed an ideological foundation on which Hitler would later build his movement. In words that foreshadowed Hitler, Paul de Lagarde, professor of oriental languages, said of the Jews: "One does not have dealings with pests and parasites; one does not rear them and cherish them; one destroys them as speedily and thoroughly as possible."[4]

It is, of course, absurd to believe that a nation of fifty million was threatened by half a million citizens of Jewish birth, or that the eleven million Jews of the world (by 1900) had organized to rule the planet. The Jewish birthrate in Germany was low, the rate of intermarriage high, and the desire for complete assimilation into German life great. Within a few generations, the Jewish community in Germany might well have disappeared. Contrary to the paranoid claims of the anti-Semites, the German Jews and the Jews in the rest of Europe were actually quite powerless. There were scarcely any Jews in the ruling circles of governments, armies, civil services, or heavy industries. As events were to prove, the Jews, with no army or state and dwelling in lands where many despised them, were the weakest of peoples. But the race mystics, convinced that they were waging a war of self-defense against a satanic foe, were impervious to rational argument. Anti-Semites, said Theodor Mommsen, the great nineteenth-century German historian, would not listen to "logical and ethical arguments. . . . They listen only to their own envy and hatred, to the meanest instincts. Nothing else counts for them. They are deaf to reason, right, morals. One cannot influence them. . . . [Anti-Semitism] is a horrible epidemic, like cholera—one can neither explain nor cure it."[5]

Racial nationalism, a major element in nineteenth-century intellectual life, attacked and undermined the Enlightenment tradition. Racial nationalists denied equality, scorned toleration, dismissed the idea of the oneness of humanity, and made myth and superstition vital forces in political life. They distorted reason and science to demonize and condemn an entire people and to justify humiliation and persecution. They presented a pathogenic racial ideology, fraught with unreason and hate, as something virtuous and

idealistic. That many people, including the educated and the elite, accepted these racial doctrines was an ominous sign for Western civilization. It made plain the tenuousness of the rational tradition of the Enlightenment and showed how receptive the mind is to dangerous myths and how easily human behavior can degenerate into inhumanity.

THE EMERGENCE OF THE NEW IMPERIALISM

The Second Industrial Revolution coincided with an age of imperialism as European states (and the United States) extended their hegemony over much of the globe. Why did Westerners strive to claim and control most of the world?

Causes

Some historians suggest that the *new imperialism* (to differentiate it from the *colonialism* of settlement and trade that flourished from the sixteenth to the eighteenth century) was a direct result of industrialization. As economic activity and competition intensified, Europeans struggled for raw materials, markets for their manufactured goods, and places to invest their capital. In the late nineteenth century, many politicians and industrialists believed that the only way for their nations to ensure their economic necessities was through the acquisition of overseas territories.

Captains of industry defended the new empires to their sometimes reluctant governments and compatriots, predicting dire consequences if their nation failed to get its share of the world markets. However, their expectations often did not materialize. Historians point to the fact that most areas claimed by Europeans and Americans did not possess profitable sources of raw materials or enough wealth to be good markets. For Europeans and Americans, the primary trading and investment areas were Europe and America rather than Asia or Africa. Some individual businesses made colonial profits, but most colonies proved unprofitable for the Western taxpayer.

The economic motivations for imperialism are inseparable from the intensely nationalistic one: the desire to win glory for the nation. Nationalists in newly unified Germany and Italy demanded colonies as recognition of their countries' Great Power status. Convinced that Britain's standing depended on colonies and naval power, they wanted their nations as well to "have a place in the sun." After its inglorious defeat by Prussia in 1870, France also turned its attention overseas, hoping to recoup some prestige and to add to its manpower (by recruiting colonials) and wealth for future European struggles. For a time, the nationalistic competition among the Europeans led them to extend their power struggles to Africa and Asia.

With its image of national vitality and competition between the fit and the unfit, Social Darwinism was the most extreme ideological expression of nationalism. Social Darwinists vigorously advocated the acquisition of empires, contending that the strong nations—by definition, those that were successful at expanding industry and empire—would survive and that others would not. To these elitists, all white men were more fit than nonwhites to prevail in the struggle for dominance, but among Europeans, some nations were deemed more fit than others for the competition. In the popular mind, survival of the fittest justified the exploitation of "lesser breeds" by superior races. This language of race and conflict, of superior and inferior people, was widely used, particularly in Germany, Britain, and the United States.

Not all advocates of empire were Social Darwinists, however. Some believed that the extension of empire, law, order, and industrial civilization would raise "backward peoples" up the ladder of civilization. Many westerners deemed it their duty as Christians to set an example and to uplift and convert Africans and Asians. Christian missionaries who went to unexplored African regions to preach against slavery, which was still carried on by Arab and African traders, believed that to end slavery, Europeans must provide law, order, and stability.

Control and Resistance

Aided by superior technology and the machinery of the modern state, Europeans established varying degrees of political control over much of the rest of the world. Control could mean outright annexation and the governing of a territory as a colony. In this way, Germany controlled Tanganyika (in east-central Africa) after 1886, and Britain ruled much of India. Control could also mean status as a protectorate, an arrangement whereby the local ruler continued to rule but was directed, or "protected," by a Great Power. That is how the British controlled Egypt after 1882 and maintained authority over their dependent Indian princes, and how France guarded Tunisia. There were also spheres of influence, where, without military or political control, a European nation had special trading and legal privileges that other Europeans did not have. At the turn of the century, the Russians and the British divided Persia (Iran), each recognizing the other's sphere of influence—Russia's in the north and Britain's in the south.

In some non-Western lands, the governing authorities granted Europeans extraterritoriality, or the right of foreigners to a trial by their own laws in other countries. Often, too, Europeans lived a segregated and privileged life in quarters, clubs, and whole sections of foreign lands or cities in which no native was allowed to live.

Many non-Europeans resisted American and European economic penetration and political control in varied ways, and the very process of resistance shaped their history and their self-awareness. Such resistance became a statement of both national and individual identity. It could be violent: the many instances of violent resistance included the Sudanese Muslims' holy war led by the Mahdi Mohammed Ahmed against both Egyptian fellow Muslims, who were regarded as agents of the European nonbelievers, and the Europeans; the Boxer Rebellion in China; and the Sepoy Mutiny in India. Some resisters, however, took a different path. Also imbued with strongly nationalistic feelings, they reacted to Western penetration by fighting to strengthen the nationalism of their people, sometimes even going to Western universities, military schools, and factories to master the West's modern ways, including advanced technology. Mohandas Gandhi, Jawaharlal Nehru, Sun Zhongshan (Sun Yat-sen), Jiang Jieshi (Chiang Kai-shek), and Mustapha Kemal Atatürk were the most famous leaders of nationalistic resistance to the West.

EUROPEAN DOMINATION OF ASIA

Western influence in Asia expanded during the middle decades of the nineteenth century. Increased contact with Western ideas and institutions had a profound impact on Asian societies.

India

In the last part of the eighteenth century, the British East India Company became a territorial power in India. It gained the upper hand by making alliances with warring princes, by carrying on trade and collecting taxes, and by commanding armies of *sepoys* (native soldiers). Parliament regulated the chartered monopoly enterprise but in fact did not control it much until the Sepoy Mutiny of 1857–58. (The Indians call this massive act of resistance the Great Rebellion.) This major popular uprising joined Muslim and Hindu soldiers with some native princes, who finally perceived that the British, rather than neighboring princes, were the true threat to their authority. With the aid of faithful troops from the Punjab, the British repressed the uprising. The rebellion caused Parliament to abolish the East India Company and to make India an integral part of the British Empire. The British ruled some states through dependent Indian princes, but about two-thirds of the subcontinent was ruled directly by about a thousand British officials in the civil service.

At first, the civil service was entirely British, its officials confident of the superiority of their people, law, and society. Later, an elite of Indians, educated in English and trained in administration, became part of it. Indian civil servants, along with soldiers recruited from peoples with military traditions, such as the Gurkhas and the Punjabis, carried out British laws, adding their interpretations, customs, and traditions. By 1900, a civil service of four thousand Europeans and half a million Indians ruled some 300 million Indians.

The British built a modern railroad and communications system and developed agriculture and industry to meet the needs of the world market. As a link to areas of food surplus, the railroad reduced the incidence and impact of local famines, which had plagued India's history.

British rule also ended internal war and disorder. Population increased as fewer people died of starvation and lives were saved by Western medical practices. But many students of history believe that the Indian masses did not benefit from economic progress because they could not pay their debts in money, as their landlords now demanded. Furthermore, the British flooded the Indian market with cheap, machine-produced English goods, driving native artisans out of business or even deeper into debt.

The racism that excluded the Indian elite from British clubs, hotels, and social gatherings and from top government positions alienated the leaders that British rule had created. Many of the older elite of princes and landlords who may have profited from British connections resented the lack of respect for Indian traditions and culture. Educated Indians, demanding equality and self-government, created the Indian National Congress in the 1880s. The Congress party ultimately organized masses of Indians to work toward independence.

In 1919, at Amritsar in Punjab, a British officer commanded his Gurkha troops to fire into a peaceful demonstration until their ammunition was exhausted; 379 Indians died and 1,200 were wounded. Women and children were among the victims. The government punished the officer, but the British community in India gave him a fortune, honoring him for what he had done. The massacre and British behavior stung Indians to action—even those Indians who had supported the British.

Out of this feverish period emerged a gentle but determined revolutionary leader, Mohandas K. Gandhi (1869–1948). He had led the resistance to the vicious system of racial discrimination faced by the Indian community in South Africa and, in the process, developed a doctrine of civil disobedience and nonviolent resistance. He believed that the power of love and spiritual purity would ultimately overthrow British rule in

Map 16.1 Asia in 1914 In addition to the lands ▶ depicted in the map under European and American domination, western states also exercised control over technically sovereign states, particularly China and Siam (Thailand).

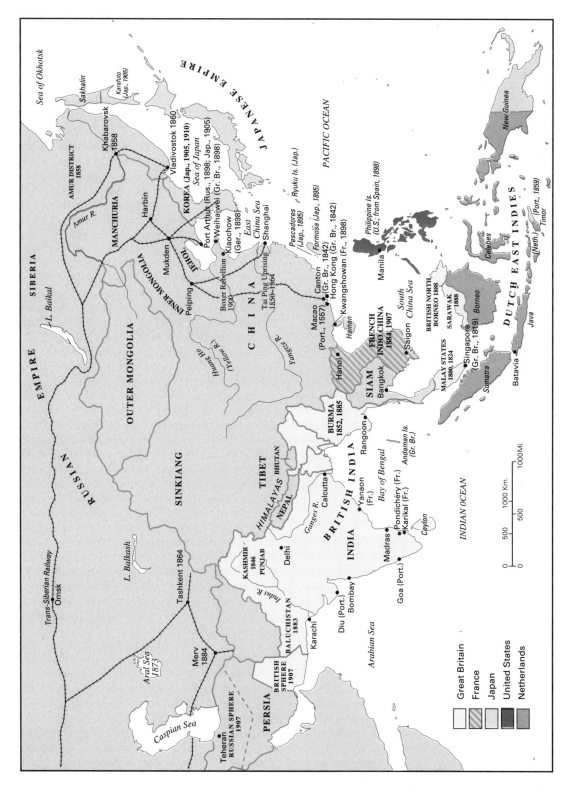

Sea of Okhotsk

Karafuto (Jap., 1905)

Sakhalin

JAPANESE EMPIRE

RUSSIAN EMPIRE

SIBERIA

AMUR DISTRICT 1858

Khabarovsk 1858

Amur R.

MANCHURIA

Harbin

Vladivostok 1860

Sea of Japan

KOREA (Jap., 1905, 1910)

Port Arthur (Rus., 1898; Jap., 1905)

Weihaiwei (Gr. Br., 1898)

L. Baikal

INNER MONGOLIA

OUTER MONGOLIA

Mukden

JEHOL

Peiping

Kiaochow (Ger., 1898)

Shanghai

East China Sea

Boxer Rebellion 1900

CHINA

Hwang Ho (Yellow) R.

Ryuku Is. (Jap.)

PACIFIC OCEAN

Pescadores (Jap., 1895)

Formosa (Jap., 1895)

Tai Ping Uprising 1850–1864

Yangtze R.

Canton (Gr. Br., 1842)

Macao (Port., 1557)

Hong Kong (Gr. Br., 1842)

Kwangshowan (Fr., 1898)

Hainan

South China Sea

Philippine Is. (U.S.; from Spain, 1898)

Manila

New Guinea

DUTCH EAST INDIES

Celebes

(Neth.) (Port., 1859)

Timor

FRENCH INDO CHINA 1884, 1907

Hanoi

SIAM

Bangkok

Saigon

BRITISH NORTH BORNEO 1888

SARAWAK 1888

Borneo

Singapore (Gr. Br., 1819)

MALAY STATES 1800, 1824

Sumatra

Batavia

Java

RUSSIAN EMPIRE

RUSSIA

L. Balkash

SINKIANG

Trans-Siberian Railway

Omsk

Tashkent 1864

Aral Sea 1873

Merv 1884

TIBET

HIMALAYAS

BHUTAN

NEPAL

BURMA 1852, 1885

Rangoon

Andaman Is. (Gr. Br.)

Bay of Bengal

Calcutta

BRITISH INDIA

Ganges R.

Yanaon (Fr.)

Pondichéry (Fr.)

Karikal (Fr.)

Ceylon

INDIAN OCEAN

KASHMIR 1846

PUNJAB

Delhi

INDIA

Madras

Indus R.

BALUCHISTAN 1883

Diu (Port.)

Bombay

Goa (Port.)

Karachi

BRITISH SPHERE 1907

PERSIA

RUSSIAN SPHERE 1907

Teheran

Caspian Sea

Arabian Sea

1000 Mi.

1000 Km.

500

500

0

0

Great Britain

France

Japan

United States

Netherlands

India. His was a spiritually uplifting message, and a shrewd political tactic as well. Gandhi called on the Indian elite to give up the privileges allotted by the British and to resign their positions, boycott British schools, and boycott all foreign goods. He dramatically rallied mass support with "the march to the sea": a mass refusal to pay taxes on salt. When imprisoned, Gandhi and his followers fasted for spiritual discipline. But their tactic also threatened the British, for if the confined leaders should starve to death, more civil disturbances might erupt. Gandhi also emphasized the boycott of foreign goods by spinning cotton and wearing simple native dress. To gain independence, Gandhi was even willing to sacrifice the higher standard of living that an industrial economy could bring to India.

Independence finally came after World War II had exhausted British resources and reduced British power. It was achieved without a war between Britain and India—an accomplishment that many credit to the strength of Gandhi's moral leadership. But even his leadership could not prevent the partition of the country into Muslim Pakistan and predominantly Hindu India. Nor could it prevent conflict between Hindus and Muslims, as bloody massacres following independence clearly revealed.

China

The defeat of the Chinese by the British in the Opium War of 1839–1842 forced the Manchu dynasty to open trade with the West. Before the war, such commerce had been limited, controlled by native monopolists to whom the emperor had granted trading privileges. When the Chinese government destroyed Indian opium being traded by the East India Company, the British aggressively asserted their right to free trade and demanded compensation. In the subsequent war, Britain seized several trading cities along the coast, including Hong Kong, and the Chinese capitulated. In the Treaty of Nanking (1842), the British insisted on determining the tariffs that the Chinese might charge them. Furthermore, British subjects in China would have the right to be tried according to their own law (the right of extraterritorial-

ity). Both provisions undermined the emperor's ability to control the foreigners in his country.

Defeat in the Opium War also forced change on the emperor. He drew on China's mandarins (high officials) to revitalize the Manchu bureaucracy by cleaning out much of the official corruption, which weighed heavily on the poorest taxpayers, and by strengthening China against the westerners, sometimes by hiring westerners to train Chinese armies. Nevertheless, widespread economic discontent, hatred of the Manchu (who were regarded by many Chinese as foreign conquerors, even though the conquest had taken place some two hundred years earlier), and religious mysticism led to the Taiping Rebellion of 1850–1864. This uprising seriously threatened the dynasty, which called on Western assistance to suppress the rebels. For this aid, Britain and France extorted additional concessions from the emperor.

For a time, the Europeans seemed content with trading rights in coastal towns and preferential treatment for their subjects. But the Sino-Japanese War of 1894–95, which Japan won easily because of China's weakness, encouraged the Europeans to mutilate China. Britain, France, Russia, and Germany all scrambled for concessions, protectorates, and spheres of influence. China might have been carved up like Africa, but each Western nation, afraid of its rivals, resisted any partition that might possibly give another state an advantage. The United States, which insisted that it be given any trading concession that any other state received, proclaimed an "Open Door" policy: that trade should be open to all and that the Great Powers should respect China's territorial integrity. The U.S. action may have restrained the Western powers from partitioning China, but it was also a way to safeguard American interests there.

Chinese traditionalists organized secret societies to expel foreigners and to punish those Chinese who accepted Christianity or any other form of westernization. In 1900, encouraged by Empress Tzu-hsi, the Society of Righteous and Harmonious Fists (called the Boxers by Europeans) attacked foreigners throughout the north of China. An international army of Europeans, Japanese, and Americans suppressed the rebellion, seized Chinese treasures, and forced China

Commodore Perry and the U.S. Squadron Meeting Japanese Imperial Commissioners at Yokohama, 1854. Commodore Matthew Perry had opened Japan, against its will, to the West the preceding year. With the Meiji Restoration of 1867, a strong central government pushed Japan until it became one of the top ten industrial nations by 1900. Japan's imperialistic expansion brought it into conflict with China, Russia, and the Western imperialist powers. (*Culver Pictures*)

to pay an indemnity. They also made China agree to the stationing of foreign troops on its soil.

Chinese discontent with the dynasty deepened, as did unrest and nationalistic opposition to the foreigners. When the Japanese defeated the Russians in 1905, many Chinese argued that the only way to protect their country was to imitate the West, as the Japanese had done. Many signs of growing nationalism appeared. In 1911, nationalist revolutionaries, strongly present among soldiers, workers, and students, overthrew the Manchu and declared a republic. Sun Zhongshan (Sun Yat-sen, 1866–1925), who was in the United States when the revolution broke out, returned to China to become the first president of the republic and the head of the Nationalist party.

Espousing the Western ideas of democracy, nationalism, and social welfare (the three principles of the people, as Sun called them), the republic struggled to establish its authority over a China torn by civil war and ravaged by foreigners. Russia was claiming Mongolia, and Britain was claiming Tibet. The northern warlords, who were regional leaders with private armies, resisted any attempt to strengthen the republic's army because it might diminish their power. In the south, however, the republic more or less maintained control. After Sun's death, the Guomindong (Kuomintang), under the authoritarian leadership of Jiang Jieshi (Chiang Kai-shek, 1887–1975), tried to westernize by using the military power of the state and introducing segments of a modern economic system. But faced with civil war, attacked both from the right and from the Communist left under Mao Zedong (Mao Tse-tung, 1893–1976), and by the Japanese after 1931, the Guomindong made slow progress. A divided China continued to be at the mercy of outside interests until after World War II.

Japan

Japan, like China, was opened to the West against its will. The Japanese had expelled Europeans in the seventeenth century, remaining isolated for the next two hundred years. By the 1850s, however, as in India and China, social dissension within Japan and foreign pressure combined to force the country to admit outside trade. Americans in particular refused to accept Japanese prohibitions on commercial and religious contacts. Like China, Japan succumbed to superior technological power. In 1853, Commodore Matthew C. Perry sailed into Tokyo Bay, making a show of American strength and forcing the Japanese to sign a number of treaties that granted westerners extraterritoriality and control over tariffs.

A flood of violence surged over Japan. Determined to preserve Japan's independence, a group of *samurai,* the warrior nobility, seized the government. This takeover—the Meiji Restoration of 1867—returned power to the emperor, or Meiji, from the feudal aristocracy, which had ruled in his name for almost seven hundred years. The new government enacted a series of reforms, turning Japan into a powerful modern unitary state. Large landowners were persuaded to give their estates to the emperor in exchange for compensation and high-level positions in the government. All classes were made equal before the law. As in France and Germany, universal military service was required, which diminished social privilege and helped to imbue Japanese of all classes with nationalism. The Japanese modeled their constitution on Bismarck's: there was a parliament, but the emperor held the most authority, which he delegated to his ministers to govern in his name without much control from the parliament.

The Meiji regime introduced modern industry and economic competition. Japanese visited factories all over the West and hired westerners to teach industrial skills. The government built de-

fense industries, backed heavy industry and mining, and developed a modern communications system of railways, roads, and telegraphs. Industry in Japan adopted traditional Japanese values and emphasized cooperation more than competition; relations between employer and employee were paternalistic rather than individualistic and deferential rather than hostile. Within little more than a generation of the Meiji Restoration, Japan moved from economic backwardness to a place among the top ten industrial nations. To underdeveloped countries, Japan became a model of a nation that borrowed from the West yet preserved its traditional values and social structure.

By 1900, Japan had ended the humiliating treaties with the West and become an imperialist power in its own right. It had won Taiwan and Korea in its war with China in 1894–95, although the Great Powers intervened, forcing the Japanese to return some of the spoils of victory while they themselves grabbed greater spheres of influence from the helpless Chinese. Their self-serving maneuvering infuriated the Japanese. Finally, in 1904, conflict over influence in Manchuria brought Japan and Russia to war, which Japan won. The victory of an Asian power over a Western power had a tremendous impact on Asian nationalists. If Japan could unite its people with nationalism and strong leadership, others should be able to do likewise. Japan's victory inspired anti-Western and nationalist movements throughout China, Indochina, India, and the Middle East.

In the 1930s, militarist and fascist groups, which were set on imperialism in Manchuria and China, gained the upper hand in Japan. To Asians in the 1930s, Japan seemed to champion Asian racial equality and to oppose Western imperialism. Many leaders of nationalist movements in Burma, India, Indochina, and Indonesia were attracted for a time by Japan's pose. World War II, however, brought Japanese occupation and exploitation, not freedom and equality for Asians.

THE SCRAMBLE FOR AFRICA

The most rapid European expansion took place in Africa. Until the 1870s, Great Power interest in Africa seemed marginal and likely to decline even

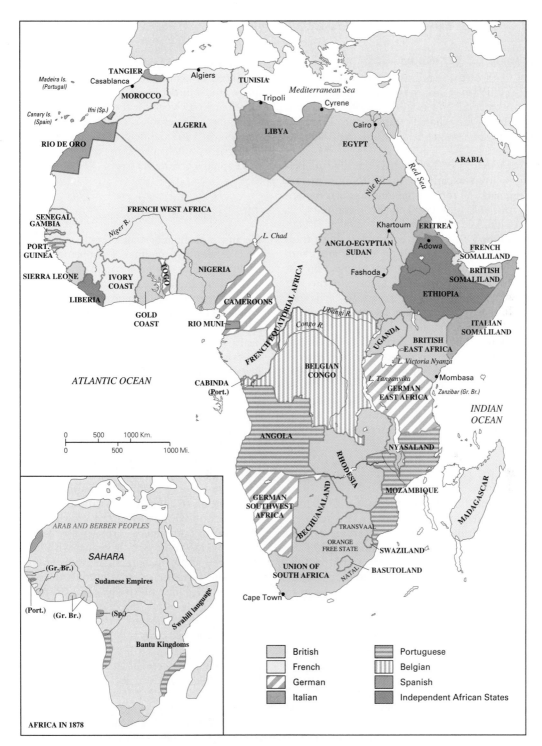

Map 16.2 Africa in 1914 Africa's rapid dismemberment is pictured in these two maps. In 1878 there were few enclaves of Europeans along the coasts. By 1914 Africa had been carved up and all but Ethiopia and Liberia had been claimed.

further. As late as 1880, European nations ruled just a tenth of the continent. Only three decades later, by 1914, Europeans had claimed all of Africa except Liberia (a small territory of freed slaves from the United States) and Ethiopia, which had successfully held off Italian invaders at Adowa in 1896.

The activities of Leopold II, the king of Belgium, spurred expansion. In 1876, as a private entrepreneur, he formed the International Association for the Exploration and Civilization of Central Africa. Leopold sent Henry Stanley (1841–1904) to the Congo River Basin to establish trading posts, sign treaties with the chiefs, and claim the territory for the association. Stanley, an adventurer and a newspaper reporter who had fought on both sides of the American Civil War, had earlier led an expedition to central Africa in search of David Livingstone, the popular missionary explorer, who was believed to be in danger. For men like Stanley, Leopold's private development efforts promised profit and adventure. For the Africans, they promised brutal exploitation. The French responded to Leopold's actions by immediately establishing a protectorate on the north bank of the Congo. The scramble was on.

The Berlin Conference

Bismarck and Jules Ferry, the premier of France, called an international conference of the Great Powers in Berlin in 1884 to lay some ground rules for the development of Africa south of the Sahara. The Berlin Conference established the rule that a European country had to occupy territory in order to claim it. This led to a mad race to the interior of Africa; it was a field day for explorers and soldiers. As Europeans rushed to claim territory, they ignored both natural and cultural frontiers. Even today, the map of Africa reveals many straight (and thus artificial) boundary lines, rather than the irregular lines of natural boundaries, such as rivers and mountains.

The conference declared that Leopold (as an individual, not as the king of Belgium) was the personal ruler of the Congo Free State. Before long, Leopold's Congo Association was trying to turn a profit with practices as vicious as those of the African slave traders. At the turn of the cen-

tury, Edward D. Morel, an English humanitarian, produced evidence that slavery, mutilation, brutality, and murder were commonly practiced to force blacks to work for the rubber plantations in the Congo. In response to the outcry of public opinion, in 1908 the Belgian parliament declared the territory a Belgian colony, thus putting an end to Leopold's private enterprise.

The British in Africa

For much of the nineteenth century, British interest in Africa was minimal. The opening, in 1869, of the Suez Canal, which Britain viewed as a vital highway to India, greatly increased the strategic value of Egypt. Officially a part of the Ottoman Empire, Egypt had, in effect, been independent of the Ottoman sultan since the 1830s. When a nearly bankrupt Egypt could not pay its foreign debts and was threatened with internal rebellion, Britain intervened as "protector" in 1882. Prime Minister Gladstone, a "little Englander" (one who opposed empire), promised to withdraw British troops once the situation stabilized.

Not only did the British fail to withdraw from Egypt, they moved further south into the Sudan to quell a Muslim holy war against Egyptian authority and British influence. In 1885, the Sudanese, led by the Mahdi, who viewed himself as the successor to Muhammad, captured Khartoum and killed the popular General Charles Gordon, the recently appointed governor-general of the Sudan. In 1898, the British, armed with machine guns, mowed down charging Muslims at Omdurman. The casualties were reported to be eleven thousand Muslims and twenty-eight Britons.

Immediately after the battle, British forces confronted the French at Fashoda in the Sudan. In the diplomatic crisis that followed, Britain and France were brought to the brink of war, and public passions were inflamed. However, since France was too divided by the Dreyfus affair at home to risk a showdown with Britain, the French cabinet ordered retreat.

The British also sought territory in South Africa. Cecil Rhodes (1853–1902), who had gone to South Africa for his health in 1870 and made a fortune in diamonds and gold, dreamed of expanding the British Empire. "The British," he de-

The Battle of Omdurman, 1898. A romanticized oil painting depicts the British lancers at the battle of Omdurman in heroic terms. The Muslim fundamentalists who followed the Mahdi in his attempts to expel the Egyptians and British from the Sudan were massacred in 1898 by General Kitchener. As many as 11,000 dervishes were killed, but the British suffered only slight casualties. Paintings such as this fed the public hunger for heroism and thirst for exotic places. (*Eileen Tweedy/The Art Archive*)

clared, "are the finest race in the world and the more of the world we inhabit the better it is for the human race."[6] Rhodes was responsible for acquiring Rhodesia (Zimbabwe), a sizable and wealthy territory, for Britain. He also plotted to involve Britain in a war with the Boers, Dutch farmers and cattlemen who had settled in South Africa in the seventeenth century.

During the Napoleonic wars, the British had gained Cape Town, at the southern tip of Africa, a useful provisioning place for trading ships bound for India. Despising British rule and refusing to accept the British abolition of slavery in 1833, the Boers moved northward in a migration called the Great Trek (1835–37), warring with African tribes along the way. They established two republics, the Transvaal and the Orange Free State, whose independence the British recognized in the 1850s. The republics' democratic practices did not extend to black Africans, who were denied political rights. In 1877, the British annexed the Transvaal, but Boer resistance forced them in 1881 to recognize the Transvaal's independence again.

The discovery of rich deposits of gold and diamonds in the Boer lands reinforced Rhodes's dream of building a great British empire in Africa. In 1895, his close friend Leander Jameson led some six hundred armed men into the

Transvaal, hoping to create a pretext for a British invasion. Although the raid failed and both Jameson and Rhodes were disgraced, tensions between Britain and the Boer republics worsened, and in 1899 the Anglo-Boer War broke out.

The Boers were formidable opponents—farmers by day and commandos by night, armed with the latest French and German rifles. To deal with their stubborn foe, the British herded, or "concentrated," thousands of Boers, including women and children, into compounds surrounded by barbed wire, where some twenty-five thousand perished. The nasty war ended in 1902. Hoping to live together in peace with the Boers, the British drew up a conciliatory treaty. In 1910, the former Boer republics were joined with the British territories into the Union of South Africa. Self-government within the British Empire for the British settlers and the Boers did not help the majority black population; it still had to cope with the Boers' deeply entrenched racist attitudes.

Other European Countries in Africa

The cost of imperialism in Africa seemed high not only to the British, but to other imperialists as well. The Italians' defeat at Adowa (1896) by Ethiopians belied Italian dreams of empire and national glory. (Bismarck scoffed that the Italians had enormous appetites but very poor teeth.) Germans could take little heart from their African acquisitions—Southwest Africa (Namibia), East Africa (Tanzania, but not Zanzibar, which was British), the Cameroons, and Togo (part of Ghana today). The German colonies were the most efficiently governed (critics said the most ruthlessly controlled), but they yielded few benefits other than pride of ownership, because they were costly to govern. And the Belgians had obviously gained no prestige from the horrors perpetrated in the Congo. Serious thinkers, contemplating the depths to which Europeans would sink in search of fortune and fame, began to suggest that barbarity characterized the Europeans more than the Africans. The Europeans seemed to be the moral barbarians, as novelist Joseph Conrad and others pointed out. For the most part, honor was fleeting and profits illusory in these new African empires.

THE LEGACY OF IMPERIALISM

World War I was a turning point in the history of imperialism, although neither mother countries nor colonies seemed aware of it at the time. The principle of self-determination, championed for European nationalities at the peace conference, was seized on by Asian and African intellectuals, who intensified their anti-imperialist efforts. After World War II, the exhausted colonial powers were reluctant to fight rebellious colonies. Moreover, after waging war to destroy Nazi imperialism and racism, European colonial powers had little moral justification to deny other peoples self-determination.

A century after the rapid division of the world among the European powers and the United States and decades after the decolonization of most of the world, the consequences of imperialism persist. Imperialism has left a legacy of deep animosity in the countries of Asia, Africa, and Latin America. Although virtually all nations have political independence, nationalists resent Western economic and cultural influences. Much of the world is still poor and suffers from insufficient capital, unskilled leaders, and unstable governments. Many people in these poor areas believe that their countries' condition has resulted from years of Western exploitation.

To former colonial peoples, imperialism has been a source of great bitterness, not only because of its economic exploitation, but also because of its encouragement of racism and callous disregard of other cultures. Thus, non-Western nationalism has often included anti-Western elements. Today, European nations and the United States must deal in the areas of economics and politics with nations acutely conscious of their nationhood and quick to condemn any policy that they perceive as imperialistic.

Imperialism accelerated the growth of a global market economy, completing the trend that started with the commercial revolution of the sixteenth and seventeenth centuries. At the beginning of the twentieth century, in many parts of Europe, even the working classes and the peasantry were able to buy goods from faraway places—goods that had previously been available only to the very wealthy. The underdeveloped areas of the world, in turn, found markets for their crops and were able to buy European goods—at least, the wealthy could.

Imperialism has also fostered the spread of Western civilization around the globe. The influence of Western ideas, institutions, techniques, language, and culture is apparent everywhere. English and, to some extent, French are international languages. African and Asian lands have adopted, often with limited success, democracy and parliamentary government from the West. Socialism, a Western ideology, has been transplanted in some Third World countries. Industrialism and modern science, both achievements of the West, have become globalized. So, too, have Western agricultural techniques, business practices, medicine, legal procedures, school curricula, architecture, music, and dress. That Turkish women are no longer required to wear the veil, that Chinese women no longer have their feet bound, that Indians have outlawed untouchability, that, with exceptions, Arabs, Africans, and Indians no longer practice slavery—all these changes have occurred under the influence of Western ideas. (To be sure, cultural forms have not moved in only one direction: African and Asian ways have also influenced Western lands.) The impact of Western ways on Asian and African lands is one of the most crucial developments of our time.

❖   ❖   ❖

NOTES

1. Cited in Edward R. Tannenbaum, *1900: The Generation Before the Great War* (Garden City, N.Y.: Doubleday, 1976), p. 337.

2. Cited in Horst von Maltitz, *The Evolution of Hitler's Germany* (New York: McGraw-Hill, 1973), p. 33.

3. Quoted in Raul Hilberg, *The Destruction of the European Jews* (Chicago: Quadrangle, 1967), pp. 10–11.

4. Quoted in Helmut Krausnick, Hans Buchheim, Martin Broszat, and Hans-Adolf Jacobsen, *Anatomy of the SS State,* trans. Richard Barry et al. (London: William Collins Sons, 1968), p. 9.

5. Quoted in Peter G. J. Pulzer, *The Rise of Political Anti-Semitism in Germany and Austria* (New York: Wiley, 1964), p. 299.

6. Joseph E. Flint, *Cecil Rhodes* (Boston: Little Brown, 1974), p. 248.

SUGGESTED READING

Brunschwig, Henri, *French Colonialism: 1871–1914. Myths and Realities* (trans. 1964). The best book on French imperialism.

Craig, Gordon, *Politics of the Prussian Army* (1955). A very valuable study, with important implications for German and European history.

Fischer, Klaus P., *The History of an Obsession* (1998). A new and superb study of German-Jewish relations, particularly the delusionary character of anti-Jewish thinking.

Ford, Colin, and Brian Harrison, *A Hundred Years Ago* (1983). An excellent social history of Britain, with fine photographs.

Hobsbawm, Eric, *The Age of Capital* (1988). A Marxist interpretation of mid-nineteenth-century Europe.

Holborn, Hajo, *A History of Modern Germany, 1840–1945,* vol. 3 (1969). A definitive work.

Joll, James, *Europe Since 1870* (1973). A valuable general survey, particularly good on socialism in the individual nations.

Katz, Jacob, *From Prejudice to Destruction* (1980). A survey of modern anti-Semitism; views modern anti-Semitism as an outgrowth of traditional Christian anti-Semitism.

Kemp, Tom, *Industrialization in Nineteenth-Century Europe* (1985). Readable general survey incorporating recent scholarship.

Mack Smith, Denis, *Italy: A Modern History,* rev. ed. (1969). An excellent survey, emphasizing the theme of the failure of Italy to develop viable liberal institutions or economic solutions.

Mosse, George L., *Toward the Final Solution* (1978). An analysis of European racism.

———, *The Crisis of German Ideology* (1964). Explores the dark side of German nationalism; an excellent study of Volkish thought.

Perry, Marvin and Frederick M. Schweitzer, *Antisemitism Myth and Hate from Antiquity to the Present* (2002). Treats anti-Semitic myths and stereotypes.

Robinson, R. E., John Gallagher, and Alice Denny, *Africa and the Victorians: The Official Mind of Imperialism* (1961). An essential book for this fascinating subject; well written and controversial.

Thornton, A. P., *The Imperial Idea and Its Enemies: A Study in British Power,* 2nd ed. (1985). An interesting study of the ideas and policies of British imperialism.

Webb, R. K., *Modern England from the Eighteenth Century to the Present* (1968). A well-informed, readable book that is balanced on controversial issues.

REVIEW QUESTIONS

1. Why is the last part of the nineteenth century called the Second Industrial Revolution?

2. What was the difference between orthodox and revisionist Marxists?

3. Characterize the domestic histories of each of the following countries in the last part of the nineteenth century: Britain, France, Germany, and Italy.

4. To whom did Volkish thought appeal? Explain.

5. Why is racial nationalism a repudiation of the Enlightenment tradition and a regression to mythical thinking?

6. Anti-Semites attributed to Jews everything that they found repellent in the modern world. Discuss this statement.

7. Anti-Semitism demonstrates the immense power and danger of mythical thinking. Discuss this statement.

8. Account for the rise of the new imperialism in the last part of the nineteenth century.

9. Why and how were Europeans able to dominate African and Asian lands?

10. What role did each of the following play in the history of imperialism: Cecil Rhodes, Sun Zhongshan, Matthew C. Perry, Henry Stanley, King Leopold II?

11. What is the legacy of imperialism for the contemporary world?

Chapter 17

Modern Consciousness: New Views of Nature, Human Nature, and the Arts

- **Irrationalism**
- **Freud: A New View of Human Nature**
- **Social Thought: Confronting the Irrational and the Complexities of Modern Society**
- **The Modernist Movement**
- **Modern Physics**
- **The Enlightenment Tradition in Disarray**

*T*he modern mentality may be said to have passed through two broad phases: early modernity and late modernity. Formulated during the era of the Scientific Revolution and the Enlightenment, early modernity stressed confidence in reason, science, human goodness, and humanity's capacity to improve society. Then, in the late nineteenth and early twentieth centuries, a new outlook took shape. Late modern thinkers and scientists achieved revolutionary insights into human nature, the social world, and the physical universe; and writers and artists opened up hitherto unimagined possibilities for artistic expression.

These developments produced a shift in European consciousness. The mechanical model of the universe, which had dominated the Western outlook since Newton, was fundamentally altered. The Enlightenment view of human rationality and goodness was questioned, and the belief in natural rights and objective standards governing morality came under attack. Rules of esthetics that had governed the arts since the Renaissance were discarded. Shattering old beliefs, late modernity left Europeans without landmarks—without generally accepted cultural standards or agreed-upon conceptions about human nature and the meaning of life.

The late modern period was marked by extraordinary creativity in thought and the arts. Yet imaginative and fruitful as these changes were for Western intellectual and cultural life, they also helped to create the disoriented, fragmented, and troubled era that characterized the twentieth century. ❖

IRRATIONALISM

While many intellectuals continued to adhere to the outlook identified with the Enlightenment, some thinkers in the late nineteenth century challenged the basic premises of the philosophes and their nineteenth-century heirs. In particular, they repudiated the Enlightenment conception of human rationality, stressing instead the irrational side of human nature. Regarding reason as sovereign, the philosophes had defined human beings by their capacity to think critically; now thinkers saw blind strivings and animal instincts as the primary fact of human existence. It seemed that reason exercised a very limited influence over human conduct, that impulses, drives, and instincts—all forces below the surface—

determined behavior much more than did logical consciousness.

The problem of irrationalism is manifold. Some thinkers, while recognizing the weakness of reason, continued to value it and sought to preserve it as an essential ingredient of civilized life. Some studied manifestations of the irrational in myth, religion, the arts, and politics in a logical and systematic way in order to gain a more complete understanding of human nature and human behavior. Others, concentrating on the creative potential of the irrational, urged nourishing the feelings, which they considered vital to artistic creativity and a richer existence. Still others celebrated violence as a healthy expression of the irrational.

The new insights into the irrational side of human nature and the growing assault on reason had immense implications for political life. In succeeding decades, these currents of irrationalism would become ideologized and politicized by unscrupulous demagogues, who sought to mobilize and manipulate the masses. The popularity of fascist movements, which openly denigrated reason and exalted race, blood, action, and will, demonstrated the naiveté of nineteenth-century liberals, who believed that reason had triumphed in human affairs.

Nietzsche

The principal figure in the "dethronement of reason" and the glorification of the irrational was the German philosopher Friedrich Nietzsche (1844–1900). Nietzsche's writings are not systematic treatises but collections of aphorisms, often containing internal contradictions. Consequently, his philosophy lends itself to misinterpretation and misapplication. For example, Nazi theorists, distorted Nietzsche to justify their notions of the German master race.

Nietzsche attacked the accepted views and convictions of his day as a hindrance to a fuller and richer existence. He denounced social reform, parliamentary government, and universal suffrage; ridiculed the vision of progress through science; condemned Christian morality; and mocked the liberal belief in man's essential goodness and rationality. Man, he said, must understand that

Friedrich Nietzsche (1844–1900) with His Mother. Possessing the intuitive genius of a great poet, Nietzsche grasped the crucial problem afflicting the modern European soul: What path should the individual take in a world where God is dead? Nietzsche's answer to this question—the overman who creates his own values—lent itself to considerable misinterpretation and distortion and had little constructive social value. (*AKG London*)

life, which is replete with cruelty, injustice, uncertainty, and absurdity, is not governed by rational principles. There exist no absolute standards of good and evil whose truth can be demonstrated by reflective reason. Nothing is true; there is no higher purpose or sense to the universe or human existence. There is only the naked individual living in a godless and absurd world.

Modern bourgeois society, said Nietzsche, was decadent and enfeebled—a victim of the excessive development of the rational faculties at the expense of will and instinct. Against the liberal-rationalist stress on the intellect, Nietzsche urged recognition of the dark, mysterious world of instinctual desires—the true forces of life. Smother the will with excessive intellectualizing, and you

snuff out the spontaneity that sparks cultural creativity and ignites a zest for living. The critical and theoretical outlook destroyed the creative instincts. To realize his multifaceted potential, man must stop relying on the intellect and nurture again the instinctual roots of human existence.

Christianity, with all its prohibitions, restrictions, and demands to conform, also stifles the human impulse for life, said Nietzsche. Christian morality must be obliterated, for it is fit only for the weak, the slave. According to Nietzsche, the triumph of Christianity in the ancient world was an attempt of the resentful slave and the slavelike plebeian to prevent their aristocratic superiors from expressing their heroic natures and to strike back at those noble spirits, whom they envied. Their way of striking back was to condemn as evil the very traits that they themselves lacked—strength, power, assertiveness, and a zest for life—and to make their own base, wretched, and life-negating values the standard of all things. Then they saddled people with guilt if they deviated from these contemptible values. This transvaluation of values engineered by Christianity, said Nietzsche, led to a deterioration of life and culture.

Although the philosophes had rejected Christian doctrines, they had largely retained Christian ethics. Unlike the philosophes, however, Nietzsche did not attack Christianity because it was contrary to reason. He attacked it because, he said, it gave man a sick soul. It was life-denying. Blocking the free and spontaneous exercise of human instincts, it made humility, weakness, and self-abnegation virtues and pride a vice. In short, Christianity extinguished the spark of life in man. This spark of life, this inner yearning that is man's true essence, must again burn.

"God is dead," proclaimed Nietzsche. God is man's own creation. Dead also are all the inherited truths based on nature and reason. There are no higher worlds, no transcendental or metaphysical truths, no morality derived from God or nature, and no natural rights, scientific socialism, or inevitable progress. We are wandering through an eternal nothing in which all the old values and truths have lost their intelligibility. This *nihilism*—the belief that moral and social values have no validity—has caused a crisis in European life. But the death of God and of all transcendental truths can mean the liberation of man, insisted Nietzsche. Man can surmount nihilism by adopting a new orientation that gives primacy to the superior man, one who creates his own values and demonstrates self-mastery. He can overcome the deadening uniformity and mediocrity of modern civilization. He can undo democracy and socialism, which have made masters out of cattle-like masses, and surmount the shopkeeper's spirit, which has made man soft and degenerate.

European society, as Nietzsche saw it, lacked heroic figures; everyone belonged to a vast herd, but there were no shepherds. Europe could be saved only by the emergence of a higher type of man—the *higher man,* or *overman*—who would not be held back by the egalitarian rubbish preached by Christians, democrats, and socialists. "A declaration of war on the masses by *higher* man is needed," said Nietzsche, to end "the dominion of *inferior* men." Europe required "the annihilation of *suffrage universal,* i.e., the system through which the lowest natures prescribe themselves as laws for the higher."[1] Europe needed a new breed of rulers, a true aristocracy of masterful men.

Nietzsche conceived of the overman as a new kind of man who breaks with accepted morality and sets his own standards. He does not repress his instincts but asserts them. He destroys old values and asserts his prerogative as master. Free of Christian guilt, he proudly affirms his own being; dispensing with Christian "thou shalt not," he instinctively says, "I will." He dares to be himself. Because he is not like other people, traditional definitions of good and evil have no meaning for him. He does not allow his individuality to be stifled. He makes his own values, those that flow from his very being. He knows that life is meaningless but lives it laughingly, instinctively, fully.

The overman understands and exemplifies the ultimate fact of life: that "the most fearful and fundamental desire in man [is] his drive for power,"[2] that human beings crave and strive for power ceaselessly and uncompromisingly. It is perfectly natural for human beings to want to dominate nature and other human beings; inherent in human nature is the desire "to overpower, overthrow, . . . to become master, a thirst for enemies and antagonisms and triumphs."[3] This will to power is not a product of rational reflection but flows from the very essence of human existence. As the motivating force in human behavior, it governs everyday life and is the determining factor in political life. The enhancement of power brings supreme enjoyment: "The love of power is the demon of men. Let them have everything—health, food, a place to live, entertainment—they are and remain unhappy and low-spirited; for the demon waits and waits and will be satisfied. Take everything from them and satisfy this and they are almost happy—as happy as men and demons can be."[4] The masses, cowardly and envious, will condemn the higher man as evil; this has always been their way. Thus, Nietzsche castigates democracy because it "represents the disbelief in great human beings and an elite society,"[5] and Christianity because it imposes an unnatural morality, one that affirms meekness, humility, and compassion.

The influence of Nietzsche's philosophy is still a matter of controversy and conjecture. Perhaps better than anyone else, Nietzsche grasped the crucial problem of modern society and culture: that with the "death of God," traditional moral values had lost their authority and binding power. In a world where nothing is true, all is permitted. Nietzsche foresaw that the future, an age without values, would be violent and sordid, and he urged individuals to face themselves and life free of illusions, pretense, and hypocrisy. Nietzsche is also part of the general nineteenth-century trend that sought to affirm the human being and earthly aspirations rather than God or salvation. Furthermore, Nietzsche's rejection of God and metaphysics, as well as of all-embracing theories of history (Hegelianism and Marxism, for example) that attempt to impose rational patterns on the past and the present, is crucial to the development of existentialism (see "Existentialism" in the chapter on "The Era of Totalitarianism") and the movement in contemporary thought called postmodernism (see the last chapter on "The West in a Global Age").

However, no social policy could be derived from Nietzsche's heroic individualism, which taught that "there are higher and lower men and that a single individual can . . . justify the existence of whole millennia."[6] Nietzsche thought only of great individuals, humanity's noblest specimens, who overcome mediocrity and the artificiality of all inherited values; the social community and social injustice did not concern him. "The weak and ill-constituted shall perish: first principle of our philanthropy. And one shall help them to do so."[7] Surely, these words offer no constructive guidelines for dealing with the problems of modern industrial civilization.

Likewise, Nietzsche had no constructive proposals for dealing with the disintegration of rational and Christian certainties. Instead, his vitriolic attack on European institutions and values helped erode the rational foundations of Western civilization. This assault appealed immensely to intellectuals in central Europe, who saw Nietzsche's philosophy as liberating an inner energy. Thus, many young people, attracted to Nietzsche, welcomed World War I; they viewed it as an esthetic experience and thought that it would clear a path to a new heroic age. They took Nietzsche's words literally: "A society that definitely and *instinctively* gives up war and conquest is in decline."[8]

Nazi theorists tried to make Nietzsche a forerunner of their movement. They sought from him a philosophical sanction for their own thirst for power, contempt for the weak, ruthlessness, and glorification of action. They also wanted this sanction for their cult of the heroic and their Social Darwinist revulsion for human equality. Recasting Nietzsche in their own image, the Nazis viewed themselves as Nietzsche's supermen: members of a master race who, by force of will, would conquer all obstacles and reshape the world according to their self-created values. Some German intellectuals were drawn to Nazism because it seemed a healthy affirmation of life, the life with a new purpose for which Nietzsche called.

Detesting German nationalism and militarism, Nietzsche himself scoffed at the notion of German racial superiority, disdained (despite some unfortunate remarks) anti-Semitism, and denounced state worship. He would have abhorred Hitler and would have been dismayed at the twisting of his idea of the will to power into a prototype fascist principle. The men that he admired were passionate but self-possessed individuals who, by mastering their own chaotic passions, would face life and death courageously, affirmatively, and creatively. Such men make great demands on themselves. Nevertheless, as Janko Lavrin points out, "Practically all the fascist and Nazi theories can find some support in

Nietzsche's texts, provided one gives them the required twist."[9]

Nietzsche's extreme and violent denunciation of Western democratic principles, including equality, his praise of power, his call for the liberation of the instincts, his elitism, which denigrates and devalues all human life that is not strong and noble, and his spurning of humane values provided a breeding ground for violent, antirational, antiliberal, and inhumane movements. His philosophy, which included loose talk about the virtues of pitiless warriors, the breeding of a master race, and the annihilation of the weak and the ill constituted, is conducive to a politics of extremes that knows no moral limits.

Bergson

Another thinker who reflected the growing irrationalism of the age was Henri Bergson (1859–1941), a French philosopher of Jewish background. Originally attracted to positivism, Bergson turned away from the positivistic claim that science could explain everything and fulfill all human needs. Such an emphasis on the intellect, said Bergson, sacrifices spiritual impulses, imagination, and intuition and reduces the soul to a mere mechanism.

The methods of science cannot reveal ultimate reality, Bergson insisted. European civilization must recognize the limitations of scientific rationalism. Our capacity for intuition, whereby the mind achieves an immanent relationship with the object—becomes one with it—tells us more about reality than the method of analysis employed by science. The intuitive experience—something like the artist's instant comprehension of a natural scene—is a direct avenue to truth that is closed to the calculations and measurements of science. Bergson's philosophy pointed away from science toward religious mysticism.

To his admirers, Bergson's philosophy liberated the person from the constraints of positivism, mechanism, and materialism. It extolled the creative potential of intuition, the mystical experience, and the poetic imagination—those forces of life that resist categorization by the scientific mind. A protest against modern technology and bureaucracy and against all the features of mass society that seemed to stifle individual uniqueness and spontaneity, it sought to reaffirm the primacy of the individual in an increasingly mechanized and bureaucratic world. The popularity of Bergson's intuitionism and vitalism, with their depreciation of reason, symptomized the unsuspected strength and appeal of the nonrational—another sign that people were searching for new alternatives to the Enlightenment world-view.

Sorel

Nietzsche proclaimed that irrational forces constitute the essence of human nature, and Bergson held that a nonrational intuition brought insights unattainable by scientific thinking. Georges Sorel (1847–1922), a French social theorist, recognized the political potential of the nonrational. Like Nietzsche, Sorel was disillusioned with contemporary bourgeois society, which he considered decadent, soft, and unheroic. Whereas Nietzsche called for the higher man to rescue society from decadence and mediocrity, Sorel placed his hopes in the proletariat, whose position made them courageous, virile, and determined. Sorel wanted the proletariat to destroy the existing order. This overthrow, said Sorel, would be accomplished through a general strike: a universal work stoppage that would bring down the government and give power to the workers.

Sorel saw the general strike as having the appeal of a great mobilizing myth. What was important was not that the general strike actually take place, but that its image stir all the anticapitalist resentments of the workers and inspire them to carry out their revolutionary responsibilities. Sorel understood the extraordinary potency of myth for eliciting total commitment and inciting heroic action. Because it appeals to the imagination and feelings, myth is an effective way of moving the masses to revolt. By believing in the myth of the general strike, workers would soar above the moral decadence of bourgeois society and bear the immense sacrifices that their struggle called for. Sorel thought that the only recourse for workers was direct action and violence, which he regarded as ennobling, heroic, and sublime—a means of restoring grandeur to a flabby world.

Sorel's pseudoreligious exaltation of violence and mass action, his condemnation of liberal democracy and rationalism, and his recognition of the power and political utility of fabricated myths would find concrete expression in the fascist movements after World War I. Sorel heralded the age of mass political movements committed to revolutionary violence and of myths manufactured by propaganda experts determined to destroy democracy.

FREUD: A NEW VIEW OF HUMAN NATURE

In many ways, Sigmund Freud (1856–1939), an Austrian-Jewish physician who spent most of his adult life in Vienna, was a child of the Enlightenment. Like the philosophes, Freud identified civilization with reason and regarded science as the avenue to knowledge. But in contrast to the philosophes, Freud focused on the massive power and influence of nonrational drives. Whereas Nietzsche glorified the irrational and approached it with a poet's temperament, Freud recognized its potential danger. He sought to comprehend it scientifically and wanted to regulate it in the interests of civilization. Unlike Nietzsche, Freud did not belittle the rational but always strove to salvage respect for reason. Better than anyone, Freud recognized reason's limitations and the power of the nonrational, but he never wavered in his support of reason.

Freud's explorations of the world of the unconscious had a profoundly upsetting impact on our conception of the self. Freud himself viewed his theories as a great blow to human pride, to "man's craving for grandiosity."

Humanity has, in the course of time, had to endure from the hands of science two great outrages upon its naive self-love. The first was when it realized that our earth was not the center of the universe, but only a tiny speck in a world-system of a magnitude hardly conceivable; this is associated in our minds with the name of Copernicus. . . . The second was when biological research robbed man of his peculiar privilege of having been specially created, and relegated him to a descent from the animal world, implying an ineradicable ani-

Freud and His Daughter, Anna, 1912. Sigmund Freud (1856–1939), the father of psychoanalysis, penetrated the world of the unconscious in a scientific way. He concluded that powerful drives govern human behavior more than reason does. His explorations of the unconscious produced an image of the human being that broke with the Enlightenment's view of the individual's essential goodness and rationality. (*Mary Evans Picture Library*)

mal nature in him: this transvaluation has been accomplished in our own time upon the investigations of Charles Darwin. . . . But man's craving for grandiosity is now suffering the third and most bitter blow from present-day psychological research which is endeavoring to show the "ego" of each of us that he is not even master in his own house, but that he must remain content with the veriest scrap of information about what is going on unconsciously in his own mind.[10]

Freud held that people are not fundamentally rational; human behavior is governed primarily by powerful inner forces, which are hidden from consciousness. These instinctual strivings, rather than rational faculties, constitute the greater part of the mind. Freud's great achievement was his exploring of the world of the unconscious with the tools and temperament of a scientist. He showed that the irrational contained a structure that could be empirically explained and rationally explored.

After graduating from medical school, Freud specialized in the treatment of nervous disorders. His investigations led him to conclude that childhood fears and experiences, often sexual in nature, accounted for neuroses: disorders in thinking, feeling, and behavior that interfere with everyday acts of personal and social life. Neuroses can take several forms, including hysteria, anxiety, depression, and obsessions. So painful and threatening were these childhood emotions and experiences that his patients banished them from conscious memory to the realm of the unconscious.

To understand and treat neurotic behavior, Freud said, it was necessary to look behind overt symptoms and bring to the surface emotionally charged experiences and fears—childhood traumas—that lie buried in the unconscious, along with primitive impulses. The key to the unconscious, in Freud's view, was the interpretation of dreams. An individual's dreams, said Freud, reveal his or her secret wishes—often socially unacceptable desires and frightening memories. Too painful to bear, they get locked up in the deepest dungeons of our unconscious. But even in their cages, the demons remain active, continuing to haunt us and to generate conflicts. Our distress is real and even excruciating, but we do not know its source.

The *id*, the subconscious seat of the instincts, said Freud, is a "cauldron full of seething excitations," which constantly demand gratification. The id is primitive and irrational. It knows no values and has no awareness of good and evil. Unable to endure tension, it demands sexual release, the termination of pain, the cessation of hunger. When the id is denied an outlet for its instinctual energy, we become frustrated, angry, and unhappy. Gratifying the id is our highest pleasure. But the full gratification of instinctual demands is detrimental to civilized life. That is why the *ego*, which stands for reason, seeks to hold the id in check, to bring it in line with reality.

Freud postulated a harrowing conflict between the relentless strivings of our instinctual nature and the requirements of civilization. Civilization, for Freud, required the renunciation of instinctual gratification and the mastery of animal instincts, a thesis he developed in *Civilization and Its Discontents* (1930). Although Freud's thoughts in this work were, no doubt, influenced by the great tragedy of World War I, the main theme could be traced back to his earlier writings. Human beings derive their highest pleasure from sexual fulfillment, said Freud, but unrestrained sexuality drains off psychic energy needed for creative artistic and intellectual life; it also directs energies away from work needed to preserve communal life. Hence society, through the family, the priest, the teacher, and the police, imposes rules and restrictions on our animal nature.

But this is immensely painful. The human being is caught in a tragic bind. Society's demand for repression of instincts in the interest of civilization causes terrible frustration. Equally distressing, the violation of society's rules under the pressure of instinctual needs evokes terrible feelings of guilt. Either way, people suffer; civilized life simply entails too much pain for people. It seems that the price we pay for civilization is neurosis. Most people cannot endure the amount of instinctual renunciation that civilization requires. There are times when our elemental human nature rebels against all the restrictions and "thou shalt nots" demanded by society, against all the misery and torment imposed by civilization.

"Civilization imposes great sacrifices not only on man's sexuality but also on his aggressivity,"[11] said Freud. People are not good by nature, as the philosophes had taught; on the contrary, they are "creatures among whose instinctual endowments is to be reckoned a powerful share of aggressiveness." Their first inclination is not to love their neighbor, but to "satisfy their aggressiveness on him, to exploit his capacity for work without compensation, to use him sexually without his consent, to seize his possessions, to humiliate him, to cause him pain, to torture and to kill him."[12]

Man is wolf to man, Freud concluded. "Who has the courage to dispute it in the face of all the evidence in his own life and in history?"[13] Civilization "has to use its utmost efforts in order to set limits to man's aggressive instincts," but "in spite of every effort these endeavors of civilization have not so far achieved very much."[14] People find it difficult to do without "the satisfaction of this inclination to aggression."[15] When circumstances are favorable, this primitive aggressiveness breaks loose and "reveals man as a savage beast to whom consideration towards his own kind is something alien."[16] For Freud, "the inclination to aggression is an original self-subsisting disposition in man" and it "constitutes the greatest impediment to civilization."[17] Aggressive impulses drive people apart, threatening society with disintegration. Freud believed that an unalterable core of human nature is ineluctably in opposition to civilized life. To this extent, everyone is potentially an enemy of civilization.

Freud's awareness of the irrational and his general pessimism regarding people's ability to regulate it in the interests of civilization did not lead him to break faith with the Enlightenment tradition, for Freud did not celebrate the irrational. He was too cognizant of its self-destructive nature for that. Civilization is indeed a burden, but people must bear it because the alternative is far worse. In the tradition of the philosophes, Freud sought truth based on a scientific analysis of human nature and believed that reason was the best road to social improvement. Like the philosophes, he was critical of religion, regarding it as a pious illusion—a fairy tale in conflict with reason. Freud wanted people to throw away what he believed was the crutch of religion: to break away from childlike dependency and stand alone.

A humanitarian like the philosophes, Freud sought to relieve human misery by making people aware of their true nature, particularly their sexuality. He wanted society to soften its overly restrictive sexual standards because they were injurious to mental health. One enduring consequence of the Freudian revolution is the recognition of the enormous importance played by childhood in the shaping of the adult's personality. The neurotic disorders that burden adults begin in early childhood. Freud urged that we show greater concern for the emotional needs of children.

Although Freud was undoubtedly a child of the Enlightenment, in crucial ways he differed from the philosophes. Regarding the Christian doctrine of original sin as myth, the philosophes had believed that people's nature was essentially good. If people took reason as their guide, evil could be eliminated. Freud, on the other hand, asserted, in secular and scientific terms, a pessimistic view of human nature. He saw evil as rooted in human nature rather than as a product of a faulty environment. Education and better living conditions would not eliminate evil, as the philosophes had expected, nor would abolition of private property, as Marx had declared. The philosophes venerated reason; it had enabled Newton to unravel nature's mysteries and would permit people to achieve virtue and reform society. Freud, who wanted reason to prevail, understood that its soft voice had to compete with the thunderous roars of the id. Freud broke with the optimism of the philosophes. His awareness of the immense pressures that civilization places on our fragile egos led him to be generally pessimistic about the future.

Unlike Marx, Freud had no vision of utopia. He saw the crude, destructive tendencies of human nature as an ever-present obstacle to harmonious social relations. That Freud was hounded out of Vienna by the Nazis and his four sisters were murdered by them simply for being Jewish is a telling footnote to his view of human nature, the power of the irrational, and the fragility of civilization.

SOCIAL THOUGHT: CONFRONTING THE IRRATIONAL AND THE COMPLEXITIES OF MODERN SOCIETY

The end of the nineteenth century and the beginning of the twentieth mark the great age of sociological thought. The leading sociological thinkers of the period all regarded science as the only valid model for arriving at knowledge, and all claimed that their thought rested on a scientific foundation. They struggled with some of the crucial problems of modern society. How can society achieve coherence and stability when the customary associations and attachments that had characterized village life have been ruthlessly dissolved by the rapidly developing industrial-urban-capitalist order and when religion no longer unites people? What are the implications of the nonrational for political life? How can people preserve their individuality in a society that is becoming increasingly regimented? In many ways, twentieth-century dictatorships were responses to the dilemmas of modern society analyzed by these social theorists. And twentieth-century dictators would employ these social theorists' insights into group and mass psychology for the purpose of gaining and maintaining power.

Durkheim

Émile Durkheim (1858–1917), a French scholar of Jewish background and heir to Comte's positivism, was an important founder of modern sociology. Like Comte, he brought the scientific method to the study of society. Durkheim tried to show that the essential elements of modern times—secularism, rationalism, and individualism—put society at risk of breaking apart. In traditional society, the social order was derived from God, and a person's place and function were determined by birth and custom. However, modern people, sceptical and individualistic, would not accept such restraints.

The weakening of the traditional ties that bind the individual to society constituted, for Durkheim, the crisis of modern society. Without collective values and common beliefs, society is threatened with disintegration and the individual with disorientation. Modern people, said Durkheim, suffer from *anomie*—a condition of anxiety caused by the collapse of values. They do not feel integrated into a collective community and find no purpose in life. In *Suicide* (1897), Durkheim maintained that "the exceptionally high number of voluntary deaths manifests the state of deep disturbances from which civilized societies are suffering and bears witness to its gravity."[18] The pathology of modern society is also demonstrated by a high level of boredom, anxiety, and pessimism. Modern people are driven to suicide by intense competition, and the disappointment and frustration resulting from unfulfilled expectations, and a lack of commitment to moral principles. People must limit their aspirations and exercise discipline over their desires and passions, said Durkheim. They must stop wanting more. Religion once spurred people to view restraint and the renunciation of desires as virtues, but it can no longer do so.

Although Durkheim approved of modernity, he noted that modern ways have not brought happiness or satisfaction to the individual. Modern scientific and industrial society requires a new set of principles that would bind the various classes into a cohesive social order and help to overcome the feelings of restlessness and dissatisfaction that torment people. Durkheim called for a secular and rational system of morality to replace Christian dogma and fulfill this need.

Durkheim focused on a crucial dilemma of modern life. On the one hand, modern urban civilization has provided the individual with unparalleled opportunities for self-development and material improvement. On the other, the breakdown of traditional communal bonds stemming from the spread of rationalism and individualism has produced a sense of isolation and alienation. Twentieth-century totalitarian movements sought to integrate these uprooted and alienated souls into new collectivities: a proletarian state based on workers' solidarity or a racial state based on ethnic "purity" and nationalism.

Pareto

Like Comte, Vilfredo Pareto (1848–1923), an Italian economist and sociologist, aimed to construct a system of sociology on the model of the physical sciences. His studies led him to conclude that social behavior does not rest primarily on reason, but rather rests on nonrational instincts and sentiments. These deeply rooted and essentially changeless feelings are the fundamental elements in human behavior. Although society may change, human nature remains essentially the same. Whoever seeks to lead and to influence people must appeal not to logic, but to elemental feelings. Most human behavior is nonrational;

nonlogical considerations also determine people's beliefs. Like Marx and Freud, Pareto was convinced that we cannot accept a person's word at face value. Instead, we find the real cause of human behavior in human instincts and sentiments. People do not act according to carefully thought-out theories; they act first from nonlogical motivations and then construct a rationalization to justify their behavior. Much of Pareto's work focused on the nonrational elements of human conduct and the various beliefs invented to give the appearance of rationality to behavior that derives from feeling and instinct.

Pareto divided society into two strata: the elite and the masses. Elites have always existed, said Pareto, because human beings are unequal by nature and because the goods that all people seek cannot be shared equally. Because struggle is a general law of life, elites and masses will exist in all societies. The belief that a democracy constitutes rule by a people is a myth, said Pareto. In actuality, a small group of party leaders controls the political system. Pareto also rejected as naive Marx's vision of the end of the class struggle.

In the tradition of Machiavelli, Pareto held that a successful ruling elite must—with cunning, and if necessary with violence—exploit the feelings and impulses of the masses to its own advantage. Democratic states, he said, delude themselves in thinking that the masses are really influenced by rational argument. Pareto predicted the emergence of new political leaders who would master the people through propaganda and force, always appealing to sentiment rather than to reason. To this extent, Pareto was an intellectual forerunner of fascism, which preached an authoritarian elitism. Mussolini praised Pareto and proudly claimed him as a source of inspiration.

Weber

Probably the most prominent social thinker of the age, the German academic Max Weber (1864–1920) was a leading shaper of modern sociology. Weber believed that Western civilization, unlike the other civilizations of the globe, had virtually eliminated myth, mystery, and magic from its conception of nature and society. This process of rationalization—the "disenchantment of the world," as Weber called it—was most conspicuous in Western science, but it was also evident in politics and economics. Weber considered Western science an attempt to understand and master nature through reason, and Western capitalism an attempt to organize work and production in a rational manner. The Western state has a rational, written constitution, rationally formulated law, and a bureaucracy of trained government officials that administers the affairs of state according to rational rules and regulations.

Weber understood the terrible paradox of reason. Reason accounts for brilliant achievements in science and economic life, but it also despiritualizes life by ruthlessly eliminating centuries-old traditions, denouncing deeply felt religious beliefs as superstition, and regarding human feelings and passions as impediments to clear thinking. The process of disenchantment shattered the basis for belief in transcendental values; in a thoroughly disenchanted world, life is without ultimate purpose and the individual is soulless. This is the dilemma of modern individuals, said Weber. Secular rationality is shaping a world in which standards cannot claim ultimate sanction. A disenchanted world contains no inherited truths, no God-given answers to the human being's desperate need for meaning. We are now confronted with an immense and unprecedented burden: how to create for ourselves values that give meaning to life in a world deprived of certainty.

Secular rationality has produced still another awesome problem, said Weber. It has fostered self-liberation, for it enables human beings to overcome illusions and take control of the environment and of themselves, but it is also a means of self-enslavement, for it produces institutions, giant public and corporate bureaucracies, that depersonalize life. Modern officials, said Weber, are emotionally detached. Concerned only with the efficient execution of tasks, they employ reason in a cold and calculating way; such human feelings as compassion and affection are ruled out as hindrances to effectiveness. In the name of efficiency, people are placed in "steel cages"—that is, treated impersonally as mere objects—and thus are deprived of their autonomy. The prospect existed that people would refuse to endure this violation of their spiritual needs and would reverse the process of disenchantment by seeking redemption in the irrational. Weber himself, however, was committed to the ideals of the Enlightenment and to perpetuating the rational scientific tradition.

Like Freud, Weber was aware of the power of the irrational in social life. One expression of the irrational that he analyzed in considerable depth was the charismatic leader who attracts people by force of personality. Charismatic leaders may be religious prophets, war heroes, demagogues, or others who possess this extraordinary personality that attracts and dominates others. People yearn for charismatic leadership, particularly during times of crisis. The leader claims a mission—a sacred duty—to lead the people during the crisis; the leader's authority rests on the people's belief in the mission and their faith in the leader's extraordinary abilities. A common allegiance to the charismatic leader unites the community. In an age that has seen its share of dictators and demagogues, the question of why people are drawn to the charismatic savior—why they succumb to his authority, and why they alter their lives in order to implement his vision—is of crucial concern to historians and social theorists.

THE MODERNIST MOVEMENT

At the same time that Freud and the social theorists were breaking with the Enlightenment view of human nature and society, artists and writers were rebelling against traditional forms of artistic and literary expression that had governed European cultural life since the Renaissance. Rejecting both classical and realist models, they subordinated form and objective reality to the inner life—to feelings, imagination, and the creative process. These avant-garde writers and artists found new and creative ways to express the explosive primitive forces within the human psyche that increasingly had become the subject of contemporary thinkers. Their experimentations produced a great cultural revolution, called *modernism;* it still profoundly influences the arts. In some ways, modernism was a continuation of the Romantic Movement, which had dominated European culture in the early nineteenth century. Both movements subjected to searching criticism cultural styles that had been formulated during the Renaissance and that had roots in ancient Greece.

Breaking with Conventional Modes of Esthetics

Even more than romanticism, modernism aspired to an intense introspection—a heightened awareness of self—and saw the intellect as a barrier to the free expression of elemental human emotions. Modernist artists and writers abandoned conventional literary and artistic models and experimented with new modes of expression. They liberated the imagination from the restrictions of conventional forms and enabled their audience, readers and viewers alike, to share in the process of creation, often unconscious, and to discover fresh insights into objects, sounds, people, and social conditions. They believed that there were further discoveries to be made in the arts, further possibilities of expression, that past masters had not realized. The consequence of their bold venture, wrote the literary critic and historian Irving Howe, was nothing less than the "breakup of the traditional unity and continuity of Western culture."[19]

Like Freud, modernist artists and writers probed beyond surface appearances for a more profound reality hidden in the human psyche. Writers such as Thomas Mann, Marcel Proust, James Joyce, August Strindberg, D. H. Lawrence, and Franz Kafka explored the inner life of the individual and the psychopathology of human relations in order to lay bare the self. They dealt with the predicament of men and women who rejected the values and customs of their day, and they depicted the anguish of people burdened by guilt, torn by internal conflicts, and driven by an inner self-destructiveness. Besides showing the overwhelming might of the irrational and the seductive power of the primitive and the instinctual, they also broke the silence about sex that had prevailed in Victorian literature.

From the Renaissance through the Enlightenment and into the nineteenth century, Western esthetic standards had been shaped by the conviction that the universe embodied an inherent mathematical order. A corollary of this conception of the outer world as orderly and

intelligible was the view that art should imitate reality, that it should mirror nature. Since the Renaissance, artists had deliberately made use of laws of perspective and proportion; musicians had used harmonic chords, which brought rhythm and melody into a unified whole; writers had produced works according to a definite pattern, which included a beginning, middle, and end.

Modernist culture, however, acknowledged no objective reality of space, motion, and time that has the same meaning to all observers. Rather, reality can be grasped in many ways; a multiplicity of frames of reference apply to nature and human experience. Consequently, reality is what the viewer perceives it to be through the prism of the imagination. "There is no outer reality," said the modernist German poet Gottfried Benn, "there is only human consciousness, constantly building, modifying, rebuilding new worlds out of its own creativity."[20] Modernism is concerned less with the object itself than with how the artist experiences it—with the sensations that an object evokes in the artist's very being and with the meaning the artist's imagination imposes on reality. Sociologist Daniel Bell makes this point in reference to painting:

> Modernism . . . denies the primacy of an outside reality, as given. It seeks either to rearrange that reality, or to retreat to the self's interior, to private experience as the source of its concerns and aesthetic preoccupations. . . . There is an emphasis on the self as the touchstone of understanding and on the activity of the knower rather than the character of the object as the source of knowledge. . . . Thus one discerns the intentions of modern painting . . . to break up ordered space.[21]

Dispensing with conventional forms of esthetics, which stressed structure and coherence, modernism propelled the arts onto uncharted seas. Modernists abandoned the efforts of realists and naturalists to produce a clinical and objective description of the external world; instead, they probed subjective views and visions and the inner world of the unconscious. Recoiling from a middle-class, industrial civilization, which prized rationalism, organization, clarity, stability, and definite norms and values, modernist writers and artists were fascinated by the bizarre, the mysterious, the unpredictable, the primitive, the irrational, and the formless. Writers, for example, experimented with new techniques to convey the intense struggle between the conscious and the unconscious and to explore the aberrations and complexities of human personality and the irrationality of human behavior. In particular, they devised a new way, the stream of consciousness, to exhibit the mind's every level—both conscious reflection and unconscious strivings—and to capture how thought is punctuated by spontaneous outbursts, disconnected assertions, random memories, hidden desires, and persistent fantasies. The stream of consciousness is not narrated memory but a flow of feelings and thoughts in which the boundary between consciousness and unconsciousness is blurred. It attempts to reveal the mystery and complexity of the inner person.

Modern artists deliberately plunged into the world of the unconscious in search of the instinctual, the fantastic, the primitive, and the mysterious, which they believed yielded a truth higher than that given by analytical thought. They embarked on a voyage into the mind's interior in the hopes of finding fantastic stimulants that would spark the creative imagination. Composers engaged in open revolt against the conventional rules and standards of musical composition. For example, the Austrian composer Arnold Schöenberg (1874–1951) purposefully abandoned traditional scales and harmonic chords to produce atonal music that "seeks to express all that swells in us subconsciously like a dream."[22] The Russian composer Igor Stravinsky (1882–1921) experimented with both atonality and primitive rhythms. When Stravinsky's ballet *The Rite of Spring* was performed in Paris in 1913, the theater audience rioted to protest the composition's break with tonality, its use of primitive, jazzlike rhythms, and its theme of ritual sacrifice.

Modern Art

The modernist movement, which began near the end of the nineteenth century, was in full bloom before World War I and would continue to flower in the postwar world. Probably the clearest expression of the modernist viewpoint is found in art. In the late nineteenth century, artists began to turn away from the standards that had characterized art since the Renaissance. No longer committed to depicting how an object appears to the eye or to organizing space mathematically, they searched for new forms of representation.

Modern painting begins with impressionism, a movement centered in Paris and spanning the years 1860 through 1886. Such impressionists as Edouard Manet, Claude Monet, Camille Pissaro, Edgar Degas, and Pierre Auguste Renoir tried to give their own immediate and personal impression of an object or an event as it appeared to the eye at a fleeting instant. In the late 1880s and 1890s, postimpressionists further revolutionized the artist's sense of space and color in order to make art a vivid emotional and personal experience. French artist Paul Cézanne (1839–1906), seeking to portray his own visual perception of an object rather than a photographic copy of it, deliberately distorted perspective. He subordinated the appearance of the individual object to the requirements of the total design. The postimpressionists produced a revolution not only of space, but also of color; thus, Vincent van Gogh (1853–1890), a Dutchman who settled in France, used color as a language in and of itself to express the artist's feelings.

After the postimpressionists, art moved still further away from reproducing an exact likeness of a physical object or human being. Increasingly, artists sought to penetrate the deepest recesses of the unconscious, which they saw as the wellspring of creativity and the dwelling place of a higher truth. Paul Klee (1879–1940), a prominent Swiss painter, described modern art in these words: "Each [artist] should follow where the pulse of his own heart leads. . . . Our pounding heart drives us down, deep down to the source of all. What springs from this source, whether it may be called dream, idea or phantasy—must be taken seriously."[23]

In France, a group of avant-garde artists, the *fauves* (wild beasts), used color with great freedom to express intense feelings and heightened energy. Between 1909 and 1914, a new style, *cubism*, was developed by Pablo Picasso (1881–1973) and Georges Braque (1882–1963).

Harmony in Red by Henri Matisse (1908). In this early example of French fauvism, Matisse (1869–1954) broke away from the representational painting of his predecessors and set the tone for much of twentieth-century expressive painting. His sparing use of line, color, and rhythmic motifs transforms the visual surface into brilliant designs and establishes a new pictorial language. (*The State Hermitage Museum, St. Petersburg*)

Exploring the interplay between the flat world of the canvas and the three-dimensional world of visual perception, they sought to paint a reality deeper than what the eye sees at first glance. One art historian describes cubism as follows: "The cubist is not interested in usual representational standards. It is as if he were walking around the object he is analyzing, as one is free to walk around a piece of sculpture for successive views. But he must represent all these views at once."[24] The cubists' effort to depict something from multiple perspectives rather than from a single point in space and their need to deliberately deform objects in order to achieve this effect mark a radical break with artistic conventions.

Throughout the period 1890 to 1914, artists were de-emphasizing subject matter and stressing the expressive power of such formal qualities as line, color, and space. It is not surprising that some artists, such as Piet Mondrian (1872–1944), a Dutch painter, and Wassily Kandinsky (1866–1944), a Russian residing in Germany, finally created abstract art, a nonobjective art totally devoid of reference to the visible world. In breaking with the Renaissance view of the world as inherently orderly and rational and stressing the power of the imagination, modern artists opened up new possibilities for artistic expression. They also exemplified the growing appeal and force of the nonrational in European life.

Black Weft, by Wassily Kandinsky. Kandinsky was a leader of a group of avant-garde painters in Munich, called *Der Blaue Reiter* (The Blue Rider), whose goal was to challenge the limits of artistic expression. In this painting, he has removed virtually all traces of the physical world, thereby creating a nonobjective artwork that bears little, or no, resemblance to the natural world. (*Musée des Beaux-Arts, Nantes, France/RMN/Art Resource, NY*)

MODERN PHYSICS

Until the closing years of the nineteenth century, the view of the universe held by the Western mind was based on the classical physics of Newton. It included the following principles: (1) time, space, and matter were objective realities that existed independently of the observer; (2) the universe was a giant machine, whose parts obeyed strict laws of cause and effect; (3) the atom, indivisible and solid, was the basic unit of matter; (4) heated bodies emitted radiation in continuous waves; and (5) through further investigation, it would be possible to gain complete knowledge of the physical universe.

Between the 1890s and the 1920s, this view of the universe was shattered by a second Scientific Revolution. The discovery of x-rays by William Konrad Roentgen in 1895, of radioactivity by Henri Bequerel in 1896, and of the electron by J. J. Thomson in 1897 led scientists to abandon the conception of the atom as a solid and indivisible particle. Rather than resembling a billiard ball, the atom consisted of a nucleus of tightly packed protons, separated from orbiting electrons by empty space.

In 1900, Max Planck (1858–1947), a German physicist, proposed the quantum theory, which holds that a heated body radiates energy not in a continuous unbroken stream, as had been believed, but in intermittent spurts, or jumps, called quanta. Planck's theory of discontinuity in energy radiation challenged a cardinal principle of classical physics: that action in nature was strictly continuous. In 1913, Niels Bohr, a Danish scientist, applied Planck's theory of energy quanta to the interior of the atom and discovered that the Newtonian laws of motion could not fully explain what happened to electrons orbiting an atomic nucleus. As physicists explored the behavior of the atom further, it became apparent that its nature was fundamentally elusive and unpredictable.

Newtonian physics says that, given certain conditions, we can predict what will follow. For example, if an airplane is flying north at four hundred miles per hour, we can predict its exact position two hours from now, assuming that the plane does not alter its course or speed. Quantum mechanics teaches that in the subatomic realm we cannot predict with certainty what will take place; we can only say that, given certain conditions, it is *probable* that a certain event will follow. This principle of uncertainty was developed in 1927 by the German scientist Werner Heisenberg, who showed that it is impossible to determine at one and the same time both an electron's precise speed and its position. In the small-scale world of the electron, we enter a universe of uncertainty, probability, and statistical relationships. No improvement in measurement techniques will dispel this element of chance and provide us with complete knowledge of the universe.

The theory of relativity, developed by Albert Einstein (1879–1955), a German-Swiss physicist of Jewish lineage, was instrumental in shaping modern physics; it altered classical conceptions of space and time. Newtonian physics had viewed space as a distinct physical reality, a stationary medium through which light traveled and matter moved. Time was deemed a fixed and rigid framework that was the same for all observers and existed independently of human experience. For Einstein, however, neither space nor time had an independent existence; neither could be divorced from human experience. Once asked to explain briefly the essentials of relativity, Einstein replied: "It was formerly believed that if all material things disappeared out of the universe, time and space would be left. According to the relativ-

Albert Einstein (1879–1955), A Principal Architect of Modern Physics. Forced to flee Nazi Germany, Einstein became a U.S. citizen. He was appointed to the Institute for Advanced study at Princeton, New Jersey. *(AP/Wide World)*

ity theory, however, time and space disappear together with the things."[25]

Contrary to all previous thinking, the relativity theory holds that time differs for two observers traveling at different speeds. Imagine twin brothers involved in space exploration, one as an astronaut and the other as a rocket designer who never leaves earth. The astronaut takes off in the most advanced spaceship yet constructed, one that achieves a speed close to the maximum attainable in our universe—the speed of light. After traveling several trillion miles, the spaceship turns around and returns to earth. According to the experience of the ship's occupant, the whole trip took about two years. But when the astronaut lands on earth, he finds totally changed conditions. His brother has long since died, for according to earth's calendars some two hundred years have elapsed since the rocket ship set out on its journey. Such an occurrence seemed to defy all commonsense experience, yet experiments supported Einstein's claims.

Einstein's work encompassed motion, matter, and energy as well. Motion, too, is relative: The only way we can describe the motion of one body is to compare it with another moving body. This means that there is no motionless, absolute, fixed frame of reference anywhere in the universe. In his famous equation, $E = mc^2$, Einstein showed that matter and energy are not separate categories, but rather two different expressions of the same physical entity. The source of energy is matter, and the source of matter is energy. Tiny quantities of matter could be converted into staggering amounts of energy. The atomic age was dawning.

The discoveries of modern physics transformed the world of classical physics. Whereas nature had been regarded as something outside the individual—an objective reality existing independently of ourselves—modern physics teaches that our position in space and time determines what we mean by reality and that our very presence affects reality itself. When we observe a particle with our measuring instruments, we are interfering with it, knocking it off its course; we are participating in reality. Nor is nature fully knowable, as the classical physics of Newton had presumed; uncertainty, probability, and even mystery are inherent in the universe.

We have not yet felt the full impact of modern physics, but there is no doubt that it has been part of a revolution in human perceptions. Jacob Bronowski, a student of science and culture, concludes:

> One aim of the physical sciences has been to give an exact picture of the material world. One achievement of physics in the twentieth century has been to prove that that aim is unattainable. . . . There is no absolute knowledge. . . . All information is imperfect. We have to treat it with humility. That is the human condition; and that is what quantum physics says. . . . The Principle of Uncertainty . . . fixed once and for all the realization that all knowledge is limited.[26]

Like Darwin's theory of human origins, Freud's theory of human nature, and the transformation of classical space by modern artists, the modifications of the Newtonian picture by modern physicists have enlarged our understanding. At the same time, they have contributed to the sense of uncertainty and disorientation that characterized the twentieth century.

THE ENLIGHTENMENT TRADITION IN DISARRAY

Most nineteenth-century thinkers carried forward the spirit of the Enlightenment, particularly in its emphasis on science and its concern for individual liberty and social reform. In the tradition of the philosophes, nineteenth-century thinkers regarded science as humanity's greatest achievement and believed that through reason society could be reformed. The spread of parliamentary government and the extension of education, along with the many advances in science and technology, seemed to confirm the hopes of the philosophes for humanity's future progress.

But at the same time, the Enlightenment tradition was being undermined. In the early nineteenth century, the romantics revolted against the Enlightenment's rational-scientific spirit in favor of human will and feeling. Romantic nationalists valued the collective soul of the nation—ancient traditions rooted in a hoary and dateless past—over reason and individual freedom. Conservatives emphasized the limitations of reason and attacked the political agenda of the Enlightenment and the French Revolution. In the closing decades of the nineteenth century, the Enlightenment tradition was challenged by Social Darwinists, who glorified violence and saw conflict between individuals and between nations as a law of nature. They considered the right of the powerful to predominate to be a right of nature, beyond good and evil, and they castigated humanitarianism as weakness. Echoing Sorel, several thinkers trumpeted the use of force in social and political controversies.

Furthermore, a number of thinkers, rejecting the Enlightenment view of people as fundamentally rational, held that subconscious drives and impulses govern human behavior more than reason does. If this is so, then the individual is not essentially autonomous, a master of his own self. Several of these thinkers urged celebrating and extolling the irrational, which they regarded as the true essence of human beings and of life. They glorified an irrational vitality, or Nietzsche's will to power, which transcended considerations of good and evil. "I have always considered myself a voice of what I believe to be a greater renaissance—the revolt of the soul against the intellect—now beginning in the world," wrote the Irish poet William Butler Yeats.[27] German advocates of "life philosophy" explicitly called the mind "the enemy of the soul."

Even the theorists who studied the individual and society in a scientific way pointed out that below a surface of rationality lies a substratum of irrationality, which constitutes a deeper reality. The conviction was growing that reason was a puny instrument when compared with the volcanic strength of nonrational impulses, that these impulses pushed people toward destructive behavior and made political life precarious, and that the nonrational did not bend very much to education. The Enlightenment's image of the autonomous individual who makes rational decisions after weighing the choices (a fundamental premise of liberalism and democracy) no longer seemed tenable. Often the individual is not the master of his or her own person; human freedom is limited by human nature.

Liberalism, which owed much to the Enlightenment, was also undermined by theorists who rejected the idea of natural rights. The view that all individuals are born with inalienable rights had provided the philosophical basis of classical liberalism. It was now argued, however, that natural rights were not a law of nature or a higher truth; rather, they were simply a human creation, a product of a specific set of circumstances at a particular stage in history, notably the emergence of the bourgeoisie. Could commitment to parliamentary government, the rule of law, and other liberal-democratic institutions and practices survive this assault on the core principle of liberalism?

Other theorists argued that the ideas of right, truth, and justice do not have an independent value; rather, they are merely tools used by elites in their struggle to gain and maintain power. Opponents of liberalism and democracy utilized the theory of elites advanced by Pareto, as well as the new stress on human irrationality, as proof that the masses were incapable of self-government and that they had to be led by their betters. Many intellectuals of the right employed the new social theories to devalue the individualist and rational bases of liberal democracy bequeathed by the Enlightenment.

At the beginning of the twentieth century, the dominant mood remained that of confidence in Europe's future progress and in the values of European civilization. However, certain disquieting trends were already evident; they would grow to crisis proportions in succeeding decades. Although few people may have realized it, the Enlightenment tradition was in disarray.

The thinkers of the Enlightenment believed in an orderly, machinelike universe; natural law and natural rights operating in the social world; objective rules that gave form and structure to artistic productions; the essential rationality and goodness of the individual; and science and technology as instruments of progress. This coherent world-view, which had produced an attitude of certainty, security, and optimism, was in the process of dissolution by the early twentieth century. The commonsense Newtonian picture of the physical universe, with its inexorable laws of cause and effect, was fundamentally altered; the belief in natural rights and objective standards governing morality was undermined; rules and modes of expression that were at the very heart of Western esthetics were abandoned; and confidence in human rationality and goodness weakened. Furthermore, science and technology were accused of forging a mechanical, bureaucratic, and materialistic world that stifled intuition and feelings, thereby diminishing the self. To redeem the self, some thinkers urged a heroic struggle, which easily was channeled into primitive nationalism and martial crusades.

This radical attack on the moral and intellectual values of the Enlightenment, as well as on liberalism and democracy, included the denunciation of reason, exaltation of force, quest for the heroic, and yearning for a new authority; it constitutes the intellectual background of the fascist movements that emerged after World War I. Holding the Enlightenment tradition in contempt and fascinated by power and violence, many people, including intellectuals, would exalt fascist ideas and lionize fascist leaders.

When the new century began, most Europeans were optimistic about the future, some even holding that European civilization was on the threshold of a golden age. Few suspected that European civilization would soon be gripped by a crisis that threatened its very survival. The powerful forces of irrationalism that had been hailed by Nietzsche, analyzed by Freud, and creatively expressed in modernist culture would erupt with devastating fury in twentieth-century political life, particularly in the form of extreme nationalism and racism that extolled violence. Confused and disillusioned people searching for new certainties and values would turn to political ideologies that openly rejected reason, lauded war, and scorned the inviolability of the human person. Dictators, utilizing the insights into the unconscious and the nonrational advanced by Freud and the social theorists, succeeded in manipulating the minds of the masses to an unprecedented degree.

These currents began to form at the end of the nineteenth century, but World War I brought them together in a tidal wave. World War I accentuated the questioning of established norms and the dissolution of Enlightenment certainties. It caused many people to see Western civilization as dying and beyond redemption. Exacerbating the spiritual crisis of the preceding generation, the war shattered Europe's political and social order. It also gave birth to totalitarian ideologies that nearly obliterated the legacy of the Enlightenment. The world wars of the twentieth century, with their millions of dead and mutilated, and the totalitarian experiments, which trampled on human dignity, bore out Nietzsche's warning that in a nihilistic world all is permitted.

❖   ❖   ❖

NOTES

1. Friedrich Nietzsche, *The Will to Power,* trans. Walter Kaufmann and R. J. Hollingdale, ed. Walter Kaufmann (New York: Vintage Books, 1968), pp. 458–459.

2. Ibid., pp. 383–384.

3. Friedrich Nietzsche, *The Genealogy of Morals,* Essay 1, sec. 13 (New York: The Modern Library, 1954), p. 656.

4. Quoted in R. J. Hollingdale, *Nietzsche* (London: Routledge & Kegan Paul, 1973), p. 82.

5. Nietzsche, *Will to Power,* p. 397.

6. Ibid., p. 518.

7. Friedrich Nietzsche, *Twilight of the Idols and The Anti-Christ,* trans. R. J. Hollingdale (New York: Penguin, 1972), p. 116.

8. Nietzsche, *Will to Power,* p. 386.

9. Janko Lavrin, *Nietzsche* (New York: Charles Scribner's Sons, 1971), p. 113.

10. Sigmund Freud, *A General Introduction to Psychoanalysis,* trans. Joan Riviere (Garden City, N.Y.: Garden City Publishing Co., 1943), p. 252.

11. Sigmund Freud, *Civilization and Its Discontents* (New York: Norton, 1961), p. 62.

12. Ibid., p. 58.

13. Ibid.

14. Ibid., p. 59.

15. Ibid., p. 61.

16. Ibid., p. 59.

17. Ibid., p. 69.

18. Émile Durkheim, *Suicide: A Study in Sociology,* trans. John Spaulding and George Simpson (New York: The Free Press, 1951), p. 391.

19. Irving Howe, ed., *The Idea of the Modern in Literature and the Arts* (New York: Horizon Press, 1967), p. 16.

20. Ibid., p. 15.

21. Daniel Bell, *The Cultural Contradictions of Capitalism* (New York: Basic Books, 1976), pp. 110, 112.

22. Excerpted in Piero Weiss and Richard Taruskin, eds., *Music in the Western World: A History in Documents* (New York: Schirmen Books, 1984), p. 428.

23. Paul Klee, *On Modern Art,* trans. Paul Findlay (London: Faber & Faber, 1948), p. 51.

24. John Canaday, *Mainstreams of Modern Art* (New York: Holt, 1961), p. 458.

25. Quoted in A. E. E. McKenzie, *The Major Achievements of Science* (New York: Cambridge University Press, 1960), vol. 1, 310.

26. Jacob Bronowski, *The Ascent of Man* (Boston: Little, Brown, 1973), p. 353.

27. Quoted in Roland N. Stromberg, *Redemption by War* (Lawrence: Regents Press of Kansas, 1982), p. 65.

SUGGESTED READING

Aschheim, Steven E., *The Nietzsche Legacy in Germany, 1890–1990* (1992). How Germans, including Nazis, interpreted Nietzsche.

Baumer, Franklin, *Modern European Thought* (1977). A well-informed study of modern thought.

Bradbury, Malcolm, and James McFarlane, eds., *Modernism, 1890–1930* (1974). Essays on various phases of modernism; valuable bibliography.

Gay, Peter, *Freud: A Life for Our Times* (1988). A highly recommended study.

Hamilton, G. H., *Painting and Sculpture in Europe, 1880–1940* (1967). An authoritative work.

Hollingdale, R. J., *Nietzsche* (1973). Lucid and insightful.

Hughes, H. Stuart, *Consciousness and Society* (1958). Good on social thinkers.

Kolocotroni, Vassiliki, Jane Goldman, and Olga Taxidou, eds., *Modernism: An Anthology of Sources and Documents* (1998). An array of selections covering the breadth and variety of modernism.

Masur, Gerhard, *Prophets of Yesterday* (1961). Studies in European culture, 1890–1914.

Nelson, Benjamin, ed., *Freud and the Twentieth Century* (1957). A valuable collection of essays.

Roazen, Paul, *Freud's Political and Social Thought* (1968). The wider implications of Freudian psychology.

Stromberg, Roland N., *European Intellectual History Since 1789* (1986). A helpful text.

Zeitlin, I. M., *Ideology and the Development of Sociological Theory* (1968). Examines in detail the thought of major shapers of sociological theory.

REVIEW QUESTIONS

1. What is meant by the term *irrationalism?*

2. Discuss Nietzsche's attitude toward reason, Christianity, and democracy.

3. Why were Nazis attracted to Nietzsche?

4. Do you find anything positive in Nietzsche's thought?

5. In what ways did Bergson reflect the growing irrationalism of the age?

6. How did Sorel show the political potential of the nonrational?

7. To what extent was Freud a child of the Enlightenment? How did he differ from the philosophes?

8. What were the standards of esthetics that had governed Western literature and art since the Renaissance? How did the modernist movement break with these standards?

9. What constituted the crisis of modern society for Durkheim? How did he try to cope with this crisis?

10. What do you think of Pareto's judgment that the masses in a democratic state are not really influenced by rational argument?

11. For Weber, what was the terrible paradox of reason?

12. Describe the view of the universe held by westerners around 1880. How was this view altered by modern physics? What is the significance of this revolution for areas beyond science?

13. In what ways was the Enlightenment tradition in disarray by the early years of the twentieth century?

Part Five

Western Civilization in Crisis: World Wars and Totalitarianism

1914–1945

The Nazi Mass Rally. The most effective means of uniting the masses, said Hitler, was the mass rally. Bombarded by the cheers of thousands of voices, by marching units, by a forest of banners, and by explosive oratory, the individual becomes convinced of the truth of the party's message. (AP/Wide World Photos)

Politics and Society

1910
World War I (1914–1918)
United States declares war on Germany (1917)
Bolshevik Revolution in Russia (1917)
Wilson announces his Fourteen Points (1918)
Treaty of Versailles (1919)

1920
Mussolini seizes power in Italy (1922)
First Five-Year Plan starts rapid industrialization in the Soviet Union (1928)
Forced collectivization of agriculture in the Soviet Union (1929)
Start of the Great Depression (1929)

1930
Hitler becomes chancellor of Germany (1933)
Stalin orders mass purges in the Soviet Union (1936–1938)
Hitler sends troops into the Rhineland (1936)
Rome-Berlin Axis (1936)
Spanish Civil War (1936–1939)
Franco establishes a dictatorship in Spain (1939)
Nazi-Soviet nonaggression pact (1939)
German troops invade Poland: World War II begins (1939)

1940
Germany invades Belgium, Holland, Luxembourg, and France (1940)
Japan attacks Pearl Harbor: United States enters war against Japan and Germany (1941)
War in Europe ends (1945)
United States drops atomic bombs on Japan; Japan surrenders (1945)

Thought and Culture

1910
Bohr: Quantum theory of atomic structure (1912)
Stravinsky, *The Rite of Spring* (1913)
Pareto, *Treatise on General Sociology* (1916)
Spengler, *The Decline of the West* (1918, 1922)
Dadaism in art (1915–1924)
Barth, *The Epistle to the Romans* (1919)

1920
Wittgenstein, *Tractatus LogicoPhilosophicus* (1921–1922)
Eliot, *The Waste Land* (1922)
Mann, *Magic Mountain* (1924)
Cassirer, *The Philosophy of Symbolic Forms* (1923–1929)
Surrealism in art (c. 1925)
Hitler, *Mein Kampf* (1925–1926)
Kafka, *The Trial* (1925)
Heidegger, *Being and Time* (1927)
Lawrence, *Lady Chatterley's Lover* (1928)
Remarque, *All Quiet on the Western Front* (1929)

1930
Freud, *Civilization and Its Discontents* (1930)
Ortega y Gasset, *The Revolt of the Masses* (1930)
Jaspers, *Man in the Modern Age* (1930)
Jung, *Modern Man in Search of a Soul* (1933)
Toynbee, *A Study of History* (1934–1961)
Keynes, *The General Theory of Employment, Interest, and Money* (1936)
Picasso, *Guernica* (1937)
Steinbeck, *The Grapes of Wrath* (1939)

1940
Hemingway, *For Whom the Bell Tolls* (1940)
Koestler, *Darkness at Noon* (1941)
Fromm, *Escape from Freedom* (1941)
Camus, *The Stranger* (1942)
Sartre, *Being and Nothingness* (1943)
Orwell, *1984* (1949)

Chapter 18

World War I:
The West in Despair

- Aggravated Nationalist Tensions in Austria-Hungary
- The German System of Alliances
- The Triple Entente
- The Drift Toward War
- War as Celebration
- Stalemate in the West
- Other Fronts
- The Collapse of the Central Powers
- The Peace Conference
- The Russian Revolution of 1917
- The War and European Consciousness

*P*rior to 1914, the dominant mood in Europe was one of

pride in the accomplishments of Western civilization and confi-

dence in its future progress. Advances in science and technology, the rising standard of living, the spread of democratic institutions, and Europe's position of power in the world all contributed to a sense of optimism, as did the expansion of social reform and the increase in literacy for the masses. Furthermore, since the defeat of Napoleon, Europe had avoided a general war, and since the Franco-Prussian War (1870–71), the Great Powers had not fought each other. Few people recognized that the West's outward achievements masked an inner turbulence that was propelling Western civilization toward a cataclysm. The European state system was failing.

By 1914, national states, answering to no higher power, were fueled by an explosive nationalism and were grouped into alliances that faced each other with ever-mounting hostility. Nationalist passions, overheated by the popular press and expansionist societies, poisoned international relations. Nationalist thinkers propagated pseudoscientific racial and Social Darwinist doctrines that glorified conflict and justified the subjugation of other peoples. Committed to enhancing national power, statesmen lost sight of Europe as a community of nations sharing a common civilization. Caution and restraint gave way to belligerency in foreign relations.

The failure of the European state system was paralleled by a cultural crisis. Some European intellectuals attacked the rational tradition of the Enlightenment and celebrated the primitive, the instinctual, and the irrational. Increasingly, young people were drawn to philosophies of action that ridiculed liberal bourgeois values and viewed war as a purifying and ennobling experience. Colonial wars, colorfully portrayed in the popular press, ignited the imagination of bored factory workers and daydreaming students and reinforced a sense of duty and an urge for gallantry among soldiers and aristocrats. These "splendid" little colonial wars helped fashion an attitude that made war acceptable, if not laudable. Yearning to break loose from their ordinary lives and to embrace heroic values, many Europeans regarded vio-

lent conflict as the highest expression of individual and national life. "If only there were a war, even an unjust one," wrote George Heym, a young German writer, in 1912. "This peace is so rotten."[1] The popular historian Heinrich von Treitschke (1834–1896), whose lectures influenced many students who were to rise to positions of importance in the German army and administration, expressed the prevailing mood: "Those who preach the nonsense about everlasting peace do not understand the life of the [German] race. . . . [T]o banish war from history would be to banish all progress."[2] Although technology was making warfare more brutal and dangerous, Europe retained a romantic illusion about combat.

While Europe was seemingly progressing in the art of civilization, the mythic power of nationalism and the primitive appeal of conflict were driving European civilization to the abyss. Few people recognized the potential crisis—certainly not the statesmen whose reckless blundering allowed the Continent to stumble into war. ❖

AGGRAVATED NATIONALIST TENSIONS IN AUSTRIA-HUNGARY

On June 28, 1914, a young terrorist, with the support of a secret Serbian nationalist society called Union or Death (more popularly known as the Black Hand), murdered Archduke Francis Ferdinand, heir to the throne of Austria-Hungary. Six weeks later, the armies of Europe were on the march; an incident in the Balkans had sparked a world war. An analysis of why Austria-Hungary felt compelled to attack Serbia and why the other powers became enmeshed in the conflict shows how explosive Europe was in 1914. And nowhere were conditions more volatile than in Austria-Hungary, the scene of the assassination.

With its several nationalities, each with its own history and traditions and often conflicting aspirations, Austria-Hungary stood in opposition to nationalism, the most powerful spiritual force of the age. Perhaps the supranational

Chronology 18.1 ❖ World War I

1882	Formation of the Triple Alliance of Germany, Austria-Hungary, and Italy
1894	Alliance between Russia and France
1904	Anglo-French Entente
1907	Anglo-Russian Entente
1908	Bosnian crisis
June 28, 1914	Archduke Francis Ferdinand of Austria is assassinated at Sarajevo
August 4, 1914	Germans invade Belgium
September 1914	First battle of the Marne saves Paris
May 1915	Italy enters the war on the Allies' side
Spring 1915	Germany launches offensive that forces Russia to abandon Galicia and most of Poland
February 1916	General Pétain leads French forces at Verdun; Germans fail to capture the fortress town
July–November 1916	Battle of the Somme: the Allies suffer 600,000 casualties
January 1917	Germany launches unrestricted submarine warfare
April 6, 1917	United States declares war on Germany
November 1917	Bolsheviks take power in Russia
March 1918	Russia signs the Treaty of Brest-Litovsk, losing territory to Germany and withdrawing from the war
March 21, 1918	Germans launch a great offensive to end the war
June 3, 1918	Germans advance to within fifty-six miles of Paris
August 8, 1918	British victory at Amiens
October 1918	Turkey is forced to withdraw from the war after several British successes
November 3, 1918	Austria-Hungary signs armistice with the Allies
November 11, 1918	Germany signs armistice with the Allies, ending World War I
January 1919	Paris Peace Conference
June 28, 1919	Germany signs the Treaty of Versailles

Austro-Hungarian Empire was obsolete in a world of states based on the principle of nationality. Dominated by Germans and Hungarians, the empire remained unable either to satisfy the grievances or to contain the nationalist aims of its minorities, particularly the Czechs and South Slavs (Croats, Slovenes, and Serbs).

Heightened agitation among the several nationalities, which worsened in the decade before 1914, created terrible anxieties among Austrian leaders. The fear that the empire would be torn apart by rebellion caused Austria to pursue a forceful policy against any nation that fanned the nationalist feelings of its Slavic minorities. In par-

Map 18.1 Ethnic Groups in Germany, Austria, and the Balkans Before World War I

ticular, this policy meant worsening tensions between Austria and small Serbia, which had been independent of the Ottoman Empire since 1878.

Captivated by Western ideas of nationalism, the Serbs sought to create a Greater Serbia by uniting with their racial kin, the South Slavs who dwelt in Austria-Hungary. Since some seven million South Slavs lived in the Hapsburg Empire, the dream of a Greater Serbia, shrilly expressed by Serbian nationalists, caused nightmares in Austria. Fearing that continued Serbian agitation would encourage the South Slavs to press for secession, some Austrian leaders urged the destruction of the Serbian menace.

The tensions arising from the multinational character of the Austro-Hungarian Empire in an age of heightened nationalist feeling set off the explosion in 1914. Unable to solve its minority problems and fearful of Pan-Serbism, Austria-Hungary felt itself in a life-or-death situation. This sense of desperation led it to lash out at Serbia after the assassination of Archduke Francis Ferdinand.

THE GERMAN SYSTEM
OF ALLIANCES

The war might have been avoided, or might have remained limited to Austria and Serbia, had Europe in 1914 not been divided into two hostile alliance systems. Such a situation contains inherent dangers. For example, knowing that it has the support of allies, a country might pursue a more provocative and reckless course and be less conciliatory during a crisis. Furthermore, a conflict between two states might spark a chain reaction, drawing in the other powers and transforming a limited war into a general war. That is what happened after the assassination. This dangerous alliance system originated with Bismarck and the Franco-Prussian War.

The New German Empire

The unification of Germany in 1870–71 turned the new state into an international power of the first rank, upsetting the balance of power in Europe. For the first time since the wars of the French Revolution, a nation was in a position to dominate the European continent. To German nationalists, the unification of Germany was both the fulfillment of a national dream and the starting point for an even more ambitious goal: extending German power in Europe and the world.

As the nineteenth century drew to a close, German nationalism became more extreme. Believing that Germany must either grow or die, nationalists pressed the government to build a powerful navy, acquire colonies, gain a much greater share of the world's markets, and expand German interests and influence in Europe. Sometimes these goals were expressed in the language of Social Darwinism: that nations are engaged in an eternal struggle for survival and domination. Decisive victories against Austria (1866) and France (1871), the formation of the German Reich, rapid industrialization, and the impressive achievements of German science and scholarship had molded a powerful and dynamic nation. Imbued with great expectations for the future, Germans became increasingly impatient to see the fatherland gain its "rightful" place in world affairs—an attitude that alarmed non-Germans.

Bismarck's Goals

Under Bismarck, who did not seek additional territory but wanted only to preserve the recently achieved unification, Germany pursued a moderate and cautious foreign policy. One of Bismarck's principal goals was to keep France isolated and friendless. Deeply humiliated by its defeat in the Franco-Prussian War and the loss of Alsace and Lorraine, France found its nationalists yearning for a war of revenge against Germany. Even though the French government, aware of Germany's strength, was unlikely to initiate such a conflict, the issue of Alsace-Lorraine increased tensions between the two countries.

Bismarck also hoped to prevent a war between Russia and Austria-Hungary, for such a conflict could lead to German involvement, the breakup of Austria-Hungary, and Russian expansion in Eastern Europe. To maintain peace and Germany's existing borders, Bismarck forged complex alliances. In the 1880s, he created the Triple Alliance, consisting of Germany, Austria-Hungary, and Italy, as well as an alliance with Russia.

Bismarck conducted foreign policy with restraint, forming alliances not to conquer new lands, but to protect Germany from aggression by either France or Russia. His aim was to preserve order and stability in Europe, not to launch war. But in 1888, a new emperor ascended the German throne. When the young Kaiser William II (1888–1918) clashed with his aging prime minister, Bismarck was forced to resign (1890). Lacking Bismarck's diplomatic skills, his cool restraint, and his determination to keep peace in Europe, the new German leaders pursued a belligerent and imperialistic foreign policy in the ensuing years—a policy that frightened other states, particularly Britain. Whereas Bismarck considered Germany a satiated power, these men insisted that Germany must have its place in the sun.

The first act of the new leadership was to permit the treaty with Russia to lapse, allowing Germany to give full support to Austria, which was considered a more reliable ally. Whereas Bismarck had warned Austria to act with moderation and caution in the Balkans, his successors not only failed to hold Austria in check, but actually encouraged Austrian aggression. This proved fatal to the peace of Europe.

THE TRIPLE ENTENTE

Fear of Germany

When Germany broke with Russia in 1890, France was quick to take advantage of the situation. Worried by Germany's increasing military strength, expanding industries, growing population, and alliance with Austria and Italy, France coveted Russia as an ally. In 1894, France and Russia entered into an alliance; the isolation forced on France by Bismarck had ended.

Germany's growing military might also alarmed Great Britain. In addition, its spectacular industrial growth had made Germany a potent trade rival of England. Britain was distressed, too, by Germany's increased efforts to become a great colonial power—a goal demanded by German nationalists. But most troubling was Germany's decision to build a great navy. Germany was already the strongest land power on the Continent. Achieving naval parity with England

would give Germany the potential to threaten Britain's overseas empire and to blockade the British Isles, depriving Britain of food and supplies. Germany's naval program was the single most important reason that Britain moved closer first to France and then to Russia. Germany's naval construction, designed to increase its stature as a Great Power but not really necessary for its security, was one indication that German leaders had abandoned Bismarck's policy of good sense. Eager to add the British as an ally and demonstrating superb diplomatic skill, France moved to end long-standing colonial disputes with Britain. The Entente Cordiale of 1904 accomplished this conciliation. England had emerged from its self-imposed isolation.

Wishing to counter Germany's Triple Alliance with a strong alliance of their own, French diplomats now sought to ease tensions between their Russian ally and their new British friend. Two events convinced Russia to adopt a more conciliatory attitude toward Britain: a disastrous and unexpected defeat in the Russo-Japanese War of 1904–1905 and a working-class revolution in 1905. Shocked by defeat, its army bordering on disintegration, and its workers restive, Russia was now receptive to settling its imperial disputes with Britain over Persia, Tibet, and Afghanistan—a decision encouraged by France. In the Anglo-Russian Entente of 1907, as in the Anglo-French Entente Cordiale of 1904, the former rivals conducted themselves in a conciliatory, if not friendly, manner. In both instances, what engendered this spirit of cooperation was fear of Germany.

Europe was now broken into two hostile camps: the Triple Entente of France, Russia, and Britain and the Triple Alliance of Germany, Austria-Hungary, and Italy. The costly arms race and the maintenance of large standing armies by all the states except Britain increased fear and suspicion between the alliances.

German Reactions

Germany denounced the Triple Entente as a hostile anti-German coalition, designed to encircle and crush Germany; to survive, Germany must break this ring. Considering Austria-Hungary to be its only reliable ally, Germany resolved to preserve the power and dignity of the Hapsburg Empire. If Austria-Hungary fell from the ranks of Great Powers, Germany would have to stand alone against its enemies. At all costs, Austria-Hungary must not be weakened.

But this assessment suffered from dangerous miscalculations. First, Germany overstressed the hostile nature of the Triple Entente. In reality, France, Russia, and Britain had drawn closer together not to wage aggressive war against Germany, but to protect themselves against burgeoning German military, industrial, and diplomatic power. Second, by linking German security to Austria, Germany greatly increased the chances of war. Growing more and more apprehensive of Pan-Serbism, Austria might well decide that only a war could prevent its empire from disintegrating. Confident of German support, Austria would be more likely to resort to force; fearing any diminution of Austrian power, Germany would be more likely to give Austria that support.

THE DRIFT TOWARD WAR

Starting in 1908, several crises tested the competing alliances, pushing Europe closer to war. Particularly significant was the Bosnian affair, which involved Russia, Austria-Hungary, and Serbia. This incident contained many of the ingredients that eventually ignited the war in 1914.

The Bosnian Crisis

Russia's humiliating defeat by Japan in 1905 had diminished its stature as a Great Power. The new Russian foreign minister, Alexander Izvolsky, hoped to gain a diplomatic triumph by compelling Ottoman Turkey to allow Russian warships to pass through the Dardanelles, fulfilling a centuries-old dream of extending Russian power into the Mediterranean.

Russia made a deal with Austria: if Austria would support Russia's move to open the Dardanelles, Russia would permit Austrian annexation of the provinces of Bosnia and Herzegovina. Officially a part of the Ottoman Empire, these provinces had been administered by Austria-Hungary since 1878. The population consisted mainly of ethnic cousins of the Serbs. A formal annexation would certainly infuriate the Serbs, who hoped one day to make the region part of a Greater Serbia.

In 1908, Austria proceeded to annex the provinces, but Russia met stiff resistance from England and France when it presented its case for opening the straits to Russian warships. Austria had gained a diplomatic victory, while Russia suffered another humiliation. Even more enraged than Russia was Serbia, which threatened to invade Bosnia to liberate its cousins from Austrian oppression. The Serbian press openly declared that Austria-Hungary must perish if the South Slavs were to achieve liberty and unity. A fiery attitude also prevailed in Vienna: Austria-Hungary could not survive unless Serbia was destroyed.

During this period of intense hostility between Austria-Hungary and Serbia, Germany supported its Austrian ally. To keep Austria strong, Germany would even agree to the dismemberment of Serbia and its incorporation into the Hapsburg Empire. Unlike Bismarck, who tried to hold Austria in check, German leadership now coolly envisioned an Austrian attack on Serbia, and just as coolly offered German support if Russia intervened.

Balkan Wars

The Bosnian crisis pushed Germany and Austria closer together, brought relations between Austria and Serbia to the breaking point, and inflicted another humiliation on Russia. The first Balkan War (1912) continued these trends. The Balkan states of Montenegro, Serbia, Bulgaria, and Greece attacked the dying Ottoman Empire. In a brief campaign, the Balkan armies captured the Turkish empire's European territory, with the exception of Constantinople. Because it was on the victorious side, landlocked Serbia gained the Albanian coast and thus a long-desired outlet to the sea. Austria was determined to keep its enemy from reaping this reward, and Germany, as in the Bosnian crisis, supported its ally. Unable to secure Russian support, Serbia was forced to surrender the territory, which became the state of Albania.

The Assassination of Archduke Francis Ferdinand. Immediately after the assassination, Austrian authorities arrest one of the assassins. *(Bettman/Corbis)*

Incensed Serbian nationalists accelerated their campaign of propaganda and terrorism against Austria. Believing that another humiliation would irreparably damage its prestige, Russia vowed to back Serbia in its next confrontation with Austria. And Austria had exhausted its patience with Serbia. Emboldened by German encouragement, Austria wanted to end the Serbian threat once and for all. Thus, the ingredients for war between Austria and Serbia, a war that might easily draw in Russia and Germany, were present. Another incident might well start a war. It came in 1914.

Assassination of Francis Ferdinand

On June 28, 1914, Francis Ferdinand was assassinated while making a state visit to Sarajevo, the capital of Bosnia. Young Gavrilo Princip, who was part of a team of Bosnian terrorists linked to the Black Hand, fired two shots at close range into the archduke's car. Francis Ferdinand and his wife died within fifteen minutes. By killing the archduke, the terrorists hoped to bring tensions in the Hapsburg Empire to a boiling point and to prepare the way for revolution.

For many years, leaders of Austria had yearned for war with Serbia in order to end the agitation for the union of the South Slavs. Now, they reasoned, the hour had struck. But war with Serbia would require the approval of Germany. Believing that Austria was Germany's only reliable ally and that a diminution of Austrian power and prestige threatened German security, German statesmen encouraged their ally to take up arms against Serbia. Germany and Austria wanted a quick strike to overwhelm Serbia before other countries were drawn into the conflict.

Germany Encourages Austria

Confident of German backing, on July 23 Austria presented Serbia with an ultimatum and demanded a response within forty-eight hours. The terms of the ultimatum were so harsh that it was next to impossible for Serbia to accept them. This reaction was the one that Austria intended, as it sought a military solution to the crisis rather than a diplomatic one. But Russia would not remain indifferent to an Austro-German effort to liquidate Serbia. Russia feared that an Austrian conquest of Serbia was just the first step in an Austro-German plan to dominate the Balkans. Such an extension of German and Austrian power in a region bordering Russia was unthinkable to the tsar's government. Moreover, after suffering repeated reverses in foreign affairs, Russia would not tolerate another humiliation. As Germany had decided to back its Austrian ally, Russia resolved not to abandon Serbia.

Serbia responded to Austria's ultimatum in a conciliatory manner, agreeing to virtually all Austrian demands. But it refused to let Austrian officials enter Serbia to investigate the assassination. Having already discarded the idea of a peaceful settlement, Austria insisted that Serbia's failure to accept one provision meant that the entire ultimatum had been rejected. It ordered the mobilization of the Austrian army.

This was a crucial moment for Germany. Would it continue to support Austria, knowing that an Austrian attack on Serbia would probably bring Russia into the conflict? Determined not to desert Austria and believing that a showdown with Russia was inevitable anyway, the German war party, with the military cajoling and persuading the civilian authorities, continued to urge Austrian action against Serbia. They argued that it was better to fight Russia in 1914 than a few years later, when the tsar's empire, which already had a huge reserve of manpower and was rapidly building strategic railroads and expanding its Baltic fleet, would be stronger. Confident of the superiority of the German army, the war party

claimed that Germany could defeat both Russia and France and that Britain's army was too weak to make a difference.

On July 28, 1914, Austria declared war on Serbia. Russia, with the assurance of French support, proclaimed partial mobilization aimed at Austria alone. But the military warned that partial mobilization would throw the slow-moving Russian war machine into total confusion if the order had to be changed suddenly to full mobilization. Moreover, the only plans the Russian general staff had drawn up called for full mobilization, that is, for war against both Austria and Germany. Pressured by his generals, the tsar gave the order for full mobilization on July 30. Russian forces would be arrayed against Germany as well as Austria.

Because the country that struck first gained the advantage of fighting according to its own plans rather than having to improvise in response to the enemy's attack, generals tended to regard mobilization by the enemy as an act of war. Therefore, when Russia refused a German warning to halt mobilization, Germany, on August 1, ordered a general mobilization and declared war on Russia. Two days later, Germany also declared war on France, believing that France would support its Russian ally. Besides, German battle plans were based on a war with both Russia and France. Thus, a war between Germany and Russia automatically meant a German attack on France.

When Belgium refused to allow German troops to march through Belgian territory into France, Germany invaded the small nation, which brought Britain, pledged to guarantee Belgian neutrality, into the war. Britain could never tolerate German troops directly across the English Channel in any case, nor could it brook German mastery of western Europe.

The Question of Responsibility

The question of whether any one power was mainly responsible for the war has intrigued historians. In assessing blame, historians have focused on Germany's role. German historian Fritz Fischer argues that Germany's ambition to dominate Europe was the underlying cause of the war.

Germany encouraged Austria to strike at Serbia knowing that an attack on Serbia could mean war with Russia and its French ally. Believing that it had the military advantage, Germany was willing to risk such a war. Hence, "her leaders must bear a substantial share of the historical responsibility for the outbreak of general war in 1914."[3]

Attracted by Social Darwinist ideas that foresaw an inevitable racial struggle between Germans and Slavs, by militarist doctrines that glorified war, and by a nationalist drive for *Lebensraum* (more living space), continues Fischer, Germany sought to become the foremost economic and political power in Europe and to play a far greater role in world politics; to achieve this goal, it was willing to go to war. Fischer supports his position by pointing to Germany's war aims, drawn up immediately after the outbreak of war, which called for the annexation of neighboring territories and the creation of satellite states. Fischer's critics stress, however, that Social Darwinism and militarism enthralled other nations besides Germany and that this was not peculiarly German, but rather part of a general European sickness. They argue further that Germany would have preferred a limited war between Austria and Serbia and before the war had no plans to annex and dominate neighboring lands.

Historians also attribute blame to the other powers. Austria bears responsibility for its determination to crush Serbia and for its insistent avoidance of a negotiated settlement. Serbia's responsibility stems from its pursuing an aggressive Pan-Serbian policy, which set it on a collision course with Austria-Hungary. In 1913, Sir Fairfax Cartwright, the British ambassador to Vienna, warned: "Serbia will some day set Europe by the ears, and bring about a universal war on the Continent. I cannot tell you how exasperated people are getting here at the continual worry which that little country causes to Austria."[4] Russia bears responsibility for instituting general mobilization, thereby turning a limited war between Austria-Hungary and Serbia into a European war; France, for failing to restrain Russia and indeed for encouraging its ally to mobilize; and England, for failing to make clear that it would support its allies. Had Germany seen plainly that

Britain would intervene, it might have been more cautious.

Some historians, dismissing the question of responsibility, regard the war as an obvious sign that European civilization was in deep trouble. Viewed in the broad perspective of European history, the war marked a culmination of dangerous forces in European life: the glorification of power, the fascination with violence and the nonrational, the general dissatisfaction and disillusionment with bourgeois society, and, above all, the explosive nationalism. It also underscored the diminishing confidence in the capacity of reason to solve the problems created by the Industrial Revolution and pointed to the flaws and perils of the alliance system.

WAR AS CELEBRATION

When war was certain, an extraordinary phenomenon occurred. Crowds gathered in capital cities and expressed their loyalty to the fatherland and their readiness to fight. It seemed as if people wanted violence for its own sake. War seemed to offer an escape from the dull routine of classroom, job, and home and from the emptiness, drabness, mediocrity, and pettiness of bourgeois society—from "a world grown old and cold and weary," as Rupert Brooke, a young British poet, put it.[5] To some, war was a "beautiful . . . sacred moment" that satisfied an "ethical yearning."[6] To many people, especially youth and intellectuals, war seemed a healthy and heroic antidote to what was regarded as an unbearably decadent and soul-destroying machine age and to the bourgeois preoccupation with work, profits, and possessions. But more significantly, the outpouring of patriotic sentiments demonstrated the immense power that nationalism exercised over the European mind. With extraordinary success, nationalism welded millions of people into a collectivity ready to devote body and soul to the nation, especially during its hour of need.

In Paris, men marched down the boulevards singing the stirring words of the French national anthem, the "Marseillaise," while women showered young soldiers with flowers. A participant in these days recalls: "Young and old, civilians and military men burned with the same excitement. . . . [T]housands of men eager to fight would jostle one another outside recruiting offices, waiting to join up. . . . The word 'duty' had a meaning for them, and the word 'country' had regained its splendor."[7] Similar scenes occurred in Berlin. "It is a joy to be alive," editorialized one newspaper. "We wished so much for this hour. . . . The sword which has been forced into our hand will not be sheathed until our aims are won and our territory extended as far as necessity demands."[8] Writing about those momentous days, the British mathematician-philosopher Bertrand Russell recalled his horror and "amazement that average men and women were delighted at the prospect of war. . . . [T]he anticipation of carnage was delightful to something like ninety percent of the population. I had to revise my views on human nature."[9]

Soldiers bound for battle and wives and sweethearts seeing them off at train stations were in a holiday mood. "My dear ones, be proud that you live in such a time and in such a nation and that you . . . have the privilege of sending those you love into so glorious a battle," wrote a young German law student to his family.[10] The young warriors yearned to do something noble and altruistic, to win glory, and to experience life at its most intense.

The martial mood also captivated many of Europe's most distinguished intellectuals. They shared Rupert Brooke's sentiments: "Now God be thanked Who has matched us with His hour, / And caught our youth, and wakened us from sleeping."[11] To the prominent German historian Friedrich Meinecke, August 1914 was "one of the great moments of my life which suddenly filled my soul with the deepest confidence in our people and the profoundest joy."[12] In November 1914, Thomas Mann (see "Intellectuals and Artists in Troubled Times" in the following chapter), the distinguished German writer, saw the war as "purification, liberation . . . an enormous hope; [it] set the hearts of poets aflame. . . . How could the artist, the soldier in the artist," he asked, "not praise God for the collapse of a peaceful world with which he was fed up, so exceedingly fed up?"[13] Besides being gripped by a thirst for excitement and a quest for the heroic, some intellectuals welcomed the war because it unified the nation in a spirit of fraternity and altruism. It was

a return, some felt, to the organic roots of human existence, a way of overcoming a sense of individual isolation. War, in the view of some intellectuals, would spiritually regenerate the nation. It would resurrect glory, nobility, and heroism; it would awaken a spirit of self-sacrifice and dedication and give life an overriding purpose.

Thus, a generation of European youth marched off to war joyously, urged on by their teachers and cheered by their delirious nations. It must be emphasized, however, that the soldiers who went off to war singing and the statesmen and generals who welcomed war or did not try hard enough to prevent it expected a short, decisive, gallant conflict. Few envisioned what World War I turned out to be: four years of barbaric, senseless slaughter. The cheers of chauvinists, deluded idealists, and fools drowned out the words of those principally socialists, labor leaders, pacifists, and left-leaning liberals, who realized that Europe was stumbling into darkness. "The lamps are going out all over Europe," said British Foreign Secretary Edward Grey. "We shall never see them lit again in our lifetime."

STALEMATE IN THE WEST

On August 4, 1914, the German army invaded Belgium. German war plans, drawn up years earlier, chiefly by General Alfred von Schlieffen, called for the army to swing through Belgium to outflank French border defenses, envelop the French forces, and destroy the enemy by attacking its rear. With the French army smashed and Paris isolated, German railroads—an extensive system of tracks, carefully planned by the general staff, had been constructed in the previous decade—would rush the victorious troops to the eastern front to bolster the small force that had been assigned to hold off the Russians. Everything depended on speed. France must be taken before the Russians could mobilize sufficient numbers to invade Germany. The Germans were confident that they would defeat France in two months or less.

But things did not turn out the way the German military had anticipated. Moving faster than the Germans expected, the Russians invaded East Prussia, which led General Helmuth von Moltke

Map 18.2 **World War I, 1914–1918** This map shows Europe divided into competing alliances and German advances into France and eastern Europe once war broke out.

Triple Entente and its Allies

Central Powers

Neutral nations

Farthest German-Austrian advance

⚔ **Major battle**

0   200   400 Km.

0   200   400 Mi.

ATLANTIC OCEAN

ICELAND

IRELAND

GREAT BRITAIN
London ●

Paris ●

FRANCE

SPAIN

PORTUGAL

NORWAY

SWEDEN

DENMARK

North Sea

NETH.

BELG.

LUX.

GERMANY
Berlin ●

Rhine R.

SWITZ.

Danube R.

ITALY
Rome ●

Mediterranean Sea

British blockade line

FINLAND

Helsinki ●

St. Petersburg ●

Baltic Sea

Riga ●

⚔ Tannenberg 1914

Warsaw ●

POLAND

Vienna ●

AUSTRIA-HUNGARY

⚔ Caporetto 1917

Sarajevo ●

MONTENEGRO

ALBANIA

SERBIA

Moscow ●

RUSSIA

Treaty of Brest-Litovsk March 1918

Kiev ●

Brest-Litovsk ●

Armistice line, Dec. 1917

GALICIA

ROMANIA

Bucharest ●

Black Sea

Constantinople ●

BULGARIA

GREECE

Dardanelles

Gallipoli 1915

OTTOMAN EMPIRE

NETHERLANDS

Cologne ●

Rhine R.

Moselle R.

LUXEMBOURG

Saar R.

Strasbourg ●

ALSACE

LORRAINE

Nancy ●

Liège ●

Antwerp ●

BELGIUM

Meuse R.

Sedan ●

Argonne Forest

Verdun ●

Brussels ●

Ypres ●

FLANDERS

Passchendaele ●

Aisne R.

Reims ●

Marne R.

Ostend ●

Calais ●

Dover ●

English Channel

Amiens ●

Somme R.

Paris ●

Seine R.

FRANCE

Germany, 1914

German offensive, 1914

Farthest German advance, Sept. 1914

Front at beginning of 1915

German offensive, Summer 1918

Armistice line, November 1918

409

Trench Warfare. Soldiers in the trenches had to endure earsplitting bombardments from heavy artillery and attacks from the enemy's trenches. They also had
to deal with rats, lice, mud, the stench of rotting corpses, and the wails of the
wounded unable to be rescued from no man's land. *(The Art Archive)*

to transfer troops from the French front, hamper-
ing the German advance. By early September, the
Germans had reached the Marne River, forty
miles from Paris. With their capital at their backs,
the regrouped French forces, aided by the British,
fought with astounding courage. Moreover, in
their rush toward Paris, the Germans had un-
knowingly exposed their flank, which the French
attacked. The British then penetrated a gap that
opened up between the German armies, forcing
the Germans to retreat. The first battle of the
Marne had saved Paris. Now the war entered a
new and unexpected phase: the deadlock of
trench warfare.

For over four hundred miles across northern
France, from the Alps to the North Sea, the opposing sides both constructed a vast network of
trenches. These trenches had underground dugouts, and barbed wire stretched for yards before
the front trenches as a barrier to attack. Behind
the front trenches were other lines to which soldiers could retreat and from which support could
be sent. Between the opposing armies lay "no
man's land," a wasteland of mud, shattered trees,
torn earth, and broken bodies. In the trenches,
soldiers were reduced to a primitive existence.
Sometimes they stood knee-deep in freezing water
or slimy mud; the stench from human waste, rotting corpses, and unwashed bodies overwhelmed
the senses; rats, made more fecund by easy access
to food, including decaying flesh, swarmed over
the dead and scampered across the wounded and

the sleeping; and ubiquitous lice caused intense discomfort and disease, which frequently required hospitalization for several weeks. After days of fearsome, earsplitting bombardments, even the most stouthearted were reduced to shivering, whimpering creatures. The agonizing cries and pleas of the wounded, left to die on the battlefield because it was too dangerous to attempt a rescue, shattered the nerves of the men in the trenches. Trench warfare was a futile battle of nerves, endurance, and courage, waged to the constant thunder of heavy artillery, which pulverized both ramparts and men. It was also butchery. As attacking troops climbed over their trenches and advanced bravely across no man's land, they were decimated by heavy artillery and chewed up by machine-gun fire. If they did penetrate the front-line trenches of the enemy, they would soon be thrown back by a counterattack.

Despite a frightful loss of life, little land changed hands. The Allied generals in particular, unfeeling and totally lacking in imagination, ordered still greater attacks, hoping to wear down German manpower, which was inferior to their own. Once German reserves could not replenish losses, they reasoned, a breakthrough would be possible. But this strategy achieved nothing. The generals ordered still greater attacks to end the stalemate; this only increased the death toll, for the advantage was always with the defense, which possessed machine guns, magazine rifles, and barbed wire. Tanks could redress the balance, but the generals, committed to old concepts, did not make effective use of them. And whereas the technology of the machine gun had been perfected, the motorized tanks often broke down. Gains and losses of land were measured in yards, but the lives of Europe's youth were squandered by the hundreds of thousands. Against artillery, barbed wire, and machine guns, human courage had no chance, but the generals—uncomprehending, unfeeling, and incompetent—persisted in their mass attacks. This futile effort at a breakthrough wasted untold lives to absolutely no purpose.

In 1915, neither side could break the deadlock. Hoping to bleed the French army dry and force its surrender, the Germans, in February 1916, attacked the town of Verdun. Knowing that the French could never permit a retreat from this ancient fortress, they hoped that France would suffer such a loss of men that it would be unable to continue the war. France and Germany suffered more than a million casualties at Verdun—including some 300,000 dead—which one military historian calls "the greatest battle in world history."[14] When the British opened a major offensive on July 1, however, the Germans had to channel their reserves to the new front, relieving the pressure on Verdun.

At the end of June 1916, the British, assisted by the French, attempted a breakthrough at the Somme River. On July 1, after seven days of intense bombardment intended to destroy German defenses, the British climbed out of their trenches and ventured into no man's land. But German positions had not been destroyed. Emerging from their deep dugouts, German machine gunners fired repeatedly at the British, who had been ordered to advance in rows. Marching into concentrated machine-gun fire, few British troops ever made it across no man's land. Out of the 110,000 who attacked, 60,000 fell dead or wounded, "the heaviest loss ever suffered in a single day by a British army or by any army in the First World War."[15] When the battle of the Somme ended in mid-November, Britain and France had lost more than 600,000 men, and the military situation remained essentially unchanged. The only victor was the war itself, which was devouring Europe's youth at an incredible rate.

In December 1916, General Robert Nivelle was appointed commander in chief of the French forces. Having learned little from past French failures to achieve a breakthrough, Nivelle ordered another mass attack for April 1917. The Germans discovered the battle plans on the body of a French officer and withdrew to a shorter line on high ground, constructing the strongest defense network of the war. Knowing that the French had lost the element of surprise and pushing aside the warnings of leading statesmen and military men, Nivelle went ahead with the attack. "The offensive alone gives victory; the defensive gives only defeat and shame," he told the president and the minister of war.[16]

The Nivelle offensive, which began on April 16, was another bloodbath. Sometimes the fire was so intense that the French could not make it out of their own trenches. Although French

Women in the Factories During World War I. Women found employment in the war industry. Their patriotism and productive labor caused opposition to women's suffrage to dissipate. *(Corbis)*

soldiers fought with courage, the situation was hopeless. Still, Nivelle persisted with the attack; after ten days, French casualties numbered 187,000. The disgraced Nivelle was soon relieved of his command.

OTHER FRONTS

While the Western front hardened into a stalemate, events moved more decisively on the Eastern front. In August 1914, the Russians, with insufficient preparation, invaded East Prussia. After some initial successes, which sent a scare into the German general staff, the Russians were soundly defeated at the battle of Tannenberg (August 26–30, 1914) and forced to withdraw from German territory, which remained inviolate for the rest of the war.

Meanwhile, Germany's ally Austria was having no success against Serbia and Russia. An in-

vasion of Serbia was thrown back, and an ill-conceived offensive against Russia cost Austria its Galician provinces. Germany had to come to Austria's rescue. In the spring of 1915, the Germans made a breakthrough that forced the Russians to abandon Galicia and most of Poland. In June 1916, the Russians launched an offensive that opened a wide breach in the Austrian lines, but they could not maintain it. A German counteroffensive forced a retreat and cost the Russians more than a million casualties.

In March 1917, food shortages and disgust with the great loss of life exploded into a spontaneous revolution in Russia, and the tsar was forced to abdicate. The new government, dominated by liberals, opted to continue the war despite the weariness of the Russian masses. In November 1917, a second revolution brought to power the Bolsheviks, or Communists, who promised "Peace, Land, Bread." In March 1918, the Bolsheviks signed the punitive Treaty of Brest-

Litovsk, in which Russia surrendered Poland, the Ukraine, Finland, and the Baltic provinces.

Several countries that were not belligerents in August 1914—among them, the Ottoman Empire and Italy—joined the war later. That autumn, the Ottoman Turks entered the conflict as allies of Germany. Before the war, Germany had cultivated the Ottoman Empire's friendship by training the Turkish army; for their part, the Turks wanted German help in case Russia attempted to seize the Dardanelles. Hoping to supply Russia and, in turn, obtain badly needed Russian grain, the Allies did decide to capture the Dardanelles. In April 1915, a combined force of British, French, Australian, and New Zealander troops stormed the Gallipoli Peninsula on the European side of the Dardanelles. Ignorance of amphibious warfare, poor intelligence, and the fierce resistance of the Turks prevented the Allies from getting off the beaches and taking the heights. The Gallipoli campaign cost the Allies 252,000 casualties, and they had gained nothing.

Although a member of the Triple Alliance, Italy remained neutral when war broke out. In May 1915, on the promise of receiving Austrian territory, Italy entered the war on the side of the Allies. The Austrians repulsed a number of Italian offensives along the frontier and in 1916 took the offensive against Italy. A combined German and Austrian force finally broke through the Italian lines in the fall of 1917 at Caporetto, and the Italians retreated in disorder, leaving behind huge quantities of weapons. Germany and Austria took some 275,000 prisoners.

THE COLLAPSE
OF THE CENTRAL POWERS

The year 1917 seemed disastrous for the Allies. The Nivelle offensive had failed, the French army had mutinied, a British attack at Passchendaele did not bring the expected breakthrough and added some three hundred thousand casualties to the list of butchery, and the Russians, torn by revolution and gripped by war weariness, were close to making a separate peace. But there was one encouraging development for the Allies. In April 1917, the United States declared war on Germany.

American Entry

From the outset, America's sympathies lay with the Allies. To most Americans, Britain and France were democracies, threatened by an autocratic and militaristic Germany. These sentiments were reinforced by British propaganda, which depicted the Germans as cruel "Huns." Since most war news came to the United States from Britain, anti-German feeling gained momentum. What precipitated American entry was the German decision of January 1917 to launch a campaign of unrestricted submarine warfare. The Germans were determined to deprive Britain of war supplies and to starve it into submission. Their resolve meant that German U-boats would torpedo both enemy and neutral ships in the war zone around the British Isles. Since the United States was Britain's principal supplier, American ships became a target of German submarines.

Angered by American loss of life and materiel, as well as by the violation of the doctrine of freedom of the seas, and fearing a diminution of prestige if the United States took no action, President Woodrow Wilson (1856–1924) pressed for American entry. Also at stake was American security, which would be jeopardized by German domination of western Europe. Leading American statesmen and diplomats worried that such a radical change in the balance of power would threaten American national interests. As German submarines continued to attack neutral shipping, President Wilson, on April 2, 1917, urged Congress to declare war on Germany. It did so on April 6.

Germany's Last Offensive

With Russia out of the war, General Erich Ludendorff prepared for a decisive offensive before the Americans could land sufficient troops in France to help the Allies. A war of attrition now favored the Allies, who could count on American supplies and manpower. Without an immediate and decisive victory, Germany could not win the war. On March 21, 1918, the Germans launched an offensive that was intended to bring victory in the west.

Suddenly, the deadlock was broken; it was now a war of movement. Within two weeks, the

Wilson and Clemenceau Arrive at Versailles, June 28, 1919. The idealism of President Wilson (center) clashed with Premier Clemenceau's (left) determination to enhance France's security. *(Hulton Deutsch Collection)*

Germans had taken some 1,250 square miles. But British resistance was astonishing, and the Germans, exhausted and short of ammunition and food, called off the drive. A second offensive against the British, in April, also had to be called off, as the British contested every foot of ground. Both campaigns depleted German manpower, while the Americans were arriving in great numbers to strengthen Allied lines and uplift morale. At the end of May, Ludendorff resumed his offensive against the French. Attacking unexpectedly, the Germans broke through and advanced to within 56 miles of Paris by June 3. However, reserves braced the French lines, and in the battle of Belleau Wood (June 6–25, 1918), the Americans checked the Germans.

In mid-July, the Germans tried again, crossing the Marne River in small boats. Although in one area they advanced nine miles, the offensive failed against determined American and French opposition. By August 3, the second battle of the Marne had ended. The Germans had thrown everything they had into their spring and summer offensives, but it was not enough. The Allies had bent, but, reinforced and encouraged by American arms, they did not break. Now they began to counterattack, with great success.

Meanwhile, German allies, deprived of support from a hard-pressed Germany, were unable to cope. An Allied army of Frenchmen, Britons, Serbs, and Italians compelled Bulgaria to sign an armistice on September 29. Shortly afterward, British successes in the Middle East forced the Turks to withdraw from the war. In the streets of Vienna, people were shouting "Long live peace! Down with the monarchy!" The Austro-Hungarian Empire was rapidly disintegrating into separate states based on nationality.

By early October, the last defensive position of the Germans had crumbled. The army's spirit collapsed as well; war-weary soldiers, sensing that the war was lost, surrendered in large numbers and refused orders to return to the front. Fearing that the Allies would invade the fatherland and shatter the reputation of the German army, Ludendorff wanted an immediate armistice. However, he needed to find a way to obtain favorable armistice terms from President Wilson and to shift the blame for the lost war from the military and the kaiser to the civilian leadership. Cynically, he urged the creation of a popular parliamentary government in Germany. But events in Germany went further than the general had anticipated. Whereas Ludendorff sought a limited monarchy, the shock of defeat and widespread hunger sparked a revolution that forced the kaiser to abdicate. On November 11, the new German Republic signed an armistice ending the hostilities.

THE PEACE CONFERENCE

In January 1919, representatives of the Allied Powers assembled in Paris to draw up peace terms; President Wilson was also there. The war-weary masses turned to Wilson as the prophet who would have the nations beat their swords into plowshares.

Wilson's Hope for a New World

For Wilson, the war had been fought against autocracy. He hoped that a peace settlement based

Map 18.3 Post–World War I: Broken Empires and Changed Boundaries World War I led to the breakup of the Russian, Austro-Hungarian, and Ottoman Empires and the creation of several new countries, including Poland, Czechoslovakia, Yugoslavia, Lithuania, Latvia, and Estonia.

Legend:
— Boundaries of German, Russian, and Austro-Hungarian empires in 1914
Demilitarized Zone
Areas lost by Austro-Hungarian Empire
Areas lost by Russia
Areas lost by Germany
Areas lost by Bulgaria
— Boundaries of 1926

Scale:
0   200   400 Mi.
0   200   400 Km.

Labels on map:
Leningrad (St. Petersburg)
SOVIET UNION
FINLAND
ESTONIA
LATVIA
LITHUANIA
Stockholm
SWEDEN
NORWAY
Baltic Sea
EAST PRUSSIA
Danzig
POLISH CORRIDOR
Vistula R.
Warsaw
POLAND
Kiev
Dniester R.
BESSARABIA
ROMANIA
Bucharest
GALICIA
CZECHOSLOVAKIA
Budapest
HUNGARY
Vienna
AUSTRIA
Prague
Berlin
Weimar
Frankfurt
GERMANY
RUHR
Cologne
Elbe R.
Kiel
DENMARK
NETH.
Amsterdam
Brussels
BELG.
LUX.
Rhine R.
Strasbourg
LORRAINE
ALSACE
SWITZ.
Geneva
Milan
ITALY
Venice
S. TYROL
Trieste
Fiume
Zagreb
CROATIA
YUGOSLAVIA
Belgrade
SERBIA
MONTENEGRO (To Yugoslavia, 1921)
ALBANIA
Rome
Naples
Sofia
BULGARIA
Black Sea
Istanbul (Constantinople)
TURKEY
GREECE
Athens
Crete
Mediterranean Sea
North Sea
ATLANTIC OCEAN
GREAT BRITAIN
IRELAND
Paris
Versailles
FRANCE
SPAIN
PORTUGAL

on liberal-democratic ideals would sweep away the foundations of war, and he expressed these hopes in several speeches, including the famous Fourteen Points of January 1918. None of Wilson's principles seemed more just than the idea of self-determination: the right of a people to have its own state, free of foreign domination. In particular, this goal meant (or was interpreted to mean) the return of Alsace and Lorraine to France, the creation of an independent Poland, a readjustment of the frontiers of Italy to incorporate Austrian lands inhabited by Italians, and an opportunity for Slavs of the Austro-Hungarian Empire to form their own states.

Aware that a harshly treated Germany might well seek revenge, engulfing the world in another cataclysm, Wilson insisted that there should be a "peace without victory." A just settlement would encourage a defeated Germany to work with the victorious Allies in building a new Europe. To preserve peace and help remake the world, Wilson urged the formation of the League of Nations, an international parliament to settle disputes and discourage aggression. Wilson wanted a peace of justice to preserve Western civilization in its democratic and Christian form.

Problems of Peacemaking

Wilson's negotiating position was undermined by the Republican party's victory in the congressional elections of November 1918. Before the election, Wilson had appealed to the American people to cast their ballots for Democrats as a vote of confidence in his diplomacy. But instead, Americans sent twenty-five Republicans and only fifteen Democrats to the Senate. Whatever the motives of the American people in voting Republican—apparently their decision rested on local and national, not international, issues—the outcome diminished Wilson's prestige at the conference table. To his fellow negotiators, Wilson was trying to preach to Europe when he could not command the support of his own country. Since the Senate must ratify any American treaty, European diplomats worried that what Wilson agreed to the Senate might reject, which is precisely what happened.

Another obstacle to Wilson's peace program was France's demand for security and revenge.

Nearly the entire war on the western front had been fought on French territory. Many French industries and farms had been ruined; the country mourned the loss of half its young men. Representing France at the conference table was Georges Clemenceau (1841–1929), nicknamed "the Tiger." Nobody loved France or hated Germany more. Cynical, suspicious of idealism, and not sharing Wilson's hope for a new world or his confidence in the future League of Nations, Clemenceau demanded that Germany be severely punished and its capacity to wage war destroyed.

Seeing Germany's greater population and superior industrial strength as a threat, and doubting that its military tradition would let it resign itself to defeat, Clemenceau wanted guarantees that the wars of 1870–71 and 1914–1918 would not be repeated. The latter war had shown that without the help of Britain and the United States, France would have been at the mercy of Germany. Since there was no certainty that these states would again aid France, Clemenceau wanted to use his country's present advantage to cripple Germany.

The intermingling of European nationalities was another barrier to Wilson's program. Because in so many regions of central Europe there was a mixture of nationalities, no one could create a Europe completely free of minority problems; some nationalities would always feel that they had been treated shabbily. And the various nationalities were not willing to moderate their demands or lower their aspirations. For example, Wilson's Fourteen Points called for the creation of an independent Poland with secure access to the sea. But between Poland and the sea lay territory populated by Germans. Giving this land to Poland would violate German self-determination; denying it to Poland would mean that the new country had little chance of developing a sound economy. No matter what the decision, one people would regard it as unjust. Similarly, to provide the new Czechoslovakia with defensible borders, it would be necessary to give it territory inhabited mostly by Germans. This, too, could be viewed as a denial of German self-determination, but not granting the territory to Czechoslovakia would mean that the new state would not be able to defend itself against Germany.

Secret treaties drawn up by the Allies during the war also interfered with Wilson's program.

These agreements dividing up German, Austrian, and Ottoman territory did not square with the principle of self-determination. For example, to entice Italy into entering the war, the Allies had promised it Austrian lands that were inhabited predominantly by Germans and Slavs. Italy was not about to repudiate its prize because of Wilson's principles.

Finally, the war had generated great bitterness, which persisted after the guns had been silenced. Both the masses and their leaders demanded retribution and held exaggerated hopes for territory and reparations. In such an atmosphere of postwar enmity, the spirit of compromise and moderation could not overcome the desire for spoils and punishment.

The Settlement

After months of negotiations, often punctuated by acrimony, the peacemakers hammered out a settlement. Five treaties made up the Peace of Paris: one each with Germany, Austria, Hungary, Bulgaria, and Turkey. Of the five, the Treaty of Versailles, which Germany signed on June 28, 1919, was the most significant.

France regained Alsace and Lorraine, lost to Germany in the Franco-Prussian War of 1870–71. The treaty also barred Germany from placing fortifications in the Rhineland. The French military had wanted to take the Rhineland from Germany and break it up into one or more republics under French suzerainty. Under this arrangement, French control would extend to the Rhine River, which was a natural defensive border; one had only to destroy the bridges to prevent a German invasion of France. With Germany deprived of this springboard for invasion, French security would be immensely improved. Recognizing that the German people would never permanently submit to the amputation of the Rhineland, which was inhabited by more than five million Germans and contained key industries, Wilson and British Prime Minister David Lloyd George (1863–1945) resisted these French demands.

Faced with the opposition of Wilson and Lloyd George, Clemenceau backed down and agreed instead to Allied occupation of the Rhineland for fifteen years, the demilitarization of the region,

and an Anglo-American promise of assistance if Germany attacked France in the future. This last point, considered vital by France, proved useless. The alliance went into effect only if both the United States and Britain ratified it. Since the Security Treaty did not get past the U.S. Senate, Britain also refused to sign it. The French people felt that they had been duped and wronged.

A related issue concerned French demands for annexation of the coal-rich Saar Basin, which adjoined Lorraine. By obtaining this region, France would weaken Germany's military potential and strengthen its own. France argued that this would be just compensation for the deliberate destruction of the French coal mines by the retreating German army at the end of the war. But here, too, France was disappointed. The final compromise called for a League of Nations commission to govern the Saar Basin for fifteen years, after which the inhabitants would decide whether their territory would be ceded to France or returned to Germany.

In Eastern Germany, in certain districts of Silesia that had a large Polish population, a plebiscite determined the future of the region. Part of Upper Silesia was ceded to Poland. The settlement also gave Poland a corridor cut through West Prussia and terminating in the Baltic port of Danzig; Danzig itself was declared an international city, to be administered by a League of Nations commission. The Germans would never resign themselves to this loss of territory that separated East Prussia from the rest of Germany.

The victorious nations were awarded control of German and Ottoman colonies. However, these nations held colonies not outright but as mandates under the supervision of the League, which would protect the interests of the native peoples. The mandate system implied the ultimate end of colonialism, for it clearly opposed the exploitation of colonial peoples and asserted independence as the rightful goal for subject nations.

Other issues revolved around the German military forces and reparations. To prevent a resurgence of militarism, the German army was limited to one hundred thousand volunteers and deprived of heavy artillery, tanks, and warplanes. The German navy was limited to a token force, which did not include submarines. The issue of war reparations caused great bitterness between

Wilson and his French and British adversaries. The American delegation wanted the treaty to fix a reasonable sum that Germany would have to pay and specify the period of years allotted for payment. But no such items were included; they were left for future consideration. The Treaty of Versailles presented Germany with an open-ended bill that would probably take generations to pay. Moreover, Article 231, which preceded the reparation clauses, placed sole responsibility for the war on Germany and its allies. The Germans responded to this accusation with contempt.

In separate treaties, the conference dealt with the dissolution of the Hapsburg Empire. During the final weeks of the war, the Austro-Hungarian Empire had crumbled as the various nationalities proclaimed their independence from Hapsburg rule. In most cases, the peacemakers ratified with treaties what the nationalities had already accomplished in fact. Serbia joined with Austrian lands inhabited by Croats and Slovenes to become Yugoslavia. Czechoslovakia arose from the predominantly Czech and Slovak regions of Austria. Hungary, which broke away from Austria to become a separate country, had to cede considerable land to Romania and Yugoslavia. Austria turned over to Italy the South Tyrol, inhabited by two hundred thousand Austrian Germans. This clear violation of the principle of self-determination greatly offended liberal opinion. Deprived of its vast territories and prohibited from union with Germany, the new Austria was a third-rate power.

Assessment and Problems

The Germans unanimously denounced the Treaty of Versailles, for in their minds the war had ended not in German defeat but in a stalemate. They regarded the armistice as the prelude to a negotiated settlement among equals, based on Wilson's call for a peace of justice. Instead, the Germans were barred from participating in the negotiations. And they viewed the terms of the treaty as humiliating and vindictive—designed to keep Germany militarily and economically weak.

When the United States had entered the war, the Germans protested, Wilson had stated that the enemy was not the German people but their government. Surely, the Germans now argued, the new German democracy should not be punished for the sins of the monarchy and the military. To the Germans, the Treaty of Versailles was not the dawning of the new world that Wilson had promised, but an abomination—a vile crime.

Critics in other lands also condemned the treaty as a punitive settlement in flagrant violation of Wilsonian idealism. The peacemakers, they argued, should have set aside past hatreds and, in cooperation with the new democratic German Republic, forged a just settlement to serve as the foundation of a new world. Instead, they burdened the fledgling German democracy with reparations that were impossible to pay, insulted it with the accusation of war guilt, and deprived it of territory in violation of the principle of self-determination. All these provisions, said the critics, would only exacerbate old hatreds and fan the flames of German nationalism. This was a poor beginning for democracy in Germany and for Wilson's new world.

The treaty's defenders, however, insisted that if Germany had won the war, it would have imposed a far harsher settlement on the Allies. They pointed to German war aims, which called for the annexation of parts of France and Poland, the reduction of Belgium and Romania to satellites, and German expansion in central Africa. They pointed also to the treaty of Brest-Litovsk, which Germany had compelled Russia to sign in 1918, as an example of Germany's ruthless appetite. An insatiable Germany gained 34 percent of Russia's population, 32 percent of its farmland, 54 percent of its industrial enterprises, and 89 percent of its coal mines. Moreover, they maintained that the peace settlement did not repudiate Wilson's principles. The new map of Europe was the closest approximation of the ethnic distribution of its peoples that Europe had ever known.

What is most significant about the Treaty of Versailles is that it did not solve the German problem. Germany was left weak but unbroken—its industrial and military power only temporarily contained, and its nationalist fervor not only undiminished but stoked higher by a peace treaty that all political parties viewed as unjust, dictated, and offensive to national pride. The real danger in

The Tsar in Exile. Nicholas II and his children, now living in reduced circumstances, take the sun on a roof in Tobolsk, Siberia. The imperial family was later transferred to Ekaterinburg and then murdered in 1918. *(Hulton Deutsch Collection)*

Europe was German unwillingness to accept defeat or surrender the dream of expansion.

Would France, Britain, and the United States enforce the treaty against a resurgent Germany? The war had demonstrated that an Allied victory depended on American intervention. But in 1920, the U.S. Senate, angry that Wilson had not taken Republicans with him to Paris and fearing that membership in the League of Nations would involve America in future wars, refused to ratify the Treaty of Versailles. Britain, feeling guilty over the treatment of Germany, lacked the will for enforcement and even came to favor revising the treaty. Therefore, the responsibility for preserving the settlement rested primarily with France, which was not encouraging. The Paris peace settlement left Germany resentful but potentially powerful, and to the east lay small and weak states—some of them with sizable German minorities—that could not check a rearmed Germany.

THE RUSSIAN REVOLUTION OF 1917

One consequence of the war that influenced the course of European and world history in momentous ways was the Russian Revolution of 1917 and the resultant triumph of the Bolsheviks. The people of Russia had initially responded to the war with a show of patriotic fervor. But the realities of war quickly dimmed this ardor. The ill-equipped and poorly led Russian armies suffered huge losses. In July 1915, the minister of war wrote this dismal report:

> *The soldiers are without doubt exhausted by the continued defeats and retreats. Their confidence in final victory and in their leaders is undermined. Ever more threatening signs of impending demoralization are evident. Cases of desertion and voluntary surrender to the*

*enemy are becoming more frequent. It is diffi-
cult to expect enthusiasm and selflessness
from men sent into battle unarmed and ordered to pick up the rifles of their dead comrades.*[17]

By 1916 the home front began to fall apart.
Shops were empty, money had no value, and
hunger and cold stalked the working quarters of
cities and towns. Factory workers, many of them
women replacements for husbands, brothers, and
sons who were at the front, toiled long hours for
wages that could not keep up with the accelerating
inflation. When they protested, the government
resorted to heavy-handed repression. By January
1917, nearly all Russians, soldiers and civilians
alike, had lost trust in their autocratic government. But Tsar Nicholas II, determined to preserve autocracy, resisted any suggestion that he
liberalize the regime for the sake of the war effort.

Autocracy was ready to collapse at the slight-
est blow. In early March (February 23 by the calendar* then in use), a strike, riots in the food
lines, and street demonstrations in Petrograd (formerly Saint Petersburg) flared into sudden, un-
premeditated revolution. The soldiers, who in 1905
had massacred peaceful protesters, now rushed to
support the striking workers. The Romanov dynasty, after three hundred years of rule (1613–
1917), came to an end. The Provisional Government was set up—provisional until a representative Constituent Assembly, to be elected as soon
as possible, could establish a permanent regime.

The Problems of the Provisional Government

The collapse of autocracy was followed by what
supporters in Russia and the West hoped would
be a liberal-democratic regime pledged to give
Russia a constitution. In reality, however, the
course of events from March to November 1917
resembled a free-for-all—a no-holds-barred fight
for the succession to autocracy, with only the

*Until March 1918, events in Russia were dated by the Ju-
lian calendar, thirteen days behind the Gregorian calendar
used in the West. By the Julian calendar, the first revolution occurred in February and the second in October.

fittest surviving. Events demonstrated the desperate state of the Russian Empire. Its vast size promoted internal disunity; increasing hardships
raised the fury of the accumulated resentments to
raw brutality among the masses. National minorities took advantage of the anarchy to dismember the country.

Among the potential successors to the tsars,
the liberals of various shades seemed at first to
enjoy the best chances. They represented the educated and forward-looking elements in Russian
society that had arisen after the reforms of the
1860s: lawyers, doctors, professional people of
all kinds, intellectuals, businesspeople and industrialists, many landowners, and even some bureaucrats. Liberals had opposed autocracy and
earned a reputation for leadership.

The liberals had joined the March revolution
only reluctantly, for they were afraid of the
masses and the violence of the streets. They
dreaded social revolution that could result in the
seizure of factories, dispossession of landowners,
and tampering with property rights. Although
most leaders of the Provisional Government had
only modest means, they were "capitalists," believing in private enterprise as the means of promoting economic progress. Their ideal was a
constitutional monarchy, its leadership entrusted
to the educated and propertied elite familiar with
the essentials of statecraft.

Unfortunately, the liberals misunderstood the
mood of the people. Looking to the Western
democracies—including, after April 1917, the
United States—for political and financial support,
the liberals decided to continue the war on the
side of the Allies. The decision antagonized the
war-weary masses, along with the Russian soldiers, almost two million of whom had deserted.
The liberals also antagonized the Russian peasants by not confiscating and redistributing the
landlords' lands free of charge. As Russian nationalists who wanted their country to remain
undivided, the liberals opposed national minorities—Finns, Ukranians, Georgians, and others—
who sought self-determination; hence, they lost
the minorities' support.

The peasants began to divide the landlords'
land among themselves, which encouraged more
soldiers to desert in order to claim a share of the
land. The breakdown of the railways stopped fac-

Women Demonstrate in Petrograd, 1917. The collapse of the tsarist regime was followed by a period of political fermentation, meetings, and concern about food shortages. Women demonstrated for increased bread supplies. The poster reads, "Comrades, workers, and soldiers, support our demands!" *(VA/Sovfoto)*

tory production; enraged workers ousted factory managers and owners. Consumer goods grew scarce and prices soared, and the peasants could see no reason to sell their crops if they could buy nothing in return. Thus, the specter of famine in the cities arose. Hardships and anger mounted. Adding to the disorder were the demands of the non-Russian nationalities for self-determination and even secession.

Freedom in Russia was leading to dissolution and chaos. The largely illiterate peasant masses had no experience with or understanding of the institutions, habits, and attitudes of a free society. Without their cooperation, Russian liberalism collapsed. This outcome demonstrated the difficulty of establishing Western liberal-democratic forms of government in countries lacking a sense of unity, a strong middle class, and a tradition of responsible participation in public affairs.

By July 1917, when Aleksandr Kerensky (1881–1970), a radical lawyer of great eloquence, took over the leadership of the Provisional Gov-

ernment, it had become clear that law and order could be upheld only by brute force. In late August and early September, a conspiracy led by an energetic young general, Lavr Kornilov, sought to establish a military dictatorship. Kornilov had the support not only of the officer corps and the tsarist officials, but also of many liberals who were fed up with anarchy. What stopped the general was not Kerensky's government (which had no troops), but the workers of Petrograd. Their agitators demoralized Kornilov's soldiers, proving that a dictatorship of the right had no mass support. The workers also repudiated Kerensky and the Provisional Government, as well as their own moderate leaders; henceforth, they supported the Bolsheviks.

Lenin and the Rise of Bolshevism

Revolutionary movements had a long history in Russia, going back to the early nineteenth

V. I. Lenin. Red Army soldiers leaving for battle are addressed by Lenin in Moscow in May 1920. *(Sovfoto)*

century, when educated Russians began to compare their country unfavorably with western Europe. They, too, wanted constitutional liberty and free speech in order to make their country modern. Prohibited from speaking out in public, they went underground, giving up their liberalism as ineffective. They saw revolutionary socialism, with its idealistic vision and compassion for the multitude, as a better ideology in the harsh struggle with the tsar's police. By the 1870s, many socialists had evolved into austere and self-denying professional revolutionaries who, in the service of the cause, had no moral scruples, just as the police had no scruples in the defense of the tsars. Bank robbery, murder, assassination, treachery,

and terror were not seen as immoral if they served the revolutionary cause.

In the 1880s and 1890s, revolutionaries had learned industrial economics and sociology from Marx; from Marxism they had also acquired a vision of a universal and inevitable progression toward socialism and communism that satisfied their semireligious craving for salvation in this world, not the next. Marxism also allied them with socialist movements in other lands, giving them an internationalist outlook. History, they believed, was on their side, as it was for all the proletarians and oppressed peoples in the world.

By 1900, a number of able young Russians had rallied to revolutionary Marxism; almost all of them were educated or came from privileged families. The most promising was Vladimir Ilyich Ulyanov, known as Lenin (1870–1924), the son of a teacher and school administrator who had attained the rank of a nobleman. Lenin had studied law but practiced revolution instead. His first contribution lay in adapting Marxism to Russian conditions; to do so, he took considerable liberties with Marx's teaching. His second contribution followed from the first: outlining the organization of an underground party capable of surviving against the tsarist police. It was to be a tightly knit conspiratorial elite of professional revolutionaries. Its headquarters would be safely located abroad, and it would have close ties to the masses, that is, to the workers and other potentially revolutionary elements.

Two other prominent Marxists close to Lenin were Leon Trotsky (1879–1940) and Joseph Stalin (1879–1953). Trotsky, whose original name was Lev Bronstein, was the son of a prosperous Jewish farmer from southern Russia and was soon known for his brilliant pen. Less prominent until after the Revolution, Stalin (the man of steel) was originally named Iosif Dzhugashvili; he was from Georgia, beyond the Caucasus Mountains. Bright enough to be sent to the best school in the area, he dropped out for a revolutionary career. While they were still young, Lenin, Trotsky, and Stalin were all hardened by arrest, imprisonments, and exile to Siberia. Lenin and Trotsky later lived abroad, while Stalin, following a harsher course, stayed in Russia; for four years before 1917, he was banished to bleakest northern Siberia and conditioned to ruthlessness for life.

In 1903, the Russian Marxists split into two factions, the moderate Mensheviks, so named after finding themselves in a minority (*menshinstvo*) at a rather unrepresentative vote at the Second Party Congress, and the extremist Bolsheviks, who at that moment were in the majority (*bolshinstvo*). They might more accurately have been called the "softs" and the "hards." The "softs" (Mensheviks) preserved basic moral scruples; they would not stoop to crime or undemocratic methods for the sake of political success. For that the "hards" (Bolsheviks) ridiculed them, noting that a dead, imprisoned, or unsuccessful revolutionary was of little use.

Meanwhile, Lenin perfected Bolshevik revolutionary theory. He violated Marxist tradition by paying close attention to the revolutionary potential of peasants (thereby anticipating Mao Zedong). Lenin also looked closely at the numerous peoples in Asia who had recently fallen under Western imperialist domination. These people, he sensed, constituted a potential revolutionary force. In alliance with the Western—and Russian—proletariat, they might overthrow the worldwide capitalist order. The Bolsheviks, the most militant of all revolutionary socialists, were ready to assist in that gigantic struggle.

Lenin was a Russian nationalist, as well as a socialist internationalist; he had a vision of a modern and powerful Russian state destined to be a model in world affairs. Russian communism was thus nationalist communism. The Bolsheviks saw the abolition of income-producing property by the dictatorship of the proletariat as the most effective way of mobilizing the country's resources. Yet the Bolshevik mission was also internationalist. The Russian Revolution was intended to set off a world revolution, liberating all oppressed classes and peoples around the world and achieving a higher stage of civilization.

Lenin's Opportunity

On April 16, 1917, Lenin, with German help, arrived in Petrograd from exile in Switzerland. (The Germans provided Lenin with a secret train to take him to Petrograd; they hoped that the Bolshevik leader, who wanted Russia to withdraw from the "capitalist" war, would initiate a revolution and gain power.) The Provisional Government, he said, could not possibly preserve Russia from disintegration. Most of the soldiers, workers, and peasants would repudiate the Provisional Government's cautious liberalism in favor of a regime expressing their demand for peace and land. Nothing would stop them from avenging themselves for centuries of oppression. Lenin also felt that only complete state control of the economy could rescue the country from disaster. The sole way out, he insisted, was the dictatorship of the proletariat backed by *soviets* (councils) of soldiers, workers, and peasants, particularly the poorer peasants.

Lenin prepared his party for the second stage of the Revolution of 1917: the seizure of power by the Bolsheviks. His slogan, "Peace, Land, and Bread," held a magnetic attraction for the desperate Russian masses. The Bolsheviks' determined effort to win over the disheartened soldiers proved particularly effective. Many of the people who supported the Bolsheviks interpreted Lenin's other powerful slogan—"All Power to the Soviets"—to mean that the Bolsheviks aimed to create a democratic socialist state that would institute needed social reforms. They did not anticipate the creation of Bolshevik dictatorship.

Conditions favored the Bolsheviks, as Lenin had predicted. The Bolsheviks obtained majorities in the soviets. The peasants were in active revolt, seizing the land themselves. The Provisional Government lost all control over the course of events. On November 6 (October 24 by the old calendar), Lenin urged immediate action: "The government is tottering. It must be *given the death blow* at all costs." On the following day, the Bolsheviks, meeting little resistance, seized power. Lenin permitted the elections for the Constituent Assembly that had been scheduled by the Provisional Government. In a free election, the Bolsheviks received only 24 percent of the vote. After meeting once in January 1918, however, the Constituent Assembly was disbanded by the Bolsheviks.

The Bolsheviks Survive

Lenin contended that he was guiding the Russian proletariat and all humanity toward a higher social order, symbolizing—in Russia and much of the world—the rebellion of the disadvantaged against Western (or "capitalist") dominance. That is why, in 1918, he changed the name of his party from Bolshevik to Communist, which implied a concern for the human community. For Lenin, as for Marx, a world without exploitation was humanity's noblest ideal.

But staggering adversity confronted Lenin after his seizure of power. In the prevailing anarchy, Russia lay open to the German armies. Under the Treaty of Brest-Litovsk, signed in March 1918—the lowest point in Russian history for over two hundred years—Russia lost Finland, Poland, and the Baltic provinces, all regions inhabited largely by non-Russians. It also lost the rebellious Ukraine, its chief industrial base and breadbasket. Yet Lenin had no choice but to accept the humiliating terms.

THE WAR AND EUROPEAN CONSCIOUSNESS

"There will be wars as never before on earth," Nietzsche had predicted. World War I bore him out. Modern technology enabled the combatants to kill with unprecedented efficiency; modern nationalism infused both civilians and soldiers with the determination to fight until the enemy was totally beaten. Exercising wide control over its citizens, the modern state mobilized its human, material, and spiritual resources to wage total war. As the war hardened into a savage and grueling fight, the statesmen did not press for a compromise peace; instead, they demanded ever more mobilization, ever more escalation, and ever more sacrifices.

The Great War profoundly altered the course of Western civilization, deepening the spiritual crisis that had produced it. How could one speak of the inviolability of the individual when Europe had become a slaughterhouse, or of the primacy of reason when nations permitted slaughter to go unabated for four years? How could the mind cope with this spectacle of a civilization turning against itself, destroying itself in an orgy of organized violence? A young French soldier, shortly before he was killed at Verdun, expressed the disillusionment that gripped the soldiers in the

trenches: "Humanity is mad! It must be mad to do what it is doing. What a massacre! What scenes of horror and carnage, I cannot find words to translate my impressions. Hell cannot be so terrible. Men are mad!"[18] The war, said British poet Robert Graves, provoked an "inward scream" that still reverberates. The agony caused by the astronomical casualty figures—some 9.4 million dead and 21 million wounded, many of them pathetically mutilated and disfigured—touched millions of homes. Now only the naive could believe in continuous progress. Western civilization had entered an age of violence, anxiety, and doubt.

The war left many with the gnawing feeling that Western civilization had lost its vitality and was caught in a rhythm of breakdown and disintegration. It seemed that Western civilization was fragile and perishable, that Western people, despite their extraordinary accomplishments, were never more than a step or two away from barbarism. Surely, any civilization that could allow such senseless slaughter to last had entered its decline and could look forward to only the darkest of futures.

European intellectuals were demoralized and disillusioned. The orderly, peaceful, rational world of their youth had been wrecked. The Enlightenment world-view, weakened in the nineteenth century by the assault of romantics, Social Darwinists, extreme nationalists, race mystics, and glorifiers of the irrational, was now disintegrating. The enormity of the war had destroyed faith in the capacity of reason to deal with crucial social and political questions. Civilization seemed to be fighting an unending and hopeless battle against the irrational elements in human nature. It appeared that war would be a recurring phenomenon in the twentieth century.

Scientific research had produced more efficient weapons to kill and maim Europe's youth. The achievements of Western science and technology, which had been viewed as a boon for humanity and the clearest testament to the superiority of European civilization, were called into question. Confidence in the future gave way to doubt. The old beliefs in the perfectibility of humanity, the blessings of science, and ongoing progress now seemed an expression of naive optimism and post-Christian myths; the war had exposed them as fraudulent. As A. J. P. Taylor concludes,

The Survivors (1922) by Käthe Kollwitz. With an estimated 9.4 million dead and twenty-one million wounded, World War I shattered the hope that western Europe had been making continuous progress toward a rational and enlightened civilization. *(National Gallery of Art, Washington, D.C., Rosenwald Collection © Estates of Käthe Kollwitz, VAGA, New York, 1991)*

> *The First World War was difficult to fit into the picture of a rational civilization advancing by ordered stages. The civilized men of the twentieth century had outdone in savagery the barbarians of all preceding ages, and their civilized virtues—organization, mechanical skill, self-sacrifice—had made war's savagery all the more terrible. Modern man had developed powers which he was not fit to use. European civilization had been weighed in the balance and found wanting.*[19]

This disillusionment heralded a loss of faith in liberal-democratic values—a loss of faith that contributed to the widespread popularity of fascist ideologies in the postwar world. Having lost confidence in the power of reason to solve the problems of the human community, in liberal doctrines of individual freedom, and in the institutions of parliamentary democracy, many people turned to fascism as a simple saving faith. Far from making the world safe for democracy, as Wilson and other liberals had hoped, World War I gave rise to totalitarian movements that would nearly destroy democracy.

The war produced a generation of young people who had reached their maturity in combat. Violence had become a way of life for millions of soldiers hardened by battle and for millions of civilians aroused by four years of propaganda. The relentless massacre of Europe's young men had a brutalizing effect. Violence, cruelty, suffering, and even wholesale death seemed to be natural and acceptable components of human existence. The sanctity of the individual seemed to be liberal and Christian claptrap.

The fascination with violence and contempt for life persisted in the postwar world. Many returned veterans yearned for the excitement of battle and the fellowship of the trenches—what one French soldier called "the most tender human experience." After the war, a young English officer reminisced: "There was an exaltation, in those days of comradeship and dedication, that would have come in few other ways."[20] A fraternal bond united the men of the trenches. But many veterans also shared a primitive attraction to war's fury. A Belgian veteran expressed it this way:

The plain truth is that if I were to obey my native animal instincts—and there was little hope for anything else while I was in the trenches—I should enlist again in any future war, or take part in any sort of fighting, merely to experience again that voluptuous thrill of the human brute who realizes his power to take away life from other human beings who try to do the same to him. What was first accepted as a moral duty became a habit . . . had become a need.[21]

The British novelist D. H. Lawrence (1885–1930) understood that the brutality and hate unleashed by the war ruined old Europe and would give rise to even greater evils. On the day the armistice was signed, he warned prophetically:

I suppose you think the war is over and that we shall go back to the kind of world you lived in before it. But the war isn't over. The hate and evil is greater now than ever. Very soon war will break out again and overwhelm you. . . . The crowd outside thinks that Germany is crushed forever. But the Germans will soon rise again. Europe is done for . . . The war isn't over. Even if the fighting should stop, the evil will be worse because the hate will be damned up in men's hearts and will show itself in all sorts of ways.[22]

The veterans who aspired to recapture the exhilaration experienced in combat made ideal recruits for extremist political movements that glorified action and promised to rescue society from a decadent liberalism. Both Hitler and Mussolini, themselves ex-soldiers imbued with the ferocity of the front, knew how to appeal to veterans. The lovers of violence and the harbingers of hate who became the leaders of fascist parties would come within a hairsbreadth of destroying Western civilization. The intensified nationalist hatreds following World War I also helped fuel the fires of World War II. The Germans swore to regain lands lost to the Poles. Some Germans, like the embittered Hitler, were consumed by anguish over a defeat that they believed never should have happened and over the humiliating Treaty of Versailles; a desire for revenge festered in their souls. Italy, too, felt aggrieved because it had not received more territory from the dismembered Austro-Hungarian Empire.

Yet, while some veterans clung to an aggressive militarism, others aspired to build a more humane world. Such veterans embraced democratic and socialist ideals and resolved that the horror should never be repeated. Tortured by the memory of the Great War, European intellectuals wrote pacifist plays and novels and signed pacifist declarations. In the 1930s, an attitude of "peace at any price" discouraged resistance to Nazi Germany in its bid to dominate Europe.

During World War I, new weapons were introduced, particularly the tank and the fighter plane, which revolutionized the future of warfare. Just prior to World War II, imaginative military planners recognized that planes and tanks, properly deployed, could penetrate and smash the enemy's defenses, circumventing the stalemate of trench warfare. Planes also meant terror from the skies, for bombs could pulverize a city, killing and maiming tens of thousands of civilians.

World War I was total war; it encompassed the entire nation and was without limits. States demanded total victory and total commitment from their citizens. They regulated industrial production, developed sophisticated propaganda techniques to strengthen morale, and exercised ever-greater control over the lives of their people, organizing and disciplining them like soldiers.

This total mobilization of nations' human and material resources provided a model for future dictators. With ever-greater effectiveness and ruthlessness, dictators would centralize power and manipulate thinking. The ruthless dictatorships that emerged in Russia, Germany, and Italy were products of the war. The war gave Communists the opportunity to seize power in Russia, and the mentality of the front helped to mold the fascist movement that emerged in Italy and Germany. The barbarism of the trenches would be eclipsed in the postwar era by the horrors inflicted on people by totalitarian regimes.

❖   ❖   ❖

NOTES

1. Quoted in Roland N. Stromberg, *Redemption by War* (Lawrence: The Regents Press of Kansas, 1982), p. 24.

2. Heinrich von Treitschke, *Politics,* excerpted in *Germany's War Mania* (New York: Dodd, Mead, 1915), pp. 222–223.

3. Fritz Fischer, *Germany's Aims in the First World War* (New York: Norton, 1967), p. 88.

4. Quoted in Joachim Remak, *The Origins of World War I* (New York: Holt, 1967), p. 135.

5. Rupert Brooke, "Peace," in *Collected Poems of Rupert Brooke* (New York: Dodd, Mead, 1941), p. 111.

6. Quoted in Joachim C. Fest, *Hitler* (New York: Harcourt Brace Jovanovich, 1973), p. 66.

7. Roland Dorgelès, "After Fifty Years," excerpted in *Promise of Greatness,* ed. George A. Panichas (New York: John Day, 1968), pp. 14–15.

8. Quoted in Barbara Tuchman, *The Guns of August* (New York: Macmillan, 1962), p. 145.

9. Bertrand Russell, *The Autobiography of Bertrand Russell, 1914–1944* (Boston: Little, Brown, 1951, 1956), vol. 2, 4–6.

10. Quoted in Robert G. L. Waite, *Vanguard of Nazism* (New York: Norton, 1969), p. 22.

11. Brooke, "Peace," p. 111.

12. Quoted in James Joll, "The Unspoken Assumptions," in *The Origins of the First World War,* ed. H. W. Koch (New York: Taplinger, 1972), p. 318.

13. Quoted in Peter Gay, *Freud: A Life for Our Time* (New York: Norton), p. 348.

14. S. L. A. Marshall, *The American Heritage History of World War I* (New York: Dell, 1966), p. 215.

15. A. J. P. Taylor, *A History of the First World War* (New York: Berkeley, 1966), p. 84.

16. Quoted in Richard M. Watt, *Dare Call It Treason* (New York: Simon & Schuster, 1963), p. 169.

17. Excerpted in Ronald Kowalski, ed., *The Russian Revolution, 1917–1921* (New York: Routledge, 1997), p. 20.

18. Quoted in Alistair Horne, *The Price of Glory* (New York: Harper, 1967), p. 240.

19. A. J. P. Taylor, *From Sarajevo to Potsdam* (New York: Harcourt, Brace & World), 1966, pp. 55–56.

20. Quoted in Modris Eksteins, *Rites of Spring: The Great War and the Birth of the Modern Age* (New York: Doubleday Anchor Books, 1989), p. 232.

21. Quoted in Eric J. Leed, *No Man's Land: Combat and Identity in World War I* (New York: Cambridge University Press, 1979), p. 201.

22. Quoted in Samuel Hynes, *A War Imagined* (New York: Atheneum, 1991), p. 266.

SUGGESTED READING

Berghahn, V. R., *Germany and the Approach of War in 1914* (1975). Relates German foreign policy to domestic problems.

Fay, Sidney, *The Origins of the World War*, 2 vols. (1966). A comprehensive study of the underlying and immediate causes of the war; first published in 1928.

Figues, Orlando, *A People's Tragedy* (1996). A recent study of the Russian Revolution: thorough, detailed, anecdotal, and comprehensive.

Fischer, Fritz, *Germany's Aims in the First World War* (1967). A controversial work, stressing Germany's responsibility for the war.

Gilbert, Martin, *The First World War* (1994). A recent survey; contains illuminating anecdotal material.

Hale, Oron J., *The Great Illusion, 1900–1914* (1971). European thought, society, and politics just prior to World War I; a volume in the distinguished Rise of Modern Europe series.

Joll, James, *The Origins of the First World War* (1984). Excellent work of synthesis.

Koch, H. W., ed. The *Origins of the First World War* (1972). Useful essays, particularly those dealing with the glorification of war before 1914.

Kowalski, Ronald, ed., *The Russian Revolution, 1917–1921* (1997). A useful collection of original sources.

Lafore, Laurence, *The Long Fuse* (1971). A beautifully written study of the causes of the conflict.

Leed, Eric J., *No Man's Land: Combat and Identity in World War I* (1979). The impact of the war on the men who participated in it.

Marshall, S. L. A., *The American Heritage History of World War I* (1966). Probably the best account available.

Panichas, George A., ed., *Promise of Greatness* (1968). Recollections of the war by people of prominence.

Remak, Joachim, *The Origins of World War I* (1967). A fine introduction.

Schmitt, Bernadotte, E., *The World in the Crucible, 1914–1919* (1984). The war and its aftermath. A volume in the distinguished *Rise of Modern Europe* series.

Service, Robert, *The Russian Revolution, 1900–1927* (1990). A brief overview.

Strachan, Hew, ed., *The Oxford Illustrated History of the First World War* (1998). Essays by an international team of specialists on many phases of the war, including causes, battles, and consequences.

Stromberg, Roland N., *Redemption by War: The Intellectuals and 1914* (1982). A superb analysis of the reasons that so many intellectuals welcomed the war.

Tuchman, Barbara, *The Guns of August* (1962). A beautifully written account of the opening weeks of World War I.

Williams, John, *The Other Battleground* (1972). A comparison of the home fronts in Britain, France, and Germany.

Winter, J. M., *The Experience of World War I* (1995). Excellent illustrations and eye-witness accounts are integrated into a gripping narrative.

REVIEW QUESTIONS

1. How did the nationality problems in Austria-Hungary contribute to the outbreak of World War I?

2. What conditions led to the formation of the Triple Entente? How did Germany respond to it?

3. After the assassination of Archduke Francis Ferdinand, what policies were pursued by Austria-Hungary, Germany, and Russia?

4. In assessing responsibility for the war, what arguments have been advanced by historians for each of the major countries involved?

5. What battle plans did Germany and France implement in 1914? What prevented Germany from reaching Paris in 1914?

6. Identify and explain the historical significance of the battles of Verdun, the Somme, and Gallipoli.

7. Why did the United States enter the war?

8. Describe Wilson's peace program. What obstacles did it face?

9. What were the provisions of the Treaty of Versailles regarding Germany?

10. Why did the tsarist regime collapse in March 1917?

11. Why did the Provisional Government and liberal democracy fail in 1917?

12. Why was World War I a great turning point in the history of the West?

Chapter 19

An Era of Totalitarianism

*I*n the 1930s, the term *totalitarianism* was used to describe the Fascist regime in Italy, the National Socialist regime in Germany, and the Communist regime in the Soviet Union. To a degree that far exceeds the ancient tyrannies and early modern autocratic states, these dictatorships aspired to and, with varying degrees of success, attained control over the individual's consciousness and behavior and all phases of political, social, and cultural life. To many people, it seemed that a crisis-riddled democracy was dying and that the future belonged to these dynamic totalitarian movements.

Totalitarianism was a twentieth-century phenomenon, for such all-embracing control over the individual and society could be achieved only in an age of modern ideology, technology, and bureaucracy. The totalitarian state was more completely established in Germany and the Soviet Union than in Italy, where cultural and historic conditions impeded the realization of the totalitarian goal of monolithic unity and total control.

The ideological aims and social and economic policies of Hitler and Stalin differed fundamentally. However, both Soviet Russia and Nazi Germany shared the totalitarian goal of total domination of the individual and institutions, and both employed similar methods to achieve it. Mussolini's Italy is more accurately called authoritarian, for the party-state either did not intend to control all phases of life or lacked the means to do so. Moreover, Mussolini hesitated to use the ruthless methods that Hitler and Stalin employed so readily. ❖

THE NATURE OF TOTALITARIANISM

Striving for total unity, control, and obedience, the totalitarian dictatorship is the antithesis of liberal democracy. It abolishes all competing political parties, suppresses individual liberty, eliminates or regulates private institutions, and utilizes the modern state's bureaucracy and technology to impose its ideology and enforce its commands. The party-state determines what people should believe—what values they should hold. There is no room for individual thinking, private moral judgment, or individual conscience. The individual possesses no natural rights that the state must respect. The state regards individuals merely as building blocks, the human material to be hammered and hewed into a new social order. It seeks to create an efficiently organized and stable society—one whose members do not raise troublesome questions or hold unorthodox opinions.

Nevertheless, the totalitarian dictatorship is also an unintended consequence of liberal democracy. It emerged in an age in which, because of the French and Industrial Revolutions, the masses had become a force in political life. The totalitarian leader seeks to gain and preserve power by harnessing mass support. Hitler, in particular, built a party within the existing constitutional system and exploited the electoral process in order to overthrow the democratic government.

Unlike previous dictatorial regimes, the dictatorships of both the left and the right sought to legitimatize their rule by gaining the masses' approval. They claimed that their governments were higher and truer expressions of the people's will. The Soviet and Nazi dictatorships established their rule in the name of the people—the German Volk or the Soviet proletariat.

A distinctive feature of totalitarianism is the overriding importance of the leader, who is seen as infallible and invincible. The masses' slavish adulation of the leader and their uncritical acceptance of the dogma that the leader or the party is always right promote loyalty, dedication, and obedience and distort rational thinking.

Totalitarian leaders want more than power for its own sake; in the last analysis, they seek to transform the world according to an all-embracing ideology, a set of convictions and beliefs, which, says Hannah Arendt, "pretend[s] to know the mysteries of the whole historical process—the secrets of the past, the intricacies of the present, the uncertainties of the future."[1] The ideology constitutes a higher and exclusive truth, based on a law of history or social development, that, says Karl Dietrich Bracher, "reduce[s] the past and the future to a single historical principle of struggle, no matter whether by state, nation, people, race, or class."[2] The ideology contains a dazzling vision of the future—a secular New Jerusalem— that strengthens the will of the faithful and attracts converts. Like a religion, the totalitarian ideology provides its adherents with beliefs that make society and history intelligible, that explain all of existence in an emotionally gratifying way.

The ideology satisfies a human yearning for complete certitude. Like a religion, it creates true believers, who feel that they are participating in a great cause—a heroic fight against evil—that gives meaning to their lives. During World War II, a German soldier fighting on the eastern front wrote to his brother that the battle "is for a new ideology, a new belief, a new life! I am glad that I can participate . . . in this war of light and darkness."[3] Also like a religion, the totalitarian party gives isolated and alienated individuals a sense of belonging, a feeling of camaraderie; it enables a person to lose himself or herself in the comforting and exhilarating embrace of a mass movement.

Not only did the totalitarian religion-ideology supply followers with a cause that claimed absolute goodness, it also provided a Devil. For the Soviets, the source of evil and the cause of all the people's hardships were the degenerate capitalists, reactionary peasants who resisted collectivization, the traitorous Trotskyites, or the saboteurs and foreign agents who impeded the realization of the socialist society. For the Nazis, the Devil was the conspirator Jew. These "evil" ones must be eliminated in order to realize the totalitarian movement's vision of the future. Thus, totalitarian regimes liquidate large segments of the population designated as "enemies of the people." Historical necessity or a higher purpose demands and justifies their liquidation. The appeal to historical necessity has all the power of a great myth. Presented as a world-historical struggle between the forces of good and the forces of evil, the myth incites fanaticism and numbs the conscience. Traditional rules of morality have no meaning; seemingly decent people engage in terrible acts of brutality with no remorse, convinced that they are waging a righteous war.

Totalitarians are utopians inspired by idealism; they seek the salvation of their nation, their race, or humanity. They believe that the victory of their cause will usher in the millennium, a state of harmony and bliss. Such a vision is attractive to people burdened by economic insecurity or spiritual disorientation. The history of the twentieth century demonstrates how easily utopian beliefs can be twisted into paranoid fantasies, idealistic sentiments transformed into murderous fanaticism, and destructive components of human nature mobilized and directed by demagogues.

Unlike earlier autocratic regimes, the totalitarian dictatorship is not satisfied with its subjects' outward obedience; it demands the masses' unconditional loyalty and enthusiastic support. It strives to control the inner person—to shape thoughts, feelings, and attitudes in accordance with the party ideology, which becomes an official creed. It does not rule by brute force alone but seeks to create a "new man," one who dedicates himself body and soul to the party and its ideology. Such unquestioning, faithful subjects can be manipulated by the party. The disinterested search for truth, justice, and goodness—the exploration of those fundamental moral, political, and religious questions that have characterized the Western intellectual tradition for centuries—is abandoned. Truth, justice, and goodness are what the party deems them to be, and ideological deviation is forbidden.

The totalitarian dictatorship deliberately politicizes all areas of human activity. Ideology pervades works of literature, history, philosophy, art, and even science. It dominates the school curriculum and influences everyday speech and social relations. The state is concerned with everything its citizens do; there is no distinction between public and private life, and every institution comes under the party-state's authority. If voluntary support for the regime cannot be generated by indoctrination, then the state unhesitatingly resorts to terror and violence to compel obedience. People live under a constant strain. Fear of the secret police is ever present; it produces a permanent state of insecurity, which induces people to do everything that the regime asks of them and to watch what they say and do.

COMMUNIST RUSSIA

In 1918, the infant Soviet government was threatened with civil war. Tsarist officers had gathered troops in the south; other anti-Communist centers rose in Siberia, and still others in the extreme north and along the Baltic coast. The political orientation of these anti-Communist groups, generally called Whites in contrast to the Communist Reds, combined all shades of opinion, from moderate socialist to reactionary, the latter usually predominating. The Whites received support from foreign governments, which freely intervened. Until their own revolution in November 1918, the Germans occupied much of southern Russia. England, France, and the United States sent troops to points in northern and southern European Russia; England, Japan, and the United States also sent troops to Siberia. At first, they wanted to offset German expansion, but later they hoped to overthrow the Communist regime. In May and June 1918, Czech prisoners of war, about to be evacuated, precipitated anti-Communist uprisings along the Trans-Siberian Railroad, bringing the civil war to fever pitch.

In July 1918, Nicholas II and his entire family were murdered by Communists. In August, a non-Communist socialist nearly assassinated Lenin, while the White forces in the south moved to cut off central Russia from its food supply. In response, the Communists speeded the buildup of their own Red Army. Recruited from the remnants of the tsarist army and its officer corps, the Red Army was reinforced by compulsory military service and strict discipline; Trotsky reintroduced the death penalty, which had been outlawed by the Provisional Government. Threatened with death if they refused, many tsarist officers served in the Red Army. They were closely watched by Trotsky's ruthless political commissars, who were also responsible for the political reliability and morale of the troops. Trotsky ordered the formation of "blocking units" to machine-gun retreating soldiers. The civil war was brutal; both sides butchered civilians and their own comrades.

In November 1918, thanks to the Allied victory and the American contribution to it, the German menace ended. Yet foreign intervention stepped up in response to the formation of the Communist International (Comintern), an organization founded by Lenin to guide the international revolutionary movement that he expected to issue from the world war. Lenin sought revolutionary support from abroad for strengthening his hand at home; his enemies reached into Russia to defeat at its source the revolution that they feared in their own countries. At the same time, the civil war rose to its climax.

Hard-pressed as Lenin's party was, by the autumn of 1920 it had prevailed over its enemies.

The Whites were divided among themselves and discredited by their association with the tsarist regime; the Communists had greater popular support, the advantage of interior communications, and superior political skills. The war-weary foreign interventionists called off their efforts to overthrow the Bolshevik regime by force.

The Communist victory in the civil war exacted a staggering price. Reds and Whites alike carried the tsarist tradition of political violence to a new pitch of horror. Some 1.2 million combatants on both sides perished. In addition, the Communists killed some 250,000 peasants who resisted grain requisitions and executed tens of thousands of political opponents. Adding to the death toll were some 100,000 Jews, victims of pogroms perpetrated largely by Whites. Compounding the nation's anguish was the famine of 1921–22, which claimed some 5 million victims.

War Communism and the New Economic Policy

Besides the extreme misery brought on by the world war and civil war, the Russian people had to endure the rigors of the policy known as War Communism. It was introduced in 1918 to deal with plummeting agricultural and economic production, rampant inflation, and desperate hunger in the cities. Under War Communism, the state took over the means of production and greatly limited the sphere of private ownership; it conscripted labor and, in effect, confiscated grain from the peasants in order to feed workers in the cities. War Communism devastated the economy even further and alienated workers and peasants. The state-run factories were mismanaged, workers stayed away from their jobs or performed poorly, and peasants resisted the food requisition detachments that the government sent to seize their grain.

There was even open rebellion. In March 1921, sailors at the Kronstadt naval base and workers in nearby Petrograd—people who in 1917 had been ready to give their lives for the Revolution—rose against the repression that had been introduced during the civil war; they called for the establishment of socialist democracy. Trotsky ruthlessly suppressed that uprising, but the lesson was clear: the Communist regime had to retreat from War Communism and to restore a measure of stability to the country.

In 1921, the Communist party adopted the New Economic Policy, called NEP, which lasted until 1928. Under a system that Lenin characterized as "state socialism," the government retained control of finance, industry, and transportation—"the commanding heights" of the economy—but allowed the rest of the economy to return to private enterprise. The peasants, after giving part of their crops to the government, were free to sell the rest in the open market; traders could buy and sell as they pleased. With the resumption of small-scale capitalism, an air of normal life returned.

One-Party Dictatorship

While the Communists were waging a fierce struggle against the Whites, they instituted a militant dictatorship run by their party. Numbering about five hundred thousand members in 1921, the Communist party was controlled by a small, tight core of professional political leaders, the best of them unusually disciplined in personal dedication to the Revolution.

Under its constitution, the "Russian Communist Party," as its formal title read, was a democratic body. Its members elected delegates to periodic party congresses; these in turn elected the membership of the central committee, which originally held the reins of leadership. However, power soon shifted to a smaller and more intimate group, the *politburo* (political bureau), which assumed a dictatorial role. The key leaders—Lenin, Trotsky, Stalin, and a few others—determined policy, assigned tasks, and appointed important officials. The party dominated all public agencies; its leaders held the chief positions in government. No other political parties were tolerated, and trade unions became agents of the regime. Never before had the people of Russia been forced into such abject dependence on their government.

Impatient with the endless disputes among righteous and strong-willed old revolutionaries, Lenin, in agreement with other top leaders, demanded unconditional submission to his decisions. He even ordered that dissidents be disciplined and political enemies be terrorized. No price was too high to achieve monolithic party unity. Believing that they were creating a new and better society that would serve as a model for the rest of humanity, the Communists felt no moral objection to the use of force or even terror, including executions and forced-labor camps. The dreaded Cheka, a ruthless secret police organization, executed some two hundred thousand people from 1919 to 1925. The means Lenin employed for ruling his backward country denied the human values that Marx had taken from the Enlightenment and put into his vision of a socialist society. Lenin was perfectly willing to use state terror to promote the class struggle.

The Communists abolished the power of the Orthodox church, which was the traditional ally of tsarism and the enemy of innovation. They were militant atheists, believing with Marx that religion was the "opium of the people"; God had no place in their vision of a better society.

The Communists also simplified the alphabet, changed the calendar to the Gregorian system prevailing in the capitalist West, and brought theater and all arts, until then reserved for the elite, to the masses. Above all, they wiped out—by expropriation, discrimination, expulsion, and execution—the educated upper class of bureaucrats, landowners, professional people, and industrialists.

In the spring of 1918, Lenin argued that the Russian workers had not yet matched capitalist performance: "The Russian worker is a bad worker compared with the workers of the advanced, i.e., western countries." To overcome this fatal handicap, Lenin relentlessly hammered home the need for "iron discipline at work" and "unquestioning obedience" to a single will, that of the Communist party. There was no alternative: "Large-scale machinery calls for absolute and strict unity of will, which directs the joint labors of hundreds and thousands and tens of thousands of people. A thousand wills are subordinated to one will."[4] In these words lay the essence of subsequent Soviet industrialization. The entire economy was to be monolithic, rationally planned in its complex interdependence, and pursuing a single goal: overcoming the weaknesses of Russia, so disastrously demonstrated in the war.

Forging Socialism. Men and women work equally in this socialist realist propanganda poster from 1921. *(Aurora Publishers, Leningrad. Reproduced by permission of N/O Vneshtorgizdat)*

In attempting to transform their Soviet Russia into a modern industrialized state that would serve as a model for the world, the Communists imposed a new autocracy even more authoritarian than the old. The minds of the people came under unprecedented government control. In education, from kindergarten through university, in press and radio, and in literature and the arts, the Communist party tried to fashion people's thoughts to create the proper "consciousness." The party made Marxism-Leninism the sole source of truth, eliminating as best it could all rival creeds, whether religious, political, or philosophical. Minds were to be as reliably uniform as machine processes and totally committed to the party and they were to be protected against all subversive capitalist influences.

Lenin molded the Soviet Union into an international revolutionary force, the champion of anticapitalism and of the liberation of colonial peoples. The Russian Revolution inspired nationalistic ambitions for political self-determination and cultural self-assertion among a growing number of peoples around the world, especially in Asia. It appealed particularly to intellectuals educated in the West (or in westernized schools), yet identifying themselves with their downtrodden compatriots.

To have a political tool for world revolution Lenin created the Communist—or Third—International (Comintern). The most radical successor to earlier socialist international associations, it helped organize small Communist parties in Western Europe, which in time became dependable, although rather powerless, agents of Soviet Russia. In Asia, where no proletariat existed, Lenin tried to work closely with incipient nationalist movements. Lenin and the Bolshevik Revolution gained the admiration and instinctive loyalty of colonial and semicolonial peoples in what would come to be called the Third World. Soviet Russia now stood out as the Communist alternative to the capitalist West.

THE STALIN REVOLUTION

Lenin died in 1924, and the task of achieving the goal that he had set was taken up by Stalin. The "man of steel" was crude and vulgar, toughened by the revolutionary underground and tsarist prisons and by the roughest aspects of Russian life. Relentlessly energetic but relatively inconspicuous among key Communists, Stalin had been given, in 1922, the unwanted and seemingly routine task of general secretary of the party. He used this position to his own advantage, building up a reliable party cadre—apparatus men, or *apparatchiki,* as they came to be called—and dominating the party as not even Lenin had done. When he was challenged, particularly by Trotsky and his associates, in the protracted struggles for the succession to Lenin, it was too late to unseat him. None of Stalin's rivals could rally the necessary majorities at the party congresses; none could match Stalin's skill in party infighting or in making rough and anarchic people into docile members of the Communist party apparatus.

Modernizing Russia: Industrialization and Collectivization

To Stalin, Russia's most pressing need was not world revolution, but the fastest possible buildup of Soviet power through industrialization. The country could not afford to risk near-annihilation again, as it had done in the world war and then in the civil war. Communist pride dictated that the country be made as strong as possible. Stalin set forth the stark reckoning of Russian history in a speech delivered in 1931, three years after launching a program of massive industrialization.

> *Those who fall behind get beaten. But we do not want to be beaten. No, we refuse to be beaten. One feature of the history of old Russia was the continual beatings she suffered for falling behind, for her backwardness. All beat her—for her backwardness, for military backwardness, cultural backwardness, political backwardness, for industrial backwardness, for agricultural backwardness. She was beaten because to do so was profitable and could be done with impunity. . . . You are backward, you are weak—therefore you are wrong, hence you can be beaten and enslaved. You are mighty, therefore you are right, hence we must be wary of you. Such is the law of the exploiters. . . . That is why we must no longer lag behind.[5]*

Stalin decided on all-out industrialization at the expense of the toiling masses. Peasants and workers, already poor, would be required to make tremendous sacrifices of body and spirit to overcome the nation's weaknesses. Abandoning the NEP, Stalin decreed a series of Five-Year Plans, the first and most experimental one commencing in 1928. The industrialization drive was heralded as a vast economic and social revolution, undertaken by the state according to a rational plan. The emphasis lay on heavy industry: the construction of railroads, power plants, steel mills, and military hardware, such as tanks and warplanes. Production of consumer goods was cut to the minimum, and all small-scale private trading, revived under the NEP, came to an end—

with disastrous results for the standard of living. Having just come within sight of their pre-1914 standard of living, Russians now found their expectations dashed for decades.

Thus, a new grim age began, with drastic material hardships and profound anguish. Harsh punishments, including denial of food cards and imprisonment, were meted out for lateness, slowness, or incompetence. But many people, particularly the young, were fired to heroic exertions. They were proud to sacrifice themselves for the building of a superior society. And many common factory workers had the opportunity to attend school and become engineers and administrators, which tied them to the regime. When the Great Depression in the capitalist countries put millions out of work, no Soviet citizen suffered from unemployment; gloom pervaded the West, but confidence and hope, artificially fostered by the party, buoyed up many people in Soviet Russia. The first two Five-Year Plans dramatically and rapidly increased Russia's industrial infrastructure as factories, mines, dams, and railroads were feverishly constructed. At no time, though, did the planning produce Western-style efficiency, and workers, who labored in a Herculean way, actually suffered a decline in real wages. The regime concentrated on heavy industry, not consumer goods or improving the standard of living.

Meanwhile, a second and far more brutal revolution overtook Soviet agriculture, for the peasants had to be forcibly integrated into the planned economy through collectivization. Agriculture—the peasants, their animals, and their fields—had to submit to the same rational control as industry. Collectivization meant the pooling of farmlands, animals, and equipment for the sake of more efficient, large-scale production. The Bolshevik solution for the backwardness of Russian agriculture had long been that the peasants should become like workers. But knowing the peasants' distaste for the factory, their attachment to their own land, and their stubbornness, the party had hesitated to carry out its ambitious scheme. In 1929, however, Stalin believed that, for the sake of industrialization, he had no choice. If the Five-Year Plan was to succeed, the government had to receive planned crops of planned size and quality at planned times. This could only be accomplished, Stalin thought, by

Forced Labor in the Gulag. All those accused of disloyalty to the party and not killed outright ended up in one of the gulags, or forced-labor camps. Forced labor was designed as a punishment and also as a means of obtaining raw materials from inhospitable regions in the far north. In this photo, deported peasants and political prisoners using primitive technology are engaged in constructing the canal linking Leningrad with the White Sea. Millions perished in the gulags. *(David King Collection, London, England)*

destroying the independent peasantry and creating huge agricultural factories. With collectivization, the ascendancy of the party over the people of Russia became almost complete.

The peasants paid a ghastly price. Stalin declared war on the Russian countryside. He ordered that the *kulaks*, the most enterprising and well-to-do peasants, be "liquidated as a class." Many were killed outright, and millions were deported to forced-labor camps in the far north, where most ultimately perished from hunger or abuse. Their poorer and less efficient neighbors

were herded onto collective farms at the point of a bayonet.

The peasants struck back, sometimes in pitched battles. The horror of forced collectivization broke the spirit even of hardened officials. "I am an old Bolshevik," sobbed a secret police colonel to a fellow passenger on a train; "I worked in the underground against the Tsar and then I fought in the civil war. Did I do all that in order that I should now surround villages with machine guns and order my men to fire indiscriminately into crowds of peasants? Oh, no, no!"[6] Typically, however, the local officials and activists who stripped the peasants of their possessions and searched for hidden grain viewed themselves as idealists building a new society that was in the best interests of a suffering humanity; they infused their own ruthlessness into the official orders. Their dedication to the triumph of communism overcame all doubts caused by the sight of starving people and the sounds of wailing women and children.

Defeated but unwilling to surrender their livestock, the peasants slaughtered their animals, gorging themselves in drunken orgies against the days of inevitable famine. The country's cattle herds declined by one-half, inflicting irreparable secondary losses as well. The number of horses, crucial for rural transport and farm work, fell by one-third. Crops were not planted or not harvested, the Five-Year Plan was disrupted, and from 1931 to 1933 millions starved to death.

The suffering was most cruel in the Ukraine, where famine killed approximately seven million people, many after extreme abuse and persecution. In order to buy industrial equipment abroad so that industrialization could proceed on target, the Soviet Union had to export food, as much of it as possible and for prices disastrously lowered by the Great Depression. Let the peasants in the Ukrainian breadbasket perish so that the country could grow strong! Moreover, Stalin relished the opportunity to punish the Ukrainians for their disloyalty during the civil war and their resistance to collectivization.

By 1935, practically all farming in Russia was collectivized. The kulaks had been wiped out as a class, and the peasants, ever rebellious under the tsars, had been cowed into permanent submission. In theory, the collective farms were run democratically, under an elected chairman; in practice, they followed as best they could the directives handed down from the nearest party office. People grumbled about the rise of a new serfdom. Agricultural development had been stifled.

Total Control

To quash resistance and mold a new type of suitably motivated and disciplined citizen, Stalin unleashed a third revolution, the revolution of totalitarianism. Only Communist regimentation, he believed, could liberate Russia from its historic inferiority. Moreover, the totalitarian state accorded with his desire to exercise total control over the party and the nation. Stalin's totalitarianism aimed at a complete reconstruction of state and society, down to the innermost recesses of human consciousness. It called for "a new man," suited to the needs of Soviet industrialism.

The revolution of totalitarianism encompassed all cultural activity. All media of communication—literature, the arts, music, the stage—were forced into subservience to the Five-Year Plan and Soviet ideology. In literature, as in all art, an official style was promulgated. Called *socialist realism*, it was expected to describe the world as the party saw it or hoped to shape it. Novels in the social realist manner told how the romances of tractor drivers and milkmaids or of lathe operators and office secretaries led to new victories of production under the Five-Year Plan. Composers found their music examined for remnants of bourgeois spirit; they were to write simple tunes suitable for heroic times. Everywhere huge, high-color posters showed men and women hard at work with radiant faces, calling others to join them; often Stalin, the wise father and leader, was shown among them. In this way, artistic creativity was locked into a dull, utilitarian straitjacket of official cheerfulness; creativity was allowed only to boost industrial productivity. Behind the scenes, all artists were disciplined to conform to the will of the party or be crushed.

Education, from nursery school to university, was likewise harnessed to train dutiful and loyal citizens, and Soviet propaganda made a cult of Stalin that bordered on deification. Thus, a writer declared in 1935:

> *Centuries will pass and the generations still to come will regard us as the happiest of mortals, as the most fortunate of men, because we . . . were privileged to see Stalin, our inspired leader. Yes, and we regard ourselves as the happiest of mortals because we are the contemporaries of a man who never had an equal in world history. The men of all ages will call on thy name, which is strong, beautiful, wise, and marvellous. Thy name is engraven on every factory, every machine, every place on the earth, and in the hearts of all men.*[7]

Stalin unleashed raw terror to break stubborn wills and compel conformity. Terror had been used as a tool of government ever since the Bolshevik Revolution (and the tsars had also used it, moderately and intermittently). After the start of the first Five-Year Plan, show trials were staged that denounced as saboteurs the engineers who disagreed with Stalin's production timetable. The terror used to herd the peasants onto collective farms was even greater. Stalin also used terror to crush opposition and to instill an abject fear both in the ranks of the party and in Russian society at large.

Purges had long been used to rid the party of weaklings. After 1934, however, they became an instrument of Stalin's drive for unchallenged personal power. In 1936, his vindictive terror broke into the open. The first batch of victims, including many founders of the Communist party, were accused of conspiring with the exiled Trotsky to set up a "terrorist center" and of scheming to terrorize the party. After being sentenced to death, they were immediately executed. In 1937, the next group, including prominent Communists of Lenin's day, were charged with cooperating with foreign intelligence agencies and wrecking "socialist reconstruction," the term for Stalin's revolution; they too were executed. Shortly afterward, a secret purge decimated the military high command—almost half the country's seventy thousand officers were either shot or sent to the camps—for which the country paid a heavy price when Germany attacked in 1941.

In 1938, the last and biggest show trial advanced the most bizarre accusation of all: sabotage, espionage, and attempting to dismember the Soviet Union and kill all its leaders (including Lenin in 1918). In the public hearings, some defendants refuted the public prosecutor, but in the end all confessed, usually after torture and threats to their family, before being executed. Western observers were aghast at the cynical charges and at the physical and mental tortures used to obtain the confessions.

The great trials, however, involved only a small minority of Stalin's victims; many more perished in silence without the benefit of legal proceedings. The terror first hit members of the party, especially the Old Bolsheviks, who had joined before the Revolution; they were the most independent-minded members and therefore the most dangerous to Stalin. But Stalin also diminished the cultural elite that had survived the Lenin revolution. Thousands of engineers, scientists, industrial managers, scholars, and artists disappeared; they were shot or sent to forced-labor camps, where most of them perished. No one was safe. To frighten the common people in all walks of life, men, women, and even children were dragged into the net of Stalin's secret police, leaving the survivors with a soul-killing reminder: submit or else.

Stalin may have orchestrated the terror, but large numbers of party members believed that terror, which was decimating their own ranks, was necessary. The memory of the vicious civil war, when domestic and foreign enemies sought to overthrow the new Bolshevik regime, and the resistance of the kulaks to collectivization created a siege mentality among the Communist leadership. Everywhere they saw anti-Soviets plotting against the party; they defined these enemies as Trotskyites, former kulaks, Whites who had fought in the civil war, members of outlawed anti-Soviet political parties, foreign agents, criminals, cattle and horse thieves, contraband smugglers, bandits, and so on. Party officials saw terror as a legitimate way both of protecting the party, to which they were ideologically committed and from which they derived prestige, power, and material benefits, and of protecting the Soviet experiment, which they viewed as humanity's best hope.

The toll of the purges is reckoned in many millions; it included Trotsky, who in 1940 was murdered in Mexico. The bloodletting was ghastly, as Stalin's purge officials themselves followed each other into death and ignominy.

Stalin was untroubled by the waste of life. He believed that without the total obedience of the Russian people, the Soviet economy could not be effectively and quickly mobilized, and that terror was necessary to compel compliance. In Stalin's mind, totalitarianism was necessary to save Russia from foreign enemies that would devour it. No doubt, the terror was also an expression of his craving for personal power and his vengeful and suspicious, some say clinically paranoid, nature. He saw enemies everywhere, took pleasure in selecting victims, and reveled in his omnipotence. By showing party officials and the Russian masses how vulnerable they were, how dependent they were on his will, Stalin frightened them into servility. For good reason, Stalin has been called a twentieth-century Ivan the Terrible. Like the sixteenth-century tsar, for whom he expressed admiration, Stalin stopped at no brutality to establish personal autocracy.

But more than a craving for personal power motivated Stalin. He regarded himself as Lenin's heir, responsible for securing and expanding the Revolution and defending it against foreign and domestic enemies. The only way to do this was to create a powerful Soviet Union through rapid modernization.

THE NATURE AND APPEAL OF FASCISM

Liberals viewed the Great War as a conflict between freedom and autocracy and expected an Allied victory to accelerate the spread of democracy throughout Europe. Right after the war, it seemed that liberalism would continue to advance as it had in the nineteenth century. The collapse of the autocratic German and Austrian Empires had led to the formation of parliamentary governments throughout Eastern and central Europe. Yet within two decades, in an extraordinary turn of events, democracy seemed in its death throes. In Spain, Portugal, Italy, and Germany, and in all the newly created states of central and Eastern Europe except Czechoslovakia, democracy collapsed, and various forms of authoritarian government emerged. The defeat of democracy and the surge of authoritarianism was best exemplified by the triumph of totalitarian fascist movements in Italy and Germany.

The emergence of fascist movements in more than twenty European lands after Word War I was a sign that liberal society was in a state of disorientation and dissolution. The cultural pessimism, disdain for reason, elitism, romantic glorification of action and heroism, and contempt for liberal values voiced by many intellectuals and nationalists before the war found expression after the war in the antidemocratic and irrational fascist ideologies, which altered European political life. Fascism marked the culmination of the dangerous trends inherent in the extreme nationalism and radical conservatism of the late nineteenth century and in the repudiation of modern Western civilization by disenchanted intellectuals.

As a Europe-wide phenomenon, fascism was a response to a postwar society afflicted with spiritual disintegration, economic dislocation, political instability, and thwarted nationalist hopes. A general breakdown of meaning and values led people to search for new beliefs and new political arrangements. Fascism was an expression of fear that the Bolshevik Revolution would spread westward. It was also an expression of hostility to democratic values and a reaction to the failure of liberal institutions to solve the problems of modern industrial society; with brutal frankness, fascist leaders proclaimed that individual freedom, a relic of a dying liberal age and a barrier to national greatness, would be dispensed with.

Fascist movements were marked by a determination to eradicate liberalism and Marxism—to undo the legacy of the French Revolution of 1789 and the Bolshevik Revolution of 1917. Fascists believed that theirs was a spiritual revolution, that they were initiating a new era in history and building a new civilization on the ruins of liberal democracy. "We stand for a new principle in the world," said Mussolini. "We stand for the sheer, categorical, definitive antithesis to the world of democracy ... to the world which still abides by the fundamental principles laid down in 1789."[8] The chief principle of Nazism, said Hitler, "is to abolish the liberal concept of the individual and the Marxist concept of humanity, and to substitute for them the Volk community, rooted in the soil and united by the bond of its common blood."[9] The fascists' uniforms, songs, flags, parades, mass rallies, and cult of physical strength and violence all symbolized this call for a reawakened and reunited people.

Fascists accused liberal society of despiritualizing human beings and transforming them into materialistic creatures whose highest ideal was moneymaking. Regarding liberalism as bankrupt and parliamentary government as futile, many people yearned for a military dictatorship. To fascists and their sympathizers, democracy seemed an ineffective and enfeebled Old Order, ready to be overthrown. Idealistic youth and intellectuals rejoiced in fascist activism. They saw fascism as a revolt against the mediocrity of the liberal state and modern mass society and a reaffirmation of the noblest human qualities: heroism and dedication to one's people. Fascists saw themselves as participants in a dynamic mass movement that would rectify the weaknesses and irresolution of parliamentary government and rid the nation of corrosive foreign influences. For them, the triumph of fascism would mark a new beginning for their nation and a new era in world history.

The fascist vision of a regenerated nation—a New Order led by a determined and heroic elite—arising from the ruins of a decadent Old Order had the appeal of great myth; it evoked belief, commitment, and loyalty. The myth of rebirth—a nation cured of evil and building a new and vigorous society—had a profound impact on people dissatisfied with liberal society and searching for new beliefs. The myth of the nation reborn answered a metaphysical yearning to give meaning to life and history. It provided an emotionally gratifying world-view at a time when many people had lost their confidence in liberal-democratic ideals and institutions.

Fascists regarded Marxism as another enemy, for class conflict divided and weakened the state. To fascists, the Marxist call for workers of the world to unite meant the death of the national community. Fascism, in contrast, would reintegrate the proletariat into the nation and end class hostilities by making people at all levels feel that they were a needed part of the nation. Fascism thus offered a solution to the problem of insecurity and isolation in modern industrial society.

Attacking the rational tradition of the Enlightenment, fascism exalted will, blood, feeling, and instinct. Intellectual discussion and critical analysis, said fascists, cause national divisiveness; reason promotes doubt, enfeebles the will, and hinders instinctive, aggressive action. Fascism made a continual appeal to the emotions as a means of integrating the national community. This flow of emotion fueled irrational and dangerous desires, beliefs, and expectations that blocked critical judgment and responsible action. Glorifying action for its own sake, fascists aroused and manipulated brutal and primitive impulses and carried into politics the combative spirit of the trenches. They formed private armies, which attracted veterans—many of them

rootless, brutal, and maladjusted men who sought to preserve the loyalty, camaraderie, and violence of the front.

Fascists exalted the leader—who, according to the fascist view, intuitively grasped what was best for the nation—and called for rule by an elite of dedicated party members. The leader and the party would relieve the individual of the need to make decisions. Convinced that the liberal stress on individual freedom promoted national divisiveness, fascists pressed for monolithic unity: one leader, one party, one ideology, and one national will.

Fascism drew its mass support from the lower middle class: small merchants, artisans, white-collar workers, civil servants, and peasants of moderate means, all of whom were frightened both by big capitalism and by Marxism. They hoped that fascism would protect them from the competition of big business and prevent the hated working class from establishing a Marxist state, which would threaten their property. The lower middle class saw in fascism a noncommunist way of overcoming economic crises and restoring traditional respect for family, native soil, and nation. Furthermore, many of these people saw fascism as a way of attacking the existing social order, which denied them opportunities for economic advancement and social prestige.

Although a radicalized middle class gave fascist movements their mass support, the fascists could not have captured the state without the aid of existing ruling elites: landed aristocrats, industrialists, and army leaders. In Russia, the Bolsheviks had to fight their way to power; in Italy and Germany, the old ruling order virtually handed power to the fascists. In both countries, fascist leaders succeeded in reassuring the conservative elite that they would not institute widespread social reforms or interfere with private property and would protect the nation from communism. Even though the old elite abhorred fascist violence and demagoguery, it entered into an alliance with the fascists to protect its interests.

In their struggle to bring down the liberal state, fascist leaders aroused primitive impulses and tribal loyalties; they made use of myths and rituals to mobilize and manipulate the masses. Organizing their propaganda campaigns with the rigor of a military operation, fascists stirred and dominated the masses and confused and undermined their democratic opposition, breaking its will to resist. Fascists were most successful in countries with weak democratic traditions. When parliamentary government faltered, it had few staunch defenders, and many people were drawn to charismatic demagogues who promised direct action.

The proliferation of fascist movements demonstrated that the habits of democracy are not quickly learned, easily retained, or even desired. Particularly during times of crisis, people lose patience with parliamentary discussion and constitutional procedures, sink into nonrational modes of thought and behavior, and are easily manipulated by unscrupulous politicians. For the sake of economic or emotional security and national grandeur, they will often willingly sacrifice political freedom. Fascism starkly manifested the immense power of the irrational; it humbled liberals, making them permanently aware of the limitations of reason and the fragility of freedom.

The fascist goal of maximum centralization of power was furthered by developments during World War I: the expansion of bureaucracy, the concentration of industry into giant monopolies, and the close cooperation between industry and the state. The instruments of modern technology—radio, motion pictures, public address systems, telephone, and teletype—made it possible for the state to indocrinate, manipulate, and dominate its subjects.

THE RISE OF FASCISM IN ITALY

Postwar Unrest

Although Italy had been on the winning side in World War I, the country resembled a defeated nation. Food shortages, rising prices, massive unemployment, violent strikes, workers occupying factories, and peasants squatting on the uncultivated periphery of large estates created a climate of crisis. Italy required effective leadership and a reform program, but party disputes paralyzed the liberal government. With several competing parties, the liberals could not organize a solid majority that could cope with the domestic crisis.

The middle class was severely stressed. To meet its accelerating expenses, the government had increased taxes, but the burden fell unevenly on small landowners, owners of small businesses, civil service workers, and professionals. Large landowners and industrialists feared that their nation was on the verge of a Bolshevik-style revolution. In truth, Italian socialists had no master plan to seize power. Peasant squatters and urban strikers were responding to the distress in their own regions and did not significantly coordinate their efforts with those in other localities. Besides, when workers realized that they could not keep the factories operating, their revolutionary zeal waned and they started to abandon the plants. The workers' and peasants' poorly led and futile struggles did not portend a Red revolution. Nevertheless, the industrialists and landlords, with the Bolshevik Revolution still vivid in their minds, were taking no chances.

Adding to the unrest was national outrage at the terms of the World War I peace settlement. Italians felt that despite their sacrifices—five hundred thousand dead and one million wounded—they had been robbed of the fruits of victory. Italy had been denied the Dalmatian coast, the Adriatic port of Fiume, and territory in Africa and the Middle East. Nationalists blamed the liberal government for what they called a "mutilated victory." In 1919, a force of war veterans, led by the poet and adventurer Gabriele D'Annunzio (1863–1938), seized Fiume, to the delirious joy of Italian nationalists and the embarrassment of the government. D'Annunzio's occupation of the port lasted more than a year, adding fuel to the flames of Italian nationalism and demonstrating the weakness of the liberal regime in imposing its authority on rightist opponents.

Mussolini's Seizure of Power

Benito Mussolini (1883–1945), a former socialist and World War I veteran, exploited the unrest in postwar Italy in order to capture control of the state. In 1919, he organized the Fascist party, which attracted converts from among the discontented, the disillusioned, and the uprooted. Many Italians viewed Mussolini as the leader who would gain Fiume, Dalmatia, and colonies and win for Italy its rightful place of honor in international affairs. Hardened battle veterans joined the

Fascist movement to escape the boredom and idleness of civilian life. They welcomed the opportunity to wear the uniforms of the Fascist militia (Black Shirts), parade in the streets, and fight socialist and labor union opponents. Squads of the Black Shirts (*squadristi*) raided socialist and trade union offices, destroying property and beating the occupants. As socialist Red Shirts responded in kind, Italy soon appeared to be drifting toward civil war.

Hoping that Mussolini would rescue Italy from Bolshevism, industrialists and landowners contributed large sums to the Fascist party. The lower middle class, fearful that the growing power of labor unions and the Socialist party threatened their property and social prestige, viewed Mussolini as a protector. Middle-class university students, searching for adventure and an ideal, and army officers, dreaming of an Italian empire and hostile to parliamentary government, were also attracted to Mussolini's party. Mussolini's philosophy of action intrigued intellectuals disenchanted with liberal politics and parliamentary democracy. His nationalism, activism, and anticommunism gradually seduced elements of the power structure: capitalists, aristocrats, army officers, the royal family, and the church. Regarding liberalism as bankrupt and parliamentary government as futile, many of these people yearned for a military dictatorship.

In 1922, Mussolini made his bid for power. Speaking at a giant rally of his followers in late October, he declared: "Either they will give us the government or we shall take it by descending on Rome. It is now a matter of days, perhaps hours." A few days later, the Fascists began their March on Rome. It would have been a relatively simple matter to crush the twenty thousand Fascist marchers, who were armed with little more than pistols and rifles, but King Victor Emmanuel III (1869–1947) refused to act. The king's advisers, some of them sympathetic to Mussolini, exaggerated the strength of the Fascists. Believing that he was rescuing Italy from terrible violence, the king appointed Mussolini prime minister.

Mussolini had bluffed his way to power. Fascism had triumphed not because of its own strength—the Fascist party had only 35 of 535 seats in parliament—but because the liberal government, indecisive and fearful of violence, did

Mussolini with His Troops. The Italian dictator deliberately tried to sustain an image of a virile warrior. Although Mussolini established a one-party state, he was less successful than Hitler or Stalin in creating a totalitarian regime. (*AP/Wide World Photos*)

not counter force with force. In the past, the liberal state had not challenged Fascist acts of terror; now it feebly surrendered to Fascist blustering and threats. No doubt, liberals hoped that once in power, the Fascists would forsake terror, pursue moderate aims, and act within the constitution. But the liberals were wrong; they had completely misjudged the antidemocratic character of fascism.

The Fascist State in Italy

Gradually, Mussolini moved toward establishing a dictatorship. In 1925–26, he eliminated non-Fascists from his cabinet, dissolved opposition parties, smashed the independent trade unions, suppressed opposition newspapers, replaced local mayors with Fascist officials, and organized a secret police to round up troublemakers. Many anti-Fascists fled the country or were deported.

Mussolini was less successful than Hitler and Stalin in fashioning a totalitarian state. The industrialists, the large landowners, the church, and to some extent even the army never fell under the complete domination of the party. Nor did the regime possess the mind of its subjects with the same thoroughness as the Nazis did in Germany. Life in Italy was less regimented and the individual less fearful than in Nazi Germany or Communist Russia.

Like Communist Russia and Nazi Germany, however, Fascist Italy used mass organizations and mass media to control minds and regulate behavior. As in the Soviet Union and the Third Reich, the regime created a cult of the leader. "Mussolini goes forward with confidence, in a halo of myth, almost chosen by God, indefatigable and infallible, the instrument employed by Providence for the creation of a new civilization," wrote the philosopher Giovanni Gentile.[10] To convey the image of a virile leader, Mussolini had himself photographed bare-chested or in a uniform and a steel helmet. Elementary school textbooks depicted him as the savior of the nation, a modern-day Julius Caesar.

Fascist propaganda urged that the grandeur of the Roman Empire be restored through conquest. It also inculcated habits of discipline and obedience: "Mussolini is always right." "Believe! Obey! Fight!" Propaganda also glorified war: "A minute on the battlefield is worth a lifetime of peace." The press, radio, and cinema idealized life under fascism, implying that fascism had eradicated crime, poverty, and social tensions. Schoolteachers and university professors were compelled to swear allegiance to the Fascist government and to propagate Fascist ideals, while students were urged to criticize instructors who harbored liberal attitudes. Millions of youths belonged to Fascist organizations, in which they participated in patriotic ceremonies and social functions, sang Fascist hymns, and wore Fascist uniforms. They submerged their own identities in the group.

Denouncing economic liberalism for promoting individual self-interest, Fascists also attacked socialism for instigating conflicts between workers and capitalists, which divided and weakened the nation. The Fascist way of resolving tensions between workers and employers was to abolish independent labor unions, prohibit strikes, and establish associations or corporations that included both workers and employers within a given industry. In theory, representatives of labor and capital would cooperatively solve their particular industry's labor problems; in practice, however, the representatives of labor turned out to be Fascists, who protected the interests of the industrialists. Although the Fascists lauded the cooperative system as a creative approach to modern economic problems, in reality it played a minor role in Italian economic life. Big business continued to make its own decisions, paying scant attention to the corporations.

Nor did the Fascist government solve Italy's long-standing economic problems. To curtail the export of capital and to reduce the nation's dependence on imports in case of war, Mussolini sought to make Italy self-sufficient. To win the "battle of grain," the Fascist regime brought marginal lands under cultivation and urged farmers to concentrate on wheat rather than other crops. While wheat production increased substantially, total agricultural output fell because wheat had been planted on land more suited to animal husbandry and fruit cultivation. To make Italy industrially self-sufficient, the regime limited imports of foreign goods, with the result that Italian consumers paid higher prices for goods manufactured in Italy. Mussolini posed as the protector of the little people, but under his regime the power and profits of big business grew and the standard of living of small farmers and urban workers slipped.

Although anticlerical since his youth, Mussolini was also expedient. He recognized that coming to terms with the church would improve his image with Catholic public opinion. The Vatican regarded Mussolini's regime as a barrier against communism and as less hostile to church interests and more amenable to church direction than a liberal government. Pope Pius XI (1922–1939) was an ultraconservative whose hatred of liberalism and secularism led him to believe that the Fascists would increase the influence of the church in the nation.

In 1929, the Lateran Accords recognized the independence of Vatican City, repealed many of the anticlerical laws passed under the liberal government, and made religious instruction compulsory in all secondary schools. Relations between the Vatican and the Fascist government remained fairly good throughout the decade of the 1930s. When Mussolini invaded Ethiopia and intervened in the Spanish Civil War, the church supported him. Although the papacy criticized Mussolini for drawing closer to Hitler and introducing anti-Jewish legislation, it never broke with the Fascist regime.

THE NEW GERMAN REPUBLIC

In the last days of World War I, a revolution brought down the German government, a semi-authoritarian monarchy, and led to the creation of a democratic republic. The new government, headed by Chancellor Friedrich Ebert (1871–1925), a Social Democrat, signed the armistice agreement ending the war. Many Germans blamed the new democratic leadership for the defeat—a baseless accusation, for the German generals, knowing that the war was lost, had sought an armistice. In February 1919, the recently elected National Assembly met at Weimar and proceeded to draw up a constitution for the new state. The Weimar Republic—born in revolution, which most Germans detested, and military defeat, which many attributed to the new government—faced an uncertain future. The legend that traitors, principally Jews and Social Democrats, cheated Germany of victory was created and propagated by the conservative right—generals, high-ranking bureaucrats, university professors, and nationalists, who wanted to preserve the army's reputation and bring down the new and hated democratic Weimar Republic.

Threats from Left and Right

Dominated by moderate socialists, the infant republic faced internal threats from both the radical left and the radical right. In January 1919, the newly established German Communist party, or

The German Inflation, 1923. As the value of the mark plummeted, many Germans lost their entire savings, which had taken a lifetime to accumulate. Here children play with now worthless banknotes. *(Hulton-Deutsch Collection/Corbis)*

Spartacists, disregarding the advice of their leaders Rosa Luxemburg and Karl Liebknecht, took to the streets of Berlin and declared Ebert's government deposed. To crush the revolution, Ebert turned to the Free Corps: volunteer brigades of ex-soldiers and adventurers, led by officers loyal to the emperor, who had been fighting to protect the eastern borders from encroachments by the new states of Poland, Estonia, and Latvia. The men of the Free Corps relished action and despised Bolshevism. They suppressed the revolution and murdered Luxemburg and Liebknecht on January 15.

The Spartacist revolt and the short-lived "soviet" republic in Munich (and others in Baden and Brunswick) had a profound effect on the German psyche. The Communists had been easily subdued, but fear of a Communist insurrection remained deeply embedded in the middle and upper classes—a fear that drove many of their members into the ranks of the Weimar Republic's right-wing opponents.

Refusing to disband as the government ordered, detachments of the right-wing Free Corps marched into Berlin and declared a new government, headed by Wolfgang Kapp, a staunch German nationalist. Insisting that it could not fire on fellow soldiers, the German army, the *Reichswehr,* made no move to defend the republic. A general strike called by the labor unions prevented Kapp from governing, and the coup collapsed. However, the Kapp Putsch demonstrated that the loyalty of the army to the republic was doubtful and that important segments of German society supported the overthrow, by violence if necessary, of the Weimar Republic and its replacement by an authoritarian government driven by a nationalist credo.

Economic Crisis

In addition to uprisings by the left and right, the republic was burdened by economic crisis. Unable to meet the deficit in the national budget, the government simply printed more money, causing the value of the German mark to decline precipitously. In 1919, the mark stood at 8.9 to the dollar; in November 1923, a dollar could be exchanged for 4 billion marks. Bank savings, war bonds, and pensions, representing years of toil and thrift, became worthless. Blaming the government for this disaster, the ruined middle class became more receptive to ultrarightist movements that aimed to bring down the republic.

A critical factor in the collapse of the German economy was the French occupation of the Ruhr in January 1923. With the economy in shambles, the republic had defaulted on reparation payments. The French premier, Raymond Poincaré (1860–1934), ordered French troops into the Ruhr—the nerve center of German industry. Responding to the republic's call for passive resistance, factory workers, miners, and railway workers in the Ruhr refused to work for the French. Paying salaries to striking workers and officials contributed to the mark's free fall.

Gustav Stresemann, who became chancellor in August 1923, skillfully placed the republic on the path to recovery. He declared Germany's willingness to make reparation payments and issued a new currency, backed by a mortgage on German real estate. To protect the value of the new currency, the government did not print another issue. Inflation receded, and confidence was restored.

A new arrangement regarding reparations also contributed to the economic recovery. In 1924, the parties accepted the Dawes Plan, which reduced reparations and based them on Germany's economic capacity. During the negotiations, France agreed to withdraw its troops from the Ruhr—another step toward easing tensions for the republic.

From 1924 to 1929, economic conditions improved. Foreign capitalists, particularly Americans, were attracted by high interest rates and the low cost of labor. Their investments in German businesses stimulated the economy. By 1929, iron, steel, coal, and chemical production exceeded prewar levels. The value of German exports also surpassed that of 1913. Real wages were higher than before the war, and improved unemployment benefits also made life better for the workers. It appeared that Germany had achieved political stability, as threats from the extremist parties of the left and the right subsided. Given time and continued economic stability, democracy might have taken firmer root in Germany. But then came the Great Depression. The global economic crisis that began in October 1929 starkly revealed how weak was the Weimar Republic.

Fundamental Weaknesses of the Weimar Republic

German political experience provided poor soil for transplanting an English democratic parliamentary system. Before World War I, Germany had been a semiautocratic state, ruled by an emperor who commanded the armed forces, controlled foreign policy, appointed the chancellor, and called and dismissed parliament. This authoritarian system blocked the German people from acquiring democratic habits and attitudes; still accustomed to rule from above, still adoring the power-state, many Germans sought to destroy the democratic Weimar Republic.

Traditional conservatives—the upper echelons of the civil service, judges, industrialists, large landowners, and army leaders—scorned democracy and hated the republic. They regarded the revolution against the monarchy in the last weeks of the war as a treacherous act and the establishment of a democratic republic as a violation of Germany's revered tradition of hierarchical leadership. Nor did the middle class feel a commitment to the liberal-democratic principles on which the republic rested. The traditionally nationalistic middle class identified the republic with the defeat in war and the humiliation of the Versailles treaty. Rabidly antisocialist, this class saw the leaders of the republic as Marxists, who would impose on Germany a working-class state. Right-wing intellectuals often attacked democracy as a barrier to the true unity of the German nation. In the tradition of nineteenth-century Volkish thinkers, they disdained reason and political freedom, glorifying instead race, instincts, and action. By doing so, they turned many Germans against the republic, eroding the popular support on which democracy depends.

The Weimar Republic also showed the weaknesses of the multiparty system. With the vote spread over a number of parties, no one party held a majority of seats in the parliament (Reichstag), so the republic was governed by a coalition of several parties. But because of ideological differences, the coalition was always unstable and in danger of failing to function. This is precisely what happened during the Great Depression. When effective leadership was imperative, the government could not act. Political deadlock caused Germans to lose what little confidence they had in the democratic system. Support for the parties that wanted to preserve democracy dwindled, and extremist parties that aimed to topple the republic gained strength. Seeking to bring down the republic were the Communists, on the left, and two rightist parties—the Nationalists and the National Socialist German Workers' party, led by Adolf Hitler.

THE RISE OF HITLER

Adolf Hitler (1889–1945) was born in Austria on April 20, 1889, the fourth child of a minor civil servant. A poor student in secondary school, although by no means unintelligent, Hitler left high school and lived idly for more than two years. In 1907 and again in 1908, the Vienna Academy of Fine Arts rejected his application for admission. Hitler did not try to learn a trade or to work steadily but earned some money by painting picture postcards. He read a lot, especially in art, history, and military affairs. He also read the racial, nationalist, anti-Semitic, and Pan-German literature that abounded in multinational Vienna. The racist treatises preached the danger posed by mixing races, called for the liquidation of racial inferiors, and marked the Jew as the embodiment of evil and the source of all misfortune.

In Vienna, Hitler came into contact with Georg von Schönerer's Pan-German movement. For Schönerer, the Jews were evil not because of their religion or because they rejected Christ, but because they possessed evil racial qualities. Schönerer's followers wore watch chains with pictures of hanged Jews attached. Hitler was particularly impressed with Karl Lueger, the mayor of Vienna, a clever demagogue who skillfully manipulated the anti-Semitic feelings of the Catholic Viennese for his own political advantage. In Vienna, Hitler also acquired a hatred for Marxism and democracy and grew convinced that the struggle for existence and the survival of the fittest were the essential facts of the social world.

When World War I began, Hitler was in Munich. He welcomed the war as a relief from his daily life, which lacked purpose and excitement. Volunteering for the German army, Hitler found battle exhilarating, and he fought bravely, twice receiving the Iron Cross. The experience of battle taught Hitler to prize discipline, regimentation, leadership, authority, struggle, and ruthlessness— values that he carried with him into the politics of the postwar world.

The shock of Germany's defeat and revolution intensified Hitler's commitment to racial nationalism. To lead Germany to total victory over its racial enemies became his obsession. Germany's defeat and shame, he said, were due to the creators of the republic, the "November criminals," and behind them was a Jewish-Bolshevik world conspiracy.

The Nazi Party

In 1919, Hitler joined a small right-wing extremist group. Displaying fantastic energy and extraordinary ability as a demagogic orator, propagandist, and organizer, Hitler quickly became the leader of the party, whose name was changed to National Socialist German Workers' party (commonly called Nazi). As leader, Hitler insisted on absolute authority and total allegiance—a demand that coincided with the postwar longing for a strong leader who would set right a shattered nation.

Like Mussolini, Hitler incorporated military attitudes and techniques into politics. Uniforms, salutes, emblems, flags, and other symbols imbued party members with a sense of solidarity and camaraderie. At mass meetings, Hitler was a spellbinder who gave stunning performances. His pounding fists, throbbing body, wild gesticulations, hypnotic eyes, rage-swollen face, and repeated, frenzied denunciations of the Versailles treaty, Marxism, the republic, and Jews inflamed and mesmerized the audience. Hitler instinctively grasped the innermost feelings of his audience—their resentments and longings. "The intense will of the man, the passion of his sincerity seemed to flow from him into me. I experienced an exaltation that could be likened only to religious conversion," said one early admirer.[11]

In November 1923, Hitler tried to seize power in Munich, in the state of Bavaria, as a prelude to toppling the republic. The attempt, which came to be known as the Beer Hall Putsch, failed miserably. Ironically, however, Hitler's prestige increased, for when he was put on trial, he used it as an opportunity to denounce the republic and the Versailles treaty and to proclaim his philosophy of racial nationalism. His impassioned speeches, publicized by the press, earned Hitler a nationwide reputation and a light sentence: five years' imprisonment, with the promise of quick parole. While in prison, Hitler dictated *Mein Kampf*, a rambling and turgid work that contained the essence of his world-view. The unsuccessful Munich Putsch taught Hitler a valuable

lesson: armed insurrection against superior might fails. He would gain power not by force, but by exploiting the instruments of democracy—elections and party politics. He would use apparently legal means to destroy the Weimar Republic and impose a dictatorship.

Hitler's World-View

Racial Nationalism Hitler's thought comprised a patchwork of nineteenth-century anti-Semitic, Volkish, Social Darwinist, antidemocratic, and anti-Marxist ideas. From these ideas, many of which enjoyed wide popularity, Hitler constructed a world-view rooted in myth, fantasy, and ritual. Nazism rejected both the Judeo-Christian and the Enlightenment traditions and sought to found a new world order based on racial nationalism. For Hitler, race was the key to understanding world history. He believed that a reawakened, racially united Germany, led by men of iron will, would carve out a vast European empire and would deal a decadent liberal civilization its deathblow. It would conquer Russia, eradicate communism, and reduce to serfdom the subhuman Slavs, "a mass of born slaves who feel the need of a master."[12]

In the tradition of crude Volkish nationalists and Social Darwinists, Hitler divided the world into superior and inferior races and pitted them against each other in a struggle for survival. For him, this fight for life was a law of nature and of history.

The Jew as Devil An obsessive and virulent hatred of Jews dominated Hitler's mental outlook. In waging war against the Jews, Hitler believed that he was defending Germany from its worst enemy, a sinister force that stood in total opposition to the new world he envisioned. In his mythical interpretation of the world, the Aryan was the originator and carrier of civilization. As descendants of the Aryans, the German race embodied creativity, bravery, and loyalty. As the opposite of the Aryan, the Jews, who belonged to a separate biological race, personified the vilest qualities. "Two worlds face one another," said Hitler, "the men of God and the men of Satan! The Jew is the anti-man, the creature of another god. He must have come from another root of the human race. I set the Aryan and the Jew over and against each other."[13] Everything Hitler despised—liberalism, intellectualism, pacifism, parliamentarianism, internationalism, Marxism, modern art, and individualism—he attributed to Jews.

Hitler's anti-Semitism served a functional purpose as well. By concentrating all evil in one enemy, "the conspirator and demonic" Jew, Hitler provided true believers with a simple, all-embracing, and emotionally satisfying explanation for their misery. By defining themselves as the racial and spiritual opposites of Jews, Germans of all classes felt joined together in a Volkish union.

The surrender to myth served to disorient the German intellect and to unify the nation. When the mind accepts an image such as Hitler's image of Jews as vermin, germs, and satanic conspirators, it has lost all sense of balance and objectivity. Such a disoriented mind is ready to believe and to obey, to be manipulated and led, to brutalize and to tolerate brutality. It is ready to be absorbed into the will of the collective community. That many people, including intellectuals and members of the elite, accepted these racial ideas shows the enduring power of mythical thinking and the vulnerability of reason. In 1933, the year Hitler took power, Felix Goldmann, a German-Jewish writer, commented astutely on the irrational character of Nazi anti-Semitism: "The present-day politicized racial anti-Semitism is the embodiment of myth,... nothing is discussed... only felt,... nothing is pondered critically, logically or reasonably,... only inwardly perceived, surmised.... We are apparently the last [heirs] of the Enlightenment."[14]

The Importance of Propaganda Hitler understood that in an age of political parties, universal suffrage, and a popular press—the legacies of the French and Industrial Revolutions—the successful leader must win the support of the masses. This could be achieved best with propaganda. To be effective, said Hitler, propaganda must be aimed principally at the emotions. The masses are not moved by scientific ideas or by objective and abstract knowledge, but by primitive feelings, terror, force, and discipline. Propaganda must reduce everything to simple slogans incessantly

repeated and must concentrate on one enemy. The masses are aroused by the spoken, not the written, word—by a storm of hot passion erupting from the speaker "which like hammer blows can open the gates to the heart of the people."[15]

The most effective means of stirring the masses and strengthening them for the struggle ahead, Hitler had written in *Mein Kampf,* is the mass meeting. Surrounded by tens of thousands of people, individuals lose their sense of individuality and no longer see themselves as isolated. They become members of a community, bound together by an esprit de corps reminiscent of the trenches during the Great War. Bombarded by the cheers of thousands of voices, by marching units, by banners, by explosive oratory, individuals become convinced of the truth of the party's message and the irresistibility of the movement. Their intellects overwhelmed, their resistance lowered, they lose their previous beliefs and are carried along on a wave of enthusiasm. Their despair over the condition of their nation turns to hope, and they derive a sense of belonging and mission. They feel that they are participants in a mighty movement that is destined to regenerate the German nation and initiate a new historical age. "The man who enters such a meeting doubting and wavering leaves it inwardly reinforced; he has become a link to the community."[16]

Hitler Gains Power

After serving only nine months of his sentence, Hitler left prison in December 1924. He continued to build his party and waited for a crisis that would rock the republic and make his movement a force in national politics. The Great Depression, which began in the United States at the end of 1929, provided that crisis. Desperate and demoralized people lined up in front of government unemployment offices. Street peddlers, beggars, and youth gangs proliferated; suicides increased, particularly among middle-class people shamed by their descent into poverty, idleness, and uselessness. As Germany's economic plight worsened, the German people became more amenable to Hitler's radicalism. His propaganda techniques worked. The Nazi party went from 810,000 votes

Art as History: The Renaissance to the Present

Michelangelo Buonarotti: *David*, 1504. A towering marble sculpture, Michelangelo's *David* is one of the crowning masterpieces of the High Renaissance. During the Middle Ages, artists depicted the nude figure for specific, often moral, reasons: tormented sinners at the Last Judgment, for example. Michelangelo's use of nudity breaks with this tradition. What does his heroic, idealized portrayal of the biblical David reveal about the secular spirit of the Renaissance? (*Scala/Art Resource, NY*)

The visual arts are a particularly rich source of information for historians of the modern West. Revolutionary changes in art styles reflect the stages and complexities of the modern age. What insights into modern history can be derived from examining these works of art?

Filippo Brunelleschi. Church of San Lorenzo.
Brunelleschi's design of the church exemplifies the
practice of Renaissance artists of modelling their art
and architecture on classical forms with clearly prescribed mathematical limits and ratios. If a temple
or church may be said to represent the universe inhabited by the gods of a people, what kind of universe did the interior of Brunelleschi's building
suggest? How does it differ from the interior of a
Gothic cathedral? (*Erich Lessing/Art Resource*)

Rembrandt van Rijn (1606–1669): *Self Portrait at Old Age,* **1669.** Rembrandt was influenced in his early years by Italian painters' use of light. He also was highly introspective and produced a series of sixty-two self-portraits during his lifetime. The portraits revealed a variety of attitudes and poses, ranging from youthful and flamboyant to aging and distraught. In this painting, the fifty-fifth of the self-portraits, Rembrandt stares back at us with the calm assurance of a man who has mastered his art and life. What words would you use to describe the emotions conveyed in this self-portrait? How does Rembrandt use light and darkness in this painting? *(Erich Lessing/National Gallery, London/Art Resource, NY)*

Jacques Louis David: *The Death of Marat,* **1793.** This painting was done during the French Revolution by David, a foremost exponent of the neo-classical style, and an ardent revolutionary. It shows Marat, a revolutionary leader, after he had been stabbed to death by a crazed woman who had handed him a personal petition to read. What does this stark depiction of the death scene reveal about David's perception of the episode, and his indebtedness to the classical style of antiquity? How does his treatment of the moment of death differ from a work such as the Laocoön group's treatment of the same theme? (*Musée d'Art Ancien, Brussels, Giraudon/Art Resource, NY*)

J. M. W. Turner (1775–1851): *Burning of the Houses of Parliament,* c. 1835.
Turner was preoccupied with shimmering light. Although he often used literary
themes for his paintings, in accordance with romantic taste, the people, buildings, and ships were often obscured. What does this painting reveal about his
temperament and perception of the world? (*Oil on canvas. H. 36¼″ W. 48½″.
Philadelphia Museum of Art: The John H. McFadden Collection*)

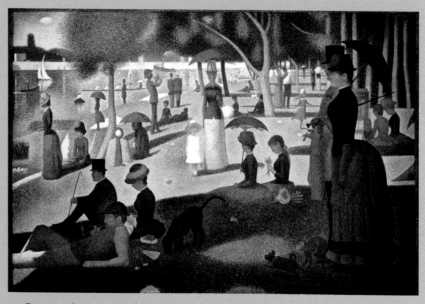

Georges Seurat: *Sunday Afternoon on the Island of La Grande Jatte,*
1884–1886. Seurat belonged to a late nineteenth century artistic movement
called impressionism, which wanted to depict objects in the instant they impress
themselves on the passive human eye. This position was opposed to the early
nineteenth century movement of romanticism, which wanted to reveal how the
act of seeing an object expresses a mood or feeling. Describe what Seurat's
painting contains. How does it compare to a romantic work, such as Turner's
Burning of the Houses of Parliament? (*Art Institute of Chicago*)

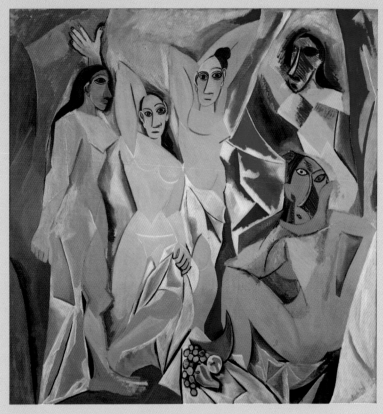

Pablo Picasso (1881–1973): *Les Demoiselles d'Avignon,* **1907.** The cubists further distorted perspective, to give viewers the feeling of seeing objects and people "in the round" and over time. In this picture, Picasso painted the female nude in the strong cubist style to express the forces of nature; he goes beyond the conscious level. Can a correlation be made between some twentieth century art and the scientific examination of the unconscious? (*Oil on canvas. 8′ × 7′8″. Collection, The Museum of Modern Art, New York. Acquired through the Lillie P. Bliss Bequest*)

Edward Hopper (1882–1967): *Nighthawks,* **1942.** American painter, Edward Hopper is one of the most notable American realist artists of the twentieth century. Set in 1942 in an all-night diner, *Nighthawks* depicts loneliness and alienation. The couple seems disconnected as the man converses with the waiter and the fourth figure sits alone at the counter. Exposed and vulnerable in the bright light, these people suffer from existential loneliness. What details does Hopper use to convey this sense of loneliness? What historical events in 1942 might Hopper have been responding to in this painting? *(Art Institute of Chicago)*

Jackson Pollock (1912–1956): *Convergence,* **1952.** American artist Jackson Pollock poured and splattered his colors on the canvas, instead of applying them with a brush or palette knife. This style of painting, known as action painting, allowed Pollock to walk around the canvas and work on it from all sides and angles. His *Convergence* may at first seem to be a canvas used as a drop cloth, but each application of color was made in a controlled and studied manner. Pollock was part of the abstract-expressionist movement, in which artists strived to express their emotions through color and abstract, nonrepresentational forms. What emotions does this painting convey to you? Why might it have been important for an abstract-expressionist like Pollock to move around the canvas instead of painting in a more traditional manner? *(Albright Knox Art Gallery, Buffalo)*

Frank O. Gehry (1929–): Guggenheim Museum at Bilbao, Spain, 1997. American architect Frank Gehry is famous for his innovative use of materials—twisting, bending, and turning metal into shapes that affect the emotions. Gehry views architecture as an art form, like painting and sculpture, which is expressive of human feeling and emotion. His Guggenheim Museum in Bilbao, Spain consists of organically interrelated contrasting shapes composed of a multiplicity of materials, ranging from limestone and glass to titanium. It provides the city of Bilbao with a dramatic architectural centerpiece that attracts thousand of visitors each year. In what ways does this museum prove Gehry's assertion that architecture is an art form capable of stirring human emotion? *(Superstock)*

in 1928 to 6,400,000 in 1930, and its representation in the Reichstag soared from 12 to 107.

To the lower middle class, the Nazis promised effective leadership and a solution to the economic crisis. But Nazism was more than a class movement. It appealed to the discontented and disillusioned from all segments of the population: embittered veterans, romantic nationalists, idealistic intellectuals, industrialists and large landowners frightened by communism and social democracy, rootless and resentful people who felt they had no place in the existing society, the unemployed, lovers of violence, and newly enfranchised youth yearning for a cause. And always there was the immense attraction of Hitler, who tirelessly worked his oratorical magic on increasingly enthusiastic crowds, confidently promising leadership and national rebirth. Many Germans were won over by his fanatical sincerity, his iron will, and his conviction that he was chosen by fate to rescue Germany.

In the election of July 31, 1932, the Nazis received 37.3 percent of the vote and won 230 seats—far more than any other party, but still not a majority. Franz von Papen, who had resigned from the chancellorship, persuaded the aging president, Paul von Hindenburg (1847–1934), to appoint Hitler as chancellor. In this decision, Papen had the support of German industrialists and aristocratic landowners, who regarded Hitler as a useful instrument to fight communism, block social reform, break the backs of organized labor, and rebuild the armament industry.

Never intending to rule within the spirit of the constitution, Hitler, who took office on January 30, 1933, quickly moved to assume dictatorial powers. In February 1933, a Dutch drifter with communist leanings set a fire in the Reichstag. Hitler persuaded Hindenburg to sign an emergency decree suspending civil rights on the pretext that the state was threatened by internal subversion. The chancellor then used these emergency powers to arrest, without due process, Communist and Social Democratic deputies.

In the elections of March 1933, the German people elected 288 Nazi deputies in a Reichstag of 647 seats. With the support of 52 deputies of the Nationalist party and in the absence of Communist deputies, who were under arrest, the Nazis now had a secure majority. Later that month, Hitler bullied the Reichstag into passing the Enabling Act, which permitted the chancellor to enact legislation independently of the Reichstag. With astonishing passivity, the political parties had allowed the Nazis to dismantle the government and make Hitler a dictator with unlimited power. Hitler had used the instruments of democracy to destroy the republic and create a totalitarian state.

NAZI GERMANY

The Nazis moved to subjugate all political and economic institutions and all culture to the will of the party. The party became the state and its teachings the soul of the German nation. There could be no separation between private life and politics and no rights of the individual that the state must respect. Ideology must pervade every phase of daily life, and all organizations must come under party control. For both Communists and Nazis, ideology was "a grand transcendent fiction [or] metamyth" that provided adherents with answers to the crucial questions of life and history.[17] Joseph Goebbels (see upcoming section, "Shaping the 'New Man'") summed up this totalitarian goal as follows: "It is not enough to reconcile people more or less to our regime, to move them towards a position of neutrality towards us, we want rather to work on people until they are addicted to us."[18] An anonymous Nazi poet expressed the totalitarian credo in these words:

> *We have captured all the positions*
> *And on the heights we have planted*
> *The banners of our revolution.*
> *You had imagined that that was all that we*
> *   wanted*
> *We want more*
> *We want all*
> *Your hearts are our goal*
> *It is your souls we want.*[19]

The Leader-State

The Third Reich was organized as a leader-state, in which Hitler, the *fuehrer* (leader), embodied and expressed the real will of the German people, commanded the supreme loyalty of the nation, and held omnipotent power. As a Nazi political theorist stated, "The authority of the Fuehrer is total and all embracing...it is subject to no checks or controls; it is circumscribed by no...individual rights; it is...overriding and unfettered."[20]

In June 1933, the Social Democratic party was outlawed, and within a few weeks, the other political parties simply disbanded on their own. In May 1933, the Nazis had seized the property of the trade unions, arrested the leaders, and ended collective bargaining and strikes. The newly established German Labor Front, an instrument of the party, became the official organization of the working class.

Unlike the Bolsheviks, the Nazis did not destroy the upper classes of the Old Regime. Hitler made no war against the industrialists. He wanted from them loyalty, obedience, and a war machine. German businessmen prospered but exercised no influence on political decisions. The profits of industry rose, and workers lauded the regime for ending the unemployment crisis.

Nazism conflicted with the core values of Christianity. "The heaviest blow that ever struck humanity was the coming of Christianity," said Hitler to intimates during World War II.[21] Because Nazism could tolerate no other faith alongside itself, the Nazis, recognizing that Christianity was a rival claimant for the German soul, moved to repress the Protestant and Catholic churches. In the public schools, religious instruction was cut back, and the syllabus was changed to omit the Jewish origins of Christianity. Christ was depicted not as a Jew, heir to the prophetic tradition of Hebrew monotheism, but as an Aryan hero. The Gestapo (secret state police) censored church newspapers, scrutinized sermons and church activities, forbade some clergymen to preach, dismissed the opponents of Nazism from theological schools, and arrested some clerical critics of the regime.

The clergy were well represented among the Germans who resisted Nazism; some were sent to concentration camps or were executed. But these courageous clergy were not representative of the German churches, which, as organized institutions, capitulated to and cooperated with the Nazi regime. Both the German Evangelical and German Catholic churches demanded that their faithful render loyalty to Hitler; both turned a blind eye to Nazi persecution of Jews. Even before World War II and the implementation of genocide, many Evangelical churches banned baptized Jews from entering their temples and dismissed pastors with Jewish ancestry. During the war, both Catholic and Evangelical churches condemned resistance and found much in the Third Reich to admire; and both supported Hitler's war. The prominent Lutheran theologian who "welcomed that change that came to Germany in 1933 as a divine gift and miracle" voiced the sentiments of many members of the clergy.[22]

The Nazis instituted many anti-Jewish measures, designed to make outcasts of the Jews. Thousands of Jewish doctors, lawyers, musicians, artists, and professors were barred from practicing their professions, and Jewish members of the civil service were dismissed. A series of laws tightened the screws of humiliation and persecution. Marriage or sexual encounters between Germans and Jews were forbidden. Universities, schools, restaurants, pharmacies, hospitals, theaters, museums, and athletic fields were gradually closed to Jews.

In November 1938, using as a pretext the assassination of a German official in Paris by a seventeen-year-old Jewish youth, whose family the Nazis had mistreated, the Nazis organized an extensive pogrom. Nazi gangs murdered scores of Jews, destroyed 267 synagogues, and burned and vandalized 7,500 Jewish-owned businesses all over Germany—an event that became known as Night of the Broken Glass (Kristallnacht). Twenty thousand Jews were thrown into concentration camps. The Reich then imposed on the Jewish community a fine of one billion marks. These measures were a mere prelude, however. During World War II, the genocidal murder of European Jewry became a cardinal Nazi objective. As a rule, German academic and clerical elites did not protest; indeed, many agreed with the National Socialists' edicts. The Jews were simply abandoned.

Shaping the "New Man"

The Ministry of Popular Enlightenment, headed by Joseph Goebbels (1897–1945), controlled the

Young Nazis Burning Books in Salzburg, Austria, 1938. Heinrich Heine, the great nineteenth-century German-Jewish poet, once said that people who burn books end up burning people. *(© Topham/The Image Works)*

press, book publishing, the radio, the theater, and the cinema. Nazi propaganda sought to condition the mind to revere the fuehrer and to obey the new regime. Its intent was to deprive individuals of their capacity for independent thought. By concentrating on the myth of race and the infallibility of the fuehrer, Nazi propaganda tried to disorient the rational mind and to give the individual new standards to believe in and obey. Propaganda aimed to mold the entire nation to think and respond as the leader-state directed.

The regime made a special effort to reach young people. All youths between the ages of ten and eighteen were urged and then required to join the Hitler Youth, and all other youth organizations were dissolved. At camps and rallies, young people paraded, sang, saluted, and chanted: "We were slaves; we were outsiders in our own country. So were we before Hitler united us. Now we would fight against Hell itself for our leader."[23] The schools, long breeding grounds of national-

ism, militarism, antiliberalism, and anti-Semitism, now indoctrinated the young in Nazi ideology. The Nazis instructed teachers how certain subjects were to be taught, and to ensure obedience, members of the Hitler Youth were asked to report teachers who did not conform.

In May 1933, professors and students proudly burned books considered a threat to Nazi ideology. Many academics praised Hitler and the new regime. Some 10 percent of the university faculty, principally Jews, Social Democrats, and liberals, were dismissed, and their colleagues often approved. "From now on it will not be your job to determine whether something is true but whether it is in the spirit of the National Socialist revolution," the new minister of culture told university professors.[24] Numerous courses on "racial science" and Nazi ideology were introduced into the curriculum.

Symbolic of the Nazi regime were the monster rallies staged at Nuremberg. Scores of thousands roared, marched, and worshiped at their leader's feet. These true believers, the end product of Nazi indoctrination, celebrated Hitler's achievements and demonstrated their loyalty to their savior. Everything was brilliantly orchestrated to impress Germans and the world with the irresistible power, determination, and unity of the Nazi movement and the greatness of the fuehrer. Armies of youths waving flags, storm troopers bearing weapons, and workers shouldering long-handled spades paraded past Hitler, who stood at attention, his arm extended in the Nazi salute. The endless columns of marchers, the stirring martial music played by huge bands, the forest of flags, the chanting and cheering of spectators, and the burning torches and beaming spotlights united the participants into a racial community. "Wherever Hitler leads we follow," thundered thousands of Germans in a giant chorus.

Terror was another means of ensuring compliance and obedience. The instrument of terror was the SS, which was organized in 1925 to protect Hitler and other party leaders and to stand guard at party meetings. Under the leadership of Heinrich Himmler (1900–1945), a fanatical believer in Hitler's racial theories, the SS was molded into an elite force of disciplined, dedicated, and utterly ruthless men.

Mass Support

The Nazi regime became a police state, characterized by mass arrests, the persecution of Jews, and concentration camps that institutionalized terror. Yet fewer heads had rolled than people expected, and in many ways life seemed normal. The Nazis skillfully established the totalitarian state without upsetting the daily life of the great majority of the population. Moreover, Hitler, like Mussolini, was careful to maintain the appearance of legality. By not abolishing parliament or repealing the constitution, he could claim that his was a legitimate government.

To people concerned with little except family, job, and friends—and this includes most people in any country—life in the first few years of the Third Reich seemed quite satisfying. Most Germans believed that the new government was trying to solve Germany's problems in a vigorous and sensible

manner, in contrast to the ineffective Weimar leadership. By 1936, the invigoration of the economy, stimulated in part by rearmament, had virtually eliminated unemployment, which had stood at six million jobless when Hitler took power. An equally astounding achievement in the eyes of the German people was Hitler's bold termination of the humiliating Versailles treaty, the rebuilding of the German war machine, and the restoration of German power in international affairs. It seemed to most Germans that Hitler had awakened a sense of self-sacrifice and national dedication among a people dispirited by defeat and economic depression.

There was some opposition to the Hitler regime. Social Democrats and Communists in particular organized small cells. Some conservatives, who considered Hitler a threat to traditional German values, and some clergy, who saw Nazism as a pagan religion in conflict with Christian morality, also formed small opposition groups. But only the army could have toppled Hitler. Some generals, even before World War II, urged resistance, but the overwhelming majority of German officers preferred the new regime or were too concerned about their careers to do anything or considered it dishonorable to break their oath of loyalty to Hitler. Most of these officers would remain loyal until the bitter end. Very few Germans realized that their country was passing through a long night of barbarism, and still fewer considered resistance.

LIBERALISM AND AUTHORITARIANISM IN OTHER LANDS

After World War I, in country after country, parliamentary democracy collapsed and authoritarian leaders came to power. In most of these countries, liberal ideals had not penetrated deeply. Proponents of liberalism met resistance from conservative elites.

The Spread of Authoritarianism

Spain and Portugal In both Spain and Portugal, parliamentary regimes faced strong opposition from the church, the army, and large landowners. In 1926, army officers overthrew the Portuguese republic that had been created in 1910, and gradually Antonio de Oliveira Salazar (1889–1970), a professor of economics, emerged as dictator. In Spain, after antimonarchist forces won the election of 1931, King Alfonso XIII (1902–1931) left the country, and Spain was proclaimed a republic. But the new government, led by socialists and liberals, faced the determined opposition of the ruling elite. The reforms introduced by the republic—expropriation of large estates, reduction of the number of army officers, dissolution of the Jesuit order, and the closing of church schools—only intensified the Old Order's hatred.

The difficulties of the Spanish republic mounted: workers, near starvation, rioted and engaged in violent strikes; the military attempted a coup; and Catalonia, with its long tradition of separatism, tried to establish its autonomy. Imitating France (see below), the parties of the left, including the Communists, united in the Popular Front, which came to power in February 1936. In July 1936, General Francisco Franco (1892–1975), stationed in Spanish Morocco, led a revolt against the republic. He was supported by army leaders, the church, monarchists, landlords, industrialists, and the Falange, a newly formed fascist party. Spain was torn by a bloody civil war. Aided by Fascist Italy and Nazi Germany, Franco won in 1939 and established a dictatorship.

Eastern and Central Europe Parliamentary government in Eastern Europe rested on weak foundations. Predominantly rural, these countries lacked the sizable professional and commercial classes that had promoted liberalism in western Europe. Only Czechoslovakia had a substantial native middle class with a strong liberal tradition. The rural masses of eastern Europe, traditionally subjected to monarchical and aristocratic authority, were not used to political thinking or civic responsibility. Students and intellectuals, often gripped by a romantic nationalism, were drawn to antidemocratic movements. Right-wing leaders also played on the fear of communism. When parliamentary government failed to solve internal problems, the opponents of the liberal state seized the helm. Fascist movements, however, had little success in eastern Europe. Rather, authoritarian regimes headed by traditional ruling elites—army leaders or kings—extinguished democracy there.

The Western Democracies

While liberal governments were everywhere failing, the great Western democracies—the United States, Britain, and France—continued to preserve democratic institutions. In Britain and the United States, fascist movements were merely a nuisance. In France, however, fascism was more of a threat because it exploited a deeply ingrained hostility in some quarters to the liberal ideals of the French Revolution.

The United States The central problem faced by the Western democracies was the Great Depression, which started in the United States. In the 1920s, hundreds of thousands of Americans had bought stock on credit; this buying spree sent stock prices soaring well beyond what the stocks were actually worth. In late October 1929, the stock market was hit by a wave of panic selling, causing prices to plummet. Within a few weeks, the value of stocks listed on the New York Stock Exchange fell by some $26 billion. A ruinous chain reaction followed over the next few years. Businesses cut production and unemployment soared; farmers who were unable to meet mortgage payments lost their land; banks that had made poor investments closed down. American investors withdrew the capital they had invested in Europe, causing European banks and businesses to fail. Throughout the world, trade declined and unemployment rose.

When President Franklin Delano Roosevelt (1882–1945) took office in 1933, more than thirteen million Americans—one-quarter of the labor force—were out of work. Hunger and despair showed on the faces of the American people. Moving away from laissez faire, Roosevelt instituted a comprehensive program of national planning, economic experimentation, and reform known as the New Deal. Although the American political and economic system faced a severe test, few Americans turned to fascism or communism; the government engaged in national planning but did not break with democratic values and procedures.

Britain Even before the Great Depression, Britain faced severe economic problems. Loss of markets to foreign competitors hurt British manufacturing, mining, and shipbuilding; rapid development of water and oil power reduced the demand for British coal, and outdated mining equipment put Britain in a poor competitive position. To decrease costs, mine owners in 1926 called for salary cuts; the coal miners countered with a strike and were joined by workers in other industries. To many Britons, the workers were leftist radicals trying to overthrow the government. Many wanted the state to break the strike. After nine days, industrial workers called it off, but the miners held out for another six months; they returned to work with longer hours and lower pay. The general strike had failed. Because the workers had not called for revolution and had refrained from violence, the fear that British workers would follow the Bolshevik path abated.

The Great Depression cast a pall over Britain. The Conservative party leadership tried to stimulate exports by devaluing the pound and to encourage industry by providing loans at lower interest rates, but in the main, it left the task of recovery to industry itself. Not until Britain began to rearm did unemployment decline significantly. Despite the economic slump of the 1920s and the Great Depression, Britain remained politically stable, a testament to the strength of its parliamentary tradition. Neither the Communists nor the newly formed British Union of Fascists gained mass support.

France In the early 1920s, France was concerned with restoring villages, railroads, mines, and forests that had been ruined by the war. From 1926 to 1929, France was relatively prosperous; industrial and agricultural production expanded, tourism increased, and the currency was stable. Although France did not feel the Great Depression as painfully as the United States and Germany, the nation was hurt by the decline in trade and production and the rise in unemployment. The political instability that had beset the Third Republic virtually since its inception continued, and hostility to the republic mounted. The rift between liberals and conservatives, which had divided the country since the Revolution and had grown worse with the Dreyfus affair (see "France:

A Troubled Nation" in the chapter entitled "Europe in the Late Nineteenth Century: Modernization, Nationalism, and Imperialism"), continued to plague France during the Depression. As the leading parties failed to solve the nation's problems, a number of fascist groups gained strength.

Fear of growing fascist strength at home and in Italy and Germany led the parties of the left to form the Popular Front. In 1936, Léon Blum (1872–1950), a socialist and a Jew, became premier. Blum's Popular Front government instituted more reforms than any other ministry in the history of the Third Republic. To end a wave of strikes that tied up production, Blum gave workers a forty-hour week and holidays with pay and guaranteed them the right to collective bargaining. He took steps to nationalize the armaments and aircraft industries. To reduce the influence of the wealthiest families, he put the Bank of France under government control. By raising prices and buying wheat, he aided farmers. Conservatives and fascists denounced Blum as a Jewish socialist who was converting the fatherland into a communist state. "Better Hitler than Blum," grumbled French rightists.

Despite significant reforms, the Popular Front could not revitalize the economy. His political support eroding, Blum resigned in 1937, and the Popular Front, always a tenuous alliance, soon fell apart. Through democratic means, the Blum government had tried to give France its own New Deal, but the social reforms passed by the Popular Front only intensified hatred between the working classes and the rest of the nation. France had preserved democracy against the onslaught of domestic fascists, but it was a demoralized and divided nation that confronted a united and dynamic Nazi Germany.

INTELLECTUALS AND ARTISTS IN TROUBLED TIMES

The presuppositions of the Enlightenment, already eroding in the decades before World War I, seemed near collapse after 1918—another casualty of trench warfare. Economic distress, particularly during the Depression, also profoundly disoriented the European mind. Westerners no longer possessed a frame of reference, a common outlook for understanding themselves, their times, or the past. The core values of Western civilization—the self-sufficiency of reason, the inviolability of the individual, and the existence of objective norms—no longer seemed inspiring or binding.

The crisis of consciousness evoked a variety of responses. Some intellectuals, having lost faith in the essential meaning of Western civilization, turned their backs on it or found escape in their art. Others sought a new hope in the Soviet experiment or in fascism. Still others reaffirmed the rational humanist tradition of the Enlightenment. Repelled by the secularism, materialism, and rootlessness of the modern age, Christian thinkers urged westerners to find renewed meaning and purpose in their ancestral religion. A philosophical movement called existentialism, which rose to prominence after World War II, aspired to make life authentic in a world stripped of universal values.

Postwar Pessimism

After World War I, Europeans looked at themselves and their civilization differently. It seemed that in science and technology they had unleashed powers that they could not control, and belief in the stability and security of European civilization appeared to be an illusion. Also illusory was the expectation that reason would banish surviving signs of darkness, ignorance, and injustice and usher in an age of continual progress. European intellectuals felt that they were living in a "broken world." In an age of heightened brutality and mobilized irrationality, the values of old Europe seemed beyond recovery. "All the great words," wrote D. H. Lawrence "were cancelled out for that generation."[25] The fissures discernible in European civilization before 1914 had grown wider and deeper. To be sure, Europe also had its optimists—those who found reason for hope in the League of Nations and in the easing of international tensions and improved economic conditions in the mid-1920s. However, the Great Depression and the triumph of totalitarianism intensified feelings of doubt and disillusionment.

Expressions of pessimism abounded after World War I. In 1919, Paul Valéry stated: "We

modern civilizations have learned to recognize that we are mortal like the others. We feel that a civilization is as fragile as life."[26] "We are living today under the sign of the collapse of civilization,"[27] declared humanitarian Albert Schweitzer in 1923. German philosopher Karl Jaspers noted in 1932 that "there is a growing awareness of imminent ruin tantamount to a dread of the approaching end of all that makes life worthwhile."[28]

T. S. Eliot's "The Waste Land" (1922) also conveys a sense of foreboding. In his image of a collapsing European civilization, Eliot creates a macabre scenario. Hooded hordes, modern-day barbarians, swarm over plains and lay waste to cities. Jerusalem, Athens, Alexandria, Vienna, and London—each once a great spiritual or cultural center—are now "falling towers." Amid this destruction, one hears "high in the air / Murmur of maternal lamentation."[29]

Carl Gustav Jung, a Swiss psychologist, stated in *Modern Man in Search of a Soul* (1933):

> *I believe I am not exaggerating when I say that modern man has suffered an almost fatal shock, psychologically speaking, and as a result has fallen into profound uncertainty. . . . The revolution in our conscious outlook, brought about by the catastrophic results of the World War, shows itself in our inner life by the shattering of our faith in ourselves and our own worth. . . . I realize only too well that I am losing my faith in the possibility of a rational organization of the world, the old dream of the millennium, in which peace and harmony should rule, has grown pale.[30]*

In 1936, Dutch historian Johan Huizinga wrote in a chapter entitled "Apprehension of Doom":

> *We are living in a demented world. And we know it. . . . Everywhere there are doubts as to the solidity of our social structure, vague fears of the imminent future, a feeling that our civilization is on the way to ruin. . . . almost all things which once seemed sacred and immutable have now become unsettled, truth and humanity, justice and reason. . . . The sense of living in the midst of a violent crisis of civilization, threatening complete collapse, has spread far and wide.[31]*

The most influential expression of pessimism was Oswald Spengler's *The Decline of the West.* The first volume was published in July 1918, as the Great War was drawing to a close, and the second volume in 1922. The work achieved instant notoriety, particularly in Spengler's native Germany, shattered by defeat. Spengler viewed history as an assemblage of many different cultures, which, like living organisms, experience birth, youth, maturity, and death. What contemporaries pondered most was Spengler's insistence that Western civilization had entered its final stage and that its death could not be averted.

To an already troubled Western world, Spengler offered no solace. The West, like other cultures and like any living organism, was destined to die; its decline was irreversible and its death inevitable, and the symptoms of degeneration were already evident. Spengler's gloomy prognostication buttressed the fascists, who claimed that they were creating a new civilization on the ruins of the dying European civilization.

Literature and Art: Innovation, Disillusionment, and Social Commentary

Postwar pessimism did not prevent writers and artists from continuing the cultural innovations begun before the war. In the works of D. H. Lawrence, Marcel Proust, André Gide, James Joyce, Franz Kafka, T. S. Eliot, and Thomas Mann, the modernist movement achieved a brilliant flowering. Often these writers gave expression to the troubles and uncertainties of the postwar period.

Franz Kafka (1883–1924), a Czech Jew, grasped the dilemma of the modern age perhaps better than any other novelist of his generation. In Kafka's world, human beings are caught in a bureaucratic web that they cannot control. They live in a nightmare society dominated by oppressive, cruel, and corrupt officials and amoral torturers: a world where cruelty and injustice are accepted facts of existence, power is exercised without limits, and victims cooperate in their own destruction. Traditional values and ordinary logic do not operate in such a world. In *The Trial* (1925), for example, the hero is arrested without

Franz Kafka (1883–1924). The troubled Czech-Jewish writer expressed the feelings of alienation and aloneness that burden people in the modern age. *(Corbis/Bettmann)*

knowing why, and he is eventually executed, a victim of institutional evil that breaks and destroys him "like a dog." In these observations, Kafka proved to be a prophet of the emerging totalitarian state. (Kafka's three sisters perished in the Holocaust.)

Kafka expressed the feelings of alienation and isolation that characterize the modern individual; he explored life's dreads and absurdities, offering no solutions or consolation. In Kafka's works, people are defeated and unable to comprehend the irrational forces that contribute to their destruction. The mind yearns for coherence, but, Kafka tells us, uncertainty, if not chaos, governs human relationships. We can be sure neither of our own identities nor of the world we encounter, for human beings are the playthings of unfathomable forces, too irrational to master.

Before World War I, German writer Thomas Mann (1875–1955) had earned a reputation for his short stories and novels, particularly *Buddenbrooks* (1901), which portrays the decline of a prosperous bourgeois family. In *The Magic Mountain* (1924), Mann reflected on the decomposition of bourgeois European civilization. The setting for the story is a Swiss sanitarium whose patients, drawn from several European lands, suffer from tuberculosis. The sanitarium symbolizes Europe, and it is the European psyche that is diseased. *The Magic Mountain* raised, but did not resolve, crucial questions. Was the epoch of rational humanist culture drawing to a close? Did Europeans welcome their spiritual illness in the same way that some of the patients in the sanitarium had a will to illness? How could Europe rescue itself from decadence?

In 1931, two years before Hitler took power, Mann, in an article entitled "An Appeal to Reason," described National Socialism and the extreme nationalism it espoused as a rejection of the Western rational tradition and a regression to primitive and barbaric modes of behavior. Nazism, he wrote, "is distinguished by . . . its absolute unrestraint, its orgiastic, radically anti-humane, frenziedly dynamic character. . . . Everything is possible, everything is permitted as a weapon against human decency. . . . Fanaticism turns into a means of salvation . . . politics becomes an opiate for the masses . . . and reason veils her face."[32]

Shattered by World War I, disgusted by fascism's growing strength, and moved by the suffering caused by the Depression, many writers became committed to social and political causes. Erich Maria Remarque's *All Quiet on the Western Front* (1929) was one of many antiwar novels. George Orwell's *The Road to Wigan Pier* (1937) recorded the bleak lives of English coal miners. In *The Grapes of Wrath* (1939), John Steinbeck captured the anguish of American farmers driven from their land by the Dust Bowl and foreclosure during the Depression. Few issues stirred the conscience of intellectuals as did the Spanish Civil War, and many of them volunteered to fight with the Spanish republicans against the fascists. Ernest Hemingway's *For Whom the Bell Tolls* (1940) expressed the sentiments of these thinkers.

The new directions taken in art before World War I—abstractionism and expressionism—continued in the postwar decades. Picasso, Mondrian, Kandinsky, Matisse, Rouault, Braque, Modigliani, and other masters continued to refine their styles. In addition, new art trends emerged, mirroring the trauma of a generation that had experienced the war and lost its faith in Europe's moral and intellectual values.

In 1915 in Zurich, artists and writers founded a movement, called Dada, to express their revulsion against the war and the civilization that spawned it. From neutral Switzerland, the movement spread to Germany and Paris. Dada shared in the postwar mood of disorientation and despair. Dadaists viewed life as essentially absurd (*Dada* is a nonsense term) and cultivated indifference. "The acts of life have no beginning or end. Everything happens in a completely idiotic way,"[33] declared the poet Tristan Tzara, one of Dada's founders and its chief spokesman. Dadaists expressed contempt for artistic and literary standards and rejected both God and reason. "Through reason man becomes a tragic and ugly figure," said one Dadaist; "beauty is dead," said another. Tzara declared:

> *What good did the theories of the philosophers do us? Did they help us to take a single step forward or backward? . . . We have had enough of the intelligent movements that have stretched beyond measure our credulity in the benefits of science. What we want now is spontaneity. . . . because everything that issues freely from ourselves, without the intervention of speculative ideas, represents us.*[34]

For Dadaists, the world was nonsensical and reality disordered; hence, they offered no solutions to anything. "Like everything in life, Dada is useless,"[35] said Tzara. Despite their nihilistic aims and "calculated irrationality," however, Dadaist artists, such as Marcel Duchamp, were innovative and creative.

Dada ended as a formal movement in 1924 and was succeeded by surrealism. Surrealists inherited from Dada a contempt for reason; they stressed fantasy and made use of Freudian insights and symbols in their art to reproduce the raw state of

Angel of Hearth and Home by Max Ernst (1891–1976). Ernst formed part of the transition from Dada to surrealism. His paintings expressed a profound anxiety. André Breton called him "the most magnificently haunted mind in Europe." *(© 2000 Artists Rights Society (ARS), New York/ADAGP, Paris)*

the unconscious and to arrive at truths beyond reason's grasp. In their attempt to break through the constraints of rationality to reach a higher reality—that is, a "surreality"—leading surrealists such as Max Ernst (1891– 1976), Salvador Dali (1904–1989), and Joan Mir— (1893–1983) produced works of undeniable artistic merit.

Like writers, artists expressed a social conscience. George Grosz combined a Dadaist sense of life's meaninglessness with a new realism to depict the moral degeneration of middle-class German society. In *After the Questioning* (1935), Grosz, then living in the United States, dramatized Nazi brutality; in *The End of the World* (1936), he expressed his fear of another impending world war. Käthe Kollwitz, also a German artist, showed a deep compassion for the sufferer: the unemployed, the hungry, the ill, and the politically oppressed. William Gropper's *Migration* (1932) dramatized the suffering of the same dis-

possessed farmers described in Steinbeck's novel *The Grapes of Wrath*. Philip Evergood, in *Don't Cry Mother* (1938–1944), portrayed the apathy of starving children and their mother's terrible helplessness.

In his etchings of maimed, dying, and dead soldiers, German artist Otto Dix produced a powerful visual indictment of the Great War's cruelty and suffering. Max Beckmann's service in the German army during World War I made him acutely aware of violence and brutality, which he expressed in *The Night* (1918–19) and other paintings. Designated a "degenerate artist" by the Nazis, Beckmann went into exile. In *Guernica* (1937), Picasso memorialized the Spanish village decimated by saturation bombing during the Spanish Civil War. In the *White Crucifixion* (1938), Marc Chagall, a Russian-born Jew who had settled in Paris, depicted the terror and flight of Jews in Nazi Germany.

Communism: "The God That Failed"

The economic misery of the Depression and the rise of fascist barbarism led many intellectuals to find a new hope, even a secular faith, in communism. They praised the Soviet Union for supplanting capitalist greed with socialist cooperation, for replacing a haphazard economic system marred by repeated depressions with one based on planned production, and for providing employment for everyone when joblessness was endemic in capitalist lands. American literary critic Edmund Wilson said that in the Soviet Union one felt at the "moral top of the world where the light never really goes out."[36] To these intellectuals, it seemed that in the Soviet Union a vigorous and healthy civilization was emerging and that only communism could stem the tide of fascism. For many, however, the attraction was short-lived. Sickened by Stalin's purges and terror, the denial of individual freedom, and the suppression of truth, they came to view the Soviet Union as another totalitarian state and communism as another "god that failed."

One such intellectual was Arthur Koestler (1905–1983). Born in Budapest of Jewish ancestry and educated in Vienna, Koestler worked as a correspondent for a leading Berlin newspaper chain. He joined the Communist party at the very end of 1931 because he "lived in a disintegrating society thirsting for faith," was moved by the misery caused by the Depression, and saw communism as the "only force capable of resisting the onrush of the primitive [Nazi] horde."[37] Koestler visited the Soviet Union in 1933, experiencing firsthand both the starvation brought on by forced collectivization and the propaganda that grotesquely misrepresented life in Western lands. While his faith was shaken, he did not break with the party until 1938, in response to Stalin's liquidations.

In *Darkness at Noon* (1941), Koestler explored the attitudes of the Old Bolsheviks who were imprisoned, tortured, and executed by Stalin. These dedicated Communists had served the party faithfully, but Stalin, fearing opposition, hating intellectuals, and driven by megalomania, denounced them as enemies of the people. In *Darkness at Noon,* the leading character, the imprisoned Rubashov, is a composite of the Old Bolsheviks. Although innocent, Rubashov, without being physically tortured, publicly confesses to political crimes that he never committed.

Rubashov is aware of the suffering that the party has brought to the Russian people:

> [I]n the interests of a just distribution of land we deliberately let die of starvation about five million farmers and their families in one year.... [To liberate] human beings from the shackles of industrial exploitation . . . we sent about ten million people to do forced labour in the Arctic regions . . . under conditions similar to those of antique galley slaves.[38]

Pained by his own complicity in the party's crimes, including the betrayal of friends, Rubashov questions the party's philosophy that the individual should be subordinated, and, if necessary, sacrificed to the regime. Nevertheless, Rubashov remains the party's faithful servant; true believers do not easily break with their faith. By confessing, Rubashov performs his last service for the revolution. For the true believer, everything—truth, justice, and the sanctity of the individual—is properly sacrificed to the party.

Reaffirming the Christian World-View

By calling into question core liberal beliefs—the essential goodness of human nature, the primacy of reason, the efficacy of science, and the inevitability of progress—World War I led thinkers to find in Christianity an alternative view of the human experience and the crisis of the twentieth century. Christian thinkers, including Karl Barth, Paul Tillich, Reinhold Niebuhr, Christopher Dawson, Jacques Maritain, and T. S. Eliot, affirmed the reality of evil in human nature. They assailed liberals and Marxists for holding too optimistic a view of human nature and human reason and for postulating a purely rational and secular philosophy of history. For these thinkers, the Christian conception of history as a clash between human will and God's commands provided an intelligible explanation of the tragedies of the twentieth century. They agreed with the leading French Catholic thinker Jacques Maritain (1882–1973), who argued that "anthropomorphic humanism," which held that human beings by themselves alone can define life's purpose and create their own values, had utterly failed. Without guidance from a transcendental source, Maritain insisted, reason is powerless to control irrational drives, which threaten to degrade human existence. Without commitment to God's values, we find substitute faiths in fanatic and belligerent ideologies and unscrupulous leaders. For democracy to survive, he said, it must be infused with Christian love and compassion.

Reaffirming the Ideals of Reason and Freedom

Several thinkers tried to reaffirm the ideals of rationality and freedom that had been trampled by totalitarian movements. In *The Treason of the Intellectuals* (1927), Julien Benda (1867–1956), a French cultural critic of Jewish background, castigated intellectuals for intensifying hatred between nations, classes, and political factions. "Our age is indeed the age of the *intellectual organization of political hatreds*," he wrote. These intellectuals, said Benda, do not pursue justice or truth but proclaim that "even if our country is wrong, we must think of it in the right." They scorn outsiders, extol harshness and action, and proclaim the superiority of instinct and will to intelligence; or they "assert that the intelligence to be venerated is that which limits its activities within the bounds of national interest." The logical end of this xenophobia, said Benda, "is the organized slaughter of nations and classes."[39]

José Ortega y Gasset (1883–1955), descendant of a noble Spanish family and a professor of philosophy, gained international recognition with the publication of *The Revolt of the Masses* (1930). According to Ortega, European civilization, the product of a creative elite, was degenerating into barbarism because of the growing power of the masses, for the masses lacked the mental discipline and commitment to reason needed to preserve Europe's intellectual and cultural traditions.

Ortega did not equate the masses with the working class and the elite with the nobility; it was an attitude of mind, not a class affiliation, that distinguished the "mass-man" from the elite.

The mass-man, said Ortega, has a commonplace mind and does not set high standards for himself. Faced with a problem, he "is satisfied with thinking the first thing he finds in his head," and "crushes . . . everything that is different, everything that is excellent, individual, qualified, and select. Anybody who is not like everybody, who does not think like everybody, runs the risk of being eliminated."[40] Such intellectually vulgar people, declared Ortega, cannot understand or preserve the processes of civilization. The fascists, for him, exemplified this revolt of the masses:

> Under Fascism there appears for the first time in Europe a type of man who does not want to give reasons or to be right, but simply shows himself resolved to impose his opinions. This is the new thing: the right not to be reasonable, the "reason of unreason." Hence I see the most palpable manifestation of the new mentality of the masses, due to their having decided to rule society without the capacity for doing so.[41]

Since the mass-man does not respect the tradition of reason, he does not enter into rational dialogue with others or defend his opinions logically, said Ortega. Rejecting reason, the mass-man glorifies violence—the ultimate expression of barbarism. As Ortega saw it, if European civilization was to be rescued from fascism and communism, the elite must sustain civilized values and provide leadership for the masses.

A staunch defender of the Enlightenment tradition, Ernst Cassirer (1874–1945), a German philosopher of Jewish lineage, emigrated after Hitler came to power, eventually settling in the United States. Just prior to Hitler's triumph, in 1932, Cassirer wrote about the need to uphold and reenergize that tradition: "More than ever before, it seems to me, the time is again ripe for applying . . . self-criticism to the present age, for holding up to it that bright clear mirror fashioned by the Enlightenment. . . . The age which venerated reason and science as man's highest faculty cannot and must not be lost even for us."[42]

In his last work, *The Myth of the State* (1946), Cassirer described Nazism as the triumph of mythical thinking over reason. The Nazis, he wrote, cleverly manufactured myths—of the race, the leader, the party, the state—that disoriented the intellect. The Germans who embraced these myths surrendered their capacity for independent judgment, leaving themselves vulnerable to manipulation by the Nazi leadership. To contain the destructive powers of political myths, Cassirer urged strengthening the rational humanist tradition and called for the critical study of political myths, for "in order to fight an enemy you must know him. . . . We should carefully study the origin, the structure, the methods, and the technique of the political myths. We should see the adversary face to face in order to know how to combat him."[43]

George Orwell (1903–1950), a British novelist and political journalist, wrote two powerful indictments of totalitarianism: *Animal Farm* (1945) and *1984* (1949). In *Animal Farm,* based in part on his experiences with Communists during the Spanish Civil War, Orwell satirized the totalitarian regime built by Lenin and Stalin in Russia. In *1984,* Orwell, who was deeply committed to human dignity and freedom, warned that these great principles were now permanently menaced by the concentration and abuse of political power. "If you want a picture of the future, imagine a boot stamping on a human face forever," says a member of the ruling elite as he tortures a victim in the dungeons of the Thought Police.[44]

The society of *1984* is ruled by the Inner Party, which constitutes some 2 percent of the population. Heading the Party is Big Brother—most likely a mythical figure created by the ruling elite to satisfy people's yearning for a leader. The Party indoctrinates people to love Big Brother, whose picture is everywhere. The Ministry of Truth resorts to thought control to dominate and manipulate the masses and to keep Party members loyal and subservient. Independent thinking is destroyed. Objective truth no longer exists. Truth is whatever the Party decrees at the moment. If the Party were to proclaim that two plus two equals five, it would have to be believed.

Anyone thinking prohibited thoughts is designated a thought-criminal, a crime punishable by death. The Thought Police's agents are everywhere, using hidden microphones and telescreens to check on Party members for any signs of deviance from Party rules and ideology. Posters displaying Big Brother's picture carry the words "BIG BROTHER IS WATCHING YOU." Convinced that "who controls the past controls the future," the Ministry of Truth alters old newspapers to make the past accord with the Party's current doctrine. In this totalitarian society of the future, all human rights are abolished, people are arrested merely for their thoughts, and children spy on their parents.

EXISTENTIALISM

The philosophical movement that best exemplified the anxiety and uncertainty of Europe in an era of world wars was existentialism. Like writers and artists, existentialist philosophers were responding to a European civilization that seemed to be in the throes of dissolution. Although existentialism was most popular after World War II, expressing the anxiety and despair of many intellectuals who had lost confidence in reason and progress, several of its key works were written prior to or during the war.

What route should people take in a world where old values and certainties had dissolved, where universal truth was rejected and God's existence denied? How could people cope in a society where they were menaced by technology, manipulated by impersonal bureaucracies, and overwhelmed by feelings of anxiety? If the universe lacks any overarching meaning, what meaning could one give to one's own life? These questions were at the crux of existentialist philosophy.

Existentialism does not lend itself to a single definition, since its principal theorists did not adhere to a common body of doctrines. For example, some existentialists were atheists, like Jean Paul Sartre, or omitted God from their thought, like Martin Heidegger; others, like Karl Jaspers, believed in God but not in Christian doctrines; still others, like Gabriel Marcel and Nikolai Berdyaev, were Christians; and Martin Buber was a believing Jew. Perhaps the following principles contain the essence of existentialism, although not all existentialists would subscribe to each point or agree with the way it is expressed.

Jean Paul Sartre and Simone de Beauvoir. Existentialism was a major philosophical movement of the twentieth century. Sartre and de Beauvoir were two of its principal exponents. *(Corbis/Sygma/G. Pierre)*

1. Reality defies ultimate comprehension; there are no timeless truths that exist independently of and prior to the individual human being. Our existence precedes and takes precedence over any presumed absolute values. The moral and spiritual values that society tries to impose cannot define the individual person's existence.

2. Reason alone is an inadequate guide to living, for people are more than thinking subjects who approach the world through critical analysis. They are also feeling and willing beings, who must participate fully in life and experience existence directly, actively, and passionately. Only in this way does one live wholly and authentically.

3. Thought must not merely be abstract speculation but must have a bearing on life; it must be translated into deeds.

4. Human nature is problematic and paradoxical, not fixed or constant; each person is like no other. Self-realization comes when one affirms one's own uniqueness. One becomes less than human when one permits one's life to be determined by a mental outlook—a set of rules and values—imposed by others.

5. We are alone. The universe is indifferent to our expectations and needs, and death is ever stalking us. Awareness of this elementary fact of existence evokes a sense of overwhelming anxiety and depression.

6. Existence is essentially absurd. There is no purpose to our presence in the universe. We simply find ourselves here; we do not know and will never find out why. Compared with the eternity of time that preceded our birth and will follow our death, the short duration of our existence seems trivial and inexplicable. And death, which irrevocably terminates our existence, testifies to the ultimate absurdity of life.

7. We are free. We must face squarely the fact that existence is purposeless and absurd. In doing so, we can give our life meaning. It is in the act of choosing freely from among different possibilities that the individual shapes an authentic existence. There is a dynamic quality to human existence; the individual has the potential to become more than he or she is.

THE MODERN PREDICAMENT

The process of fragmentation in European thought and arts, which had begun at the end of the nineteenth century, accelerated after World War I. Increasingly, philosophers, writers, and artists expressed disillusionment with the rational-humanist tradition of the Enlightenment. They no longer shared the Enlightenment's confidence in either reason's capabilities or human goodness, and they viewed perpetual progress as an illusion.

For some thinkers, the crucial problem was the great change in the European understanding of truth. Since the rise of philosophy in ancient Greece, Western thinkers had believed in the existence of objective, universal truths: truths that were inherent in nature and applied to all peoples at all times. (Christianity, of course, also taught the reality of truth as revealed by God.) It was held that such truths—the natural rights of the individual, for example—could be apprehended by the intellect and could serve as a standard for individual aspirations and social life. The recognition of these universal principles, it was believed, compelled people to measure the world of the here-and-now in the light of rational and universal norms and to institute appropriate reforms. It was the task of philosophy to reconcile human existence with the objective order.

During the nineteenth century, the existence of universal truth came into doubt. A growing historical consciousness led some thinkers to maintain that what people considered truth was merely a reflection of their culture at a given stage in history—their perception of things at a specific point in the evolution of human consciousness. These thinkers held that universal truths were not woven into the fabric of nature. There were no natural rights of life, liberty, and

property that constituted the individual's birthright; there were no standards of justice or equality inherent in nature and ascertainable by reason. Rather, people themselves elevated the beliefs and values of an age to the status of objective truth. The normative principles—the self-evident truths proclaimed by Jefferson—which for the philosophes constituted a standard for political and social reform and a guarantee of human rights, were no longer linked to the natural order, to an objective reality that could be confirmed by reason. As Hannah Arendt noted, "We certainly no longer believe, as the men of the French Revolution did, in a universal cosmos of which man was a part and whose natural laws he had to imitate and conform to."[45]

This radical break with the traditional attitude toward truth contributed substantially to the crisis of European consciousness that marked the first half of the twentieth century. Traditional values and beliefs, whether those inherited from the Enlightenment or those taught by Christianity, no longer gave Europeans a sense of certainty and security. People were left without a normative order to serve as a guide to living—and without such a guide might be open to nihilism. For if nothing is fundamentally true—if there are no principles of morality and justice that emanate from God or can be derived from reason—then it can be concluded, as Nietzsche understood, that everything is permitted. Some scholars interpreted Nazism as the culminating expression of a nihilistic attitude grown ever more brutal.

By the early twentieth century, the attitude of westerners toward reason had undergone a radical transformation. Some thinkers, who had placed their hopes in the rational tradition of the Enlightenment, were distressed by reason's inability to resolve the tensions and conflicts of modern industrial society. Moreover, the growing recognition of the nonrational—of human actions determined by hidden impulses—led people to doubt that reason played the dominant role in human behavior. Other thinkers viewed the problem of reason differently. They assailed the attitude of mind that found no room for Christianity because its teachings did not pass the test of reason and science. Or they attacked reason for fashioning a technological and bureaucratic society that devalued and crushed human passions and stifled individuality. These thinkers insisted that human beings cannot fulfill their potential, cannot live wholly, if their feelings are denied. They agreed with D. H. Lawrence's critique of rationalism: "The attribution of rationality to human nature, instead of enriching it, now seems to me to have impoverished it. It ignored certain powerful and valuable springs of feeling. Some of the spontaneous, irrational outbursts of human nature can have a sort of value from which our schematism was cut off."[46]

While many thinkers focused on reason's limitations, others, particularly existentialists, pointed out that reason was a double-edged sword: it could demean, as well as ennoble and liberate, the individual. These thinkers attacked all theories that subordinated the individual to a rigid system. They denounced positivism for reducing human personality to psychological laws and Marxism for making social class a higher reality than the individual. They rebelled against political collectivization, which regulated individual lives according to the needs of the corporate state. They also assailed modern technology and bureaucracy, creations of the rational mind, for fashioning a social order that devalued and depersonalized the individual, denying people an opportunity for independent growth and a richer existence. According to these thinkers, modern industrial society, in its drive for efficiency and uniformity, deprived people of their uniqueness and reduced flesh-and-blood human beings to mere cogs in a mechanical system.

Responding to the critics of reason, its defenders insisted that it was necessary to reaffirm the rational tradition first proclaimed by the Greeks and given its modern expression by the Enlightenment. Reason, they maintained, was indispensable to civilization. What these thinkers advocated was broadening the scope of reason to accommodate the insights into human nature advanced by the romantics, Nietzsche, Freud, modernist writers and artists, and others who explored the world of feelings, will, and the subconscious. They also stressed the need to humanize reason so that it could never threaten to reduce a human being to a thing—a mere instrument used to realize some socioeconomic blueprint.

In the decades shaped by world wars and totalitarianism, intellectuals raised questions that went to the heart of the dilemma of modern life. How can civilized life be safeguarded against human irrationality, particularly when it is channeled into political ideologies that idolize the state, the leader, the party, or the race? How can individual human personality be rescued from a relentless rationalism that organizes the individual as it would any material object? Do the values associated with the Enlightenment provide a sound basis on which to integrate society? Can the individual find meaning in what many now regarded as a meaningless universe? World War II and the Holocaust gave these questions a special poignancy.

❖   ❖   ❖

NOTES

1. Hannah Arendt, *The Origins of Totalitarianism* (New York: World, Meridian Books, 1958), p. 469.

2. Karl Dietrich Bracher, *The Age of Ideologies*, trans. Erwald Osers (New York: St. Martin's Press, 1984), p. 83.

3. Quoted in Omer Bartov, *Hitler's Army: Soldiers, Nazis, and War in the Third Reich* (New York: Oxford University Press, 1992), p. 166.

4. V. I. Lenin, "The Immediate Tasks of the Soviet Government," in *The Lenin Anthology,* ed. Robert C. Tucker (New York: Norton, 1975), pp. 448 ff.

5. J. V. Stalin, "Speech to Business Executives" (1931), in *A Documentary History of Communism from Lenin to Mao*, ed. Robert V. Daniels (New York: Random House, 1960), 2:22.

6. Quoted in Isaac Deutscher, *Stalin: A Political Biography* (New York: Oxford University Press, 1966), p. 325.

7. Excerpted in T. H. Rigby, ed., *Stalin* (Englewood Cliffs, N.J.: Prentice-Hall, 1966), p. 111.

8. Quoted in Zeev Sternhill, "Fascist Ideology," in *Fascism: A Reader's Guide,* ed. Walter Laqueur (Berkeley: University of California Press, 1976), p. 338.

9. Quoted in John Weiss, *The Fascist Tradition* (New York: Harper & Row, 1967), p. 9.

10. Quoted in Max Gallo, *Mussolini's Italy* (New York: Macmillan, 1973), p. 218.

11. Quoted in Joachim C. Fest, *Hitler,* trans. Richard and Clara Winston (New York: Harcourt Brace Jovanovich, 1974), p. 162.

12. *Hitler's Secret Conversations, 1941–1944,* with an introductory essay by H. R. Trevor Roper (New York: Farrar, Straus & Young, 1953), p. 28.

13. Quoted in Lucy S. Dawidowicz, *The War Against the Jews 1933–1945* (New York: Holt, Rinehart & Winston, 1975), p. 21.

14. Quoted in Uri Tal, "Consecration of Politics in the Nazi Era," in *Judaism and Christianity Under the Impact of National Socialism,* ed. Otto Dov Kulka and Paul R. Mendes Flohr (Jerusalem: Historical Society of Israel, 1987), p. 70.

15. Adolf Hitler, *Mein Kampf* (Boston: Houghton Mifflin, 1962), p. 107.

16. Ibid., p. 479.

17. Quoted in Zbigniew Brzezinski, *Out of Control* (New York: Charles Scribner's Sons, 1993) p. 19.

18. Quoted in David Welch, ed., *Nazi Propaganda* (Totowa, N.J.: Barnes & Noble, 1983), p. 5.

19. Quoted in J. S. Conway, *The Nazi Persecution of the Churches* (New York: Basic Books, 1968), p. 202.

20. Quoted in Helmut Krausnick, Hans Buchheim, Martin Broszart, and Hans-Adolf Jacobsen, *Anatomy of the SS State* (London: Collins, 1968), p. 128.

21. *Hitler's Secret Conversations,* p. 6.

22. Quoted in Hermann Graml et al., *The German Resistance to Hitler* (Berkeley: University of California Press, 1970), p. 206.

23. Quoted in T. L. Jarman, *The Rise and Fall of Nazi Germany* (New York: New York University Press, 1956), p. 182.

24. Quoted in Karl Dietrich Bracher, *The German Dictatorship,* trans. Jean Steinberg (New York: Praeger, 1970), p. 268.

25. Quoted in Barbara Tuchman, *The Guns of August* (New York: Macmillan, 1962), p. 489.

26. Quoted in Hans Kohn, "The Crisis in European Thought and Culture," in *World War I: A Turning Point in Modern History,* ed. Jack J. Roth (New York: Alfred A. Knopf, 1967), p. 28.

27. Quoted in Franklin L. Baumer, "Twentieth-Century Version of the Apocalypse," *Cahiers d'Histoire Mondiale (Journal of World History),* 1 (January 1954): 624.

28. Ibid.

29. T. S. Eliot, "The Waste Land," in *Collected Poems, 1909–1962* (New York: Harcourt, Brace, 1970), p. 67.

30. Carl Gustav Jung, *Modern Man in Search of a Soul,* trans. W. S. Dell and Cary F. Baynes (New York: Harcourt, Brace, 1933), pp. 231, 234–235.

31. Johan Huizinga, *In the Shadow of Tomorrow* (London: Heinemann, 1936), pp. 1–3.

32. Thomas Mann, "An Appeal to Reason," excerpted in *Sources of the Western Tradition,* ed. Marvin Perry et al., 5th ed. (Boston: Houghton Mifflin, 1991), vol. 2, 366–367.

33. Tristan Tzara, "Lecture on Dada (1922)," trans. Ralph Mannheim, in *The Dada Painters and Poets,* ed. Robert Motherwell (New York: Witterborn, Schultz, 1951), p. 250.

34. Ibid., p. 248.

35. Ibid., p. 251.

36. Quoted in David Caute, *The Fellow Travellers* (New York: Macmillan, 1973), p. 64.

37. Richard Crossman, ed., *The God That Failed* (New York: Bantam Books, 1951), pp. 15, 21.

38. Arthur Koestler, *Darkness at Noon* (New York: Macmillan, 1941), pp. 158–159.

39. Julien Benda, *The Betrayal of the Intellectuals,* trans. Richard Aldington (Boston: Beacon,

1955), pp. 21, 38, 122, 162. The book is commonly known by its first translation, *The Treason of the Intellectuals.*

40. José Ortega y Gasset, *The Revolt of the Masses* (New York: Norton, 1957), pp. 63, 18.

41. Ibid., p. 73.

42. Ernst Cassirer, *The Philosophy of the Enlightenment,* trans. Fritz C. A. Koelln and James P. Pettegrove (Boston: Beacon, 1955), pp. xi–xii.

43. Ernst Cassirer, *The Myth of the State* (New Haven, Conn.: Yale University Press, 1946), p. 296.

44. George Orwell, *1984* (New York: Harcourt, Brace, 1949; paperback, The New American Library, 1961), p. 220.

45. Cited in Harry S. Kariel, *In Search of Authority* (Glencoe, Ill.: The Free Press, 1964), p. 246.

46. Quoted in Anthony Arblaster, *The Rise and Decline of Western Liberalism* (Oxford: Basil Blackwell, 1984), p. 81.

SUGGESTED READING

Allen, William Sheridan, *The Nazi Seizure of Power* (1965). An illuminating study of how the people of a small German town reacted to Nazism during the years 1930–1935.

Barrett, William, *Irrational Man* (1958). Especially good on the intellectual and cultural roots of existentialism.

Bissel, Richard, ed., *Life in the Third Reich* (1987). Essays dealing with various aspects of life in Hitler's Germany; good overviews.

Blackham, H. J., *Six Existentialist Thinkers* (1952). Useful analyses of Kierkegaard, Nietzsche, Jaspers, Marcel, Heidegger, and Jean Paul Sartre.

———, ed., *Reality, Man and Existence* (1965). Essential works of existentialism.

Bracher, Karl Dietrich, *The German Dictatorship* (1970). A highly regarded analysis of all phases of the Nazi state.

Broszat, Martin, *The Hitler State* (1981). A detailed anatomy of the internal structure of the Third Reich.

Bullock, Alan, *Hitler: A Study in Tyranny* (1964). An excellent biography.

Burleigh, Michael, and Wolfgang Wippermann, *The Racial State: Germany 1933–1945* (1991). Persecution of Jews, Gypsies, mentally handicapped, and homosexuals; analysis of racially motivated social policies of the Nazi regime.

Cassels, Alan, *Fascist Italy* (1968). A clearly written introduction.

Conquest, Robert, *The Harvest of Sorrow: Soviet Collectivization and the Terror-Famine* (1986). The human consequences of collectivization.

Cruickshank, John, ed., *Aspects of the Modern European Mind* (1969). A useful collection of sources in modern intellectual history.

Fest, Joachim C., *Hitler* (1974). An excellent biography.

Fischer, Klaus, *Nazi Germany: A New History* (1995). An excellent synthesis.

Jackel, Eberhard, *Hitler's Weltanschauung* (1972). An analysis of Hitler's world-view.

Kershaw, Ian, *The Nazi Dictatorship: Problems of Interpretation* (2000). A masterful work of synthesis. Kershaw is also the author of an internationally acclaimed two-volume biography of Hitler.

Laqueur, Walter, ed., *Fascism: A Reader's Guide* (1976). A superb collection of essays.

Mack Smith, Denis, *Mussolini* (1982). By a leading historian of modern Italy.

Macquarrie, John, *Existentialism* (1972). A lucid discussion of existentialism.

Mandelstam, Nadezhda, *Hope Against Hope: A Memoir* (1976). A searing account of life during Stalin's purges by the widow of one of the victims.

Medvedev, Roy, *Let History Judge: The Origins and Consequences of Stalinism,* rev. ed. (1990). Includes newly available material on Stalin's crimes of the 1930s.

Paxton, Robert O., *Europe in the Twentieth Century* (1975). A first-rate text, with an excellent bibliography.

Peukert, Detlev J. K., *Inside Nazi Germany* (1982). How ordinary citizens responded to Nazi rule.

Razgon, Lev, *True Stories* (1997). A survivor's account of Stalin's camps.

Rees, Laurence, *The Nazis: A Warning from History* (1997). A companion volume to the BBC documentary, its principal virtue lies in the testimonies of former Nazis.

Reuth, Ralf Georg, *Goebbels* (1993). A highly acclaimed biography newly translated into English.

Rosenbaum, Ron, *Explaining Hitler* (1998). Interviews with leading historians about Hitler's life and career. The author knows how to ask questions and interpret answers.

Rosenthal, Bernice Glatzer, *New Myths, New World: From Nietzsche, to Stalinism* (2002). This pioneering work shows how Nietzsche's thought became part of Russian culture and influenced Bolshevism and Stalinism.

Spielvogel, Jackson J., *Hitler and Nazi Germany* (1988). Clearly written, up-to-date survey.

Volkogonov, Dmitri, *Stalin: Triumph and Tragedy* (1991). The first Soviet biography based on hitherto unavailable archive material.

Von Laue, Theodore H., *Why Lenin? Why Stalin? Why Gorbachev?* 3rd ed. (1993). A brief survey of the rise and fall of the Soviet Union.

Wagar, W. Warren, ed., *European Thought Since 1914* (1968). A valuable collection of sources.

REVIEW QUESTIONS

1. How does twentieth-century totalitarianism differ from earlier autocracies?

2. Why did the tsarist regime collapse in March 1917?

3. Why did the Provisional Government and liberal democracy fail in 1917?

4. Why, by contrast, were the Bolsheviks successful in seizing and holding power from 1917 to 1921?

5. What were the purpose and the effects of the Five-Year Plans?

6. How did the Soviet leaders view the position of Russia in the world? What were their aims and ambitions? How did their goals compare with those of other states?

7. What were Stalin's motives and justifications for the terror purges?

8. How did fascist principles "stand for the sheer, categorical, definitive antithesis to the world of democracy . . . to the world which still abides by the fundamental principles laid down in 1789"?

9. Why did some Italians support Mussolini? In what ways was Mussolini less effective than Hitler in establishing a totalitarian state?

10. How was Hitler's outlook shaped by his experiences in Vienna? What were his attitudes toward democracy, the masses, war, the Jews, and propaganda?

11. How did the Nazis extend their control over Germany?

12. How did Nazism conflict with the core values of Christianity? What was the general policy of the Nazis toward the churches? Why did the German churches by and large fail to take a stand against the Nazi regime?

13. By 1939, most Germans were enthusiastic about the Nazi regime. Discuss this statement.

14. After World War I, in country after country, parliamentary democracy collapsed and authoritarian leaders came to power. Explain.

15. How did the United States, Britain, and France try to cope with the Great Depression?

16. What factors contributed to the mood of pessimism in the period after World War I?

17. Better than any other novelist of his time, Franz Kafka grasped the dilemma of the modern age. Discuss this statement. Do his insights still apply?

18. In *The Magic Mountain*, Thomas Mann reflected on the decomposition of bourgeois European civilization. Discuss this statement.

19. In what ways were both Dada and surrealism an expression of the times?

20. Why were many intellectuals attracted to communism in the 1930s?

21. What did Ortega y Gasset mean by the "mass-man"? What dangers did the mass-man present?

22. Why did Julien Benda entitle his book *The Treason of the Intellectuals*?

23. What was Ernst Cassirer's attitude toward the Enlightenment? How did he interpret Nazism?

24. What were some of the conditions that gave rise to existentialism? What are the basic principles of existentialism?

Chapter 20

World War II: Western Civilization in the Balance

- ■ **The Road to War**
- ■ **The Nazi Blitzkrieg**
- ■ **The New Order**
- ■ **The Turn of the Tide**
- ■ **The Legacy of World War II**

*F*rom the early days of his political career, Hitler dreamed of forging a vast German empire in central and eastern Europe. He believed that only by waging a war of conquest against Russia could the German nation gain the living space and security it required and, as a superior race, deserved. War was an essential component of National Socialist ideology, and it accorded with Hitler's temperament. For the former corporal from the trenches, the Great War had never ended. Hitler aspired to political power because he wanted to mobilize the material and human resources of the German nation for war and conquest.

Although historians may debate the question of responsibility for World War I, few would deny that World War II was Hitler's war: "It appears to be an almost incontrovertible fact that the Second World War was brought on by the actions of the Hitler government, that these actions were the expression of a policy laid down well in advance in *Mein Kampf*, and that this war could have been averted up until the last moment if the German government had so wished."[1] Western statesmen had sufficient warning that Hitler was a threat to peace and to the essential values of Western civilization, but they failed to rally their people and take a stand until Germany had greatly increased its capacity to wage aggressive war. ❖

THE ROAD TO WAR

After consolidating his power and mobilizing the nation, Hitler moved to implement his foreign policy objectives: the destruction of the Versailles treaty, the conquest and colonization of Eastern Europe, and the domination and exploitation of racial inferiors. In foreign affairs, Hitler demonstrated the same blend of opportunism and singleness of purpose that had brought him to power. Here, too, he displayed an uncanny understanding of his opponents' weaknesses; and here, too, his opponents underestimated his skills and intent. As in his climb to power, he made use of propaganda to undermine his opponents' will to resist. The Nazi propaganda machine, which had effectively won the minds of the German people, became an instrument of foreign policy. To promote social and political disorientation in other lands, the Nazis propagated anti-Semitism worldwide. Nazi propagandists also tried to draw international support for Hitler as Europe's best defense against the Soviet Union and Bolshevism.

British and French Foreign Policies

As Hitler had anticipated, the British and the French backed down when faced with his violations of the Versailles treaty and threats of war. Haunted by the memory of World War I, Britain and France went to great lengths to avoid another catastrophe—a policy that had the overwhelming support of public opinion. Because Britain believed that Germany had been treated too severely by the Versailles treaty and knew that its own military forces were woefully unprepared for war, from 1933 to 1938 the British were amenable to making concessions to Hitler. Although France had the strongest army on the Continent, it was prepared to fight only a defensive war—the reverse of its World War I strategy. France built immense fortifications, called the Maginot Line, to protect its borders from a German invasion, but it lacked a mobile striking force that could punish an aggressive Germany. The United States, concerned with the problems of the Great Depression and standing aloof from Europe's troubles, did nothing to strengthen the resolve of France and Britain. Since both France and Britain feared and mistrusted the Soviet Union, the grand alliance of World War I was not renewed. There was an added factor: suffering from a failure of leadership and political and economic unrest that eroded national unity, France was experiencing a decline in morale and a loss of nerve. It consistently turned to Britain for direction.

British statesmen championed a policy of appeasement: giving in to Germany in the hope that a satisfied Hitler would not drag Europe through another world war. British policy rested on the disastrous illusion that Hitler, like his Weimar predecessors, sought peaceful revision of the Versailles treaty and that he could be contained through concessions. Accepting the view that Nazi propaganda cleverly propagated and exploited, some British appeasers also regarded Hitler as a defender of European civilization and the capitalist economic order against Soviet communism. Appeasement, which in the end was capitulation to blackmail, failed. Germany grew stronger and the German people more devoted to the fuehrer. Hitler did not moderate his ambitions, and the appeasers did not avert war.

Breakdown of Peace

To realize his foreign policy aims, Hitler required a formidable military machine. Germany must

Appeasement. Haunted by the memory of World War I, many French and British officials and ordinary citizens would go to great lengths to appease Germany in order to avoid a second world war. Soon after Hitler's remilitarization of the Rhineland, cartoonist David Lowe called the leaders of England and France spineless. (*London Evening/Solo Standard*)

rearm. The Treaty of Versailles had limited the size of the German army to a hundred thousand volunteers; restricted the navy's size; forbidden the production of military aircraft, heavy artillery, and tanks; and disbanded the general staff. In March 1935, Hitler declared that Germany was no longer bound by the Versailles treaty. Germany would restore conscription, build an air force (which it had been doing secretly), and strengthen its navy. France and Britain offered no resistance.

A decisive event in the breakdown of peace was Italy's invasion of Ethiopia in October 1935. The League of Nations called for economic sanctions against Italy, and most League members restricted trade with the aggressor. But Italy continued to receive oil, particularly from American suppliers, and neither Britain nor France sought to restrain Italy. Mussolini's subjugation of Ethiopia discredited the League of Nations, which had already been weakened by its failure to deal effectively with Japan's invasion of the mineral-rich Chinese province of Manchuria in 1931. The fall of Ethiopia, like that of Manchuria, evidenced the League's reluctance to check aggression with force.

Remilitarization of the Rhineland On March 7, 1936, Hitler marched troops into the Rhineland, violating the Versailles treaty, which called for the demilitarization of these German border lands. German generals had cautioned Hitler that such a move would provoke a French invasion of Germany, which the German army could not repulse. But Hitler gambled that France and Britain, lacking the will to fight, would take no action.

Hitler had assessed the Anglo-French mood correctly. The remilitarization of the Rhineland did not greatly alarm Britain. After all, Hitler was not expanding Germany's borders but only sending soldiers to its frontier. Such a move, reasoned British officials, did not warrant risking a war, and France would not act alone. Moreover, the French general staff overestimated German military strength and thought only of defending French soil from a German attack, not of initiating a strike against Germany.

Spanish Civil War The Spanish Civil War of 1936–1939 was another victory for fascism. Nazi Germany and Fascist Italy aided Franco (see "Liberalism and Authoritarianism in Other Lands" in the preceding chapter); the Soviet Union supplied the Spanish republic. By October 1937, some sixty thousand Italian "volunteers" were fighting in Spain. Hitler sent between five thousand and six thousand men and hundreds of planes, which proved decisive in winning the war. By comparison, the Soviet Union's aid was meager. Viewing the conflict as a struggle between democracy and fascism, thousands of Europeans and Americans volunteered to fight for the republic.

Without considerable help from France, the Spanish republic was doomed, but Prime Minister Léon Blum feared that French intervention might lead to war with Germany. Moreover, supplying the republic would have dangerous consequences at home because French rightists were sympathetic to Franco's conservative-clerical authoritarianism. In 1939, the republic fell, and Franco established a dictatorship, imprisoning or banishing to labor camps more than one million Spaniards and executing another two hundred thousand. The Spanish Civil War provided Germany with an opportunity to test weapons and pilots and demonstrated again that France and Britain lacked the determination to fight fascism.

Anschluss with Austria One of Hitler's aims was incorporation of Austria into the Third Reich, but the Treaty of Versailles had expressly prohibited the union (Anschluss) of the two German-speaking countries. In March 1938, under the pretext of preventing violence, Hitler ordered his troops into Austria, which was made a province of the German Reich.

Many Austrians welcomed the Anschluss. The idea of a Greater Germany appealed to their Pan-German sentiments, and they hoped that Hitler's magic would produce economic recovery. Moreover, depriving Jews of their rights, property, and occupations had widespread appeal among traditionally anti-Semitic Austrians. The Viennese celebrated by ringing church bells, waving swastika banners, and spontaneously beating, robbing, and humiliating Jews, including tearing torah scrolls, shearing the beards of rabbis, and forcing whole families to scrub sidewalks. The Austrians' euphoria over the Anschluss and their treatment of Jews astonished many observers, including the German occupiers.

Sudetenland, Munich, Prague Hitler obtained Austria merely by threatening to use force. Another threat would give him the Sudetenland of Czechoslovakia. Of the 3.5 million people living in the Sudetenland, some 2.8 million were ethnic Germans. Encouraged and instructed by Germany, the Sudeten Germans, led by Konrad Henlein, shrilly denounced the Czech government for "persecuting" its German minority and depriving it of its right to self-determination. The Sudeten Germans agitated for local autonomy and the right to profess the National Socialist ideology. Behind this demand was the goal of German annexation of the Sudetenland and the destruction of Czechoslovakia.

While negotiations between the Sudeten Germans and the Czech government proceeded, Hitler's propaganda machine accused the Czechs of hideous crimes against the German minority and warned of retribution. Hitler also ordered his generals to prepare for an invasion of Czechoslovakia. Fighting between Czechs and Sudeten Germans heightened the tensions. Seeking to preserve peace, Prime Minister Neville Chamberlain (1869–1940) of Britain offered to confer with Hitler, who then extended an invitation.

Britain's position regarding Czechoslovakia—the only democracy in Eastern Europe—was somewhat different from that of France. In 1924, France and Czechoslovakia had concluded an agreement of mutual assistance in the event that either was attacked by Germany. Czechoslovakia had a similar agreement with Russia, but with the provision that Russian assistance depended on

France first fulfilling the terms of its agreement. Britain had no commitment to Czechoslovakia. Swallowing Hitler's propaganda, some British officials believed that the Sudeten Germans were indeed a suppressed minority, entitled to self-determination, and that the Sudetenland, like Austria, was not worth a war that could destroy Western civilization. Hitler, they said, only wanted to incorporate Germans living outside Germany; he was only carrying the principle of self-determination to its logical conclusion. Once these Germans lived under the German flag, argued these British officials, Hitler would be satisfied. In any case, Britain's failure to rearm between 1933 and 1938 weakened its position. The British chiefs of staff believed that the nation was not prepared to fight and that it was necessary to sacrifice Czechoslovakia to buy time.

Czechoslovakia's fate was decided at the Munich Conference (September 1938), attended by Chamberlain, Hitler, Mussolini, and Prime Minister Édouard Daladier (1884–1970) of France. The Munich Pact gave the Sudetenland to Germany. Both Chamberlain and Daladier were showered with praise by the people of Britain and France for keeping the peace.

Chamberlain's critics have insisted that the Munich agreement was an enormous blunder and tragedy. Chamberlain, they say, was a fool to believe that Hitler, who sought domination over Europe, could be bought off with the Sudetenland. Hitler regarded concessions by Britain and France as signs of weakness; they only increased his appetite for more territory. Furthermore, argue the critics, it would have been better to fight Hitler in 1938 than a year later, when war actually did break out. To be sure, in the year following the Munich agreement, Britain increased its military arsenal, but so did Germany, which built submarines, planes and heavy tanks, strengthened western border defenses, and trained more pilots. The Czechs had a sizable number of good tanks, and the Czech people were willing to fight to preserve their nation's territorial integrity. While the main elements of the German army were battling the Czechs, the French, who could mobilize a hundred divisions, could have broken through the German West Wall, which was defended by only five regular and four reserve divisions; then they could have invaded the Rhineland and devastated German industrial centers in the Ruhr.

After the annexation of the Sudetenland, Hitler plotted to crush Czechoslovakia out of existence. He encouraged the Slovak minority in Czechoslovakia, led by a fascist priest, Josef Tiso, to demand complete separation. On the pretext of protecting the Slovak people's right of self-determination, Hitler ordered his troops to enter Prague. In March 1939, Czech independence ended.

The destruction of Czechoslovakia was a different matter from the remilitarization of the Rhineland, the Anschluss with Austria, and the annexation of the Sudetenland. In all these previous cases, Hitler could claim the right of self-determination, Woodrow Wilson's grand principle. However, the occupation of Prague and the end of Czech independence showed that Hitler really sought European hegemony. Outraged statesmen now demanded that the fuehrer be deterred from further aggression.

Poland After Czechoslovakia, Hitler turned to Poland and demanded, among other things, that Danzig be returned to Germany. Poland refused to restore the port which was vital to its economy. On May 22, 1939, Hitler and Mussolini entered into the Pact of Steel, promising mutual aid in the event of war. The following day, Hitler told his officers that Germany's real goal was the destruction of Poland. "Danzig is not the objective. It is a matter of expanding our living space in the East, of making our food supplies secure. . . . There is therefore no question of sparing Poland, and the decision remains to attack Poland at the first suitable opportunity."[2]

Britain, France, and the Soviet Union had been engaged in negotiations since April. The Soviet Union wanted a mutual assistance pact, including joint military planning, and demanded bases in Poland and Romania in preparation for a German attack. Britain was reluctant to endorse these demands, fearing that a mutual assistance pact with Russia might cause Hitler to embark on a mad adventure that would drag Britain into war. Moreover, Poland would not allow Russian troops on its soil, fearing Russian expansion.

At the same time, Russia was conducting secret talks with Nazi Germany. Unlike the Allies, Germany could tempt Stalin with territory that would serve as a buffer between Germany and Russia. Besides, a treaty with Germany would give Russia time to strengthen its armed forces.

On August 23, 1939, the two totalitarian states signed a nonaggression pact, stunning the world. A secret section of the pact called for the partition of Poland between Russia and Germany and Russian control over Lithuania, Latvia, and Estonia (later the agreement was amended to include Lithuania). By signing such an agreement with his enemy, Hitler had pulled off an extraordinary diplomatic coup: he blocked the Soviet Union, Britain, and France from duplicating their World War I alliance against Germany. The Nazi-Soviet Pact was the green light for an invasion of Poland, and at dawn on September 1, 1939, German troops crossed the frontier. When Germany did not respond to their demand for a halt to the invasion, Britain and France declared war.

THE NAZI BLITZKRIEG

The Conquest of Poland

Germany struck at Poland with speed and power. The German air force, the *Luftwaffe,* destroyed Polish planes on the ground, attacked tanks, pounded defense networks, and bombed Warsaw, terrorizing the population. Tanks opened up breaches in the Polish defenses, and mechanized columns overran the foot-marching Polish army, trapping large numbers of soldiers. The Polish high command could not cope with the incredible speed and coordination of German air and ground attacks. By September 8, the Germans had advanced to the outskirts of Warsaw. On September 17, Soviet troops invaded Poland from the east. On September 27, Poland surrendered. In less than a month, the Nazi *blitzkrieg* (lightning war) had vanquished Poland.

The Fall of France

For Hitler, the conquest of Poland was only the prelude to a German empire stretching from the Atlantic to the Urals. When weather conditions were right, he would unleash a great offensive in the west. In early April 1940, the Germans struck at Denmark and Norway. Denmark surrendered within hours. A British-French force tried to assist the Norwegians, but the landings, badly coordinated and lacking in air support, failed.

On May 10, 1940, Hitler launched his offensive in the west with an invasion of neutral Belgium, Holland, and Luxembourg. On May 14, after the Luftwaffe had bombed Rotterdam, destroying the center of the city and killing many people, the Dutch surrendered. Meeting almost no resistance, German panzer divisions had moved through the narrow mountain passes of Luxembourg and the dense Forest of Ardennes in southern Belgium. Thinking that the Forest of Ardennes could not be penetrated by a major German force, the French had only lightly fortified the western extension of the Maginot Line. But on May 12, German units were on French soil near Sedan. Then the Germans raced across northern France to the sea, which they reached on May 20, cutting the Anglo-French forces in two.

The Germans now sought to surround and annihilate the Allied forces converging on the French seaport of Dunkirk, the last port of escape. But probably fearing that German tanks would lose mobility in the rivers and canals around Dunkirk, Hitler called them off just as they prepared to take the port. Instead, he ordered the Luftwaffe to wipe out the Allied troops, but fog and rain prevented German planes from operating at full strength and British pilots inflicted heavy losses on the attackers. While the Luftwaffe bombed the beaches, some 338,000 British and French troops were ferried across the English Channel by destroyers, merchant ships, motorboats, fishing boats, tugboats, and private yachts. Hitler's personal decision to hold back his tanks made "the miracle of Dunkirk" possible.

Meanwhile, the battle for France was turning into a rout. With authority breaking down, demoralization spreading, and resistance dying, the French cabinet appealed for an armistice. It was signed on June 22, in the same railway car in which Germany had agreed to the armistice ending World War I.

How can the collapse of France be explained? The French had as many planes and tanks as the Germans, but their military leaders, unlike the German command, had not mastered the psychology and technology of motorized warfare. Put succinctly, the French were badly outgeneraled. One senses also that there was a loss of will among the French people—the result of internal political disputes, poor leadership, the years of appeasement and lost opportunities, and German propaganda, which depicted Nazism as irresistible and the fuehrer as a man of destiny. It was France's darkest hour.

According to the terms of the armistice, Germany occupied northern France and the coast. The French military was demobilized, and the French government, now located at Vichy, in the south, would collaborate with the German authorities in occupied France even to the point of passing racial laws and deporting Jews, including two thousand orphans under the age of six, to Nazi murder factories. The leaders of Vichy and their supporters, many of them prominent intellectuals and anti-Dreyfusards in their youth, shared in the antidemocratic, anti-Marxist, and anti-Semitic tradition of the radical right that had arrayed itself against the Third French Republic since the late nineteenth century. Refusing to recognize defeat, General Charles de Gaulle (1890–1970) escaped to London and organized the Free French forces. The Germans gloried in their revenge; the French wept in their humiliation; and the British gathered their courage, for they now stood alone.

The Battle of Britain

Hitler expected that, after his stunning victories in the West, Britain would make peace. The British, however, continued to reject Hitler's peace overtures, for they envisioned only a bleak future if Hitler dominated the Continent. After the German victory in Norway, Chamberlain's support in the House of Commons had eroded, and he had been replaced by Winston Churchill, who had opposed appeasement. Dynamic, courageous, and eloquent, Churchill had the capacity to stir and lead his people in the struggle against Nazism. "The Battle of Britain is about to begin," Churchill told them. "Upon this battle depends the survival of Christian civilization. . . . [I]f we fail, then . . . all we have known and cared for will sink into the abyss of a new Dark Age."[3]

Finding Britain unwilling to come to terms, Hitler proceeded in earnest with invasion plans. But a successful crossing of the English Channel and the establishment of beachheads on the English coast depended on control of the skies. Mar-shal Hermann Goering assured Hitler that his Luftwaffe could destroy the British Royal Air Force (RAF), and in early August 1940, the Luftwaffe began massive attacks on British air and naval installations. Virtually every day during the battle of Britain, weather permitting, hundreds of planes fought in the sky above Britain. Convinced that Goering could not fulfill his promise to destroy British air defenses and unwilling to absorb more losses in planes and trained pilots, Hitler called off the invasion. The development of radar by British scientists, the skill and courage of British fighter pilots, and the unwillingness of Germany to absorb more losses in planes saved Britain in its struggle for survival. With the invasion of Britain called off, the Luftwaffe concentrated on bombing English cities, industrial centers, and ports, in the hopes of eroding Britain's military potential and undermining in civilian morale. Every night for months, the inhabitants of London sought shelter in subways and cellars to escape German bombs, while British planes rose time after time to make the Luftwaffe pay the price. British morale never broke during the "Blitz."

Britain, by itself, had no hope of defeating the Third Reich. What ultimately changed the course of the war were Germany's invasion of the Soviet Union in June 1941 and Japan's attack on the United States in December 1941. With the entry of these two powers, a coalition was created that had the human and material resources to reverse the tide of battle.

The Invasion of Russia

The obliteration of Bolshevism and the conquest, exploitation, and colonization of Russia by the German master race were cardinal elements of Hitler's ideology. To prevent any interference with the forthcoming invasion of Russia, the Balkan flank had to be secured. On April 6, 1941, the Germans struck at both Greece, where an Italian attack had failed, and Yugoslavia. Yugoslavia was quickly overrun, and Greece, although aided by fifty thousand British, New Zealander, and Australian troops, fell at the end of April.

Stalingrad, February 1943. In the photograph, the Russians are rescuing the bombed-out city of Stalingrad from the Nazi invaders. *(Sovfoto)*

For the war against Russia, Hitler had assembled a massive force: some four million men, 3,300 tanks, and 2,000 planes. Evidence of the German buildup abounded, but a stubborn Stalin ignored these warnings. Desperate to avoid war with Nazi Germany, Stalin would take no action that he feared might provoke Hitler. Consequently, the Red Army was vulnerable to the German blitzkrieg. In the early hours of June 22, 1941, the Germans launched their offensive over a wide front. Raiding Russian airfields, the Luftwaffe destroyed 1,200 aircraft on the first day. The Germans drove deeply into Russia, cutting up and surrounding the disorganized and unprepared Russian forces. The Russians suffered horrendous losses. In a little more than three months, 2.5 million Russian soldiers had been killed, wounded, or captured and 14,000 tanks destroyed. Describing the war as a crusade to save Europe from "Jewish Bolshevik subhumans," German propaganda claimed that victory was assured.

But there were also disquieting signs for the Nazi invaders. The Russians, who had a proven capacity to endure hardships, fought doggedly and courageously for the motherland, and the government would not consider capitulation. Russian reserve strength was far greater than the Germans had estimated. Far from its supply lines, the Wehrmacht (German army) was running short of fuel, and trucks and cars had to contend with primitive roads that turned into seas of mud when the autumn rains came. Early and bitter cold weather hampered the German attempt to capture Moscow. The Germans advanced to within twenty miles of Moscow, but on December 6, a Red Army counterattack forced them to postpone the assault on the Russian capital.

By the end of 1941, Germany had conquered vast regions of Russia but had failed to bring the country to its knees. There would be no repetition of the collapse of France. Moreover, by moving machinery and workers east far beyond the German reach, the Soviets were able to replenish their military hardware, which was almost totally destroyed during the first six months of the war. Driven by patriotic fervor—and by fear of the omnipresent NKVD agents searching for malingerers—Russian factory workers toiled relentlessly, heroically. Soon many of them, the wives and daughters of soldiers at the front, were producing more planes and tanks than Germany.

The Russian campaign demonstrated that the Russian people would make incredible sacrifices for their land and that the Nazis were not invincible.

THE NEW ORDER

By 1942, Germany ruled virtually all of Europe, from the Atlantic to deep into Russia. Some conquered territory was annexed outright; other lands were administered by German officials; in still other countries, the Germans ruled through local officials sympathetic to Nazism or willing to collaborate with the Germans. On this vast empire, Hitler and his henchmen imposed a New Order.

Exploitation and Terror

The Germans systematically looted the countries they conquered, taking gold, art treasures, machinery, and food supplies back to Germany and exploiting the industrial and agricultural potential of non-German lands to aid the German war economy. The Nazis also made slave laborers of conquered peoples. Some seven million people from all over Europe were wrested from their homes and transported to Germany. These forced laborers, particularly the Russians and Poles, whom Nazi ideology classified as a lower form of humanity, lived in wretched, unheated barracks and were poorly fed and overworked; many died of disease, hunger, and exhaustion.

The Nazis ruled by force and terror. The prison cell, the torture chamber, the firing squad, and the concentration camp symbolized the New Order. In the Polish province annexed to Germany, the Nazis jailed and executed intellectuals and priests, closed all schools and most churches, and forbade Poles to hold professional positions. In the region of Poland administered by German officials, most schools above the fourth grade

◀ Map 20.1 World War II: The European Theater By 1942 Germany ruled virtually all of Europe from the Atlantic to deep into Russia. Germany's defeat in Stalingrad in Russia and in El Alamein in North Africa were decisive turning points.

were shut down. The Germans were especially ruthless toward the Russians. Soviet political officials were immediately executed; many prisoners of war were herded into camps and deliberately starved to death. In all, the Germans took prisoner some 5.5 million Russians, of whom about 3.5 million perished, primarily from starvation.

Extermination

Against the Jews of Europe, the Germans waged a war of extermination. The task of imposing the "Final Solution of the Jewish Problem" was given to Himmler's SS. Himmler fulfilled his grisly duties with fanaticism and bureaucratic efficiency. He and the SS believed that they had a holy mission to rid the world of worthless life—a satanic foe that was plotting to destroy Germany. Regarding themselves as righteous and courageous idealists who were writing a glorious chapter in the history of Germany, the SS tortured and murdered with immense dedication.

Special squads of the SS—the *Einsatzgruppen,* trained for mass murder—followed on the heels of the German army into Russia. Entering captured villages and cities, they rounded up Jewish men, women, and children, herded them to execution grounds, and slaughtered them with machine-gun and rifle fire at the edge of open trenches, which sometimes were piled high with thousands of victims, including severely wounded people, who would suffocate to death when the pit was filled with earth. Aided by Ukrainian, Lithuanian, and Latvian auxiliaries, the Einsatzgruppen massacred some 1.3 million Russian Jews. Units of the regular German army, the Wehrmacht, actively participated in the rounding up of Jews and sometimes in the shootings. Despite the denials of staff officers after the war, evidence from their own files reveals that they knew full well that the extermination of the Jews was state policy that units of the Wehrmacht were helping to implement. To speed up the Final Solution, extermination camps were built in Poland. Jews from all over Europe were rounded up, jammed into sealed cattle cars, and shipped to Treblinka, Auschwitz, and other death camps, where they entered another world:

Corpses were strewn all over the road; bodies were hanging from the barbed wire fence; the sound of shots rang in the air continuously. Blazing flames shot into the sky; a giant smoke cloud ascended about them. Starving, emaciated human skeletons stumbled forward toward us, uttering incoherent sounds. They fell down right in front of our eyes gasping out their last breath.

Here and there a hand tried to reach up, but when this happened an SS man came right away and stepped on it. Those who were merely exhausted were simply thrown on the dead pile. . . . Every night a truck came by, and all of them, dead or not, were thrown on it and taken to the crematory.[4]

SS doctors quickly inspected the new arrivals—"the freight," as they referred to them. Those unfit for work, including children, were immediately exterminated in gas chambers. Those not gassed faced a living death in the camp, which also included non-Jewish inmates. The SS took sadistic pleasure in humiliating and brutalizing their Jewish victims. When exhausted, starved, diseased, and beaten prisoners became unfit for work, generally within a few months, they were sent to the gas chambers.

Many of the SS were true believers, committed to racist and Social Darwinist fantasies. To realize their mythic vision of ultimate good, they had to destroy the Jews, whom Nazi ideology designated as less than human and the source of all evil. Other SS, and their army of collaborators, were simply ordinary people doing their duty as they had been trained to do, following orders the best way they knew how. They were morally indifferent bureaucrats, concerned with techniques and effectiveness, and careerists and functionaries seeking to impress superiors with their ability to get the job done. These people quickly adjusted to the routine of mass murder. Thus, as Konnilyn G. Feig notes, thousands of German railway workers "treated the Jewish cattle-car transports as a special business problem that they took pride in solving so well."[5] German physicians who selected Jews for the gas chambers were concerned only with technical problems and efficiency, and those doctors who performed unspeakable med-

ical experiments on Jews viewed their subjects as laboratory animals. German industrialists who worked Jewish slave laborers to death considered only cost-effectiveness in their operations. So, too, did the firms that built the gas chambers and the furnaces, whose durability and performance they guaranteed.

An eyewitness reports that engineers from Topf and Sons experimented with different combinations of corpses, deciding that "the most economical and fuel-saving procedure would be to burn the bodies of a well-nourished man and an emaciated woman or vice versa together with that of a child, because, as the experiments had established, in this combination, once they had caught fire, the dead would continue to burn without any further coke being required."[6] Rudolf Hoess, the commandant of Auschwitz, who exemplified the bureaucratic mentality, noted that his gas chambers were more efficient than those used at Treblinka because they could accommodate far more people. The Germans were so concerned with efficiency and cost that—to conserve ammunition or gas and not slow down the pace from the time victims were ordered to undress until they were hurried into the gas chambers—toddlers were taken from their mothers and thrown live into burning pits or mass graves.

When the war ended, the SS murderers and those who had assisted them returned to families and jobs, resuming a normal life, free of remorse and untroubled by guilt. "The human ability to normalize the abnormal is frightening indeed," observes sociologist Rainer C. Baum.[7] Mass murderers need not be psychopaths. It is a "disturbing psychological truth," states Robert Jay Lifton, that "ordinary people can commit demonic acts."[8]

There have been many massacres during the course of world history. And the Nazis murdered many non-Jews in concentration camps and in reprisal for acts of resistance. What is unique about the Holocaust—the systematic extermination of European Jewry—was the Nazis' determination to murder without exception every single Jew who came within their grasp, and the fanaticism, ingenuity, and cruelty with which they pursued this goal. Despite the protests of the army, the SS murdered Jews whose labor was needed for the war effort, and when Germany's military position was desperate, the SS still diverted mili-

Concentration Camp Survivors. Thousands of emaciated and diseased inmates of German concentration camps died in the weeks after liberation by the Allies. These camps will forever remain a monument to the capacity of human beings for inhumanity. *(© Topham/The Image Works)*

tary personnel and railway cars to deport Jews to the death camps.

The Holocaust was the grisly fulfillment of Nazi racial theories. Believing that they were cleansing Europe of a lower and dangerous race that threatened the German people, Nazi executioners performed their evil work with dedication and resourcefulness, with precision and moral indifference—a gruesome testament to human irrationality and wickedness. Using the technology and bureaucracy of a modern state, the Germans killed approximately 6 million Jews—*two-thirds* of the Jewish population of Europe. Some 1.5 million of the murdered were children; almost 90 percent of Jewish children in German-occupied

lands perished. Tens of thousands of entire families were wiped out without a trace. Centuries-old Jewish community life vanished, never to be restored. Burned into the soul of the Jewish people was a wound that could never entirely heal. Written into the history of Western civilization was an episode that would forever cast doubt on the Enlightenment conception of human goodness, rationality, and the progress of civilization.

Resistance

Each occupied country had its collaborators who welcomed the demise of democracy, saw Hitler as

Japanese Empire, 1931
Japanese Empire, 1942
Extent of Japanese expansion
Allied advances

SOVIET UNION

ASIA

MONGOLIA

MANCHURIA

Peiping
(Peking)

KOREA

JAPAN

Hiroshima

Tokyo

CHINA

Shanghai

Nagasaki

PACIFIC OCEAN

Taiwan

Iwo Jima
1945

Midway 1942

Okinawa
1945

Mariana Is.

Hawaiian Is.

BURMA

Hong
Kong

Wake

Pearl Harbor

THAILAND

FRENCH
INDOCHINA

Manila

Philippine Is.

Saipan

Leyte 1944

Guam
1944

Marshall
Is.

MALAYA

Singapore

Borneo

Caroline Is.

Tawara
1943

Sumatra

Dutch East Indies

New
Guinea

Java

Solomon Is.

Gilbert Is.

INDIAN OCEAN

Guadalcanal
1942

AUSTRALIA

Attu

Kiska
1943

Aleutian Is.

Brisbane

0   500   1000 Km.

0   500   1000 Mi.

Europe's best defense against communism, and profited from the sale of war materiel. Each country also produced a resistance movement that grew stronger as Nazi barbarism became more visible and the prospects of a German defeat more likely. The Nazis retaliated by torturing and executing captured resistance fighters and killing hostages—generally fifty for every German killed.

In western Europe, the resistance rescued downed Allied airmen, radioed military intelligence to Britain, and sabotaged German installations. Norwegians blew up the German stock of heavy water needed for atomic research. The Danish underground sabotaged railways and smuggled into neutral Sweden almost all of Denmark's eight thousand Jews just before they were to be deported to the death camps. After the Allies landed on the coast of France in June 1944, the French resistance delayed the movement of German reinforcements and liberated sections of the country.

In eastern Europe, resistance took the form of guerrilla warfare and sabotage. In August 1944, with Soviet forces approaching Warsaw, the Poles staged a full-scale revolt against the German occupiers. The Poles appealed to the Soviets, camped ten miles away, for help. Thinking about a future Russian-dominated Poland, the Soviets did not move. After sixty-three days of street fighting, remnants of the Polish underground surrendered, and the Germans destroyed what was left of Warsaw. In the Soviet Union, Russian partisans numbered several hundred thousand men and women. Operating behind the German lines, they sabotaged railways, destroyed trucks, and killed scores of thousands of German soldiers in hit-and-run attacks. In Yugoslavia, the mountains and forests provided excellent terrain for guerrilla warfare. The leading Yugoslav resistance army was headed by Josip Broz (1892–1980), better known as Tito. Moscow-trained, intelligent, and courageous, Tito organized his partisans into a disciplined fighting force that tied down a huge

◀ Map 20.2 World War II: The Pacific Theater The battle of Midway was a major turning point in the Pacific Theater. The map also shows the island hopping of the Americans that brought them closer to Japan. The battles of Iwo Jima and Okinawa were particularly brutal.

German army and ultimately liberated the country from German rule. Jews participated in the resistance in all countries and were particularly prominent in the French resistance. Specifically Jewish resistance organizations emerged in eastern Europe and revolts took place in the ghettos and concentration camps. In the spring of 1943, the surviving Jews of the Warsaw ghetto, armed with only a few guns and homemade bombs, fought the Germans for several weeks.

Italy and Germany also had resistance movements. After the Allies landed in Italy in 1943, bands of Italian partisans helped to liberate Italy from fascism and the German occupation. In Germany, army officers plotted to assassinate the fuehrer. On July 20, 1944, Colonel Claus von Stauffenberg planted a bomb at a staff conference attended by Hitler, but the fuehrer escaped serious injury. In retaliation, some five thousand suspected anti-Nazis were tortured and executed in an exceptionally barbarous fashion.

THE TURN OF THE TIDE

While Germany was subduing Europe, its ally, Japan, was extending its dominion over much of Asia. Seeking raw materials and secure markets for Japanese goods and driven by a xenophobic nationalism, Japan in 1931 had attacked Manchuria in northern China. Quickly overrunning the province, the Japanese established the puppet state of Manchukuo in 1932. After a period of truce, the war against China was renewed in July 1937. Japan captured leading cities, including China's principal seaports, and inflicted heavy casualties on the poorly organized Chinese forces, obliging the government of Jiang Jieshi (Chiang Kai-shek) to withdraw to Chungking in the interior.

The Japanese Offensive

In 1940, after the defeat of France and with Britain standing alone against Nazi Germany, Japan eyed Southeast Asia—French Indochina, British Burma and Malaya, and the Dutch East Indies. From these lands, Japan planned to obtain the oil, rubber, and tin vitally needed by Japanese industry and enough rice to feed the nation. Japan hoped that a quick strike against the

American fleet in the Pacific would give it time to enlarge and consolidate its empire. On December 7, 1941, the Japanese struck with carrier-based planes at Pearl Harbor in Hawaii. Taken by surprise—despite warning signs—the Americans suffered a total defeat: the attackers sank 17 ships, including 7 of the 8 battleships; destroyed 188 airplanes and damaged 159 others; and killed 2,403 men. The Japanese lost only 29 planes. After the attack on Pearl Harbor, Germany declared war on the United States. Now the immense American industrial capacity could be put to work against the Axis powers—Germany, Italy, and Japan. American factories produced planes, tanks, and ships at a pace and scale that astonished both friend and foe. The American arsenal supplied Britain and the Soviet Union with badly needed equipment.

Defeat of the Axis Powers

By the spring of 1942, the Axis powers held the upper hand. The Japanese empire included the coast of China, Indochina, Thailand, Burma, Malaya, the Dutch East Indies, the Philippines, and other islands in the Pacific. Germany controlled Europe almost to Moscow. When the year ended, however, the Allies seemed assured of victory. Three decisive battles—Midway, Stalingrad, and El Alamein—reversed the tide of war.

In June 1942, the main body of the Japanese fleet headed for Midway, eleven hundred miles northwest of Pearl Harbor; another section sailed toward the Aleutian Islands, in an attempt to divide the American fleet. But the Americans had broken the Japanese naval code and were aware of the Japanese plan. On June 4, 1942, the two navies fought a strange naval battle; it was waged entirely by carrier-based planes, for the fleets were too far from each other to use their big guns. American pilots destroyed four Japanese aircraft carriers stacked with planes. The battle of Midway cost Japan the initiative. With American industrial production accelerating, the opportunity for a Japanese victory had passed.

After being stymied at the outskirts of Moscow in December 1941, the Germans renewed their offensive in the spring and summer of 1942. Hitler's goal was Stalingrad, the great industrial center located on the Volga River; con-

trol of Stalingrad would give Germany command of vital rail transportation and access to the oil fields of the Caucasus. The battle of Stalingrad was an epic struggle, in which Russian soldiers and civilians fought for every building and street of their city. In this urban battlefield, scarred by mile after mile of destroyed buildings and mountains of rubble, the combatants were separated by mere yards, snipers lurked in the maze of ruins, and tough Russian soldiers stealthily and ceaselessly attacked at night with bayonets and daggers; here the blitzkrieg, which had brought the Germans immense success in their earlier offensives, did not apply. So brutal was the fighting that at night half-crazed dogs sought to escape the city by swimming across the river. One German soldier wrote in his diary at the end of December: "The horses have already been eaten . . . the soldiers look like corpses or lunatics looking for something to put in their mouths. They no longer take cover from Russian shells; they haven't the strength to walk, run away and hide."[9]

A Russian counterattack in November, planned by General (later Marshal) Georgi Zhukov, caught the Germans in a trap. With his soldiers exhausted and desperately short of food, medical supplies, weapons, and ammunition, Friedrich Paulus, commander of the Sixth Army, urged Hitler to order a withdrawal before the Russians closed the ring. The fuehrer refused. After suffering tens of thousands of additional casualties, their position hopeless, the remnants of the Sixth Army surrendered on February 2, 1943. Some 260,000 German soldiers had perished in the battle of Stalingrad, and another 110,000 were taken prisoner.

The Soviet high command, which had performed terribly in the early days of the German offensive, distinguished itself at Stalingrad. At the battle of Kursk in July 1943, Russian military leaders again demonstrated an increasing ability to master the technique of modern warfare. Analyzing correctly that the Germans would attack the Kursk salients, Marshal Georgi Zhukov turned the area into a fortress. In an epic encounter, over three hundred German tanks were destroyed in one day. After the battle of Kursk, the initiative passed to the Russians.

In January 1941, the British were routing the Italians in northern Africa. Hitler assigned Gen-

Hiroshima After the Atomic Bomb. The mass destruction of Hiroshima ushered in a new age. Nuclear weapons gave humanity the capacity to destroy civilization. *(Corbis/ Bettmann)*

eral Erwin Rommel (1891–1944) to halt the British advance. Rommel drove the British out of Libya and, with strong reinforcements, might have taken Egypt and the Suez Canal. But Hitler's concern was with seizing Yugoslavia and Greece and preparing for the invasion of Russia. Early in 1942, Rommel resumed his advance, intending to conquer Egypt. The British Eighth Army, commanded by General Bernard L. Montgomery, stopped him at the battle of El Alamein in October 1942. The victory of El Alamein was followed by an Anglo-American invasion of northwest Africa in November 1942. By May 1943, the Germans and Italians were defeated in northern Africa.

After securing northern Africa, the Allies, seeking complete control of the Mediterranean, invaded Sicily in July 1943 and quickly conquered the island. Mussolini's fellow Fascist leaders turned against him, and the king dismissed him as prime minister. In September, the new government surrendered to the Allies, and in the

following month, Italy declared war on Germany. Italian partisans—their number would grow to three hundred thousand—resisted the occupying German troops, who were determined to hold on to central and northern Italy. At the same time, the Allies fought their way up the peninsula. Captured by partisans, Mussolini was executed (April 28, 1945), and his dead body, hanging upside down, was publicly displayed.

On June 6, 1944, D-Day, the Allies landed on the beaches of Normandy in France. They had assembled a massive force for the liberation of Europe: two million men and five thousand vessels. The success of D-Day depended on securing the beaches and marching inland, which the Allies did despite stubborn German resistance. On some beaches the soldiers struggled ashore in the face of intense enemy fire. At Omaha Beach, the Americans almost did not make it. Weighed down by heavy equipment, men drowned as they were tossed by high waves; others were killed or wounded by machine-gun fire before reaching the beach. Much of the heavy armor was lost. Those who stumbled ashore hugged the embankment and sheltered themselves behind whatever barrier they could find to escape the German guns firing from the cliffs. Traumatized by the devastation and death surrounding them, and often leaderless, the soldiers, many of them facing combat for the first time, seemed paralyzed. But amid the chaos, says the official army account, enough soldiers rallied:

> At half-a-dozen or more points on the long stretch, they found the necessary drive to leave their cover and move out over the open beach flat toward the bluffs . . . . [T]he decisive factor was leadership. Wherever an advance was made, it depended on the presence of some few individuals, officers and noncommissioned officers, who inspired, encouraged, or bullied their men forward by making the first forward moves . . . . Colonel [George A. Taylor] summed up the situation in a terse phrase: "Two kinds of people are staying on this beach, the dead and those who are going to die—now let's get the hell out of here."[10]

By the end of July, the Allies had built up their strength in France to a million and a half. In the middle of August, Paris rose up against the German occupiers and was soon liberated.

As winter approached, the situation looked hopeless for Germany. Brussels and Antwerp fell to the Allies; Allied bombers were striking German factories and mass-bombing German cities in terror raids that took a horrendous toll of life. The air war eroded Germany's industrial potential and caused morale to plummet. Desperate, Hitler made one last gamble. In mid-December 1944, he launched an offensive to split the Allied forces and regain the vital port of Antwerp. The Allies were taken by surprise in the battle of the Bulge, but a heroic defense by the Americans at Bastogne helped stop the German offensive. While their allies were advancing in the west, the Russians were continuing their drive in the east, advancing into the Baltic states, Poland, and Hungary. By February 1945, they stood within one hundred miles of Berlin.

By April 1945, British, American, and Russian troops were penetrating into Germany from east and west. From his underground bunker near the chancellery in Berlin, Hitler, physically exhausted

and emotionally unhinged, engaged in wild fantasies about new German victories. On April 30, 1945, with the Russians only blocks away, the fuehrer took his own life. On May 7, 1945, a demoralized and devastated Germany surrendered unconditionally.

In the Pacific war, after the victory at Midway in June 1942, American forces attacked strategic islands held by Japan. American troops had to battle their way up beaches and through jungles tenaciously defended by Japanese soldiers, who believed that death was preferable to the disgrace of surrender. In March 1945, twenty-one thousand Japanese perished on Iwo Jima; another hundred thousand died on Okinawa in April 1945 as they contested for every inch of the island.

On August 6, 1945, the United States dropped an atomic bomb on Hiroshima, killing more than seventy-eight thousand people and demolishing 60 percent of the city. President Harry S Truman said that he ordered the atomic attack to avoid an American invasion of the Japanese homeland, which would have cost hundreds of thousands of lives. Truman's decision has aroused considerable debate. Some analysts maintain that dropping the bomb was unnecessary. They say that Japan, deprived of oil, rice, and other essentials by an American naval blockade and defenseless against unrelenting aerial bombardments, was close to surrender and had indicated as much. It has been suggested that because the Soviet Union was about to enter the conflict against Japan, Truman wanted to end the war immediately, thus depriving the U.S.S.R. of an opportunity to extend its influence in East Asia. On August 8, Russia did enter the war against Japan, invading Manchuria. After a second atomic bomb was dropped on Nagasaki on August 9, the Japanese asked for peace.

THE LEGACY OF WORLD WAR II

World War II was the most destructive war in history. The total war waged by the combatants also enveloped civilians, who were victims of reprisals, genocide, slave labor, and aerial bombardment of cities. Estimates of the number of dead range as high as fifty million, including some twenty-five million Russians, who sacrificed more than the other participants in both population and material resources. The war produced a vast migration of peoples unparalleled in modern European history. The Soviet Union annexed the Baltic lands of Latvia, Lithuania, and Estonia, forcibly deporting many of the native inhabitants into central Russia. The bulk of East Prussia was taken over by Poland, and Russia annexed the northeastern portion. Millions of Germans fled the invading Russians, who, bent on revenge for the misery the Nazis had inflicted on their kin and country, committed numerous atrocities, including indiscriminate killing and mass rape, before Soviet authorities ended the mayhem. Millions more Germans were driven out of Poland, Czechoslovakia, Yugoslavia, Romania, and Hungary, places where their ancestors had lived for centuries, by vengeful eastern Europeans. Moreover, leaders in these countries, driven by nationalist aspirations, welcomed an opportunity to rid their nations of an ethnic minority, particularly since so many of these Germans had aided the Nazi occupiers. In 1945–46, some twelve million to thirteen million Germans were driven westward. Expelled from their homes, often with only a few minutes' warning, they had to leave almost everything behind. Herded into internment camps, they were brutalized by Polish and Czech guards who relished the opportunity to torment Germans. Tens of thousands died from malnutrition, disease, exposure, and mistreatment; thousands more committed suicide.

Material costs were staggering. Everywhere cities were in rubble; bridges, railway systems, waterways, and harbors destroyed; farmlands laid waste; livestock killed; coal mines wrecked. Homeless and hungry people wandered the streets and roads. Europe faced the gigantic task of rebuilding. Yet Europe did recover from this material blight, and with astonishing speed.

The war produced a shift in power arrangements. The United States and the Soviet Union emerged as the two most powerful states in the world. The traditional Great Powers—Britain, France, and Germany—were now dwarfed by these *superpowers*. The United States had the atomic bomb and immense industrial might; the Soviet Union had the largest army in the world and was extending its dominion over Eastern Europe. With Germany defeated, the principal incentive for Soviet-American cooperation had evaporated.

After World War I, nationalist passions had intensified. After World War II, Western Europeans progressed toward unity. The Hitler years had convinced many Europeans of the dangers inherent in extreme nationalism, and fear of the Soviet Union prodded them toward greater cooperation.

World War II accelerated the disintegration of Europe's overseas empires. The European states could hardly justify ruling over Africans and Asians after they had fought to liberate European lands from German imperialism. Nor could they ask their people, exhausted by the Hitler years and concentrating all their energies on reconstruction, to fight new wars against Africans and Asians pressing for independence. In the years just after the war, Great Britain surrendered India, France lost Lebanon and Syria, and the Dutch departed from Indonesia. In the 1950s and 1960s, virtually every colonial territory gained independence. Where a colonial power resisted granting the colony independence, the price was bloodshed.

The consciousness of Europe, already profoundly damaged by World War I, was again grievously wounded. Nazi racial theories showed that even in an age of advanced science, the mind remains attracted to irrational beliefs and mythical imagery; Nazi atrocities proved that people will torture and kill with religious zeal and machinelike indifference. This regression to mythical thinking and savagery bears out Walter Lippmann's contention that "men have been barbarians much longer than they have been civilized. They are only precariously civilized, and within us there is the propensity, persistent as the force of gravity, to revert under stress and strain, or under temptation, to our first natures."[11] And the behavior of German intellectuals also contained a painful lesson, says German historian Karl Dietrich Bracher: "The intellectuals who supported the Nazis in one way or another all document that the mind can be temporarily seduced, that people can be bribed with careers and fame, that thinking people, especially, are tempted by an irrational cult of action and are peculiarly susceptible to ('one-dimensional') answers and promises of salvation."[12]

The Nazi assault on reason and freedom demonstrated anew the fragility of Western civilization.

This assault would forever cast doubt on the Enlightenment conception of human goodness, secular rationality, and the progress of civilization through advances in science and technology.

The Holocaust was heightened irrationality and organized evil on an unprecedented scale. Auschwitz, Treblinka, Sobibor, and the other death factories represent the triumph of human irrationality over reason—the surrender of the mind to a bizarre racial mythology that provided a metaphysical and pseudoscientific justification for mass murder. They also represent the ultimate perversion of reason. A calculating reason manufactured and organized lies and demented beliefs into a structured system with its own inner logic, and employed sophisticated technology and administrative techniques to destroy human beings spiritually and physically. Science and technology, venerated as the great achievement of the Western mind, had made mass extermination possible. The philosophes had not foreseen the destructive power inherent in reason.

Both the Christian and the Enlightenment traditions had failed the West. Some intellectuals, shocked by the irrationality and horrors of the Hitler era, drifted into despair. To these thinkers, life was absurd, without meaning; human beings could neither comprehend nor control it. In 1945, only the naive could have faith in continuous progress or believe in the essential goodness of the individual. The future envisioned by the philosophes seemed more distant than ever. Nevertheless, this profound disillusionment was tempered by hope. Democracy had, in fact, prevailed over Nazi totalitarianism and terror. Perhaps, then, democratic institutions and values would spread throughout the globe, and the newly established United Nations would promote world peace.

❖   ❖   ❖

NOTES

1. Pierre Renouvin, *World War II and Its Origins* (New York: Harper & Row, 1969), p. 167.

2. *Documents on German Foreign Policy, 1918–1945,* vol. 6 (London: Her Majesty's Stationery Office, 1956), series D, no. 433.

3. Winston S. Churchill, *The Second World War: Their Finest Hour* (Boston: Houghton Mifflin, 1949), vol. 2, pp. 225–226.

4. Judith Sternberg Newman, *In the Hell of Auschwitz* (New York: Exposition, 1964), p. 18.

5. Konnilyn G. Feig, *Hitler's Death Camps* (New York: Holmes & Meier, 1979), p. 37.

6. Quoted in Steven T. Katz, "Technology and Genocide: Technology as a 'Form of Life,'" in *Echoes from the Holocaust*, eds. Alan Rosenberg and Gerald E. Meyers (Philadelphia: Temple University Press, 1988), p. 281.

7. Rainer C. Baum, "Holocaust: Moral Indifference as the Form of Modern Evil," in *Echoes from the Holocaust,* ed. Rosenberg and Meyers, p. 83.

8. Robert Jay Lifton, *The Nazi Doctors* (New York: Basic Books, 1968), p. 5.

9. Richard Overy, *Why the Allies Won* (New York: W. W. Norton, 1955), p. 82.

10. *Omaha Beachhead,* prepared by the War Department Historical Division (Washington, D.C., 1945), pp. 58, 71.

11. Walter Lippmann, *The Public Philosophy* (Boston: Little Brown, 1955), p. 86.

12. Karl Dietrich Bracher, *Turning Points in Modern Times,* trans. Thomas Dunlap (Cambridge, Mass.: Harvard University Press, 1995), p. 198.

SUGGESTED READING

Adams, R. J. Q., *British Politics and Foreign Policy in the Age of Appeasement, 1935–1939* (1993). The nature, purpose, and meaning of appeasement.

Ambrose, Stephen E., *D-Day* (1994). Based on oral histories from people who were there.

Bartow, Omer, *Hitler's Army* (1992). Excellent material on the indoctrination of the German soldier.

Bauer, Yehuda, *A History of the Holocaust* (1982). An authoritative study.

Baumont, Maurice, *The Origins of the Second World War* (1978). A brief work by a distinguished French scholar.

Bell, P. M. H., *The Origins of the Second World War in Europe* (1986). An intelligent survey.

Calvocoressi, Peter, and Guy Wint, *Total War* (1972). A good account of World War II.

Dear, I. C. B., *The Oxford Companion to World War II* (1995). A superb reference work.

Des Pres, Terrence, *The Survivors* (1976). A sensitive analysis of life in the death camp.

Hildebrand, Klaus, *The Foreign Policy of the Third Reich* (1973). A brief assessment of Nazi foreign policy.

Keegan, John, *The Second World War* (1989). A recent survey by a leading military historian.

Klee, Ernst, Willi Dressen, and Volker Riess, eds., *The Good Old Days* (1988). Documents show perpetrators and bystanders not only as indifferent to the suffering of Jews, but also deriving pleasure from it.

Marrus, Michael R., *The Holocaust in History* (1987). An excellent summary of key issues and problems.

Michel, Henri, *The Shadow War* (1972). An analysis of the European resistance movement, 1939–1945.

———, *The Second World War,* 2 vols. (1975). Translation of an important study by a prominent French historian.

Murray, Williamson and Allen R. Miller, *A War to Be Won* (2000). An analysis of the operations and tactics employed by the belligerents.

Overy, Richard, *Why the Allies Won* (1995). A brilliant analysis.

Remak, Joachim, *The Origins of the Second World War* (1976). A useful essay, followed by documents.

Weinberg, Gerhard L., *A World at Arms* (1994). A recent study based on extraordinary knowledge of the sources.

Wiesel, Elie, *Night* (1960). A moving personal record of the Holocaust.

REVIEW QUESTIONS

1. What were Hitler's foreign policy aims?
2. Why did Britain and France practice a policy of appeasement?
3. Discuss the significance of each of the following: Italy's invasion of Ethiopia (1935); Germany's remilitarization of the Rhineland (1936); the Spanish Civil War (1936–1939); Germany's union with Austria (1938); the occupation of Prague (1939); and the Nazi-Soviet Pact (1939).
4. What factors made possible the quick fall of France?
5. Describe the New Order that the Nazis established in Europe.
6. In your opinion, what is the meaning of the Holocaust for Western civilization? For Jews? For Christians? For Germans?
7. Discuss the significance of each of the following battles: Midway (1942), Stalingrad (1942–43), El Alamein (1942), and D-Day (1944).
8. What is the legacy of World War II?

Part Six

The Contemporary World

The Destruction of the World Trade Center's Twin Towers. (AP/World Wide Photos)

Politics and Society	Thought and Culture
1940	
Yalta agreement (1945)	Wiener, *Cybernetics* (1948)
United Nations established (1945)	Orwell, *1984* (1949)
Marshall Plan for recovery of Europe (1947)	de Beauvoir, *The Second Sex* (1949)
Cold war starts (1947)	
State of Israel established (1948)	
North Atlantic Treaty Organization (NATO) established (1949)	
Division of Germany (1949)	Camus, *The Rebel* (1951)
Triumph of communism in China (1949)	Discovery of DNA by Crick and Watson (1951–1953)
	Djilas, *The New Class* (1957)
1950	
Korean War (1950–1953)	Chomsky, *Syntactic Structures* (1957)
European Economic Community (EEC) established (1957)	Grass, *The Tin Drum* (1959)
Sputnik launched: space age begins (1957)	Snow, *The Two Cultures and the Scientific Revolution* (1959)
1960	
Berlin Wall built (1961)	Carson, *Silent Spring* (1962)
Cuban missile crisis (1962)	Pope John XXIII, *Pacem in Terris* (Peace on Earth) (1963)
Vietnam War (1963–1973)	McLuhan, *Understanding Media* (1964)
	Levi-Strauss, *The Savage Mind* (1966)
1970	
Détente in East-West relations (1970s)	Solzhenitsyn, *The Gulag Archipelago* (1974–1978)
	Wilson, *Sociobiology* (1975)
1980	
Gorbachev becomes leader of Soviet Union (1985)	Creation of the Internet (1983)
Explosion at Chernobyl nuclear power plant (1986)	Gorbachev, *Perestroika* (1987)
Peaceful overthrow of Communist governments in Eastern Europe (1989)	
Berlin Wall demolished (1989)	
1990	
Reunification of Germany (1990)	
Charter of Paris for a New Europe (1990)	
Official end of cold war (1990)	
Persian Gulf War (1991)	
Yugoslav federation breaks up and war begins (1991)	
Collapse of the Soviet Union (1991)	
European Union ratifies the Maastricht Treaty (1993)	
Dayton Agreement ends civil war in former Yugoslavia (1995)	
2000	
Terrorist attack on World Trade Center (2001)	
U.S.-led war in Iraq; fall of Sadaam Hussein (2003)	

Chapter 21

The West in a Global Age

- ■ **The Cold War**
- ■ **Decolonization**
- ■ **Building a New Europe: Unity and Recovery**
- ■ **The Soviet Bloc**
- ■ **The Post-Cold War World**
- ■ **Our Global Age: Tensions and Concerns**

*A*t the end of World War II, Winston Churchill described Europe as "a rubble heap, a charnel house, a breeding ground for pestilence and hate."[1] Millions had perished. Industry, transportation, and communication had come to a virtual standstill; bridges, canals, dikes, and farmlands were ruined. Ragged, worn people picked among the rubble and bartered their valuables for food.

Europe was politically cut in half, for in pursuing Hitler's armies, Soviet troops had overrun Eastern Europe and penetrated into the heart of Germany. Europe's future now depended on two countries, the United States and the Soviet Union, which soon became embroiled in a bitter cold war. The Soviet Union, exhausted by World War II and anxious about security, imposed its grim tradition of dictatorship on Eastern Europe, while the United States, virtually unharmed by the war, brought the boon of its wealth and power to help rebuild Western Europe. Henceforth, the United States stood out as the heir to and guardian of the Western tradition, a political giant come into its own. ❖

THE COLD WAR

The cold war (the American financier Bernard Baruch coined the phrase in 1947) stemmed from the divergent historical experiences and the incompatible political ambitions of the United States and the Soviet Union, which clashed head-on as the new global order began to take shape. During the war, the basic disparities between the West and the U.S.S.R. had been glossed over, but once the common danger receded, the differences between political institutions and ideologies pushed again to the fore.

As the Red Army moved through Eastern Europe, the fate of the peoples of that region hung in the balance. The Yalta agreement of February 1945, signed by Roosevelt, Churchill, and Stalin on Stalin's home ground in the Crimean peninsula, turned the prevailing military balance of power into a political settlement. The American bargaining position at Yalta was weakened by the expectation that Soviet help would be needed for victory over Japan. Soviet promises of free elections in Soviet-dominated Eastern Europe were not kept.

Ever worried about the security of Russia's western boundaries, Stalin sought to incorporate the countries of Eastern Europe into a buffer zone for protection against Western attack. The Western allies, advancing from the Atlantic against Hitler's armies, were in no position to stop Stalin from doing as he wished. As the Red Army fought its way west in 1944–45, Eastern European Communists, trained in the Soviet Union,

followed. The Baltic states (Lithuania, Latvia, Estonia), seized after the Nazi-Soviet Pact of 1939 and then lost to Hitler, were reincorporated into the Soviet Union as "soviet socialist republics." Elsewhere, Stalin respected, at least outwardly, the national sovereignty of the occupied countries by ruling through returning native Communists and whatever sympathizers he could find. In the Soviet-occupied zone of Germany, Stalin arranged for the establishment of Communist rule. This area became the German Democratic Republic, while the three other zones combined as the democratic Federal Republic of Germany. The local populations and their sympathizers in Western European nations and the United States viewed the Soviet occupation of Eastern Europe as a calamity. But short of starting another war, Western countries were powerless to intervene. For the next forty-five years or so, the two parts of the Continent, Eastern Europe and Western Europe, would constitute two camps of opposing ideologies, Communist and anti-Communist.

By the end of 1948, the lands of Eastern Europe had become Soviet satellites. The puppet regimes leveled the formerly privileged classes, socialized the economy, and implemented hasty plans for industrialization and for the collectivization of agriculture. Religion and the churches were repressed, and political liberty and free speech were stamped out. Even the "proletarian masses" derived few benefits from the artificial revolution engineered from Moscow because Stalin drained Eastern Europe of its resources in order to rebuild the Soviet Union. Contact with Western Europe or the United States was banned. Each satellite country existed in isolation, its borders fortified with barbed wire and watchtowers set along mined corridors cut through the landscape. Fear reached deep into every house and into individual souls as little Stalins copied their mentor's style in East Berlin, Warsaw, Prague, Budapest, Sofia, and Bucharest. All Communist parties (whatever their name) were guided by Moscow; Soviet troops remained strategically stationed in the area.

An exception to this trend was Yugoslavia under the leadership of the pugnacious Marshal Tito, who became a symbol of defiance to Stalin. During World War II, he had led the Yugoslav resistance movement against Nazi occupation. A

Chronology 21.1 ❖ Europe After 1945

1945	United Nations founded; Eastern Europe occupied by Red Army
1947	Cold war starts; Marshall Plan inaugurated
1948	Stalinization of Eastern Europe; Tito's Yugoslavia breaks with the Soviet Union
1949	NATO formed
1953	Stalin dies
1956	Khrushchev's secret speech on Stalin's crimes; the Polish October; the Hungarian uprising crushed
1957	*Sputnik* launched: the space age begins; the EEC established
1961	Berlin Wall built, dividing the city of Berlin
1962	Cuban missile crisis
1963–1973	Vietnam War
1964	Khrushchev ousted; Brezhnev and Kosygin installed as leaders in U.S.S.R.
1968	Czechoslovakia's "Prague Spring": Dubček's "socialism with a human face"
1971	Détente in East-West relations
1979	Soviet Union invades Afghanistan
1980	Solidarity trade union formed in Poland
1982	Brezhnev dies, succeeded by Andropov (d. 1984) and Chernenko (d. 1985)
1985	Gorbachev becomes U.S.S.R. leader
1988	Soviet Union withdraws from Afghanistan
1989	Year of liberation in Eastern Europe
1990	Reunification of Germany; Charter of Paris for a New Europe: official end of the cold war
1991	Persian Gulf War; Yeltsin elected Russian president; collapse of Soviet Union; Yugoslav federation breaks up and war begins
1993	Czechoslovakia splits into Czech Republic and Slovakia; elections for new Russian constitution and parliament; European Union ratifies Maastricht Treaty
1994	South Africa elects multiracial government; war breaks out between Russia and Chechnya
1995	Dayton Agreement ends civil war in Bosnia
1996	Yeltsin reelected president of Russia; truce ends hostilities in Chechnya
1999	NATO invades Kosovo; Russia again attacks Chechnya
2001	Terrorist attack on World Trade Center; War on terrorism in Afghanistan
2003	United States and Britain crush regime of Saddam Hussein

Map 21.1 Western Europe After 1945 To counter the communist threat from the Soviet Union, Western European countries, formerly enemies, cooperated for their mutual protection. The majority of countries joined NATO for security against communist attack, and six countries within Europe formed the Common Market (the forerunner of the European Union) to facilitate trade and economic integration.

hardened Communist, Tito was also a Yugoslav patriot committed to rebuilding and unifying his country. Thus, Yugoslavia escaped Soviet occupation. Backed by his party and his people, Tito guided his country on an independent course.

Deepening Tensions

Farther afield, in the eastern Mediterranean, Stalin was suspected of aiding Communist guerrillas in the Greek civil war of 1946–47. The guerrillas were supported by the neighboring Soviet-dominated countries of Albania, Bulgaria, and Yugoslavia; Stalin's influence on the course of the war was in fact minimal. He did, however, lay claim to the Straits of Constantinople, and he unduly prolonged the wartime Soviet occupation of northern Iran.

In March 1947, fearing Soviet penetration into the eastern Mediterranean and aware of British weakness in that area, President Harry S. Truman proclaimed the Truman Doctrine: "It must be the policy of the United States to support free peoples who are resisting attempted subjugation by armed minorities or by outside pressures."[2] The Truman Doctrine was the centerpiece of the new policy of *containment*—of holding Soviet power within its then current boundaries. The United States soon furnished military and economic support to Greece and Turkey. Thus, American foreign policy underwent a sharp reversal: prewar isolation gave way to worldwide vigilance against any Soviet effort at expansion. In June 1947, the United States took another step toward strengthening the West. Secretary of State George C. Marshall announced an impressive program of economic assistance to Europe. Formally called the European Recovery Program, it became widely known as the Marshall Plan. Between 1947 and 1951, it supplied Europe with more than $12 billion in aid—a modest pump-priming for the subsequent record upswing in U.S., Western European, and even global prosperity. Western Europe recovered, and the United States gained economically strong allies and trading partners. These measures were accompanied by a massive ideological mobilization of American opinion against communism and a new apprehension about national security.

A spectacular test between the two superpowers took place from June 1948 to May 1949, after the Soviet authorities severed all overland access to the western sectors of Berlin. The Soviets aimed to starve into submission a half-city of about two million inhabitants who, because of their freedom, were "a bone in the Communist throat" (as Nikita Khrushchev later put it). West Berlin was saved by an impressive airlift: under U.S. direction, the French, British, and Americans flew in supplies around the clock in all kinds of weather.

The year 1949 was a turning point in the cold war, which spread from Europe into the world at large, intensifying as it did so. The victory of the Chinese Communists under Mao Zedong seemed more threatening to the United States than the Berlin blockade. Now another Communist giant had joined the Soviet Union. Even more alarming was the fact that the Soviet Union had exploded its first atomic bomb sooner than expected, breaking the U.S. monopoly of that all-powerful weapon, which had inspired American self-confidence in the immediate postwar years. Now Americans felt that they had to keep ahead of the Soviet Union in nuclear weapons as well.

The Growth of Military Alliances

The United States and the countries of Western Europe established the North Atlantic Treaty Organization (NATO) in 1949 to prevent the widely dreaded westward expansion of Soviet communism. NATO combined the armed forces of the United States, Canada, Portugal, Norway, Iceland, Denmark, Italy, Britain, France, and the Benelux countries (an acronym for Belgium, the Netherlands, and Luxembourg). Greece and Turkey soon joined; West Germany was included in 1955, and Spain in 1982. The postwar rebuilding of Western Europe proceeded under the protection of U.S. military power.

The Soviet Union had its own alliance system: the Warsaw Pact, or Warsaw Treaty Organization (WTO), created in 1955. It coordinated the armies of the satellite countries with the Red Army so that they might serve as a military instrument for preserving the ideological and political unity of the bloc and for counterbalancing NATO.

Confrontations

Korean War In June 1950, war broke out in Korea, a country divided in 1945 between a pro-Soviet Communist regime in the north and a pro-American regime in the south. Eager to restore Korean national unity and mistakenly assuming U.S. nonintervention, the North Korean army invaded South Korea, possibly with Stalin's approval. Immediately, the United States took countermeasures, gaining U.N. backing for a war against North Korea. Under the command of General Douglas MacArthur, South Korean and U.S. troops, assisted by a token force from other U.N. members, fought their way north toward the Chinese border. Fearing for his own security, Mao Zedong dispatched Chinese "volunteers" to drive back the approaching enemy in a surprise attack. Forced to retreat, General MacArthur's troops eventually withdrew from North Korea. Peace was restored in 1953, with the division of Korea reaffirmed. South Korea became an outpost of U.S. power.

Cuban Missile Crisis Confrontation between the superpowers rose to a terrifying climax in 1962 during the Cuban missile crisis. In 1959, the infamous dictatorship of Fulgencio Batista had been toppled by Fidel Castro (b. 1927), a left-wing revolutionary who turned Cuba into a Communist-style dictatorship. After an American attempt to overthrow him—the bungled Bay of Pigs operation—Castro was ready to turn his country into an outpost of Soviet power. Khrushchev planned to exploit this foothold in the Western Hemisphere by installing Soviet nuclear missiles in Cuba. Although the United States had for some time stationed nuclear weapons in Turkey, within easy reach of Soviet targets, the reverse situation—allowing a major Soviet threat close to home—alarmed the country. President John F. Kennedy demanded that Khrushchev withdraw the Soviet missiles from Cuba. The cold war confrontation threatened to turn into a very hot nuclear war. However, Khrushchev backed down—a move that contributed to his fall from power two years later. No Soviet missiles were stationed in Cuba.

Vietnam War The new countries emerging from colonial rule in Asia and Africa offered seductive opportunities for Soviet global ambitions. From the U.S. perspective, the biggest challenge arose in Vietnam, where the Communist regime in the north threatened to take over South Vietnam as well. The threat had started with the partition of the country in 1954. From the north, the authoritarian regime of Ho Chi Minh (1890–1969), backed by indigenous nationalism and Soviet aid, cast its shadow over a disorganized south. Providing South Vietnam with the stability and strength needed to resist Communist infiltration required increasing U.S. aid—including troops to fight off the Communist guerrillas, the Vietcong. If the Communists prevailed, the argument ran, all the other countries in East and Southeast Asia emerging from colonial rule would fall like dominoes to Communist rule. Under President Lyndon B. Johnson, who assumed office in 1963, U.S. intervention in South Vietnam became the undeclared Vietnam War.

The U.S. government shipped to Vietnam nearly half a million soldiers, equipped with the most advanced chemical weapons and electronic equipment available. Yet victory eluded the American forces. The North Vietnamese government and its people withstood the cruelest punishment of bombs and chemical weapons ever inflicted on human beings. Nor was South Vietnam spared; virtually every South Vietnamese family saw relatives killed or maimed, and their farms and livelihoods ruined.

As domestic opposition to the war increased and Vietcong resistance could not be broken, President Richard M. Nixon, elected in 1968, realized that the war had to be ended by "peace with honor." While he initiated negotiations with North Vietnam, U.S. forces put pressure on the enemy by attacking Communist bases and supply routes in neighboring Cambodia and Laos. Civilians were bombed more fiercely than in World War II. In 1973, by agreement with North Vietnam, the United States withdrew its forces from the area. In 1975, the North Vietnamese swept aside the inept South Vietnamese army and unified the country under a Communist dictatorship. Ho Chi Minh had triumphed against the mightiest nation in the world.

In the wake of the American withdrawal, Cambodian Communists—the Khmer Rouge—seized power under their leader, Pol Pot. He

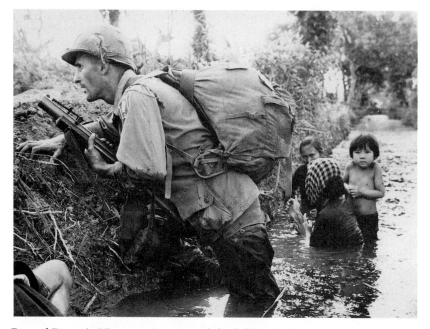

Bogged Down in Vietnam. Americans defended South Vietnam against a threatened takeover by Communist North Vietnam. Between 1964 and 1973, U.S. involvement in the unsuccessful Vietnam War cost tens of thousands of Vietnamese and American lives, ruined South Vietnam, and polarized U.S. public opinion over the morality of the war. *(AP/Wide World Photos)*

drove more than two million people from the capital city of Phnom Penh and tried to establish a new order based on ideologically regimented rural communes. The result was genocide in which hundreds of thousands of people perished.

DECOLONIZATION

The cold war between the two superpowers had spread into Asia and Africa—into the Third World, as it came to be known. Western imperialism had everywhere introduced Western institutions, goods, and ideals. World War II had stirred up the non-Western peoples living under Western colonial rule to liberate themselves. When World War II ended, the militancy of anticolonial movements increased. The political agitation of the war, in which many colonial soldiers had loyally fought for their masters, sparked the desire for

political independence. After all, freedom and self-determination had been prominent Allied war slogans. Exhausted by the war, European colonial powers had little strength left for colonial rule.

In this setting, a mighty groundswell of decolonization, supported by the superpowers and the ideals of the United Nations, eventually abolished all overseas empires and propelled their former subjects into independent statehood. Decolonization quickly became a major issue in the cold war as the two superpowers competed with each other for influence in the emerging states of Africa and Asia. The Soviet Union, proclaiming an ideology that called for the liberation of all oppressed peoples, tried to steer the colonial independence movements into its orbit, supporting them with advisers and weapons. The Western powers, with their superior resources, tried to guide their former colonial subjects toward a pro-Western allegiance, likewise offering military, political, and financial assistance. In their ignorance of local cultures, both sides found themselves entangled in the intricacies of local power struggles, especially in tropical Africa, which was frequently involved in protracted civil wars bordering on anarchy.

Decolonization everywhere sparked protracted and often brutal struggles to build modern states among peoples who had been utterly unprepared for this effort by their colonial rulers and who were also divided by their past animosities, as well as by the competition between the superpowers. Given these countries' lack of preparation, Western practices like capitalism and democracy proved too complex. The Soviet model seemed more suitable; besides, it offered the new leaders the attraction of absolute power. Yet how long could that model hold its own against the capitalist rival, whose riches exerted an even stronger attraction? Decolonization inevitably expanded the influence of Western ways of life in the newly independent nations, even though one-party governments and dictatorships remain in power in many countries.

BUILDING A NEW EUROPE: UNITY AND RECOVERY

Although Europeans share a common cultural heritage, the diversity of their history and national temperaments has burdened them in the past with incessant warfare. After two ruinous world wars, many people at last began to feel that the price of violent conflict had become excessive; war no longer served any national interest. And the extension of Soviet power made some form of Western European unity attractive, if not imperative.

In 1951, the chief Continental consumers and producers of coal and steel, the two items most essential for the rebuilding of Western Europe, created the European Coal and Steel Community (ECSC). Its six members, France, West Germany, the Netherlands, Belgium, Luxembourg, and Italy, intended to put the Ruhr industrial complex, the heart of German industrial power, under international control, thereby promoting cooperation and reconciliation, as well as economic strength.

Emboldened by the success of the ECSC, in 1957 the six countries established the European Economic Community (EEC), also known as the Common Market, a customs union that created a free market among the member states and sought to improve living conditions in them. In 1973, Great Britain, Ireland, and Denmark joined the original members in what was now called the European Community (EC); in 1981, Greece and in 1986, Spain and Portugal became members. The EC constituted the largest single trading bloc, conducting more than one-fifth of the world's commerce. In this framework of growing cooperation, the major countries of Western Europe experienced a political and economic revival, which contributed to Western superiority in the cold war.

A most striking fact of recent history in the West has been the unprecedented economic advance. Between the early 1950s and the late 1970s, production in Western Europe and the United States surpassed all previous records. The rapid postwar economic boom suffered a setback in the 1970s due in part to the drastic increase in oil prices imposed by the Organization of Petroleum Exporting Countries (OPEC). Recovery revived and prosperity continued throughout the 1980s. However, unemployment in Western Europe remained high, even in West Germany, the strongest country economically.

Stimulated by the expansion of U.S. multinational corporations into Western Europe and by the opportunities offered by the European Community, many European companies have turned multinational and grown bigger than any nationalized industry. The Western European economy came to be dominated by gigantic private and public enterprises tied to other parts of the world.

Boosted by rising standards of living and by U.S. power, the overall trend of political life in the West since World War II has been toward constitutional democracy. Although Spain and Portugal retained their prewar dictatorships until the mid-1970s and Greece for a time wavered between democracy and dictatorship, by the late 1970s even these countries had conformed to the common pattern.

Great Britain and France

Impoverished by the war and vulnerable in its dependence on imported food and raw material,

Great Britain lost its leading role in world politics after World War II. It peacefully dismantled its colonial empire, and British seapower was replaced by the American navy and air force. The postwar Labour government, allied with powerful trade unions, provided Britons with a measure of economic security through social programs and extensive government control over important branches of the economy. Such controls, however, placed Britain at a disadvantage vis-à-vis its European competitors.

In 1979, at a low point in the economy, the voters elected a Conservative government, led by Margaret Thatcher, the "Iron Lady" and the first woman prime minister. She dominated English politics for the next decade, fighting inflation and rigorously encouraging individual initiative and free enterprise. During the Thatcher years, the British economy improved, and London regained its former luster as a financial center. Still, industries were declining, causing a rise in unemployment. Civic tensions—terrorism by the Irish Republican Army, which sought to drive Britain from Northern Ireland, and resentment at the influx of Indians, Pakistanis, West Indians, and other people from former colonies—also took their toll. In addition, despite their EC membership, the English clung to their traditional insular detachment from their neighbors on the Continent.

Across the English Channel, France, liberated from German occupation, was reorganized democratically under the Fourth Republic and soon achieved respectable economic growth, despite frequent changes of government (twenty-six in twelve years). A major problem that France faced in these years was decolonization. In Indochina, the colonial liberation movement inflicted a resounding defeat on the French army in 1954. In Algeria, French settlers and soldiers were determined to thwart independence. The long and bloody Algerian conflict had serious repercussions.

In 1958, the agitation to keep Algeria under French control, supported by certain army circles, reached a dangerous point. To prevent a right-wing coup aided by the army, General Charles de Gaulle stepped forward. He had been the leader of the Free French forces in World War II and president for a brief period after the war ended.

De Gaulle established the Fifth Republic, with a strong executive authority, and sought to raise the country again to prominence by building its nuclear strength, making France independent of NATO, and renewing French influence in Africa. In 1962, he arranged a cease-fire in Algeria, allowing it to achieve independence. In 1968, demonstrations by students and workers demanding educational reform and social justice, which were supported by the Communist party, greatly alarmed de Gaulle. He quickly called a general election, in which a frightened electorate gave him a landslide victory. However, unable to revise the constitution in his favor, he resigned in 1969.

The Fifth Republic continued under a government firmly based on a stable centrist majority, flanked by two radical parties. On the left, the Communist party gradually lost credibility because of its loyalty to Moscow. On the extreme right, the ultranationalist *Front National* took hold, stirring up hatred against the increasing number of immigrants from North Africa. Under the pressure of the newcomers, the French, even more than the English, feared for their national identity.

Amid the economic and political uncertainties of the times, François Mitterrand, a moderate socialist who became president in 1981, maintained the Gaullist tradition. His country was the third largest nuclear power and the fourth largest economy in the world, deriving 70 percent of its energy from nuclear power plants. All along, France was a leading architect of European unity without surrendering its French character.

Italy and Germany

Italy, half the size of France, yet larger in population by a few million, became a democratic republic in 1946. Its government, however, has been weak and unstable. The average life span of an Italian cabinet to the present has been less than a year. A lengthy peninsula stretching out into the Mediterranean, the country offered a sharp contrast between north and south. The north was efficient and prosperous, whereas the south was backward and infiltrated by the Mafia. Centered in Sicily, the Mafia was a source of political corruption and even occasional terror against the government.

Division also characterized the political parties, from Communists to Christian Democrats. The Italian Communists, relatively free from corruption, well organized, and oriented toward Europe rather than Moscow, usually gained a quarter of the vote. On the other hand, the Christian Democrats—allied with the Vatican and constituting the majority party—were poorly disciplined, like the other non-Communist parties, and riven by corruption.

Yet the Italian economy proved to be a surprising success, despite the fact that the government was perennially in debt and unemployment ran high, especially in the south. Even more than France, Italy has been overrun by legal and illegal immigrants from Asia and Africa, straining the country's resources. It has been the most unruly of the major European countries, but no troublemaker for its neighbors.

In 1945, its cities in ruins, Germany had been defeated, occupied, and branded as a moral outcast. Divided among the four occupying powers—the United States, Britain, France, and the Soviet Union—the German nation was politically extinct. Extensive eastern lands were lost to Poland and the Soviet Union; some territory was returned to France. By 1949, two new and chastened Germanys had emerged. West Germany (the Federal Republic of Germany), formed from the three western zones of occupation, faced the hostile, Soviet-dominated East Germany (the German Democratic Republic). The former capital city of Berlin, inside East Germany, was similarly divided into western and eastern zones of occupation. The partition of Germany signified the destruction of Germany's traditional identity and ambition. The national trauma reached a climax in August 1961, when the East German government suddenly threw up a wall between East and West Berlin and tightly sealed off East from West Germany. West Germany thus became the crucial frontier of the cold war, radiating Western superiority into the Soviet bloc.

The cold war proved a boon to the West Germans; it contributed to their integration into the emerging new Europe and to the reduction of old hatreds. Located next door to the Red Army, the West Germans, along with the Western armed forces stationed on their soil, were in a strategic position for defending Western Europe. Moreover, German industrial expertise was indispensable for rebuilding the Western European economy. On this basis, West Germany (far larger than its Communist counterpart to the east and the most populous of all Western European countries) began to build a new political identity.

The architect of the new West Germany was Konrad Adenauer, its chancellor from 1949 to 1963. He sought to restore respect for Germany in cooperation with the leading states of Western Europe and the United States. As a patriot, he reestablished a cautious continuity with the German past. He also had Germany shoulder responsibility for the crimes of the Nazi regime and assume the payment of indemnifications and pensions to the Jewish victims and survivors of the Nazi era, as well as the payment of reparations to the state of Israel, which had been established in 1948. Under Adenauer's guidance, the West Germans also threw themselves into rebuilding their economy; the whole world soon admired the German "economic miracle." As a result, democracy put down roots among the West German people, strengthening their solidarity with their former European enemies. West Germany was admitted to NATO in 1957 and, together with East Germany, to the United Nations in 1972. It joined France in promoting the European Community.

After the Adenauer era, German voters shifted from center-right to center-left. Chancellor Willy Brandt (1969–1974) took the initiative for an "opening toward the East," contributing to a temporary relaxation of tensions between the superpowers. During these years, West German prosperity and a generous admission policy attracted ambitious immigrants, many from Turkey; the booming economy needed additional workers. Political extremists did not endanger political stability, except for one party, the Greens, which called attention to the destruction of the environment, industrial pollution, and the dangers of nuclear power. Loosely organized, the Greens expressed a romantic alienation from contemporary society and politics but achieved no lasting success. In 1982, the voters turned conservative, electing the leader of the Christian Democratic Union, Helmut Kohl, chancellor. Kohl continued Adenauer's policy of integrating West

Germany, now the most prominent country in Western Europe, into the cold war alliance against Soviet Communism.

THE SOVIET BLOC

Stalin's Last Years

For the Soviet Union, World War II was another cruel landmark in the long succession of wars, revolutions, and crises that had afflicted the country since 1914. Nothing basically changed after the war. The liberation from terror and dictatorship that many soldiers had hoped for as a reward for their heroism never occurred.

Corrupted by unlimited power and unrestrained adulation, Stalin displayed in his last years an unrelenting ruthlessness and a suspiciousness that turned into paranoia. He found no reason to relax control. The country still had immense problems: the large anti-Soviet populations in Eastern Europe; the destruction wreaked by the war; the political unreliability of returning soldiers and prisoners of war; and the overwhelming strength of the United States. Stalin's indomitable ambition, undiminished by age (he was sixty-six years old in 1945), was to build up Soviet power in his lifetime, whatever the human cost. More Five-Year Plans and more terror were needed.

On this familiar note, the Soviet Union slid from war into peace, staggering through the hardships and hunger of the war's aftermath, mourning its dead, and desperately short of men. Planning, much selfless hard work, manpower released from the army, and resources requisitioned from all occupied territories brought industrial production back to prewar levels within three years—no mean achievement.

In his last years, Stalin withdrew into virtual isolation, surrounded by a few fawning and fearful subordinates, and his paranoia worsened. Before he died, he "recognized" a plot among the doctors, most of them Jews, who treated him and personally issued orders for their torture (which killed one of them). When on March 5, 1953, the failing dictator died of a stroke, his advisers sighed with relief, but many people wept. To them, Stalin was the godlike leader and savior of the nation. The human costs of his regime were immense, but of his achievements in raising Soviet power there can be no doubt. By 1949, Soviet Russia possessed the atomic bomb. By 1953, at the same time as the United States, it had the hydrogen bomb as well.

Khrushchev

After Stalin's death, leadership was assumed by a team headed by Nikita Khrushchev (1954–1964), who breathed fresh air into Soviet life. Khrushchev was the driving force behind the "thaw" that emptied the forced-labor camps and allowed most of the nationalities forcibly resettled during the war to return to their native regions. In a speech at the Twentieth Party Congress in February 1956, Khrushchev even dared to attack Stalin himself. His audience gasped with horror as he recited the facts: "Of the 139 members and candidates of the Party Central Committee who were elected at the 17th Congress (1934), 98 persons, i.e., 70 percent, were arrested and shot."[3] In this vein, Khrushchev cited example after example of Stalin's terror. Without criticizing the Soviet system, Khrushchev acknowledged and rejected the excesses of Stalinism.

Khrushchev's revelations created a profound stir around the world and prompted defection from Communist ranks everywhere. Among the Soviet satellite countries, Poland was on the brink of rebellion by 1956; a workers' uprising forced a change of leadership. In Hungary in 1956, the entire Communist regime was overthrown, but the Soviet army reoccupied the country and crushed the uprising.

In foreign policy, Khrushchev professed to promote peace. But while trying to reduce the role of the army, he also made some provocative moves by threatening Western access to West Berlin and placing missiles in Cuba; U.S. pressure forced him

Map 21.2 Eastern Europe After 1945 ▶
During and after World War II the Soviet Union extended its rule halfway across Europe. Repressive communist governments in Eastern Europe were controlled by Moscow. Yugoslavia, under President Tito, defied Moscow and became a communist state with links to Western Europe and the United States.

ICELAND

ATLANTIC
OCEAN

IRELAND
Dublin

GREAT
BRITAIN
London

NORWAY
Oslo

SWEDEN
Stockholm

FINLAND
Helsinki

SOVIET UNION

Leningrad

Moscow

Volga R.

Caspian Sea

North Sea

Baltic Sea

DENMARK
Copenhagen

G. of Finland

ESTONIA
LATVIA
LITHUANIA

BELORUSSIA

Kiev

Dnieper R.

UKRAINE

CRIMEA

Black Sea

IRAN

IRAQ

SYRIA

TURKEY
Ankara

Istanbul

NETHERLANDS
Amsterdam

Brussels
BELGIUM

Paris

LUX.

Hamburg
Elbe R.

Berlin
EAST
GERMANY

Prague

Gdańsk
(Danzig)

Vistula R.

Warsaw

POLAND

CZECHOSLOVAKIA

BESSARABIA

ROMANIA
Bucharest

Danube R.

BULGARIA
Sofia

Budapest
HUNGARY

Vienna
AUSTRIA

Belgrade

YUGOSLAVIA

Tirane
ALBANIA

GREECE
Athens

Bonn

WEST GERMANY

Munich

Rhine R.

SWITZERLAND

Po R.

ITALY
Rome

Adriatic Sea

Corsica

Sardinia

Sicily

Mediterranean Sea

FRANCE

Rhône R.

Seine R.

Ebro R.

SPAIN
Madrid

PORTUGAL

Lisbon

400 Mi.

400 Km.

200

200

0

0

German territory to Poland

Acquired by Soviet Union,
1939–1945

Soviet satellites

Communist, nonsatellite nation

"Iron Curtain" after 1950

to withdraw in both cases. In 1960, not wishing to help Communist China build atomic weapons, he withdrew, after mutual recrimination, all Soviet advisers, causing a break between the two Communist nations. Mao then charged him with "revisionism," as well as imperialism.

Eager to prod his country toward a higher level of Marxist-Leninist ideology, Khrushchev presented a new party program and impatiently pressed for reforms in industry, agriculture, and party organization. His ceaseless reorganizations, impatient manner, and extravagant promises antagonized wide sections of state and party administration. In October 1964, while he was on vacation, his comrades in the Politburo unceremoniously ousted him for "ill health" or, as they later added, his "hare-brained schemes." He was retired and allowed to live out his years in peace.

Khrushchev was succeeded by a group of leaders acting in common. Among these men, Leonid Brezhnev (1906–1982) gradually rose to the fore. Under his leadership, the government of the U.S.S.R. turned from a personal dictatorship into an oligarchy: the collective rule of a privileged minority. Brezhnev's style stressed reasoned agreement rather than command. Soviet officials breathed more easily, and Soviet society in turn grew less authoritarian.

Never before in Soviet history had the country enjoyed such external security. As a result, the rigors of totalitarian rule could be relaxed, and the country could be opened, cautiously, to the outside world. For instance, young people were allowed access to Western styles of music and dress. More issues of state policy were opened to public debate, and more latitude was granted to artistic expression. Interest in religion revived.

Changes in Eastern Europe

Realizing that continued repression of the satellite countries would provoke trouble, Stalin's successors began to relax their controls. A new era dawned for Eastern Europe. The Soviet satellites began to move toward greater national self-determination, searching for their own forms of industrialization, collectivization of agriculture, and Communist dictatorship. The history of the region after 1953 was thus a series of experiments to determine what deviations from Soviet practice in domestic politics and what measure of self-assertion in foreign policy the Kremlin would tolerate.

No event proved more crucial than Khrushchev's attack on Stalin in 1956. It set off a political earthquake throughout the bloc, discrediting Stalinists and encouraging moderates in the parties, reviving cautious discussions among intellectuals, and even arousing visions of national self-determination.

The first rumbles of protest were heard in June 1956 in Poland—the largest and most troublesome of the satellite countries. The crisis came to a head in October: would Poland revolt, inviting invasion by the Red Army, or would Khrushchev ease Soviet control? The Soviet boss yielded in return for a Polish pledge of continued loyalty to the Soviet Union. Thereafter, Poland breathed more freely, clinging to its Catholicism as a cornerstone of its national identity.

Although the "Polish October" ended peacefully, events moved to a brutal showdown in Hungary. The Stalinists had suppressed national pride in Hungary for too long. On October 20, 1956, anti-Soviet feeling boiled over in an uprising in Budapest, forcing Soviet troops to withdraw from the country. A moderate Communist government took over the reins. Eager to capture popular sentiment, it called for Western-style political democracy and Hungary's withdrawal from the Warsaw Pact. Thoroughly alarmed, and supported by Mao and even Tito, the Soviet leaders struck back. On November 4, 1956, Soviet troops reentered Hungary and crushed all opposition.

But the bold uprising left its mark. The new Communist leader of Hungary, János Kádár, was a moderate. With Khrushchev's approval, he built a pragmatic regime of consumer-oriented "goulash communism" that granted considerable opportunity to private enterprise. Kádár's regime also allowed non-Communists to participate extensively in public affairs. Relaxation and decentralization of planning made possible in the 1970s a remarkable increase in popular prosperity and individual freedom. The Hungarian experiment became the envy of all other Soviet-bloc countries.

After 1956, Soviet leaders grew more circumspect in their approach to the satellite countries' internal affairs, allowing increasing diversity of political development. The post-Stalin permissiveness was never without risks, however, even under the milder regime of Brezhnev, as was shown in Czechoslovakia in 1968. A new group of Czech Communists, led by Alexander Dubček, sought to liberalize their regime to include non-Communists, permit greater freedom of speech, and rid the economy of the rigidities that for so long had prevented prosperity. Their goal was a "humanist democratic socialism," or "socialism with a human face": a Communist party supported by public goodwill rather than by the secret police.

This program panicked the governments of East Germany, Poland, and the Soviet Union. On August 21, East German, Polish, Hungarian, and Soviet troops, under the provisions of the Warsaw Pact, carried out a swift and well-prepared occupation of Czechoslovakia but failed to break the rebellious will of its reformers. While Soviet tanks rumbled through Prague, an extraordinary Czechoslovak party congress met secretly in choked fury. Never had the Soviet leaders encountered such united resistance by a Communist party. Nonetheless, the revolt ended in failure. The party was purged, all reforms were canceled, and the country was reduced to abject hopelessness. But the Soviet Union paid a high price. A cry of moral outrage resounded around the world; protests were heard even in Moscow.

Extraordinary events occurred in Poland. Industrial workers, theoretically the real masters in Communist regimes, embarrassed their government by taking the lead in pressing for freedom and a better standard of living. When a Polish cardinal became Pope John Paul II in 1978, patriotism surged. In 1980, workers, under the leadership of an electrician named Lech Walesa, succeeded, with the blessing of the church, in forming an independent labor union. Called Solidarity, the union engaged in numerous strikes. In 1981, matters came to a head: some of Solidarity's more radical members spoke of bringing free elections to Poland. In December, a military dictatorship, formed suddenly under General Wojciech Jaruzelski, imposed martial law. Walesa and other leaders of Solidarity were arrested, and protesting workers were dispersed by force.

The German Democratic Republic (East Germany) at first shared the fate of all Soviet satellites. Under the leadership of German Communists who had spent the Nazi years in the Soviet Union, industry was nationalized, agriculture collectivized, and the people regimented under the Communist party (here called the Socialist Unity party). But protests against Stalinism appeared earlier here than elsewhere. In June 1953, the workers of Berlin staged an uprising, gaining some concessions. Then followed a steady exodus of skilled manpower to West Germany, mostly through West Berlin. More than three million people escaped before the East German government, in August 1961, suddenly constructed the infamous "Berlin Wall" and built equally deadly barriers along the entire border with West Germany. For a time, all contact between East and West Germany ceased.

With renewed control over their people, the Communist leaders—first Walter Ulbricht and then, starting in the early 1970s, Erich Honecker—successfully advanced the economy. The East Germans enjoyed the highest standard of living in the Soviet bloc. In 1972, détente opened diplomatic relations with West Germany and promoted closer economic ties. After 1985, East Germans cheered the progress of reform in the Soviet Union—their leader, Honecker, denounced it as "a march to anarchy"—and hoped for similar benefits at home.

The Gorbachev Years

Brezhnev died in 1982; his immediate successors, chosen by agreement among top party officials, were old men who survived in office only for a short time. Former KGB chief Yuri Andropov (aged sixty-eight), in poor health from the start, died in early 1984. He was replaced by Konstantin Chernenko, a man of Brezhnev's generation, likewise in poor health, who lasted until early 1985. In that year, Mikhail Gorbachev (b. 1931) took over, representing a younger and more sophisticated age group, whose members had started their careers in the calmer times after Stalin's death.

Self-confident, energetic, and articulate, Gorbachev was keenly aware of his country's problems and eager to confront them. He knew that the Soviet Union had to update its industrial and

Mikhail Gorbachev. Soviet leader Gorbachev and his wife visit Vilnius, the capital of Lithuania, following the declaration of independence by the Lithuanian Communist party. Gorbachev warned demonstrators, "If we should separate, it is the end of perestroika." *(Corbis/Sygma/Alain Nogues)*

agricultural productivity to compete with Japan, South Korea, Taiwan, the countries of Western Europe, and the United States; in particular, the Soviet Union lagged in the design and production of computers. A sobering demonstration of inefficiency and mismanagement occurred in late April 1986 when, because of staff misjudgment, a reactor at the nuclear power plant at Chernobyl exploded, spewing dangerous radiation high into the atmosphere; poisonous fallout covered much of Europe. Wherever Gorbachev looked, the mismanagement caused by rigid, centralized planning stifled innovation.

Gorbachev demanded no less than a fundamental reorganization—*perestroika*—of the Soviet system, with the party in charge but responding more readily to the plans and hopes of Soviet citizens. Even more than his predecessors, he advocated "the democratization of society," hoping to stimulate participation by ordinary citizens, especially at their place of work and in local administration. He called for multiple candidates for elected posts, a novel experience for Soviet voters. To loosen up administrative rigidity, he also granted greater freedom to local entrepreneurs in agriculture, industry, and consumer services, demanding that supply and demand be closely coordinated, as in a free market.

Gorbachev promoted a new policy, *glasnost* (openness), in the discussion of public affairs. Let all the problems of Soviet society, hitherto kept under cover, be openly discussed: corruption, abuse of power, disregard for legality, and stifling of criticism. Domestic news began to depict Soviet reality more accurately. There was also a new candor about the Soviet past. During the seventieth anniversary of the Bolshevik Revolution, Gorbachev asserted that "the guilt of Stalin . . . for the wholesale repressive measures and acts of lawlessness is enormous and unforgivable."[4] Gorbachev then assured Soviet citizens that they should not hesitate to speak out freely. Academics, writers, and artists responded enthusiastically. As contacts with the outside world increased, Western ideals, culture, and respect for human rights entered Soviet minds as never before. Far-reaching economic changes designed to loosen the restraints of central planning and to promote a market economy accompanied the political reforms.

The End of the Cold War

Gorbachev also sought to ease international tensions. National security in the nuclear age, he stressed, called for superpower cooperation for the sake of common survival. Moreover, the high cost of the cold war impeded the reforms that he so urgently promoted. In the spirit of glasnost, Gorbachev frankly admitted that the adverse prospects of his country's economy forced him to advocate not only "normal international relations," but also an end to the arms race. Setting an example, with a touch of Western sartorial elegance, he traveled abroad and cautiously lifted the restrictions barring access to the outside world. Jewish emigration was eased; foreign firms were invited to help stimulate the Soviet economy; and high-level discussions between Russians and Americans became commonplace.

By the end of 1988, Gorbachev withdrew the Soviet army from Afghanistan, admitting that the 1979 invasion had been a mistake. He liberated Eastern Europe from Soviet domination, permitting the dissolution of the Warsaw Pact, the Soviet military alliance in the area, and gave approval to German reunification. He surrendered the Leninist claim to the superiority of Soviet communism and stopped support for Marxist regimes in the Third World. Unilaterally demobilizing sizable units of the Red Army in 1988, he also stopped nuclear testing. At summit meetings—with President Reagan and later with President George Bush—Gorbachev successfully pressed for strategic arms reduction. In late 1991, both the United States and the Soviet Union agreed to scrap a significant part of their nuclear arsenals.

The Collapse of Communism

1989: The Year of Liberation Perestroika and glasnost spread among the peoples of Eastern Europe, resentful of Soviet domination and worried by growing economic hardships. During 1989 and 1990, Eastern Europeans showed their distaste for Communist leadership and demanded democratic reforms. Faced with a rising tide of popular discontent, Communist leaders resigned or agreed to reforms. People around the world cheered the opening of a new era in Eastern Europe.

In Poland, public pressure had forced General Jaruzelski to end his dictatorship and appoint a civilian government. Struggling with a deteriorating economy, Jaruzelski legalized the highly popular Solidarity union in 1989. Permitted to run against Communist party candidates in a free election, Solidarity won an overwhelming victory. The once jailed Solidarity members now sat in the Polish parliament next to their former jailers. In December 1990, Lech Walesa, who was instrumental in forming Solidarity, was elected president.

Encouraged by events in Poland, Hungary abolished its Communist bureaucracy in May 1989. By the end of the year, a multiparty system was in place, with two non-Communist parties, the Democratic Forum and the Alliance of Free Democrats, competing for leadership. Hungary had shaken off Soviet domination and embraced the ideals of democracy and free enterprise.

An even more momentous upheaval occurred in 1989 in East Germany. More than 340,000 people voted for freedom and prosperity with their feet, escaping to West Germany across the recently opened borders of Hungary and Czechoslovakia. Far larger numbers took to the streets in protest against the regime. Hoping to restore calm, Honecker's colleagues deposed their sickly, old, hard-line boss, but antigovernment demonstrations continued. On November 6, when almost a million demonstrators crammed the streets of East Berlin, the Communist government resigned. On November 9, in an explosion of patriotic fervor, the Berlin Wall was breached; tens of thousands of East Germans flocked into West Berlin, where they were welcomed with flowers and champagne. Liberated East Germany was soon reunited with West Germany, with Gorbachev's ultimate approval.

In Bulgaria, the dramatic events in Berlin led to the resignation of Tedor Zhivkov, the longest-serving Communist dictator in the Soviet bloc and an opponent of reform. Bulgaria had joined the quest for democratic government and private enterprise.

While democratic reforms triumphed elsewhere, Romania's Nicholae Ceausescu, long bent on pursuing his own dictatorial course and hostile to Gorbachev's reforms, ruthlessly enforced his own rule, ordering his soldiers to shoot into a crowd of antigovernment demonstrators. But popular resentment was too powerful to contain, and even the army turned against the dictator. On December 25, 1989, Ceausescu and his wife were tried and executed. The most hardened symbol of Communist rule, defying to the last the common trend toward democratic freedom, had ignominiously fallen.

Faced with massive demonstrations in Prague and urged by Gorbachev himself to institute democratic reform, Czechoslovakia's Communist leaders resigned on November 24, 1989. Václav

The Wall Came Tumbling Down. The Berlin Wall, symbol of the division of Germany, was breached in November 1989. Young people excitedly clambered onto the partially demolished wall, while East and West Berliners thronged the streets. *(Corbis/Regis Bossu/Sygma)*

◀ Map 21.3 Post–Cold War Europe and the Former Soviet Union Instead of the stark postwar division of Europe into three blocs—Western Europe, Eastern Europe, and the Soviet Union—the Continent is now a patch work of independent countries, some with new names. Russia remains the largest country, but the former Soviet Republics have claimed their territory on Russia's eastern and southern borders. Within Europe, East and West Germany have reunited, while Yugoslavia has split up.

Havel, a leading dissident writer and outspoken advocate of democracy who had been jailed for his views, was chosen president on December 25.

Shocked by the news of Ceausescu's execution and Havel's election, the Yugoslav Communist party caved in. Its central committee suggested the formation of a multiparty system, which was fully adopted in January 1990.

Except for Albania, where the Communist party held on until free elections in February

1991, all of Eastern Europe had liberated itself from Soviet domination—a breathtaking change, accomplished unexpectedly within a single year. Viewed as a whole, events in Eastern Europe had taken a surprisingly peaceful course, prompted by a number of favorable factors. First, Gorbachev had been willing to let the satellite peoples go their own way. Second, led by intellectuals and clergy, the people united against repression, foreign domination, and economic misery, which so vividly contrasted with the prosperity of Western Europe. Third, like Gorbachev, the Communist rulers had lost confidence in their Marxist-Leninist ideology; they knew that they had forfeited their legitimacy. Finally, the evidence of progress under freedom and democracy in the West had penetrated deep into eastern lands and had heightened popular expectations. The revolutionary changes of 1989 constituted an overwhelming victory for Western forms of government and ways of life.

The Disintegration of the Soviet Union The transformation and spiritual rebirth that Gorbachev hoped for the Soviet Union did not occur. In October 1990, Gorbachev conceded that "unfortunately, our society is not ready for the procedures of a law-based state. We don't have that level of political culture, those traditions. All that will come in the future."[5] Meanwhile, the Soviet Union was experiencing a breakdown of effective government, economic collapse, corruption, and spiraling crime. In response to the mounting crisis, the liberals, most strongly represented in Moscow and Leningrad among the young generation open to Western ways, pressed, under Boris Yeltsin's guidance, for speedy westernization, including a multiparty system and a market economy. On the opposite side, the Communist hard-liners prepared to revive the old system, relying on the army and the security forces to restore order and hold the country together. In August 1991, they staged a coup, imprisoning Gorbachev and deposing him as president of the Soviet Union. Their aim was to establish a new Communist dictatorship.

However, the conspirators, all of them high officials appointed by Gorbachev, grossly misjudged the people's revulsion against the Communist party. The KGB's vanguard forces defected to

Yeltsin, who led a fervent popular protest at a risk to his life. The emotional outburst in favor of democracy quickly spread from Moscow to other cities, and the coup collapsed within three days. The chief victim of the coup, apart from its leaders, was the Communist party, now repudiated by Gorbachev himself and swept aside by public fury. Racked by the deteriorating economy and the growing nationalist sentiments among the various ethnic groups, the Soviet Union fell to pieces. The Baltic nations—Lithuania, Latvia, and Estonia—established their independence shortly after the coup, and a new Commonwealth of Independent States, consisting of eleven former republics of the collapsed Soviet Union, was proclaimed in December 1991. At the end of the month, Gorbachev, the last leader of the Soviet Union, resigned as president of a now defunct country. Boris Yeltsin, president of Russia, the most powerful of the new independent states, became the informal leader of the commonwealth. Its ideology discredited, its economy shattered, and its government transformed into a confederation of sovereign states, the Soviet Union had collapsed as a major force in world affairs. Only one superpower remained.

The Death of an Ideal?

The sudden and unexpected collapse of communism in Eastern Europe in 1989 seemed to discredit Marxism irrevocably. Reformers in Eastern European lands liberated from Communist oppression expressed revulsion for the socialist past and a desire to regenerate their countries with an infusion of Western liberal ideals and institutions. Havel, the newly elected president of a free Czechoslovakia, expressed this disillusionment with the past and hope for a new democratic future:

> *The worst of it is that we live in a spoiled moral environment. We have become morally ill because we are used to saying one thing and thinking another. We have learned not to believe in anything, not to care about each other, to worry only about ourselves. . . . The*

previous regime, armed with a proud and intolerant ideology, reduced people into the means of production. . . . Many of our citizens died in prison in the 1950's. Many were executed. Thousands of human lives were destroyed.

Perhaps you are asking what kind of republic I am dreaming about. I will answer you: a republic that is independent, free, democratic, a republic with economic prosperity and also social justice.[6]

Marxism is a failed ideology propped up only by force in the few surviving Communist regimes. "Scientific socialism," which claimed to have deciphered the essential meaning and direction of history, is neither scientific nor relevant to current needs. It is merely another idea that was given too much credence and is now ready to be swept into the dustbin of history. Political theorist Francis Fukuyama suggests that the decline of communism and the end of the cold war reveal a larger process at work, "the ultimate triumph of Western liberal democracy":

The twentieth century saw the developed world descend into a paroxysm of ideological violence, as liberalism contended first with the remnants of absolutism, then bolshevism and Fascism, and finally an updated Marxism that threatened to lead to the ultimate apocalypse of nuclear war. But the century that began full of self-confidence in the ultimate triumph of Western liberal democracy seems at its close to be returning full circle to where it started . . . to an unabashed victory of economic and political liberalism. The triumph of the West, of the Western idea, is evident first of all in the total exhaustion of viable systematic alternatives to Western liberalism. . . . What we may be witnessing . . . is the end point of mankind's ideological evolution and the universalization of Western liberal democracy as the final form of government.[7]

THE POST-COLD WAR WORLD

The end of the cold war marked a sharp break with the past. The competition between the two superpowers and their rival ideologies, which had polarized world politics, now gave way to a new affirmation of the world's political diversity, encouraged by the victorious ideals of democratic freedom and self-determination. Ethnic and religious minorities began to struggle for recognition and independence; political tensions within and between states, hitherto subdued by superpower rivalry, flared up. The collapse of the Communist dictatorships was followed by the agonies of liberation among the peoples of Eastern and Central Europe and the former Soviet Union.

Eastern Europe After 1989

At the start, hopes ran high in Eastern and Central Europe. The Western ideal of freedom and democracy had penetrated deep into the eastern lands and had heightened popular expectations. By 1990, however, the euphoria of the previous year began to vanish. How could democratic government and market economies be adapted to the tension-ridden traditions of that troubled area, now suspended between the remnants of Communist rule and the glittering promise of Western life? In 1991, Václav Havel summed up those strains of the transition as follows:

We are witnesses to a bizarre state of affairs: society has freed itself, true, but in some ways it behaves worse than when it was in chains. Criminality has grown rapidly, and the familiar sewage that in times of historical reversal always wells up from the nether regions of the collective psyche has overflowed into the mass media, especially the gutter press. But there are . . . more serious and dangerous symptoms: hatred among nationalities, suspicion, racism, even signs of Fascism; politicking, an unrestrained, unheeding struggle for purely particular interests, unadulterated ambition, fanaticism of every conceivable kind, new and unprecedented varieties of robbery, the rise of different mafias; and a prevailing lack of tolerance, understanding, taste, moderation, and reason.[8]

How under these conditions could people follow the Western model? Yet after 1995, the economic prospects began to improve, with the help of Western aid. Now people in Poland, Hungary, and the Czech Republic anticipate political stability and prosperity through their integration into NATO in 1999 and future membership in the European Union. Life greatly improved after Havel's speech. Farther east, Bulgaria and Romania also began to emancipate themselves from their Communist heritage, although they are still beset by poverty. Albania fell deeper into economic misery, resembling a Third World country. In many parts of Eastern Europe ethnic tensions simmered.

Conditions were worst in Yugoslavia. Cobbled together after World War I as an artificial state, and composed of sharply different ethnic groups dominated by Serbia, Yugoslavia was torn apart by the nationalist ambitions set off by the collapse of the Soviet Union. In July 1991, Slovenia and Croatia voted for independence; in April 1992, Bosnia seceded, ending Serbian control. Now ethnic hatred exploded, centered on Bosnia, a splintered mountainous region. Its major ethnic groups—44 percent Muslim, 32 percent Catholic Croat, and 11 percent Orthodox Serb—were scattered in multiethnic communities, with few ethnically consolidated areas.

The three ethnic groups ruthlessly fought each other, the Bosnian Serbs attempting to join with Serbia in a Greater Serbia. They conquered 70 percent of Bosnia, conducting a brutal "ethnic cleansing" of Muslims, while submitting Sarajevo, Bosnia's capital, to bloody bombardment. All sides, but most of all the Serbs, committed heinous atrocities, provoking moral outrage.

A U.N. force vainly tried to prevent further ethnic cleansing, especially by Serbs. In November 1995, the United States stepped forward, in negotiations held in Dayton, Ohio, to promote peace. The Dayton Agreement proposed a Bosnian government equally shared by Muslims, Croats, and Serbs. As the fighting died down, the U.N. forces were replaced by smaller NATO units, including American troops and even some Russian soldiers. A measure of normality returned to Sarajevo. Yet can a foreign military presence soften deeply entrenched local hatreds?

Europeans and Americans were forced to reconsider this question when violence erupted between Serbs and ethnic Albanians in the Yugoslav province of Kosovo. This is a sacred place for Serbs, the site of Orthodox shrines and of the battle of Kosovo in 1389, in which the Ottoman Turks defeated the Serbs, ruling Kosovo until 1912. The Serbs regard this battle as the birth of the Serb nation. Ethnic antagonism has persisted between Serbs and the predominantly Muslim Albanians, who form 90 percent of the population of two million. In 1989, Yugoslav president Slobodan Milosevic, seeking to shore up his power by manipulating Serbian nationalist feelings, revoked political autonomy for the ethnic Albanians in Kosovo. This loss of self-government combined with mistreatment at the hands of Serbian officials radicalized more Albanians, who now pressed for Albanian separatism. In 1998, when armed bands of the Kosovo Liberation Army (KLA) began to attack Serbs in Kosovo, Milosevic sent Serbian forces to crush the KLA. Repelled by the forced expulsions and massacres of innocent villagers, NATO felt compelled to intervene, launching air strikes on Serbia in March 1999. At the same time special Serbian forces, determined to drive Albanians out of Kosovo, stormed into the region. Carrying the practice of ethnic cleansing to a new level of brutality, they terrorized and murdered Albanians, systematically burned villages, confiscated valuables, and compelled their victims to flee the province. Hundreds of thousands of Albanian refugees streamed out of the country into neighboring lands, creating a massive humanitarian crisis. The NATO bombardment of Yugoslavia, expected to be brief and decisive, continued for eleven weeks—so too did the ethnic cleansing of Kosovo—until Milosevic capitulated. Eventually the Kosovo Albanians were allowed to return to their ravaged country. A force of forty thousand NATO and U.N. troops remained in Kosovo to assist with relief efforts, prevent revenge attacks on the remaining Serb population, and enable an administration to be put in place to guarantee Kosovo's autonomy.

The U.N. International Criminal Tribunal for the Former Yugoslavia indicted President Milosevic and Bosnian Serb and Croatian leaders and military commanders on charges of genocide and crimes against humanity. President Milosevic ran for reelection in a fraudulent campaign in September 2000. This brazen act sparked massive protests in Belgrade and forced him from office. Facing the threat of a cutoff of Western aid for rebuilding the shattered country, Serbia eventually arrested him and transferred him to the custody of the U.N. Tribunal to face charges. His trial began in 2002.

Post-Communist Russia and the Former Soviet Republics

Throughout the 1990s and into the new century, the Russian Federal Republic has been struggling to bring its political and economic systems into conformity with the Western model while coping with its loss of territory and superpower status. The collapse of the Soviet Union revealed Russia to be a weak, poorly developed society, beset by profound problems.

Yeltsin's "Shock Therapy." Marred by mismanagement, waste, and lack of incentives, the Soviet economic system had failed miserably in comparison with Western capitalism. In order to reform the economy and improve the standard of living of the Russian people, which lagged far behind living standards in Western lands, President Yeltsin, emerging in 1990 as the leader of the new Russia, made a sudden switch in 1992 from a state-run economy to private ownership and a capitalist market system. This precipitous transfer of state firms to private ownership—"shock therapy"—in many ways proved a disaster. The chief beneficiaries of privatization were often the same inefficient managers who had controlled the economy during the Soviet era and amassed wealth by unscrupulous means. As a result of industrial decline and the withdrawal of government subsidies, ruinous inflation reduced millions of people dependent on pensions to hand-to-mouth subsistence. Many working Russians also sank into poverty as real wages plummeted some 40 percent from 1992 to 1998. Workers often had to wait two to six months for their paychecks, and unemployment soared. In sum, the achievement of economic security, no less than the attainment of participatory democracy, was likely to be a long and painful process.

With popular unrest mounting and facing opposition from Communist hardliners, Yeltsin was forced to slow his liberalization of the economy; the social costs—public confusion over bewildering changes, a sharp decline in the standard of living, and the loss of productivity leading to shortages—were too high. "No more experiments," advised slogans spray-painted on walls.

Adding to the intractable problems of the new Russia were soaring crime and corruption. Yeltsin consolidated his power by making alliances with a small group of businessmen, the "oligarchs," who had grown wealthy by acquiring former state-owned enterprises at extremely low prices. They plundered the firms for assets, concentrating Russia's wealth in their own hands, and they gained control of banks that operated like crime organizations. As law enforcement deteriorated, organized crime became a major force in Russian life.

In August 1998 everything changed. The dysfunctional banking system precipitated a second currency collapse, wiping out Russians' savings and livelihoods. Among the casualties were the majority of the oligarchs. Some were ruined by the collapse of their banks, others went abroad, and the remainder backed out of public life. Suddenly their political influence, which had been paramount since 1995, diminished dramatically, and a new generation of businessmen began to emerge.

Yeltsin resigned on New Year's Eve 1999. His grasp of events had become increasingly uncertain, and he was obviously incapable of ruling. He thus became the first Russian leader to give up power voluntarily. In his demoralized, bankrupt, and corrupt post-Communist country, Yeltsin contended with problems beyond the capacity of the most astute politician. He made appalling mistakes by selling major state enterprises to private individuals—often unscrupulous oligarchs—at ridiculously low prices. However, he made the restoration of communism in Russia impossible. It was no mean achievement.

Putin: Clamping Down and Reaching Out. Yeltsin's chosen successor, Vladimir Putin, determined to make his mark as a strongman during his short term as Yeltsin's prime minister by reopening the war in Chechnya, a small Islamic enclave in the Caucasus, at war for centuries with the conquering Russians. After two years of ruthless fighting, at great political damage to Yeltsin, the defeated Russian armies withdrew in 1996, leaving the burden of the final settlement of Chechnya's independence to the future. The war resumed in 1999 when Chechen rebels invaded neighboring Dagestan in an effort to establish a united Islamic state in the Caucasus. At the same time a terrorist attack on apartment blocks in Russian cities killed more than three hundred people and maimed many more. Putin put the blame for the attack on Chechens and stormed into the Caucasus to force the invaders out of Dagestan. The Chechen capital, Grozny, was razed; the main victims were elderly Russian residents, the rebels having already escaped to the mountains. Russian troops took control of the war-devastated Caucasus region, but the Chechen leaders remained at large and continued guerrilla attacks on Russian soldiers.

Putin became president of Russia at a time when modest economic stability was beginning to emerge. His objective has been to establish a strong centralized state under the rule of law. He destroyed the remaining political influence of the oligarchs in order to reassert executive power. The oligarchs have been succeeded by eight large business groups who have created monopolies by systematically buying up entire sectors of Russian industry. Private companies in the coal, steel, automobile, aluminum, and timber industries have been aggressively taken over by business tycoons. The new tycoons, four of whom are under forty, differ from the oligarchs in that they are beginning to modernize the industries that they control; they invest in their companies, pay taxes, and forge connections with Western industry. A growing body of new business law circumscribes their tactics to a limited extent.

By 2003, cautious optimism was visible. Russia's oil and gas are in demand abroad, and a nascent middle class is emerging. Profits are still leaving the country, but at a slower rate, and more money is being reinvested in the economy. Foreign investment, which dried up during the corrupt and chaotic Yeltsin years, is returning.

Despite misgivings about Western intentions toward Russia and sensitivity about their loss of superpower status, Russians are adopting more positive feelings toward the West. The emergence of this new attitude has coincided with Putin's policies, which clearly indicate his conviction that Russia's future lies westward. In the spring of 2002 Putin set a course of strategic integration with the United States and Europe. With President George W. Bush he signed a bilateral arms control treaty to reduce nuclear arsenals, and at the same time Russia was made a junior member of NATO. Because NATO's historical mission had been a military alliance against the Soviet Union, Russia had hitherto regarded NATO as a threat. But Putin evidently regards the prestige of membership in NATO as an opportunity for integration with the West and as a means of maintaining Russia's image as a great power.

The gap between Russia and the West remains enormous. Russia is still a huge poor country riddled with crime and corruption; it is burdened with a crumbling infrastructure, high inflation, and desperate rural poverty. Its health and social services are in disarray, and drug addiction, AIDS, drug-resistant tuberculosis, and alcoholism run rampant. Life expectancy has declined over the past decade, and deaths outnumber births. Real incomes of Russians are only now starting to approach the levels reached in 1990.

Unrealistic optimism at the time of the Soviet collapse that Russia would emerge as a free, democratic, and market-oriented state changed to pessimism during the 1990s. Building a democratic civic society took centuries in the West; Russia in its weakened state cannot achieve that in one generation. But there are positive signs, and it is in the interests of the West to assist Russia; for if Russia unravels, the whole Eurasian continent will be destabilized.

The Former Soviet Republics Deep uncertainty prevails in the states that succeeded the former Soviet republics: Belarus, Ukraine, Moldova, Georgia, and the Muslim states of central Asia, which include Azerbaijan, Kazakhstan, Turkmenistan, and Uzbekistan. Reorganized through dubious elections, the majority of the states are still dominated by the Communist legacy of over-regulated, centrally planned economies. The precipitous breakdown of trading patterns after the Soviet collapse resulted in economic turmoil. The privatization of major industries has proceeded slowly, if at all, and government corruption and regulation have hampered foreign investment, leading to continued impoverishment of the populations of the states.

The Muslim countries are governed by repressive one-party governments, and the growth of Islamic extremism has destabilized the region. The Muslim states clustered around the Caspian Sea have extensive oil and gas reserves. Cooperative ventures with western European and American oil companies have given these states access to potential wealth.

Central Asia, located at the intersection of Europe, Asia, and the Middle East, provides porous borders for traffic in weapons, terrorists, and narcotics. After centuries of compulsory unity imposed by tsars and commissars, the diverse and divided inhabitants in the huge area between Europe and East Asia have to learn how to manage by themselves. This is no small task for people untrained in the techniques of civic cooperation required for effective modern states.

Western Europe

Since the end of World War II, the Western European states have engaged in a slow process of economic, political, and cultural integration. The collapse of the Soviet power supplied a sudden jolt for accelerating this trend. In 1991 in the Dutch city of Maastricht, the twelve members of the European Community negotiated the Maastricht Treaty, designed to shape Europe into a unified economic and political union. By 1993 the member states had ratified the Treaty and, in recognition of its aims, the European Community transformed itself into the European Union (EU). This organization is shaping Europe into a unified political and economic force, with the help of a common monetary unit, the euro, which competes with the U.S. dollar as a currency for worldwide use. Tied to the global economy with an impact second only to the United States, this new Europe is emerging as a powerful presence in world affairs. EU countries are also members of NATO, which in 2002 admitted its former adversary, Russia, as a junior partner.

Implementing the EU's objectives has proved no easy task. Many Europeans have unanswered questions about the future of their countries. Are they surrendering their identity, along with their sovereignty, to the EU? Are Europeanization and globalization (the latter frequently defined as "American imperialism") going to change irrevocably their national status?

Center-left governments in EU countries are being challenged by the resurgent right wing, which champions an anti-immigration platform. Many Europeans feel that immigration is a legitimate cause for alarm, for every year thousands of illegal immigrants enter the EU area from all over the world. Some are genuinely fleeing oppression and danger in their own countries; others are in search of jobs; most are unskilled. Unlike the United States, European nations have very limited immigration, so people entering countries illegally have to apply for asylum—that is, they have to prove that they would be in danger if forced to return to their countries of origin. Asylum may be granted on humanitarian grounds, but rarely for immigrants just looking for jobs.

Both Germany and England, which have the greatest number, forbid asylum seekers to work but give them housing and welfare checks while they wait for their applications to be considered; this wait can take up to two years. Asylum seekers are bitterly resented by citizens who perceive them to be living idly on the generosity of the welfare state. Although European countries are comparatively prosperous, unemployment is high, and when jobs are few, immigration is seen as a threat. Right-wing rhetoric is complicating attempts to liberalize the myriad asylum laws. Throughout Europe, right-wing parties exploit the immigration issue by charging that immigrants cause crime. By playing on fears for personal safety, these parties hope to win people to their cause.

Because the EU is integrating politically as well as economically, any country applying for membership has not only to demonstrate economic progress toward a market economy but also to conform to acceptable standards of democracy and human rights. By 2000, applications for admission had been received from twelve countries: Bulgaria, Cyprus, the Czech Republic, Estonia, Hungary, Latvia, Lithuania, Malta, Poland, Romania, Slovakia, and Slovenia. If all are admitted, the population of the EU will approach five hundred million. A major concern is that most of these candidates have weak economies and would

Growing Ethnic Diversity in Europe. In recent decades, Western Europe has become the home for an increasing number of people from outside the Continent. Turkish guest workers have settled in Germany; millions of people from former colonial possessions in North Africa and sub-Saharan Africa now reside in France; immigrants from India, Pakistan, and the Caribbean, regions once part of the British Empire, now live in Britain. Cultural clashes, competition for employment, criminality, and pressure on welfare services have, at times, led to a xenophobic reaction against immigrants. *(AP/World Wide Photos)*

be in need of financial assistance at enormous expense to the EU. Hitherto, countries accepted into membership were fully democratic with mature market economies. Can the EU choose to neglect countries that fall short of this ideal, or should it help them to achieve it?

In the United Kingdom, Prime Minister Margaret Thatcher resigned in 1990 in the face of conservative criticism. Her successor, John Major, maintained an uncertain majority in Parliament, increasingly troubled by political scandals and the rising popularity of the Labour party. In the election of 1997, that party, revitalized by Tony Blair, its young and lively leader in

close touch with the people, scored an impressive victory. Under his leadership, the Labour party has moved to the political center. It endorsed a pro-business, pro-enterprise policy, limiting benefits for the poor, and jettisoned the old working-class/state-ownership image. This policy has given the country an unusually strong economy, and London is a vibrant worldwide financial center. Socially, however, the picture is less bright; educational standards in schools have fallen, the health service is in crisis, and crime (in a formerly law-abiding country) has increased. The industrial north of England has been neglected and is currently the largest ricipient of EU structural funds, which makes this region one of the most deprived in Europe. Looking across the Channel to Europe, the English wonder why their public services are so inferior to those in other EU countries.

In Northern Ireland, where Protestants and Catholics had long been at war with each other, Blair helped to end the conflict and create an elected assembly. After three difficult years, the peace process was finally on track. It was a huge gamble that terrorists and bigots, who have spent decades trying to destroy each other, could act rationally in a democratic assembly. The potential for violence in Northern Ireland still remains high.

Britain continues to play an important role in international affairs. It aided the United States, its close ally, in the Gulf War of 1991, when an international coalition led by the United States prevented Saddam Hussein from annexing Kuwait to Iraq. Britain also participated in NATO actions to counter Serbian aggression in the Balkans, and in the war against the Taliban in Afghanistan following the tragic events of September 11, 2001. In 2003 it joined with the United States to overthrow Saddam Hussein's dictatorship.

France has a population of fifty-eight million and is the largest territorial state in western Europe. Cherishing their historical tradition, the French are uneasy about the intrusion of alien ways, especially from the United States. Following de Gaulle, the French goverment still wants to play its part in world affairs, for instance, in opposing American policies in the Mideast. At the same time, however, it works closely with NATO to reduce violence in the Balkans. Its chief concern is cooperation with Germany in creating an effective European Union that balances French and German aspirations. France also wants to preserve its influence in Africa, generously donating financial aid to economic development.

At home, French politics are in reasonably stable order. The socialist François Mitterrand, president until 1995, named Jacques Chirac, a moderate conservative, as his prime minister in 1986. Succeeding Mitterrand as president, Chirac was forced to name a socialist, Lionel Jospin, to head the goverment. The two men were each suited to their jobs, but personal rivalry made for a difficult relationship, especially when Jospin

challenged Chirac for the presidency in 2002. A fragmented vote resulted in an upset when Jean Marie Le Pen, the far-right leader of the National Front party, qualified for a runoff election against Chirac. The result sent shock waves through France, where demonstrations against Le Pen gathered force and Chirac campaigned vigorously, claiming that international respect for France would be wrecked if Le Pen—an anti-immigration, anti-EU, antiglobalization, anti-Semitic, racist candidate—won a large proportion of the vote. He received only 18 percent of the vote, but the affair revealed a troubling undercurrent in French society.

With its eighty-three million people, Germany has the largest population in Europe. It enjoys the third largest economy in the world and is proud of the peaceful reunification of its western and eastern parts in 1990. Helmut Kohl, as chancellor of West Germany, was the architect of the reunited Germany; he poured huge amounts of West German money into what had been the Communist German Democratic Republic, hoping for quick integration. However, attitudes and habits developed under communism have persisted; the seventeen million former East Germans, with no experience of democracy, still feel themselves to be second-class citizens. More than a decade after reunification, a sour mood of disillusionment persists. Unemployment is at 20 percent because communist-era factories have closed and no new industries have been established. East Germans feel sidelined by reunification. The rise in right-wing violence since reunification is particularly severe in the old East Germany, where neo-Nazis and skinheads, usually underemployed and alienated youth, have been responsible for outbreaks of lawlessness and brutality against "outsiders"—immigrants and Jews—whom they regard as parasites draining away the country's resources and diluting its national character.

Kohl's conservative chancellorship ended after sixteen eventful years. In 1998, Germans elected Gerhard Schröder, leader of the Social Democrats, as his successor. Schröder's party formed a coalition with the Greens, who scaled down their environmental and pacifist radicalism. Like England and France, Germany is now ruled by a moderate left-wing government. And like his

French colleague, Schröder has to balance the customary high level of social benefits against the pressures of global economic competition, while unemployment remains high.

OUR GLOBAL AGE: TENSIONS AND CONCERNS

In the twenty-first century, globalization continues relentlessly; the world is being knit ever closer together by the spread of Western ideals, popular culture (particularly American), free-market capitalism, and technology. Government officials and business and professional people all over the world dress in Western clothes. Women follow Western fashions in dress and makeup. People line up to eat at McDonald's, see a Hollywood movie, or attend a rock concert. Everywhere people are eager to adopt the latest technology that originated in the West but is now also manufactured in other, particularly Asian, lands. Advanced technology intensifies the means of communication, not only through television and radio but also with faxes, e-mail, cellular phones, or the Internet—all means of instantaneous individual communication that have become commonplace in the past decade.

These developments promote shared interests among individuals and businesses, some of them multinational corporations, throughout the globe, reducing the importance of national frontiers. All these factors combined are reshaping non-Western societies in a relentless adjustment that causes both deep hardships and possibilities for a better life.

The ideals of freedom and democracy, historical accomplishments of Western civilization, exert a powerful influence worldwide; they are also part of the process of westernization. Unlike technology, they cannot be easily put into practice outside the countries of their origin. However, they inspire human ambitions everywhere. They have even become part of the rhetoric of dictatorships.

At the same time, strong cultural traditions still divide the world. Traditional ways of life, often at odds with the demands of modernization, remain deeply ingrained in many lands.

Among people deeply committed to their own cultural traditions or feeling left behind by modernization, the process of globalization has provoked a powerful backlash, nowhere more so than in the Muslim world. The hatred of radical Muslim fundamentalists for the West, which they see as a threat to traditional Islam, is a striking example of the clash of cultures in a world being increasingly connected.

On September 11, 2001, nineteen Muslim Arabs, most of them from Saudi Arabia, hijacked four planes: two of them they crashed into the World Trade Center in New York, bringing down both towers; a third plane rammed into the Pentagon in Washington, D.C., causing severe damage; the fourth plane, apparently headed for the White House, crashed in a field in Pennsylvania when passengers attacked the hijackers. In all, more than three thousand people perished in the worst terrorist attack in history. The meticulously planned operation was the work of Al Qaeda, an international terrorist network of militant Muslims, or Islamists as they call themselves. In 1998, it was responsible for the deadly bombings of the American embassies in Kenya and Tanzania, which killed hundreds, and in 2000, it detonated a bomb next to the U.S. destroyer *Cole* in the harbor of Aden, costing the lives of seventeen American sailors.

The leader of Al Qaeda, Osama bin Laden, scion of an immensely wealthy Saudi family, operated from Afghanistan with the protection of the radical fundamentalist Taliban, who ruled the country, transforming it into a repressive regime based on a rigid interpretation of Islamic law. In particular, the Taliban imposed oppressive rules for women, permitting beatings by male relatives, prohibiting females from working, barring them from schools, and demanding that they wear a garment—the burka—that covered them from head to foot. Violators could be severely beaten, imprisoned, or executed.

When Taliban leaders refused to turn bin Laden over to the United States, President George W. Bush, supported by an international coalition, launched a military campaign whose ultimate goal was the destruction of international terrorism. The United States showed a fierce resolve unexpected by bin Laden, who thought that the Americans would not risk sending troops to fight

Afghanistan After the Taliban. After the defeat of the Taliban, which had harbored and encouraged Al Qaeda terrorists, Hamid Karzai became president of an interim government in Afghanistan with the support of the United States. President Karzai struggled to deal with his nation's immense problems: local warlords who resisted the Kabul government, pockets of surviving Taliban fighters, the return of hundreds of thousands of refugees after the ouster of the Taliban, and the destruction, caused by years of warfare and drought, of great stretches of once fertile land. *(Reuters New Media Inc./Corbis)*

in the forbidding Afghan terrain and against people who had defeated the Soviet Union. Local Afghan forces opposed to the Taliban, assisted by American airpower—which proved decisive—defeated the Taliban in a few weeks. The new leaders of Afghanistan no longer permit their country to serve as a haven and training center for radical Islamic terrorists. But Taliban fighters, who found refuge in Pakistan, waged guerrilla war against the American-backed government; accelerating violence at the end of 2003 threatened Afghan stability.

On numerous occasions President Bush and his chief advisers declared that the attack on Afghanistan was directed against "evil doers" and not against Muslims in general or their faith. However, bin Laden and his followers view their struggle against the United States as a holy war against the infidel. Bin Laden and other Arabs from Morocco to Yemen who were devoted to a militant Islam had fought in Afghanistan to drive out the Soviets. During that conflict, bin Laden and his cohorts drew up plans for the creation of an Islamic world-state governed by Islamic law, a revival of the medieval caliphate. In 1998, bin Laden told his followers that the stationing of American troops in Saudi Arabia, "the land of the two holy Mosques," demonstrated that

America "had spearheaded the crusade against the Islamic nation." A religious fanatic and absolutist who cannot tolerate pluralism, bin Laden wants to drive westerners and Western values out of Islamic lands; he is also a theocrat, who would use the state's power to impose a narrow, intolerant version of Islam on the Muslim world. He and his followers are zealots who are convinced that they are doing God's will. Recruits for suicide missions are equally convinced that they are waging holy war against the enemies of God and their centers of evil, for which they will be richly rewarded in Paradise.

To be sure, the actions of bin Laden and his followers violate core Islamic teachings against killing civilians. At the same time, however, terrorists find religious justification for their actions in Islamic tradition. The early followers of Muhammad, says Bernard Lewis, divided the world

> into two houses: the House of Islam, in which a Muslim government ruled and Muslim law prevailed, and the House of War, the rest of the world . . . ruled by infidels. Between the two, there was to be a perpetual state of war until the entire world either embraced Islam or submitted to the rule of the Muslim state. . . . For Osama bin Laden, 2001 marks the resumption of the war for the religious dominance of the world that began in the seventh century. For him and his followers, this is the moment of opportunity. Today America exemplifies the civilization that embodies the leadership of the House of War, and it . . . has become degenerate and demoralized, ready to be overthrown.[9]

The hatred of radical Muslims for the West shows that in an age of globalism the world is still divided by strong cultural traditions. It also reveals how the problems confronting the Middle East—authoritarian governments, the suppression of human rights, rampant corruption, mushrooming populations, high unemployment, and the ongoing Arab-Israeli conflict—have a global impact. All of these factors have led many disillusioned young Muslims to place their hopes for a better life not in democratic reforms but in a radical Islam that promises to restore a glorious past and guarantee entrance to Paradise. Fostering this

outlook are the numerous religious schools financed by Saudi Arabia that have been established in many parts of the Muslim world. In these schools youngsters are given no secular education and from an early age are indoctrinated in the tenets of radical Islamism: hatred of the West, holy war against the infidel, the Jew as Devil, and the virtue of martyrdom for the faith.

Before September 11, Al Qaeda operated in Muslim lands from Indonesia to Morocco with little fear of government interference and received huge sums from wealthy Arabs in the Persian Gulf and from worldwide Muslim organizations purporting to be raising funds only for charitable purposes. Al Qaeda members also found a haven in western European lands, where they coordinated their operations generally unrestrained by the authorities. The successful engagement in Afghanistan, American pressure on other lands that had harbored terrorists, the tracking down, capture, and killing of Al Qaeda leaders, and rigorous international efforts to destabilize Al Qaeda's vast financial network greatly weakened the terrorist organization. But thousands of Al Qaeda fighters crossed from Afghanistan into Pakistan, and the seething discontent in the Muslim world, particularly among Arabs, provides Al Qaeda with recruits, including zealots willing to inflict maximum casualites on civilians, even if doing so means blowing themselves up in the process. After September 11, several Al Qaeda operations were thwarted, including attempts to explode airplanes. But in 2002, an Al Qaeda affiliate rammed a fuel truck into a historic Tunisian synagogue, killing nineteen people, most of them German tourists. And it is believed that in the same year the Al Qaeda network was responsible for a bus attack in Karachi that killed eleven French engineers, a bombing of the U.S. consulate in Karachi that took the lives of twelve Pakistanis, the kidnapping and beheading of the American journalist Daniel Pearl—he was singled out because he was Jewish—the blowing up of a French oil tanker off Yemen, the killing of an American marine in Kuwait, the bombing of a nightclub in Bali, Indonesia, that killed more than 200 people, most of them westerners on holiday, and an attack in Kenya on an Israeli resort that killed twelve Kenyans, three Israelis, and at least two suicide bombers (missles directed against an airliner transporting Israelis home from Kenya missed their target). In May 2003 militants affiliated with Al Qaeda bombed residential compounds in Riyadh, the capital of Saudia Arabia, killing thirty-four people, including nine suicide bombers. A short while later, a quick succession of five suicide bombings in Casablanca, Morocco killed forty-one people, including ten terrorists who may have been loosely connected with the Al Qaeda network. The targets consisted of a Jewish community center, an old Jewish cemetery, an upscale Spanish social club, the Belgian consulate, and a major hotel. November was a particularly bloody month. Another car bomb blast against a residential neighborhood in Riyadh killed seventeen, including five children, and wounded one hundred twenty-two others. A series of truck-bomb explosions in Istanbul wrecked two Jewish synagogues, the British consulate, and a British bank killing more than fifty people and wounding hundreds. These terrorist acts were designed to disrupt Muslim Turkey's pro-Western stance and secular orientation.

With Al Qaeda cells located in numerous countries, with many affiliated groups and freelancers, inspired by bin Laden's ideology, eager to attack Western interests, and with bin Laden unaccounted for, international terrorism remains a threat to world stability. Making the situation more ominous is the uncovering of evidence that Al Qaeda has sought to obtain weapons of mass destruction.

The events of September 11 may have signaled a new type of warfare for a new century. Free and open societies like the United States are vulnerable to attack, less from states that are deterred by America's might—as in the cold war—than by stateless conspiratorial groups employing modern computers and communications and difficult to trace financial operations to organize and finance terrorism. Such groups are not deterred by America's arsenal. And there is the fearful prospect that a rogue state will supply these groups with biological, chemical, and eventually nuclear weapons to wage war by proxy.

It was just such a fear that led President Bush in March 2003 to order an invasion of Iraq. The war was supported by Great Britain, who provided military assistance, but France, Germany, and Russia strongly opposed the decision. In about three weeks, U.S. and British forces, in an awesome display of operational planning and

Tyrant of Iraq. In 2002 President George W. Bush threatened to go to war in order to remove Saddam Hussein, the ruthless dictator of Iraq. In the past, Saddam attacked Iran and Kuwait and used poison gas against the rebellious Kurdish minority. In April 2003 U.S. soldiers and Iraqi citizens toppled this statue of Saddam Hussein in a square in central Baghdad. The destruction of the statue symbolized the end of a tyrannical regime. *(AP/World Wide Photos)*

precision weaponry and suffering minimum casualties, destroyed Iraq's military hardware and decimated its armies. The victorious coalition forces uncovered torture chambers, where "enemies" of Hussein's regime were brutalized, and mass graves, where thousands were slaughtered at the tyrant's command. But vexing problems remained. Could the United States install a democratic regime in a country torn by ethnic, religious, and tribal hatreds, where some Iraqis regarded the Americans as hated occupiers, and where democratic traditions and attitudes were largely lacking? The United States had declared that it invaded Iraq to overthrow a ruthless dictator who was feverishly amassing an arsenal of biological and chemical weapons and was also seeking a nuclear capability. America reminded the world that Saddam had used poison gas against Iranian forces and Kurdish rebels in the 1980s; UN inspection teams had destroyed huge stockpiles of chemical and biological weapons in the 1990s; and Saddam's regime had not complied with a Security Council resolution ordering Iraq to account fully for its weapons of mass destruction (WMD) program and to cooperate with UN inspectors. Now, warned the United States, there was a danger that Hussein would supply weapons to be used against Americans. However, when no such weapons were found in the months after Iraq's defeat—although significant amounts of equipment for preparing these weapons have been discovered and vast arsenals remain to be examined—critics in several lands accused the United States of pursuing a reckless foreign policy. Moreover, coalition forces faced armed opposition from hard-liners loyal to Hussein and his Baath party and from militant Islamists, many of them Arabs from other lands, who saw themselves engaged in a holy war against hated Americans. American soldiers were confronted with numerous daily guerrilla attacks, but they did succeed in killing and capturing many of the top leadership of the Baath party, including Hussein's two notorious sons, Uday and Qusay, who had routinely imprisoned, tortured, and murdered many Iraqis. In the closing months of 2003, attacks by Hussein loyalists—including suicide bombings—increased in scope, frequency, intensity, and sophistication; the insurgents, who demonstrated effective organization and seemed well financed, targeted both coalition forces and Iraqi officials and police working with the coalition in a deliberate attempt to demoralize and destabilize the new government and its supporters. The continued loss of American lives after President Bush had declared victory, the spiraling cost of pacifying and reconstructing Iraq, and the failure to find weapons of mass destruction led more Americans to question President Bush's policies. But there were also positive signs. Many Iraqis welcomed the end of Hussein's terror and the thousands of reconstruction projects initiated by the United States, including the renovation of 1500 schools and the greatly improved medical care. Moreover, it is hoped that the stunning capture of Saddam Hussein in December 2003, combined with increasingly more successful American counterinsurgency operations, will overcome resistance to the occupation, permitting coalition forces to proceed with constructing a free, democratic, and viable Iraq.

International terrorism is a major source of concern in today's interconnected world. There are others. Western science, medicine, humanitarianism, and economic progress have produced an unprecedented population explosion in Asia, Africa, the Middle East, and Latin America. For countless millennia the world's population remained almost stationary, slowly beginning to grow in the eighteenth century. At the height of Western imperialism, in 1900, the world's population reached 1.6 billion. Fifty years later, it reached 2.5 billion, and by the year 2000 it skyrocketed to 6.1 billion. Despite immense losses of life in two world wars, totalitarian terror, local famines, and other calamities, the world's population nearly quadrupled within a century.

The economic disparity between the rich and the poor, which sharply separates the industrialized from the developing countries, is further cause for concern. By all accounts, the trend will get worse. As a U.N. report of 1996 concluded, the gap between rich and poor "will move from inequitable to inhuman."[10]

The growth of the urban population is equally alarming. Megacities of 10 million and more people have multiplied in developing countries, the biggest being Mexico City, with 16.6 million inhabitants. Within a quarter of a century, 61 percent of the world's population is expected to live in cities. One billion urban households are too poor to feed their crowded people; Guangzhou, the biggest city in southern China, averages 5.7 people per room. These cities often contain vast, squalid slums, lack sewage facilities, clean water, and clean air, and are infected with mosquitoes that spread malaria. Crime, violence, and corruption add to the misery of the world's slum dwellers.

Violence is escalating throughout the world. In the first half of the 1990s, at least 3.2 million people were killed in local political conflicts, most of them civilians, not counting the untold number of victims of daily crime. Most frightening for the future is the development of weapons of mass destruction by states that do not share Western democratic values. North Korea, a ruthless Communist dictatorship, possesses nuclear weapons. Iran, headed by Islamic fundamentalists who support terrorism against the infidel, is also moving ahead with weapons of mass destruction.

How can peaceful global interdependence be advanced, given the persistent cultural and political differences that divide the world, promoting hatred and inciting violence? How can tiny individuals on our crowded planet gain a sense of control over their personal circumstances, as well as over the ever more complex institutions under which they live? How is it possible to gain the world-mindedness that would enable us to be co-operative citizens of our earthly habitat even under grave adversity? Can the present generation of Western peoples help shape the development of the global community in accordance with the highest ideals of Western civilization: reason, freedom, and respect for human dignity?

❖ ❖ ❖

NOTES

1. Quoted in Walter Laqueur, *Europe Since Hitler* (Baltimore: Penguin Books, 1970), p. 118.

2. "The Truman Doctrine," in *Major Problems in American Foreign Policy: Documents and Essays,* ed. Thomas G. Paterson (Lexington, Mass.: Heath, 1978), 2:290.

3. Nikita S. Krushchev in *The Crimes of the Stalin Era: Special Report to the 20th Congress of the Communist Party of the Soviet Union,* annotated by Boris I. Nicolaevsky (New York: The New Leader, 1956), p. 20.

4. Gorbachev's speech at the seventieth anniversary of the Bolshevik Revolution, quoted in *The New York Times,* November 3, 1987, p. A3.

5. Quoted in Anthony Lewis, "Et Tu Eduard," *The New York Times,* December 21, 1990, p. A39.

6. *The New York Times,* January 2, 1990, p. A13.

7. Francis Fukuyama, "The End of History," *The National Interest* (Summer 1989):3–4.

8. Václav Havel, *Summer Meditations* (New York: Alfred A. Knopf, 1992), p. 2.

9. Bernard Lewis, "Revolt of Islam," *The New Yorker,* November 19, 2001, pp. 52, 62.

10. United Nations Development Programme, *Human Development Report, 1996* (New York: Oxford University Press, 1996), p. iii.

SUGGESTED READING

Cohen, Leonard J., *Serpent in the Bosom: The Rise and Fall of Slobodan Milosevic* (2000). Violence and genocide in pursuit of an ethnic vision.

Freeland, Chrystia, *Sale of the Century: Russia's Wild Ride from Communism to Capitalism* (2000). A colorful account of the takeover of state-owned firms by Russian oligarchs.

Friedman, Thomas L., *The Lexus and the Olive Tree: Understanding Globalization* (1999). The rules and logic of the new international system.

Garron-Ash, Timothy, *The Magic Lantern: The Revolution of '89 Witnessed in Warsaw, Budapest, Berlin and Prague* (1990). A lively account of the death of communism in eastern Europe, conveying the exhilaration of the time.

Geddes, Andrew P., *Immigration and European Integration: Toward Fortress Europe* (2000). Migration into and within the European Union countries.

Gorbachev, Mikhail S., *Memoirs* (1996). The tumultuous years of reform in the Soviet Union.

Gordon, Philip, and Sophie Meunier, *The French Challenge: Adapting to Globalization* (2001). The problems of French hostility to globalization.

Havel, Václav, *Summer Meditations* (1992). An excellent selection of essays by the president of the Czech Republic.

Hodge, James F., and Gideon Rose, eds., *How Did This Happen: Terrorism and the New War* (2001). Wide-ranging essays on the attack of September 11, 2001.

Pond, Elizabeth *Beyond the Wall: Germany's Road to Unification* (1993). An account of the new Germany by a veteran journalist with anoptimistic view of the future of Europe.

Rashid, Ahmed, *Jihad: The Rise of Militant Islam in Central Asia* (2002). Analysis of Islamic movements in a volatile area.

Remnick, David, *Lenin's Tomb* (1993). A superb, Pulitzer prize–winning account of the last years of the Soviet Union.

———, *Resurrection: The Struggle for a New Russia* (1997). A vivid portrait of Russia's post-1991 problems.

Rieff, David, *Slaughterhouse: Bosnia and the Failure of the West* (1995). The responsibility of the Western nations for the Bosnian genocide.

REVIEW QUESTIONS

1. What do you consider the biggest changes to have taken place in Western Europe after World War II?

2. Discuss the major problems of government in France and Britain since 1945.

3. What problems in the Soviet Union did Stalin face after the end of World War II? How did he try to cope with them?

4. What happened to Stalinism after Stalin's death? Under Khrushchev? Under Gorbachev?

5. List the major events in Eastern Europe in 1989. Why was the "revolution of 1989" a relatively peaceful one?

6. What is your attitude regarding the conflict between modernization and the preservation of traditional cultures?

7. Why has lethal terrorism arisen in the Muslim world?

Epilogue

REAFFIRMING THE CORE VALUES OF THE WESTERN TRADITION

In recent years, modern Western civilization, whose core values were articulated during the Enlightenment, has come under severe attack from several quarters, including religious thinkers, intellectuals loosely called postmodernists, advocates of the poor and oppressed, and militant Muslims. Some religious thinkers deplore the modern age for its espousal of secular rationality, the central legacy of the Enlightenment. These thinkers argue that reason without God degenerates into an overriding concern for technical efficiency—an attitude of mind that produces Auschwitz, Stalin's labor camps, weapons of mass destruction, and the plundering and polluting of the environment. The self without God degenerates into selfish competition, domination, exploitation, and unrestrained hedonism. Human dignity conceived purely in secular terms does not permit us to recognize the *thou* of another human being, to see our neighbor as someone who has been dignified by God; and removing God from life ends in spiritual emptiness and gnawing emotional distress. These critics of the Enlightenment tradition urge the reorientation of thinking around God and transcendent moral absolutes. Without such a reorientation, they argue, liberal democracy cannot resist the totalitarian temptation or overcome human wickedness.

Postmodernists argue that modernity founded on the Enlightenment legacy, which once was viewed as a progressive force emancipating the individual from unreasonable dogmas, traditions, and authority, has itself become a source of repression through its own creations: technology, bureaucracy, consumerism, materialism, the nation-state, ideologies, and a host of other institutions, procedures, and norms. Aversion to a technoscientific culture and to its methodology leads postmodernists to devalue the principle of objectivity in the social sciences and to give greater weight to the subjective, to feelings, intuition, fantasy, to the poetry of life. Postmodernists contend that the evaluation of data and reasoned arguments, no matter how logical they seem, reveal only personal preferences and biases. In their view, science has no greater claim to truth than does religion, myth, or witchcraft. In a world marked by cultural diversity and individual idiosyncrasies, there are no correct answers, no rules that apply everywhere and to everyone. Moreover, like those who point out the dangers of reason not directed by spiritual values, postmodernists argue that reason fosters oppressive governments, military complexes, and stifling bureaucracies. Nor has it solved our problems.

Expressing disdain for Western humanism, which ascribes an inherent dignity to human beings, urges the full development of the individual's potential, and regards the rational, self-determining human being as the center of existence, postmodernists claim that humanism has failed. The humanist vision of socialist society ended in Stalinism, and liberal humanism proved no more effective a barrier to Nazism than did Christianity. In our own day, they ask, has the rational humanist tradition been able to solve the problems of overpopulation, worldwide pollution, world hunger, poverty, and war that ravage our planet? Closer to home, has reason coped successfully with urban blight, homelessness, violence, racial tensions, or drug addiction? Moreover, postmodernists contend that the Western tradition, which has been valued as a great and creative human achievement, is fraught with gender, class, and racial bias. In their view, it is merely a male, white, Eurocentric interpretation of things, and the West's vaunted ideals are really a cloak of hypocrisy intended to conceal, rationalize, and legitimate the power, privileges, and preferences of white, European, male elites.

People who identify with victims of exploitation, discrimination, and persecution throughout the globe also attack the Western tradition. They point to the modern West's historic abuses: slavery, imperialism, racism, ethnocentrism, sexism, class exploitation, and the ravaging of the environment. They accuse westerners of marginalizing the poor, women, and people of color by viewing them as the "other." Furthermore, they condemn the West for arrogantly exalting Western values and achievements and belittling, or even destroying, indigenous peoples and cultures. Finding Western civilization intrinsically flawed, some critics seek a higher wisdom in non-Western traditions—African, Asian, or Native American.

Radical Muslims, who were responsible for or identify with the events of September 11, view Western civilization as a threat to traditional Islam. Their vision of an Islamic society based on a strict interpretation of the Koran clashes head on with core principles of Western democracy—separation of church and state, religious toleration, protection of basic rights, and female equality.

Defenders of the Enlightenment heritage argue that this heritage, despite its flaws, still has a powerful message for us. They caution against devaluing and undermining the modern West's unique achievements: the tradition of *rationality*, which makes possible a scientific understanding of the physical universe and human nature, the utilization of nature for human betterment, and the identification and reformation of irrational and abusive institutions and beliefs; the tradition of *political freedom*, which is the foundation of democratic institutions; the tradition of *inner freedom*, which asserts the individual's capacity for ethical autonomy, the ability and duty to make moral choices; the tradition of *humanism*, which regards individuals as active subjects, with both the right and the capacity to realize their full human potential; the tradition of *equality*, which demands equal treatment under the law; and the tradition of *human dignity*, which affirms the inviolable integrity and worth of the human personality and is the driving force behind what is now a global quest for social justice and human rights.

The modern struggle for human rights—initiated during the Enlightenment, advanced by the French Revolution, and embodied in liberalism—continues in the contemporary age. Two crucial developments in this struggle are the civil rights movement in the United States and the feminist movement. Spokespersons for these movements have used ideas formulated by Western thinkers in earlier struggles for liberty and equality. Thus, one reason for the success of Martin Luther King's policy of direct action was that he both inspired and shamed white America to live up to its Judeo-Christian and democratic principles. Although written more than twenty-five years ago, the insights of French social theorist Jacques Ellul still apply:

[T]he essential, central, undeniable fact is that the West was the first civilization in history to focus attention on the individual and on freedom. . . . The West, and the West alone, is responsible for the movement that has led to the desire for freedom. . . . Today men point the finger of outrage at slavery and torture. Where did that kind of indignation originate? What civilization or culture cried out that slavery was unacceptable and torture scandalous? Not Islam, or Buddhism, or Confucius, or Zen, or the religions and moral codes of Africa and India! The West alone has defended the inalienable rights of the human person, the dignity of the individual. . . . The West attempted to apply in a conscious, methodical way the implications of freedom. . . . [T]he West discovered what no one else had discovered: freedom and the individual. . . . I see no other satisfactory model that can replace what the West has produced.*

The roots of these ideals are ultimately found in the West's Greek and Judeo-Christian heritage, but it was the philosophes of the Enlightenment who clearly articulated them for the modern age. To be sure, these ideals are a goal, not a finished achievement, and nothing should make westerners more appreciative of the preciousness of these ideals and more alert to their precariousness than examining the ways they have been violated and distorted over the course of centuries. It is equally true that every age has to rethink and revitalize this tradition in order to adapt it to the needs of its own time.

Therefore, it is crucial in this age of globalism, with its heightened sense of ethnic and cultural diversity, that westerners become sensitized to the histories and traditions of all cultures. But it is equally crucial in an era of global interdependence and tension that westerners continuously affirm and reaffirm the core values of their heritage and not permit this priceless legacy to be dismissed or negated. As the history of the twentieth century demonstrates, when we lose confidence in this heritage, we risk losing our humanity, and civilized life is threatened by organized barbarism.

---

*Jacques Ellul, *The Betrayal of the West*, trans. J. O'Connell (New York: Seabury, 1978), pp. 17–19, 29.

Index